LANDSLIDE

THE 2025 AUSTRALIAN FEDERAL ELECTION

LANDSLIDE

THE 2025 AUSTRALIAN FEDERAL ELECTION

EDITED BY
MARIAN SAWER,
JILL SHEPPARD AND
JOHN WARHURST

ANU PRESS

AUSTRALIAN FEDERAL ELECTION

ANU PRESS

Published by ANU Press
The Australian National University
Canberra ACT 2600, Australia
Email: anupress@anu.edu.au

Available to download for free at press.anu.edu.au

ISBN (print): 9781760467258
ISBN (online): 9781760467265

WorldCat (print): 1553683234
WorldCat (online): 1553697286

DOI: 10.22459/L.2026

Cover design and layout by ANU Press.

Cover photograph: Australian Prime Minister Anthony Albanese speaks at the Labor Election Night function at Canterbury-Hurlstone Park RSL Club on Election Day of the 2025 federal election campaign, 3 May 2025, Sydney. Source: AAP Image/Lukas Coch.

This book is published under the aegis of the Social Sciences editorial board of ANU Press.

Contents

List of illustrations

Figures

Map and plates

Tables

Abbreviations

2CP	two-candidate-preferred
2PP	two-party-preferred
3CP	three-candidate-preferred
ABC	Australian Broadcasting Corporation
ACL	Australian Christian Lobby
ACT	Australian Capital Territory
ACTU	Australian Council of Trade Unions
AEC	Australian Electoral Commission
AI	artificial intelligence
ALP	Australian Labor Party
CI	Community Independent
CIM	Community Independents Movement
CLP	Country Liberal Party
DEI	diversity, equity and inclusion
DOGE	Department of Government Efficiency
HECS	Higher Education Contribution Scheme
LNP	Liberal National Party of Queensland
LPA	Liberal Party of Australia
MAGA	'Make America Great Again'
MLA	Member of the Legislative Assembly
MP	Member of Parliament
MRP	multilevel regression with post-stratification
MVM	Muslim Votes Matter
NSW	New South Wales

NT	Northern Territory
PHON	Pauline Hanson's One Nation
PM	Prime Minister
SA	South Australia
TAFE	technical and further education
TMV	The Muslim Vote
TOP	Trumpet of Patriots
UAP	United Australia Party
UK	United Kingdom
UN	United Nations
US	United States
WA	Western Australia
WFH	work from home

Acknowledgements

Many people contribute to the success of the federal election series and our thanks are due to all of them.

First and foremost is the Academy of the Social Sciences in Australia, which has supported the federal election series since 1996. We acknowledge again the help of its Chief Executive Officer, Chris Hatherly, and Events Coordinator, Ellen Scott. In 2025 the election workshop was held at The Australian National University (ANU) and Maria Mendoza Rozo of the ANU Research School of Social Sciences also played a vital role in the organising team.

In addition to the academy, we are grateful for funding support for the workshop from the Australian Political Studies Association and the School of Politics and International Relations at ANU. There was a day of intense discussion (with only 10-minute coffee breaks) of the draft chapters and key election themes. We owe much to the formal discussants, who were: Anika Gauja, Patrick Leslie, Natalie Barr, Pandanus Petter, Andrew Hughes, Stephen Mills, Chris Wallace, Frank Bongiorno, Mark Kenny and Joshua Black. They, along with other participants, made key observations that have helped shape the book.

Immediately after the workshop, we held a public lecture by Antony Green, titled 'Bungee Jumping on Election Night: Into the void tethered by only a thin stream of data'. Almost 500 people attended this highly successful event, which was designed to honour Antony's 36-year career as the ABC's chief election analyst. After Antony's highly amusing address, Jill Sheppard hosted the Q and A and Andrea Carson, as President of the Australian Political Studies Association, paid a tribute to his career and contribution.

We owe much to ANU Press for their support of the federal election series and to Teresa Prowse for the cover design. The book has benefited once again from the immaculate copyediting of Jan Borrie and from her patience and persistence in dealing with authors.

Contributors

Andrea Carson is Professor of Political Communication and Associate Dean of Research at La Trobe University, Melbourne. She studies election campaigns and the ways in which political actors use the media to reach voters with their election messages. She is the author of several books and journal articles about politics and the media, public trust, election campaigns, misinformation and how to manage it.

Emily Foley is a Postdoctoral Research Fellow at Flinders University, Adelaide, and the University of Canberra. Her research interests include centre-left political parties and labour migration policies.

Zareh Ghazarian is the Head of Politics and International Relations at Monash University, Melbourne. He holds a PhD in Political Science from Monash University and has published widely in the field. Zareh was awarded an E.G. Whitlam Research Fellowship for 2025 and is regularly called upon by national and international media to provide political analysis.

Murray Goot is Emeritus Professor of Politics at Macquarie University, Sydney, and a Fellow of the Academy of the Social Sciences in Australia. His main publications cover opinion polls, the media and electoral behaviour. His next book (with Tim Rowse), on Indigenous recognition and the Voice referendum, is scheduled for publication in 2026.

Antony Green is Chief Election Analyst Emeritus at the Australian Broadcasting Corporation. He is also an Adjunct Professor in the Department of Government and International Relations at the University of Sydney.

Phoebe Hayman is a PhD candidate in the Department of Politics, Media and Philosophy at La Trobe University, Melbourne. Her doctoral research examines volunteer participation in the 2022 Teal Independent campaigns. Phoebe's broader research interests and publications include political organisations, election campaigns and political communication.

Carolyn M. Hendriks is a Professor at the Crawford School of Public Policy at The Australian National University. She undertakes social research on democratic aspects of contemporary governance, including public engagement, community organising, listening and representation. Carolyn is the author of four books, the latest of which examines citizen-led efforts to solve practical governance problems (*Democracy in Action*, with Albert Dzur, Oxford University Press, 2025).

Josh Holloway is a Lecturer in Government in the College of Business, Government and Law at Flinders University, Adelaide. His research covers political parties, party finance and democratic resilience to crisis. His most recent publications can be found in *Perspectives on Politics*, *Armed Forces & Society* and the *European Political Science Review*.

Simon Jackman is an Honorary Professor at the University of Sydney and a Fellow of the Academy of the Social Sciences in Australia. He studies public opinion, elections and electoral systems. He consults for a wide variety of clients in politics, advocacy, media and academia, utilising his expertise in data science and research methods.

Stewart Jackson is a Senior Lecturer in the Discipline of Government and International Relations at the University of Sydney. His research focuses on green politics in Australia and the Asia-Pacific, specialising in party development. Further interests extend to green political theory, including environmental feminism and the intersection of social movements and parliamentary politics.

Carol Johnson is an Emerita Professor in the Department of Politics and International Relations at the University of Adelaide and a Fellow of the Academy of the Social Sciences in Australia. She has published extensively on Australian politics, with a particular interest in issues of ideology, gender, sexuality and the politics of emotion. Her most recent book is *The Politics of Gender Equality: Australian Lessons in an Uncertain World* (Palgrave Macmillan, 2024).

Lucien Leon is an independent researcher who writes on political satire and contemporary news media. His publications include 'Talking pictures (and cartoons, videos, memes etcetera)' (with Richard Scully) in *Watershed: The 2022 Australian Federal Election* (ANU Press, 2023) and 'In memes we trust? Co-option of democratisation of graphic political satire', in *Moral Dimensions of Humour: Essays on Humans, Heroes and Monsters* (edited by Benjamin Nickl and Mark Rolfe, Tampere University Press, 2024). Since 2021, he has been a judge for the Museum of Australian Democracy's annual 'Behind the Lines' political cartoons exhibition.

Michael Maley had a 30-year career at the Australian Electoral Commission, retiring in 2012 as special adviser for electoral reform and international services. He has also worked as a consultant to the United Nations, the International Foundation for Electoral Systems, the International Institute for Democracy and Electoral Assistance and the Commonwealth Secretariat. He is a member of the Editorial Board of the *Election Law Journal*, was awarded the Public Service Medal in 2001 and received the International Foundation for Electoral Systems' Joe C. Baxter Award in 2015.

Rob Manwaring is an Associate Professor of Politics at Flinders University, Adelaide. Rob researches political parties, comparative politics and the centre-left. He was President of the Australian Political Studies Association in 2024.

Justin Phillips is a Senior Lecturer in Politics at the University of Waikato, New Zealand. He specialises in a wide range of political communication research on social media data, including election campaigns, fact-checking, conspiracy beliefs and online extremism. This research has received funding from, among others, the New Zealand Government, Meta and the Royal Society Te Apārangi.

Ben Raue is an independent election analyst who writes about elections in Australia for his website *The Tally Room* and hosts the associated podcast. Ben has been a regular commentator and analyst on Australian election nights for ABC Radio and the *Guardian*.

Richard Reid is a Research Fellow at the Crawford School of Public Policy at The Australian National University. He researches contemporary political representation and party politics and has published on the Australian Senate, the UK House of Lords and broader issues of political representation, public administration, public policy and citizen-led democratic innovation.

Mark Riboldi is a Lecturer in Social Impact and Social Change at the UTS Business School at the University of Technology Sydney. Mark studies the role of civil society within democracy. His research includes how Australian not-for-profits responded to the Covid-19 pandemic, the democratic relationships between organisations and communities and the rise of Independents and minor parties in Australian politics.

Marian Sawer AO is an Emeritus Professor in the School of Politics and International Relations at The Australian National University and a Fellow of the Academy of the Social Sciences in Australia. She has led the Democratic Audit of Australia and has a longstanding interest in electoral regulation. Her most recent book is *Toxic Parliaments and What Can Be Done About Them* (with Maria Maley, Palgrave, 2024).

Richard Scully is Professor in Modern History and Head of the Department of Archaeology, Classics and History at the University of New England. His main field of research is the global history and function of political cartoons and he is the chief investigator on the Australian Research Council Discovery Grant 'Cartoon Nation: Australian editorial cartooning—Past, present, and future'. He is the author of *Eminent Victorian Cartoonists* (three volumes, Political Cartoon Society, 2018) and the co-editor of *Cartoon Conflicts: Contemporary Controversies and Historical Precedents* (with Paulo Jorge Fernandes and Ritu Gairola Khanduri, Springer Nature, 2025).

Kurt Sengul is a Macquarie University Research Fellow in the School of Communication, Society and Culture. His research centres on populist and far-right media and communication. His book *Far-Right Populism in Australia: Communication, Discourse, Performance* is forthcoming from Bloomsbury.

Jill Sheppard is an Associate Professor in Politics at The Australian National University. She is an investigator on the Australian Election Study, an election analyst for the ABC and researches public opinion, political participation and political parties in Australia.

Josh Sunman is an Associate Lecturer in Public Policy at Flinders University, Adelaide. His current research looks at the intersection of electoral management, policy agendas and democratic health. He also has a keen research and commentary interest in South Australian and federal politics.

Marija Taflaga is a Senior Lecturer at The Australian National University. Marija is a comparative political institutionalist specialising in Australian politics and holds two Australian Research Council Grants on Australian political careers and parliamentary speech. She is co-host of the *Democracy Sausage* podcast.

Ariadne Vromen is Head of the Division of Political and International Studies at the University of Glasgow and a Fellow of the Academy of the Social Sciences in Australia. She has long-term research interests in citizen engagement and campaigning organisations, and her latest book is *Story Tech: Power, Storytelling, and Social Change Advocacy* (with Filippo Trevisan and Michael Vaughan, University of Michigan Press, 2025).

John Warhurst AO is Emeritus Professor of Political Science in the School of Politics and International Relations, The Australian National University. His special interest in all church–state issues includes religion and elections. He has co-edited many of the books in this federal election series and his involvement as an author began with the 1980 election.

Finley Watson is a PhD candidate in the Department of Politics at La Trobe University, Melbourne. He studies the politics of new media with a focus on political influencers and alternative news media. His broader research interests include platformed political communication, participatory culture, interest groups and misinformation.

Blair Williams is a Lecturer in Australian Politics at UNSW Canberra. She has published widely on the gendered media coverage of women in politics, gender and sexuality in Australian politics, political leadership masculinities and the politics of Covid-19. Her most recent publications can be found in *Men and Masculinities*, the *European Journal of Politics and Gender* and the *Australian Journal of Politics and History*.

1

Landslide: The 2025 Australian federal election

Marian Sawer, Jill Sheppard and John Warhurst

Abstract

This chapter introduces the themes of the 2025 federal election campaign, the main campaign events and the dramatis personae. It notes the changing demography of the electorate and the need for parties to take their campaigns to different social media platforms to pursue the votes of Millennials and Generation Z. The 'Trump effect' is examined as is related campaigning around 'Australian values'. The chapter covers regulatory issues including those arising from the new importance to the campaign of social media influencers. It finishes with an overview of the three parts of the book: Part 1 on the campaign and context, Part 2 on the actors and Part 3 on the results.

Keywords: campaign themes; Trump effect; demographic change; social media; regulatory issues

On election night, 3 May 2025, commentators found it difficult to believe the results. While Labor had been gaining in the polls and seemed likely to retain at least minority government, no-one anticipated the landslide that occurred. Labor had won a higher proportion of seats than at any time since their wartime victory in 1943.

Table 1.1 Federal election timetable, 2025

Date	Event
28 March	Prime Minister calls the election
31 March	Writs issued for the House of Representatives and half-Senate elections
7 April	Close of rolls
10 April	Close of nominations
22 April	Early voting begins
3 May	Election day
13 May	The new Albanese ministry sworn in
12 June	Return of writs

Source: The authors.

How did this happen? The authors in our book explore what contributed to this result, the nature of party and third-party campaigns, the changing demography of the electorate and external factors including the 'Trump effect'. The main cast of characters—apart from US President Donald Trump—is introduced in Table 1.2.

Table 1.2 2025 federal election: *Dramatis personae*

Australian Labor Party	
Anthony Albanese	Prime Minister
Jim Chalmers	Treasurer
Jason Clare	Election spokesperson
Senator Katy Gallagher	Election spokesperson
Paul Erickson	National Secretary
Liberal Party	
Peter Dutton	Opposition Leader
Senator Jane Hume	Shadow Minister for Finance and the Public Service
Senator James Paterson	Election spokesperson
Andrew Hirst	Federal Director
Topham Guerin	Liberal Party advertising agency
Nationals	
David Littleproud	Leader
Senator Bridget McKenzie	Senate Leader
Senator Jacinta Nampijinpa Price	Shadow Minister for Indigenous Affairs and Government Efficiency

Greens	
Adam Bandt	Leader
Senator Larissa Waters	Deputy Leader
Stephen Bates	MP for Brisbane
Max Chandler-Mather	MP for Griffith
Independents and minor parties	
Monique Ryan	Community Independent MP
Zoe Daniel	Community Independent MP
Dai Le	Independent MP
Senator Jacqui Lambie	Leader, Jacqui Lambie Network
Senator Pauline Hanson	Leader, Pauline Hanson's One Nation
Clive Palmer	Billionaire funder, Trumpet of Patriots
Others	
Sandra Bourke	Advance spokesperson
Sally McManus	Secretary, Australian Council of Trade Unions
Peta Credlin	*Sky News* presenter
Gina Rinehart	Mining billionaire

Source: The authors.

While there was a landslide of seats, we must point to the disproportionality of the result. Labor gained 35 per cent of the primary vote for the House of Representatives but 63 per cent of the seats. Such disproportionality is characteristic of Westminster electoral systems based on single-member constituencies. In the 2024 UK general election, for example, the Labour Party won 34 per cent of the vote and 63 per cent of the seats in the House of Commons.

In Australia, the preferential system at least ensures that seats are won by those with majority support in the seat, even if this majority is only achieved through the distribution of preferences. Labor won 55 per cent of the 'two-party-preferred' vote, meaning it won more preferences as well as more primary votes than the Coalition. In 2025, the trend that we observed in 2022—the shift away from Australia's traditional two-party system—continued. While in 1980 more than 90 per cent of the primary vote was for the major parties, by 2025, this had shrunk to about two-thirds and the vote for minor parties and Independents reached a record high.

The era of life-long party loyalties was coming to an end, along with the dominance of baby boomers in the electorate. The baby boomers (born between 1946 and 1964), were outnumbered in 2025 by Millennials (born 1981–96) and Gen Z (born 1997–2012). These new generations related to politics in a different way from the baby boomers, and Gen Z in particular received news through social media rather than newspapers or online news websites. Gen Z spent most time on social media—apparently almost four and a half hours a day. Those pursuing their votes had to do so through social media, including Facebook, Instagram, YouTube and TikTok. The enormous followings of social media 'influencers' meant that being interviewed on their podcasts could be of great value to political leaders; the Coalition, however, appears to have been particularly unsuccessful in its social media strategy and in winning votes from Gen Z.

Apart from the new political importance of Millennials and Gen Z (see Chowdhury 2025), other demographic shifts influenced the campaign. More than 30 per cent of the population was born overseas, with the most important source country continuing to be the United Kingdom but the next largest numbers coming from India and China. Labor engaged a multicultural marketing agency in its attempt to reach out to these communities. However, celebrating Bengali New Year on its Facebook page (15 April) had mixed responses, including: 'This is exactly why no true blue Aussies are voting for Labor.'

The Coalition had difficulty trying to attract back Chinese Australians' votes lost in 2022 while also presenting itself as stronger than the government on standing up to China. At the same time, Labor was challenged by new efforts to mobilise Muslim voters over the war in Gaza and the future of Palestine, while Jewish voters were mobilised over a rise in anti-Semitism. This new involvement of Muslim and Jewish communities in the campaign overshadowed religious communities mobilised politically in the past, such as the much larger Catholic community.

Another outstanding feature of the 2025 election was the 'Trump effect'. While Opposition leader Peter Dutton (Table 1.2) was at first keen to be associated with Trump and his successful campaign for the US presidency, this association quickly became a liability as Trump pursued policies harmful to Australia such as the tariffs announced on 2 April ('Liberation Day'). The labelling of Dutton as 'Temu-Trump' went viral on social media after Greens MP Stephen Bates used the term in Question Time the day before the election was called.

The Coalition continued to enjoy the backing of the Murdoch media including *Sky News Australia*. All News Corp mastheads endorsed a Coalition government except the Adelaide *Advertiser*, which endorsed majority government by either major party. However, populist attacks on the 'wokeness' of Labor, the Greens and Community Independents (generally known as Teals)—whether by the Murdoch media or the well-financed digital campaign organisation Advance—appeared to have little traction beyond the conservative base.

In this introductory chapter, we highlight key themes of the 2025 federal election campaign, look briefly at the 'Trump effect' and then outline new regulatory issues. We finish with a brief overview of the structure of the book and its place in the federal election series.

Election themes

Campaigning began well before the Prime Minister finally called the 2025 election. Labor's campaign could be dated to 3 November 2024, when it announced that if re-elected its first piece of legislation would cut student loan debt by 20 per cent, benefiting three million Australians 'doing it tough', particularly Millennials and Gen Z, who had become the largest voting bloc since the previous election. In January 2025, Anthony Albanese visited Queensland for the announcement of major funding for improvement of the Bruce Highway.

Meanwhile, the Coalition re-engaged New Zealand–based advertising agency Topham Guerin and, on 8 January 2025, launched its campaign message: 'Let's get Australia back on track.' Topham Guerin had earlier helped the New Zealand National Party win government with the slogan 'Get our country back on track'.

At the same time, Opposition leader Dutton echoed several of the themes of Trump's successful campaign for the US presidency, attacking government waste and Canberra-based public servants, and telling Sydney radio station 2GB that the Albanese government was 'more interested in pronouns and a $500 million Voice campaign' than the cost of living. After Trump's inauguration on 20 January and his executive order of that day establishing the Department of Government Efficiency (DOGE), the Coalition appointed Senator Jacinta Nampijinpa Price as Shadow Minister for Government Efficiency.

The formal 2025 election campaign began on Friday, 28 March, when the Prime Minister called on the Governor-General at Government House (Table 1.1). Treasurer Jim Chalmers had delivered the Budget on Tuesday, 25 March and Dutton gave his budget reply speech on Thursday, 27 March.

The trip to Government House was later than originally planned (Evans 2025) after Tropical Cyclone Alfred delayed an earlier election. During the cyclone emergency, Albanese appeared business-like alongside Queensland Liberal National Party (LNP) Premier, David Crisafulli.

Chalmers' well-received 'cost-of-living' budget included a small income tax cut that the Opposition decided to oppose. Chalmers otherwise emphasised support for Medicare, housing and defence spending, and gave every taxpayer $300 towards their energy bill—just weeks before the Reserve Bank of Australia cut interest rates for the first time in three years, although Trump's tariff plans threatened to increase global economic uncertainty.

Dutton's reply was more a pre-election speech than an alternative budget. New housing policies, such as tax concessions on interest repayments for the first five years, were a major ingredient. He also promised an east coast gas reservation scheme and a reduction in public service numbers of 41,000, claiming to save $7 billion per year once operational. His vote sweetener, which became a centrepiece of his campaign, was a proposal to halve the fuel excise for 12 months. Dutton only made passing reference to his existing promise to build seven government-funded nuclear power stations. The speech also accused the Prime Minister of being weak in relation to crime and anti-Semitism.

Economists were unenthusiastic about both speeches, wanting restraint rather than a 'spendathon' given the growing size of the national debt. Yet, the parties were matching each other's spending promises.

Some matters were off the table between the major parties despite wider community concern. These included the huge commitment to the AUKUS (Australia, United Kingdom, United States) defence agreement, miserly treatment of the unemployed, cautious policies on border protection and refugees, regulation of gambling advertising and general commitment to net-zero emissions by 2050. The defeat of the October 2023 Voice referendum cast a shadow over Indigenous policies, as did the recent big Coalition victories in the Northern Territory and Queensland elections. Likewise, both major parties refused to condemn Israel's actions in the Middle East, despite international and local pressure. Each of these policies was left to others to advocate, including the Greens and community protest groups.

A close election was anticipated, with a general expectation of either a Labor or a Coalition minority government. This perception impacted party strategies. The Liberals warned against a 'Labor–Green–Teal extremist minority government'. Labor was pressed on a possible minority government supported by the Greens, and the Teal Independents were pressed on whom they would support. Labor emphasised that its goal was majority government even when that seemed unlikely. The Greens saw such a minority government as an opportunity for progressive policies and described their role as 'keeping Dutton out'.

As in 2022, it was an interrupted campaign. The two-week pre-polling period began on Tuesday, 22 April, while the campaign encompassed two weeks of school holidays, the Easter holiday from Friday, 18 April to Monday, 21 April and Anzac Day on Friday, 25 April. Subsequently, the unexpected death of Pope Francis on Easter Monday forced another pause in campaigning.

The campaign was punctuated by a record four televised debates between the two major-party leaders and numerous debates between ministers and shadow ministers. The leaders' debates were uneventful and relatively even, with the Prime Minister a nose in front (Mills 2025). Neither leader made a major error. The official campaign spokespeople were Jason Clare MP and Senator Katy Gallagher for Labor and Senator James Paterson for the Coalition. The official Labor and Coalition launches came late in the campaign—within an hour of each other on Sunday, 13 April in Perth and Western Sydney, respectively. The Greens finally officially launched their campaign, in Melbourne, on the final Sunday before the election, 30 April (Table 1.3).

Table 1.3 Key campaign events, 2025

Date	Event
3 November 2024	Launch in Adelaide of Labor's election commitment to 20 per cent reduction in student loan debt
12 January 2025	Soft launch in Melbourne of 'Let's get Australia back on track: The priorities of a Dutton Coalition government'
7 March 2025	Tropical Cyclone Alfred makes landfall, delays election announcement
28 March 2025	Election called
2 April 2025	Announcement of global tariffs on US imports ('Liberation Day')
7 April 2025	Peter Dutton says Coalition's work-from-home policy was 'a mistake'
8 April 2025	First leaders' debate, Sky News

Date	Event
13 April 2025	Labor campaign launch in Perth; Coalition launch in Sydney
16 April 2025	Second leaders' debate, ABC TV
22 April 2025	Third leaders' debate, Nine Network
27 April 2025	Fourth leaders' debate, Seven Network
30 April 2025	Greens campaign launch in Melbourne; Albanese speech to National Press Club

Source: The authors.

The party leaders and their spokespeople were the major figures during the campaign. Each leader travelled widely. Albanese provocatively—but, as it turned out, realistically—campaigned in Dutton's own electorate of Dickson. He campaigned hard on health and his signature flourish became waving his green Medicare card. He also criticised Dutton for not campaigning in the electorates in which the Coalition's proposed nuclear power stations were to be located. Dutton's signature campaign gesture was to fill up at a petrol station to emphasise his proposed cut to the fuel excise. Neither leader visited Indigenous communities.

The Liberals called on all their former prime ministers for campaign assistance, especially John Howard. Albanese campaigned with popular Labor State premiers, especially Peter Malinauskas in South Australia. He seemed to avoid Victorian Premier Jacinta Allen because of her apparent unpopularity in what was predicted to be a difficult State for Labor to defend seats. Noticeably quiet figures included shadow defence minister Andrew Hastie, whose policies were not launched until the second last week, and minister for the environment Tanya Plibersek, overseeing a sensitive area for the government. The Nationals did not call on out-of-favour former leader Barnaby Joyce.

The Liberal Party lost several candidates during the campaign to revelations of historical gaffes and the Greens candidate for Franklin in Tasmania withdrew after it was discovered he had New Zealand citizenship.

The leaders' campaign interactions were generally polite despite personal attacks. Liberal advertising made a deliberate attempt to soften Dutton's 'hard-man' image. When his father suffered a heart attack just before the first leaders' debate, Albanese was gracious, but Dutton chose not to withdraw. The politeness appeared not to extend to the campaign trail itself, however. Social division around the Israel–Gaza war formed a large part of the breakdown of civility. Other incidents included theft of corflutes and personal abuse.

Several policy themes were at the core of major-party disagreements: competing cost-of-living measures (who could offer bigger bribes), different approaches to cutting immigration (who could cut more heavily), energy policy including the nuclear option and gas reservation (the clearest difference) and competing housing policies (alternative approaches).

Labor's slogan was 'Building Australia's future'. Its campaign was led by a stronger performance by Albanese than he managed in 2022, while Chalmers also featured more heavily. It was a tightly scripted and focused campaign, which grew in confidence as the polls improved for the government and victory seemed highly likely. As time went on, the government was able to feast on Opposition mistakes and contradictions. By the time Albanese addressed the National Press Club in the final week, his relaxed confidence was obvious.

The Liberals emphasised their strong leadership, an immediate 50 per cent cut to the fuel excise, spending cuts including to the federal public service and national security. It promised to cut fuel emission regulations, describing them as 'Albo's ute tax'. Its campaign ally, the advocacy group Advance, campaigned against the 'ute tax' on Facebook and YouTube from 2024, describing it as 'slugging Aussies in the regions and suburbs with more expensive cars while inner city elites get cheaper Teslas'. In an extensive digital campaign, Advance described the government and its leader as 'weak, woke, and sending us broke'.

Ultimately, the Liberals' campaign organisation undermined its prospects: lack of detail, overkill, confusion, backflips and apologies, and poor timing. The nuclear policy, led by shadow minister for energy Ted O'Brien, was weakened by lack of detail on cost and the timing of implementation. The overkill included Trump-like attacks on diversity, equity and inclusion (DEI) policies and labelling of 'hate media', with the ABC and the *Guardian* singled out. The confusion was related to the meaning and implementation of its public service cuts policy. The main backflip involved Senator Jane Hume's extremely unpopular 'work-from-home' policy, which led to excruciating apologies by Dutton and other ministers. The poor timing included the late release of Hastie's increased defence spending policy (which also lacked detail).

The Nationals' campaign was largely out of sight in the cities. It was happy with nuclear energy, claiming the policy as its own. The party opposed renewable energy and supported road user charges for electric vehicles on grounds of rural–urban equity.

The Greens campaigned to 'Keep Dutton out', with leader Adam Bandt featured in podcasts with well-known influencers including Abbie Chatfield. Substantive policies included rental price freezes, removing negative gearing and free school lunches. Late in the campaign Bandt toted a human-sized toothbrush to promote his free dental care policies.

The widespread Community Independents campaigns were local and community-focused and hard to summarise other than by a general emphasis on accountability and transparency. This time they lacked the target provided in 2022 by unpopular Liberal leader Scott Morrison.

An exchange of preferences between the Coalition and Pauline Hanson's One Nation (PHON), abandoning previous Coalition practice of putting One Nation last or at least below Labor, caused a damaging perception that the Coalition was moving further to the right. Clive Palmer's new Trumpet of Patriots party sent millions of SMS text messages and advertised extravagantly in the mass media to little effect.

By the end of the campaign, the verdict was clear. The government had successfully defended its right to carry on for a second term, while the Opposition had failed to demonstrate that it was ready to govern.

The Trump factor

Three leaders are fighting out this campaign and only one of them is definitely not Trump.

—Niki Savva on *Insiders*, ABC TV, 6 April 2025

The shadow of Trump was such an important part of the 2025 campaign that one seasoned observer labelled it 'Australia's Trump election' (Megalogenis 2025). The delay caused by Tropical Cyclone Alfred helped maximise the Trump effect. In the first two weeks of the campaign, which included 'Liberation Day', Trump was featuring in 13 per cent of front-page stories. Initially the Coalition had tried to depict itself as closer to Trump and hence able to obtain a better deal on the tariffs he was threatening. The Coalition also identified with several themes of the successful Trump campaign, including opposition to 'woke' government waste such as DEI programs, as well as support for nuclear energy and fossil fuels.

However, Trump's erratic behaviour in relation to the war in Ukraine and announcement of sweeping and seemingly arbitrary tariffs on trading partners including Australia meant that the Trump factor became a liability rather than an asset. Already by 4 March the negative association of Dutton with Trump was evident in tropes such as 'Donald Dutton' seen in comments on the Liberal Party's Facebook page.

The Coalition then sought to distance itself from Trump but not always successfully. Some of its donors, such as mining billionaire Gina Rinehart, continued to call for Australia to follow Trump (Burton 2025). And the Coalition itself returned to Trump-like populist themes at the end of the campaign, attacking Welcome to Country ceremonies and suggesting Labor was in thrall to 'activist elites'. The zigzags of the Coalition's association with Trump are summarised in Table 1.4.

Table 1.4 The shadow of Trump, 2024–2025

Date	Event
9 November 2024	The *Weekend Australian* reports that the Coalition is soliciting advice on messaging and advertising from Trump campaign strategists.
11 November 2024	Mining billionaire Gina Rinehart calls on the Liberal Party to 'watch and learn' from Donald Trump's successful 2024 election campaign.
20 January 2025	Trump sworn in as US President, issues executive orders establishing Department of Government Efficiency and ending DEI programs and remote work for all federal employees.
25 January 2025	Senator Jacinta Nampijinpa Price appointed Shadow Minister for Government Efficiency.
6 February 2025	Opposition leader Peter Dutton praises Donald Trump as 'shrewd', 'reasonable' and 'a big thinker and deal maker'.
19 February 2025	Billionaire Clive Palmer announces his Trump-inspired Trumpet of Patriots party, vowing to 'make Australia great again'.
3 March 2025	Senator Jane Hume announces a Coalition government would end work-from-home arrangements for federal public servants.
27 March 2025	Greens MP Stephen Bates calls Dutton 'Temu-Trump' in Question Time.
31 March 2025	Dutton says DEI does nothing to improve the lives of everyday Australians and he will cut back the public service.
2 April 2025	Trump announces sweeping tariffs, including on Australia.

Date	Event
3 April 2025	Dutton says that he could successfully negotiate tariff exemptions for Australia.
7 April 2025	Dutton says work-from-home policy a mistake.
12 April 2025	Senator Jacinta Nampijinpa Price vows to 'make Australia great again' at campaign event.
16 April 2025	Dutton asked at the second leaders' debate whether he trusts Donald Trump, responds: 'I don't know the president; I've not met him.'
21 April 2025	The *Australian*'s political editor Simon Benson reports that Donald Trump has crafted 'a diabolical situation' for Peter Dutton.
23 April 2025	Canadian Conservative Party Opposition leader Pierre Poilievre publishes platform commitment to end 'woke' ideology in the public service and in funding for university research.
28 April 2025	Trump repeats threat to make Canada the fifty-first State of the United States. Canadian Conservative Party loses election and Poilievre loses seat.
3 May 2025	Anthony Albanese wins re-election in a landslide of seats. Opposition leader Peter Dutton loses his seat.
3 May 2025	National Party Senate leader Bridget McKenzie says the 'Trump factor' played a significant role in Coalition's defeat.

Source: Compiled by Kurt Sengul and Marian Sawer.

Meanwhile, Labor was careful to avoid appearing directly antagonistic to Trump while at the same time wary of seeming too 'soft' on him—a difficult balancing act. It portrayed itself as standing up for Australian values instead of borrowing from America. For example, when the Coalition announced its intention of ending work from home (WFH), Minister for Finance and the Public Service Katy Gallagher claimed that most of the Coalition's policy platform was 'stolen from the United States'. Labor also put increasing emphasis on resisting 'Americanisation' of Australia's health system and industrial relations and described the imposition of tariffs on Australia as 'not the act of a friend'.

The negative association of Dutton with Trump became a feature of the campaign, as seen in the Victorian Trades Hall Council's 'Donald Dutton' image posted on Facebook (Plate 1.1). A TikTok post by Greens MP Stephen Bates calling Dutton 'Temu-Trump' attracted more than two million views.

Plate 1.1 'Protect Australia from Donald Dutton' poster
Source: Victorian Trades Hall Council.

The Coalition's opponents were so successful at identifying Dutton with Trump that senior Coalition figures, including Nationals Senate leader Senator Bridget McKenzie, blamed the Trump effect for the election landslide (9News 2025). As Simon Jackman observes in Chapter 19, the election narrative shifted from the handling of the cost-of-living crisis to assessments as to which leader would be less like Trump.

Clive Palmer's Trumpet of Patriots party also suffered from its association with Trump, despite spending $60 million on campaign advertisements. And in the last week of the campaign, the Canadian election provided a similar warning. The Conservative Party of Canada, committing to end 'woke' ideology in the public service and research funding, lost its election and, as in Australia, the Opposition Leader lost his seat.

Regulatory issues

Two new regulatory and administrative challenges characterised the Australian election: political commentary among online influencers and a long and uniquely complex vote count. Other challenges—such as expectations of convenience voting, candidate defections and party registration requests, electoral misinformation and disinformation and donation disclosures—were the same as in previous years, but no less acute. Reforms to political funding and disclosure passed the parliament in January 2025 for implementation in July 2026, making this the last (for now) federal election with unlimited donations and expenditure.

Electoral matter and authorisations

On the back of the 2024 US presidential election in which Trump conducted 14 (often hours-long) interviews with different podcasters, Australian leaders and candidates sought to leverage local content creators' significant audiences in 2025. On paper, this was standard politicking, akin to giving a sit-down interview with a newspaper or television reporter. In such cases, electoral authorisations are not required, as the purpose (and funding source) of the interview is clear to most audiences.

Less common is politicians sharing those interviews via their own social media accounts. In February and March 2025, both Albanese and Bandt appeared on Abbie Chatfield's podcast *It's a Lot* at Chatfield's request. As unpaid and voluntary, the interviews did not require electoral authorisation (for example, 'Authorised by A. Chatfield, Sydney') as per the *Commonwealth Electoral Act 1918*. When the leaders reposted the interviews on their own campaign accounts, with authorisations, questions emerged (in Senate estimates hearings and the media) about the content creators' responsibilities under the Act. The advice of the Australian Electoral

Commission (AEC) to both parties and creators was that, although the original podcast did not require authorisation due to the voluntary and unpaid nature of the interview, if creators 'are in doubt, authorise'.

Independent candidates also pushed against the bounds of the *Electoral Act* on several occasions. Member for Wentworth Allegra Spender paid content creators to endorse her without appropriate electoral authorisation and Monique Ryan, Independent member for Kooyong, equivocated on ABC TV's *Insiders* program about whether paid content should require authorisation (the AEC confirmed that it must, as per the Act).

Several Teal candidates benefited from *Gazette News*, a digital newspaper ostensibly created in June 2024 and covering eastern Melbourne, Sydney's North Shore, the mid-north coast of New South Wales, Gippsland and western Victoria. All these regions centred on electorates where Climate 200–backed candidates were challenging Liberal incumbents, and the newspaper's founder had disclosed previous donations to Independent Senator David Pocock and Climate 200. While the AEC found that *Gazette News* constituted actual news content and not electoral matter, and so did not require authorisation, the ability for third-party actors to quickly and cheaply create news outlets portends an increasingly blurred line between news and electoral matter.

Anonymous opponents of Spender's campaign in Wentworth also found themselves on the wrong side of the *Electoral Act*: 47,000 unauthorised flyers were distributed across the electorate, with the AEC identifying the publisher privately but not publicly. Spender criticised the AEC for not releasing the person's identity—a rare example of public disagreement between high-profile candidates and the commission.

Clive Palmer's Trumpet of Patriots did not breach the Act but did test voters' patience with daily spam texts on issues ranging from free university education to limiting immigration. With the introduction of donation and expenditure caps before the next election, and Palmer indicating that his political ambitions have now waned, voters can expect fewer unsolicited texts in future.

Complex vote counts

The AEC's other major challenge for this election came after 3 May: no Australian election has seen so many 'maverick seats' nor so many non-traditional contests (see also Ben Raue's Chapter 17, this volume). Before each federal election, the AEC (very discreetly) nominates which two candidates they expect will be in the final round of counting after preference distribution. This allows returning officers to start estimating preference flows on election night itself; this is the kind of forward projection that allows TV analysts to 'call' seats with only 10 per cent of all votes counted. In total, 22 seats had to restart their estimated preference counts on election night as initial primary vote counts revealed that the nominated two candidates appeared to be incorrect. This does not change final vote counts, but it certainly makes election night and the following days much more difficult for AEC staff and scrutineers (and candidates!).

The continued rise in primary votes for non–major-party candidates has also led to more complex preference distributions. In Calwell—where Independents collectively received 40 per cent of primary votes—the AEC could not estimate preference distributions until they had finished counting every primary vote. Preference distributions only began on 20 May—17 days after the election. At that point, there was still no clear winner in Bradfield and Goldstein had only just produced an apparent winner (with the caveat that the result could change once the final preference distribution was complete).

Large numbers of candidates, combined with comparatively low rates of English literacy, led to record high rates of informal voting throughout Western Sydney and some parts of Melbourne. The national informal vote rate was 5.6 per cent—in line with recent elections. The seats of Watson and Werriwa saw informal vote rates of 17 per cent—up significantly (7 and 6 percentage points, respectively) from 2022. Of the 21 seats with the most informal votes, 20 were in New South Wales.

Redistributions during the Forty-Seventh Parliament

Between the 2022 and 2025 elections, the parliament lost the seats of North Sydney and Higgins and gained a new Western Australian seat in Bullwinkel. These changes abolished one Independent-held seat, one Labor-held seat and created one notionally Labor seat. Boundary changes shifted Menzies to marginally Labor-held and Bennelong to marginally Liberal-held.

While the redistributions had little electoral effect, they produced additional headaches for the AEC. Traditionally, the AEC has been able to estimate new electoral margins after a redistribution based on polling place results from the previous election—for example, if a polling place in the suburb of Blackburn produced a 54–46 per cent two-party-preferred result for Labor in 2022, we can generally assume that the polling place would produce similar results even when boundaries mean it sits inside a new electorate. It is much more difficult to estimate these new margins if the previous election's results include a successful Independent or if a viable Independent candidate is standing in the new electorate. While the AEC's estimated margins are not necessary to the electoral process and have little impact on commentary or outcomes, it is another sign of the changing electoral landscape.

Early voting and the National Rugby League 'Magic Round'

As in 2022, in 2025, the early voting period was two weeks and the number of voters not waiting until election day continued to grow. On every day of early voting, turnout eclipsed the equivalent day in 2022, culminating in one million votes cast on Friday, 2 May. By election day, 37.5 per cent of those eligible had already voted. Combined with postal votes (which fell slightly after the Covid-19–era highs of 2022), more than 56 per cent of voters cast their vote before or outside election day proper. This creates additional strain on the AEC's temporary workforce and it is reasonable to suspect that the commission, major parties, minor parties and Independents will unite in seeking shorter pre-poll periods in future elections.

An external factor did not help matters: the National Rugby League's 'Magic Round' in Brisbane from 1 to 4 May enticed more than 150,000 voters into the city on election day. The AEC encouraged fans to vote before travelling and put in place additional capacity at Brisbane polling places on election day.

Reforms to the *Commonwealth Electoral Act 1918*

Although the Albanese government successfully reformed the *Electoral Act* in January 2025, major changes to the political finance regime (including donation and expenditure caps, lowered threshold for disclosures and seven-day timelines) will not be in place until the 2028 federal election. Other elements of the January 2025 legislation did impact this election—namely, prohibition of unauthorised filming inside a polling place and additional provision of convenience voting for people with a disability and their carers. Despite advocacy from some civil society groups, the provision to remove voters of 'unsound mind' from the electoral roll to prevent voter fraud was not removed, but the language was updated to modern standards.

Overview of the book

Landslide is the nineteenth in the series of federal election studies, which originated in 1987 and has been supported by the Academy of the Social Sciences in Australia since 1996. The series has evolved over time, along with the changing nature of federal elections: the erosion of the two-party system and the shift to digital campaigning. Authorship has also evolved to keep pace with techniques required by the new electoral landscape. Established scholars team up with early career researchers at home with the digital domain where so much campaigning now takes place.

The first part of the book has chapters comparing the campaign strategies of the major parties, the way the campaigns were reported in print and digital media and campaign commentary through memes, videos and cartoons. Podcasts with social media influencers were a new campaign tool in 2025 and parties also engaged in more humorous and satirical messaging on social media platforms such as TikTok and Instagram. Negative advertising appeared under the rubric of accounts such as 'Dutton cuts, you pay', 'Don't risk Dutton' and 'Teals revealed'.

The media chapter provides extensive evidence of how, in 2025, political actors had to navigate both legacy media (print, radio, television) and digital media platforms. The chapter analyses front-page stories as well as the issues prioritised in both traditional and digital media. Crucially, it measures online audience engagement with different topics and how the communication logic of social media influencers compounds the personalisation of politics.

The re-entry of religion into Australian electoral politics also features in Part 1, with new players and issues arising from the war in Gaza. Emotions ran high in some Sydney and Melbourne electorates, leading to unaccustomed incivility at polling places.

Another chapter analyses the familiar subject of political leadership in newer terms of competing models of protective masculinity: the 'strongman' who would keep Australia safe contrasted with a leader emphasising kindness and inclusion ('weak and woke', according to the Opposition). Also on a gender theme is a chapter contrasting the record number of women and Australians from diverse backgrounds elected to parliament with the failure of the Coalition to address gender issues, to their electoral detriment.

The populist discourse associated with the defeat of the Voice referendum in 2023 and with Donald Trump's successful presidential campaign played an interesting role in the 2025 election. The main vectors of this discourse are looked at here: the Murdoch media including Sky News, the digital campaigning organisation Advance, the minor parties Trumpet of Patriots and Pauline Hanson's One Nation and, intermittently, the Coalition.

The first part of the book ends with the management of disinformation by the AEC. Before the election there was considerable apprehension that its integrity might be threatened by artificial intelligence (AI)—in particular, by foreign actors. Fortunately, this threat did not materialise and the preventative work undertaken by the AEC continued to be widely admired.

Despite fears about the role AI might play in spreading disinformation, its main contribution was in repurposing popular culture content. The sharing and posting of memes remained a staple form of participation by citizen and partisan actors in 2025. And, as usual, the election book has a rich sample of visual material from the campaign.

The second part of the book discusses the campaign from the perspective of the four major political parties—Labor, Liberals, Nationals and Greens—together with the Community Independents (also known as Teals), other Independents and minor parties, and third-party organisations. Despite the exogenous factors such as Donald Trump, the landslide result for the Labor government can be primarily attributed to three interconnected endogenous factors: institutional learning from the 2019 defeat, the new Labor government's cautious, incremental record and its disciplined campaign strategy. The government followed a range of targeted, labourist strategies that served it well in difficult economic times.

The failure of the Liberals' campaign was also a factor. The Liberals went backwards again and suffered a disastrous election result, including the defeat of their leader, Peter Dutton. Their campaign demonstrated the party's lack of a coherent policy agenda and a failure to effectively prosecute its individual policies, including its 'big picture' policy proposals for nuclear and gas energy.

The Nationals were more successful than their Coalition partners, losing just a single seat in each of the House of Representatives and the Senate. Their electoral steadiness did not enable the Coalition to return to office, however, and raised bigger questions, such as their representativeness of rural and regional Australia and whether the party has reached a ceiling through which they are unable to break.

The Greens entered the campaign with significant ambitions. Their subnational performance had been solid since the 2022 election. Their campaign is evaluated here in relation to institutional context, interparty dynamics, policy consistency, narrative framing and organisational execution. The chapter explores the interaction between the party and ideologically adjacent, left-leaning Community Independents and the challenge of turning national support into local success.

The 2025 vote was an electoral test for the Community Independents Movement, in the absence of some of the key issues of 2022 such as anti-Morrison sentiment and a focus on climate change. The Community Independent campaigns were shaped by the specific dynamics of the electorates in which they were standing, making it difficult to present an overall summary. This chapter discusses the performance of incumbent MPs, repeat challengers and newcomers, and speculates about the future impact of movement fatigue and new campaign spending limits.

Other Independents included apostates from the major parties, established Independents and newer entrants, including pro-Palestinian Muslim candidates supported by Muslim community groups. Minor parties included Pauline Hanson's One Nation, which campaigned on immigration while not mentioning Trump and tried to soften Hanson's right-wing image. Clive Palmer's new Trumpet of Patriots party was big-spending and openly pro-Trump. Smaller minor parties represented lifestyle issues, local concerns and various ideological positions, mostly left-wing.

There was extensive digital campaigning by third-sector organisations, with Advance on the right and the Australian Council of Trade Unions (ACTU) on the left standing out. Despite progressive media outlets concentrating on Advance, it is argued here that the ACTU emerged as the dominant third-sector organisation, with its theme of 'Don't risk Dutton'. Other third-sector organisations active in the campaign included pro-nuclear and anti-nuclear organisations and bodies opposing the Greens and the Teals.

The final part of the book discusses how Australians voted on 3 May: from opinion polling throughout the campaign to analyses of the House and Senate results and of the sociodemographic factors, campaign dynamics and policy issues that shaped voters' decisions.

Major polling companies all correctly predicted the winner in 2025, but drastically underestimated Labor's two-party-preferred vote share. Despite continued growth in the number of published polls, including multilevel regression post-stratification (MRP) polls, there was little variation in results, both over the course of the campaign and between different companies. This might have reflected 'herding' among pollsters—one of the main criticisms of incorrect predictions at the 2019 election—but also possibly shared pessimism that Labor was really that far ahead. The Liberal Party's contracted pollster, Freshwater Strategy, was among the most pessimistic and was subsequently blamed for the Coalition's obliviousness to voter sentiment. Systemic errors in underestimating Labor's vote will likely be forgotten with time due to the overall 'correct' prediction but the polling industry's challenges, particularly with a more fragmented party system, will continue to mount.

That fragmentation was obscured by one of the great landslide wins in Australian elections: Labor won 94 seats in the House of Representatives, the Coalition won 43, Independents won 10, the Greens one, Katter's Australian Party (Bob Katter) one and Centre Alliance (Rebekha Sharkie) one. The result was clear early on election night (ABC chief election analyst Antony Green's last on air), although counting in individual seats continued for a full month post election.

The result was the most disproportionate outcome in an Australian federal election since 1943 and the advent of the current (mostly) two-party system. Labor won 34.6 per cent of the national primary vote and 63 per cent of seats in the House of Representatives. The result was simultaneously the party's best in terms of seat share in the modern period and its fourth worst in terms of primary vote. The Coalition's result was bleak all round: its worst primary vote share and its fourth worst seat share.

More than one-third of voters chose minor-party or Independent candidates in the House. While the Greens' primary vote was stable from 2022, the party lost three seats. The rest of the crossbench grew only by one seat in the House, despite a swing of 2.7 percentage points (and total vote share of 21.4 per cent). In total, 20 house seats changed hands, with 16 of those shifting from the Coalition to Labor (including Bennelong, which was notionally a Liberal-held seat after redistributions).

The large minor-party and Independent vote paid dividends in the Senate: the Greens retained all their seats, David Pocock was re-elected with an 18 per cent primary-vote swing, Jacqui Lambie was re-elected for her fourth term and One Nation gained two new senators. The Coalition was decimated, with 18 senators seeking re-election and only 13 winning. Labor gained three of the Coalition's Senate seats and One Nation the other two. One Nation appears to have benefited from its preference deal with the Coalition: the minor party received preferences from surplus Coalition votes that in previous years would have been exhausted. Additionally, by helping to normalise One Nation via the preference deal, the Coalition might have lost voters to the more conservative, less mainstream minor party.

Survey data on voters' decision-making suggest that the Coalition's focus on 'culture war' issues was damaging on both the right and the left. Although Dutton arguably scored a mid-term win with the defeat of the government's Voice referendum, Voice supporters who had previously supported the Coalition defected to Labor in large numbers. Labor successfully activated dissatisfaction with the Liberals' leadership and platform among moderate ex-Liberal voters. On the flipside, One Nation performed remarkably well and gained two Senate seats, leaving the Coalition stranded in between.

References

9News. 2025. 'Is the "Trump factor" to blame for election result?' *YouTube*, 3 May.

Burton, Melanie. 2025. 'Trump style governance? Australia's richest says yes, voters seem to disagree.' *Reuters*, 1 May. www.reuters.com/sustainability/climate-energy/australias-richest-person-says-she-wants-trump-like-reforms-election-nears-2025-05-01/.

Chowdhury, Intifar. 2025. 'This election young people held the most political power. Here's how they voted.' *The Conversation*, 16 May. theconversation. com/this-election-young-people-held-the-most-political-power-heres-how-they-voted-255769. doi.org/10.64628/AA.d5tncntqj.

Evans, Jake. 2025. 'Prime Minister leaves door open to calling election in days after Tropical Cyclone Alfred.' *ABC News*, 6 March. www.abc.net.au/news/2025-03-06/albanese-prime-minister-call-election-cyclone-alfred/105013996.

Megalogenis, George. 2025. 'Australia's Trump election.' *The Monthly*, April. www. themonthly.com.au/issue/2025/april/george-megalogenis/australia-s-trump-election.

Mills, Stephen. 2025. 'In an election that played out on social media as much as TV, do leaders' debates still matter?' *The Conversation*, 7 May. theconversation.com/in-an-election-that-played-out-on-social-media-as-much-as-tv-do-leaders-debates-still-matter-255771. doi.org/10.64628/AA.h9usda39j.

Part 1.
Campaign and context

2

Competing models of political leadership

Carol Johnson

Abstract

The 2025 Australian federal election highlighted the leadership contest between Labor's Anthony Albanese and the Coalition's Peter Dutton. Both leaders mobilised forms of identity politics. Dutton's strongman leadership competed with Albanese's softer, kinder image. Both leaders denigrated the other, evoking different conceptions of masculine identity. Dutton suggested Albanese was weak and woke and incapable of protecting Australians, uniting them or providing a prosperous future. Dutton argued Albanese had been neglecting the working class to pursue his woke objectives and failed to tackle the cost-of-living crisis. Albanese suggested that Dutton was aggressive, risky, fostered social division, picked on vulnerable Australians and had opposed Labor's cost-of-living measures. This rhetorical contest positioned a weak male against a rogue male. Dutton's top-down style of leadership contributed to campaign missteps. Albanese's more collaborative style was praised by his colleagues. Meanwhile, US President Trump's disruptive actions caused problems for Dutton's strongman image.

Keywords: Peter Dutton; Anthony Albanese; political leadership; gender; identity politics; Trump

The 2025 election campaigns highlighted the leadership contest between two leaders who had been honing their identities for several years and articulating different forms of identity politics. Anthony Albanese's image reflected a 'new politics' that emphasised inclusion, diversity, wellbeing and kindness. Peter Dutton's image projected a strong leader, who would make the tough decisions, keep Australia safe and emphasise unity over diversity. Both promised a prosperous future, albeit Albanese's was built on renewable energy and Dutton's on nuclear power. Dutton depicted Albanese as divisive, weak and woke. Albanese depicted Dutton as fostering fear, division and picking on vulnerable minorities. Both leadership images evoked forms of protective masculinity in which a male leader promises to protect Australians, albeit taking significantly different forms.

Dutton's strongman persona initially appeared to be cutting through in the polls. Although a minority Labor government remained the most likely outcome, there were times when a minority Coalition government also appeared possible (see Chapter 19, this volume). Albanese's image had been damaged by the Voice referendum defeat. Government attempts to tackle the cost-of-living crisis were being undermined by inflation and high interest rates. It will be argued here that various issues, from a poor Liberal campaign to the impact of Trump, had major implications for the leadership contest and contributed to the Liberals' massive defeat. Meanwhile, the exceptional result appeared to vindicate Albanese's leadership image and strategy, confirming his place in the pantheon of Labor leaders (despite Labor's low primary vote). The discussion in this chapter will begin by focusing on Peter Dutton as leader before progressing to discuss Anthony Albanese's leadership.

The importance of leadership

The analysis in this chapter reinforces international and Australian research demonstrating the important role of political leadership, although policy continues to play a significant, albeit interconnected, role (Rhodes and 't Hart 2014; Kefford 2013: 140–43). It reinforces longstanding research indicating that party leaders have 'become symbols of who we are, personifications of our way of life and our deepest beliefs' (Little 1988: 2) and that, as prime minister Alfred Deakin noted more than a century ago, the 'personality of the leader' becomes a major issue (Walter 2010: 110). The image, personality and discourse of political leaders are therefore particularly important as they mobilise competing visions and emotions (see, for example, Feldman 2020; Walter 2010: 341). Furthermore, while there is a long history of gender playing an important role in Australian political leadership contests (Johnson 2021), the 2025 election saw a particularly overt contest between different forms of masculine leadership, at a time when debates about the nature of masculinity are part of the cultural zeitgeist (see Chapter 6, this volume).

Peter Dutton's leadership image and style

Dutton built his authoritarian strongman image long before becoming leader (emphasising his former role as a police officer rather than as a successful property developer). His previous Liberal government ministerial roles in Immigration, Border Protection, Home Affairs and Defence saw him depicted as the Coalition's authoritarian 'hard man'. Dutton targeted ethnic minorities, from Lebanese Muslim migrants to African gangs, introduced tough measures against asylum-seekers, urged tougher policing of climate change protesters and deported criminal non-citizens (Blaine 2024). Dutton was a longstanding China hawk, despite (unsuccessfully) trying to not alienate Chinese Australian voters during the campaign (Sun 2025). Although promising to show a broader, smiling persona when first becoming leader (Evans 2022), Dutton increasingly contrasted his claimed strong, tough leadership with Albanese's claimed weak one.

In short, Dutton depicted himself as a strong male leader who would make the tough decisions that were necessary to ensure a bright economic future for Australians, while also ensuring their personal and national security. His conservative identity politics potentially evoked both fear of and resentment towards outgroups while making socially conservative Australians feel protected. Like John Howard, whose influence Dutton (Clennell 2025) acknowledged, Dutton disagreed with views emphasising the structural disadvantage experienced by groups ranging from women to Indigenous Australians (see further Johnson 2025). For Dutton (2025a), 'egalitarianism' involved 'pushing back on identity politics' (which he identified only with the left) and largely treating people the same. Consequently, the proposed Indigenous Voice to Parliament was depicted as an anti-egalitarian measure that would give some Australians more political rights than others (Commonwealth of Australia 2023). Similarly, Howard government Indigenous affairs policy interpreted 'social unity as a form of equality based on identical treatment and uniform political processes' (Robbins 2007).

Dutton therefore depicted himself as a leader who supported the unity of the Australian people, while Labor policies fostered division. He declared that he would only stand in front of one Australian flag, rather than including the Aboriginal and Torres Strait Islander flags, because: 'We are united as a country when we gather under one flag', while multiple flags involved 'dividing our country unnecessarily' (Evans 2024). Similarly, Dutton claimed Welcome to Country ceremonies were overdone and potentially divisive (Butler and Belot 2025).

Such culture war identity politics strategies were central to Dutton's plan for winning workers in the outer suburbs away from Labor. He declared: 'Just as we are the party of small and family businesses, we are also the party of the worker. In this, we represent two constituencies who have been forgotten and forsaken by the modern Labor Party' (Dutton 2024a). He claimed that Labor had supported elite 'woke advocates' while neglecting the economic concerns of ordinary Australians:

> [F]or the first 16 months of their term, the Prime Minister and his Government were fixated on winning the Voice referendum. They spent $450 million on the 'Yes' campaign but did nothing to alleviate cost-of-living pressures for Australian families or businesses when they were crying out for help. (Dutton 2024a)

Furthermore, he said, such government spending increased inflation (Dutton 2024a).

Consequently, Dutton claimed to be more in touch with working-class values as a leader than was Albanese:

> [P]eople in areas like Kallangur and Strathpine … they're working class Australians, many of them voted for the Labor Party at the last election, but they're not going to vote for the Labor Party at the next election because the Labor Party has left them and their ideals and their values … The Prime Minister has a seat, unlike mine, where he's listening constantly to elites. (Dutton 2023)

The arguments evoking the people versus elites reflected the populism at the heart of Dutton's leadership strategy (see Chapter 4, this volume).

Dutton also tried to address the Coalition's 'women problem' by depicting himself as a strongman protector of women, arguing that 'I've always been serious in my public life as a police officer and since I've been in Parliament … in protecting people', particularly 'women and children' (Albanese and

Dutton 2025). Dutton's protective masculinity (Johnson 2021) also took other forms, including protecting Australians generally from the claimed depredations of wokeness, ranging from Indigenous issues to transgender women in sport. He would protect Australians from China, criticising Albanese's claimed weak response to Chinese warships being close to Australian waters. He would protect Australians from asylum-seekers, including refugees from Gaza, whom he claimed had not been screened properly by the government for possible terrorist sympathies. He would protect Australians from criminal asylum-seekers being released from detention after a High Court decision. He would protect Australians from the cost of renewable energy, from high government debt and the resulting inflation. Overall, he would protect Australians from a weak Australian government that was incapable of standing up for them. He would be a good cop to those Australians he favoured and a bad cop to those he opposed. In short, Dutton (Lipson 2025) would be the strong male leader who would get Australia 'back on track'—in the words of a slogan used in the 2023 New Zealand election, but also reminiscent of Trump's 'Make America great again'.

Dutton's leadership and Trump

Dutton's electoral leadership strategy was also reminiscent of John Howard's campaigns against political correctness and 'black-armband history' to wean 'Howard's battlers' away from Labor. Blaine (2024: 7), however, argues that where Howard used a 'dog whistle', Dutton used a 'foghorn' and Bongiorno (2025) suggests that Dutton's vision was a particularly bleak one. Howard's approach had longer-term US roots in Richard Nixon's so-called Southern strategy and its subsequent developments (Maxwell and Shields 2019). The more recent US influence of Donald Trump was reflected in Dutton's claim during the Voice referendum campaign that the AEC's referendum process was 'rigged' (Basford Canales 2023). His opposition to multiple flags and work from home (WFH) also revealed Trump-style influences (Gedeon and Roth 2025; The White House 2025). Similarly, echoing the Trump campaign's slogan against so-called gender ideology— 'Kamala's for they/them. President Trump is for you' (McLaughlin 2024)— Dutton announced:

> [W]hen I see a Government that is more interested in pronouns than they are in people, it starts to become a real problem. If you can't pay your mortgage and you can't pay your electricity bill, and there's uncertainty at work, or you own a small business and numbers are down by 30 per cent, and you hear the Government talking about the Voice and all of these sorts of issues, well you get angry and you respond. I think that has happened in the United States and I think there's a big likelihood that it happens here in Australia as well. (Dutton 2024b)

Dutton therefore initially positioned himself as a Trump-style leader. He claimed there would be 'a near revolution' against political correctness 'that comes with the Trump administration' because 'a lot of the woke issues that might be fashionable in universities and at the ABC … just aren't cutting it around kitchen tables at the moment where people can't pay their bills' (cited in Maiden 2025a). In other Trumpian moves, as well as appointing Jacinta Nampijinpa Price to a shadow government efficiency portfolio, Dutton initially advocated cutting 'culture, diversity and inclusion adviser' positions in the public service, claiming they 'do nothing to improve the lives of everyday Australians' (Dutton 2025b). Dutton also claimed that young men in the United States and elsewhere were angry and had 'had enough' of missing out to diversity hires and being depicted as 'ogres' (cited in Maiden 2025b; see further Chapter 6, this volume).

Dutton wanted the Albanese government to have a 'man problem' (see further Johnson 2024a) that would help counter the Coalition's 'women problem', both by appealing to men directly and by emasculating Albanese. Similarly, Howard had tried to emasculate then Labor leader Kim Beazley by suggesting he 'lacked a ticker' (Johnson 2021: 15). However, the chaos, economic disruption and uncertainty arising from the Trump tariffs early in the election campaign soon made Dutton's association with Trump's form of strongman politics less desirable. Senator Michaelia Cash (2025) initially claimed that Trump's trade policies showed 'he's a man of action' and Australians would 'get the exact same attitude under a Peter Dutton government'. Nonetheless, Dutton soon distanced himself from Trump, instead emphasising Howard's influence (Albanese and Dutton 2025). Liberal advertisements belatedly—and largely unsuccessfully—tried to soften Dutton's image (ABC 2025). A few days before the election, a senior Liberal MP claimed that 'the single biggest factor is Trump … He has just smashed us' (Maiden 2025c)—an analysis endorsed by some independent commentators (Brent 2025).

Here, as elsewhere, Dutton's vision of protecting Australia from weakness and wokeness and getting Australia 'back on track' to being a unified, economically prosperous society failed to cut through.

Labor and Albanese's leadership

While Dutton projected a tough, strongman version of protective masculinity, Albanese projected a softer, kinder version of masculinity like that of some other male leaders internationally such as Barack Obama, David Cameron and Joe Biden (Johnson 2022). Closer to home, he was also channelling Bob Hawke's focus on bringing people together and Jacinda Ardern's emphasis on kindness (Johnson 2021, 2022). He was, in the words of Blair Williams, a 'state daddy' (see Chapter 6, this volume). He emphasised his backstory as the son of a disabled mother who grew up in social housing and could therefore empathise with others less fortunate than himself.

Albanese explained how he saw his leadership role early in his period of office in interviews for a *Quarterly Essay* written by Katharine Murphy (2022). Albanese depicted himself as a leader who would best represent the 'new politics' of Australia. That 'new politics' involved a decline in primary votes for major parties but valued inclusion, diversity, aspiration and positivity, championed dialogue over division and acted on issues such as climate change.

Albanese (2025a) emphasised that Labor's agenda did not mimic overseas developments, as he suggested the Coalition's did, but would draw on Australia's values to create a strong future in which there would be '[n]o-one held back, no-one left behind. Every one of us, Building Australia's Future, together.' Meanwhile, Labor projected Albanese as being a calm, considered and steady leader who was methodically fixing the economy, addressing cost-of-living issues and pressing ahead with a plan for Australia's future in uncertain times (ALP 2025).

Labor introduced a raft of related policies covering areas including manufacturing, climate change, education, Medicare, building homes, foreign relations, social diversity, skills training for tradies and men's mental health (ALP 2025). Consequently, Albanese (2025c) contrasted his government's plans with the Liberals, who offered '[n]o proposals of their own, just militant opposition to our cost of living measures and mindless negativity'.

Albanese also repeatedly criticised Dutton's leadership, countering Coalition accusations that he was weak and woke and promoting an alternative version of masculine leadership in the process:

> Peter Dutton seems to think that bluster and yelling and interrupting and being rude is strength. It's not. One of the things that you have to do as a leader is show kindness and compassion to the vulnerable. That's part of who I am. It's part of my character. That's not weakness. Strength is having the capacity to go to the National Press Club, as I did, and say we are going to change the tax cuts that have been legislated because we don't want some people to be left behind. (Albanese 2025b)

When asked, 'What do you say to the opposition claims that you're too soft, that you're too wishy washy? Do we need more of a hard man in such uncertain times?', Albanese responded: '[I]t's just rhetoric. Kindness isn't weakness' (Albanese and Dutton 2025). Albanese also emphasised that he had made tough decisions to bring in a budget surplus, deal with Trump, Chinese President Xi Jinping and Russian President Vladimir Putin, and 'you don't get to be Prime Minister and to lead the Labor Party without a toughness' (Albanese and Dutton 2025). In contrast, Albanese (2025c) accused Dutton of not being tough enough to face the National Press Club while making derogatory comments about journalists—for example, calling the ABC 'hate media', which 'say[s] more about his temperament than anything else'.

When asked whether Donald Trump had advantaged him and disadvantaged Dutton by 'darkening the brand of hardman leaders', Albanese accused Dutton of divisively attacking the vulnerable, while he tried to bring people together:

> I think Peter Dutton has darkened his own brand. He has made a career out of promoting division, about punching down on vulnerable people, about seeking to divide the community, engaging in culture wars. What I've done is to try and bring people together. (Albanese 2025b)

Nonetheless, despite his support for social diversity, Albanese also attempted to counter Dutton's accusations that he was woke by defusing some potential culture war issues. For example, Albanese ruled out measures that would prevent religious organisations discriminating against LGBTQIA+ persons in the absence of bipartisan support (Razik 2025). Albanese initially tried to cancel proposed Australian Bureau of Statistics census questions on sexuality and gender identity, although eventually partially backed down (ABS 2024). Albanese was also accused of reneging on previous commitments regarding the Indigenous Makarrata commission process of Treaty and Truth-Telling after the Voice referendum defeat (Allam 2024).

However, Albanese highlighted his support for women while suggesting that Dutton was out of touch:

> [L]ook at their proposal to ban Working from Home. Last month, Peter Dutton said that women who couldn't be in the office 5 days a week should just 'job share'. A statement that is so out of touch with the lives of modern families and the flexibility that working from home gives parents in particular. It also fundamentally misunderstands the national productivity benefit of supporting greater opportunity for women and the essential right of women to make their own choices about their own careers. (Albanese 2025c)

Albanese also repeatedly countered Dutton's arguments that the government had not been standing up for workers, suggesting that the Liberals posed a major (American-style) threat:

> [W]e've understood that we don't want to go down the American road of people having to rely on tips to get by … A Labor government will always stand up for fairness in the workplace, not undermining wages and conditions. Or … sacking public servants so you can hire more consultants at higher rates, which seems to be their vision. (Albanese 2025d)

Labor campaign material suggested that Australians would 'be worse off under Dutton', who had opposed multiple government cost-of-living measures, and that 'he cuts, you pay' (Giles 2025).

In short, Labor's campaign message emphasised that Albanese would protect all Australians and build a stronger future, while Dutton was depicted as a risky social and economic threat.

The outcome

As late as 3–4 March, Newspoll (Benson 2025) was showing a two-party-preferred vote for Labor of 49 per cent and 51 per cent for the Coalition. Australian Labor Party (ALP) National Secretary and campaign director Paul Erickson (2025) acknowledged such initial poll concerns but put

Labor's victory down to two key leadership messages: 'Anthony Albanese was the only leader with a plan to make Australians better off over the next three years … And in uncertain times Peter Dutton was not a risk worth taking.' Erickson also argued that Dutton's attempt to frame the leadership contest as strength versus weakness highlighted issues with Dutton's own character, and 'the very aggressive approach in some of the debates actually turned a lot of people off' (Boscaini 2025). Erickson claimed:

> [E]ven before our campaign amplified these facts, our research identified some deeper reservations about Peter Dutton. One year ago, our target voters already believed they would be worse off under a Dutton government because of the risk posed by Peter Dutton's character. His recklessness concerned them and made them worry about what kind of Prime Minister he would be. His aggression and intolerance unsettled people. And above all his hard-headedness, his lack of empathy and his lack of understanding of ordinary people's lives kept coming to the fore. (Erickson 2025)

It was a message that Labor repeatedly hammered home, along with suggesting that Dutton was trying to introduce foreign ideas. In Erickson's (2025) words:

> Was he focused on Australians who were looking for the party with the best plan to make them better off over the next three years? Or was his priority winning over voters who were looking for an Australian variation on MAGA [Make America Great Again]?

In contrast, Erickson (2025) claimed that the 'Prime Minister offered authentic, measured and firm leadership' that was also 'steady', whereas Dutton's 'back on track' slogan meant taking Australia 'backwards':

> Back to the cuts of the Coalition's decade in power, with a promise to slash billions that would put the Abbott–Hockey budget in the shade. Back to the relentless, confected division of culture wars and punching down. And back to the evidence-free, politics-first approach to energy that held the country back the last time the Coalition were in power. (Erickson 2025)

Erickson was not alone in praising Albanese. Treasurer Jim Chalmers gave a significant tribute to Albanese's leadership qualities both in office, by facilitating 'effective cabinet government', and during the campaign:

> [O]ne of the defining characteristics of our government is Anthony sets a tone of being an inclusive leader and we all enjoy working in that context … It's probably never been a better time to be a senior minister … Anthony … has led from the front and when things were looking dicey towards the end of last year … he came out of the blocks … I think in 10 or 20 years' time they will be writing about this Albanese effort in this campaign. (Chalmers 2025)

Admittedly, such sentiments may not have been shared by those Labor figures Albanese did not favour, such as Tanya Plibersek. Nonetheless, such celebrations were very different from many comments made about Dutton's leadership. Dutton did make key mistakes (discussed elsewhere in this book) that undermined his own leadership pitch—for example, flying out of Queensland to attend a Sydney fundraiser in the days before Cyclone Alfred was projected to hit and saying he wanted to live in Sydney in Kirribilli House rather than the Lodge in Canberra. In particular, the WFH policy debacle—meant to be a populist attack on public servants—just made him seem out of touch with women and modern families, while the subsequent backtracking made him seem indecisive and weak. He admitted wrongly attributing comments to the Indonesian President regarding Russian bases. The failure to adequately justify, explain or cost his nuclear policy similarly counted against him as Labor repeatedly suggested that Dutton's nuclear plan was not only risky but also would need massive cuts to fund it; as did backflips on energy policies such as tax breaks for electric vehicles. Admittedly, other members of the Liberal leadership team, such as shadow treasurer Angus Taylor, also failed to present Dutton with ideas and a persuasive narrative. Furthermore, any leader's strategy would have been hampered by spectacularly poor Coalition polling.

Nonetheless, some errors were related to Dutton's strongman leadership persona. A Liberal insider reportedly complained that Dutton 'wanted to steer the ship. He wanted to design the ads. He wanted to set the agenda. He wanted to run the campaign. He basically steered the ship onto the rocks' (Campbell 2025b). Other insiders complained that shadow ministers had been excluded from decision-making (Chambers and Brown 2025); that the culture in Dutton's office encouraged a bunker mentality and groupthink, while Dutton 'surrounded himself with uber right-wing advisers and blokes. It's all monotone opinion in the leader's office … no one challenges or puts an alternative view' (Campbell 2025a). Even allowing for senior Liberals wishing to distance themselves from such a spectacular campaign loss, it seems clear that there were dysfunctional elements in both

Dutton's leadership style and his office, although admittedly, lack of policy detail may sometimes have resulted from Dutton's unenviable task of trying to hold together a very divided party room.

Meanwhile, according to one insider, staff did not want to tell Dutton that his own seat was at risk because Dutton performed best when he was confident and 'we didn't want to make Dutton nervous and he was already a nervous wreck. We were trying to manage him' (Campbell 2025b). That comment resonates with Lech Blaine's (2024: 114) claim that Dutton was '[t]all and strong at first glance. But when you watch him for a long time, you can see that the man is small and scared.' Dutton may not have been quite as tough a leader as he tried to portray.

Dutton's strongman leadership played particularly poorly with women (see Chapter 6, this volume). However, Dutton's strategy of using culture war arguments to try to win over working-class voters in the outer suburbs (thereby neglecting inner-city Teal seats) also did not work. This may not just be due, as pollsters such as Kos Samaras suggest, to WFH policies alienating working women and their families or to demographic changes, from the increasingly multicultural nature of working-class communities (Giannini 2025) to the increasing youth vote. After all, not only are some similar demographic changes taking place overseas with different electoral outcomes (Chowdhury 2025), they also cannot fully explain the Coalition's more favourable position in earlier polls. So, while such factors may partly explain what happened, another part of the answer may lie in a key difference between the Howard era and Dutton's.

Howard did use culture war identity politics strategies to try to lure socially conservative working-class voters away from Labor. However, Howard-era Labor was committed to a neoliberal-influenced policy that had resulted in wage restraint and real wage cuts—albeit with claimed compensatory 'social wage' government benefits (Johnson 2019: 119–20). This enabled Howard to boast that wages had risen more under the Coalition than under Labor (Howard 2005), thereby making it easier for him to argue that Labor had neglected workers by favouring politically correct policies and minority groups. By contrast, wages had stagnated under the most recent Coalition governments and Dutton had opposed key Albanese government attempts to improve wages and conditions (Johnson 2024b: 207–12).

The reasons for the Coalition's defeat were therefore varied and complex. However, Albanese's election night victory speech suggested that the result was an outcome of the 'new politics', and his leadership strategy for addressing it, which he had outlined to Katharine Murphy back in 2022. His vision, message and values had triumphed over Dutton's:

> Today, the Australian people have voted for Australian values. For fairness, aspiration and opportunity for all. For the strength to show courage in adversity and kindness to those in need … A future built on everything that brings us together as Australians and everything that sets our nation apart from the world. In this time of global uncertainty, Australians have chosen optimism and determination …
>
> [N]o matter who you voted for, no matter where you live, no matter how you worship, or who you love. Whether you belong to a culture that has known and cared for this continent for 65,000 years or you have chosen our nation as your home and enriched our society with your contribution. We are all Australians. (Albanese 2025e)

In short, Albanese argued that his vision of a present and future Australia had soundly defeated Dutton's retrograde vision of getting Australia 'back on track' and that he was advocating an inclusionary identity politics versus a claimed exclusionary one. (While this chapter focuses on the Labor–Liberal leadership contest, Dutton's socially conservative leadership strategy clearly also had implications for the Liberals' poor performance against the Teals, with only one seat being won back and another lost.)

Conclusion

Election outcomes are determined by numerous factors. Nonetheless, this was an election in which the issue of leadership was emphasised by both the Coalition and Labor. The leaders also evoked different forms of the politics of identity, ranging from contrasting masculine personas to attitudes to social diversity. Both leaders depicted themselves as protecting Australians in ways that their opponent would not. Dutton's leadership strategy and style were derivative of Howard and Trump but arguably lacked Howard's skill and nuance, while his evocation of Trump eventually proved a liability. Dutton attempted to sell himself as a strongman leader, facing a 'weak and woke' opponent. However, his leadership pitch was unsuccessful, sometimes due to own goals as policy vacuums and backflips undermined a sense of reassuring consistency and sometimes due to Labor's attempts to frame Dutton as not a strong leader but a cruel, bullying one who punched down on vulnerable groups, backflipped on policy, was out of touch with ordinary Australians, particularly women, was reckless and did not have the temperament, including calmness and stability, that was required for a leader in uncertain times.

Dutton had wanted Albanese to have a 'man problem'. However, in the end, it was Dutton who had a 'man problem', in terms of both a protective masculinity failure that saw him constructed as risky and being too closely associated with an increasingly alarming US strongman leader. By contrast, Albanese framed himself as an inclusive male leader who was kind, not weak; a protective leader, who would stand up for all Australians in their diversity while sensibly and calmly managing uncertain, uncharted times. Furthermore, his leadership style had facilitated an incredibly disciplined and competent Labor campaign, whereas Dutton's had contributed to a dysfunctional one. Meanwhile, Albanese seems convinced that his strategic vision of a new politics, so badly dented by the Voice referendum defeat, is alive and well again.

The Liberals are now potentially moving away from strongman leaders, with new leader Sussan Ley proclaiming: 'Peter Dutton and I have different styles, we're different personalities, and I will bring a different approach to my leadership' (cited in Maiden 2025d). Whether that leadership style can help rebuild the Liberals after a disastrous election defeat remains to be seen, particularly given ongoing policy and ideological divisions within the party and Coalition, including over the effectiveness of Howard-era culture war strategies. It also remains to be seen whether Albanese's assessment of the 'new politics' is correct and whether it will help consolidate a long period of Labor rule. The answers depend on multiple factors, including how much Labor's victory was due to its own efforts and demographic change or how greatly factors such as an unpopular leader, a poor campaign and Trump contributed to the Coalition's massive defeat.

References

Albanese, Anthony. 2025a. 'Address to Labor campaign launch: Building Australia's future.' Speech, 13 April. Transcript available: anthonyalbanese.com.au/media-centre/address-to-labor-campaign-launch-building-australias-future.

Albanese, Anthony. 2025b. 'Interview.' *7.30*, [*ABC TV*], 28 April. Transcript available: anthonyalbanese.com.au/media-centre/television-abc-7-30.

Albanese, Anthony. 2025c. 'National Press Club speech.' Canberra, 30 April. Transcript available: anthonyalbanese.com.au/media-centre/new-article-1746058885351.

Albanese, Anthony. 2025d. 'National Press Club Q&A.' Canberra, 30 April. Transcript available: anthonyalbanese.com.au/media-centre/national-press-club-q-a.

Albanese, Anthony. 2025e. 'Election night speech.' 3 May. Transcript available: www.pm.gov.au/media/election-night.

Albanese, Anthony, and Peter Dutton. 2025. 'The great debate.' *Nine Network*, 22 April. 9now.com.au/the-great-debate [page discontinued].

Allam, Lorena. 2024. 'What is makarrata and has Albanese broken an election promise?' *The Guardian*, 5 August. www.theguardian.com/australia-news/article/2024/aug/05/what-is-makarrata-anthony-albanese-controversy-indigenous-leaders.

Australian Broadcasting Corporation (ABC). 2025. 'Should the Liberal Party be softening Peter Dutton's image?' *Gruen Nation*, [*ABC TV*], 1 May. www.youtube.com/watch?v=MxOJ1kuILXw.

Australian Bureau of Statistics (ABS). 2024. 'New questions for the 2024 census test.' Media release, 13 September. Canberra: Australian Bureau of Statistics. www.abs.gov.au/census/census-media-hub/releases-and-statements/on-the-record/new-questions-2024-census-test [page discontinued].

Australian Labor Party (ALP). 2025. *Building Australia's Future*. [Online]. Canberra: Australian Labor Party. alp.org.au/policies.

Basford Canales, Sarah. 2023. 'AEC hits back after Peter Dutton suggests Voice referendum rules are "rigged".' *The Guardian*, 25 August. www.theguardian.com/australia-news/2023/aug/25/indigenous-voice-to-parliament-referendum-aec-poll-unfairness-claims-rejected.

Benson, Simon. 2025. 'Final Newspoll: PM to defy historic major party slump.' *The Australian*. 2 May. www.theaustralian.com.au/nation/politics/final-newspoll-pm-to-defy-historic-major-party-slump/news-story/4589224ac1b653daecc5057e1138e0cc?amp&nk=a78267e86c9267167cae4a5a36151049-1746182148.

Blaine, Lech. 2024. 'Bad cop: Peter Dutton's strongman politics.' *Quarterly Essay*, no. 93.

Bongiorno, Frank. 2025. 'Uncertainty and pessimism abound. Will fear be enough to push Dutton into office?' *The Conversation*, 31 March. theconversation.com/uncertainty-and-pessimism-abound-will-fear-be-enough-to-push-dutton-into-office-247360. doi.org/10.64628/AA.gjfr6kjxv.

Boscaini, Joshua. 2025. 'ICYMI: Paul Erickson explains Labor's campaign success at National Press Club.' *ABC News*, 21 May. www.abc.net.au/news/2025-05-21/federal-politics-may-21-coalition-liberal-nationals-labor/105315946?utm_campaign=abc_news_web&utm_content=link&utm_medium=content_shared&utm_source=abc_news_web#live-blog-post-182453.

Brent, Peter. 2025. 'Labor's Trump card goes missing.' *Inside Story*, 27 May. insidestory.org.au/trump-goes-missing/.

Butler, Josh, and Henry Belot. 2025. 'Dutton claims majority of veterans don't want welcome to country at Anzac Day ceremonies.' *The Guardian*, 28 April. www.theguardian.com/australia-news/2025/apr/28/dutton-claims-majority-of-veterans-dont-want-welcome-to-country-at-anzac-day-ceremonies-ntwnfb.

Campbell, James. 2025a. 'Where the Libs went off track.' *Advertiser*, 1 May: 6.

Campbell, James. 2025b. '"A nervous wreck": What Dutton's inner circle didn't tell him.' *Herald Sun*, 5 May. www.heraldsun.com.au/news/national/federalelection/already-a-nervous-wreck-what-peter-duttons-inner-circle-didnt-tell-him-about-dickson/news-story/c9aadcaf127017b89c97291fc58ddce3.

Cash, Michaelia. *2025*. Response to question on the *Today Show*, [*Nine Network*], 3 February. Transcript available: www.michaeliacash.com.au/federal-news/transcript/transcript-the-today-show-4/.

Chalmers, Jim. 2025. 'Video: Jim Chalmers pays tribute to Anthony Albanese's leadership.' *ABC Election Panel*, [*ABC TV*], 3 May. www.abc.net.au/news/2025-05-03/jim-chalmers-pays-tribute-to-anthony-albanese/105248320.

Chambers, Geoff, and Greg Brown. 2025. 'Sleepwalking to disaster: How Coalition missed all the warnings.' *The Australian*, 5 May: 1.

Chowdhury, Intifar. 2025. 'I looked at 35 years of data to see how Australians vote. Here's what it tells us about the next election.' *The Conversation*, 21 February. theconversation.com/i-looked-at-35-years-of-data-to-see-how-australians-vote-heres-what-it-tells-us-about-the-next-election-249368. doi.org/10.64628/AA.gm4r7nwar.

Clennell, Andrew. 2025. 'Interview with Peter Dutton.' *Sunday Agenda*, [*Sky News*], 16 February. Transcript available: webarchive.nla.gov.au/awa/20250224010559/https://peterdutton.com.au/leader-of-the-opposition-transcript-interview-with-andrew-clennell-sunday-agenda-sky-news/.

Commonwealth of Australia. 2023. *Parliamentary Debates*. House of Representatives, 22 May: 3237.

Dutton, Peter. 2023. 'Address to the Liberal National Party (LNP) State Convention, Eatons Hill.' 21 October. Brisbane: Peter Dutton Media. www.peterdutton. com.au/leader-of-the-opposition-transcript-address-to-the-liberal-national-party-lnp-state-convention-eatons-hill/ [page discontinued].

Dutton, Peter. 2024a. 'Address to the Council of Small Business Organisations Australia National Small Business Summit 2024, Sydney.' April. Brisbane: Peter Dutton Media. www.peterdutton.com.au/leader-of-the-opposition-transcript-address-to-the-council-of-small-business-organisations-australia-national-small-business-summit-2024-sydney/ [page discontinued].

Dutton, Peter. 2024b. 'Interview with Ray Hadley, 2GB.' [Radio interview]. 7 November. Brisbane: Peter Dutton Media. www.peterdutton.com.au/leader-of-the-opposition-transcript-interview-with-ray-hadley-2gb-29/ [page discontinued].

Dutton, Peter. 2025a. 'Address to the Coalition campaign rally Mount Waverley.' 12 January. Brisbane: Peter Dutton Media. peterdutton.com.au/leader-of-the-opposition-transcript-address-to-the-coalition-campaign-rally-mount-waverley/ [page discontinued].

Dutton, Peter. 2025b. 'The echoes of history.' Economic address to the Menzies Research Centre, Sydney, 31 January. Transcript available: web.archive.org/web/20250216173309/https://www.peterdutton.com.au/leader-of-the-opposition-transcript-economic-address-to-the-menzies-research-centre-sydney/.

Erickson, Paul. 2025. 'Campaign director's address: Paul Erickson, ALP National Secretary.' National Press Club, Canberra, 21 May. Transcript available: alp.org.au/national-secretary-media/250521-campaign-directors-address-to-the-national-press-club/.

Evans, Jake. 2022. 'Peter Dutton becomes the new Liberal Party leader, as the Coalition enters the wilderness.' *ABC News*, 30 May. www.abc.net.au/news/2022-05-30/who-is-new-liberal-leader-peter-dutton/101091410.

Evans, Jake. 2024. 'Peter Dutton won't stand beside Indigenous flags at press events if elected prime minister.' *ABC News*, 10 December. www.abc.net.au/news/2024-12-10/dutton-wont-use-indigenous-flags-at-press-as-prime-minister/104706118.

Feldman, Ofer, ed. 2020. *The Rhetoric of Political Leadership: Logic and Emotion in Public Discourse*. Cheltenham: Edward Elgar. doi.org/10.4337/9781789904581.

Gedeon, Joseph, and Andrew Roth. 2025. 'Trump administration bans non-US flags from being flown at embassies.' *The Guardian*, 24 January. www.theguardian.com/us-news/2025/jan/23/trump-administration-bans-non-us-flags-from-being-flown-at-embassies.

Giannini, Dominic. 2025. 'Why history might hold the answer for stricken Liberals.' *The Canberra Times*, 17 May. www.canberratimes.com.au/story/8969273/why-history-might-hold-the-answer-for-stricken-liberals/.

Giles, Andrew. 2025. 'You'll be worse off under Dutton.' Instagram post. www.instagram.com/reel/DFlyCCOssiI/.

Howard, John. 2005. 'Address to the Liberal Party Victorian Division State Council Melbourne University, Hawthorn.' 2 April. Canberra: Department of the Prime Minister and Cabinet. Transcript available: pmtranscripts.pmc.gov.au/release/transcript-21663.

Johnson, Carol. 2019. *Social Democracy and the Crisis of Equality: Australian Social Democracy in a Changing World*. Singapore: Springer. doi.org/10.1007/978-981-13-6299-6.

Johnson, Carol. 2021. 'The gendered identities of Australian political leaders: From Hawkie to ScoMo.' In *Gender Politics: Navigating Political Leadership in Australia*, edited by Zareh Ghazarian and Katrina Lee-Koo, 11–23. Sydney: NewSouth Publishing.

Johnson, Carol. 2022. 'Feeling protected: Protective masculinity and femininity from Donald Trump and Joe Biden to Jacinda Ardern.' *Emotions and Society* 4, no. 1: 7–26. doi.org/10.1332/263169021X16310949038420.

Johnson, Carol. 2024a. 'Good cop, bad cop.' *Inside Story*, 20 March. insidestory.org.au/good-cop-bad-cop/.

Johnson, Carol. 2024b. *The Politics of Gender Equality: Australian Lessons in an Uncertain World*. Cham: Palgrave Macmillan. doi.org/10.1007/978-3-031-64816-8.

Johnson, Carol. 2025. 'When "equal" does not mean "the same": Liberals still do not understand their women problem.' *The Conversation*, 24 April. doi.org/10.64628/AA.hfgatpsck.

Kefford, Glenn. 2013. 'The presidentialisation of Australian politics? Kevin Rudd's leadership of the Australian Labor Party.' *Australian Journal of Political Science* 48, no. 2: 135–46. doi.org/10.1080/10361146.2013.786676.

Lipson, David. 2025. 'Dutton launches election pitch.' *AM*, [*ABC Radio*], 13 January. www.abc.net.au/listen/programs/am/dutton-launches-election-pitch/104809970.

Little, Graham. 1988. *Strong Leadership: Thatcher, Reagan and an Eminent Person*. Melbourne: Oxford University Press.

Maiden, Samantha. 2025a. '"Had enough": Peter Dutton predicts anti-woke revolution for Australia.' *News.com.au*, 22 January. www.news.com.au/national/had-enough-peter-dutton-predicts-antiwoke-revolution-for-australia/news-story/f71438a3a3b328256a2acb6a061bcb07.

Maiden, Samantha. 2025b. 'Peter Dutton warns men have "had enough" of diversity hires.' *News.com.au*, 24 January. www.news.com.au/national/politics/peter-dutton-warns-men-have-had-enough-of-diversity-hires/news-story/8826192e181e20d007242c1ce0dd2295.

Maiden, Samantha. 2025c. 'If Dutton is done, they will blame it on Trump.' *Advertiser*, 1 May: 13.

Maiden, Samantha. 2025d. '"Sexist": Karl Stefanovic grills new Liberal leader.' *News.com.au*, 16 May. www.news.com.au/national/politics/sexist-karl-stefanovic-grills-new-liberal-leader/news-story/21bcdd6d007f31057e8794d369c179cb.

Maxwell, Angie, and Todd Shields. 2019. *The Long Southern Strategy: How Chasing White Voters in the South Changed American Politics*. Oxford: Oxford University Press. doi.org/10.1093/oso/9780190265960.001.0001.

McLaughlin, Dan. 2024. 'This is the political ad that could win Trump the election.' *New York Post*, 22 October, [Updated 23 October 2024]. nypost.com/2024/10/22/opinion/this-is-the-political-ad-that-could-win-trump-the-election.

Murphy, Katharine. 2022. 'Lone wolf: Albanese and the new politics.' *Quarterly Essay*, no. 88.

Razik, Naveen. 2025. 'Albanese rules out renewing religious discrimination law push without "broad support".' *SBS News*, 1 May. www.sbs.com.au/news/article/albanese-rules-out-renewing-religious-discrimination-law-push-without-broad-support/udl5hr4ns.

Rhodes, R.A.W., and Paul 't Hart, eds. 2014. *The Oxford Handbook of Political Leadership*. Oxford: Oxford University Press. doi.org/10.1093/oxfordhb/9780199653881.001.0001.

Robbins, Jane. 2007. 'The Howard government and Indigenous rights: An imposed national unity?' *Australian Journal of Political Science* 42, no. 2: 315–28. doi.org/10.1080/10361140701320042.

Strangio, Paul, and James Walter. 2024. 'Australian governance in an era of leadership instability and the potential of "new politics".' In *Australian Politics at a Crossroads: Prospects for Change*, edited by Matteo Bonotti and Narelle Miragliotta, 40–54. London: Routledge. doi.org/10.4324/9781003394686-5.

Sun, Wanning. 2025. 'Dutton's "hawk–dove–hawk" seesaw on China keeps Labor on its toes.' *Crikey*, 16 April. www.crikey.com.au/2025/04/16/peter-dutton-anthony-albanese-china-defence-2025-election/.

The White House. 2025. 'Return to in-person work.' *Presidential Actions*, 20 January. Washington, DC: The White House. www.whitehouse.gov/presidential-actions/2025/01/return-to-in-person-work/.

Walter, James. 2010. *What Were They Thinking? The Politics of Ideas in Australia*. Sydney: UNSW Press.

3

Strategy and leadership in the Labor and Liberal campaigns

Phoebe Hayman and Emily Foley

Abstract

This chapter compares the campaign strategies of the Labor and Liberal parties, considering whether the result of the 2025 federal election can be attributed to campaign effects. The political context leading into the election shaped the development of the parties' strategies as they attempted to adapt to the fragmented political landscape. Overseeing these efforts were teams of campaign professionals and firms. While Labor assembled an experienced team to run the campaign, the Liberal campaign proved less well coordinated. This asymmetry was reflected in the strength of the parties' campaign strategies and narratives. Digital advertising continued to grow, but the 2025 election marked a substantial shift in the strategic use of new mediums, as Albanese and Dutton embraced influencers and podcasts. Ultimately, we argue, the election result demonstrated the ongoing professionalisation of campaigning in an increasingly fragmented landscape and the effect these efforts have when a strong campaign meets a weak one.

Keywords: election campaigning; campaign strategy; campaign effects; Liberal Party; Labor Party

In the final days of the campaign, Peter Dutton argued that the election would be 'a referendum, not about the election campaign, but about the last three years of government' (Cassidy and Dhanji 2025). In most elections, he may have been right, but in 2025, the campaigns appeared decisive as voters shifted in the early months of the year. This chapter addresses a central question: to what extent can the result of the 2025 federal election be attributed to campaign effects? Drawing on digital advertising data, media coverage and discussions with those within the campaigns' respective organisations, this chapter analyses the campaign strategies and how they may have contributed to the election result.

Campaigns aim to influence the issues about which voters think, provide them with information on new topics and, most ambitiously, shape how voters view these political problems and their potential solutions, persuading them to the parties' perspective (Farrell and Schmitt-Beck 2006: 186). Despite the importance parties and campaign professionals place on these efforts, whether campaigns have an impact on the outcomes of elections is often dismissed in favour of macro or contextual explanations. Many contend that campaigns have little or no effect, particularly on the voter persuasion required in Australian election campaigns. Campaign effects are difficult to demonstrate, but for those who argue that campaigns can shape outcomes, they are credited with informing voters, shaping their understanding of the issues, influencing their engagement with political news, mobilising or demobilising their participation and impacting their trust in political institutions—all of which may ultimately influence their vote (Farrell and Schmitt-Beck 2006: 13).

However, campaign effects may be fleeting, reinforcing rather than swaying votes and neutralising the other's influence. They should be most influential when a weak campaign meets a strong one in an election with many undecided voters—a succinct summary of the 2025 election. The asymmetry between the Labor and Liberal campaigns was a rare event in contemporary professionalised campaigning. Through analysing these campaigns, this chapter considers to what extent the election result can or should be attributed to campaign effects.

Political context

The government appeared to be at a disadvantage in the leadup to the 2025 federal election. Following the unsuccessful Voice referendum in 2023, the Albanese government was defined by consistently declining poll results (Beaumont 2025). Globally, voters had been punishing incumbents and rallying behind populist figures. Dutton had dabbled in positioning himself as an Australian Trump-lite, appointing Jacinta Nampijinpa Price to the portfolio of 'Government Efficiency'—equivalent to the US Department of Government Efficiency headed by Elon Musk (see Chapter 4, this volume; Cassidy and Jervis-Bardy 2025). Under Dutton's leadership, the Opposition had effectively framed the government as ineffectual and unfocused. This characterisation was aided by the broader economic context: inflation had led to successive interest rate hikes by the Reserve Bank of Australia, ratcheting up the cost of living; the price of housing hit new highs, substantially impacting renters and mortgage holders, and day-to-day expenses such as groceries and bills had risen steeply. Labor's technocratic approach to addressing these issues did little to boost its popularity.

Before the official start of the campaign, YouGov polling in February predicted a minority government (Shepherd 2025). The loudness of the ensuing discussion compelled the major-party leaders to address with which Independents or minor parties they would be willing to negotiate in the event of a hung parliament (Coorey 2025). The major parties' popularity has declined over decades and the 2022 federal election marked a watershed. The dealignment of voters and declining party loyalties were noted in both the ALP and the Liberal 2022 federal election review summaries—made public for the first time in more than a decade.

Both parties faced a more complex political landscape, with shrinking and unstable voter bases in what were once safe seats. The Greens threatened Labor in Victorian seats such as Wills and Macnamara, while highly organised and well-supported Independent campaigns presented a challenge to the Coalition across both rural and urban electorates. In response, the Liberal Party planned a pivot to the suburbs but faced an uphill battle to reach a majority. Labor split its efforts between battling the Liberals for marginal suburban seats and reclaiming urban Brisbane seats from the Greens. The electorate itself had also changed and the dominant voting bloc (47 per cent) of voters are either Millennials or Gen Z (Chowdhury 2025). These younger voters were more likely to be unaligned and to show an interest in minor-party or Independent candidates. As a product of this fragmentation and dealignment, it appeared unlikely that either Labor or the Coalition would be able to form a majority.

This was the backdrop to the major parties' planning for the federal election campaign. By 12 March, Labor was ready to launch the campaign officially, but Cyclone Alfred and the fear of repeating Scott Morrison's tone-deaf response to natural disasters delayed matters. Dutton's absence from his own electorate in Queensland as it faced Cyclone Alfred was deeply unpopular. The delay meant that the Albanese government had to submit a final budget before the campaign, presenting some promises in advance of the campaign proper. Later that week, Albanese's planned trip to the Governor-General to start the campaign was leaked to the media during Dutton's budget reply speech, effectively wiping it from the media coverage.

Labor used the additional two weeks to fine-tune their strategy. The result was a well-organised and tightly run campaign, although derided as boring by some. Conversely, gaffes, apologies and a revolving door of policy ideas would mark the ensuing Coalition campaign.

Campaign organisation and leadership

Labor campaign organisation

The Labor campaign exemplifies the electoral success that can accompany a well-organised, disciplined and experienced campaign. As in the 2022 election, the Labor Party's campaign headquarters was in Surry Hills, an inner-city suburb of Sydney. National secretary and campaign strategist Paul Erickson again served as national director of Labor's 2025 campaign, overseeing an assemblage of returning figures and agencies.

Like the 2022 election, in 2025, assistant national secretary Jennifer Light led a team within Labor producing tailored advertising for targeted electorates while Dee Madigan returned as creative lead of Labor's advertising strategy through her agency, Campaign Edge. The Moss Group was engaged again specifically for advertising in Western Australia, while GroupM's Mindshare and Sparro by Brainlabs were brought in to handle offline and digital media, respectively. The use of three agencies was unprecedented and, although Erickson (2025) noted the 'risk of overcomplication', their work was carefully delineated and coordinated. Member for Blaxland Jason Clare and ACT Senator Katy Gallagher reprised their 2022 roles as campaign spokespeople, tasked with holding regular press briefings and other public-facing responsibilities.

There were also new additions to Labor's campaign resourcing and strategy, in line with recommendations from Labor's 2022 election review. For example, the review recommended that Labor should 'consider increasing the central investment in CALD [culturally and linguistically diverse] engagement during the formal election campaign period' (Combet and Oshalem 2022: 11). In 2025, Labor partnered with Sydney multicultural marketing agency Diverse Communications to assist with engaging strategically with multicultural communities nationwide.

The review also acknowledged the growing electoral threat posed by the Greens and the development of three-cornered contests. In response, it recommended that Labor 'should actively contest the policy and political positions advocated by the Greens and dedicate resources for this purpose' (Combet and Oshalem 2022: 9). Therefore, for the first time, Labor's secretariat engaged with advertising recruitment agency Shannon Company, which worked alongside a team within the party secretariat to target the Greens (Mizen 2025a).

Liberal campaign organisation

The Liberal Party campaign was populated by both familiar, experienced faces and newer consultancies. Ultimately, its efforts were poorly coordinated across the assemblage of consultancies and campaigners. Andrew Hirst returned as Liberal Party director, overseeing his third consecutive federal campaign. The party set up shop in the Western Sydney suburb of Parramatta—a change from 2022's Brisbane campaign headquarters and indicative of changes in the key battleground States in 2025 (Bourke 2025). The party assembled similarly well-experienced consultants, re-enlisting advertising agency 'kwpx' and media-buying outfit Atomic 212º (Hickman 2025). The Liberals again secured the services of Topham Guerin, a digital consultancy firm with experience across successful centre-right campaigns in Australia, New Zealand and the United Kingdom.

Similarly, Senator James Paterson reprised his role as Liberal campaign spokesperson. Notably, Paterson was visible across major mainstream broadcasters on shows Dutton appeared to avoid, such as the *Today Show*, *Sunrise* and ABC *Radio National*. With Paterson selling the Liberal message through these avenues, Dutton instead focused his media appearances on Sky News and sympathetic talkback radio stations such as 2GB, referring to the ABC and the *Guardian* as the 'hate media' at a Liberal Party rally.

Other associations were new, and tumultuous. Following strategy and polling firm Crosby Textor's involvement in the 'Yes' campaign during the Voice referendum, the Liberal Party broke ties with the firm it had engaged in every election since 2002 (Galloway 2023). Instead, Freshwater

Strategy was hired by the party to run polling and focus groups during the campaign. Freshwater was founded in 2022 by Michael Turner, the Liberal Party's chief pollster at Crosby Textor in the 2019 and 2022 federal election campaigns (Turner 2025a). In the wake of the Liberals' loss, this decision was described by some as 'disastrous'. The quality of polling was maligned by party insiders (Nilsson 2025) and Turner responded with an explanation in the *Australian Financial Review* (Turner 2025b). Dutton's insistence that he was polling well in the final weeks of the campaign, including in his own seat of Dickson, and the apparent surprise at the scale of Labor's victory were blamed on the quality of polling (see Chapter 11, this volume).

Despite the experience within the national campaign assemblage, many decisions appeared to come directly from the less-experienced team around Dutton. Heading this team was former politician Jamie Briggs, returning to politics nine years after his departure (Galloway 2024). His return was not without controversy and, while experienced, Briggs had a chequered record of campaign success, famously losing his own seat of Mayo to Rebekha Sharkie in 2016 (Maiden 2025a).

Strategy and leadership

Successive election analyses have highlighted the growing importance and prominence of party leaders in Australian election campaigns—often referred to as the personalisation of politics (Gauja 2015). The 2025 campaigns sought to frame their leader in a positive light, while disparaging their opponent. For the Liberal Party, the effort to rebrand Peter Dutton began long before the election campaign, from the moment he assumed leadership of the party. However, the potential for a minority government necessitated careful narrative work to make Dutton and the Liberals appealing not only to Liberal voters but also to Independents and their constituencies.

Dutton was reintroduced to the electorate as misunderstood by voters who had only seen the hard-man side before. However, the strong, tough health and home affairs minister who made cuts and enforced strict border security was difficult to reconcile with the humanised, softer image they were attempting to portray (see Chapter 2, this volume). Other cabinet figures were largely sidelined, reinforcing the centrality of Dutton's persona to the party's electoral strategy. This was also complicated by Dutton's earlier experimentations with aligning himself with Trump. By the time the campaign began, association with Trump was viewed as politically toxic. Dutton later attempted to distance himself from support for Trumpian politics, but with limited success.

In stark contrast to the Liberals, Labor consolidated Anthony Albanese's image as a stable and responsible national leader, drawing on longstanding Labor traditions of egalitarianism and fairness. Albanese was portrayed as the custodian of Medicare and a respectable global citizen. This portrayal of the Prime Minister as a trustworthy figure offering secure and steady governance aligned with a campaign narrative centred on continuing the economic and social agendas begun in Labor's first term in office.

Labor also successfully framed Peter Dutton's role as party leader as a risk to Australian values and its economic future. While events on the world stage such as Trump's tariffs were influential, campaigns play a role in directing attention and informing voter interpretations (Jacobson 2015: 34). In this case, Labor used the Liberals' plans to significantly reduce the public service to paint Dutton as 'Trump-lite' or 'Temu-Trump'—a term coined by Greens MP Stephen Bates (see Chapters 1 and 8, this volume) but adopted and amplified by the ALP—to try to undermine trust in the Liberals, particularly within inner-city electorates. This portrayal contributed to a larger Labor narrative of risk management, casting Dutton as a threat to public institutions such as Medicare. In fact, one of Labor's key slogans, 'Don't risk Dutton', not only sought to raise concern among the electorate about a return to radical conservatism but also invoked Labor's traditions of investing in social services such as health care to consolidate its moral and political authority and legitimacy. This theme dominated the party's advertising, discussed below. Similar Liberal attempts to define Albanese as untrustworthy, weak and a poor performer did not seem to stick in the same way, lacking the narrative consistency and policy alignment of Labor's argument.

In terms of policy narratives, in the months before the election was announced, the Liberals pursued a small-target 'me too' strategy, matching Labor's election commitments in areas such as health care, attempting to neutralise any division. However, this strategy allowed Labor to frame the main issues of the campaign. The issue ownership literature suggests the role of campaigns is to set the agenda, placing the issue areas that are favourable to their party at the top of voters' minds when voting. In Australia, this has meant the ALP focuses its messaging on areas of perceived strength, such as health and education.

However, the Liberal Party's 'me too' period did not extend to all policy areas. The party did not support Labor's flagship education commitment of a 20 per cent reduction in student Higher Education Contribution Scheme (HECS) debts or fee-free TAFE (technical and further education) commitments. Most surprisingly, the Liberals also opposed Labor's plan to lower income taxes. This stance appeared to contradict the Liberal Party's focus on lower taxes, and the justification for opposing them did not resonate with voters or some within the party, who publicly regretted this choice after the election (see Chapter 11, this volume).

Policy inconsistencies became increasingly evident throughout the Liberal campaign. Dutton floated a series of what Albanese derided as 'thought bubbles' and backtracked on policy announcements, such as the plan to end work-from-home arrangements for public servants. Despite the Coalition having a nuclear energy policy for nearly a year, the campaign period featured very little discussion of nuclear and a greater focus on gas policies. Dutton visited only one proposed nuclear site on his campaign trail, signalling a lack of consideration and commitment to the proposal itself.

Policy announcements also seemed inconsistent and disorganised. Accounts from party elites and grassroots members after the election suggested that announced policies were conceived on the campaign trail, while developed proposals were left on the shelf (Kehoe 2025; Maiden 2025b). The disjointed coordination between Dutton's team and the campaign headquarters contributed to these issues. The impacts of a poorly managed campaign appeared to overshadow Dutton's efforts to promote other key policies, such as the plan to halve the fuel excise. The fuel tax was the cornerstone of Dutton's campaign in the month leading up to the May election. Despite visiting 17 petrol stations throughout the campaign, there was insufficient time to convince the electorate that this cost-of-living relief measure would outweigh those Labor had already proposed and campaigned for over several months. Ultimately, Dutton failed to persuade voters of his party's economic merits.

In sharp contrast, Labor' s key policy commitments were a tightly planned continuation of priorities established between 2022 and 2025. Commitments in health, education and tax reform were built on measures already initiated, indicating a well thought out and achievable two-term strategy, with developed economic costings and reasonable policy offerings. For example, Labor' s promise to wipe 20 per cent off student HECS loans was both popular and made sense to voters, given that during its first term in government, it had already removed $3 billion worth of student debt.

Presenting a policy agenda that aligned with its tradition and track record in government, Labor gained control of the broader narrative by positioning itself as a ready and responsible government in contrast to an opportunistic and policy-light Opposition. Labor successfully portrayed the Liberals' campaign policies as lacking vision and substance, highlighting underdeveloped policy platforms, the absence of costings for major proposals and Dutton's history of cuts to social services as health minister. The Liberals' lack of policy announcements, coupled with the underdeveloped 'thought bubble' policies, suggested a poorly prepared campaign that was intended to neutralise the government's advantages rather than articulate a robust alternative vision. A small-target strategy may have worked if the positive polling from 2024 had held, but as the popularity of Dutton and the Liberal Party waned throughout the campaign, the strategy meant the absence of a substantive alternative. The result was that the Labor Party effectively set the 2025 campaign agenda, while the Liberal Party strove to respond as the tide changed.

Resource allocation

One of the most limited resources in any political campaign is the time of the party leader. In 2025, it was more limited than ever, truncated by Easter and Anzac Day public holidays. Analysing which candidates the leaders visited, the settings they favoured and the policies announced on the campaign trail gives insights into the strategies and narratives in use.

Labor entered the election with 78 electorates to retain, while the Coalition needed to gain 20 seats nationally. This encouraged an aggressive strategy for the Liberals that focused their polling and efforts on seats they hoped to win, perhaps to the detriment of retaining marginal seats. The contest was fiercest in metropolitan Melbourne, Western Sydney and inner Brisbane, where each party sought to regain ground lost in the 2022 federal election. The Liberal Party focused their Victorian efforts in Aston, Chisholm, Kooyong and Goldstein, while Labor sought to regain Brisbane and Griffith from the Greens and to win marginal seats such as Leichhardt from the Liberal National Party of Queensland (LNP). The larger task for the Labor Party, however, was to retain its existing majority. Ultimately, Labor was successful and, in addition to swings across the country, the party retained every seat it already held (Table 3.1). The Liberal Party had its best result in Victoria (net neutral), but lost ground in every other State.

Table 3.1 Electorates held and gained in 2025

State/Territory	Labor		Coalition	
	Held	Result	Held	Result
NSW	25	28 (+3)	16	12 (–4), *6 Lib., 6 Nats*
Vic.	25	27 (+2)	9	*9, 6 Lib., 3 Nats*
Qld	5	12 (+7)	21	16 (–5), *LNP*
WA	10	11 (+1)	5	4 (–1), *Lib.*
SA	6	7 (+1)	3	2 (–1), *Lib.*
Tas.	2	4 (+2)	2	0 (–2)
NT	2	2	–	–
ACT	3	3	–	–
Total	78	94 (+16)	56	43

Source: Compiled by authors using AEC data.

Although the election was not formally called until 28 March, the Labor campaign kicked off early, fuelling the sense that the election was likely to be called sooner rather than later. From 6 to 10 January, Albanese toured electorates across northern Queensland, the Northern Territory and Western Australia. Rather than focusing efforts on strategically important areas, this first foray tested Albanese's form and readiness for the campaign. It triggered a similar early effort from the Liberal Party. Peter Dutton and Senator Michaelia Cash were on the ground in the key Victorian seats of Aston, Chisholm and Kooyong the following week, setting the scene for the campaign to come, in which Victoria would be a key battleground. At the first rally of the campaign in Melbourne on 12 January, Dutton launched the party's campaign slogan: 'Let's get Australia back on track'—borrowed directly from the successful 2023 New Zealand National Party's campaign (see Chapter 1, this volume; Manch 2025).

From 1 January to polling day, Dutton and Albanese travelled constantly and were visiting multiple States every day by the final weeks of the campaign. Albanese started the campaign proper on the offensive in Dickson and was most often found in targeted seats such as Leichhardt and Bullwinkel. His campaign visits typically aligned with key policies, and community health centres were the preferred backdrop for Albanese's photo shoots and local funding announcements. Albanese was also frequently found sitting at the kitchen table in voters' homes or in settings that emphasised his leadership and incumbency, showcasing his responses to disasters or productive relationships with State governments. Reflecting the Liberals' incoherent policy offerings, aside from service stations, Dutton's campaign events signalled few strong themes and locations ranged from vineyards to brickworks. Once the campaign proper was under way, Dutton was notably absent from inner metropolitan seats now held by Independents. Instead, figures such as Senator Jane Hume represented the Liberal Party in these key electorates.

Alongside these scheduled electorate visits, campaigns are punctuated by high-profile media events such as leaders' debates and campaign launches. Four debates were held at this election and, while they compounded the personalisation of the campaign, none was decisive. Launches rally the party base and are a key moment in the election campaign, attracting significant attention and media coverage. It was, therefore, unfortunate that both major parties held theirs on 13 April with what amounted to the same policy offering. The Labor launch was held in Perth, while the Liberal Party's event was hosted in south-western Sydney. All living former Liberal prime ministers, apart from Malcolm Turnbull, were present at the Liberal Party launch. Coupled with a video feature introducing Dutton, the impression was one of presidentialised succession.

While the Liberal Party foregrounded past glory, Labor's line-up focused on the present, with a packed front bench in attendance. Popular WA Premier Roger Cook was the warm-up act and Julia Gillard alone represented previous leaders, seated between prominent Labor women ministers Katy Gallagher and Penny Wong. As he had with Dutton's budget reply, Albanese stole the media attention from Dutton, giving his campaign launch speech one hour after Dutton's (Rawling et al. 2025). The speeches themselves addressed their respective policy commitments and campaign narratives: Albanese spoke about continuing the work started in his first term, focusing on health and framing Dutton as a threat to Medicare, while Dutton blamed sustained cost-of-living pressures on the incumbent Labor government.

In Australian elections, launches usually occur late in the campaign due to a longstanding convention that, before the official launch, staff and ministerial travel expenses to and from campaign headquarters are covered by parliamentary allowances rather than party funds (Sawer and Maley 2020). These events are typically used as a point of focus leading into polling day, as parties direct disengaged voters' attention to key policies or new announcements. In 2025, both parties launched early, as campaigns continue to adapt to the increase in early voting. The parties used their launches to champion their pitch to first homebuyers, with policies that appeared remarkably similar at first glance.

Digital ads

Spending on digital advertising has grown across successive elections, reaching into the millions by 2025. Between 28 March and polling day, Labor's Meta accounts spent more than $3 million, while the Liberal Party's official accounts came in at just over $2 million for the same period (Figure 3.1). The disparity was mirrored in Google advertising spending and was largest in the final two weeks of the campaign, when Labor spending peaked. Overall, Labor showed a stronger commitment to digital advertising across platforms as a key part of their electoral strategy, in both scale and coordination (Table 3.2).

Table 3.2 Top 10 political advertisers on Google Ads, 1 January – 3 May 2025

Advertiser	Sum of spending (A$)
Labor Party	10,711,200
Trumpet of Patriots	8,934,900
Liberal Party	7,795,650
ACTU	1,188,300
Greens	1,002,750
The Nationals	374,250
Advance Australia Ltd	319,500
Australian Taxpayers' Alliance Pty Ltd	277,350
Nixs Run Pty Ltd (Nicolette Boele)	220,350
Climate 200	211,950

Source: Compiled by authors using Google Ads data.

Both parties broadly focused their efforts on the eastern States. The Liberal Party came *closer* to matching Labor's efforts in Victoria, New South Wales and Western Australia than in the other States, suggesting a comparatively stronger effort in these areas as they struggled to make up ground lost to Independents in 2022. Liberal Party advertisements were also more likely to be disseminated via the accounts of the constituent State parties than the more coordinated national Labor effort.

While party accounts made up a significant proportion of the overall spending, individual candidates also committed substantial resources to their campaigns, with Coalition candidates Jacinta Nampijinpa Price and Dan Tehan the biggest spenders of the campaign (Figure 3.2). Incumbents were more likely to spend big on digital advertising, indicating a defensive strategy from candidates' own accounts.

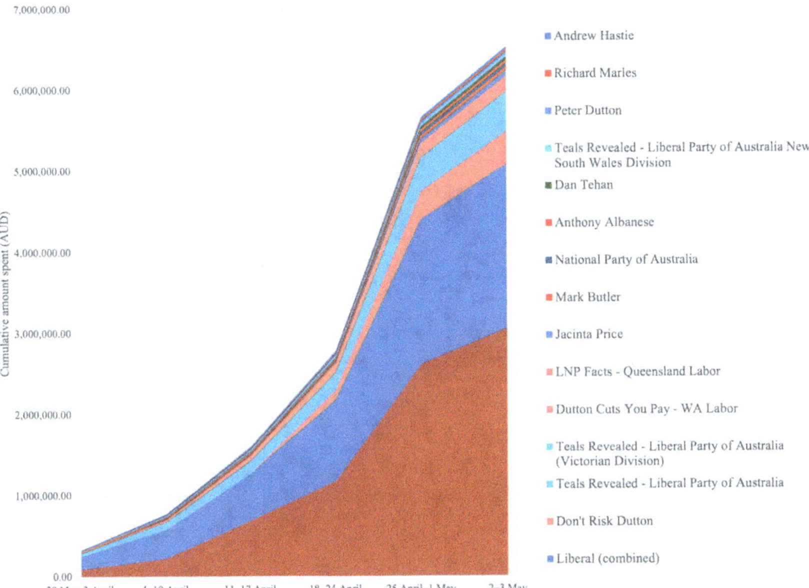

Figure 3.1 Labor and Liberal Meta advertising spending, 28 March – 3 May 2025

Source: Compiled by authors using Meta Ad Library data.

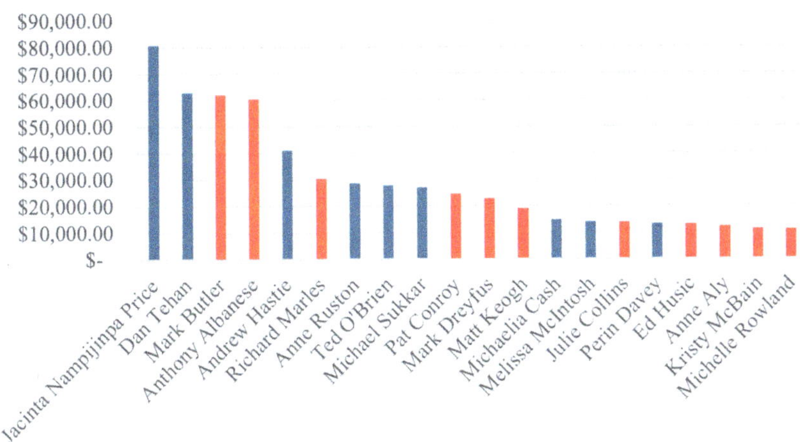

Figure 3.2 Meta advertising spending by individual major-party politicians' accounts, 28 March – 3 May 2025

Source: Compiled by authors using Meta Ad Library data.

Advertising themes aligned with the narratives and strategies employed across the campaigns. Labor's ads were numerous, but the messages were focused, homing in on Dutton's cuts, while centring on their own policy successes and future offerings. In response, the Liberals attempted to humanise Dutton while also maintaining the impression of him as a strong leader in contrast to the 'weak' Albanese. Liberal advertisements were unsurprisingly light in terms of policy offerings, focusing instead on the negative, such as those blaming the cost-of-living crisis on the Albanese government. Overall, the party's messages were numerous and inconsistent. The Liberal Party embraced artificial intelligence (AI) to spruik their fuel excise cut, putting out the first and second fully AI-generated political advertisements in Australia, developed by Topham Guerin (9News 2024; Kirk 2025).

Negative advertisements, while considered effective, are found to be unpopular with voters, leading to the hypothesised backlash effect where voters may instead punish the party putting out such ads (Dowling and Wichowsky 2015). By disseminating their attack ads through third-party accounts, each with their own messages, targeted audiences and preferred platforms, the major parties distanced themselves from any potential fallout.

From Labor, 'Dutton cuts, you pay' and 'Don't risk Dutton' paid negative ads targeted the Opposition Leader, while the Liberal campaign instead targeted Community Independents through accounts such as 'Teals Revealed'. These were also targeted based on geography and voter demographics. 'Don't risk Dutton' was primarily aimed at women in Victoria as Labor sought to capitalise on Dutton's perceived women problem.

Influencers, TikTok and podcasts

AI-generated ads and third-party accounts were not the only ways in which the 2025 election demonstrated a further shift towards a radically different media environment (see Chapter 7, this volume). With growing news avoidance, the collapse of traditional media audiences and the loss of incidental exposure to political content, reaching voters requires new strategies. In response, parties have been attempting to engage with new social media platforms and strategies to expand visibility and connect with a fragmented electorate.

The increased use of TikTok by both major parties in 2025 demonstrates the growing importance of short-form social media videos as a 'serious campaign strategy' (Grantham 2025). Parties have engaged in creating more humorous and satirical messaging to promote policies, criticise their opponents and appeal to users of platforms such as TikTok and Instagram (Oates and Chowdhury 2025; Grantham 2024). As parties recognised the ability of influencers to shape political narratives, build trust and influence opinion, influencers played a more significant role in the 2025 election than ever before.

With a federal budget taking place just days before the election campaign was due to formally begin, the Labor government invited social media influencers and online political commentators to attend the pre-budget media lockup, which traditionally included only journalists and mainstream media outlets (Mizen 2025b). Once the campaign was under way, Labor invited social media influencers to cover their election campaign. For the first time, Canberra press gallery members were no longer the only group allowed to join the travelling media pack following Anthony Albanese on the campaign trail.

The second innovation was the use of podcasts throughout the election. MPs and political candidates turned to this medium to connect with younger audiences who are less likely to encounter campaign messages and framing through traditional media channels such as television and radio. There was also a noticeable gendered element to podcast engagement, with Albanese appearing on podcasts with predominantly female audiences, while Dutton targeted podcasts with a greater male listenership (see Chapter 6, this volume). Podcasts hosted by social media influencers provided a platform for long-form informal conversations that were free from the usual journalistic ethical practices and standards of neutrality and balance.

However, this trend has also prompted scrutiny. In response to a query from Liberal Senator Jane Hume regarding the extent to which a podcast host who shares the ideological leanings of the party or candidate is in breach of political advertising laws, the AEC clarified that such appearances do not breach political advertising laws, as long as the politicians or their parties make no payment for participation (AEC 2025).

By investing in and adapting to emerging digital media platforms, major parties not only extended their reach in a fragmented media environment but also reshaped how political messages are consumed. While these tactics were effective in engaging new and younger audiences, they also contributed to an increased blurring of boundaries between journalism, advocacy and entertainment, signalling a new phase in the evolution of political campaigning.

Conclusion

The major parties were tasked with strengthening party identity and voter confidence within a volatile electoral landscape and an expected minority government. While the economic and international context were important, the strength of the Labor campaign and the weakness of the Liberal campaign contributed to the outcome in 2025. Both parties attempted to frame their leaders in a positive light and their opponents in a negative one during the campaign.

Labor's campaign was well run by an experienced team, who built a well-organised and tightly coordinated effort that played to the party's strengths. Messaging and timing were tightly coordinated between key campaign figures and aligned across mediums. As a result, the party effectively weathered international events and methodically prosecuted the need for stable, steady leadership. The inconsistent messaging and gaffes from the Liberal Party allowed Labor to set the agenda, leading to a campaign that was fought on issues such as health. Labor effectively cemented the electorate's understanding of Dutton as a hard man and a risky proposition. Finally, the Liberal Party overextended, aggressively pursuing suburban seats with few policy offerings in a strategy that did not adapt to the changing political landscape.

Campaign effects are considered strongest when a weak campaign faces a strong one (Farrell and Schmitt-Beck 2006). This was exemplified in the 2025 federal election. Optimistically interpreted, this election result could be seen as an argument in favour of policy substance. More cynically, we suggest it indicates the continuing professionalisation of Australian campaigns and the influence that a well-run campaign can have in the right circumstances.

References

9News. 2024. 'Liberal Party launches Australia's first entirely AI-generated political ad.' *9News*, 13 October. www.9news.com.au/national/liberal-party-launches-australias-first-entirely-ai-political-ad/f17cbea7-4e69-4fba-a8e8-346dc9fd699a.

Australian Electoral Commission (AEC). 2025. 'AEC statement: Authorisation statements for social media content.' Media release, 7 April. Canberra: Australian Electoral Commission. www.aec.gov.au/media/2025/04-07b.htm.

Beaumont, Adrian. 2025. 'Newspoll steady but Albanese's ratings jump; swing to Labor in marginal seats.' *The Conversation*, 13 April. theconversation.com/news poll-steady-but-albaneses-ratings-jump-swing-to-labor-in-marginal-seats-254445. doi.org/10.64628/AA.qq9vxeamt.

Bourke, Latika M. 2025. 'Federal election 2025: Key spokespeople, ad gurus and pollsters in Labor and Coalition campaigns revealed.' *The Nightly*, 27 February. thenightly.com.au/politics/australia/federal-election-2025-key-spokespeople-ad-gurus-and-pollsters-in-labor-and-coalition-campaigns-revealed--c-17864971.

Cassidy, Caitlin, and Krishani Dhanji. 2025. 'Coalition plans to have two nuclear power plants operating by mid-2030s—As it happened.' *The Guardian*, 1 May. www.theguardian.com/australia-news/live/2025/may/01/australia-election-2025-live-anthony-albanese-peter-dutton-campaign-policies-economy-inflation-cost-of-living-coalition-labor-ntwnfb.

Cassidy, Caitlin, and Dan Jervis-Bardy. 2025. 'Peter Dutton appoints Jacinta Nampijinpa Price to Musk-style government efficiency role in new frontbench.' *The Guardian*, 25 January. www.theguardian.com/australia-news/2025/jan/25/peter-dutton-reveals-new-coalition-frontbench-before-2025-federal-election.

Chowdhury, Intifar. 2025. 'This election, Gen Z and Millennials hold most of the voting power. How might they wield it?' *The Conversation*, 23 April. theconversation.com/this-election-gen-z-and-millennials-hold-most-of-the-voting-power-how-might-they-wield-it-252803. doi.org/10.64628/AA.ja69ur9yc.

Combet, Greg, and Lenda Oshalem. 2022. *Election 2022: An Opportunity to Establish a Long-Term Labor Government*. Report of the review of Labor's 2022 federal election campaign. Canberra: Australian Labor Party. alp-assets.s3.ap-southeast-2.amazonaws.com/documents/ALP+CAMPAIGN+REVIEW+2022.pdf.

Coorey, Phillip. 2025. 'Dutton willing to negotiate minority government, PM rules out deals.' *Australian Financial Review*, 24 January. www.afr.com/politics/federal/dutton-willing-to-negotiate-minority-government-pm-rules-out-deals-2025 0124-p5l6wn.

Dowding, Keith. 2013. 'Presidentialisation again: A comment on Kefford.' *Australian Journal of Political Science* 48, no. 2: 147–49. doi.org/10.1080/10361146.2013. 787960.

Dowling, Conor M., and Amber Wichowsky. 2015. 'Attacks without consequence? Candidates, parties, groups, and the changing face of negative advertising.' *American Journal of Political Science* 59, no. 1: 19–36. doi.org/10.1111/ajps. 12094.

Edison Research. 2024. 'In the "podcast election", Trump talked to vastly more people.' *US Election Research*, 14 November. Somerville: Edison Research. www.edison research.com/in-the-podcast-election-trump-talked-to-vastly-more-people/.

Erickson, Paul. 2025. 'Campaign director's address: Paul Erickson, ALP National Secretary.' National Press Club, Canberra, 21 May. Transcript available: alp. org.au/national-secretary-media/250521-campaign-directors-address-to-the-national-press-club/.

Farrell, David M., and Rudiger Schmitt-Beck, eds. 2006. *Do Political Campaigns Matter? Campaign Effects in Elections and Referendums*. London: Routledge.

Galloway, Anthony. 2023. 'Inside the growing rift between the Liberals and Crosby Textor.' *Capital Brief*, 5 October. www.capitalbrief.com/newsletter/inside-the-growing-rift-between-the-liberals-and-crosby-textor-a3e661fc-4111-4016-bc76-9394cec93958/.

Galloway, Anthony. 2024. 'Peter Dutton hires former minister Jamie Briggs as "chief advisor".' *Capital Brief*, 19 September. www.capitalbrief.com/article/dutton-hires-former-minister-jamie-briggs-as-chief-advisor-e00b8ece-3014-4db0-8da0-5ec2872e63c6/.

Gauja, Anika. 2015. 'The presidentialization of parties in Australia.' In *The Presidentialization of Political Parties: Organizations, Institutions and Leaders*, edited by Gianluca Passarelli, 160–77. London: Palgrave Macmillan. doi.org/ 10.1057/9781137482464_9.

Grantham, Susan. 2024. 'The rise of TikTok elections: The Australian Labor Party's use of TikTok in the 2022 federal election campaigning.' *Communication Research and Practice* 10, no. 2: 181–99. doi.org/10.1080/22041451.2024.2349451.

Grantham, Susan. 2025. 'Thought the election campaign was boring? Maybe you're just not on TikTok.' *The Conversation*, 5 May. theconversation.com/thought-the-election-campaign-was-boring-maybe-youre-just-not-on-tiktok-255847. doi.org/10.64628/AA.a4wdnwyqm.

Hickman, Arvind. 2025. 'Who are the agencies supporting Labor and the Coalition in the election?' *B&T*, 21 February. www.bandt.com.au/who-are-the-agencies-supporting-labor-and-the-coalition-in-the-election/.

Jacobson, Gary C. 2015. 'How do campaigns matter?' *Annual Review of Political Science* 18: 31–37. doi.org/10.1146/annurev-polisci-072012-113556.

Kehoe, John. 2025. 'How the Liberals got it so wrong.' *Australian Financial Review*, 4 May. www.afr.com/politics/federal/how-the-liberals-got-it-so-wrong-202505 04-p5lwd6.

Kirk, Emma. 2025. 'The Liberal Party release a new election campaign video made entirely with AI.' *News.com.au*, 9 April. www.news.com.au/national/federal-election/the-liberal-party-release-a-new-election-campaign-video-made-entirely-with-ai/news-story/61646660ca385d4a514a98e521f4cf73.

Maiden, Samantha. 2025a. '"Sh*tshow": How the Voice blew up Peter Dutton and the Liberal Party's polling.' *News.com.au*, 5 May. www.news.com.au/national/federal-election/shtshow-how-the-voice-blew-up-peter-dutton-and-the-liberal-partys-polling/news-story/e7d381980023a0e725635a67a7e218d9.

Maiden, Samantha. 2025b. 'How Peter Dutton destroyed the Liberal Party.' *News. com.au*, 7 May. www.news.com.au/national/federal-election/how-peter-dutton-destroyed-the-liberal-party/news-story/450493ff8a3ffb7c37849ac759516ca5.

Manch, Thomas. 2025. 'Australian Opposition borrows National Party's "Back on track" slogan.' *The Post*, 13 January. www.thepost.co.nz/politics/360546184/australian-opposition-borrows-national-partys-back-track-slogan.

Mizen, Ronald. 2025a. 'Labor ramps up campaign in Greens battlegrounds.' *Australian Financial Review*, 16 January. www.afr.com/politics/federal/labor-ramps-up-campaign-in-greens-battlegrounds-20250113-p5l405.

Mizen, Ronald. 2025b. 'Influencers invited on campaign trail in election first.' *Australian Financial Review*, 26 March. www.afr.com/politics/federal/social-media-influencers-invited-on-campaign-trail-in-election-first-20250326-p5lml7.

Nilsson, Anton. 2025. 'Was Dutton dishonest about his internal polling, or misled? Liberals believe it's the latter.' *Crikey*, 5 May. www.crikey.com.au/2025/05/05/peter-dutton-coalition-polling-ct-group-freshwater-strategy/.

Oates, Hannah, and Intifar Chowdhury. 2025. 'What did the parties say on TikTok in the election, and how? Here's the campaign broken down in 5 charts.' *The Conversation*, 13 May. theconversation.com/what-did-the-parties-say-on-tiktok-in-the-election-and-how-heres-the-campaign-broken-down-in-5-charts-254793. doi.org/10.64628/AA.uspcfw5e7.

Rawling, Caitlin, Andrew Thorpe, Daniela Pizzirani, and Claudia Long. 2025. 'Albanese launches campaign in Perth after Dutton's pitch to voters in Sydney— As it happened.' *ABC News*, 13 April. www.abc.net.au/news/2025-04-13/ federal-election-live-updates-albanese-dutton-campaign-2025/105169880.

Rising, David, Jill Lawless, and Nicholas Riccardi. 2024. 'The "super year" of elections has been super bad for incumbents as voters punish them in droves.' *AP News*, 17 November. apnews.com/article/global-elections-2024-incumbents-defeated-c80fbd4e667de86fe08aac025b333f95.

Sawer, Marian, and Michael Maley. 2020. 'The rules of the game.' In *Morrison's Miracle: The 2019 Australian Federal Election*, edited by Anika Gauja, Marian Sawer, and Marian Simms, 47–69. Canberra: ANU Press. doi.org/10.22459/ MM.2020.03.

Shepherd, Tory. 2025. 'All signs point to a hung parliament: What does this mean, and what should crossbenchers do?' *The Guardian*, 30 March. www.theguardian. com/australia-news/2025/mar/30/australian-election-2025-hung-parliament-chances-what-happens.

Turner, Mike. 2025a. 'Dr Michael Turner.' [Homepage]. *Pollster Mike Turner*. www. pollstermiketurner.com/.

Turner, Mike. 2025b. 'Three reasons we missed Labor's landslide.' *Australian Financial Review*, 4 May. www.afr.com/politics/federal/three-reasons-we-missed-labor-s-landslide-20250504-p5lwf8.

4

Swimming with or against the tide of populism

Kurt Sengul and Marian Sawer

Abstract

Populist discourses were ubiquitous during the 2025 election campaign, with the spectre of Donald Trump once again looming large. Drawing on content analysis data from 2024 and 2025, this chapter explores the key vectors of populist discourse in the 2025 election, including the roles of Sky News Australia, conservative digital campaigning group Advance and right-wing populist minor parties Trumpet of Patriots and Pauline Hanson's One Nation. It critically examines how the Peter Dutton–led Coalition initially found itself swimming with the tide of populism, buoyed by the defeat of the Indigenous Voice to Parliament and the success of anti-elite discourses in Trump's presidential campaign. However, as the association with Trump became a political liability, the Coalition found itself unable to pivot effectively in a new direction. The chapter concludes by arguing that Labor's emphatic victory highlights the contingent nature of populism in the Australian political landscape.

Keywords: populism; anti-elitism; woke; Sky News Australia; Advance

The background to the 2025 federal election was a rising tide of populism in many parts of the world. The re-election of Donald Trump to the American presidency in 2024 seemed to confirm the power of populist discourse, mobilising resentment against 'out-of-touch elites' and their supposed contempt for the values and interests of ordinary people. Populist discourse had a long history in Australia but in its modern form had been disseminated by the Murdoch media since the 1990s.

This chapter examines vectors of populist discourse in the 2025 election, including the important roles of Sky News Australia and the digital campaign organisation Advance, and draws on content analysis conducted in 2024 and 2025. It looks at the extent to which such discourse was adopted by the Coalition and the attempt to depict the Albanese government as driven by inner-city elite agendas that disregarded everyday Australians.

Constructing elites

The essence of populist politics has been a discourse mobilising the people against elites, creating an 'us and them' frame of reference. From the 1990s, the way that 'elites' have been constructed in this discourse has undergone a dramatic change, thanks to the Murdoch media and particularly the *Australian* newspaper (Scalmer and Goot 2004). Today, those at the forefront of disseminating anti-elite discourse still include the *Australian*, but it has been joined by Sky News Australia and the digital campaigning organisation Advance.

While social scientists from Pareto to Mosca have understood 'elites' in different ways, one crucial factor has been the idea that elites hold some kind of power. In the older version of rural populism in Australia, elites were seen as bankers, corrupt politicians and big businessmen. In the more recent version, elites are not necessarily rich or powerful but have values acquired from university education that are different from those of ordinary people. This newer version of populist discourse has itself been evolving and, since 2018, the term 'woke' has become the favoured shorthand for elite values, whether that is concern about climate change, gender equality, the treatment of refugees and asylum-seekers, Indigenous issues or other progressive causes. In the Murdoch media over the past 20 years or so, elite membership has been defined by such concerns rather than by economic power or assets.

However, elites are not only identified by their opinions. In this discourse, they are also characterised by their contempt for ordinary people. While they may not directly exploit ordinary people, they lecture and preach at them rather than respecting their values. Examples given of such disrespect include attitudes towards the flag or Australia Day and the 'mini-lectures' involved in Acknowledgements of Country.

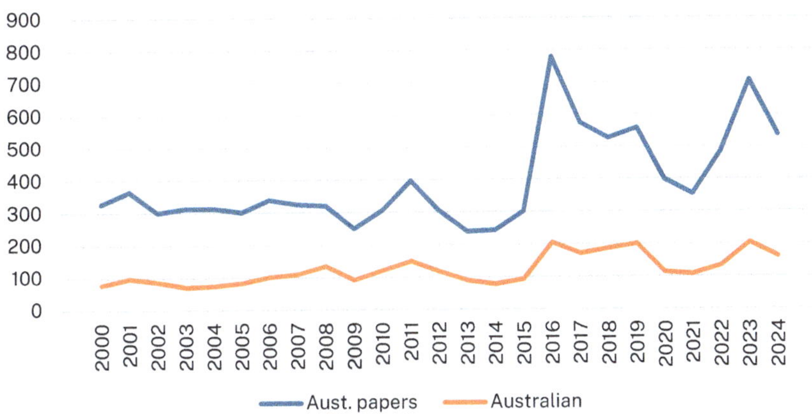

Figure 4.1 Items on elites in Australian newspapers, 2000–2024

Source: Compiled by Marian Sawer using Factiva data, 5 July 2025.

There is certainly a gap in political attitudes and behaviour between those with a university education and other Australians, and populist discourse helps to fuel resentment across this education gap. This resentment contributed to the defeat of the Voice referendum in 2023, which was framed as a 'divisive elite project' (Kelly 2024). This framing resulted in a peak of items on elites in Australian newspapers in 2023, particularly in Murdoch mastheads, although not as high as the peak in 2016 when both Brexit and Trump's successful bid for the US presidency were framed as defeats for the elites (see Figure 4.1).

An older feature of anti-elite discourse still to the fore in the 2025 election campaign was the spatial dimension. There is a long history of rural populism in Australia mobilising resentment of city-based elites. Today this spatial dimension has shifted slightly, so that elites are now located in the inner city, as contrasted with everyday Australians in the suburbs as well as in rural and regional Australia. 'Canberra' and 'Canberra-based bureaucrats' also continue to be particular targets as do international bureaucrats; in 2024, Peter Dutton made it clear he was not going to try to please 'people in Paris' over climate policies.

The role of Murdoch mastheads

In the runup to the 2025 federal election, the Murdoch media continued to play a leading role in disseminating anti-elite discourse as they had done since the 1990s (see Table 4.1). When the Nine newspapers ran items on elites, they used the term in a more traditional sense to refer to those with socioeconomic power rather than in the Murdoch sense of those with progressive values.

Table 4.1 Items on elites in the Australian and other newspapers, 2003 and 2024

Date (1 January – 31 December)	Newspaper	No.	Percentage
2003	*Australian*	70	22.4
2003	All 17 Australian newspapers in Factiva	313	100.0
2024	*Australian*	159	29.7
2024	*Australian Online*	180	33.7
2024	All 17 Australian newspapers in Factiva	535	100.0

Source: Factiva, 4 April 2025.

Liberal leader Peter Dutton was increasingly framed as a hero of the struggle against elites over issues such as identity politics, immigration, the flag and Australia Day: '[H]e is becoming a symbol for people who feel disenfranchised, overlooked by the system, denied a voice and patronised by the elites' (Kelly 2024).

In November 2024 the success of Donald Trump in the US presidential election resulted in a record number of items on elites in Australian newspapers, with Murdoch columnists blaming the Democrats' defeat on elites being out of touch and too concerned with minority rights (Sawer and Sengul 2025). The lesson they drew was that elites needed to listen to ordinary people rather than sneering at them. A good example was the *Courier-Mail* editorial with the headline 'Lessons for Labor as sneering elites trumped again'. The message was that 'Labor … needs to urgently rid its inner sanctum of the elite sneering class' (6 November 2024). The Adelaide *Advertiser* also editorialised about how Trump's win over the elites meant wokeism was dead and that everyday Australians did not like to be lectured to (8 November 2024).

As found in a study of the Murdoch press 20 years before, elites were primarily defined in cultural terms: holding 'progressive values' was sufficient to make one a member of the elite (Scalmer and Goot 2004).

However, even corporations could now attain elite membership for non-profit-making activities such as support for the Indigenous Voice. But elites were characterised not only by their progressive views but also by their attitude towards ordinary Australians—expressed by lecturing them. The main example provided of objectionable lecturing by elites was the Acknowledgement of Country at the start of meetings. At the Sky News anti-Semitism summit in February 2025, then attorney-general Mark Dreyfus was booed as he began his speech with such an acknowledgement.

Further insight into how elites were being constructed was provided by reporting of a CT Group (Crosby Textor) survey conducted in October 2024 that split respondents into mainstream and elite voters. The elite group comprised voters with a postgraduate degree, earning more than $120,000 in household income and living in metropolitan areas. The minimum household income of these elite voters is immediately noticeable, being far less than the household income of a nurse married to a primary schoolteacher. The findings were that gaps between mainstream Australia and elites were growing on issues including migration, trust in government and climate change (Chambers and Ferguson 2024).

The role of Advance

The online campaigning organisation Advance was created in 2018 in response to the role of GetUp! on the other side of politics or, as its website put it: in response to 'woke politicians and elitist activist groups taking Aussies for a ride'. During the 2025 campaign, it described its mission as being 'to give voice to the mainstream Australians who are silenced and ignored by the elite-run media and institutions in Australia' (Advance Update, 11 April 2025).

Advance had campaigned in the 2019 and 2022 federal elections—for example, in Warringah—but became nationally prominent in 2023 for its role in defeating the Voice referendum. Reflecting on this success a year later, Advance spokeswoman Sandra Bourke said: 'So many Australians came out to fight with Advance to stop the elites and activists cementing division in our Constitution. It has become the biggest grassroots movement in Australian political history' (Advance Update, 4 October 2024). By this time, Advance already had more than 300,000 online 'supporters', rising to 355,000 in 2025.

Plate 4.1 Advance Facebook advertisement: Weak woke sending us broke
Photo: Meta Ad Library, 4 April 2025.

In the wake of its referendum success, Advance received a record amount of income in 2023–24. According to the AEC's Transparency Register, it tripled its income—receiving $15.7 million, including $500,000 from Liberal Party affiliate the Cormack Foundation. It enabled the hiring of 23 full-time staff and paid for ongoing culture wars to 'save' Australia Day and the national flag from elites and activists, and two election campaigns described below, the 'Greens truth' and the 'Weak, woke and sending us broke' campaigns. The overriding message of its email updates and Facebook ads was that inner-city elites were out of touch with mainstream or 'real' Australians and thought they were better than them (for detailed content analysis, see Sawer and Sengul 2025). Characteristic of this discourse was a Facebook summons to 'say no to the elites' with images of Greens leader Adam Bandt, Labor leader Antony Albanese and Independent Zali Steggall (posted 14 August 2024).

Plate 4.2 Advance Facebook advertisement: Activists and elites are pushing 'Welcome to Country' ceremonies
Photo: Meta Ad Library, 16 April 2025.

Advance's most significant expenditure from 2024 was on its 'Greens truth' campaign, targeting six electorates and aiming to persuade voters that the Greens were 'not who they used to be' (Koutsoukis 2024). It suggested the Greens had turned into a 'malignant political force' promoting immigration, decriminalisation of drugs and 'death taxes'. Sometimes this campaign resulted in the odd formulation of 'extreme elites and activists' juxtaposed with 'mainstream Australians like you' (Advance Update, 11 March 2025). By February 2025, Advance claimed that its 'Greens truth' ads had been seen 2.2 million times on Facebook and seven million times on Google and YouTube and that 70 large billboards had been placed in seats held by the Greens or targeted by them. Advance claimed credit for the Greens losing a State seat in Melbourne in February and later for 'smashing the Greens' in the federal election.

From March 2025, Advance's 'Greens truth' campaign was joined by its 'Weak, woke and sending us broke' campaign targeting the Albanese government. During the campaign, the most popular of the Advance online petitions—more popular than 'Stop immigration'—was its 'End Welcome to Country' petition, endorsing Senator Jacinta Nampijinpa Price's call to stop spending taxpayer dollars on 'elite and activist ceremonies that divide us by race'. Advance ran 14 different ads attacking woke ceremonies in April, with messages such as 'Don't welcome me to my own country'. In the last week of the campaign, the Opposition Leader had a similar message—that Welcome to Country ceremonies had been 'overdone' and were divisive.

Another example of discursive sharing by Advance, the Murdoch media and the Coalition was triggered by an unguarded comment by senior minister Senator Penny Wong during a *Betoota Talks* podcast on 30 April, three days before the election. Wong responded to a question about the Voice referendum by saying, 'I think we'll look back on it in ten years' time and it'll be a bit like marriage equality … [I]t'll be like … did we even have an argument about that.' Sky News and the *Australian* promptly claimed Wong had resurrected the Voice and had declared it would be 'inevitable' (Crotty 2025). On the same day, Advance put out five different ads with the *Australian*'s headline 'A resurrected Voice is inevitable, says Penny Wong' and messages such as 'You voted NO, but Labor didn't get the memo'.

By 1 May, the LNP had also put out ads comparing Wong's alleged statement with the percentage of 'No' voters in different electorates. On the same day, Wong's musing became a 'stunning admission' in an article by Price, which began: 'Albanese's response to the question of welcomes to country this week, along with Penny Wong's comments, show that Labor has refused to learn from its failure of [sic] listening to the activist elites' (Price 2025). By 2 May, Advance was saying, 'Once again, mainstream Australians are being dismissed, talked down to, and pushed aside', while Dutton was claiming Labor had 'a plan' to bring the Voice back despite Australians having voted against it (Advance Update, 2 May 2025; Tingle 2025).

Sky News Australia

As one of Australia's only rolling news channels—alongside the ABC's 24-hour news channel—Sky News Australia continued to play a prominent role in the election (Carson and Jackman 2023). Despite its small domestic viewership, Sky secured the first leaders' debate, which was hosted in conjunction with its Murdoch stablemate the *Daily Telegraph*. Sky has always maintained an outsized influence on the Australian political and media landscape despite its marginal audience share (Young 2009). Rupert Murdoch's News Corp Australia gained full ownership of Sky in 2016, which signalled an aggressive rightward shift in the network's opinion side—pejoratively referred to as 'Sky After Dark' by its critics. The network has also invested heavily in its digital media strategy and has become one of Australia's largest digital news organisations. Boasting 5.5 million subscribers on its YouTube channel and 1.7 million Facebook followers, Sky's digital footprint now exceeds its commercial and public service rivals, including the ABC, 9News and 7News Australia.

Since 2016, Sky's opinion programs have embraced the unabashed right-wing populist style of its American sister network Fox News. Its nightly roster of conservative opinion hosts, including Andrew Bolt, Rowan Dean, Paul Murray, Rita Panahi and Peta Credlin, are textbook examples of media populism, characterised by anti-elitism, appeals to common sense, in-group favouritism and out-group antagonism, and highly emotionalised, personalised and tabloid-style rhetoric (Krämer 2014). In recent years, Sky has leaned heavily into culture war issues, vigorously prosecuting the Australian iteration of the 'war on woke' on issues including climate change, LGBTQIA+ rights and the Indigenous Voice to Parliament (Sawer and Sengul 2025). Sky's brand of media populism very much mirrors the style of right-wing populism endemic to Australia: hostility towards cultural and political elites, privileging socio-cultural issues over socioeconomic concerns and a spatial divide between the cities and the regions (Moffitt and Sengul 2023).

Unsurprisingly, Sky's editorial content throughout the election was highly critical of the Labor Party, the Greens and the so-called Teal or Community Independents. Opposition leader Peter Dutton appeared on the network several times throughout the campaign and was openly endorsed by several of Sky's evening hosts, including Sharri Markson and Murray. In the leadup to the election campaign, Sky host and editor of the *Spectator Australia*, Rowan Dean, urged Australians to 'vote out woke garbage at the next election'. In the early stages of the campaign, the term 'woke' was prominent in Sky's digital election content.

The Coalition was initially praised for its commitment to 'remove the woke agenda in the education system'. On the other hand, Labor and the Greens were derided as 'woke' on the issues of gender and climate change.

Outsiders host Rowan Dean accused Foreign Affairs Minister Penny Wong of 'ramming woke garbage' such as gender studies and climate change down the throats of Papua New Guineans. Fellow *Outsiders* host Rita Panahi ridiculed Labor's election commitment to invest $10 million into 'inclusive and culturally safe' LGBTQIA+ primary healthcare training, commenting, '[W]ho knew it was this expensive to enforce pronouns?' Several hosts defended shadow defence spokesman Andrew Hastie from 'insane political correctness' after he came under fire during the campaign due to resurfaced comments suggesting that women should not be allowed to serve in close-combat roles in the Australian Defence Force.

As the campaign progressed, however, several Sky hosts became increasingly frustrated with the Coalition's campaign for a perceived lack of attention to culture war issues. Indeed, in late April, Dean criticised Dutton for not attacking Labor 'for being woke' and, ironically, accused the Liberal Party 'of going woke'. Much of this criticism concerned the Coalition's decision to centre cost-of-living concerns over culture war issues in its campaign materials. In particular, several evening hosts suggested that the Coalition had 'missed an opportunity' to campaign against transgender rights in the wake of the UK Supreme Court's ruling to define women based on 'biological sex'.

As previously mentioned, while Price was roundly criticised for her Trumpian call to 'make Australia great again', the senator's comments were celebrated on Sky, with one host referring to Price as 'a rockstar'. Indeed, several hosts were critical of Peter Dutton for distancing himself from Donald Trump throughout the campaign as well as forcing Price to walk back her comments. As Sawer and Sengul (2025) have discussed, Sky's digital content is heavily geared towards international audiences with pro-Trump and 'anti-woke' content generating significant views. Despite Trump being widely unpopular in Australia, the network's primetime hosts are overwhelmingly supportive of Trump's right-wing populist agenda, creating tension with the Coalition's desire to distance itself from the US President. As the Coalition found itself swimming against the tide of populism, 'Sky After Dark' became increasingly dissatisfied. This tension was seized upon by Australia's most successful populist politician, Pauline Hanson, who became a frequent fixture on the network throughout the campaign and used her appearances to attack the Coalition's strategic retreat from Trumpism.

Post-election media narratives highlighted Dutton's affinity with Trump as a factor contributing to his loss (for example, Knott 2025). Sky's brand of right-wing media populism (Sawer and Sengul 2025) presents an ongoing challenge for the Liberal Party as it seeks to modernise and recapture support in major cities. While former Liberal ministers such as George Brandis have urged the party to move away from so-called culture war issues that alienated women, multicultural communities and inner-city voters (Karvelas 2025), on Sky, the post-mortem consensus was that the Coalition should have embraced Trump-style populist policies and rhetoric even further. Indeed, during Sky's election-night coverage, both Credlin and Bolt attributed the Coalition's loss to their apparent refusal to fight 'wokeness' and the culture wars.

Several commentators interpreted Labor's landslide victory as a sign of News Corp's waning influence over Australian politics (Simons 2025). While there may be some truth to this, the influence of the Murdoch media within the conservative side of politics should not be understated. In a post-election interview with Barrie Cassidy for the *Guardian Australia*, RedBridge pollster and former Liberal Party strategist Tony Barry reflected on the influence of Sky News Australia on the party membership: 'Our branch members love "Sky after Dark". It's their newsletter. And they are incredibly influential over pre-selections and over our membership' (Barry 2025).

The Coalition's populist campaigning

After the success of Trump's presidential campaign, the Coalition appeared keen to identify with his attacks on elites and the government waste for which they were responsible—such as diversity, equity and inclusion (DEI) projects. Trumpian themes that surfaced during the Australian campaign, particularly when the Opposition Leader was speaking on Sky News, included hostility to 'woke agendas' in universities and schools, which taught students to be ashamed of their country (for example, Sky News, 24 January 2025).

University education had become a key characteristic of elites as identified by the Murdoch media and some Coalition politicians: 'One of the most important shared characteristics of elites across the West is their university education and qualifications' (Alston 2024: 33). In November 2024, Labor made an election commitment to a one-off 20 per cent reduction in student loan debt—cost-of-living relief for three million Australians with university or vocational education and training loans, the majority of whom are women. This was labelled by the Coalition as 'elitist' and unfair to young tradies or those who had paid off their student debt—a response like that of Donald Trump to president Joe Biden's student loan forgiveness plans (Minsky 2024).

Another aspect of the Trump campaign taken up by Opposition leader Peter Dutton was mockery of 'woke' personal pronouns and concern for minorities. At the time of his 'Let's get Australia back on track' launch in January 2025, he said on Sydney radio station 2GB that the Albanese government was 'more interested in pronouns and a $500 million Voice campaign than it was in the cost of living' (Barlow 2025). In addition to the portrayal of the Voice campaign as dividing Australians by race, related themes concerned the display of flags on official occasions and Welcome to Country ceremonies. Dutton's commitment on flags echoed campaigning by Advance as well as the Trump administration's 'one flag policy'.

In January, Senator Jacinta Nampijinpa Price became shadow minister for government efficiency—a portfolio echoing the Trump administration's Department of Government Efficiency (DOGE) led by Elon Musk. As part of the targeting of government waste, she outlined her plans to redirect funding currently used for Welcome to Country ceremonies—something heartily endorsed by Advance, for whom she was previously spokeswoman. Along with Advance, Senator Price continued to echo Trump campaign themes after the imposition of US tariffs made identification with Trump a liability for conservative parties. One example was her call to 'Make Australia great again', uttered at a campaign event in Perth the day before the Coalition campaign launch. Dutton also returned to anti-woke themes in the last week of the campaign, suggesting Welcome to Country ceremonies were 'overdone' and divisive.

The theme of government waste on woke projects had been highlighted in March with the release of *Stop the Bloat* by the Liberal Party's Menzies Research Centre (Louw 2025). Top of its list of wasteful expenditure was a 'decolonising breastfeeding' project, intended to help increase breastfeeding rates among Indigenous Australians. Advance said such projects showed that 'Albo is the PM for the inner-city, not the suburbs or the regions' and the breastfeeding project became a lead item in Advance's 'Weak, woke and sending us broke' video (Advance 2025). The Opposition Leader's theme of the Prime Minister being 'weak' (rather than a strongman who would keep Australians safe) was also highlighted in the Advance video.

The calls to slash woke government waste—for example, Andrew Hastie's Facebook ad of 7 April—were combined with the traditional spatial dimension of Australian populism. In 2023 Dutton had called the Voice proposal an elite 'Canberra voice'. At the soft launch of its 2025 campaign, the Coalition depicted itself as standing up for 'for everyday Australians from our suburbs to our regions' and foreshadowed a major campaign theme of attacking government waste in Canberra. The main target was the '36,000 extra Canberra-based bureaucrats' employed by Labor—a number later updated to 41,000 (LPA 2025).

Regardless of statistics showing most of the additional public servants were employed outside Canberra (APSC 2024), the Coalition pressed on with the anti-Canberra theme. Dutton underlined the message by saying at the end of March that he would not move to Canberra if elected to government. On 24 April, he confirmed that the proposed cut of 41,000 public servants would be in Canberra only, amounting to about two-thirds of federal public servants employed there (Bell and Crowley 2025). Other frontbenchers qualified this slightly by saying the cuts would be 'Canberra focused'. Advance had justified the hostility towards Canberra on the grounds that the Australian Capital Territory's 'Yes' vote to the Voice showed it had 'no understanding of real Australians or the struggles you face' (Advance Update, 15 January 2025).

A spatial dimension also underlay the Coalition's promised fuel excise cut, particularly benefiting ute-drivers in the outer suburbs and regions, unlike Labor policies supposedly benefiting inner-city elites. As Advance had said about Labor's fuel efficiency standards, '[M]ake no mistake: it's about slugging Aussies in the regions and suburbs with more expensive cars while the inner-city elites get cheaper Teslas' (Advance Update, 8 September 2024). Despite the failure of the anti-elite campaign to resonate with the electorate, after the election, Senator Price was still repeating it, lamenting that Labor had walked away with 'three more years to ignore mainstream Australians and listen to the elites and activists' (Advance Update, 26 May 2025).

Swimming with the populist tide: Trumpet of Patriots and One Nation

While the Coalition campaign attempted to eschew comparisons with Trump, minor parties on the populist right were vying for the mantle of Australia's most Trumpian party. The two most significant of these parties,

Pauline Hanson's One Nation (PHON) and Clive Palmer's Trumpet of Patriots (TOP), openly embraced Trumpism as a panacea for a range of social, cultural and economic woes. Unsurprisingly, given its salience in Trump discourse, immigration formed the centrepiece of both campaigns. Both parties framed 'out of control' immigration as the root cause of Australia's cost-of-living and housing crises. Trumpet of Patriots campaigned on an 80 per cent cut to immigration while PHON promised to cut immigration by 570,000 from current levels as part of its Trump-like 'Australia first housing policy'. Moreover, both parties sought to scapegoat immigrants and international students as the cause of the housing affordability crisis. TOP committed to doubling tuition fees for international students and 'restricting foreigners from buying homes'. Interestingly, while Pauline Hanson has always campaigned for lower net migration (Moffitt and Sengul 2025), PHON's anti-immigration rhetoric was amplified in this election. In addition to drastically scaling back Australia's migrant intake, Hanson campaigned heavily on her party's plan to deport 75,000 illegal immigrants. PHON's emphasis on deportations was a significant development in the party's immigration approach (Sengul 2023), particularly in the context of the Trump administration's aggressive deportation efforts in the United States and its popularity with the Make America Great Again (MAGA) base.

Although Clive Palmer's previous personal parties (United Australia Party and Palmer United Party) were noted for their ideological promiscuity (Kefford and McDonnell 2016), there is little doubt that Trumpet of Patriots is a distinctly right-wing, populist party. The party leaned into its MAGA bona fides, claiming that 'Trump-like policies were needed to secure the nation's future' and promising to 'drain the swamp'. Its first televised campaign advertisement featured an interview between Palmer and prominent far-right commentator and Trump-aligned former Fox News host Tucker Carlson. The party's campaign materials were replete with far-right populist discourses and grievances, railing against 'unelected bureaucrats' and 'the scourge of globalist bodies' such as the World Health Organization and the World Economic Forum. Both PHON and TOP committed to withdrawing from the Paris Climate Agreement and ending Australia's commitment to achieve net-zero carbon emissions by 2050. Like the Coalition, both PHON and TOP took inspiration from the Trump administration's DOGE led by Elon Musk with his chainsaw, promising to cut wasteful government spending and inefficiencies.

Consistent with the 2022 election, anti-elitism and 'anti-wokeness' played a key role in the campaigns of both populist parties (Johnson 2023). In the first week of the campaign, the Trumpet of Patriots invested heavily in 'anti-woke' advertisements across print, digital, television and radio media markets. Part of this campaign was a front-page ad in the *Newcastle Herald* featuring the slogan: 'There are only two genders: male and female.' The paper's decision to feature the ad on its front page generated backlash from the *Herald*'s editorial staff, and its publisher, Australian Community Media (ACM), issued an apology to staff and readers (Muller 2025). Both PHON and TOP railed against the so-called woke indoctrination of children in schools, with a particular focus on 'gender ideology' (see Chapter 6, this volume). In populist fashion, TOP promised 'common sense solutions' to 'get the woke agenda out of schools' while PHON argued that 'there should be no room for Western, white, gender, guilt shaming in any classroom'.

Anti-Indigenous rhetoric was a feature of both campaigns. Trumpet of Patriots and PHON both attempted to leverage the rejection of the Indigenous Voice to Parliament in 2023. Indigenous Acknowledgement and Welcome to Country ceremonies were singled out by both parties and TOP ran several campaign ads featuring the slogan 'We don't need to be welcomed to our own country', including unsolicited text messages. PHON has been consistently critical of the 'Aboriginal industry', promising to abolish the National Indigenous Australians Agency and calling for Indigenous land recognition ceremonies to be 'ended altogether'.

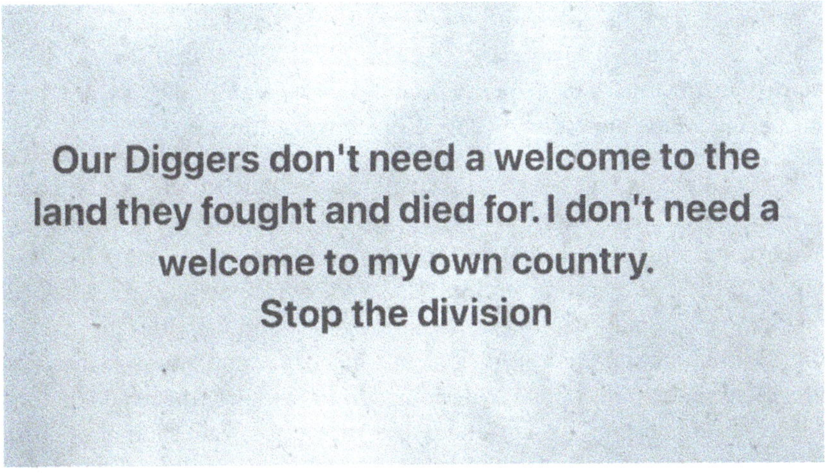

Plate 4.3 A meme posted on Pauline Hanson's One Nation Facebook page, 28 April 2025
Photo: Pauline Hanson's Please Explain Facebook account.

In the final week of the campaign, several neo-Nazi agitators booed and jeered Bunurong man Uncle Mark Brown as he delivered a Welcome to Country at an Anzac Day dawn service in Melbourne (Thompson and Sengul 2025). While the stunt was widely condemned, Hanson instead used it as an opportunity to call for such ceremonies to be abolished. Post election, PHON has doubled down on its opposition to Acknowledgement and Welcome to Country ceremonies. Hanson and fellow PHON senators were widely condemned for turning their backs during the Acknowledgement of Country ceremony in the Senate on the first day of the Forty-Eighth Parliament.

Concluding discussion

Populist discourse was ubiquitous during the 2025 campaign, whether the 'Weak, woke and sending us broke' campaign of Advance or the front-page messages from the Trumpet of Patriots telling readers, 'We don't need to be welcomed to our own country'. As we have seen, in the leadup to the 2025 campaign, the Coalition appeared buoyed by the populist tide associated with the re-election of Donald Trump and the defeat of the Indigenous Voice. However, when the association with Trump became a negative, the Coalition campaign found itself swimming against a tide that was going out.

Ironically, the political editor of *The Australian* published an article immediately after the election blaming the Liberal Party for its 'untested and superior assumption that Labor was out of touch and unaligned with the mainstream values of Australians' (Benson 2025). The *Australian* had done more than any other newspaper to promote this assumption that Labor and the Greens were dominated by out-of-touch woke elites.

Labor's emphatic victory was a reminder of the unpredictable and contingent nature of populism. While attacks on inner-city elites appeared to be a winning card during the Indigenous Voice referendum, this was not so in the 2025 election. Indeed, the hostility to inner-city elites helped rewrite the electoral map, with the Liberal Party ending with only two of the 43 inner metropolitan seats. Dutton's inconsistent attempts to distance himself from Trumpism were undermined by his own frontbench, including Senator Jacinta Nampijinpa Price. Despite the electoral landslide, anti-elitist rhetoric has been normalised within conservative politics thanks in large part to the influence of the Murdoch media.

References

Advance. 2025. 'Weak, woke and sending us broke.' Facebook video, 6 April. Brisbane: Advance. www.facebook.com/watch/?v=443649655478278.

Alston, Richard. 2024. *The Trouble with Elites: Elitism and the Anti-Democratic Impulse.* Brisbane: Connor Court.

Australian Public Service Commission (APSC). 2024. *State of the Service Report 2023–24.* Canberra: Australian Public Service Commission. www.apsc.gov. au/initiatives-and-programs/workforce-information/research-analysis-and-publications/state-service/state-service-report-2023-24.

Barlow, Karen. 2025. '"They're excited by Trump": Dutton's inclusion strategy.' *The Saturday Paper*, 25 January. www.thesaturdaypaper.com.au/news/politics/2025/01/25/theyre-excited-trump-duttons-inclusion-strategy.

Barry, Tony. 2025. 'Back to back Barries: The brutal aftermath of a shock election result.' *Full Story*, [*The Guardian*], 10 May. www.theguardian.com/australia-news/audio/2025/may/10/back-to-back-barries-the-brutal-aftermath-of-a-shock-election-result-podcast.

Bell, Patrick, and Tom Crowley. 2025. 'Dutton confirms public service cuts limited to Canberra, which Labor says is "impossible".' *ABC News*, 24 April. www.abc.net.au/news/2025-04-24/dutton-confirms-public-service-cuts-limited-to-canberra/105211946.

Benson, Simon. 2025. 'Out of touch and out of time: Libs were told Australia had changed but decided not to listen.' *The Australian*, 5 May.

Carson, Andrea, and Simon Jackman. 2023. 'Media coverage of the campaign and the electorate's responses.' In *Watershed: The 2022 Australian Federal Election*, edited by Anika Gauja, Marian Sawer, and Jill Sheppard, 121–44. Canberra: ANU Press. doi.org/10.22459/W.2023.07.

Chambers, Geoff, and Richard Ferguson. 2024. 'Mainstream v elites chasm widens ahead of federal election fight.' *The Australian*, 1 November. www.theaustralian.com.au/nation/politics/mainstream-v-elites-chasm-widens-ahead-of-federal-election-fight/news-story/d9f61a5aadaf85dea18bf22dd86a865f.

Courier-Mail. 2024. 'Lessons for Labor as sneering elites trumped again.' [Editorial], *The Courier-Mail*, 6 November. www.couriermail.com.au/news/opinion/editorial-lessons-for-labor-as-sneering-elites-trumped-again/news-story/6cef283df7e062e2f9a0ca853986844d.

Crotty, Gemma. 2025. 'Federal election: Penny Wong resurrects Voice to Parliament three days out from federal election, declaring the plan inevitable.' *Sky News*, 30 April. www.skynews.com.au/australia-news/politics/penny-wong-suggests-indigenous-voice-will-be-inevitable-as-foreign-minister-equates-issue-to-marriage-equality-vote/news-story/e27110338c88abb5ab261a437439d709.

Johnson, Carol. 2023. 'Variants of populism.' In *Watershed: The 2022 Australian Federal Election*, edited by Anika Gauja, Marian Sawer, and Jill Sheppard, 59–78. Canberra: ANU Press. doi.org/10.22459/W.2023.04.

Karvelas, Patricia. 2025. 'Decimated and divided Liberal Party insiders at odds over what went wrong and what they stand for.' *ABC News*, 26 May. www.abc.net.au/news/2025-05-26/liberal-party-insiders-election-campaign-divided-four-corners/105313660.

Kefford, Glenn, and Duncan McDonnell. 2016. 'Ballots and billions: Clive Palmer's personal party.' *Australian Journal of Political Science* 51, no. 2: 183–97. doi.org/10.1080/10361146.2015.1133800.

Kelly, Paul. 2024. 'Note to Labor: Beware the "unpopular" Liberal leader.' *The Australian*, 18 December. www.theaustralian.com.au/commentary/note-to-labor-beware-the-unpopular-liberal-leader/news-story/f3ef45bfaa7239001674b969d9d64cc4.

Knott, Matthew. 2025. 'Dutton was never a Trump clone. But he fell for the trap of MAGA-style politics.' *The Sydney Morning Herald*, 4 May. www.smh.com.au/politics/federal/first-it-was-canada-then-cyclone-donald-crashed-through-australia-s-election-20250503-p5lwbt.html.

Koutsoukis, Jason. 2024. 'Advance's plan to destroy the Greens.' *The Saturday Paper*, 17 August. www.thesaturdaypaper.com.au/news/politics/2024/08/17/advances-plan-destroy-the-greens.

Krämer, Benjamin. 2014. 'Media populism: A conceptual clarification and some theses on its effects.' *Communication Theory* 24, no. 1: 42–60. doi.org/10.1111/comt.12029.

Liberal Party of Australia (LPA). 2025. *Our Plan*. Canberra: Liberal Party of Australia. www.liberal.org.au/our-plan.

Louw, Nico. 2025. *Stop the Bloat: Delivering a More Efficient and Effective Government*. MRC Report, March. Canberra: Menzies Research Centre. www.menziesrc.org/latest-reports-and-submissions/stop-the-bloat.

Minsky, Adam S. 2024. 'Trump Slams Biden's Student Loan Forgiveness Plans, Suggests Reversal.' *Forbes*, 20 June. www.forbes.com/sites/adamminsky/2024/06/20/trump-knocks-bidens-vile-student-loan-forgiveness-plans-suggests-reversal/.

Moffitt, Benjamin, and Kurt Sengul. 2023. 'The populist radical right in Australia: Pauline Hanson's One Nation.' *Journal of Language and Politics* 22, no. 3: 306–23. doi.org/10.1075/jlp.22132.mof.

Molloy, Shannon. 2024. '"Australia's Trump": The push for Peter Dutton to embrace Donald Trump's campaign style.' *News.com.au*, 11 November. www.news.com.au/national/politics/australias-trump-the-push-for-peter-dutton-to-embrace-donald-trumps-campaign-style/news-story/a918a1fc94dc268d506bb16850668b6e.

Muller, Dennis. 2025. 'Newspapers cannot justify running Clive Palmer's Trumpet of Patriots ads as freedom of speech.' *The Conversation*, 12 March. theconversation.com/newspapers-cannot-justify-running-clive-palmers-trumpet-of-patriots-ads-as-freedom-of-speech-252024. doi.org/10.64628/AA.kvkqdynnt.

Price, Jacinta Nampijinpa. 2025. 'Labor won't take "No" to their Voice.' *Australian Financial Review*, 1 May. www.afr.com/politics/federal/labor-won-t-take-no-to-their-voice-20250430-p5lvbp.

Sawer, Marian, and Kurt Sengul. 2025. 'The war on woke: Continuity and change in Australian anti-elitist discourses.' *Australian Journal of Political Science* 60, no. 3: 1–18. doi.org/10.1080/10361146.2025.2507312.

Scalmer, Sean, and Murray Goot. 2004. 'Elites constructing elites: News Limited's newspapers 1996–2002.' In *Us and Them: Anti-Elitism in Australia*, edited by Marian Sawer and Barry Hindess, 137–59. Perth: API Network.

Sengul, Kurt. 2023. 'The shameless normalization of debasement performance: A critical discourse analysis of Pauline Hanson's Australian, far-right, populist communication.' In *Debasing Political Rhetoric: Dissing Opponents, Journalists, and Minorities in Populist Leadership Communication*, edited by Ofer Feldman, 107–23. Singapore: Springer Nature. doi.org/10.1007/978-981-99-0894-3_7.

Simons, Margaret. 2025. 'As Australia's election result reminds us, News Corp no longer has the power to sway voters.' *The Guardian*, 6 May. www.theguardian.com/commentisfree/2025/may/06/as-australias-election-result-reminds-us-news-corp-no-longer-has-the-power-to-sway-voters.

Thompson, Jay Daniel, and Kurt Sengul. 2025. 'The far-right is becoming more brazen—this poses profound ethical challenges for media coverage.' *ABC News*, 6 May, [Updated 9 May 2025]. www.abc.net.au/religion/ethical-challenges-media-covering-far-right-propaganda/105259670.

Tingle, Laura. 2025. 'Just before election night, Trumpian politics rears its head.' *ABC News*, 3 May. www.abc.net.au/news/2025-05-03/penny-wong-campaign-end-trumpian-politics-crisis-era/105243162.

Young, Sally. 2009. 'Sky News Australia: The impact of local 24-hour news on political reporting in Australia.' *Journalism Studies* 10, no. 3: 401–16. doi.org/10.1080/14616700802636250.

5

Religion: Christians, Muslims and Jews

John Warhurst

Abstract

Religion once again played a role in this election, though this time with a new twist. The unfinished business of 2022 was balancing anti-discrimination for minorities and freedom of religion for faith communities. This chapter addresses the campaign interventions of representatives of three faith communities: Catholics, Muslims and Jews. The study of the extensive Catholic campaign reveals a complex community with a variety of aspirations and demands for the major parties, ranging from self-interest to social justice.

The second and third cases of the smaller Muslim and Jewish communities begin mid-term with the October 2023 Hamas attack on Israel. The domestic reactions to the subsequent war dominated Australian electoral politics for the next 18 months. Both diverse communities tried to hold the parties and Independent candidates to account. The target seats were held by Labor, the Greens or the Teals. Religion-based campaigning was one factor, though the electoral impact did not match the intensity of the social division.

Keywords: religion; Catholics; Jews; Muslims; campaigning

The interaction of religion with politics takes many forms—mostly Christian—during Australian election campaigns. In recent federal elections, it included John Howard and Kevin Rudd offering competing interpretations of their faith to the evangelical Australian Christian Lobby (ACL) in 2007, the conservative Catholic Tony Abbott battling the atheist Julia Gillard in 2010, the prominence of Scott Morrison's personal Pentecostal faith in the 'miracle' election of 2019 and the advocacy role of the ACL in 2022 (Warhurst 2010, 2012; Vromen and Rutledge-Prior 2023).

This interaction takes place in a secular society in which Christianity is the largest religious group. But the numbers of those with no religious affiliation are growing, as are other religious groups. Table 5.1 shows this. The 2021 Census reported that Christians were almost 44 per cent of the population and, among Christians, the largest denomination was Catholic (20 per cent). Those reporting 'no religion' were just under 39 per cent. Other religious groups were much smaller. Islam made up 3.2 per cent, Hinduism 2.7 per cent and Buddhism 2.4 per cent. Judaism was even smaller.

Table 5.1 Religious affiliation in Australia, 2021 Census

Religion	Percentage of national population reporting affiliation
Christianity	43.9
No religion	38.9
Islam	3.2
Hinduism	2.7
Buddhism	2.4
Judaism	0.4

Source: ABS (2022).

There is considerable variation in religious affiliation, including no religion, across Australia. Therefore, the politics of religion shows marked geographical variation. Each electorate has its distinct religious composition (see Table 5.2). Almost always those with 'no religion' are among the two largest sections by 'religion' of each electorate. But in some electorates, including Blaxland and Calwell, 'no religion' fell below 14 per cent (Table 5.2).

Table 5.2 Religious composition of selected House of Representatives electorates

Electorate	Sitting MP	Religious affiliation
Blaxland	Jason Clare (ALP)	Islam, 29.2% Catholic, 19.2% No religion, 13.4% Buddhism, 8.2%
Calwell	Retiring ALP member	Catholic, 26.6% Islam, 23.8% No religion, 13.9% Hinduism, 5.9%
Goldstein	Zoe Daniel (Ind.)	No religion, 34.8% Catholic, 21% Anglican, 11.7% Judaism, 6.8%
Kooyong	Monique Ryan (Ind.)	No religion, 40.6% Catholic, 20.2% Anglican, 15.1% Judaism, 5.3% Uniting Church, 5.1%
Macnamara	Josh Burns (ALP)	No religion, 45.2% Catholic, 15.2% Judaism, 9.9% Anglican, 5.0%
Watson	Tony Burke (ALP)	Islam, 23.4% Catholic, 23.4% No religion, 15.6% Eastern Orthodox, 8.1%
Wentworth	Allegra Spender (Ind.)	No religion, 33.0% Catholic, 20.1% Judaism, 12.5% Anglican, 10.6%
Wills	Peter Khalil (ALP)	No religion, 39.7% Catholic, 23.5% Islam, 10.3% Eastern Orthodox, 6.1%

Source: ABS (2022).

Religious affiliation also interacts with the political party system in different ways. The bulk of the religiously affiliated Christian community operates within the mainstream, the Labor Party and the Coalition. Some are also active on the left within the most secular of all parties, the Greens, while a small number feature among the parties of the general right, Pauline Hanson's One Nation and the United Australia Party/Trumpet of Patriots, and the religious right, Family First and Australian Christians. The ultraconservative Plymouth Brethren made a late entry into this election by campaigning for the Liberal Party at Sydney polling booths (Maddison and Sakkal 2025).

The 2025 election once again involved religion and politics, but it had significant new elements involving other faiths. The unfinished 'religion and politics' business from the previous federal election in 2022 was the matter of religious discrimination (Grattan 2022). Prime minister Scott Morrison was unable to achieve parliamentary reconciliation between the competing claims of faith-based schools and minority groups such as LGBTQIA+ students and teachers. Several Liberal MPs crossed the floor and the legislation was withdrawn after months of wrangling. The faith-based claims were largely prosecuted by Christian organisations, such as Christian Schools, Catholic leaders and the ACL, but there were non-Christian supporters, too.

The new Prime Minister, Anthony Albanese, promised to resolve the stand-off but was unable to do so. He could not achieve bipartisanship with the Coalition and refused to proceed without it, claiming that it would be too divisive. It would also be difficult and probably unproductive. This disappointed both sides (Warhurst 2024).

This issue was highly contested and very public during the first half of Labor's term. Although it did not disappear entirely, after the Israel–Hamas Gaza conflict began in October 2023, it was almost completely overshadowed despite News Corp's support. Instead, news was dominated by events in Gaza, political party responses, pro-Palestinian protests, anti-Israel and anti-Semitic violence, Australian positioning at the United Nations on Middle East votes, Palestinian and Jewish advocacy, State and federal parliamentary legislation curtailing vilification and hate speech and protecting religious worship properties, while addressing social division and protecting freedom of speech.

The emphasis turned to the specific social and political roles of the Jewish and Muslim communities. By mid-2024, the freedom of religion legislation was 'dead in the water', to the regret of the 'faith lobby'. Others, like the Greens, equality groups, Jewish groups and the LGBTQIA+ community regretted the Labor government's abandonment of anti-vilification legislation (for example, Grattan 2024; Lewis 2024a, 2024b; Chrysanthos 2024). *CathNews* reported: 'Broken election promise sparks community anger' (14 August 2024). By the time of the 2025 election, small conservative political parties such as Family First and Australian Christians, neither of which was successful, were the only ones strenuously advocating for such freedom of religion.

The personal faith of the two major-party leaders was originally thought to not be an election issue, though it was noted that both identified as Catholic (Cook 2025; Wimmer 2025). But from the time of Pope Francis's death on Easter Monday, it may have advantaged Albanese, 'who in recent years has strongly re-embraced his Catholic faith' (Tillett and Read 2025).

The premise behind the attention given to religion and elections is that religious identity claims matter when voters determine their vote and that such voters take their lead from their religious groups and leaders. If religious communities are divided, their adherents are less politically important because they cancel each other out. The historical idea of the 'Catholic vote', for instance, depended on the community following church leadership and speaking with 'one voice'. It also presumed that the community was large enough to make a difference.

Some of these assumptions no longer apply to the Catholic community: it is smaller, less cohesive and less inclined to support its own leadership. Whether these assumptions still applied to the much smaller Muslim and Jewish communities was moot. Was there a potential 'Jewish' and/or 'Muslim' vote?

Evolution of social division

The social and political division in Australia following the attack on Israel by Hamas on 7 October 2023, and the military response of the Israeli Government, became the context for the dramatic evolution of religion and electoral politics. The governmental and legislative responses involved the Albanese government and various State governments. The broader political framework drew in all the political parties and many existing faith groups and generated new actors. Religion and politics grew from a somewhat boutique issue to a whole-of-community mass panic.

Table 5.3 Key moments in Jewish–Muslim social division in Australia, post 7 October 2023

Event	Date
Hamas attacks Israel	October 2023
Anti-Semitic attacks	October 2023
Pro-Palestinian rallies	October 2023
Government ministers Ed Husic and Anne Aly defend protesters	October 2023
ABC cancels contract of journalist Antoinette Lattouf	December 2023
Senator Fatima Payman defects from Labor	July 2024
PM Albanese condemns 'faith-based' parties	July 2024
Muslim Independents announce campaigns	July 2024
Albanese appoints anti-Semitism envoy	July 2024
Albanese appoints anti-Islamophobia envoy	September 2024
Firebombing of Adass Synagogue in Melbourne	December 2024
State bans on protests at places of worship	December 2024
New State hate speech legislation	February 2025
United Nations votes on Middle East issues	Various
Attacks on MPs' electorate offices	Various
Eightieth anniversary of liberation of Auschwitz	January 2025
Independent Allegra Spender's motion on hate crimes legislation	February 2025
Alleged Dural 'caravan' terrorist plot	February 2025
Opposition leader Peter Dutton's budget reply speech refers to anti-Semitism	March 2025
Dutton attacks Greens as 'anti-Semitic'	April 2025

Source: Compiled by author.

Table 5.3 identifies some key moments in Jewish–Muslim social division in Australia after 7 October 2023. Initially, large pro-Palestinian protests, especially outside the Opera House in Sydney, became controversial amid allegations of anti-Semitic chants. Governments, under media pressure, rushed to respond. Cracks appeared within Labor ranks at State and national levels. Ed Husic, Labor minister and member for Chifley in Western Sydney, spoke for his Palestinian constituents while maintaining cabinet solidarity, alleging that they were being 'collectively punished for Hamas's barbarism'. He was supported by fellow Muslim minister Anne Aly. Liberal deputy leader Sussan Ley accused Husic of 'freelancing on foreign policy' (Basford Canales and Karp 2023).

When new Western Australian Labor Senator Fatima Payman defected from the Labor Party in July 2024 over the Palestinian issue, Albanese warned against the emergence of another 'faith-based' political party (Sakkal 2024). In the same month, Albanese appointed a new government anti-Semitism envoy, Jillian Segal, and, in September, an anti-Islamophobia envoy.

So-called hate speech legislation, extending existing offences, began to be discussed in the federal parliament. The same divisions in the community quickly arose and harked back to the earlier deadlock over religious discrimination/freedom. Generally, conservative faith groups warned of dangers to freedom of speech from strong anti-hate laws. These included the ACL, Christian Schools and the Australian Catholic Bishops Conference. The ACL saw the potential for 'viewpoint suppression on ideological grounds' (Karp 2024). On the other hand, according to *CathNews* (the official Catholic media hub), 'Greens, LGBT, equality groups and Jewish groups have criticised the bill for abandoning the Government's commitment to outlaw vilification' (21 November 2024).

A similar story was unfolding at the State level with anti-vilification legislation in New South Wales and Victoria (Le Grand 2024). Victorian attempts to lower the acceptable 'hate' threshold led Melbourne Catholic Archbishop Peter Comensoli to warn that a lower threshold 'could erode freedom of religious expression'.

In early December 2024, the Adass Israel Synagogue in Ripponlea in south-eastern Melbourne was firebombed. Widespread criticism of Albanese for being anti-Israel, including by the Israeli Government, followed. The anti-Semitism envoy called for stronger national leadership. The Opposition Leader, building on his consistent narrative, condemned Albanese as 'weak' and attacked the local federal Labor MP Josh Burns, who is Jewish, for having 'lost his voice'. The churches joined in condemnation of the attack (*CathNews*, 9 December 2024; 11 December 2024). The Prime Minister responded: 'To attack a synagogue is an act of anti-Semitism. It's attacking the right that all Australians should have to practise their faith in peace and security.'

The attack on the synagogue generated further moves by the three largest States to ban protests at places of worship (*CathNews*, 10 December 2024). Albanese, who was in Perth, was criticised for taking four days to visit the Melbourne synagogue. There was further anti-Israel and anti-Jewish violence in Sydney. Some voices called for calm and greater balance

(Hamilton 2024). Church leaders backed tough new laws, but then clergy abuse survivors objected to bans on protests outside places of worship (Knaus and Rachwani 2024).

In January 2025, the eightieth anniversary of the liberation of the Auschwitz Nazi concentration camp in Poland was commemorated, with Australia represented by the Foreign Minister Penny Wong and Attorney-General Mark Dreyfus. The Opposition declared that Wong's attendance was inappropriate because of Australia's stance at the United Nations on the issue of Israel–Gaza–Palestine (*7.30*, ABC TV, 27 January). Speaking from Poland, Dreyfus called politicisation of anti-Semitism 'grotesque' (Harris 2025). The Opposition Leader, after Nazi demonstrations in Adelaide, equated those on the extreme right and white supremacists with the Greens as purveyors of 'hate speech'.

February 2025 was a frantic month. There were federal and State legislative manoeuvrings, anti-Semitic attacks, arrests by police, terror warnings from the Australian Security Intelligence Organisation (ASIO), a Sky News anti-Semitism summit, the parliamentary gagging of Dreyfus, allegedly anti-Semitic NSW nurses, a Venice Biennale controversy over the dropping of the Australian representative and the continuing legal case against former ABC journalist Antoinette Lattouf.

The Australian Federation of Islamic Councils called attention to double standards (*Canberra Times*, 18 February 2025). The NSW Parliament passed 'hate speech' laws, but Faith NSW called the legislation flawed and the Rabbi of the Great Synagogue in Sydney asked for LGBTQIA+ people to be included (Maddison 2025). Creative Australia dropped Khaled Sabsabi as the Australian representative at the Venice Biennale amid controversy over some of his previous artwork (Papastergiadis 2025; SMH 2025a). Adding to discord within the arts community, Judith Chand, chair of the Sydney Writers Festival, resigned.

At the federal level, community sensitivities were such that 12 April, Passover, was ruled out as insensitive for an election date. Community Independent member for Wentworth Allegra Spender played an active role in parliamentary discussions, called on the government to defund the UN Relief and Works Agency and threatened to sue her Liberal opponent for alleging that the Spender team placed a campaign poster over an Israeli image (Chrysanthos et al. 2025). Both candidates later appeared at an election forum hosted by the Executive Council of Australian Jewry and the NSW Board of Deputies (Buckley 2025).

The Opposition Leader promised free trade with Israel and the European Union, reiterating his earlier promise of a referendum on citizenship and anti-Semitism. With an election in the air, Dutton's budget reply speech on 27 March included several items that focused on electorally sensitive anti-Semitism.

Election campaign controversies

Commentary now focused more directly on the possible role of the Muslim and Jewish communities in the election. Often this development was decried as contributing to unwanted social division.

The Sydney Morning Herald editorialised, for instance, that:

> The fading divide between religion and politics in Australia's outer suburbs is a *new, confusing and corrosive development* in Australian politics. Politicians courting the votes of Muslim communities in Sydney and Melbourne have encountered a bewildering range of responses, including threats of violence. Identity-based tribalism invaded the opening days of the election campaign with an attack on both Labor and Coalition stances on the Israel–Hamas conflict. (SMH 2025b; emphasis added)

The campaigning proceeded on the untested assumption adopted by some commentators that such faith-based tribalism would indeed have an electoral impact. The ABC's Jacob Greber, for instance, concluded that the Community Independents might be electoral victims:

> Labor has found itself squeezed between the outrage of pro-Palestinian Australians wanting stronger condemnation of Israel's government and local Jewish communities suffering antisemitism …

> Inner-city Teal or community independents are equally challenged, especially with MPs like Zoe Daniel, Monique Ryan in Melbourne and Allegra Spender in Sydney defending electorates with large Jewish populations. *It's almost conventional wisdom among analysts that fears about antisemitism will send a wave of Teal voters back to the Liberal Party, even though Peter Dutton is more socially conservative than many voters in these seats.* (Greber 2025; emphasis added)

The Christian advocate the Reverend Tim Costello assumed an unlikely unity within both faith communities:

> For the first time in living memory *Australia's Jewish and Muslim communities will largely vote as blocs* based on Australian foreign policy. (Costello 2025; emphasis added)

> I think *the Coalition have absolutely doubled down and now have pocketed every Australian Jewish vote in this next election* and that means the Prime Minister is sort of a meat in the sandwich, flailing at both. (Hawley 2025; emphasis added)

There were, however, some early doubters of the likely negative impact of the Muslim vote on Labor (Henderson 2024). The Sydney Institute's Gerard Henderson had claimed in August 2024 that it was 'most unlikely' that an Independent Muslim candidate would defeat a Labor MP.

Mid-campaign, political scientist Murray Goot approached the question through an analysis of recent polls, including YouGov (Goot 2025; see also Chapter 20, this volume). He suggested that:

> [while] the government's policy on the war in Gaza is likely to be of concern to the large number of Muslim voters in Labor seats in Melbourne (Calwell especially) and Sydney (Watson and Blaxland especially) and to Jewish voters in Labor seats, especially in the Melbourne seat of Macnamara) [ultimately, these voters would have little impact].

According to YouGov, though not the Freshwater poll, these Labor seats would not change hands, nor would the Teal seats. Goot concluded: 'On these figures, neither Muslim nor Jewish voters will even come close to changing the outcomes.'

Nevertheless, the issue continued to attract campaign attention among Muslims and Jews as well as the major parties and Independent candidates. Bagshaw and Olaya (2025) discussed four 'Muslim' seats in Sydney, concentrating on the two main 'Muslim' Independents, Ziad Basyouny in Watson and Ahmed Ouf in Blaxland, while Dumas (2025) canvassed multiple electorates in which 'Muslims aim to exert new political power at the election'.

Unauthorised flyers alleged that Labor's Tony Burke in Watson was 'a racist' and a banner claimed he supported 'genocide' (McSweeney 2025). The Stand4Palestine group called on mosques to not host politicians who supported Israel, and some visits immediately became controversial

(Duffin 2025). Local Muslim leader Jamal Rifi defended Burke and Labor. He later launched 'Friends of Tony Burke'. Attendance at mosques by politicians became an issue in Melbourne and Sydney during the Eid al-Fitr festival at the end of Ramadan (Truu 2025). The local Greens campaign against Labor MP Peter Khalil in Wills used extreme language, linking him with the 'Zionist lobby' and claiming that he was 'complicit in war crimes' (Durkin and McCubbing 2025). Earlier, Greens Senator Mehreen Faruqi had alleged Labor was 'complicit' in genocide (Olbrycht-Palmer and Wang 2024).

In Melbourne, former Liberal MP Tim Wilson hoped that angry Jewish voters would help him regain Goldstein from Community Independent MP Zoe Daniel (Knott 2025). Meanwhile, an official Jewish forum in Macnamara engendered controversy within the Jewish community by banning the Greens candidate on the grounds that the party had 'intentionally fuelled antisemitism' (in the words of Jewish leader Jeremy Liebler) (Belot and Kolovos 2025). The Zionist Federation of Australia and the Executive Council of Australian Jewry lobbied the Prime Minister and the Opposition Leader to preference each other above the Greens.

In Sydney, prominent Community Independent candidate Nicolette Boele (Bradfield) apologised at a Jewish-organised event for an anti-Semitic social media post in 2022 (*Sydney Morning Herald*, 24 April 2025). In Wentworth, 47,000 copies of an anonymous 12-page pamphlet, titled 'Allegra Spender exposed', were distributed, alleging that the Community Independent MP was weak on anti-Semitism (*Guardian*, 22 April 2025). The Opposition Leader ramped up his rhetoric against the Greens, describing the party as an 'antisemitic, Jew-hating party' (*Canberra Times*, 28 April 2025).

The Catholic voice and vote

The Christian case study is of the extensive Catholic community. The Catholic community is the best example of a large Christian faith successfully integrated into the political debate. A plethora of official and unofficial Catholic groups intervened during the election campaign (for general background, see Warhurst 2008). These advocacy efforts included the traditional statement from the Australian Catholic Bishops Conference (ACBC 2025), a more extensive Catholic Religious Australia statement and contributions from major agencies such as the National Catholic Education Commission (NCEC), Catholic Social Services Australia and Catholic Health Australia. Some local dioceses played an electoral role, as did lay groups such as the St Vincent de Paul Society (known as Vinnies).

Each of these groups had a potential audience and the networks to try to reach them: dioceses, parishes, schools, hospitals, Centacare agencies and Vinnies' conferences. Yet, in many cases, it is a diminishing audience and, in some cases, ageing. Catholic school communities were the biggest and most likely receptors of church messages though the lines of communication through school principals to parents and staff were long, contentious and unreliable.

The type of Catholic interventions varied between many different perspectives and techniques. There was the 'social justice' church and the 'professional' church—sometimes overlapping.

Some interventions were examples of hard-nosed and hard-hitting modern lobbying techniques that essentially advised Catholics whom to vote for and whom to avoid. The NCEC, representing the powerful Catholic education interest, supported the two major parties, while strongly criticising the Greens. In other statements, the NCEC and its affiliates and associates leant towards the Coalition's 'anti-woke' agenda. Its five priorities were funding certainty, support for faith-based schools, sector neutrality, addressing disadvantage and early childhood education.

Conversely, the St Vincent de Paul Society's policy scorecard strongly supported the Greens and partially supported the Labor government, while finding little or no merit in the Coalition Opposition. Its four priorities were supporting a safety net for all Australians, housing security across the country, meeting the needs of First Nations peoples and rising to the refugee challenge. Vinnies also offered a webinar and supported the 'Say yes to refugees' theme of the Palm Sunday rallies held during the election campaign.

Muslim and Jewish faith voices

The domestic Australian aftermath of October 2023 switched attention from Christian voters to the smaller Muslim and Jewish communities (about 800,000 and 120,000 people, respectively; see Table 5.1). 'Religion' in the election became 'ethno-religion'.

These two Australia-wide ethnic communities shared the same political limitations as the larger Catholic community with quite diverse voices, sometimes based on contradictory values. Unlike Catholics and other Christians, however, they were concentrated in a small number of electorates, mostly in Sydney and Melbourne, where the number of Muslims and Jews is a substantial proportion of the voting population (see Table 5.2). This may have been just high enough to make a difference.

These 'Muslim' electorates, as discussed in the media, included the Labor-held, largely working-class seats of Blaxland and Watson in Western Sydney and Calwell and Wills in Melbourne. The two Sydney seats were targeted by Independent candidates with backing from Muslim advocacy groups. The two Melbourne seats were ones that the Greens hoped to win from Labor (Kolovos 2025).

The 'Jewish' electorates included the relatively marginal middle-class seats of Wentworth in Sydney and Kooyong and Goldstein in Melbourne held by Community Independents elected in 2022. These were the 'Jewish' targets. Labor-held Macnamara in Melbourne also had a large Jewish population.

The Muslim voice and vote

The second case study is the Muslim community. The generally working-class Muslim community has traditionally been ethnically fragmented and politically disorganised. Despite some national organisations, it lacked recognised national leaders—contributing to less political effectiveness. Muslim voters in the past largely supported the Labor Party. Sitting Labor MPs were being challenged by pro-Palestine Muslim Independents, supported by various groups including Muslim Votes Matter (MVM) (Krayem 2025) and The Muslim Vote (see also Chapter 15, this volume).

MVM also generally allocated preferences to the Greens over both Labor and Liberal candidates. It handed out how-to-vote cards in targeted electorates (campaigning in 32 seats) and offered online advice in others. It believed that in certain electorates an 'organised, informed and principled' Muslim vote could be 'decisive' but outlined larger goals beyond the election. It also saw the campaign not as 'religious' but as 'a political one grounded in ethics'. Its national spokesperson Ghaith Krayem (2025) argued:

> MVM is not simply about voter turnout or civic engagement. It is about carving out a place for our voice in the political discourse of this country—asserting that we exist not only as objects of commentary, but as agents of influence …

> MVM is not an election campaign—it is the foundation of a long-term strategy to platform Muslim voices and demands in Australian political life.

The Australian Palestine Advocacy Network (APAN) distributed an election scorecard on 'how the major parties have responded to Israel's genocide in Gaza during the past 18 months' (APAN 2025). On the answers to 12 questions, the Greens ranked first, ahead of Labor, with the Liberal Party trailing far behind. Stand4Palestine called on mosques to not host politicians who had supported Israel. The minor Australia's Voice party, led by Senator Payman, also campaigned for Independents and Greens against Labor.

The driving force behind these campaigns was Muslim anger that the government was insufficiently supportive of the Palestinian cause. Other issues were secondary. MVM recognised that the Muslim community also supported the rights of its faith-based schools to determine the hiring of staff. This put them at odds with Greens policy, but the difference was accommodated through consultation and the promise by Greens leader Adam Bandt of his party's respect for conflicting rights on matters of freedom of religion (Belot 2025).

Muslim voters had established party allegiances and tended in the past to support Labor in working-class electorates, though in the 2017 same-sex marriage plebiscite and in 2023 in the Voice referendum—notably, in Western Sydney—they appeared to express a different view. Ministers Husic and Aly were advocating within the government. Yet, some Muslim voters may have been ready for change. In both the 2024 UK and the 2024 US elections, there was some evidence that Muslim voters were mobilised to desert their traditional Labour and Democrat allegiances.

The Jewish voice and vote

The equally complex third case study is the even smaller Jewish community. Historically, it was pro-Labor, but in recent years shifted to being pro-Coalition (Walker 2024; see also Patrick 2025). It contained many groups highly critical of the Albanese Labor government for being insufficiently pro-Israel, both domestically in not tackling anti-Semitism strongly enough and through its even-handed voting in the United Nations. These groups include the established peak organisations, often known colloquially as the 'Jewish lobby' or 'Israel lobby', which were well resourced, highly professional and well organised with an established profile (Lyons 2019; Gawenda 2023; see, in general, Mendes and Brahm Levy 2004).

Such older groups included the advocacy-oriented Australian Israel & Jewish Affairs Council (AIJAC, founded in 1997), the major umbrella group, the Executive Council of Australian Jewry (ECAJ, founded in 1944), the Zionist Federation of Australia and the Anti-Defamation Commission. All were active pro-Israel campaigners and generated a profusion of pro-Israel articles in the mainstream media. There were other anti-government Jewish groups, too.

An informal group known as 'Lawyers for Israel' allegedly criticised the ABC over the hiring of journalist Antoinette Lattouf in December 2023 (APAN 2024). In Macnamara, another new group, called J-United, was active (Kolovos 2025).

A new and alternative more pro-Palestinian view was represented by another, more 'progressive' body, the Jewish Council of Australia, which supported the government's position; it emerged mid-term in February 2024 to offer a fresh voice opposed to both anti-Semitism and Israel's conduct (Dumas 2024). Jewish Labor MPs, including Dreyfus and the member for Macnamara, Josh Burns, also defended the government against Jewish criticism.

Jewish groups also clashed with Climate 200, the main funder of Community Independents, alleging it contained anti-Semitic elements (Adno 2025). AIJAC executive director Colin Rubenstein asserted that Community Independent MPs, 'especially those in electorates with large Jewish communities', should 'distance themselves' from Climate 200 and its leader, Simon Holmes à Court. This stance was taken up in Wentworth by Allegra Spender's Liberal opponent.

Intra-community tensions were notably intense within the Jewish community. At its initiation, the new Jewish Council declared that it was 'ashamed that some Jewish organisations had been lobbying to refuse entry to people seeking safety' from Gaza (Jewish Council of Australia 2024). It labelled ECAJ as a 'right-wing Zionist group'. In turn, ECAJ described the Jewish Council as 'far left' and ridiculed it as a 'micro-group'.

Conclusion

Religious voices affirmed group identity and supported democratic participation as well as addressing party choice. It was the last, however, which attracted more media attention. Yet, often the faith voices deliberately steered clear of party choice. Catholic voters were divided, and this probably applied to the Muslim and Jewish voters, too.

Christianity, the majority faith, has diverse representation in the Australian polity. Traditional centrist and progressive denominations such as the Anglican and Uniting churches were now matched by the ACL, the activist evangelical lobby group, and by the influence of the growing Pentecostal community, as well as the small far-right Christian parties.

The Catholic community, the largest Christian denomination, probably spoke with too many different voices to be effective. While not explicitly disagreeing with one another in public, they certainly demonstrated their political differences vividly through their scorecards rating the parties. This method often failed to adequately consider minor parties, Community Independents and Independents, despite their increasing prevalence and attractiveness to voters.

Christians shared the stage with Muslims and Jews. The Israel–Hamas Gaza confrontation elevated the latter to new prominence. The faith groups generally represented an 'older style' of campaigning, often conducted in and around places of worship, including churches, mosques and synagogues, as well as in newspapers and community forums and meetings.

Journalist David Crowe (2025) concluded that the Greens' campaigning on Gaza was one factor in its loss of seats (see also Chapter 13, this volume). The Jewish vote appears to have been one factor in the comeback by the Liberal Party in the Melbourne electorate of Goldstein (Hayman and Nethery 2025; see also Chapter 14, this volume). Several of the Muslim Independents produced solid performances by finishing second against leading Labor figures in Western Sydney (see also Chapter 15, this volume).

After the election many 'religious' threads were kept alive. Catholic voters probably joined the general swing towards the government. Its leadership was glad to protect education funding. The unfinished war in Gaza meant that both the Muslim and the Jewish communities continued to advocate their concerns to the government.

Dreyfus and Husic, Jewish and Muslim, respectively, were both dropped from the new Labor ministry in a factional carve-up (to the dismay of Labor loyalist Jamal Rifi in the case of Husic). New Liberal leader, Sussan Ley, reiterated in her first media conference the Opposition's claim that the government was anti-Jewish. Jewish community leader Alex Rychin (ECAJ) celebrated the defeat of Greens leader Adam Bandt. Both the faith groups and Equality Australia quickly returned religious discrimination legislation to the table for the new parliamentary term.

References

Adno, Carly. 2025. 'Teals urged to cut ties with Climate 200.' *Australian Jewish News*, 3 April. www.australianjewishnews.com/teals-urged-to-cut-ties-with-climate-200/.

Australian Bureau of Statistics (ABS). 2022. 'Religious Affiliation in Australia: Exploration of the changes in reported religion in the 2021 Census.' Media release, 4 July. Canberra: Australian Bureau of Statistics. www.abs.gov.au/articles/religious-affiliation-australia.

Australian Catholic Bishops Conference (ACBC). 2025. 'Called to bring hope in the year of jubilee.' Election statement. Canberra: Australian Catholic Bishops Conference. www.catholic.au/s/article/Election-Statement-2025.

Australian Palestinian Advocacy Network (APAN). 2024. 'Pro-Israel lobby influence over ABC threatens journalistic ethics, independence.' Media release, 27 January. Canberra: Australian Palestinian Advocacy Network. apan.org.au/media_release/pro-israel-lobby-influence-over-abc-threatens-journalistic-ethics/.

APAN. 2025. 'Vote with Palestine.' *Pearls and Irritations*, 25 April. johnmenadue.com/post/2025/04/vote-with-palestine/.

Bagshaw, Eryk, and Kayla Olaya. 2025. 'Hostile and deeply divided: In south-west Sydney, it's an election campaign like never before.' *The Sydney Morning Herald*, 20 April. www.smh.com.au/politics/federal/hostile-and-deeply-divided-in-south-west-sydney-it-s-an-election-campaign-like-never-before-20250408-p5lq2l.html.

Basford Canales, Sarah, and Paul Karp. 2023. 'Albanese government accused of "deep division" and "confusion" over Israel–Hamas conflict stance.' *The Guardian*, 19 October. www.theguardian.com/australia-news/2023/oct/19/albanese-government-accused-of-deep-division-and-confusion-over-israel-hamas-conflict-stance.

Belot, Henry. 2025. 'Muslim advocacy group to preference Greens above Labor in some seats despite disagreement on religious freedom.' *The Guardian*, 16 April. www.theguardian.com/australia-news/2025/apr/16/muslim-advocacy-group-to-preference-greens-above-labor-in-some-seats-despite-disagreement-on-religious-freedom.

Belot, Henry, and Benita Kolovos. 2025. 'Jewish leaders unhappy at decision to block Greens candidate from Melbourne community forum.' *The Guardian*, 5 April. www.theguardian.com/australia-news/2025/apr/05/jewish-leaders-unhappy-at-decision-to-block-greens-candidate-from-melbourne-community-forum-ntwnfb.

Buckley, Penry. 2025. 'Handshake, strong words: First public face-off for Spender and Knox after legal threat.' *The Sydney Morning Herald*, 7 April. www.smh.com.au/politics/federal/handshake-strong-words-first-public-face-off-for-spender-and-knox-after-legal-threat-20250406-p5lpki.html.

CathNews. 2024a. 'Melbourne Archdiocese condemns firebomb attack on synagogue.' *CathNews*, 9 December. cathnews.com/2024/12/09/melbourne-archdiocese-condemns-firebomb-attack-on-synagogue/.

CathNews. 2024b. 'Catholic Religious Australia condemns arson attack on synagogue.' *CathNews*, 11 December. cathnews.com/2024/12/11/catholic-religious-australia-condemns-arson-attack-on-synagogue/.

Chrysanthos, Natassia. 2024. '"Injustices ignored": LGBTQ and faith groups fume at PM's broken promise.' *The Sydney Morning Herald*, 13 August. www.smh.com.au/politics/federal/injustices-ignored-lgbtq-and-faith-groups-fume-at-pm-s-broken-promise-20240813-p5k1zp.html.

Chrysanthos, Natassia, Olivia Ireland, and Matthew Knott. 2025. 'Teal MP Allegra Spender threatens to sue challenger over "disgraceful accusation".' *The Sydney Morning Herald*, 7 March. www.smh.com.au/politics/federal/teal-mp-allegra-spender-threatens-to-sue-challenger-over-disgraceful-accusation-20250307-p5lhof.html.

Cook, Michael. 2025. 'This is going to be a unique contest between two Catholics.' *Catholic Weekly*, 7 April. catholicweekly.com.au/unusual-dynamics-at-play-in-federal-election/.

Costello, Tim. 2025. 'Antisemitism and Islamophobia are not the only things rupturing our communities.' 17 January. Sydney: Centre for Public Christianity. [First published, *The Sydney Morning Herald*, 15 January]. publicchristianity.org/article/antisemitism-and-islamophobia-are-not-the-only-things-rupturing-our-communities/.

Crowe, David. 2025. 'The Greens bet on Gaza, now they may have lost the House.' *The Sydney Morning Herald*, 7 May. www.smh.com.au/politics/federal/the-greens-bet-on-gaza-and-may-have-lost-the-house-20250507-p5lxen.html.

Duffin, Perry. 2025. '"Interrupt, disrupt, expose": Plan to drive MPs from Sydney's mosques.' *The Sydney Morning Herald*, 30 March. www.smh.com.au/national/nsw/interrupt-disrupt-expose-plan-to-drive-mps-from-sydney-s-mosques-2025 0330-p5lnmp.html.

Dumas, Daisy. 2024. 'A fresh Jewish voice: The new Australian group opposing antisemitism—and Israel's conduct.' *The Guardian*, 1 April. www.theguardian.com/world/2024/apr/01/progressive-australian-jews-opposing-antisemitism-israel-gaza-war.

Dumas, Daisy. 2025. 'Sick of being ignored: Galvanised by Gaza, Australian Muslims aim to exert new political power at the election.' *The Guardian*, 24 April. www.theguardian.com/australia-news/2025/apr/24/sick-of-being-ignored-galvanised-by-gaza-australian-muslims-aim-to-exert-new-political-power-at-the-election.

Durkin, Patrick, and Gus McCubbing. 2025. 'The Melbourne seats where Israel–Gaza has become ugly campaign fight.' *Australian Financial Review*, 1 May. www.afr.com/politics/federal/the-melbourne-seats-where-israel-gaza-has-become-ugly-campaign-fight-20250429-p5lv3p.

Gawenda, Michael. 2023. 'Truths and myths about Australia's "Israel lobby".' *The Jewish Independent*, 6 October, [Updated 19 March 2024]. thejewish independent.com.au/michael-gawenda-truths-and-myths-about-australias-israel-lobby.

Goot, Murray. 2025. 'Which are the polls to watch?' *Inside Story*, 14 April. insidestory.org.au/which-are-the-polls-to-watch/.

Grattan, Michelle. 2022. 'With the sex and religious discrimination bills, Scott Morrison made three foolish assumptions.' *ABC News*, 11 February. www.abc.net.au/news/2022-02-11/religious-discrimination-bill-morrison-backfired/100820422.

Grattan, Michelle. 2024. 'Hate speech moves fan fire.' *Canberra Times*, 1 June.

Greber, Jacob. 2025. 'Donald Trump and Middle East chaos have up-ended Australia's politics in a way not seen "since the Vietnam War".' *ABC News*, 9 February. www.abc.net.au/news/2025-02-09/trump-gaza-foreign-issues-upend-politics-as-usual/104909980.

Hamilton, Andrew. 2024. 'The horror of synagogue burning.' *Eureka Street*, 12 December. www.eurekastreet.com.au/article/the-horror-of-synagogue-burning.

Harris, Rob. 2025. 'Dreyfus calls out left and right in antisemitism fight.' *The Sydney Morning Herald*, 28 January.

Hawley, Samantha. 2025. 'How politicians are failing on anti-Semitism.' [Interview with Tim Costello]. *ABC News Daily*, 23 January. www.abc.net.au/listen/programs/abc-news-daily/how-politicians-are-failing-on-anti-semitism/104847682.

Hayman, Phoebe, and Amy Nethery. 2025. 'Liberal Party reclaims Goldstein—How Tim Wilson turned back the Teal tidal wave.' *The Conversation*, 12 May. theconversation.com/liberal-party-reclaims-goldstein-how-tim-wilson-turned-back-the-teal-tidal-wave-256201. doi.org/10.64628/AA.jexaqf5nt.

Henderson, Gerard. 2024. 'Preference system no help to "divisive" Muslim candidates.' *The Australian*, 17 August. www.theaustralian.com.au/subscribe/news/1/?sourceCode=TAWEB_WRE170_a_GGL&dest=https%3A%2F%2Fwww.theaustralian.com.au%2Finquirer%2Fpreference-system-no-help-to-divisive-muslim-candidates%2Fnews-story%2Fd36fce4b378ec4de71ff8c9f09e7253a&memtype=anonymous&mode=premium&v21=GROUPA-Segment-1-NOSCORE&V21spcbehaviour=append.

Jewish Council of Australia. 2024. 'Jewish Council of Australia urges the Australian government to reject racism against Palestinian people fleeing persecution in Gaza.' Media release, 27 February. Sydney: Jewish Council of Australia. www.jewishcouncil.com.au/2024/02/reject-racism-against-palestinian-fleeing-persecution-gaza.

Karp, Paul. 2024. 'Labor's "thought crime" hate speech laws will turn nation into "police state", Australian Christian Lobby says.' *The Guardian*, 21 November. www.theguardian.com/world/2024/nov/21/labors-thought-hate-speech-laws-will-turn-nation-into-police-state-australian-christian-lobby-says-ntwnfb.

Knaus, Christopher, and Mostafa Rachwani. 2024. 'Clergy abuse survivors hit out at moves to ban protests outside Australian places of worship.' *The Guardian*, 13 December. www.theguardian.com/australia-news/2024/dec/13/clergy-abuse-survivors-hit-out-at-moves-to-ban-protests-outside-australian-places-of-worship.

Knott, Matthew. 2025. 'The numbers game.' *The Sydney Morning Herald*, 29 March.

Kolovos, Benita. 2025. 'Israel–Gaza war looms large over Labor's hold on Melbourne seats of Macnamara and Wills.' *The Guardian*, 14 April. www.theguardian.com/australia-news/2025/apr/14/israel-gaza-war-looms-large-over-labors-hold-on-melbourne-seats-of-macnamara-and-wills.

Krayem, Ghaith. 2025. 'From margins to movement: Why Muslim votes matter.' [Blog]. *Pearls and Irritations,* 14 April. johnmenadue.com/post/2025/04/from-margins-to-movement-why-muslim-votes-matter/.

Le Grand, Chip. 2024. 'Allan government faces showdown with faith groups over hate laws.' *The Age*, 18 November. www.theage.com.au/politics/victoria/allan-government-faces-showdown-with-faith-groups-over-hate-laws-20241115-p5k qz2.html.

Lewis, Rosie. 2024a. '"We're fast losing faith", community groups warn Anthony Albanese.' *The Australian*, 4 July. www.theaustralian.com.au/subscribe/news/1/?sourceCode=TAWEB_WRE170_a_GGL&dest=https%3A%2F%2Fwww.theaustralian.com.au%2Fnation%2Fpolitics%2Fwere-fast-losing-faith-community-groups-warn-anthony-albanese%2Fnews-story%2Fa2ab0d596e2d9a2ff0b97d3b5a35c2ca&memtype=anonymous&mode=premium&v21=GROUPA-Segment-1-NOSCORE&V21spcbehaviour=append.

Lewis, Rosie. 2024b. 'Redraft laws "with input from faiths".' *The Australian*, 15 July. www.theaustralian.com.au/nation/politics/redraft-religious-discrimination-laws-with-input-from-faiths-says-michaelia-cash/news-story/4ea3c21ad5e462b8b129b8fa43772a61.

Lyons, John. 2019. *Balcony over Jerusalem*. Sydney: HarperCollins.

Maddison, Max. 2025. 'Hate speech laws pushed through.' *The Sydney Morning Herald*, 19 February.

Maddison, Max, and Paul Sakkal. 2025. 'Exclusive Brethren made nearly a million calls for the Liberal Party.' *The Age*, 14 May. www.theage.com.au/politics/federal/exclusive-brethren-made-nearly-a-million-calls-for-the-liberal-party-20250508-p5lxml.html.

McSweeney, Jessica. 2025. 'Unauthorised flyers label Burke a racist.' *The Sydney Morning Herald*, 29 March.

Mendes, Philip, and Geoffrey Brahm Levy, eds. 2004. *Jews and Australian Politics*. Brighton: Sussex Academic Press.

Olbrycht-Palmer, Joseph, and Jessica Wang. 2024. 'Greens senator accuses Labor of "complicity" in "genocide" in Gaza.' *The Australian*, 8 October. www.theaustralian.com.au/breaking-news/greens-senator-accuses-labor-of-complicity-in-genocide-in-gaza/news-story/1761198c0b3f32dad219aa52c6cbfe61.

Papastergiadis, Nikos. 2025. 'This is the most shameful act of political intervention in the arts that I have seen.' *The Sydney Morning Herald*, 17 February. www.smh.com.au/national/this-is-the-most-shameful-act-of-political-intervention-in-the-arts-that-i-have-seen-20250217-p5lcrj.html.

Patrick, Aaron. 2025. 'The inside story of how Labor destroyed its deep ties with Australia's Jewish community in just 18 months.' *The Nightly*, 20 March. thenightly.com.au/politics/australia/how-prime-minister-anthony-albanese-and-penny-wong-lost-the-australian-jewish-community-c-17945032.

Sakkal, Paul. 2024. 'PM warns against faith-based political movements as Payman hints at next move.' *The Sydney Morning Herald*, 6 July. www.smh.com.au/politics/federal/pm-warns-against-faith-based-political-movements-as-payman-hints-at-next-move-20240705-p5jrc0.html.

Sydney Morning Herald (SMH). 2025a. 'Venice Biennale backflip could turn pride into embarrassment.' [Editorial], *The Sydney Morning Herald*, 17 February. www.smh.com.au/national/nsw/venice-biennale-backflip-could-turn-pride-into-embarrassment-20250217-p5lcpy.html.

Sydney Morning Herald (SMH). 2025b. 'The separation of the political and the tribal.' [Editorial], *The Sydney Morning Herald*, 2 April.

Tillett, Andrew, and Michael Read. 2025. 'Papal pause comes at worst time for Dutton.' *Australian Financial Review*, 22 April. www.afr.com/politics/federal/papal-pause-comes-at-worst-time-for-dutton-20250422-p5ltax.

Truu, Maani. 2025. 'Leaders missing from Eid events, as split over politicians at prayers becomes heated.' *ABC News*, 6 April. www.abc.net.au/news/2025-04-06/muslim-community-split-over-politicians-at-prayers/105122024.

Vromen, Ariadne, and Serrin Rutledge-Prior. 2023. 'Third-party campaigning organisations.' In *Watershed: The 2022 Australian Federal Election*, edited by Anika Gauja, Marian Sawer, and Jill Sheppard, 305–31. Canberra: ANU Press. doi.org/10.22459/W.2023.15.

Walker, Tony. 2024. 'Labor goes one way, Israel goes another.' *Inside Story*, 6 December. insidestory.org.au/labor-goes-one-way-israel-the-other/.

Warhurst, John. 2008. 'The Catholic lobby: Structures, policy styles and religious networks.' *Australian Journal of Public Administration* 67, no. 2: 213–30. doi.org/10.1111/j.1467-8500.2008.00583.x.

Warhurst, John. 2010. 'Religion.' *Australian Cultural History* 28, no. 1: 31–37. doi.org/10.1080/07288430903165329.

Warhurst, John. 2012. 'Religion and the 2010 election: Elephants in the room.' In *Julia 2010: The Caretaker Election*, edited by Marian Simms and John Wanna, 303–11. Canberra: ANU E Press. doi.org/10.22459/J2010.02.2012.

Warhurst, John. 2024. 'The Greens, the Church and freedom of religion.' *Eureka Street*, 1 May. www.eurekastreet.com.au/the-greens-the-church-and-freedom-of-religion.

Wimmer, A.C. 2025. 'Australia election features rare contest between Catholic candidates.' *CNA (Catholic News Agency)*, 11 April. www.catholicnewsagency.com/news/263235/faith-at-the-ballot-australia-s-election-sees-rare-contest-between-catholic-candidates.

6

Gender and diversity in the 2025 election: Policies and presence

Blair Williams and Marian Sawer

Abstract

As with previous elections, gender was again a key factor in the 2025 federal election. The Coalition continued to alienate women voters while Labor campaigned on the care economy and young women favoured the Greens. Despite the resurgence of Donald Trump and the 'war on woke', the Forty-Eighth Parliament is the most representative to date. This chapter reviews issues and representations of gender and diversity in the 2025 election and analyses the nature of party discourses and audiences addressed. It examines the policy offerings of the major parties and how they were received by gender equality advocates. Finally, it presents the Coalition's work-from-home policy as a case study of the consequences of ill-considered policy borrowing and failure to apply a gender lens in policy development.

Keywords: gender; LGBTQIA+; women politicians; women's policy; work from home

In an election that brought a record number of women into the Australian Parliament, gender again proved the Coalition's undoing. Liberal leader Peter Dutton was encouraged by the defeat of the Voice referendum and the election of Donald Trump as US President to believe that 'wokeism' was on the wane globally. The Coalition's lack of attention to women voters resulted in the most spectacular policy failure of the campaign: the work-from-home (WFH) policy received so badly in the electorate that it had to be withdrawn as a 'mistake' and proved a turning point in the campaign.

This chapter reviews the increase in gender and diversity brought by the 2025 election and analyses the nature of party discourses and the audiences addressed. It examines the policy offerings of the major parties and how they were received by gender equality advocates. Finally, it presents the Coalition's WFH policy as a case study of the consequences of ill-considered policy borrowing and failure to apply a gender lens in policy development.

Candidates

The Forty-Eighth Parliament has greater representation of women than any other. It is the first to almost reach gender parity, with women making up 49.6 per cent of the parliament. As recently as 2021, the Inter-Parliamentary Union (IPU) ranked Australia 73 of 193 countries for women in the lower house of national parliaments. The ranking improved with the 2022 federal election (to 35) and the influx of women in 2025 saw Australia rise to twelfth place in the lower house and first place in the upper house (IPU 2025).

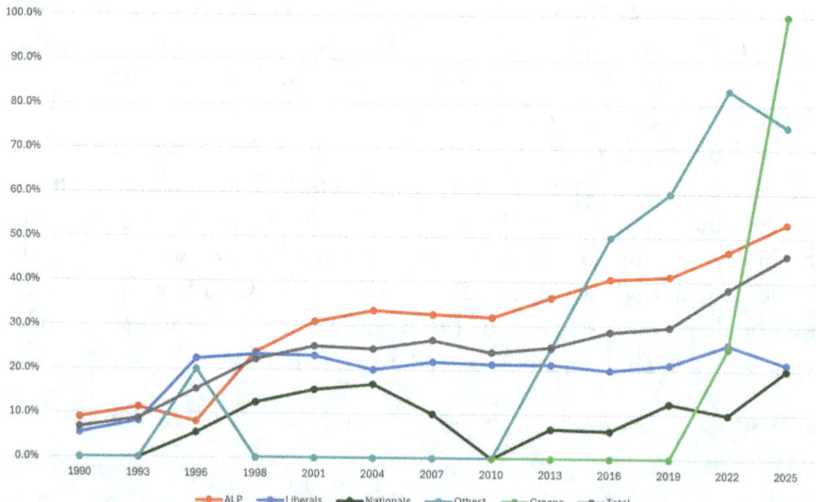

Figure 6.1 Women as a percentage of MPs in the House of Representatives
Note: * Includes Independents, Centre Alliance party and Katter's Australian Party.
Source: Compiled by Blair Williams, based on Parliamentary Library figures.

This rise in Australia's international ranking is largely due to the Labor Party's landslide electoral win. Half the seats won by Labor were women defeating incumbent Liberal or Greens men. The most memorable example was third-time candidate Ali France finally winning the Opposition Leader's seat on election night. However, Labor also chose women to replace five departing male MPs, which further increased the parliamentary representation of women. This record number of women is a testament to the effectiveness of gender quotas when integrated effectively into party rules and with ongoing oversight. In 2015 Labor increased its gender quota to 50 per cent of winnable seats by 2025, with 45 per cent by 2022. The 30-year-long gender quota strategy has now come to fruition with women outnumbering men in the parliamentary Labor Party in both houses, making up 53.7 per cent of Labor MPs in the House of Representatives and 63.3 per cent of Labor senators.

On the other side of the aisle, women continue to be critically underrepresented in the parliamentary Liberal and National parties. While women make up only 21.4 per cent of Liberals in the House of Representatives, the percentage of women Liberal senators is at a record high of 47.8 per cent. Despite Senator Jacinta Nampijinpa Price defecting from the Nationals to the Liberals after the election, the percentage of Nationals women has slightly increased, with women now making up 50 per cent of Nationals senators, though only 20 per cent of members in the lower house. The number of Liberal women across both houses has decreased to its lowest since 1993, reflecting, in part, the party's worst electoral loss in its history. Women made up only 29.4 per cent of candidates from the Liberals and LNP combined (AEC 2025), with many in marginal seats. This has sparked renewed calls from some moderate Liberals to introduce quotas, despite a longstanding refusal to do so on the grounds of 'merit'.

On the crossbench, the percentage of women in the Greens increased to 100 as Elizabeth Watson-Brown was the sole Greens MP to keep her seat, with Labor winning the other three. Women continue to make up the majority of Independent MPs, with the loss of Zoe Daniel to Tim Wilson in Goldstein balanced by the win of Nicolette Boele in the previously blue-ribbon Liberal seat of Bradfield.

Table 6.1 Gender breakdown of the Senate after the 2025 election

Party	Female	Male	Female (percentage)
Labor	19	10	65.5
Liberal	11	12	47.8
Nationals	2	2	50.0
Greens	7	4	63.6
Other	5	5	50.0
Total	**43**	**33**	**56.6**

Source: Compiled by Blair Williams, based on Parliamentary Library figures.

While the Forty-Eighth Parliament has the highest proportion of women, it is also both more and less diverse. The number of politicians with non-European heritage has significantly increased, from 15 in 2022 to 37 in 2025. This is in large part due to the rise in Asian Australian politicians, from 10 in 2022 to 17, representing 7.5 per cent of all politicians, predominantly Labor (Pearlman 2025). This includes newly elected Labor politicians Zhi Soon, Gabriel Ng, Ash Ambihaipahar and Julie Campbell and the Liberals' Leon Rebello. Labor's Basem Abdo became the first Palestinian Australian MP when he replaced outgoing MP Maria Vamvakinou in the seat of Calwell. Home to one of the largest Muslim populations in Australia, Calwell became the nation's 'most unpredictable seat', with 13 candidates including two Independents and a Greens candidate highly critical of Labor's response to the war in Gaza. While the number of non-European parliamentarians increased, the number of Indigenous politicians remained the same with Matt Smith elected in Leichhardt.

Table 6.2 Diversity in the Australian Parliament, 2025

	ALP	Lib.	Nats	Greens	Other	Total[a]
First Nations	6	2	0	0	2	10
Non–English-speaking ancestry[b]	37	12	3	2	10	64
Non-European	24	5	0	2	5	36
LGBTQIA+	5	3	0	0	0	8
Disabled[c]	2	1	0	1	0	4
Aged under 35	7	2	0	1	1	11
Aged over 70	3	0	0	1	4	8

Notes: [a] The Independents are notably non-diverse, apart from Dai Le in Fowler. The two First Nations parliamentarians in the 'Other' column are Senator Lidia Thorpe and Senator Jacqui Lambie. [b] As defined in Richards (2023). [c] Openly disabled.
Source: Compiled by Blair Williams, based on Parliamentary Library figures.

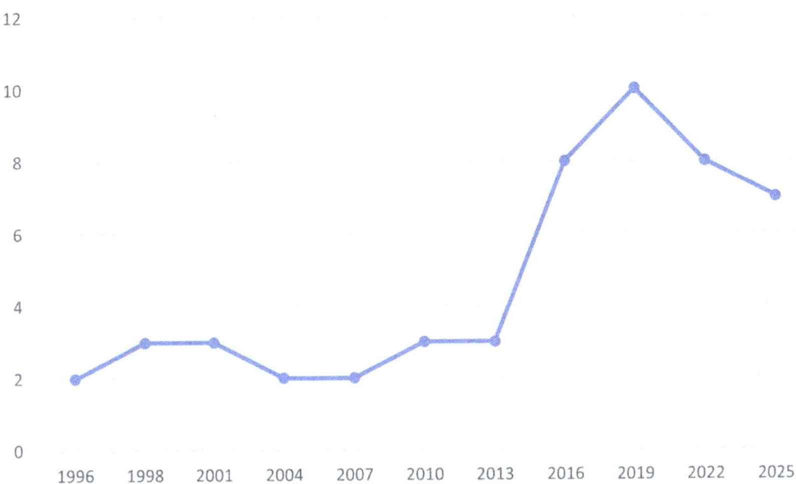

Figure 6.2 Number of LGBTQIA+ politicians in the Australian Parliament, 1996–2025

Source: Compiled by Blair Williams, based on Parliamentary Library figures.

There was an increase in the number of openly disabled politicians, with Labor's Ali France, a disability activist and proud woman with a disability, taking Dutton's seat of Dickson. The number of 'out' LGBTQIA+ representatives remained the same, despite Greens MP Stephen Bates losing his seat and Greens Senator Janet Rice retiring from politics, as the Liberals' Tim Wilson narrowly regained the seat of Goldstein after losing it in 2022 and Labor's Josh Dolega filled the Tasmanian Senate vacancy. Yet, LGBTQIA+ Australians remain underrepresented. This is perhaps a reflection of the age of parliamentarians; the Australian Bureau of Statistics (ABS) estimates that those aged 16–34 are most likely to identify as LGBTQIA+ (ABS 2024).

This is the first election in which Millennials and Gen Z made up a larger share of the electorate than baby boomers. Yet, only 10 members across the House and Senate are under the age of thirty-five. Charlotte Walker, who turned 21 on election day, is the first federal politician born in the new millennium, winning the third Labor Senate spot in South Australia. While the average age of MPs is 51.7 years and senators, 52.95, the average Australian is 38.3 years old (Centre for Population at Treasury 2025).

Despite the recent progress towards greater diversity, parliament still fails to mirror the people it represents. In 2024, more than 30 per cent of the Australian population was born overseas, yet we are not seeing this same diversity filter through to parliament. Likewise, people with disability are underrepresented, making up more than 20 per cent of the population but not yet elected to parliament in similar numbers.

Table 6.3 Gender breakdown of Federal Cabinet, 2010–25

Cabinet	Female	Male	Female (percentage)
Gillard August 2010	4	16	20.0
Rudd 2013	6	14	30.0
Abbott 2013	1	18	5.2
Turnbull 2016	6	17	26.1
Morrison 2019	7	16	30.4
Albanese 2022	10	13	43.5
Albanese 2025	12	11	52.2

Source: Compiled by Blair Williams, based on Parliamentary Library figures.

The Albanese ministry sworn in on 13 May 2025 has again broken records for the number of women in Cabinet, with women making up the majority (52 per cent) of cabinet ministers for the first time (see Table 6.4).

Table 6.4 Diversity in Albanese's second Cabinet

	Number	Percentage
Indigenous	1	4.3
CALD	5	21.7
LGBTQIA+	1	4.3
Aged under 40	1	4.3
Disabled	0	0
Women	12	52.1

Note: CALD = culturally and linguistically diverse.
Source: Compiled by Blair Williams.

Albanese's first ministry was the most diverse in Australia to date, but his second has failed to break this record due to a mix of resignations and reshuffles. Linda Burney, the first Indigenous woman cabinet minister and minister for Indigenous Australians, announced her political retirement before the 2025 election, reducing the number of First Nations ministers. However, Ed Husic, the first Muslim elected to federal parliament and the first Muslim minister, and Jewish attorney-general Mark Dreyfus were both dumped from Cabinet because of factional decisions, decreasing the number of culturally and linguistically diverse (CALD) ministers. Penny Wong is still the lone 'out' LGBTQIA+ minister and there are currently no openly disabled people in the ministry. Only two ministers are under the age of 40, Communications Minister Anika Wells and newcomer Sam Rae, appointed Minister for Aged Care and Seniors.

Campaign discourses

Before and throughout the election campaign, Dutton borrowed from Donald Trump in his language, policies and strongman persona. He positioned himself as the traditional masculine protector of the nation, vowing to defend Australians by being tough on crime, immigration and 'wokeness' (see Chapter 2, this volume). This strongman persona extended to protection of women and children from family violence as in the Coalition's related policy launch. In contrast, Albanese's more compassionate 'state daddy' masculinity focused on issues such as health and the care economy (Williams 2025). While Albanese was seen holding babies at hospitals, Dutton was seen filling up at 17 different petrol stations. Albanese's more socially inclusive leadership model was attacked by Dutton as a sign of 'weakness' and he repeatedly portrayed the Prime Minister as a weak leader, responsible for weakening Australia.

In the final leadership debate, Albanese was asked by the host, 7News political editor Mark Riley, whether he was 'too soft', to which he answered that 'kindness isn't weakness'—something he repeated in his victory speech. By embracing kindness and portraying it as an asset during a globally unstable time dominated by strongmen, Albanese effectively defused the claim by Dutton and campaign ally Advance that he was a 'weak' and 'woke' prime minister who would 'send us broke'.

As explored in other chapters, podcasts were more central in both Albanese's and Dutton's campaigns in 2025. However, their social media strategies targeted very different parts of the electorate. Like Trump—who, in the 2024 presidential race, appeared on 14 major podcasts with predominantly male audiences—Dutton appeared on podcasts mainly targeting men. On the Mark Bouris podcast on 23 January, he sympathised with young men who felt disenfranchised and ostracised, suggesting they were fed up with 'woke' practices (Bouris 2025).

In contrast, Albanese appeared on podcasts targeting mainly women audiences, including Abbie Chatfield's *It's A Lot* and Hannah Ferguson's *Big Small Talk* (Chatfield 2025a; Big Small Talk 2025a). He spoke about Labor's policies supporting women's health in areas including endometriosis care, contraceptives and menopause. Likewise, Greens leader Adam Bandt was interviewed by both Chatfield and Ferguson about his party's stance on housing, health care, women's health and safety (Big Small Talk 2025b; Chatfield 2025b).

The Greens have long led the way with their use of social media. TikTok was a key battleground (see Chapter 7, this volume) and, though the Greens had a smaller post volume on this platform than Labor or the Coalition, they had the highest engagement rating (14.4 per cent) and the highest share of women and young followers (Oates and Chowdhury 2025). They also had the highest share of policy-oriented TikToks, focusing predominantly on their policies to tackle climate change, tax reform and education.

In the previous election, Greens candidate for Brisbane Stephen Bates used the gay dating app Grindr to advertise his campaign using sexually suggestive slogans (Williams and Sawer 2023). In 2025, Bates became the first political candidate in Australia to take his campaign to OnlyFans, an 18+ online subscription service that is infamous for its popularity with sex workers and its pornography. His first video featured the Greens' plan to make HIV-prevention drugs pre-exposure prophylaxis (PrEP) and post-exposure prophylaxis (PEP) free with a script. Commenting on this approach, Bates remarked, 'I campaign on OnlyFans and Grindr because it gets attention. Sometimes you have to make a splash to make people pay attention to the things that matter' (Greens 2025). The seat of Brisbane is home to many LGBTQIA+ voters and the second-highest percentage of voters aged 18–29 in the country. However, Bates failed to hold his seat in a three-way contest with Labor and the Liberals.

The Coalition generally stayed away from the 'gender debate' since it backfired for Scott Morrison and his anti-trans 'captain's pick', Katherine Deves, in the previous election. Before the campaign, Dutton shut down deputy Coalition leader David Littleproud's assertion that Australia should 'lean into' this culture war after Trump's executive order attacking trans people. However, there was a new party to pick up this fight: Clive Palmer's Trumpet of Patriots (TOP). In his National Press Club address outlining the party's vision, Palmer stoked the 'gender debate' by raising topics such as trans women's participation in sport and children's safety from 'gender ideology' at school. Trumpet of Patriots ran an anti-trans advertising blitz, 'There are only two genders, male and female', on television and in newspapers, such as on the front page of the Melbourne *Age*. In the televised ads, TOP leader Suellen Wrightson stated:

> We don't want men in women's sports, we don't want males dressed as females confusing our children in schools.
>
> All children should be entitled to a normal safe environment in our schools and in our public toilets. (Deor 2025)

This ad campaign received widespread backlash from transgender organisations and from *Age* staff. Pauline Hanson's One Nation (PHON) campaigned on a similar anti-trans platform. Hanson said on Sky News (later posted to her Facebook page) that PHON would 'not stop fighting to protect our children and defend women from the dangers of radical gender ideology'. Borrowing language from the 2021 March4Justice protests, she critiqued the major political parties for turning their backs on the issue and argued that 'enough is enough'.

Issues: The Coalition

In 2022, the Liberal Party's post-election review referred to 'a sense that the Liberal Party is failing to adequately represent the values and priorities of women in modern Australia' (Loughnane and Hume 2022: 32). It recommended a target of 50 per cent female representation both in the parliamentary party and in the party membership by 2025 (subsequently extended to 2032).

The lack of any progress in achieving this target was evident. Former staffer Charlotte Mortlock described the consequences like this: 'The average Australian is a 37-year-old woman, our average party member is a male in his 70s.' The result of this disconnect was policy that might 'placate party membership but repel broader society' (Mortlock 2025a).

The 2022 Liberal Party review recommended the creation of the Dame Margaret Guilfoyle Network (MGN) to promote female representation in the party. This repeated the recommendations of previous reviews into declining support from women, such as the *Room for Movement* review of 2015. Senator Jane Hume, co-author of the 2022 review, suggested that such a network would be fundamental to the future success of the party and must be financed by a levy on parliamentarians (Smethurst 2023). Given lack of support for diversity measures by some in the parliamentary party, such a levy was never likely. The MGN was not launched until March 2024 and, with annual membership fees ranging up to $150 for non-members of the party, there was little evidence of activity.

Meanwhile, Mortlock went ahead to found Hilma's Network, named after suffragist Hilma Molyneux Parkes. Mortlock was a former Sky News anchor as well as Liberal staffer and was determined to keep the network free of party control, unlike the MGN. Its independence meant that Mortlock was able to take on a very public role in support of Liberal women parliamentarians and candidates. Assistance provided for women candidates in the 2025 federal election included featuring 10 of them in a podcast called *Madame Speaker*. After the election defeat, Mortlock was regularly in the media, campaigning for the party to adopt gender quotas and supporting the election of Sussan Ley as Liberal leader (for example, Mortlock 2025b).

And, as Mortlock pointed out, the Liberal Party needed to pay attention not only to increasing female representation but also to presenting policies likely to attract women voters (ABC Sydney, 14 May 2025). While there were big gender gaps on issues of climate change and the care economy (Biddle 2025), Coalition policies did not correspond to women's policy preferences and there was little evidence that their impact on women was ever considered. For example, Labor's commitment to a 20 per cent reduction in student loan debt was labelled by the Coalition as 'elitist', with seemingly no recognition that women were 60 per cent of the three million Australians with a Higher Education Contribution Scheme (HECS) debt.

There was no Coalition women's policy document, although a plan was released with commitments on family violence. As in 2022, the frontbencher with responsibility for women did not participate in debates on women's policy during the campaign and the *Let's Get Australia Back on Track* policy document mentioned women only in relation to health policy. Workforce issues such as childcare were generally neglected in Coalition campaigning, apart from its plan for regional Australia, and there was an avoidance of social media platforms for which women formed a large part of the audience.

Plate 6.1 *Women's Agenda* election debate advertisement, 24 April 2025
Photo: *Women's Agenda*.

Interestingly, while absent from women's policy debates, the Coalition was represented by Senator Andrew Bragg at the Rainbow Votes Election Forum organised by Equality Australia at the Tom Mann Theatre in Surry Hills in Sydney, which was livestreamed around the country.

While Dutton presented himself as the thin blue line protecting women and children from harm, he was not as comfortable with structural issues impacting gender equality. For example, the Coalition's WFH policy, discussed below, ignored the importance of flexible work for women or the gendered effects of its withdrawal.

Another policy with unexamined gender implications was the Coalition's commitment to end multi-employer wage bargaining. Enterprise-level bargaining has disproportionately disadvantaged female-dominated care industries such as aged care and early childhood education. This was anticipated at the time the enterprise-bargaining principle was adopted under a previous Labor government (Sawer 2008: 199–200). The Albanese government legislated industrial relations changes to improve access by workers in low-paid industries to multi-employer bargaining and this was one aspect of its strategy to close the gender gap in pay. Other aspects of the Albanese government's gender pay gap strategy are discussed below.

Plate 6.2 'Liberal Party reveals new female-focused, pink nuclear reactor', from satirical news-site *The Shovel*

Photo: *The Shovel*, 16 May 2025.

There were also big gender gaps in approval for the Coalition's nuclear energy policy. For example, Vote Compass found that, based on more than 290,000 responses, 41.9 per cent of women strongly disagreed with the Coalition's nuclear policy (compared with 29 per cent of men). Only 11.8 per cent strongly agreed with the policy, compared with 30.5 per cent of men (Higgins and Williams 2025). To undertake 'targeted education' to address women's concerns, the Women's Council of the NSW Nationals sponsored a YouTube 'Women in Nuclear' series hosted by the president of Women in Nuclear Australia and featuring Coalition senators such as Bridget McKenzie and Jane Hume. After the election, *The Shovel* satirised this kind of approach (Plate 6.2).

The work-from-home policy fiasco

The lack of gender analysis when preparing the WFH policy resulted in such a negative response that it became a turning point in the election campaign. The policy was not only gender blind but also borrowed from the recently elected US President, Donald Trump (Table 6.4). In November 2024, Elon Musk had co-written an op-ed in the *Wall Street Journal* saying:

> Requiring federal employees to come to the office five days a week would result in a wave of voluntary terminations that we welcome: If federal employees don't want to show up, American taxpayers shouldn't pay them for the Covid-era privilege of staying home. (Kelly 2025)

One of Trump's first actions after being sworn in as president on 20 January 2025 was to issue an executive order ending 'remote work' for federal employees.

In the runup to International Women's Day 2025, Senator Jane Hume as Opposition spokeswoman on the public service announced in a speech to the Menzies Research Centre that under a Coalition government WFH arrangements would be ended for federal public servants. She cited productivity reasons for requiring workers to be in the office five days a week and provided an anecdote about a public servant working from home who was frequently uncontactable because they were travelling around Australia with their family in a campervan (Hume 2025). On Sky News, Peta Credlin applauded Hume's statement that WFH was detracting from productivity and matched her campervanning story with one of her own about a Canberra-based public servant moving to the Sunshine Coast (Credlin 2025).

Outside Sky News, the policy was not so well received. Association with President Trump's administration was increasingly a liability, quite apart from the implications for women's employment of removing flexible work provisions. The fact that more than 60 per cent of federal public servants are women might have rung alarm bells if the Coalition had been running a gender lens over policies. Such a policy lens had become routine for Labor, and minister Katy Gallagher was quick to point out the disproportionate impact of ending WFH on women and their access to the workforce (Gallagher 2025). In contrast, Opposition leader Peter Dutton made the improbable claim that the policy did not discriminate based on gender.

In statements echoing Trump's and Musk's hostility to federal public servants, Dutton said the priority had to be taxpayer money; he was not going to tolerate a situation where taxpayers were working harder than ever to pay their own bills and were seeing public servants in Canberra refuse to go to work. If women could not be in the office five days a week there were 'plenty of job-sharing opportunities' (Evans 2025). There was further uproar over this proposal—that women who had been able to work full-time because of WFH should instead become part-time workers. Reminiscent of Coalition clumsiness over gender in 2022, Dutton appeared oblivious to the importance of women's earnings in a cost-of-living crisis.

Table 6.5 Evolution of the Coalition's work-from-home policy, 2025

Date	Event
20 January	President Trump issues executive order ending remote work for federal employees.
3 March	Senator Jane Hume announces a Coalition government will end WFH arrangements for federal public servants.
4 March	Opposition leader Peter Dutton says the policy does not discriminate based on gender and there are 'plenty of job-sharing arrangements' for women unable to get back to the office five days a week.
4 April	Dutton says the policy will only apply to Canberra-based public servants.
5 April	RedBridge poll finds Labor now has two-party-preferred lead, 52–48 per cent.
6 April	Senator Hume announces the Coalition no longer plans to end WFH arrangements.
7 April	Peter Dutton says the policy was a mistake.
19 April	Senator Hume says ending WFH was good policy that had not found its appropriate time.

Source: Compiled by Marian Sawer.

On 5 April, the latest RedBridge poll of voting intentions showed Labor back in front in the campaign, with a lead in the two-party-preferred vote of 52–48 per cent. There was a large gender gap in reactions to the Coalition's WFH policy, with a net favourability rating among men of +7 but a net rating among women of −19 (Campbell 2025). In the face of concerted reaction to what had easily been depicted as yet another anti-woman policy on the part of the Coalition, Dutton first restricted the policy to Canberra-based public servants before admitting it was a mistake and dropping it. This led to social media memes such as 'Dutton reboots campaign after advisor explains existence of voter group called "women"'. Later analysis of ABS data on areas where people were most likely to work from home during the Covid pandemic found that Dutton's own seat of Dickson, which he lost, was one of those with above-average numbers of flexible workers (Crabb 2025).

Issues: Labor and the Greens

The greater comfort of Labor, the Greens and the Teals with gender policy was on display in the election debate hosted by *Women's Agenda*, a digital news service with 35,000 readers daily and up to 800,000 each month. As we have seen (Plate 6.1), the Liberal Party did not participate in this debate.

The Labor Party had released a women's policy on 22 April and Senator Katy Gallagher, as Minister for Women, had the advantage of strengthened machinery-of-government arrangements and solid policy achievements in the gender equality area. This included the first national Gender Equality Strategy since the Hawke government. The Albanese government had increased the capacity of its Office for Women, now headed by a high-profile deputy secretary (Padma Rahman), to undertake such cross-governmental work. Importantly, the reporting framework for the new Gender Equality Strategy included gender-responsive budgeting—now reintroduced across government.

Progress on gender equality in the workplace included increasing the capacity of the Fair Work Commission to address undervaluation of work in the care economy, resulting in pay rises for aged-care and childcare workers. Initiatives relating to the care economy also included introducing income support payments for students undertaking mandatory placements as part of their nursing, midwifery, teaching or social work degrees or diplomas (something not supported by the Coalition).

Progress on equal pay beyond the care economy included the banning of pay secrecy clauses and the requirement for companies to report publicly on their gender pay gaps. Paid parental leave was extended to six months and now included superannuation payments and one month's 'use it or lose it' leave for fathers. Other workplace improvements included the legislating of 10 days' paid family violence leave and a positive duty of employers to protect women against sexual harassment.

In the social policy area, Labor built on its home ground of Medicare and early childhood education and care. These were policies directly related to the cost-of-living concerns of voters as well as priority issues for women. The commitment was underlined by Albanese nominating universal childcare as his hoped-for political legacy: children to have the same right of access to early childhood education and care as to the school system.

Apart from its big commitments to Medicare and the Women's Health Strategy, Labor also announced during the campaign an extra $10 million for its National Action Plan for the Health and Wellbeing of LGBTQIA+ Australians (with all its health promises being matched by the Coalition). In another crucial area, there had been record funding for gender-based violence services under the National Action Plan to End Violence against Women and Children 2022–2032. However, the increases were insufficient to meet the challenge of this national crisis and refuges still had to turn away many women and children escaping violence. The Women's Electoral Lobby described violence against women in Australia as 'an emergency on a par with a pandemic', while the *The Sydney Morning Herald* editorialised that 'all sides of politics have failed to grasp the sheer scale of domestic and gender-based violence' (2 May 2025). The Coalition's promise to criminalise technology-facilitated abuse of an intimate partner was one of the best-received parts of its domestic violence package.

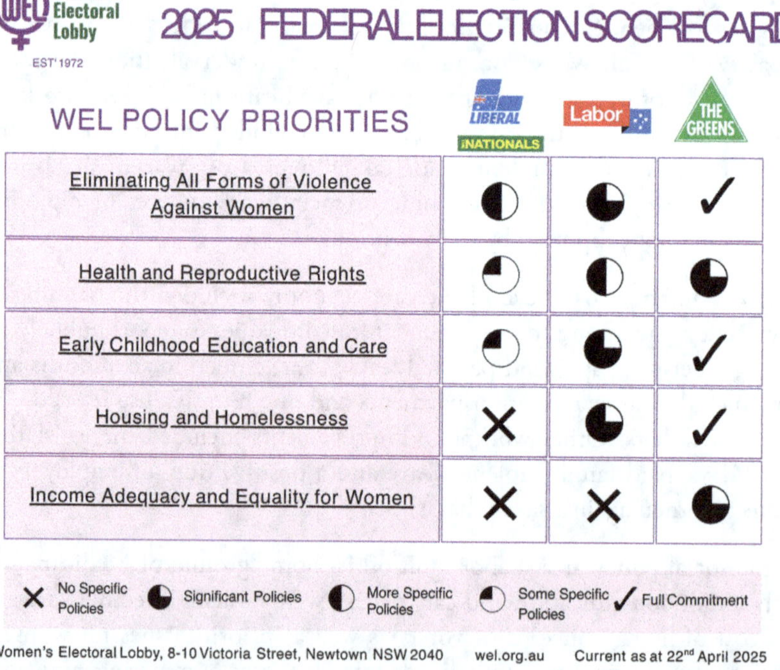

WEL POLICY PRIORITIES	LIBERAL NATIONALS	Labor	THE GREENS
Eliminating All Forms of Violence Against Women	Significant Policies	Significant Policies	Full Commitment
Health and Reproductive Rights	Some Specific Policies	More Specific Policies	Significant Policies
Early Childhood Education and Care	Some Specific Policies	Significant Policies	Full Commitment
Housing and Homelessness	No Specific Policies	Significant Policies	Full Commitment
Income Adequacy and Equality for Women	No Specific Policies	No Specific Policies	Significant Policies

Plate 6.3 Women's Electoral Lobby election scorecard

Photo: Women's Electoral Lobby (www.wel.org.au/2025_federal_election_scorecard).

Labor's election policies received a relatively positive rating from women's equality groups that produced scorecards, such as the Women's Electoral Lobby, Fair Agenda and the Australian Gender Equality Council. However, ratings were generally less positive in relation to income support, and this was also true of election material produced by the National Foundation for Australian Women, the Working for Women Alliance and Chief Executive Women. Women remained a majority of those affected by inadequate rates of Centrelink payments and punitive compliance mechanisms.

The Greens continued to receive the highest ratings for their women's and climate policies, inheriting the mantle of the Australian Democrats. Senator Larissa Waters, the Greens spokeswoman on women (and Greens leader after the election), had made an important contribution to integrity and parliamentary workplace reforms, as well as applying a gender lens to many other policy areas. The only debates about women's policy during the campaign were those hosted by *Women's Agenda* and the Australian Gender Equality Council. A new fund set up to support female Independent candidates, the Vida Fund, argued the major parties were not prioritising gender issues and its goal was to 'strengthen the cross bench, demand more from the major parties and empower candidates running on strong gender-equity platforms' (Boecker 2025).

The small parties on the right, most importantly PHON and TOP, were consistently opposed to what they labelled diversity, equity and inclusion policies.

Aftermath

In the aftermath of a crushing electoral defeat, which saw Dutton lose his own seat on election night, Sussan Ley was narrowly elected leader of the Liberal Party—the first woman leader in its 80-year history. After narrowly beating conservative shadow treasurer Angus Taylor 29 votes to 25, the more moderate Ley vowed to 'rebuild trust with all sections of Australian society' and argued that her election as leader would 'send a very strong signal that we understand that things must be done differently' (Ireland 2025).

Ley will not have an easy task as she steers a deeply divided party through its greatest crisis to date. She faces what has been termed a 'glass cliff': the tendency for women to finally break through the glass ceiling during times of crisis. Further to the left, the Greens also elected a woman leader,

Queensland Senator Larissa Waters, although this is not a first for them. But although women now make up a majority in Cabinet, Labor's leader, deputy leader and treasurer are all men and there is no sign of a woman likely to take the reins any time soon.

Conclusion

The 2025 election has resulted in the most diverse parliament to date, with the number of women almost reaching parity and the number of politicians of non-European heritage more than doubling. However, gender issues again underlay the failure of the Liberal Party to 'connect with modern Australia'. For the first time, Millennials and Gen Z voters overtook baby boomers as the largest voting bloc, now making up almost half the electorate. At the 2022 election, young women had shifted to the left at a faster rate than young men, with only about 20 per cent of young women voting for the Coalition compared with 34 per cent of young men (Chowdhury 2024). The nature of the Coalition's 2025 campaign appears to have exacerbated this disconnect with women in general and young women in particular. The failure to engage with the reality of women's lives was highlighted by the policy of ending work from home, while the Coalition also failed to persuade in other areas such as its nuclear policy. One silver lining from the massive loss of seats was the opportunity opened up for women candidates. But whether or not the Coalition is finally persuaded under Ley's leadership to do something about quotas, it must also grapple with policy issues of major concern to young women such as climate change if it is to remain electorally competitive into the future.

References

Australian Bureau of Statistics (ABS). 2024. 'Estimates and characteristics of LGBTI+ populations in Australia, 2022.' Media release, 19 December. Canberra: Australian Bureau of Statistics. www.abs.gov.au/statistics/people/people-and-communities/ estimates-and-characteristics-lgbti-populations-australia/latest-release.

Australian Electoral Commission (AEC). 2025. 'Nominations by gender.' *Tally Room: 2025 Federal Election*. Canberra: Australian Electoral Commission. results.aec. gov.au/31496/Website/HouseNominationsByGender-31496.htm.

Biddle, Nick. 2025. 'Hope, hardship, and democratic confidence: Social wellbeing and political sentiment in election-year Australia.' March/April. Canberra: School of Politics and International Relations, The Australian National University. politicsir.cass.anu.edu.au/files/docs/2025/4/Hope-Hardship-and-Democratic-Confidence.pdf.

Big Small Talk. 2025a. 'Interview: Prime Minister Anthony Albanese.' *Big Small Talk*, [Podcast], 30 March. open.spotify.com/episode/3xyISYKzEbRwjTB46O8SMV.

Big Small Talk. 2025b. 'Interview: Greens leader Adam Bandt.' *Big Small Talk*, [Podcast], 1 April. open.spotify.com/episode/7bHne0c5Pi8qCpUlGAkRHm.

Boecker, Brianna. 2025. '"Correcting the imbalance": New $100,000 Vida Fund created to support female independents.' *Women's Agenda*, 10 March. womens agenda.com.au/politics/local/correcting-the-imbalance-new-100000-vida-fund-created-to-support-female-independents/.

Bouris, Mark. 2025. 'The Peter Dutton podcast—Housing crisis, Australia Day & why he should be the next Prime Minister.' *Straight Talk with Mark Bouris*, [Podcast], 22 January. www.youtube.com/watch?v=eBEgWeeQmfY.

Campbell, James. 2025. 'WFH is working for Labor.' *Herald Sun*, 7 April.

Centre for Population at Treasury. 2025. *Profile of Australia's Population*. Article, 15 April. Canberra: Australian Institute of Health and Welfare. www.aihw.gov. au/reports/australias-health/profile-of-australias-population.

Chatfield, Abbie. 2025a. 'Prime Minister Albanese: The extended version.' *It's A Lot with Abbie Chatfield*, [Podcast], 21 February, season 7, episode 11. podcasts.apple. com/au/podcast/prime-minister-albanese-the-extended-version/id1500849438? i=1000694350921.

Chatfield, Abbie. 2025b. 'Adam Bandt (leader of the Australian Greens): The shorter version.' *It's A Lot with Abbie Chatfield*, [Podcast], 10 March. open.spotify.com/ episode/1EHSMxCquOnGEqxHPVQJcU.

Chowdhury, Intifar. 2024. 'Australia's young people are moving to the left— though young women are more progressive than men, reflecting a global trend.' *The Conversation*, 2 February. theconversation.com/australias-young-people-are-moving-to-the-left-though-young-women-are-more-progressive-than-men-reflecting-a-global-trend-222288. doi.org/10.64628/AA.5xkh6h6c4.

Crabb, Annabel. 2025. 'Peter Dutton's platform infuriated women—and it likely lost him the election.' *ABC News*, 4 May. www.abc.net.au/news/2025-05-04/did-peter-dutton-nuke-himself-with-female-voters-/105249444.

Credlin, Peta. 2025. 'Work from home rights for public servants are "detracting" from productivity.' *Sky News Australia*, 3 March. www.skynews.com.au/opinion/ peta-credlin/work-from-home-rights-for-public-servants-are-detracting-from-productivity/video/ba8d4a01e381eeb150b28515b9b88fdf.

Deor, Antimony. 2025. 'Here's everything you need to know about Clive Palmer's anti-trans "Trumpet of Patriots" party.' *Star Observer*, 27 February. www.star observer.com.au/news/national-news/heres-everything-you-need-to-know-about -clive-palmers-anti-trans-trumpet-of-patriots-party/235638.

Evans, Jake. 2025. 'Demanding a return to office, Dutton says women seeking flexible work can find job-sharing arrangements.' *ABC News*, 4 March. www. abc.net.au/news/2025-03-04/coalition-order-return-to-office-deny-women-disadvantage/105007422.

Gallagher, Katy. 2025. 'Peter Dutton's tone-deaf WFH ban will take women back to the 1950s: Katy Gallagher.' *Women's Agenda*, 6 March. womensagenda.com. au/latest/peter-duttons-tone-deaf-wfh-ban-will-take-women-back-to-the-1950s-katy-gallagher/.

Higgins, Isabella, and Claudia Williams. 2025. 'Coalition's nuclear power pitch falling flat with some voters, Vote Compass data suggests.' *ABC News*, 12 April. www.abc.net.au/news/2025-04-12/vote-compass-data-2025-nuclear-power-renewables/105127902.

Hume, Jane. 2025. 'Back to work and back to basics: An efficient government for all Australians.' Address to the Menzies Research Institute, Sydney, 3 March. www.senatorhume.com/mediafolder/latest-news/back-to-work-and-back-to-basics-an-efficient-government-for-all-australians.

Inter-Parliamentary Union (IPU). 2025. *Monthly Ranking of Women in National Parliaments*. [Online]. July. Geneva: Inter-Parliamentary Union. data.ipu.org/ women-ranking/.

Ireland, Olivia. 2025. 'Ley releases video pitch for Lib leadership as senator backs rival.' *The Sydney Morning Herald*, 10 May. www.smh.com.au/politics/federal/ ley-releases-video-pitch-for-lib-leadership-as-senator-backs-rival-20250510-p5ly4b.html.

Kelly, Jack. 2025. 'Trump ends remote work for federal employees, hoping to shrink the federal workforce.' *Forbes*, 21 January. www.forbes.com/sites/jackkelly/ 2025/01/21/trump-ends-remote-work-for-federal-employees-hoping-to-shrink-the-federal-workforce/.

Loughnane, Brian, and Jane Hume. 2022. *Review of the 2022 Federal Election*. Canberra: Liberal Party of Australia. cdn.liberal.org.au/2022/2022_election_ review.pdf.

Mortlock, Charlotte. 2025a. 'This party may be over for women.' *The Sydney Morning Herald*, 6 May.

Mortlock, Charlotte. 2025b. 'Finally, Libs listen to women, with Ley only the beginning.' *The Sydney Morning Herald*, 14 May.

Oates, Hannah, and Intifar Chowdhury. 2025. 'What did the parties say on TikTok in the election, and how? Here's the campaign broken down in 5 charts.' *The Conversation*, 13 May. theconversation.com/what-did-the-parties-say-on-tiktok-in-the-election-and-how-heres-the-campaign-broken-down-in-5-charts-254793. doi.org/10.64628/AA.uspcfw5e7.

Pearlman, Jonathan. 2025. 'Number of Asian-Australian MPs to rise in Canberra as parliament make-up changes.' *The Straits Times*, 24 May, [Updated 25 May 2025]. www.straitstimes.com/asia/australianz/number-of-asian-australian-mps-to-rise-in-canberra-as-parliament-make-up-changes.

Richards, Lisa. 2023. *Cultural Diversity in the 47th Parliament: A Quick Guide*. Research Paper Series 2023–24, 4 September. Canberra: Parliamentary Library. www.aph.gov.au/About_Parliament/Parliamentary_departments/Parliamentary_Library/Research/Quick_Guides/2023-24/CulturalDiversity47thParliament.

Sawer, Marian. 2008. *Making Women Count: A History of the Women's Electoral Lobby*. Sydney: UNSW Press.

Smethurst, Annika. 2023. 'Senator calls for a Liberal Party fundraising levy to "give women a chance".' *The Sydney Morning Herald*, 8 January. www.smh.com.au/politics/federal/senator-calls-for-a-liberal-party-fundraising-levy-to-give-women-a-chance-20230107-p5cayx.html.

The Greens. 2025. 'First Australian politician launches OnlyFans to announce The Greens' plan to make PrEP free.' Media release, 16 April. Canberra: The Greens. greens.org.au/news/media-release/first-australian-politician-launches-onlyfans-announce-greens-plan-make-prep.

Williams, Blair. 2025. 'Daggy dads and state daddies: Theorising the masculinities of Australian men political leaders.' *Men and Masculinities*: March. doi.org/10.1177/1097184X251328266.

Williams, Blair, and Marian Sawer. 2023. 'High-vis and hard hats versus the care economy.' In *Watershed: The 2022 Australian Federal Election*, edited by Anika Gauja, Marian Sawer, and Jill Sheppard, 79–100. Canberra: ANU Press. doi.org/10.22459/W.2023.05.

7

How the media reported: From headline to hashtag

Andrea Carson, Finley Watson and Justin Phillips

Abstract

This chapter analyses media coverage of the 2025 Australian federal election, focusing on how traditional and digital platforms framed the campaign. It examines challenges faced by Prime Minister Anthony Albanese—poor polling, economic strain, floods in Queensland and Trump's tariff wars— and their mediation in public discourse. Drawing on agenda-setting theory and mixed methods, manual and computational, it explores strategic communication tactics and the influence of social media influencers and short-form video platforms such as TikTok and YouTube. While highlighting the fragmentation of the media environment, the chapter challenges claims that the mainstream media has lost agenda-setting power, showing instead its continued influence—especially on digital platforms. By comparing the agenda-setting power of legacy media with the speed and reach of digital platforms, it reveals the hybrid media ecosystem that adept campaigners must understand if they are to be effective at reaching voters through their political communications.

Keywords: agenda-setting; social media; influencers; hybrid media; brain rot

As the Forty-Seventh Parliament of Australia was coming to an end, Prime Minister Anthony Albanese was looking like the political underdog. Polling numbers for the Labor leader and his party were dismal. In January 2025, polls suggested the party was at least 2 percentage points behind the Coalition on a two-party-preferred (2PP) tally (Jackman 2025).

Australians were also doing it tough amid a housing crisis and cost-of-living pressures, with many households bearing the strain of 13 consecutive interest rate hikes. Labor's polling hit its lowest point just before the Reserve Bank of Australia reversed its direction and cut interest rates, on 18 February 2025 (Jackman 2025).

By 8 March, Tropical Cyclone Alfred had struck South-East Queensland, giving the government media airtime to speak about the perils of climate change—a vexed issue for the Coalition, with a long history of policy turmoil for the party. The natural disaster enabled the embattled Albanese government to shape the public narrative and show its responsiveness, quickly getting aid to flood victims; what followed was a steady rise in polling support.

The floods also delayed any planned election date announcement and forced the government to deliver a national budget that might have been postponed if the election were earlier. The allocation of $785.7 billion was an opportunity not to be missed by Treasurer Jim Chalmers to directly target voters feeling cost-of-living pressures and to reinforce key government messages: interest rates were coming down, unemployment was low and inflation had been tamed. Labor's polling numbers continued to rise, hitting an election-winning 51 per cent 2PP by the day the election was called on 28 March (Jackman 2025). It was a promising start for a government that had begun the year poorly according to the pundits and polls.

Then, international mayhem struck. Within days of the election writs being issued, US President Donald Trump upended global stability with his so-called 'Liberation Day', launching a tariff war that targeted 'friends and foes' alike. Albanese described it as 'not the act of a friend', appearing calm and resolute as stock markets around the world crashed. Trump's tariff fiasco posed a dilemma for Opposition leader Peter Dutton: would he be seen as too closely aligned with Trumpian ideas at a time when the US President appeared to be unpopular with Australians (Australia Institute 2025)?

Dutton had already embraced an Elon Musk–inspired war on government spending, promising his own version of the Department of Government Efficiency (DOGE), led by Jacinta Nampijinpa Price—the public face of the 2023 Voice referendum 'No' campaign—with extensive public service cuts if the Coalition won office. As this chapter will show, these issues set the scene for a bumpy five-week media campaign that was interrupted by Easter, school holidays and Anzac Day, and truncated by early voting. Most Australians opted to pre-poll, with many casting ballots before all policies were released,[1] intensifying the challenge for campaigners to grab the public's attention in a vast, fragmented media environment.

Background

Australia's contemporary media landscape, like that of most advanced democracies, is highly fragmented and best characterised as hybrid, encompassing both traditional (television, radio, print) and digital media platforms (Chadwick 2017). The 2025 Australian federal election campaign was further evidence of how politicians, candidates, political parties and third-party campaigners must navigate this complex environment, combining free 'earned' and paid political communications to reach as many voters as possible with their messages.

Campaigners' goals are both to persuade undecided voters and to mobilise supporters. To do this, adept political actors use a mix of real-time media (social media, live radio and TV) and scheduled media (newspapers, TV and radio news bulletins, podcasts) to convey their policies to diverse audiences. They combine the affordances of interactivity and immediacy that characterise the digital sphere (Karlsson and Strömbäck 2010) with the agenda-setting power of legacy media (Langer and Gruber 2020). To neglect one platform, such as TikTok, can mean specific cohorts who gravitate to that platform, like Gen Z first-time voters, miss key messages. Modern election campaigns are, by necessity, diverse, requiring a range of communication and digital skills to reach voters in a multimodal communication environment.

Agenda-setting scholarship is well developed and refers to the relationship between media coverage and what audiences perceive as important. McCombs and Shaw's (1972: 177) seminal study of the 1968 US presidential election famously identified a 'near perfect correlation' between front-page news and key voter concerns. While some argue that the traditional media's

---

1   For example, the Coalition's $21-billion defence policy was released after early voting began, just 10 days before election day (Glover 2025).

agenda-setting power is diminishing in the digital age with reference to this election result (Predavec et al. 2025), this chapter contends that mainstream media continues to play an important role in election campaign coverage across media spheres.

We analyse traditional and digital media election coverage to pinpoint which issues political actors and professional gatekeepers prioritised and, crucially, audience engagement on social media leading up to the 3 May election. We agree in part with Predavec et al. (2025) that, notwithstanding News Corp Australia's extensive holdings and audience reach across print, radio and television, the Murdoch-owned outlet's influence in shifting voter support towards the conservative cause—through favourable coverage of Opposition leader Peter Dutton—appears limited. However, as will be shown, this does not capture the full story of the mainstream media's influence.

Another key finding of the chapter is that the centre-right Liberal–Nationals Coalition combined traditional and digital media in innovative ways, investing heavily in social media strategies such as memes, artificial intelligence (AI) and emotional appeals rooted in fear and negativity. However, as Chapter 8 of this volume observes, this emphasis on style—through AI-driven content, slogans such as Dutton's 'Let's get Australia back on track' and attacks (such as 'hate media')—highlights the campaign's lack of policy depth and dependence on negative messaging. Labor's approach presented a contrast in style and substance. Benefiting from the early release and reiteration of their cost-of-living education (for example, HECS debt relief and free TAFE) and health–focused policy agenda, underpinned by the pre-election budget, the incumbent's messaging appeared more consistent and disciplined. This was especially important as a record number of Australians voted before the end of the five-week campaign.

This chapter examines these divergent messaging strategies, scrutinising their intended targets and methods of dissemination. Echoing findings from the 2023 Indigenous Voice to Parliament referendum, we find that key messages circulate across both online and offline platforms to show intermedia agenda-setting between old and new media, revealing a symbiotic relationship (Carson et al. 2025; Meraz 2011). While we do not make causal claims about the election outcome in relation to campaign effects, we critically examine *how* and *where* political actors and media outlets prioritise their efforts with the purpose of shaping public discourse.

We use qualitative and quantitative methods, both manual and computational, and a range of data sources to scrutinise key facets of Australia's media ecosystem during the election. We begin our analysis focusing on the front-page press coverage of Australia's 13 major daily newspapers to identify the stories that editors deemed most important and to compare news coverage across the country. We shift to examine Facebook users' engagement with mainstream election stories on that platform, offering insights into how audiences interact with political coverage online. We then turn to older digital platforms (YouTube) and the next generation (TikTok) to explore the rise of social media influencers, comparing the political actors and narratives that gained traction. We conclude with a discussion about what this multi-platform analysis of the five-week campaign reveals about the strategic decisions of major parties and the choices of news editors that shaped the election discourse.

Mainstream media: Front-page analysis

Newspaper front pages feature the stories that editors and journalists—acting as professional gatekeepers—believe will most engage readers (Boydstun 2013). We tracked the frequency, focus and tone of press coverage. Following previous Australian (Carson and Jackman 2023; Carson and Zion 2019; Carson and McNair 2018) and international (Kahn and Kenney 2002) studies, we coded front pages for the presence of election stories, the topic of the lead story and its tone: neutral, positive or negative. Election coverage was more inconsistent than in previous campaigns, partly due to major global news events such as the death of Pope Francis on 21 April 2025 and extensive reporting on Trump's 'Liberation Day', which diverted front-page media attention from the election. Mainstream outlets published 424 front pages over the 36-day campaign, with 273 or 64 per cent of these including at least one election story.[2] This represented a slight decrease in front-page coverage, from 68 per cent in 2022 and 69 per cent in 2019.[3] As alluded to, what was unusual in 2025 were the number of page-one stories featuring international issues. In the first two weeks of the campaign, 13 per cent of front-page headlines were about Trump, showing his outsized role in public discourse during the Australian election.

---

2   This count now includes the *Guardian*'s static Monday–Friday digital front page, collected from 'FrontPages.com', to ensure consistency in data collection.

3   The *Guardian* was not included in these prior studies, though the overall decrease in coverage remains accurate across the subsequent mastheads.

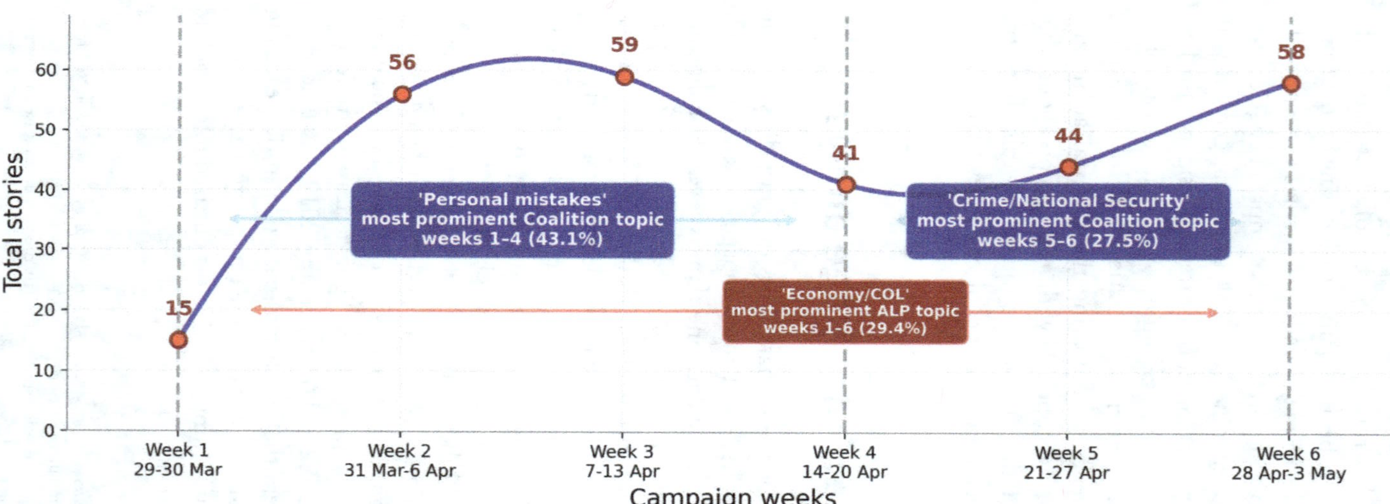

Figure 7.1 Fluctuations in election coverage on front pages during the campaign

Note: N = 273 stories; COL = cost of living.

Source: Compiled by authors using front-page coverage of 13 daily mastheads.

Unlike previous elections, front-page election coverage peaked in week two and then declined over the next two weeks before a rally in the final week (see Figure 7.1). This mid-campaign drop may reflect disruptions from school holidays and non-election events. The death of Pope Francis on 21 April and Anzac Day (25 April) captured a large proportion of front-page attention over this period. Election coverage lifted in week five, coinciding with the opening of early voting (in week four), along with a flurry of late policy announcements from the major parties. Coverage was also spread more evenly across different mastheads in 2025 than previously, with Perth's *West Australian* for the first time providing the most stories, followed closely by national broadsheet the *Australian* and the Melbourne-based *Age* (see Figure 7.2). But, as in past elections, the Hobart *Mercury* and *NT News* featured fewer front-page election stories.

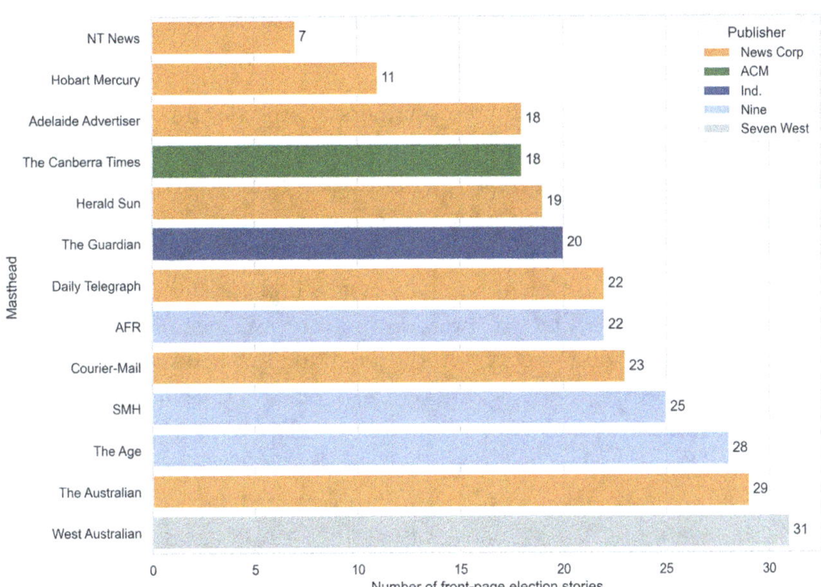

Figure 7.2 Number of front-page election stories by masthead and publisher

Notes: N = 424 front pages; election coverage n = 273 election stories; AFR = *Australian Financial Review*; SMH = *The Sydney Morning Herald*.

Source: Compiled by authors analysing front-page newspaper data.

Media-commissioned polling was among the most prominent of front-page topics, as expected, as it allows the press to shape the news agenda with 'exclusive' content. These poll-based stories consistently favoured Labor and highlighted perceived Coalition missteps. Economic issues dominated overall coverage, followed by related concerns such as the cost of living, national security and campaign process stories.

However, these topics showed high agenda volatility (McCombs and Zhu 1995), with coverage largely contextual or explanatory journalism (Fink and Schudson 2013). Rather than reinforcing clear party 'issue ownership' (Konstantinidis 2008), reporting focused on the shifting dimensions of each issue. For instance, the unexpected announcement of major tax concessions at the party campaign launches was met with an almost universal press cynicism concerning the likely economic consequences. *The Sydney Morning Herald*'s headline argued 'They treat us like mugs' (14 April 2025), while the *Australian* suggested that the policies threatened defence spending (15 April 2025).

Stories about President Trump were another key aspect of this volatility, with much front-page coverage given to the 'Trump effect' in the campaign. This term defined not only the economic uncertainty caused by a global tariff policy, but also broader concerns about how prospective prime ministers would manage Australia's international relations. This 'Trump effect' proved to be an issue for the Coalition, as coverage emphasised an unfavourable likeness between Peter Dutton's proposed ministry of government efficiency and the recently instituted US DOGE (Butler 2025). Then shadow minister for Indigenous Australians and for government efficiency, Jacinta Nampijinpa Price, contributed to such comparisons, with calls to 'make Australia great again' the day before the Coalition party launch. *The Sydney Morning Herald* questioned whether there was a 'MAGA problem for Libs?' (13 April 2025), while the *Age* wrote: 'Opposition Leader Peter Dutton has tried to distance himself from Donald Trump, only to stand next to Jacinta Nampijinpa Price yesterday, as she vowed to "make Australia great again"' (13 April 2025).

It was the first of several Coalition miscalculations that shaped page-one coverage. Within a week, Dutton reversed a key public service efficiency policy on work-from-home (WFH) arrangements, after it was criticised as unpopular and disproportionately affecting women. This decision alone made up 4 per cent of total front-page stories, including 11 of the 18 'Dutton' stories in Figure 7.3. It preceded Dutton's reversal on tax concessions for electric vehicles and a gaffe involving false claims that the Indonesian President was considering Russia's use of a Papuan airbase.

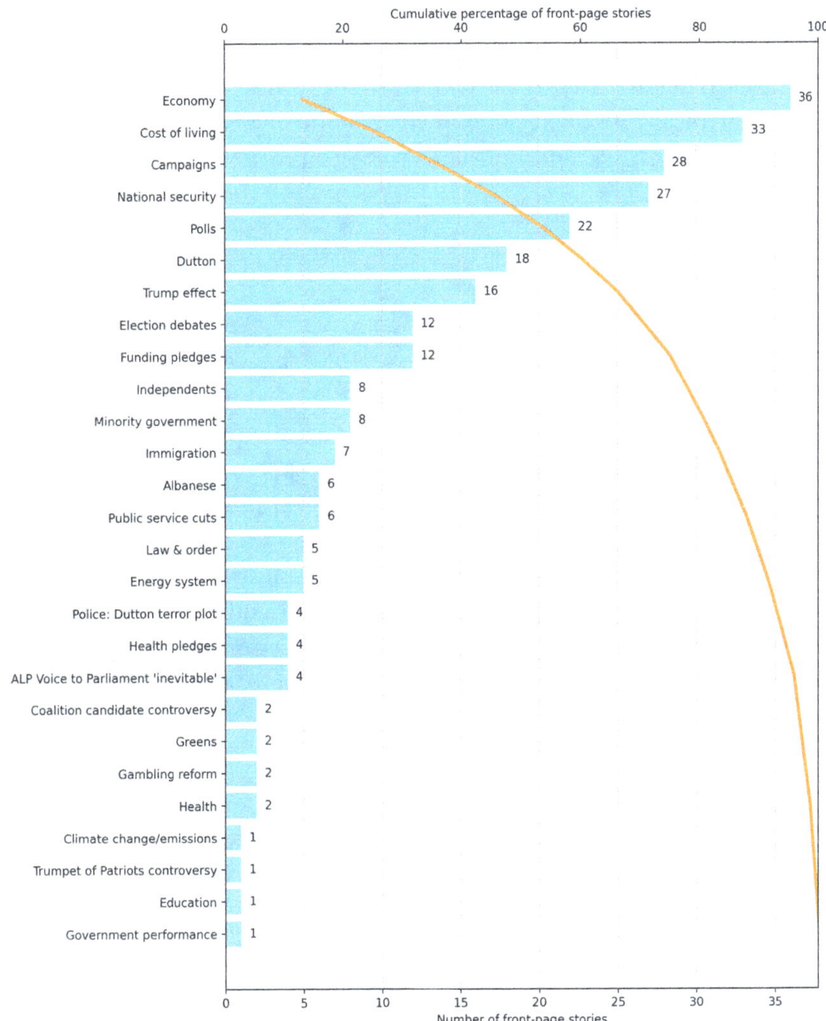

Figure 7.3 Prevalence of front-page election topics in the daily press

Notes: N = 424; election coverage n = 273.

Source: Authors' analysis of front-page newspaper data.

The remainder of campaign coverage followed similarly, with a fragmented agenda comprising both temporarily salient policy proposals, particularly regarding tax cuts and defence spending, and gaffes. Anthony Albanese falling from a stage at a campaign event and denying it (despite being caught on camera) made headlines as did the Sydney 'corflute war' and, more seriously, an alleged terror plot perpetrated by a 16-year-old student against Dutton. Meanwhile, front-page coverage of Independents was noticeably lower (about half that of the 2022 election) despite a record number serving in the Forty-Seventh Australian Parliament. Headlines did, however, typically speculate about the possibility of a minority government in the final stages of the campaign, making up 3 per cent of front-page coverage.

Partisan sentiment

Like in previous campaigns, front-page stories adopted a mostly neutral tone in coverage (Carson and Jackman 2023), although, as expected, when sentiment was expressed, it was mostly negative, particularly towards Labor (see Figure 7.3). Media tycoon Kerry Stokes, owner of Seven West Media, Australia's largest diversified media business, which includes the *West Australian*, contributed to this negativity—as did News Corp's the *Australian*, owned by Rupert Murdoch. Each published more than double the number of negative Labor stories compared with other outlets. The *West Australian* was consistently critical of Albanese's personality, headlining an 'awkward moment' with former environment minister Tanya Plibersek (15 April 2025), his 'confidence turning to arrogance' (16 April 2025) and his fall off a stage (25 April 2025).

News Corp's and the *West Australian*'s front pages were similarly critical of Labor following speculation about a future Voice to Parliament in the last week of the campaign (see Chapter 4, this volume). The *Daily Telegraph*, the *Herald Sun* and the *West Australian* ran headlines suggesting Labor's campaign had been 'thrown into chaos' by the revealing of a 'secret plan' (1 May 2025).

These headlines represented a broader agenda shift to culture war issues, particularly following the neo-Nazi–led heckling of a Welcome to Country (WTC) ceremony at the Anzac Day dawn service in Melbourne. This event prompted Dutton to assert that, while he disavowed the incident, WTC ceremonies should not be part of Anzac Day services. He reaffirmed this position during the final leaders' debate, televised on Stokes's Seven Network, suggesting WTC ceremonies were 'overdone' (Dick 2025). We return to how this issue tracked on social media shortly.

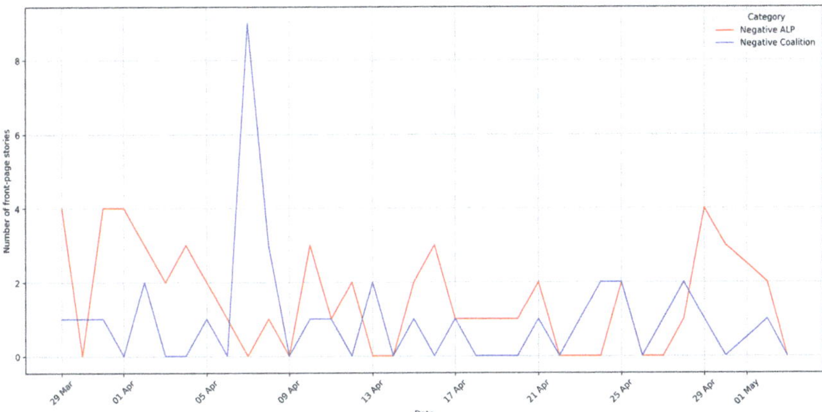

Figure 7.4 Comparison of negative major-party stories across election front pages

Note: N = 92.

Source: Data collected and coded by the authors in accordance with previous studies (Kahn and Kenney 2002).

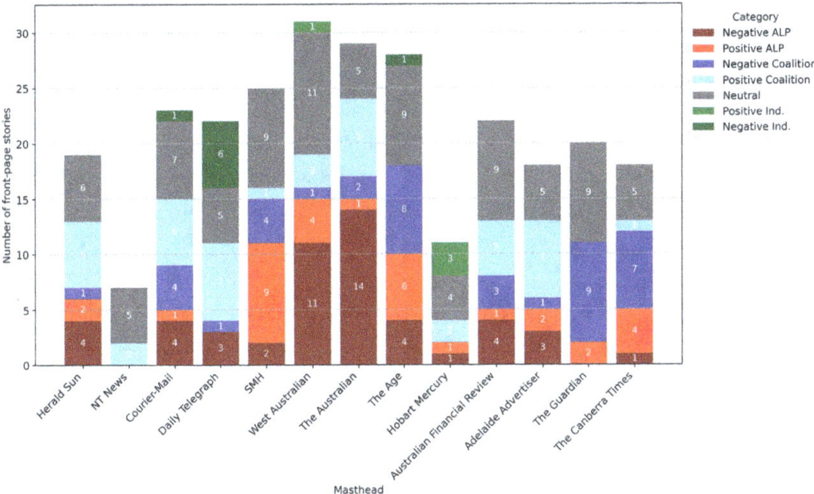

Figure 7.5 Tone of front-page election stories by masthead

Note: N = 273.

Source: Front-page data collected and coded by the authors.

Overall, negative coverage of Labor had increased slightly from 2022, equalling the 2019 campaign at 18 per cent of front-page stories. Sentiment split in accordance with ownership—giving insight into Australian media polarity—as News Corp newspapers covered the Coalition more positively, while stories from Nine (formerly Fairfax) were more favourable to Labor. The *Guardian* was just as often critical of the Coalition as it was neutral (see Figures 7.4 and 7.5). As displayed in Figure 7.4, negative coverage of the Coalition spiked on 7 April. This was due to both Dutton's WFH policy reversal and the dis-endorsement of a Liberal candidate over controversial comments to exclude women from combat roles in the Australian Defence Force. Daily negative coverage of the ALP peaked on 28 March and 29 April with criticism of Labor's contribution to the cost-of-living crisis, its 'campaign of fear' in likening Dutton to Trump (*Australian*, 28 March 2025) and allegedly risking Australia's AAA credit rating.

Social media

Political campaigners seek to build audiences on social media so they can effectively bypass traditional media gatekeepers and speak directly to voters. Building on the success of their 2023 Voice to Parliament referendum campaigns, Australia's political leaders, parties and third-party campaigners such as right-wing lobby group Advance (see Chapters 4 and 16, this volume) have developed their digital infrastructure by amassing followers and 'likes' across the major platforms to target specific voter groups. Broadly, this digital infrastructure includes X (formerly Twitter), to reach the political commentariat; Facebook, for voters over 35 years of age; Instagram, for voters under 35; and TikTok, for 18–24-year-olds (Carson et al. 2025). But, as the 2025 election result indicates, likes, followers and audience reach on social media platforms do not necessarily equate to election victory.

Take, for example, the success of the Liberal Party in infiltrating the online space. It hired Sean Topham and Ben Guerin (see Chapter 8, this volume), two Millennials known for their sharp social media strategies in political campaigns. Their approach uses humour and emotionally charged content to provoke feelings such as anger, pride and fear. In 2025, they experimented with AI content and coopted popular culture into their political messaging. For instance, several videos featured elements of 'Italian brain rot' (see Katz 2025). At face value, the Liberal Party ('liberalaus') had great success in building a youthful online following, with 15.7 million views on TikTok posts during the campaign, although it fell short of Labor's ('australianlabor') 19.4 million TikTok views over that period. Nonetheless, it was an important group to reach given that, combined, Gen Z and Millennials were the largest voting bloc (Chowdhury 2025).

A diverse range of digital strategies was used to reach voters on social media. One common technique was the dual use of partisan hashtags (for example, #alp and #liberals) to broaden visibility across ideological divides. Candidates used AI tools to redub scenes from popular culture, such as the Liberals' use of the movie *The Grinch*, to mock opponents. They also produced generative AI clips with exaggerated imagery (for example, aliens, fighter jets) to promote policies such as their proposed cut to the fuel excise.

Gaming culture was also appropriated for political outreach. Greens Senator Nick McKim used *Fortnite* to attract young male voters (88 per cent of players are men aged 18–35), while Labor used *Zelda*-themed content to attract younger voters. Politicians repurposed mainstream media appearances—for instance, the Greens' Max Chandler-Mather's segments on ABC TV's *Q&A* became short-form content for TikTok and Instagram. Debate footage was similarly cut into engaging clips for social platforms.

Social media is, however, a double-edged sword for campaigners; it can amplify traditional media reportage of gaffes and to large online audiences. For example, Dutton's failure to guess the price of eggs at the fourth leaders' debate was shared on TikTok by the Seven Network and repurposed by others, generating 4.3 million views in the final week of the campaign. Ironically, despite declining free-to-air TV audiences and falling TV viewership for election debates, reproducing segments online attracts very large secondary audiences.

Podcasts are another medium to reach non-traditional audiences, as seen with politicians' appearances on podcasts such as influencer Abbie Chatfield's show, *It's A Lot*. YouTube also remains a key site for traditional media reposts and independent creators, including influencers such as friendlyjordies' election commentary. Finally, peer-to-peer networks such as WhatsApp are employed by campaigners and mainstream media to reach specific voter groups, offering more intimate forms of political communication.

The news media has also recognised the power of colonising the online sphere. Front-page print stories are reposted on social media to increase audience reach. To understand how political news from mainstream media is shared on Facebook, the next section uses computational methods to address this question.

News stories on Facebook

We assessed political news engagement by analysing nearly 40,000 Facebook posts from Australia's top 25 news producers during the five-week election campaign. We show that domestic politics made up only 10 per cent of user engagement, even amid an intense campaign (Figure 7.6). Rather, topics such as court cases, human interest and entertainment were what featured prominently. Still, campaign-specific instances did overlap with larger topics such as economic coverage and President Trump's tariffs.

As expected, there were clear election campaign topics, which we categorised more broadly under the (domestic) politics theme in Figure 7.6. These election topics ranged widely, including Albanese's and Dutton's campaign stops, their debates, voting procedure and polling, Teal politics, the Coalition, a potential hung parliament and media advertisements about upcoming campaign coverage. Still, this collectively represents a small proportion of the overall modelled media data, indicating that campaign politics commands only minor attention from news media (and audiences), at least on Facebook.

As the wealth of game-framing literature suggests, some of this coverage fixated on the horserace aspect of the election campaign, typically using newly released poll data as evidence of *who* was ahead or behind. For example: 'Labor has secured an early lead in the election race … according to the latest Newspoll', with '[f]resh polling [that] has shown the damage done by Peter Dutton's shaky start', or post-debate undecided-voter analysis anointing candidate performance as something that might 'swing the election'. Leaders aside, frontbenchers on the verge of losing seats received similar game-framing attention, as did previous electorate strongholds now experiencing tough battles. Framing the election campaign in terms of carefully considered strategy (for example, Aalberg et al. 2012) was also apparent, with policy 'backflips' framed as 'designed to reboot the Opposition Leader's campaign [to] win back female voters'.

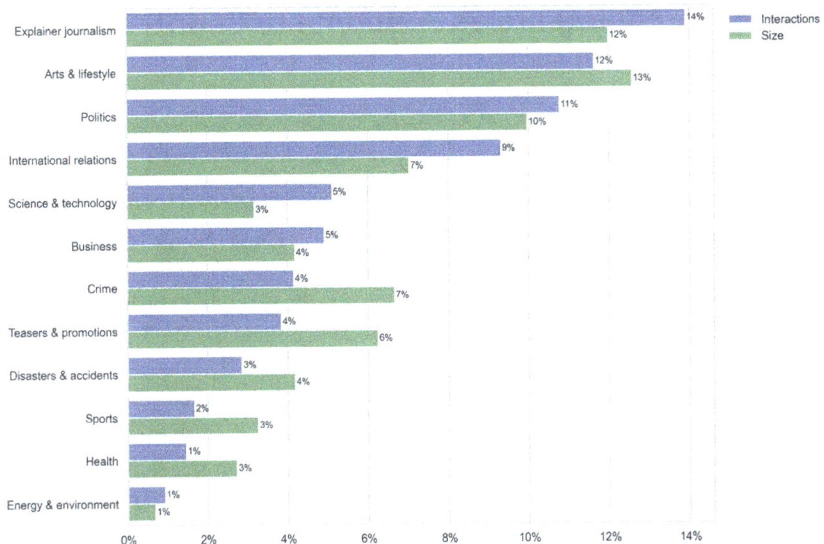

Figure 7.6 Top news topics and audience interaction with mainstream media outlets' content on Facebook

Notes: N = 38,787 posts from 25 Australian news publishers; Interactions represent the percentage of total likes, reactions, shares and comments each topic received as reported by MCL. Size is represented as a percentage of all topics. Percentages do not include noise, meaning they will not sum to 100 per cent.

Source: The authors via Meta Content Library.

Finally, Figure 7.6 also shows the interactions each topic received, which appear roughly equivalent to the size of each cluster. The figure therefore shows not only what these news media outlets considered important, but also what the users themselves valued. In other words, online content that generates more likes, reactions, shares and comments partially reflects what audiences find important, unlike content that is met with apathy. Put another way, if audiences were so deeply engaged with the election campaign, we might expect to see more interactions that reflected such interest. Instead, much like coverage of the campaign itself, online interactions tend to indicate that politics only commands a minority of public interest.

Facebook comments on Welcome to Country news posts

Given the prominence of WTC in the final week of the campaign, we map Facebook stories about it. Between 22 April and 2 May, 101 WTC news stories were published on Facebook by the 25 major news organisations, generating more than 55,000 public comments and a surge of emotional responses, both supportive and critical. As Chapter 4 of this volume notes, Advance was also ramping up its attacks on WTC with multiple ads at this time.

This public outpouring supports claims that Dutton's attack on WTC was an opportunistic one aimed at leveraging Voice to Parliament negative sentiment. It echoed the divisive rhetoric he and figures such as Price and Advance effectively employed during the 2023 Voice to Parliament referendum to shift the issue agenda using a divisive framing strategy (Phillips et al. 2024).

Notably, the stories attracted nearly 15,000 'ha ha' reactions—a troll-like emoji often used to mock supporters or signal political disagreement; in this case, supporters of WTC (Phillips 2024). Public comments using the emoji included inflammatory lines like: 'If it's not white it's not right 🤣, 😂' (25 April 2025). Many echoed Voice-era tensions, using emotionally charged language to pit military veterans against Indigenous Australians: 'Yep wrong place, the sacrifices made by the veterans & families past and present to be welcome [sic] to Country is totally wrong on Anzac Day' (26 April 2025).

This was despite RSL Victoria explicitly rejecting such a framing, with RSL president Dr Robert Webster noting that 'the spontaneous applause from the 50,000-strong crowd attending the service drowned out those who disrupted' (RSL Victoria 2025). Some Facebook users also rejected the divisive framing: 'Both my grandfathers fought in WW2, they would be so happy for a welcome to country!' (25 April 2025).

In the campaign's final days, Dutton returned to Trump-style rhetoric and negative campaigning exploiting the WTC issue, which intensified social media debate. But as Chapter 19 of this volume suggests, the failure to shift the election result highlights the limits of using a single-issue referendum— especially one that did not neatly cleave along party lines—as a guide for campaigning in a federal election context.

TikTok and YouTube

TikTok and YouTube were key election news sources, used by more than one-third of Australians (Park et al. 2024). This increases to 55 per cent for Gen Z (1997–2012) users, leading some scholars to suggest the rise of 'TikTok elections' is a key feature of Australian politics (Grantham 2024). We queried YouTube and TikTok application programming interfaces (APIs) to track key accounts and topics during the election using custom tools (Rieder 2015; Teather 2024).

While commentators highlighted that political influencers were prominent voices on these platforms (Hurcomb 2025), we find that mainstream content still dominated. While Figure 7.7 shows top influencers on TikTok consistently outperforming major parties in terms of viewership, Figure 7.8 shows that these influencers were in turn consistently *exceeded* by mainstream outlets in terms of viewership.

Influencer content still shaped coverage on the platform, though rarely by drawing attention to specific issues. Greens-aligned influencers such as Hannah Ferguson and Holly MacAlpine directed users to claims that a Coalition government would cut the minimum wage and access to childcare. In return, Liberal member Freya Leach emphasised the failure of the Voice referendum and rising power costs under Labor. More commonly, influencers tended to exaggerate existing campaign dynamics, offering direct opportunities for the leaders to express themselves in informal settings (Watson 2025). For example, clips from a 'pub chat' interview between Ethan Marrell aka 'Ozzy Man' and Albanese garnered close to 1.5 million views, compared with a short reaction to the Seven Network's coverage of Liberal campaigning that garnered more than 150,000 views.

Influencers gained traction by framing the election as personal drama using their own media style. Chatfield, for example, drew nearly a million views critiquing Olympian-turned-influencer Sam Fricker, while MacAlpine and Leach successfully engaged with Liberal campaign tactics during their 'Influencers Debate' on SBS's *The Feed*.

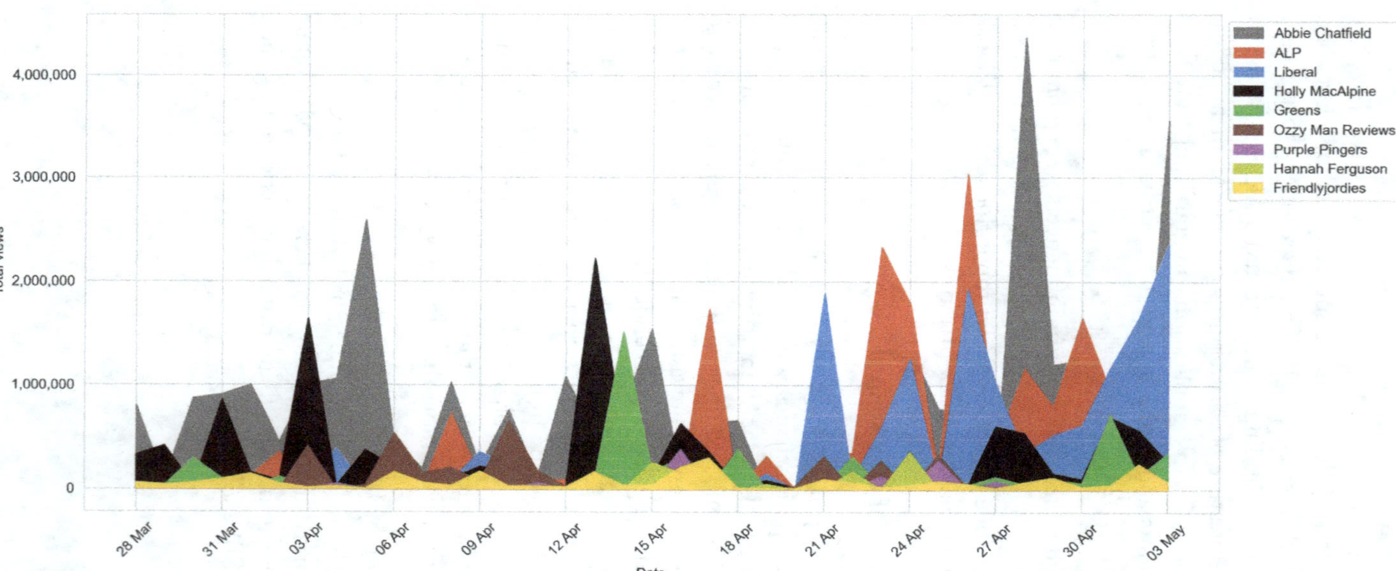

Figure 7.7 Comparison of total TikTok video views between top influencers and political party accounts

Note: N = 1,067 TikTok posts.

Source: Data collected through an unofficial researcher-developed TikTok API (Teather 2024) and analysed by the authors.

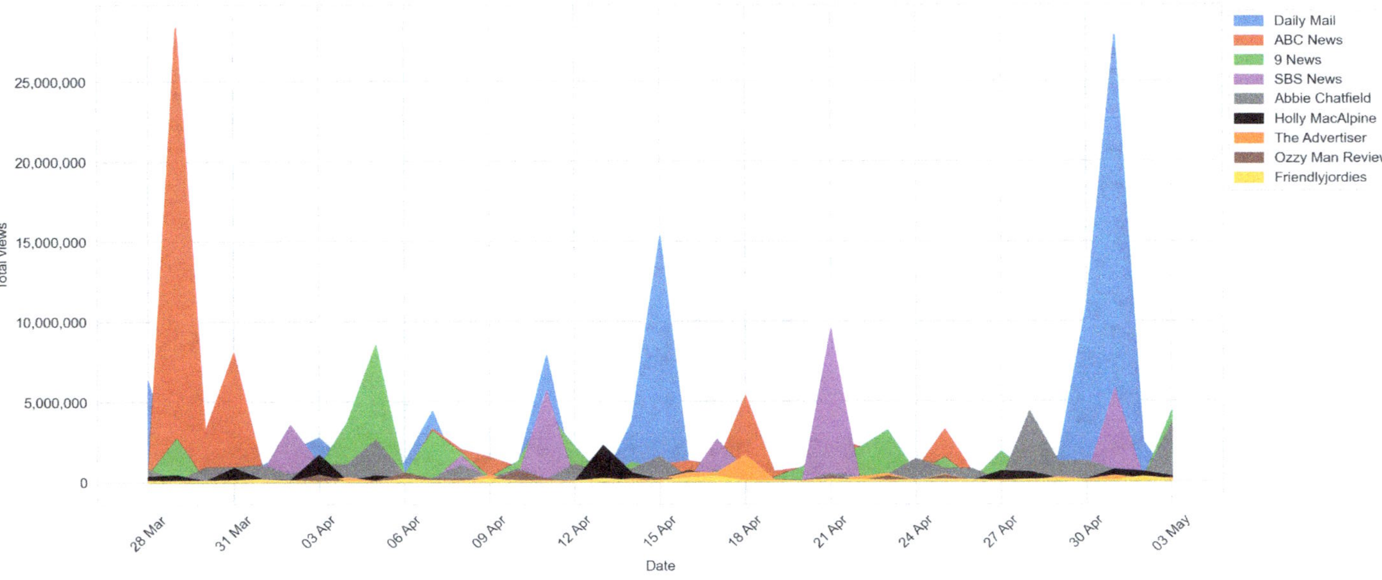

Figure 7.8 Comparison of total TikTok video views between top influencers and selected mainstream media accounts

Note: N = 1,567 TikTok posts.

Source: Data collected through an unofficial researcher-developed TikTok API (Teather 2024) and analysed by the authors.

YouTube coverage differed from that on TikTok, with the former platform affording longer productions, less algorithmic curation and catering to a male-dominated audience (Park et al. 2024). Here, several influencers, including Jordan Shanks-Markovina aka friendlyjordies, produced extended, issue-specific content that delivered large audiences. Friendlyjordies' 29 videos on topics such as housing, Dutton and the Greens drew nearly six million views during the campaign.

Further, influencers including YouTuber Konrad Benjamin, Australian correspondent for the far-right *Rebel News* network Avi Yemini and former deputy prime minister-turned-podcaster John Anderson also attracted a combined six million views (see Figure 7.9). These productions tended to feature extended discussions of specific policies, covering housing, gas royalties, renewable energy costs and immigration, averaging between three and 15 minutes.

This combination of YouTube vernacular content (Burgess and Green 2018), featuring video essays, vox-pops and podcast excerpts, was consistently more successful than the soft influencer–leader interactions seen on TikTok. For instance, Fricker's interviews with Dutton, Clive Palmer and cabinet minister Chris Bowen garnered just 12,000 of a total of 5.6 million views across the campaign. Ozzy Man's interview with Albanese similarly had a view count fewer than one-third of that on TikTok, despite a total viewership of more than 16 million.

Overall, on YouTube as on TikTok, the mainstream media still dominates this attention economy, as illustrated in Figure 7.10. While publishers such as News Corp observe a declining print readership, their digital productions are increasingly a key facet of the hybrid media system. Sky News productions alone generated 107 million YouTube views, while *News.com.au* had a larger total audience than Ozzy Man and that of 9News was close to double again.

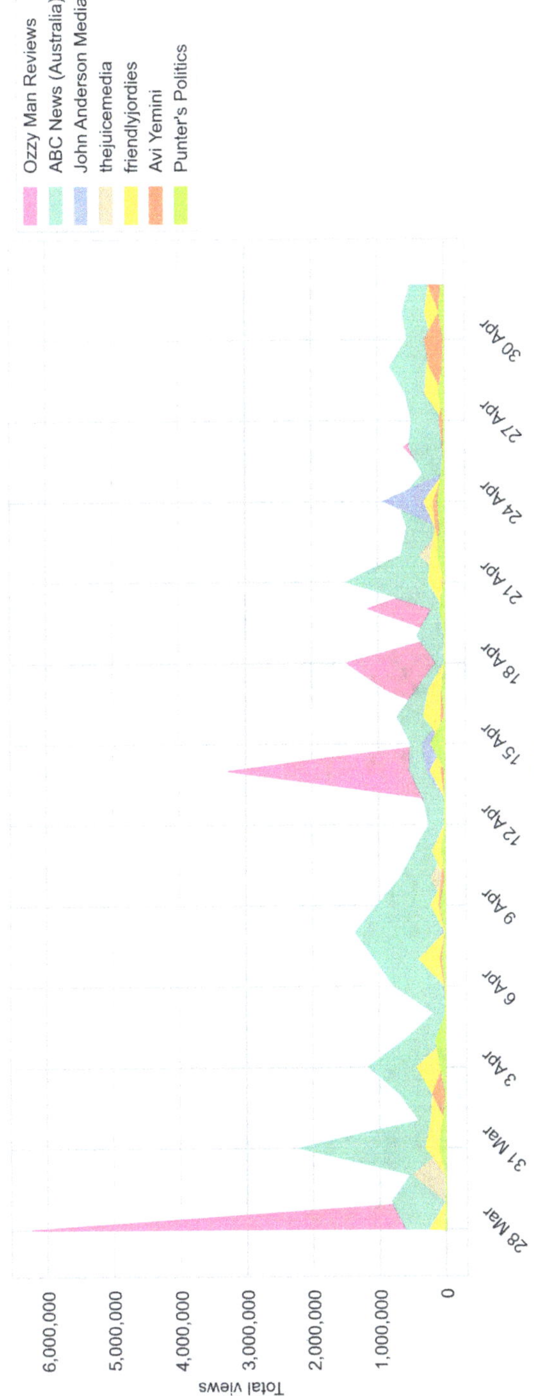

Figure 7.9 Comparison of total daily YouTube views between selected top Australian influencers and *ABC News*

Note: N = 1,577 YouTube posts.

Source: Data collected through researcher-developed tools (Rieder 2015) and analysed by the authors.

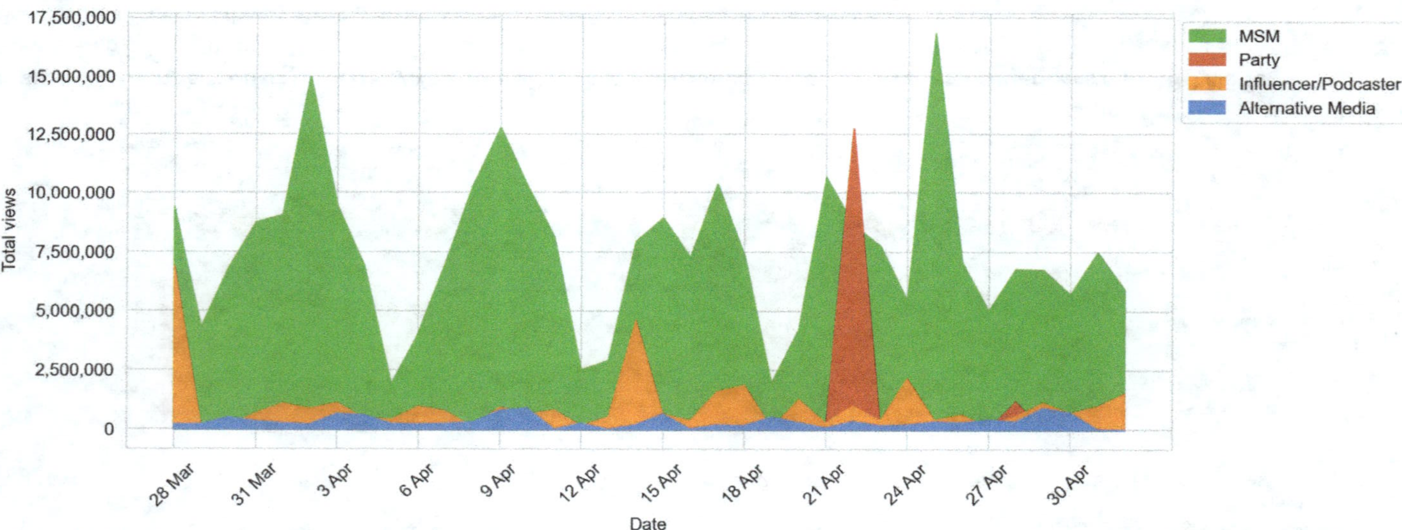

Figure 7.10 Comparison of total daily YouTube views between 27 Australian influencers and podcasters, mainstream media, alternative media and political party accounts

Note: N = 11,642 YouTube posts from 27 accounts; MSM = mainstream media.

Source: Data collected through researcher-developed tools (Rieder 2015) and analysed by the authors.

Conclusion

The 2025 federal election coverage reveals a complex interplay between mainstream and social media. While some argue that favourable conservative press coverage had little impact on the election, suggesting a decline in the influence of traditional media, we contend that it remains difficult to pinpoint the media's exact influence on election outcomes. As our data show, claims that the mainstream media no longer matters in election campaigns seem premature. The legacy media effectively expanded its reach beyond traditional forms and, in fact, dominated 2025 election coverage on digital platforms such as YouTube, TikTok and Facebook and private spaces such as WhatsApp. Facebook data also confirm previous research showing that, despite the large volume of election coverage, politics makes up a small portion of news consumers' overall media consumption (Carson and Jackman 2023).

While we cannot make causal claims about how the campaigns deliver outcomes, we can highlight the role that the media plays in issue agenda-setting and framing of the election. Broadly speaking, the mainstream media plays a complicit role in reinforcing a narrow issue agenda—dominating front pages and broadcast bulletins with coverage aligned to the major parties' priorities and horserace journalism focused on polling data and who is ahead. Also noticeable was minimal front-page attention to critical policy areas such as the National Disability Insurance Scheme, climate change, domestic violence against women and the concerns of regional and rural Australians. While scholarship on agenda-setting and framing has evolved for the digital age, the media's narrow attention to a handful of policies reinforces Bernard Cohen's 1963 insight on media influence: 'The press may not be successful much of the time in telling people what to think, but it is stunningly successful in telling its readers what to think about' (p. 13).

Initially trailing in the polls, Albanese's Labor Party capitalised on media opportunities arising from Cyclone Alfred, a well-timed Reserve Bank interest rate cut and Trump's tariff chaos, using these events to frame the election and set the agenda in its favour, positioning its leadership as both reliable and stable. In contrast, Peter Dutton's Coalition struggled to maintain narrative cohesion. The external shock of the US President's renewed tariff war had complicated their messaging, forcing difficult decisions about alignment with Trump's unpopular policies in Australia. Their emphasis on public service cuts and forcing workers back to the office backfired, leading to policy walk-backs and subsequent negative media coverage outside the conservative press. Dutton's return to negative campaigning—mirroring tactics that proved effective during the 2023 Voice referendum and focusing on WTC ceremonies and 'hate media'—garnered widespread attention across traditional and digital platforms but appears to have ultimately failed to sway most voters.

Social media, particularly TikTok and YouTube, emerged as a key site of political engagement during this campaign, with influencers, memes and emotional appeals reaching large audiences in real time. The Liberal Party's playful use of generative AI and affective messaging showed the tactical possibilities of digital media in campaigning, though, like its traditional media counterparts, this attention yielded limited electoral benefit, with Dutton losing his own seat—the first Opposition Leader to do so. Remarkably, Dutton was the first of two political leaders to fall at this election. Despite promotion by influencers such as Chatfield and others, Greens' leader Adam Bandt was unable to save his own seat of Melbourne.

Labor's campaign, by contrast, was marked by greater message discipline with its focus on the cost of living, housing and health. Early policy announcements about HECS debt relief in late 2024 and tax cuts in the March 2025 Budget before the official campaign ensured early voters had time to encounter ALP positions before filling out their ballots. Labor's pre-campaign policy releases reflected former Liberal prime minister John Howard's (2006) warning that political messaging must be re-enforced over time, captured in his vivid phrase: 'You can't fatten the pig on market day.' Labor's clear focus on core policies amid international instability gave voters a reason to stick with the status quo. The data in this chapter illustrate how legacy and digital media interact in both competitive and complementary ways. Together with the major parties' differing approaches to messaging, it reveals the fragmented and fiercely contested nature of campaigning in Australia's complex hybrid media system where a perceived underdog can produce a landslide election win.

References

Aalberg, Toril, Jesper Strömbäck, and Claes H. de Vreese. 2012. 'The framing of politics as strategy and game: A review of concepts, operationalizations and key findings.' *Journalism* 13, no. 2: 162–78. doi.org/10.1177/1464884911427799.

Australia Institute. 2025. 'Poll: Trump a greater threat to world peace than Putin or Xi.' Media release, 4 March. Canberra: The Australia Institute. australiainstitute. org.au/post/poll-trump-a-greater-threat-to-world-peace-than-putin-or-xi.

Boydstun, Amber E. 2013. *Making the News: Politics, the Media, and Agenda Setting.* Chicago: University of Chicago Press. doi.org/10.7208/chicago/97802260656 01.001.0001.

Burgess, Jean, and Joshua Green. 2018. *YouTube: Online Video and Participatory Culture.* Newark: Polity Press.

Butler, Josh. 2025. 'From Doge to Smoge, Peter Dutton's Coalition is an eerie echo of Trump (and Musk's) America.' *The Guardian,* 27 January. www.theguardian. com/australia-news/2025/jan/27/from-doge-to-smoge-peter-duttons-coalition-is-an-eerie-echo-of-trump-and-musks-america-ntwnfb.

Carson, Andrea, Phoebe Hayman, and Justin Phillips. 2025. 'Australian civic engagement: A case study of the 2023 Voice to Parliament referendum.' In *Civic Engagement in Australian Democracy,* edited by Sarah Murray and Lachlan Umbers, 119–41. Melbourne: Anthem Press. doi.org/10.2307/jj.28697674.12.

Carson, Andrea, and Simon Jackman. 2023. 'Media coverage of the campaign and the electorate's responses.' In *Watershed: The 2022 Australian Federal Election,* edited by Anika Gauja, Marian Sawer, and Jill Sheppard, 121–44. Canberra: ANU Press. doi.org/10.22459/W.2023.07.

Carson, Andrea, and Brian McNair. 2018. 'Still the main source: The established media.' In *Double Disillusion: The 2016 Australian Federal Election,* edited by Anika Gauja, Peter Chen, Jennifer Curtin, and Juliet Pietsch, 421–51. Canberra: ANU Press. doi.org/10.22459/DD.04.2018.19.

Carson, Andrea, and Lawrie Zion. 2019. 'Media coverage.' In *Morrison's Miracle: The 2019 Australian Federal Election,* edited by Anika Gauja, Marian Sawer, and Marian Simms, 431–53. Canberra: ANU Press. doi.org/10.22459/MM.2020.22.

Chadwick, Andrew. 2017. *The Hybrid Media System: Politics and Power.* Oxford: Oxford University Press. doi.org/10.1093/oso/9780190696726.001.0001.

Chowdhury, Intifar. 2025. 'This election, Gen Z and Millennials hold most of the voting power. How might they wield it?' *The Conversation,* 23 April. the conversation.com/this-election-gen-z-and-millennials-hold-most-of-the-voting-power-how-might-they-wield-it-252803. doi.org/10.64628/AA.ja69ur9yc.

Cohen, Bernard C. 1963. *The Press and Foreign Policy.* Princeton: Princeton University Press.

Dick, Samantha. 2025. 'Peter Dutton suggests Anzac Day dawn services should not involve Welcomes to Country.' *ABC News*, 28 April. www.abc.net.au/news/2025-04-28/peter-dutton-questions-welcome-to-country-at-anzac-dawn-services/105224902.

Fink, Katherine, and Michael Schudson. 2013. 'The rise of contextual journalism, 1950s–2000s.' *Journalism* 15, no. 1: 3–20. doi.org/10.1177/1464884913479015.

Glover, April. 2025. '"Pathetic whimper": Richard Marles takes aim at Coalition's $21 billion defence war chest.' *9News*, 23 April. www.9news.com.au/national/federal-election-2025-peter-dutton-announces-coalition-defence-spending-extra-21-billion/44ef126b-5b27-4d3f-80ee-73ae69ba35ec.

Grantham, Susan. 2024. 'The rise of TikTok elections: The Australian Labor Party's use of TikTok in the 2022 federal election campaigning.' *Communication Research and Practice* 10, no. 2: 181–99. doi.org/10.1080/22041451.2024.2349451.

Howard, John. 2006. 'Address to the 10th anniversary dinner Westin Hotel, Sydney.' Speech Transcript, 2 March. Canberra: Department of the Prime Minister and Cabinet. pmtranscripts.pmc.gov.au/release/transcript-22150.

Hurcombe, Edward. 2025. 'In the age of the influencer, does the political backing of News Corp matter anymore?' *The Conversation*, 8 May. theconversation.com/in-the-age-of-the-influencer-does-the-political-backing-of-news-corp-matter-anymore-255876. doi.org/10.64628/AA.agmw7htvp.

Jackman, Simon. 2025. 'Poll averages since the 2022 federal election.' [Online]. 3 May. astounding-horse-28b844.netlify.app/.

Kahn, Kim Fridkin, and Patrick J. Kenney. 2002. 'The slant of the news: How editorial endorsements influence campaign coverage and citizens' views of candidates.' *American Political Science Review* 96, no. 2: 381–94. doi.org/10.1017/S0003055402000230.

Karlsson, Michael, and Jesper Strömbäck. 2010. 'Freezing the flow of online news: Exploring approaches to the study of the liquidity of online news.' *Journalism Studies* 11, no. 1: 2–19. doi.org/10.1080/14616700903119784.

Katz, Leslie. 2025. 'What is "Italian brain rot"? The surreal TikTok obsession, explained.' *Forbes*, 3 May. www.forbes.com/sites/lesliekatz/2025/05/03/what-is-italian-brain-rot-the-surreal-tiktok-obsession-explained/.

Konstantinidis, Ioannis. 2008. 'Who sets the agenda? Parties and media competing for the electorate's main topic of political discussion.' *Journal of Political Marketing* 7, nos 3–4: 323–37. doi.org/10.1080/15377850802008350.

Langer, Ana Ines, and Johannes B. Gruber. 2020. 'Political agenda setting in the hybrid media system: Why legacy media still matter a great deal.' *The International Journal of Press/Politics* 26, no. 2: 313–40. doi.org/10.1177/1940161220925023.

McCombs, Maxwell E., and Donald L. Shaw. 1972. 'The agenda-setting function of mass media.' *The Public Opinion Quarterly* 36, no. 2: 176–87. doi.org/10.1086/267990.

McCombs, Maxwell E., and Jian-Hua Zhu. 1995. 'Capacity, diversity, and volatility of the public agenda: Trends from 1954 to 1994.' *Public Opinion Quarterly* 59, no. 4: 495–525. doi.org/10.1086/269491.

Meraz, Sharon. 2011. 'Using time series analysis to measure intermedia agenda-setting influence in traditional media and political blog networks.' *Journalism & Mass Communication Quarterly* 88, no. 1: 176–94. doi.org/10.1177/10776990 1108800110.

Park, Sora, Caroline Fisher, Kieran McGuinness, Jee Young Lee, Kerry McCallum, and Shengnan Yao. 2024. *Digital News Report: Australia 2024*. Canberra: News & Media Research Centre, University of Canberra. doi.org/10.60836/fxcr-xq72.

Phillips, Justin Bonest. 2024. 'Laughing at death: Facebook, the "haha" reaction, and death coverage on local US news pages.' *Popular Communication* 22, no. 1: 17–32. doi.org/10.1080/15405702.2023.2287738.

Phillips, Justin, Andrea Carson, and Simon Jackman. 2024. 'Issue agenda-setting in the Voice to Parliament referendum: Using big data to explain voice discourse on traditional and social media.' *Australian Journal of Political Science* 59, no. 3: 344–59. doi.org/10.1080/10361146.2024.2409113.

Predavec, Skye, Joshua Black, and Rod Campbell. 2025. *Declining Legacy Media Influence on Australian Elections: Yesterday's Kingmakers, Today's Spectators.* Canberra: The Australia Institute. australiainstitute.org.au/report/declining-legacy-media-influence-on-australian-elections/.

Rieder, Bernhard. 2015. 'YouTube data tools (version 1.42).' [Online]. ytdt.digital methods.net.

RSL Victoria. 2025. 'Statement on dawn service.' Media release, 25 April. Melbourne: RSL Victoria. rslvic.com.au/news/statement-on-dawn-service.

Teather, David. 2024. 'Unofficial TikTok API in Python.' [Online]. GitHub. github.com/davidteather/TikTok-Api.

Watson, Finley. 2025. 'Participatory propaganda and politics from the bedroom (studio): The semiotics of conservative influencers on YouTube.' *Television & New Media* 26, no. 8: 894–913. doi.org/10.1177/15274764251350062.

8

Satire and social media: Cartoons, memes and videos

Lucien Leon and Richard Scully

Abstract

There were multiple satirical voices competing for audiences in the 2025 election, including political cartoonists, citizen satirists and the major political parties. This chapter examines how the mosaic of cartoons, videos and memes circulating throughout the campaign responded to and illuminated a selection of key themes and events. The scope of the content highlights the divide between legacy media and new media and the respective cultural distinctions inherent in these audiences. The chapter also explores the extent to which the major political parties succeeded as digital content creators and how they sought to mitigate voter perceptions of inauthenticity. It observes a disciplined and focused approach by the Labor Party, while the Liberal Party's social media campaign reflected the misfortunes of its broader campaign.

Keywords: political cartoons; memes; TikTok; social media; video

In 2025 it seemed like more than three years since the previous federal election, given the number of cultural and technological shifts that had occurred in the social mediascape. Much was expected but, ultimately, little realised from this brave new world. With the cartoonists once again reliably consistent in their craft and confident in their purpose, citizen satirists surrendered much of the space they occupied three years ago to influencers and explainers. Among the political parties, Labor, the Greens and the Liberals produced and disseminated humorous memes and videos in their attempt to persuade voters. Despite a prolific output that leveraged contemporary meme and TikTok trends, the Liberal Party failed to achieve the cut-through of previous elections. Beneath a veneer of Gen Z slang and AI slop, their satirical offerings betrayed a lack of both policy substance and—perhaps more egregiously with respect to online culture—authenticity.

Elon Musk's (brief) support of a newly elected US President Trump and the amplification of right-wing content on X (formerly Twitter) prompted an exodus of left-leaning progressives (including the *Guardian*) from Musk's platform to Bluesky (Hinsliff 2024; Perez 2024; Robertson 2024). X/Twitter used to be a genuine 'town square', supporting voices from across the political spectrum, despite the vagaries of its algorithms. By 2025 this has largely been replaced with two political echo chambers—for the right and the left, along with a few others—where relatively little exchange of competing ideas occurs.

The sensational and *sensationalised* appearance of ChatGPT in 2022 introduced generative AI technology to the mainstream, enabling users with minimal technological proficiency to easily create and distribute fake content. Today, there is a plethora of generative AI tools capable of producing audiovisual content that is, to the untrained eye, indistinguishable from documentary. Especially in the wake of a 2024 deep-fake video of the Queensland Premier produced and disseminated by the LNP Opposition (Messenger 2024), some commentators (Barnes et al. 2024) had warned that deep-fake AI images might exacerbate misinformation and disinformation during the 2025 federal election. However, this imagery was largely absent from the contributions of citizen satirists and avoided altogether by the political parties. AI-generated content did, however, feature prominently throughout the campaign in the form of repurposing or recontextualising popular culture content and leveraging AI trends such as action figures, Studio Ghibli generators and 'brain rot'—the last a deliberately purposeless, repetitive and trivial low-quality digital media content (Butler et al. 2025). One deeply disturbing imagining of Peter Dutton as an out-of-touch ancien régime monarch proffering 'Let them eat yellow cake' did the rounds on Facebook, care of Spud Gun/Reunion Media (29 April 2025).

Despite the proliferation and much-vaunted potential of AI tools and imagery, the pool of satirical imagery has shrunk dramatically since 2022 (though it must be said that the total volume of visual satirical material remains vast). There were few satirical videos circulating throughout the campaign compared with previous elections, with historically reliable satirical video producers such as the ABC and *The Chaser* absent from this space in 2025. Similarly, meme aggregator sites on Facebook—a prominent feature of elections since 2010—have now largely disappeared. For example, while Australian Green Memes for Actually Progressive Teens continues, the Simpsons Against the Liberals, ALP Spicy Memes Stash and Innovative and Agile Memes—once the most prolific of meme creators and distributors—are no longer active. Toilet Paper Australia tended to be haphazard in its posting of Coalition missteps (such as a slew of Facebook comments by authors supposedly 'new to the area' but coming directly from friendly MPs' and Young Nationals' accounts), but memes nonetheless remain a staple in online political discourse and are posted in their thousands to Facebook timelines, Instagram feeds and Reddit forums.

What has remained unchanged is the staple content of 'legacy media': political cartoons, whether hand-drawn or technology-assisted, from the stalwarts of the main mastheads. These are published on the newspaper websites, the personal websites of the cartoonists or—as they have been for at least a century—in newsprint itself. As the Francophone president of the Australian Cartoonists' Association might say: '*Plus ça change, plus c'est la même chose.*'

In this chapter, we examine how the satirical cartoons, videos and memes circulating throughout the campaign responded to and illuminated a selection of key themes and events. In determining which images should be included for analysis, we have given preference to content with broad public reach (rather than the 'dark web' of internal party communications). Current newspaper readership and viewing figures validate the inclusion here of cartoons published in the editorial pages and webpages of the nation's metropolitan daily newspapers and video content broadcast or streamed on network media platforms. Also included are selected videos from independent satirists—for example, The Juice Media and friendlyjordies have subscriber bases that number in the hundreds of thousands. The sample also captured TikTok videos from political party accounts as well as content by citizen satirists identified by 'scraping' the top 100 results returned from each of the trending hashtags '#auspol', '#auspol2025', '#ausvotes', '#albanese', '#albo' and '#dutton'.

In the absence of a broad political spectrum of meme aggregators in this election, the memes in this analysis were drawn from a pool of 1,128 images mediated by official political party Facebook and Instagram accounts (n = 516) and the two best-subscribed political discourse forums on Reddit (r/AusMemes and r/AustralianPolitics, with a combined 600,000 users). The sharing and posting of memes, as well as their intermediation with legacy news media (traditional cartoons were also shared extensively), extend the reach of these images beyond their partisan base to a wider mainstream audience. Using Shifman's (2014) taxonomy for the categorisation of memes, the images in this sample were selected from a deeper pool that included photographs, graphics and political advertising material. For ease of codification, only advertising images that leveraged traditional meme formats and styles (especially satire) were categorised as a meme. This means the many hundreds of images posted to the social media accounts of the Nationals, Pauline Hanson's One Nation, Trumpet of Patriots, Independent candidates and affiliated political activist groups (such as the progressive GetUp! and conservative Advance) do not feature prominently in this analysis.

In aligning the satirical responses with the election outcome, the images collectively frame a narrative of voters who, although underwhelmed by Labor's response to the cost-of-living and housing crises, were even less impressed by the Coalition's threadbare policy platform and recent track record on the economy, energy and health care. Against a backdrop of global tumult including wars in Ukraine and Gaza, China flexing its military muscles and the United States upending decades of socio-cultural, political and economic conventions, Australians voted for familiar, stable and empathetic government.

The same old new media

Amid this dynamic and fast-moving socio-technological space, the Liberal Party once again recruited digital marketing agency Topham Guerin to drive their social media content strategy (Koutsoukis 2024). The 'water dripping on a stone' strategy that the firm executed so effectively during the Coalition's 2019 election campaign—when they produced and disseminated hundreds of negative 'boomer memes' on Facebook—failed to resonate with online communities in 2025 (Carbone 2025). This was despite Ben Guerin and Sean Topham's contribution to the victory of their alma mater, the New Zealand National Party, in 2023, and their boast that their digital advertising helped win the Queensland State election for the LNP and more besides:

> We're proud to have led the digital advertising efforts during the LNP's recent victory in Queensland, and here are two top takeaways:
>
> 1. Embracing AI Technology: The team created an impressive 744 unique pieces of creative for paid advertising, including 465 custom video ads. That's significantly greater volume than Labor and enabled more bespoke, targeted creative for the audiences. AI tools enabled the LNP to produce over half of these videos rapidly, allowing the LNP to easily speak to local issues in many marginal seats.
>
> 2. Video Dominance in Political Advertising: Nearly 80% of all advertising spend was video-first. By utilising clever hooks and modern techniques, the LNP's digital video strategy exceeded industry benchmarks for video advertisements. Video content often results in better message retention which is why this tactic was critical. (Topham Guerin 2024)

It's a fine pitch, but in recruiting Topham Guerin, and the contingent decision to 'sacrifice veracity for virality' (Hattotuwa 2025), the Coalition seems to have been the victim of its own hype and its own marketing (or, at least, the hype fed to them by those making money *through* marketing, regardless of the outcome).

Topham Guerin essentially did a very good job of convincing their client that they were on to something major when they announced 'an Australian election first' with a 'fully AI-generated ad' (Butler et al. 2025). Deploying a mix of Midjourney, Sora and Runway AI tools, the ad focused on the Opposition's promise to halve the fuel excise, which would save motorists about 25 cents a litre. The ad, however, seems to have dropped like a stone, as did Matt Canavan's and other Coalition MPs' brief flirtation with the Studio Ghibli–style meme generators that were popular just as the election was announced (Australian Green Memes for Actually Progressive Teens, 28 March 2025).

'Elsewhere in AI land' (as the *Guardian* columnists noted), there was more happening, with the trend of creating virtual action figurines being applied to politicians. The meme format persists in failing to render a lifelike portrait or to include the individual's legs (a bit like all those six-toed animations in earlier AI generation) but, apart from that, the ALP decided to get in first with their 'Albo: Building Australia's Future' figure (mint on card) on 10 April 2025 on Facebook, complete with Medicare Card and *bánh mì*, Toto the dog and a Rabbitohs jersey. 'Barely a day later' (according to the *Guardian*, but in fact posted to Facebook on the same day), the Liberals created and disseminated an 'In Action' figure of their own, laden with accessories: a 'Cheaper Power' signboard, a 'Vote Yes' sticker from the failed referendum, light globe and duct tape. The packaging screamed the $450-million bill for the Voice referendum, labelled the figure a 'Broken Promises Edition', with a '3 year lie guarantee' and '18% more for rent' and included a 'never falls over' slogan.

For the *Guardian* columnists, 'the obvious question' was 'what accessories would a Peter Dutton action figure come with'? Right on cue the answer appeared from GetUp! But Dutton *was* the accessory—to a 'Mining Magnate Gina' figurine (Vested Interest Edition), complete with wads of cash, yellow hardhat, fork and pickaxe. Thereafter, there were further attempts at action figure memes in the form of Ali France's supporter base producing an 'I ❤ Free Healthcare' edition (10 April 2025); live export lobby group Keep the Sheep and their Albanese 'Destroying Rural Communities' edition (13 April 2025); and then—as the seat of Dickson appeared to be even more marginal—the United Workers Union finally gave Peter Dutton his own 'Limited Edition' 'Dickson Dud' figure, with a MAGA 'Thinking Cap', dog whistle, nuclear briefcase dripping green radioactive waste and a 'Plan' with all the entries scrubbed out. Sadly, for collectors, a plan to fix childcare was 'not included'.

These were action figure memes produced either by the political parties themselves or by pressure groups aligned with one or the other side. There were also those produced by citizen satirists, either for full, open consumption or circulated more privately. That the Coalition campaign in Kooyong could come up with a frowning, 'insulting' Monique Ryan action figure indicates that this could be deployed locally (*Age*, 16 April 2025), but the most notable was 'John Smith' on their 'Albo is a Joke' Facebook page (24 April 2025). The standard symbolism of the Pride and Aboriginal flags, a wind farm and solar panel, as well as a T-shirt emblazoned with the Chinese flag is a good indicator of the conservative constituency the meme was intended to reach. The result: 34 likes and other reactions, four comments and nine shares seem like a pretty standard payoff for a few seconds' work by an AI bot.

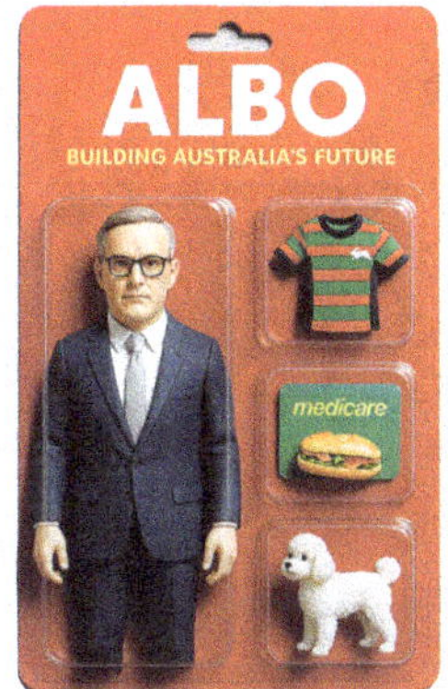

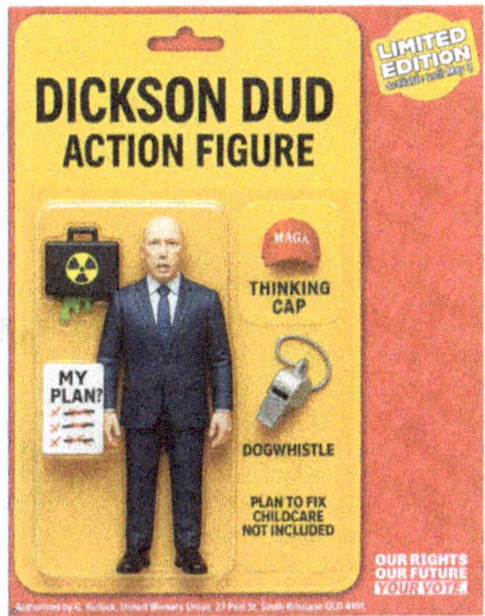

Plate 8.1 AI-generated 'action figure' images: The ALP's 'Albo: Building Australia's Future'; the Liberals' 'In Action Albo'; 'Mining Magnate Gina' by GetUp!; 'Anthony Albanese: Destroying Rural Communities' by Keep the Sheep WA; 'Ali France Action Figure' by Ali France; 'Dickson Dud Action Figure' by the United Workers Union

Sources: ALP Facebook page, 10 April 2025 (www.facebook.com/photo.php?fbid=1207819777369195&set=pb.100044235528995.-2207520000&type=3); Liberal Party Facebook page, 10 April 2025 (www.facebook.com/photo.php?fbid=1229378591879798&set=pb.100044230069311.-2207520000&type=3); GetUp! Instagram account, 11 April 2025 (www.instagram.com/p/DITB4xhTb3L/); Ali France Instagram account, 10 April 2025 (www.instagram.com/p/DIQp_0cNWLp/?img_index=1); Keep the Sheep Instagram account, 13 April 2025 (www.instagram.com/p/DIXfqNyuZEv/); United Workers Union Instagram account, 29 April 2025 (www.instagram.com/p/DJBrcU-PWrU/).

Plate 8.2 AI-generated 'Albo In Action' figure by John Smith
Source: John Smith, Albo is a Joke Facebook page, 24 April 2025.

With AI-generated satire failing to launch, this was a campaign that tended to highlight a divide between legacy media and new media, but not in the way many would have imagined. The staff cartoonists of the main mastheads, and those employed on a more ad hoc basis or as freelancers, maintained a standard and quality of art-cum-journalism very much in keeping with previous election campaigns. Readers were treated to the usual suite of Mark Knight brilliance in the *Herald Sun*; Cathy Wilcox was at her usual insightful best for the Nine newspapers stable (*Age*, *The Sydney Morning Herald*); Johannes Leak was able to stab the Liberals in the front like no other (the *Australian*); and Fiona Katauskas displayed her usual cheeky delight in the backflipping of left-leaning and right-leaning pollies for the *Guardian*. That there is still more great and real cartooning talent in the likes of Chris Downes (Hobart *Mercury*), Matt Golding (Nine), Brett Lethbridge

(*Courier-Mail*) and Peter Broelman and David Pope (*Canberra Times*) was never in doubt. They have all seen enough elections and commented on enough politics to have honed their skills to a fine art. The 2025 election was a reminder, too, that Harry Bruce (*Townsville Bulletin* and *Cairns Post*) is still formidable after 30-odd years of work; Dean Alston (*West Australian*) continues to fly the flag for cartooning across the Nullarbor; and the campaign has also reinforced the status of David Macarthur (*Mercury*) as one of the rising stars. That Megan Herbert (the *Age*) and David Rowe (*Australian Financial Review*) are just as good as ever only underscores the way legacy media is still the gold standard when it comes to satire.

Reviewing five weeks' worth of 'Talking Pictures' from the 2025 campaign is a reassuring experience. Despite this being something originally televised, and now viewable on ABC iView or YouTube, one wonders: Where was YouTube during the campaign? Where were the sensational influencers and independent news bulletins on Dailymotion, TikTok or via the podcasts as news information and opinion sources? The highlight of most Facebook feeds was the new content aggregated by Political Cartoons Australia and the Australian Cartoonists' Association, and the feeds of mastheads and cartoonists. The real shock of the new seems largely to have been how unshocking it was.

Pre-campaign

Heading into the campaign, there were some positive signs for the Coalition. Just 18 months earlier, Peter Dutton had prosecuted a successful 'No' case for the Voice referendum that had galvanised the Coalition and shored up Dutton's leadership credentials. In early March, the Coalition maintained a slight but stubborn two-party-preferred lead in all but one of the major polls (outlier YouGov showed a 51:49 lead for Labor). The electorate, fatigued by cost-of-living pressures and uninspired by Albanese's leadership, seemed primed to boot out a first-term government for the first time in nearly a century. All that was needed from the Coalition, presumably, was a little reassurance in the form of a workmanlike campaign and a sprinkling of positive policy announcements. What transpired instead was one of the worst campaigns in Liberal Party history (Kehoe 2025; Savva 2025; Tingle 2025). Meanwhile, the incumbent—albeit assisted somewhat by global events—delivered one of Labor's best.

Temu-Trump

In the last Question Time before the campaign, Greens MP Stephen Bates asked the Prime Minister, 'Why would you invite Donald Trump to Australia when you've got a Temu-Trump sitting right opposite you?' (Australian Greens 2025). A video of the exchange uploaded to the Greens' TikTok account attracted more than 2.1 million views during the campaign period. Cartoonist James Hillier (aka Nordacious) released a range of 'Temu-Trump' merchandise (Plate 8.3), while #temutrump became a trending hashtag on all the major social media platforms. A reference to the popular website offering cut-price unbranded goods, 'Temu-Trump' was effectively employed by the Coalition's opponents as shorthand for Peter Dutton's leadership style and policy ambitions. In a campaign in which an increasingly unpopular US President and seemingly dysfunctional American politics dominated the news cycle, the perception that Peter Dutton would deliver similar leadership and governance proved disastrous for the Coalition.

This perception was driven by the Coalition themselves, at a time when the global conservative brand looked to have been enhanced by the US Republican Party's ascendancy at the 2024 election. In a television interview in early February 2025, Liberal Senator Michaelia Cash declared in relation to Trump's leadership style that Australians would 'get the exact same attitude under a Peter Dutton government' (Abo 2025). Interviewed by Radio 2GB and *60 Minutes* just over a week later, Dutton offered his own praise of Trump, saying, '[H]e's a deal-maker, he's a thinker, he brings people together' (Stefanovic 2025). These sentiments were reflected in a swathe of rhetoric and policy proposals that, contrary to assuring voters, deeply concerned them (see Chapter 4, this volume).

The appointment of Country Liberal Party Senator Jacinta Nampijinpa Price in January as shadow minister for government efficiency echoed Trump's Elon Musk–led Department of Government Efficiency, which presided over a program of government employee redundancies. The parallel was reinforced by Dutton's announcement in the campaign's opening week that his government would sack 41,000 public servants. A week later, Senator Price introduced Peter Dutton to supporters gathered at a Perth bowling club with the promise that the Coalition would 'make Australia great again'. In denying that the expression was 'an ode' to the US President, Price insisted that the media was 'obsessed with Donald

Trump' (ABC News 2025)—a claim that was undermined somewhat the following day with circulation in the media of an image of Price celebrating Christmas wearing a totemic 'MAGA' cap and holding a Donald Trump Christmas tree ornament (Plate 8.4).

Plate 8.3 A selection of 'Temu-Trump' merchandise by Nordacious

Source: Nordacious (nordacious.com/products/temu-trump-australian-printed-womens-the-boyfriend-tee?variant=49960216920366).

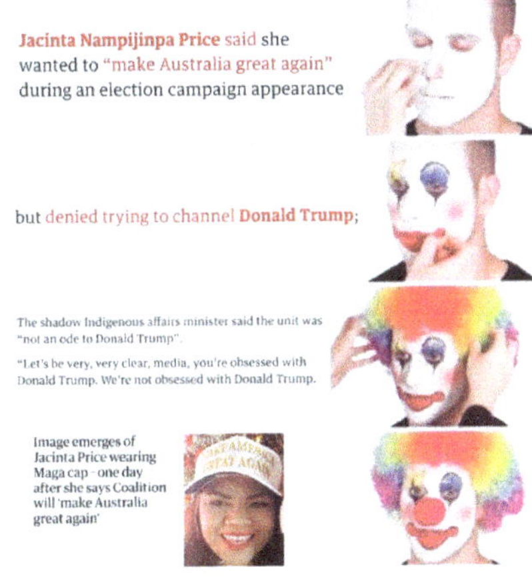

Plate 8.4 'Imagine if these absolute clowns got back into office': Meme about Jacinta Nampijinpa Price by u/TinySmugCnuts

Source: Reddit subforum r/AusMemes, April 2025 (www.reddit.com/r/Aus Memes/comments/1jxzrbm/imagine_if_ these_absolute_clowns_got_back_into/).

Plate 8.5 'Don't do it Australia!' meme by u/Broomfondl3

Source: Reddit r/AusMemes forum, 26 April 2025 (www.reddit.com/r/Aus Memes/comments/1k8akmi/dont_do_it_ australia/).

Plate 8.6 'Don't risk Dutton' pamphlet by Victorian Trades Hall Council
Source: Victorian Trades Hall Council Instagram account, 1 April 2025 (www.instagram.com/p/DH5e2ZlP3i7/).

Dutton's earlier reservations about the integrity of the AEC's Voice referendum process (Cassidy and Barry 2025) and floating of the idea for a referendum to allow the government to deport dual national citizens (McIlroy 2025) were followed in the campaign proper by promises to fix the 'woke' school curriculum and complaints about the 'hate media'. The presence of billionaire mining magnate Gina Rinehart—the Liberal party's second-largest donor—loomed over the Coalition campaign as she urged Australia to 'follow the US' lead', raising comparisons with Musk's influence in the Trump administration (Reuters 2025) and inviting questions about her influence in a future Australian one (Plate 8.5). This relationship inspired the Victorian Trades Hall Council to create pamphlets that unfolded to reveal Dutton as Rinehart's puppet, which volunteers distributed at 100 Victorian train stations (Plate 8.6).

Plate 8.7 Images showing Peter Dutton as winner of the first leaders' debate

Sources: Nationals Facebook page, 8 April 2025 (www.facebook.com/photo.php?fbid= 1204143204400020&set=pb.100044130549325.-2207520000&type=3); LNP Queensland Instagram account, 8 April 2025 (www.instagram.com/p/DlLrMrtzGZT/).

Then, in early April, President Trump unveiled a tariff plan that imposed a blanket 10 per cent import levy on most countries—including Australia— and global market chaos ensued. As Australian voters nervously contemplated the impact on their mortgage interest rates and superannuation balances, Albanese's response that the tariffs were 'not the act of a friend' threw into sharp relief the cultural and political differences that separate Australia from the United States—and, by extension, Albanese from Dutton. With a succession of US allies failing to secure tariff exemptions, Dutton's claim that he alone would be able to secure a favourable deal with the United States presented a decidedly Trumpesque recasting of fantasy as fact. A similar grandiosity was evident one week later when the Coalition triumphantly declared Peter Dutton the winner of a debate the audience had awarded convincingly to Albanese (Plate 8.7). Meanwhile, Albanese was conflating Labor values with Australian values and Liberal values with American values and applying this contrast to almost every policy issue: wages, student debt, education, defence, health, housing, superannuation, women's rights and diversity.

Cartoonists were even gifted a little bit of Commonwealth cross-fertilisation with the victory of the 'other' Liberals—the liberal ones—in the Canadian election and the clear rejection of Trumpian conservatism by our fellow subjects of King Charles (28 April 2025). This repudiation of a recently favoured conservative Opposition seems to have reflected on all the Coalition 'baggage': its women problem, minorities (transgender people, Asians, Muslims) and the environment. Aggressive posturing was scorned as the electorate seemed much more desirous of kindness, and the notion that in a world of chaos, one should choose the safe, boring option, seemed to be common sense.

Medicare 2.0

Labor successfully portrayed itself in this campaign as the creator and enduring custodian of Medicare (Plate 8.8), while casting the Coalition as opponents of bulk-billing and urgent care clinics. With Albanese brandishing a Medicare card at every photo opportunity and a giant toothbrush accompanying Adam Bandt to studio interviews as he spruiked the Greens' 'dental into Medicare' policy, Dutton was left defending his track record as health minister and playing catchup in matching Labor's health initiatives. Dutton's alignment with Trump also blunted his protestations about Labor's 'Mediscare' campaign, with Labor happy to remind voters that 'we don't want American-style politics or American-style healthcare' (Plate 8.9).

Plate 8.8 Image sequence from Labor Instagram reel

Source: ALP Instagram account, 26 April 2025.

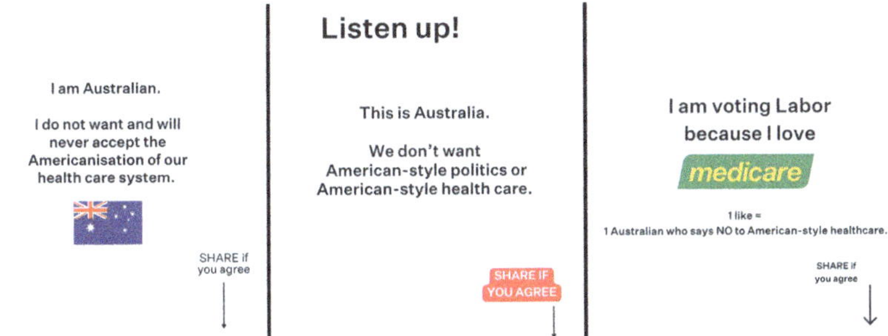

Plate 8.9 Medicare images from Labor Facebook account

Sources: ALP Facebook page, 29 April 2025 (www.facebook.com/photo.php?fbid=1223076472510192&set=pb.100044235528995.-2207520000&type=3); 30 April 2025 (www.facebook.com/photo.php?fbid=1224366712381168&set=pb.100044235528995.-2207520000&type=3); 1 May 2025 (www.facebook.com/photo.php?fbid=122471360567 9812&set=pb.100044235528995.-2207520000&type=).

Plate 8.10 Medicare memes from the Australian Labor Party

Sources: ALP Facebook page, 28 March 2025 (www.facebook.com/photo.php?fbid=1197 138905103949&set=pb.100044235528995.-2207520000&type=3); 2 May 2025 (www.facebook.com/photo.php?fbid=1225389642278875&set=pb.100044235528995.-220 7520000&type=3); 14 April 2025 (www.facebook.com/photo.php?fbid=1211225220361 984&set=pb.100044235528995.-2207520000&type=3); 12 April 2025 (www.facebook.com/photo.php?fbid=1209226720561834&set=pb.100044235528995.-2207520000&type=3); 22 April 2025 (www.facebook.com/photo.php?fbid=1217326819751824&set=pb.100044235528995.-2207520000&type=3); 30 April 2025 (www.facebook.com/photo/?fbid=1224235582394281&set=pcb.1224235809060925).

The politics of caring—not just *medi*-caring—was manifest in this kind of messaging. Although percentage terms are impossible to calculate, support for Medicare on social media via memes and TikToks was massive, and probably constituted the single biggest message in those forums. Albanese could quite easily pivot on this to stake a firm claim that the ALP was more purely Australian than its opponents, because—as he said at the Labor campaign launch—'Medicare is a declaration of Australian values' (13 April 2025).

The ALP was then able to sit back and watch the memes being generated, as Dutton's record as health minister and his comments and soundbites about 'free GP visits being unrealistic' hardly needed embellishment by the party or citizen satirists. The contrast was with Albanese flourishing a Medicare card—'the only card you'll need when you visit the GP'.

Not everyone was sold on the messaging, of course. Megan Herbert (the *Age*) made as much clear in her cartoon showing both Albanese and Dutton as dodgy doctors pedalling bandaid solutions to the real problems facing Australia.

Plate 8.11 'How about a third opinion?', cartoon by Megan Herbert, Nine newspapers

Source: 'Talking Pictures', *Insiders*, ABC TV, 6 April 2025.

Delulu with no solulu

In the days ahead of announcing an election in which younger voters in the Gen Z and Millennial cohorts would outnumber their Gen X and boomer counterparts for the first time, the Prime Minister presented as a guest on a popular youth podcast. The two Millennial hosts of *Happy Hour with Lucy and Nikki* schooled the PM on Gen Z slang, daring him to say 'delulu with no solulu' in parliament. The day the podcast went to air, the PM was in Question Time attacking the Opposition's nuclear policy (26 March 2025). The idea that the taxpayer-funded plan would not result in cuts to education, services, housing, public servants or 'cuts to everything' was, according to the Prime Minister, 'delulu with no solulu'. Now immortalised in *Hansard*, the line received substantial coverage in the legacy media, with the clip of Albanese channelling his inner Gen Z published by major news outlets and breakfast television. On social media, creator Candy Moore remixed the line into an electronic dance music or 'EDM banger' that was viewed more than 100,000 times.

Acutely aware of the fast-growing youth audience share commanded by podcasts, Labor contracted satirical news publication the *Betoota Advocate* to run an election podcast strategy for the Prime Minister (King 2025). Between January and the election, Albanese had popped up as a guest on more than a dozen youth podcasts. In March he invited 13 influencers to the Budget lockup. The contrast could not have been more stark: Albanese was strategically and positively engaging with influencers while Dutton was all but ignoring them. The fact that almost all the high-rating influencers are young women resulted in Dutton ignoring two key demographics at once. The podcast interviews in which Dutton did participate were aimed at a predominantly male audience—or, in the case of an interview with Olympic diver Sam Fricker, predominantly male athletes.

Albanese was also signalling that he understood that the shift in electoral demographics was accompanied by a shift in modes of media engagement. Cheek Media CEO (and Senate candidate) Hannah Ferguson noted the way legacy media bodies seemed obsessed with the supposed flaws and failings of their counterparts in the digital space: 'While new media is busy making content which speaks directly to Australians about how parliament works and what the budget means for them, legacy media is spending its time focused on us' (Ireland 2025).

That new media was turning out information on how Australian democracy works, rather than playing politics, was a point of difference that aligned with youth-friendly Labor policies such as 'free' TAFE, HECS debt reduction and a promise of $1 billion for mental health.

Where Labor was speaking directly to Millennials with Albanese's podcast appearances, and the Greens were speaking to Gen Z via authentic TikTok videos—such as Nick McKim's *Fortnite* Twitch streams—the Liberals appeared hostile to youth and, consequently, inauthentic in their social media engagement. In the last round of Senate estimates, Liberal Senator Jane Hume raised questions about influencer Abbie Chatfield's interviews with Albanese and Adam Bandt and whether they constituted 'political content' that had violated campaign laws in not publishing accompanying electoral authorisations. The AEC later issued a statement saying that Chatfield's videos required no such authorisation (see Chapter 1, this volume). In late March, Holly MacAlpine (handle 'HollyUnmuted') posted a video interview with Greens Senator Larissa Waters to her TikTok and Instagram accounts (MacAlpine 2025). The interview was edited into a video posted to the Liberal Party's TikTok account that made it appear that MacAlpine was critical of the Greens. The video was removed only after MacAlpine's legal representatives issued the Liberal Party with a concerns notice.

Plate 8.12 'Dropping a diss track to stay revenant hahaaha': image by u/Accomplished-Role95

Source: Reddit subforum r/AusMemes, 9 April 2025 (www.reddit.com/r/Aus Memes/comments/1jyr67n/dropping_a_ diss_track_to_stay_revenant_hahaaha/).

The Liberal Party's first salvo in the online battle to capture the youth demographic was the release of 'Leaving Labor', a 'diss track' performed in the style of rap artist Drake. First released on SoundCloud as a music track and subsequently featured in several Liberal Party TikTok and Instagram videos throughout the campaign, the track not only failed to resonate with young people, it also presented the Liberal Party as inauthentic, tone deaf and out of touch in their engagement with youth culture (Plate 8.12). Leaving aside the optics of appropriating North American culture to prosecute their case for election, the first error the Liberal Party made was the presumption that their audience would embrace the style of a rapper whose suspected grooming behaviour and paedophilia had just been publicly called out in a diss track performed by rapper Kendrick Lamar at the Superbowl half-time show. Albanese appeared very much aware of Drake's problematic conduct when offering his own critique in an interview with 9News, saying, 'The Liberal Party channelling Drake … I'm not sure they're aware of Drake and his whole background, but I don't think that's a very wise thing to do' (15 April 2025).

A second miscalculation was the appropriation of a protest culture that is famously anti-establishment and deployed by minority voices by a conservative party led by someone with a history of hostility towards minorities (and one that directed preferences to One Nation late in the campaign). This contradiction was roundly mocked by TikTok users including Mates Rates, who leveraged the design and format of song analysis account 'Genius' in a video that was viewed more than 250,000 times during the campaign. In the video (see Plate 8.14), a Peter Dutton impersonator with masking tape eyebrows and a silicone bald cap explains that:

> everybody knows that the Liberal Party is the more hip hop, the more cool, the more street credited party in this nation … so I think it was really our place to use this genre that, you know, has given a voice to the disenfranchised, to give a voice to us, the very privileged.

A final nail in this particular satirical coffin came courtesy of the fourth and final leaders' debate, in which Dutton famously underestimated the retail price of a dozen eggs even as the song lyrics of one of his party's most prominent social media incursions complain: '[J]ust wanna buy some eggs and cheese, a hundred bucks you kidding me?'

Then, in the final days of the campaign, the Liberal Party posted a video featuring Senator Jane Hume that replicated the graphic and narrative style of US TikTok-er Ray William Johnson (Plate 8.14). Appropriating another creator's video aesthetic is generally accepted practice in TikTok culture, though etiquette demands the original creator be credited, which the Liberal Party failed to do. But where the Liberal Party egregiously transgressed the sensibilities of TikTok natives was when they inexplicably decided to block Johnson from viewing the video they had just ripped off without attribution. Within hours, the video was flooded with hundreds of comments defending Johnson and mocking the Liberal Party. Tellingly, the comments received more likes than the video, with one comment liked more than 37,000 times. It only got worse from there: after Johnson posted a video calling them out for their conduct, the Liberals responded with another video that claimed they had 'accidentally blocked' Johnson—an implausible excuse that was predictably rejected by users, who piled into the comments to ridicule them for once again failing to read the room. As one commenter observed, 'Just fire the PR team at this point' (3 May 2025).

The failure of the Liberals on TikTok in particular, and its youth messaging more broadly, lay not in the cringe use of Gen Z slang ('Labor is mid') or the appropriation of contemporary TikTok trends ('Tim Cheese', 'Italian brain rot') or the dated popular culture references (*Star Wars*, *Shrek*), but in the fact that these images did not augment positive youth policies and rhetoric, and therefore lacked credibility. While Labor's promise to cut HECS debts, make TAFE free and generously fund youth mental health initiatives spoke directly to young people, Dutton was musing about young people being more inclined to vote Labor because they were renters whose political views had not yet sufficiently matured to vote Liberal (29 April 2025). The Liberal Party's social media video and meme strategy comprised in large part disguising home and car ownership as youth issues.

Plate 8.13 Still showing image sequence from Liberal Party TikTok video 'This guy is in real trouble'

Source: Liberal Party TikTok account, 1 May 2025 (www.tiktok.com/@liberalaus/video/7499384820829621522).

Plate 8.14 Still showing image sequence from Mates Rates TikTok video 'This is a real song released by the Liberal Party …'
Source: Mates Rates TikTok account, 17 April 2025 (www.tiktok.com/@mates.rates/video/7494163655446056210).

Working from home

In their review of the 2022 federal election loss, the Liberal Party devoted nearly five pages to identifying how the party might address its 'women problem' (Loughnane and Hume 2022: 31–35). Yet, the Liberals not only failed to promote policy that spoke directly and positively to women, they also proposed measures that were openly hostile to them (see Chapter 6, this volume). That disaffected well-to-do women would continue to support the Teal candidates seemed obvious to the likes of the *Betoota Advocate* (2 May 2025) and others. For them, Teal candidate Caz Heise as a 'Coffs Harbour midwife' with 'experience of telling unhelpful blokes to get out of the way' seemed an ideal summary of the 'Cowper curveball' that nearly unseated Nationals incumbent Pat Conaghan (2 May 2025).

Plate 8.15 'My fellow public servants', cartoon by David Pope,
Canberra Times

Source: 'Talking Pictures', *Insiders*, ABC TV, 6 April 2025.

Even as the Liberal Party rolled out its policy to ban work from home (WFH)—a flexible work arrangement employed more by women than men—Dutton signalled that the ban would not apply to him as he prematurely mused that his preferred prime ministerial residence would be the harbourside Kirribilli House and not the Lodge in Canberra (Plate 8.15). Speaking directly to his local readership in the 'Canberra bubble', David Pope took Dutton to task for this and reminded everyone of the Trump connection one more time (Plate 8.15).

Meanwhile, in the leadup to the election, Labor had supported a wage increase for early childhood education and care workers and a guaranteed 72 hours of subsidised childcare. An election pledge to establish a $1-billion fund to build and expand childcare centres positioned Labor as the party most responsive to the challenges faced by working mothers.

A video by one TikTok user, viewed more than 575,000 times, paired a trending audio sample of misogynistic comments made by far-right live-streamer Nick Fuentes in the wake of Donald Trump's election with the caption, 'Anyone voting liberal please block me' (the irony being that, in the United States, 'liberal' equates to left-wing).

Plate 8.16 Work-from-home image by Australian Unions
Source: Australian Unions Facebook page, 31 March 2025.

Social media strategy

The array of memes and videos produced and disseminated by political parties throughout this campaign points to a well-targeted and future-positive social media strategy on the part of Labor and the Greens and a poorly devised one focused on the past by the Liberal Party. In an election in which the three issues of most concern to voters were the cost of living, housing and health care (Smith 2025), the Liberal Party's social media offerings almost completely ignored two of them. As a post-election washup from the *Australian* noted, 'Their policies were based around the fuel pump and owning houses and nuclear power plants' (Carbone 2025), but the casual observer could have been forgiven for assuming the Coalition's single biggest policy was fuel excise relief for 12 months (while Labor stood for free GP visits and the Greens for placing dental care in Medicare). In terms of defining imagery, Labor and the Greens opted for positive portraits of their leaders brandishing policy props (the green-and-gold Medicare card and a giant toothbrush, respectively) while the Liberals focused on petrol bowsers.

In line with their consultant Topham Guerin's preferred approach, the Liberal Party outposted Labor and the Greens, but their policies did not align with the satire. In any case, Topham Guerin's saturation did not really resonate with an audience. Aside from a handful of videos showing Peter Dutton in a sympathetic light, their strategy was largely negative in tone. While 25 per cent of the Liberal Party's TikTok videos were devoted to the cost of living and the economy, these predominantly attacked Labor rather than offering alternative policy. Just less than 15 per cent of Liberal Party videos spruiked their fuel excise policy, with the second most frequent topic being Albanese's denial that he fell over after speaking at a Mining and Energy Union event in the first week of the campaign (Plate 8.17). The attempt to insist that this showed he was a liar, not to be trusted (Plate 8.18), was perhaps clumsier than the Prime Minister's own footing during the incident. On Facebook and Instagram, the fuel excise policy was reduced to the third most frequent topic, with memes attacking Albanese's role in the failed Voice referendum accounting for just more than 20 per cent of the content.

fyi here is the next 3 years if Labor wins....

Plate 8.17 Liberal Party memes related to Albanese's fall off a stage

Sources: Liberal Party Facebook page, 13 April 2025 (www.facebook.com/photo.php?
fbid=1231832051634452&set=pb.100044230069311.-2207520000&type=3); 11 April
2025 (www.facebook.com/photo.php?fbid=1229906998493624&set=pb.10004423
0069311.-2207520000&type=3); 23 April 2025 (www.facebook.com/photo.php?fbid=
1239609760856681&set=pb.100044230069311.-2207520000&type=3); 8 April 2025
(www.facebook.com/photo.php?fbid=1227894838694840&set=pb.100044230069311.
-2207520000&type=3).

Plate 8.18 Liberal Party memes about Albanese lying

Sources: Liberal Party Facebook page, 11 April 2025 (www.facebook.com/photo.php?fbid=1229881085162882&set=pb.100044230069311.-2207520000&type=3); 16 April 2025 (www.facebook.com/photo.php?fbid=1234280598056264&set=pb.100044230069311.-2207520000&type=3); 24 April 2025 (www.facebook.com/photo.php?fbid=1240449320772725&set=pb.100044230069311.-2207520000&type=3); 27 April 2025 (www.facebook.com/photo.php?fbid=1242598473891143&set=pb.100044230069311.-2207520000&type=3).

Plate 8.19 'Is the hate media really to blame?', cartoon by Fiona Katauskas, the *Guardian*, 19 April 2025

Source: 'Talking Pictures', *Insiders*, ABC TV, 4 May 2025.

There was a not inconsiderable irony when, late in the campaign, Peter Dutton pointed the finger at what he called the 'hate media'—something Fiona Katauskas took pleasure in pointing out (in the *Guardian*), as did David Pope in the *Canberra Times* (1 May 2025) and *The Chaser* via Facebook, imagining Dutton slamming the 'hate media' for 'making him look bad by publishing the things he says and does' (1 May 2025).

Interestingly, despite the big dollars shelled out by the Coalition for Topham Guerin, it seems the ALP made their investments in a cannier fashion. This was something noted by commentators:

> While Labor has brought in experienced operators such as Dee Madigan, Darren Moss, The Shannon Company and two separate research agencies, Talbot Mills and Campbell White's Pyxis Polling & Insights, the Liberal set-up is more stripped back, the Labor insider says. (Koutsoukis 2025)

Other Labor insiders deployed their Facebook feeds on an individual basis, with Jason Clare 'complaining' on 1 May about 'getting old texts' (from Peter Dutton, from 2014: 'There are too many free Medicare services') and Clare O'Neil reposting a sequence of 'cuts' memes (based on films such as *Love, Actually, You've Got Mail, Notting Hill, 50 First Dates, Crazy Stupid Love, My Big Fat Greek Wedding* and the like—all with the main noun or other form replaced with 'Cuts') (29 April 2025).

Election fatigue

As it became ever clearer that the ALP was in for re-election, cartoonists and satirists tended to express the exhaustion that many felt at the seemingly interminable nature of the campaign. Speaking with one voice with *Guardian* stablemate First Dog on the Moon ('Is this the worst most boring election campaign ever? Will voting make any difference?', 15 April 2025), Fiona Katauskas started relatively early, in the first week of the campaign, detailing just how far voters had to go before the democracy sausage of 3 May.

Plate 8.20 'It sure looks like familiar territory', cartoon by Fiona Katauskas, the *Guardian*, 1 April 2025

Source: 'Talking Pictures', *Insiders*, ABC TV, 6 April 2025.

Plate 8.21 Cartoon by Brett Lethbridge in Brisbane's *Courier-Mail*
Source: 'Talking Pictures', *Insiders*, ABC TV, 27 April 2025.

By the time polling day was in sight, Brett Lethbridge (*Courier-Mail*) could point to a few hazards that had appeared along the way, apart from those that had determined Albanese's choice of a polling date in the first place (Easter, Anzac Day).

The alternative view, from Matt Golding, was that 'five weeks of a depressingly negative, simplistic, chaotic and reactive election campaign' would 'be a welcome distraction' from Trump's antics.

No doubt this was something shared across the political spectrum, but it is worth noting (as Katauskas had done) that a week is a long time in politics. Or, at least, two weeks is. By the week of 20 April, Golding was convinced that Australians were completely over the repetition of campaigning, the high-vis clothing and the endless recourse of mainstream media to following the leaders around.

Plate 8.22 'Petty politics is stopping us from building a city', cartoon by Matt Golding, Melbourne *Age*, 1 April 2025

Source: 'Talking Pictures', *Insiders*, ABC TV, 6 April 2025.

Plate 8.23 'If an election were held now ...', cartoon by Matt Golding, Nine newspapers

Source: 'Talking Pictures', *Insiders*, ABC TV, 20 April 2025.

It is worth noting, too, just how many of the cartoonists employed legacy media devices in their work throughout 2025—once again confounding the notion that this would be an election dominated by new media and AI. Golding again seemed uniquely suited to this, using the notion of put-upon voters hiding, like *Doctor Who* fans, behind or under the sofa to avoid witnessing the horror.

Plate 8.24 'I will keep you safe' and 'Where to watch the election', cartoons by Matt Golding, Nine newspapers

Source: 'Talking Pictures', *Insiders*, ABC TV, 27 April and 4 May 2025.

The TV loomed large as well for Mark Knight, who imagined the leaders' respective housing commitments turning the election campaign into an episode of the Nine Network's *The Block*; and both he and Golding saw the televised leaders' debate, and the whole campaign, being largely overshadowed by other issues (whether the ubiquitous Trump and a cameo from Putin or the death of the Pope). Sean Leahy made much the same point: the timing of Francis's funeral broadcast from St Peter's was something to feel grateful for: 'Only one more week of election ads!' (*Courier-Mail*, 28 April 2025).

Likewise, microphone-wielding journos and protestors (of the anti–salmon farming and anti-coal as well as anti-nuclear variety) were the ones Chris Downes saw as the culprits in prolonging the '2025 federal race', pursuing both Dutton and Albanese to the point of exhaustion.

Plate 8.25 'Did you see US Senator #senatormarkwarner stand up for Australia ...', cartoon by Mark Knight, *Herald Sun*

Source: 'Talking Pictures', *Insiders*, ABC TV, 13 April 2025.

Plate 8.26 'Could I have your attention', cartoon by Mark Knight, *Herald Sun*

Source: 'Talking Pictures', *Insiders*, ABC TV, 20 April 2025.

**Plate 8.27 'Pope's passing cuts across election', cartoon by Mark Knight,
*Herald Sun***

Source: 'Talking Pictures', *Insiders*, ABC TV, 27 April 2025.

The fact that something as 'legacy' as corflutes could also be the focal point
of cartoons is also apparent from Matt Golding's output, with Liberal
dynastic scion Amelia Hamer a particular target in Kooyong (25 April
2025). Hamer's team had apparently manufactured and disseminated a
record number of posters and promotional items. Yet, the fact that this
did not seem to be resulting in the royal-blue wave against Teal incumbent
Monique Ryan was pretty telling, especially when so many of Hamer's
posters were fixed to the gates of mansions in Kew and surrounds, thus
making for a perfect meme. So perfect that it required no real satire at all
was the legacy media image of James Brickwood's old-fashioned photograph
of Hamer 'enjoying' a drink with Senator Jane Hume and Peter Dutton at
the Tower Hotel in Hawthorn (30 April 2025).

So, too, Tim Wilson's outlay in trying to win back Goldstein was targeted by
the *Betoota Advocate* (1 May 2025): mock concern for his superannuation
balance was accompanied by photos of Wilson standing proudly in front
of a blue-painted campaign minivan (not a full bus) or in obviously posed
conversation with a 'genuine tradie' (1 May 2025).

Plate 8.28 'Half-bakery', cartoon by Johannes Leak, *The Australian*

Source: 'Talking Pictures', *Insiders*, ABC TV, 27 April 2025.

**Plate 8.29 'Has the Coalition finally found the perfect slogan?',
cartoon by Fiona Katauskas, the *Guardian*, 22 April 2025**

Source: 'Talking Pictures', *Insiders*, ABC TV, 27 April 2025.

That the party (and the Coalition) was out of ideas was also something apparent to Leak's ideological opposite at the *Guardian*, as the theme of exhaustion and fatigue manifested itself once again (Plate 8.29).

Liberal Party–leaning cartoonists such as Knight and Johannes Leak had largely given up on Dutton's campaign by the final week and were just as nonplussed as they had been in 2022 by the pie-in-the-sky promises, policy turnovers and ham-fisted approach. Leak's 'Half-bakery' (the *Australian*; Plate 8.28) is the epitome of that feeling, from a conservative side of politics utterly disenchanted by its political representatives.

The Chaser | John Delmenico

Labor secures bigger majority, excited to do nothing with it

Plate 8.30 'You wanted action and we promise to deliver tinkering around the edges', John Delmenico, *The Chaser*

Source: Facebook, 3 May 2025.

When all was (almost) said and done, the *Betoota Advocate* proclaimed: 'This election shit is pretty much done and it's Friday afternoon. Here's a photo of Sydney Sweeney' (2 May 2025); and then, when the washup began, it was—again—more of the same.

Matt Golding, however, provided a reminder of perhaps the most significant thing about election night 2025: Antony Green's last outing for the ABC (Plate 8.31).

Plate 8.31 'Antony Green did it his way', cartoon by Matt Golding, Nine newspapers
Photo: Facebook, 4 May 2025.

Conclusion

Political satire in the social mediascape has matured to the point where, like political cartoons, pundits and scholars are no longer seduced by the empirically impossible question of the impact of memes and videos on election outcomes. A more pertinent question is how this material, in conjunction with political cartoons and the 'Temu-satire' produced by partisan players, reveals and amplifies the prevailing mood of the electorate and the success or failure of a given party's campaign. Among the political cartoonists, citizen satirists and political parties, only the Liberal Party failed comprehensively to understand their audience. Ignoring the lessons from the previous election, and seemingly oblivious to the evolution of the social mediascape into a venue for news and information as well as entertainment, the Liberal Party's satirical offerings cynically and ineffectively privileged style over substance. As any political cartoonist will attest, satire contains a kernel of truth. Unfortunately for the Liberal Party, the kernel nestled in their content was that they were bereft of ideas and out of touch with the electorate—and they were duly punished for it by voters who demanded better.

References

6 News Australia. 2025. 'Live: Question Time in the House of Representatives in Canberra.' *6 News Australia*, 27 March. www.youtube.com/live/WZ66P2irkVs.

9News. 2025. 'Prime Minister responds to diss track.' *9News*, 15 April. www.youtube.com/shorts/GfLUgIH_-c8.

ABC News. 2025. 'Coalition frontbencher's "MAGA" moment prompts Trump comparison.' *ABC News*, 12 April. www.youtube.com/watch?v=zfMPn2jOl48.

Abo, Sarah. 2025. 'Interview with Michaelia Cash.' *The Today Show with Sarah Abo*, 3 February. Transcript available: www.michaeliacash.com.au/federal-news/transcript/transcript-the-today-show-4/.

Australian Greens. 2025. 'Think @StephenBatesMP struck a nerve with this one.' *TikTok*, 27 March. www.tiktok.com/@australiangreens/video/7486372411571522824.

Barnes, Renee, Aimee Riedel, Lucas Whittaker, and Rory Mulcahy. 2024. 'Disinformation and deepfakes played a part in the US election. Australia should expect the same.' *The Conversation*, 21 November. theconversation.com/disinformation-and-deepfakes-played-a-part-in-the-us-election-australia-should-expect-the-same-243373. doi.org/10.64628/AA.qaexfv33g.

Butler, Josh, Dan Jervis-Bardy, Krishani Dhanji, and Elias Visontay. 2025. 'AI ads, action figures and Auto-Tuned raps: Australian election campaigns battle on social media.' *The Guardian*, 12 April. www.theguardian.com/australia-news/2025/apr/12/ai-ads-action-figures-and-auto-tuned-raps-australian-election-campaigns-battle-on-social-media.

Carbone, Joseph. 2025. 'Why Coalition election social media campaign failed.' *The Australian*, 13 May: 20.

Cassidy, Barry, and Tony Barry. 2025. 'The Trump effect has left Dutton exposed and Albanese in poll position in this atypical election race.' *The Guardian*, 1 May. www.theguardian.com/commentisfree/2025/may/01/the-trump-effect-left-dutton-exposed-and-albanese-in-poll-position-in-this-atypical-election-race-ntwnfb.

Guardian Australia. 2025. 'Delulu with no solulu: PM channels Gen Z in attack on Coalition economic and energy plan.' *Guardian Australia*, 26 March. www.youtube.com/watch?v=OAq7pPPhjWI&t=3s.

Hattotuwa, Sanjana. 2025. 'Sacrificing veracity for virality: Topham Guerin's influence operations, and democratic implications.' *LinkedIn*, 5 March. www.linkedin.com/pulse/sacrificing-veracity-virality-topham-guerins-sanjana-hattotuwa-ph-d--mqvcf/.

Hinsliff, Gaby. 2024. 'The exodus from X to Bluesky has happened—the era of mass social media platforms is over.' *The Guardian*, 15 November. www.theguardian.com/commentisfree/2024/nov/15/x-bluesky-social-media-platforms.

Ireland, Olivia. 2025. 'Australian Labor Party paid content creators' travel costs for budget.' *The Sydney Morning Herald*, 26 March. www.smh.com.au/politics/federal/lululemon-brand-ambassador-finance-advisers-13-content-creators-get-advance-budget-reading-20250325-p5lmdc.html.

Kehoe, John. 2025. 'How the Liberals got it so wrong.' *Australian Financial Review*, 4 May. www.afr.com/politics/federal/how-the-liberals-got-it-so-wrong-20250504-p5lwd6.

King, Tynan. 2025. 'Company associated with Betoota Advocate contracted to run PM's re-election podcast strategy.' *ABC News*, 17 April. www.abc.net.au/news/2025-04-17/prime-ministers-secret-podcast-strategists-albanese-betoota/105180156.

Koutsoukis, Jason. 2024. 'Exclusive: Dutton hires Morrison's "disinformation" team.' *The Saturday Paper*, 7 December. www.thesaturdaypaper.com.au/news/politics/2024/12/07/exclusive-dutton-hires-morrisons-disinformation-team.

Koutsoukis, Jason. 2025. 'This is going to stick: Inside Dutton's Trump thump.' *The Saturday Paper*, 5 April. www.thesaturdaypaper.com.au/news/politics/2025/04/05/this-going-stick-inside-duttons-trump-thump.

Loughnane, Brian, and Jane Hume. 2022. *Review of the 2022 Federal Election*. Canberra: Liberal Party of Australia. cdn.liberal.org.au/2022/2022_election_review.pdf.

MacAlpine, Holly. 2025. 'True or false with Greens Senator for Queensland @LarissaWaters.' *HollyUnmuted*, [TikTok video], 24 March. www.tiktok.com/@hollyunmuted/video/7485289508146105616.

McIlroy, Tom. 2025. 'Dutton wants deportation referendum to fix "restrictive" Constitution.' *Australian Financial Review*, 18 March. www.afr.com/politics/federal/dutton-wants-deportation-referendum-to-fix-restrictive-constitution-20250318-p5lkct.

Messenger, Andrew. 2024. 'Queensland premier rules out AI-generated election material after LNP releases dancing TikTok attack advertisement.' *The Guardian*, 23 July. www.theguardian.com/australia-news/article/2024/jul/23/queensland-premier-steven-miles-ai-generated-qld-election-video-lnp-tiktok-attack-ad?utm_term=Autofeed&CMP=soc_568&utm_medium=Social&utm_source=Twitter#Echobox=1721703938.

Perez, Sarah. 2024. 'Bluesky is benefitting from an exodus of unhappy X users following the election.' *TechCrunch*, 12 November. techcrunch.com/2024/11/12/bluesky-is-seeing-an-exodus-of-unhappy-x-users-following-the-election/.

Reuters. 2025. 'Australia's richest person Gina Rinehart says she wants Trump-like reforms as election nears.' *The Straits Times*, 1 May. www.straitstimes.com/asia/australianz/australias-richest-person-gina-rinehart-says-she-wants-trump-like-reforms-as-election-nears.

Robertson, Craig. 2024. 'What does the X exodus to Bluesky mean for journalism?' *The Conversation*, 20 December. theconversation.com/what-does-the-x-exodus-to-bluesky-mean-for-journalism-246296. doi.org/10.64628/AB.nruajvw94.

Savva, Niki. 2025. 'Dutton has led one of the worst election campaigns in living memory.' *The Sydney Morning Herald*, 1 May. www.smh.com.au/politics/federal/dutton-has-led-one-of-the-worst-election-campaigns-in-living-memory-20250429-p5lv7q.html.

Shifman, Limor. 2014. *Memes in Digital Culture*. Cambridge: MIT Press. doi.org/10.7551/mitpress/9429.001.0001.

Smith, Michael. 2025. 'How Labor weaponised Medicare (again) to take on Peter Dutton.' *Australian Financial Review*, 1 May. www.afr.com/companies/healthcare-and-fitness/how-labor-weaponised-medicare-again-to-take-on-peter-dutton-20250423-p5ltox.

Stefanovic, Karl. 2025. 'Is Peter Dutton Australia's Donald Trump?' [Interview with Peter Dutton]. *60 Minutes Australia*, 16 February. www.youtube.com/watch?v=6IT5_OkSj2w.

Tingle, Laura. 2025. 'Laura Tingle on Dutton's "shockingly bad" campaign.' *ABC News Daily*, 1 May. www.abc.net.au/listen/programs/abc-news-daily/laura-tingle-on-peter-duttons-shockingly-bad-campaign/105235634.

Topham Guerin. 2024. LinkedIn post. www.linkedin.com/posts/topham-guerin_clientwork-digitaladvertising-politics-activity-7259055966267006976-iIns/?utm_source=share&utm_medium=member_desktop.

9

Managing electoral disinformation

Michael Maley

Abstract

While electoral disinformation did not have a significant effect on the outcome of the 2025 election, there have been increasing concerns about its dangers. Its defining characteristic is the deliberate intention to deceive. It can take several different forms, including targeting of a particular candidate or party, spreading false information about the electoral process (either to induce a person to vote in a particular way or to discredit an electoral outcome) and creating a general atmosphere of distrust and/or confusion. Contextual factors that can influence the impact of disinformation include the transparency of electoral processes, the degree of public trust in election management bodies, levels of political polarisation and a country's political and electoral history. This chapter describes various mitigating measures already in place for federal elections in Australia and discusses challenges for the future, especially relating to 'truth in political advertising'.

Keywords: electoral disinformation; transparency and trust; electoral integrity assurance; disinformation register; truth in political advertising

Although the 2025 federal election saw its fair share of claims by various contestants that others had told lies or misled voters, there was no false claim that stood out as having a decisive or even substantial effect on the overall election result. That said, there was an unusual level of attention paid during the life of the preceding parliament to what was seen as the looming challenge of dealing with disinformation, driven not least by the discourse surrounding the 2023 Voice referendum, patterns observed in other countries' electoral events, concerns about the rising influence of social media and the possible use of artificial intelligence (AI) tools to produce materials the counterfeit character of which would not be immediately obvious.

This chapter therefore seeks to take stock of the status of the management of disinformation at federal elections in Australia as of 2025 and to outline various measures that have been adopted or proposed to mitigate its impact. The discussion that follows addresses how disinformation is defined and the forms it can take, contextual factors in Australia that can influence its impact, current legal provisions and processes aimed at controlling or mitigating disinformation at federal elections, the role played by the AEC in dealing with the problem and some policy proposals that have not yet been adopted.

What is electoral disinformation and what forms can it take?

The definition of disinformation adopted by the Australian Government's Electoral Integrity Assurance Taskforce (EIAT 2025a) is 'knowingly false information designed to deliberately mislead and influence public opinion or obscure the truth for malicious or deceptive purposes'. That distinguishes disinformation from 'misinformation': false or misleading material passed on by mistake, without the intention to mislead. In practice, however, the distinction can be a difficult one to make, as the originator of a particular piece of information, and his or her motivations, may not be readily identifiable; such information will often pass through many hands, especially now that social media entries can be widely shared with a single mouse click, and between the two categories, there may be information recklessly disseminated with motives that are neither wholly malicious nor entirely innocent. Therefore, mitigation measures must often be constructed to be effective against both misinformation and disinformation.

As highlighted in Table 9.1, electoral disinformation can take many forms, giving rise to different threats and risks to the process depending on context, and calls for different remedies.

Table 9.1 Forms of electoral disinformation

'Micro'-level disinformation, affecting politicians, candidates or parties	
Disinformation to influence a person to vote for (or against) a particular party or candidate	This can range from lies about policy through to false attacks on the personal character or conduct of a candidate. A prominent case of targeted electoral disinformation in Australia was the distribution in the division of Lindsay, before the 2007 federal election, of unauthorised pamphlets from a fake Islamic group that supposedly praised the ALP for supporting terrorism. Several people with Liberal Party connections subsequently faced court and were convicted over the matter.
Disinformation not directly targeted at a particular party or candidate, but intended to highlight issues in a way that will benefit the political player(s) spreading the disinformation	A classic example of this was candidate Donald Trump's allegation during the 2024 US election campaign that people of Haitian background in Springfield, Ohio, were eating other residents' dogs and cats.
Disinformation passed on with the aim of leading a political player to discredit himself/herself	An episode of this type occurred in the last week of the 1996 federal election campaign, when the then treasurer Ralph Willis released two letters purporting to be between the Premier of Victoria and the Leader of the Federal Opposition. The revelation that both letters were forgeries proved to be highly embarrassing both for Willis and for the incumbent government.
Disinformation with political impact, the intentions of which may be obscure	A case of this type arose in 2009 when Opposition leader Malcolm Turnbull was embarrassed by having criticised the government based on a leaked email that turned out to have been forged by a public servant, Godwin Grech.
'Meso'-level disinformation, relating to a specific electoral process	
Disinformation about the voting process, spread with the aim of inducing a person to vote for a particular candidate or party	A recent example of this arose in the divisions of Chisholm and Kooyong at the 2019 federal election, when signs were displayed at polling booths in Chinese script but with colouring similar to that typically used by the AEC bearing text that was held by the Federal Court to breach the prohibition in the *Commonwealth Electoral Act 1918* of the publication of matter likely to mislead or deceive an elector in relation to the casting of a vote.

Disinformation about the voting process, spread with the aim of depriving a party or candidate of a vote which they otherwise could have received	This encompasses, for example, the distribution of bogus 'how-to-vote' cards, designed to appear to have been issued by a candidate who in fact had not done so and recommending a preference ordering different from the one recommended by that candidate.
Disinformation about the overall electoral process, spread with the intention of casting doubt on the legitimacy of a particular election or referendum result	The statements and actions of Donald Trump following the US presidential election of 2020 exemplify this. Complaints preceding the 2023 Voice referendum about the AEC's legally correct handling of ballots marked with ticks or crosses also fell into this category.
'Macro'-level disinformation, intended to undermine democratic processes and trust on a large scale	
Disinformation spread by or on behalf of malevolent foreign state actors, intended to undermine confidence in a country's system of government	Concerns about Russian attempts to influence the United Kingdom's 'Brexit' referendum in 2016 were sufficiently well formed to give rise to a lengthy parliamentary committee inquiry. Australia's *Foreign Influence Transparency Scheme Act 2018* seeks to create a mechanism for making more readily identifiable attempts by foreign actors at influence (covering much more than just the spreading of disinformation).
Disinformation spread by malevolent foreign non-state actors, intended either to undermine confidence in a country's system of government or to influence the outcomes of political or electoral processes	Such actors could include foreign media proprietors with a record of spreading disinformation; surrogates acting on behalf of foreign states or corporations; and foreign oligarchs.
Large-scale disinformation intended to sow confusion on a grand scale	This strategy, described by former Trump presidential adviser Steve Bannon as 'flooding the zone with shit', has become a feature of public discourse in the United States, and reflects an insight propounded long ago by Hannah Arendt (1951: 474), who said: 'The ideal subject of totalitarian rule is not the convinced Nazi or the convinced Communist, but people for whom the distinction between fact and fiction (i.e., the reality of experience) and the distinction between true and false (i.e., the standards of thought) no longer exist.'

Source: Compiled by author.

Australian contextual factors

First and foremost, Australians clearly are not indifferent to the dangers of electoral disinformation. Carson and Grömping (2025) report having 'surveyed more than 7,000 people during March and April [2025] when the election campaign was heating up', finding that a least 'two-thirds of respondents said they had already encountered false or misleading election information'. They note also that an 'overwhelming majority of respondents (94%) viewed political misinformation as a problem; more than half regarded it as a "big" or "very big problem"'.

The impact of an item of electoral disinformation will be much influenced by the immediate context in which it is disseminated. In some cases, it may be relatively innocuous—for example, if it is blatantly false but obviously posted online from a 'parody' account; is so wildly implausible on the face of it as to be unlikely to have much impact; has only very limited distribution; or is of significance to only a small class of voters. At the other end of the scale, claims amounting to disinformation could be the centrepiece of the campaign of a major political party.

In Australia several more enduring contextual factors are also significant. First, federal electoral processes and management have from the very outset been highly transparent, not only because candidates have a right to deploy scrutineers to monitor the voting and counting on election day, but also because those activities predominantly use simple manual processes, based on a paper ballot, which are intrinsically easier to observe, even by people with relatively little specialist expertise, than complex processes involving technology (such as electronic or internet voting).

Second, there exists a strong and longstanding political and public consensus on the role and trustworthiness of the AEC (Carson et al. 2025). Public expressions to the contrary are rare and the Opposition Leader's ill-founded criticisms of the AEC's approach to the handling of ballots marked with ticks or crosses at the 2023 Voice referendum probably gained a degree of public attention precisely because they were so unusual as well as irresponsible. If anything, there has been a decline in recent years in the volume of targeted criticism attempting to motivate distrust in the electoral system, and the H.S. Chapman Society, a civil society body that actively pursued such issues over several decades, now appears to be moribund. More typical was the statement issued by the Liberal candidate for the division of Bradfield on 14 July 2025 when announcing her intention to mount a court challenge to her narrow defeat (Kapterian 2025):

> To be clear, there is no question regarding the integrity of our electoral system. In fact, this process has only served to reaffirm my faith in Australia's democratic institutions. I am grateful for the AEC's tireless work in delivering two very close counts.

Third, Australia to date has largely been free of the political tribalism, sustained by media 'echo chambers', which has been so destructive of democratic practice in the United States (where disinformation has thrived, purveyed by 'news' sources that reflect the intrinsic biases of a polarised population). On the contrary, Australian voters' identification with political parties has been in long-term decline and the major parties' share of the vote in 2025 was at a postwar record low.

Finally, Australia is not yet a country where politically 'anything goes'. Political players still face some risk that proven engagement in disinformation (or other sharp practices) could lose rather than gain them votes.

Current legal provisions and mitigation processes

As of 2025, measures for limiting electoral disinformation and mitigating its effects on federal elections fall into two broad categories: those specifically focused on the electoral process and those with a broader focus but which may nevertheless be beneficial in the electoral context.

Electorally focused statutory requirements at the federal level

Electoral advertisements are subject to authorisation requirements, so that the persons or organisations responsible for them can be readily identified. The phenomenon of social media has given rise to a need for more complex legal provisions: where authorisation of printed material was at one time covered by a single section (328) of the *Electoral Act*, there is now an entire part (XXA) of the Act, comprising eight sections, addressing a range of different forms of advertising, as well as conferring various information-gathering powers on the Electoral Commissioner. Those provisions are supplemented by the nine-page instrument known as the Commonwealth Electoral (Authorisation of Voter Communication) Determination 2021, while the overall authorisation requirements are spelt out in a 32-page AEC better practice guide on authorisation placement, formatting and language (AEC 2025a). The *Broadcasting Services Act 1992* and the *Special Broadcasting Service Act 1991* also set out authorisation requirements for broadcast political advertisements. During the 2025 campaign, the AEC had to act in response to inadequately authorised corflutes and signs in the divisions of Bendigo, Bennelong, Blair, Boothby, Calare, Chisholm, Hawke and Menzies, and unauthorised leaflets in the division of Wentworth.

As noted above, Section 329 of the *Electoral Act* deals with misleading information in relation to the casting of a vote. However, as construed by the High Court in the leading case of *Evans v Crichton-Browne*, it does not apply to matter that could mislead a voter in his or her process of deciding for whom to vote, but only to the process by which that decision is given effect.

Section 330 of the Act also makes it an offence to make a knowingly false or materially misleading statement to an elector on polling day with respect to the elector's enrolment. That section is clearly in need of revision, given that it provides no protection to the many people who now vote before polling day.

A distinctive feature of Australian elections is the election blackout: a prohibition on the broadcast of political advertisements in the two days immediately preceding polling day. Its aim has been to prevent the last-minute dissemination of disinformation that in practice could not be answered, as well as to give voters an opportunity for quiet reflection before voting; when enacted in 1942, it applied not just to advertisements, but also to virtually any broadcast comment on the election, candidates or issues in the campaign. However, it is now generally seen as an anachronism— first, because the ready availability of pre-poll and postal voting means that many voters will have cast their ballots before the blackout even comes into effect and, second, because it does not apply to social or print media. In the light of those trends, the Federal Parliament's Joint Standing Committee on Electoral Matters (JSCEM 2023b: 124) recommended that 'contingent on the Australian Government introducing truth in political advertising laws … the media blackout, known as the relevant period in the Broadcasting Services Act 1992, be removed'.

Amendments to that effect were included in the government's Electoral Legislation Amendment (Electoral Communications) Bill 2024, which was introduced but not brought on for debate, and which lapsed with the dissolution of the parliament before the 2025 election.

Beneficial measures with a broader focus

Recent legislation to limit social media access for persons under the age of 16, though not enacted with the explicit aim of restricting the impact of electoral disinformation, could well assist in that, by limiting the opportunity to embed falsehoods in the minds of an upcoming cohort of voters whose understanding of politics and government, and ability to evaluate information critically, may not always be fully developed.

Tools for limiting the effect of foreign purveyors of disinformation include the Foreign Influence Transparency Scheme mentioned above and the power of governments to prohibit certain known purveyors of disinformation from entering Australia by application of the character test set out at Section 501 of the *Migration Act 1958*. The latter mechanism, for example, saw the notorious Holocaust denier David Irving refused entry on multiple occasions.

Electoral communications containing disinformation will also generally be subject to the law of defamation. Defamation, however, is, with very limited exceptions, a civil wrong, so while aggrieved persons may be able to sue for damages, there is no enforcement role played by a body such as the AEC. For almost 90 years, the *Electoral Act* contained a provision (Section 350) prohibiting the making of 'any false and defamatory statement in relation to the personal character or conduct of a candidate', but it was repealed in 2007 on the recommendation of the JSCEM. More generally, some electoral disinformation may fall foul of statute laws with a general application, such as the Commonwealth Criminal Code or the *Racial Discrimination Act 1975*.

One response to the problem of disinformation is the rise of nonpartisan fact-checking. In the United States, this has been required on an almost industrial scale: at the end of President Trump's first term of office, the Fact Checker webpage maintained by the *Washington Post* (Kessler et al. 2021) stated that Trump had 'made 30,573 false or misleading claims as president'. (This finding, of course, was not accepted by Trump and his supporters.) While a fact-checking operation run jointly by the ABC and the Royal Melbourne Institute of Technology (RMIT) closed in June 2024 after 11 years of operation (RMIT ABC Fact Check 2024), the Australian Associated Press (AAP) website still includes a 'FactCheck' page (AAP 2025), on which were published numerous entries addressing misleading and/or false claims that had been made about the 2025 election process.

There has, however, been a reversal of some high-level support for such operations. While Meta had in the past provided grants to partners AAP, RMIT and Agence France-Presse to support their fact-checking activities (Gauja et al. 2023), Meta's head, Mark Zuckerberg, has more recently expressed concerns about 'censorship' and is moving to defund fact-checking programs, starting with those in the United States (Rushton 2025).

For its part, the Digital Industry Group Inc. (DIGI 2022) has developed the Australian Code of Practice on Disinformation and Misinformation, which has been adopted by Adobe, Apple, Facebook, Google, Legitimate, Microsoft, Redbubble, TikTok and Twitch, and which commits the signatories 'to safeguards to protect Australians against harm from online disinformation and misinformation, and to adopting a range of scalable measures that reduce its spread and visibility'.

The role of the AEC

The AEC, as the body responsible for the conduct of federal elections in Australia, has been playing an increasingly prominent role in addressing the problem of disinformation. It was established on 21 February 1984 with bipartisan support on the unanimous recommendation of the Federal Parliament's Joint Select Committee on Electoral Reform (JSCER). Paragraph 2.30 of the committee's September 1983 *First Report* (JSCER 1983: 39) stated, among other things:

> The Committee sees great merit in the existence of an Australian Electoral Commission with a statutory basis and which is seen to operate independent of political influence. Accordingly, the Committee recommends the establishment of an Australian Electoral Commission as an independent statutory authority.

The AEC's regulatory powers in relation to electoral processes are primarily derived from the *Electoral Act*. Paragraph 7(1)(c) of the Act also makes it a function of the AEC 'to promote public awareness of election and ballot matters, and Parliamentary matters, by means of the conduct of education and information programs and by other means'. While this provision is sufficiently broad to enable the commission to play an active role in combating electoral disinformation, the extent to which it will in fact do so is in practice determined by its chief executive, the Electoral Commissioner. Over time, different holders of that office have brought varying perspectives to bear on what should be the organisation's priorities: some have been inclined to focus primarily on the mechanics of the electoral process, while others have taken a more expansive view. Under the leadership of Tom Rogers, who by the time of his retirement in late 2024 had served longer in the position than any of his predecessors, the commission played a more active role in seeking to address the problem of disinformation than at any time in its history, and that approach was continued by Jeff Pope, who acted in the position of Electoral Commissioner at the 2025 election.

At the strategic level, the AEC has given enhanced recognition to the importance of fostering electoral integrity as well as ensuring the conduct of mechanical election processes to a high standard; this joint emphasis is clearly stated in its 2024–25 *Corporate Plan* (AEC 2024), which now lists, as the first of the commission's 'key activities', maintaining 'the integrity of electoral and regulatory processes'. To that end, the AEC has undertaken several significant initiatives.

First, the Electoral Integrity Assurance Taskforce mentioned earlier, chaired at the operational level by the AEC, has been established as a whole-of-government body:

> [It is] responsible for ensuring that federal electoral events are unaffected by interference … [which] is achieved by:
>
> - Monitoring the information environment for potential interference including mis and disinformation on the electoral process
> - Sharing information on potential risks or threats with relevant agencies
> - Advising the Electoral Commissioner on how identified risks or threats can be mitigated. (AEC 2025b)

In January 2025, the taskforce published an 'Election Security Environment Overview' (EIAT 2025b), which noted that electoral disinformation and misinformation constituted a potential threat to the integrity of Australia's electoral system. On 1 July 2025, however, the taskforce board, in a document that put on the public record advice it had given to the acting Electoral Commissioner (EIAT 2025c), stated:

> Electoral Integrity Assurance Taskforce (EIAT) agencies did not identify any foreign interference, or any other interference, that compromised the delivery of the 2025 federal election and would undermine the confidence of the Australian people in the results of the election.

Organisationally, the AEC has established its Defending Democracy Unit, which constitutes the key repository within the organisation for corporate knowledge of issues of electoral integrity and disinformation, serves as a focal point for AEC liaison with other government bodies and with international counterparts focusing on similar problems and works with the AEC's Media and Digital Engagement Section to monitor disinformation and misinformation on a day-to-day basis, and responds as appropriate.

In recent years, and particularly in the runup to the 2025 election, the AEC pursued an active, multifaceted and at times 'edgy' social media strategy, much of which involved responding rapidly to items of misinformation and disinformation. An 'AEC TV' YouTube channel has been a significant initiative in this area. Up-to-date mechanisms are used to monitor key social media channels so that public posts relating to electoral issues can be rapidly identified.

The AEC's website now contains a Disinformation Register (AEC 2025c), on which specific items of disinformation relating to the administration and mechanics of the electoral process are debunked. The organisation follows a structured process for determining what items of disinformation are to be addressed and for ensuring that responses are clear and accurate and have been approved at a high level. For the 2025 election, the following specific pieces of disinformation were included and addressed:

> Six million ballot papers went missing and weren't counted in the 2025 federal election.

> There are substantial inconsistencies or errors in the electoral roll that make voter fraud and 'vote rigging' easier.

> There is a formula to casting a 'Vote of No Confidence' (VONC)—people leave the ballot paper blank and instead write 'no suitable candidate to meet my will'. This can cause an election to be re-run if enough people cast their vote that way.

A video circulated online shows an AEC polling official rubbing out votes marked with pencil.

Prior to February 2025, the AEC has never attended citizenship ceremonies to enrol new citizens.

The AEC can compel a group to become a registered political party.

The AEC should check, and are empowered to check, the constitutional eligibility of candidates during an election.

The AEC knows the date of the election before voters do.

Your preferences are controlled by political parties.

In each case, the AEC provided a succinct and clear response. For example, in relation to the claim that an AEC official had been filmed rubbing out votes marked with a pencil, the Disinformation Register entry read as follows:

Correct information

The video that was shared on social media is from the 2023 NSW state election—this is an election that is not run by the AEC. The NSW Electoral Commission explained at the time that their polling official featured in the video was completing the paperwork required to run the polling place.

AEC ballot paper handling processes include the use of uniquely coded security seals, weatherproof packaging and tamper proof tape. Multiple officers are involved in the sign off of the packaging and receipt of materials. AEC counting processes are also highly transparent and manual. Around 100,000 staff—members of the community—count the votes and candidate appointed scrutineers observe the process. Results data is then published to the tally room in real time so people at each count can verify that the information published is what they saw for themselves.

The AEC supplies pencils for voting because they don't smudge when ballot papers are folded, they are cheaper than pens and they don't run dry in tropical conditions. Voters are welcome to bring a pen to a polling place and use it to mark their ballot paper if they wish.

AEC action

The AEC responded to social media commentary on multiple channels. An AEC TV video about the issue was used in the communication. (AEC 2025b)

More generally, the AEC has been pursuing a range of information initiatives united by the slogan 'Stop and Consider', the fundamental aim of which is to encourage people to think critically about things they are told, rather than routinely accepting possibly dubious claims at face value. Advice on useful ways of reflecting on information was included in the AEC document entitled *Your Official Guide to the 2025 Federal Election* (AEC 2025d), which was distributed to households across the country.

The AEC also distributed messages through a range of social media channels, including AEC TV, emphasising (using the slogan 'Your vote, your choice') that a secret ballot is a guaranteed individual right and a key feature of the Australian electoral process.

Finally, the AEC in the late 1990s initiated, and continues to support in partnership with four international bodies, the BRIDGE electoral capacity-building project—a unique set of learning resources that now includes a module on cybersecurity and disinformation. BRIDGE courses have now been taught in more than 100 countries.

Taking stock of all the measures and initiatives outlined above, the problem of electoral disinformation has been addressed seriously in Australia and significant steps are being taken to try to deal with it. There are, however, some notable challenges and constraints that administrators and policymakers face.

First, enforcement of Australian laws against foreign entities such as X or Meta may in practice be difficult and may give rise to pushback at the political level (a notable theme from the Trump administration).

Second, the increasing dissemination of election-related material in languages other than English gives rise to the need for translation, which at the very least has the potential to slow the process for responding to disinformation, thereby giving greater opportunities for falsehoods to proliferate. Any such translation must also be sensitive to the complexity of metaphors and figurative usage in languages other than English.

Third, certain material may be of an official nature, which takes it outside the scope of potential official responses to disinformation. The Yes/No pamphlets published before a referendum are an example of such material, as are accurate reports of statements made in parliaments, which are covered by parliamentary privilege.

Finally, any legislative provisions aimed at curbing disinformation must be carefully crafted to ensure that they do not exceed a parliament's powers because of the constitutionally implied freedom of political communication.

Policy proposals not yet adopted

Among the smorgasbord of mechanisms for managing electoral disinformation connected with Australian federal elections, there is one conspicuous absence: a legal requirement for political advertising to be truthful. Legislative initiatives to that end have a history going back more than 100 years (Maley 2019) and were pursued during the previous parliament by several Independent MPs. Their efforts were buttressed by the work of various academics (Ng 2024; Hill et al. 2022) and advocacy bodies (Australia Institute 2025); and the JSCEM (2023a: 106–7), in its June 2023 interim report on the *Conduct of the 2022 Federal Election and Other Matters*, recommended:

> that the Australian Government develop legislation, or seek to amend the Commonwealth Electoral Act 1918, to provide for the introduction of measures to govern truth in political advertising, giving consideration to provisions in the Electoral Act 1985 (SA) … and that the Australian Government consider the establishment of a division within the Australian Electoral Commission, based on the principles currently in place in South Australia, to administer truth in political advertising legislation, with regard to ensuring proper resourcing and the need to preserve the Commission's independence as the electoral administrator.

The government, while nominally accepting those recommendations, thereafter gave no particular priority to their implementation. Legislation to give effect to them, the Electoral Legislation Amendment (Electoral Communications) Bill 2024, was introduced only on 18 November 2024 and, as noted above, was never brought on for debate and lapsed with the dissolution of the Forty-Seventh Parliament. That was probably no bad thing, as the bill was problematical in several respects, including the following:

- It would have established a system of civil penalties for false and misleading advertising, rather than specifying an offence. One consequence of that would have been that a transgressor would not face the risk of being disqualified from membership of parliament by Section 44(ii) of the Constitution, which comes into play only when a person has been 'convicted' of an 'offence'.

- Communications from parliamentarians that were funded via their parliamentary allowances would have been exempted from the 'truth' requirements set out in the bill.

- It would have been explicitly stated that a contravention of the civil penalty provisions could not be a ground for the Court of Disputed Returns to overturn a candidate's election.

- A regulatory role would have been played by an Electoral Communications Panel, a majority of the members of which would be appointed on the recommendation of the incumbent minister. There would have been no prohibition of the appointment of persons with known partisan political backgrounds.

- From the membership of the Electoral Communications Panel, smaller 'Decision Panels' would have been constituted to deal with specific issues and complaints. A Decision Panel would have been required to decide within two days of having a complaint referred to it, except in the case of complaints made on the Thursday or Friday before polling day or on polling day itself, when a decision would have been required within 24 hours. Such deadlines would have been manifestly absurd, given the steps that would typically be needed to investigate even simple complaints properly (Maley 2024), let alone those involving complex issues.

Overall, the bill appeared to have been crafted to give the impression of putting in place an effective scheme for guaranteeing truth in political advertising without cramping the style of current political campaigners to any great extent. In that respect, it had overtones of the approach taken to the creation of the National Anti-Corruption Commission—now seen in some quarters as having failed to live up to expectations.

Final reflections

The experience of the 2025 election suggests that the problem of electoral disinformation is yet to become critical in Australia, in contrast to the situation prevailing in some other democracies—most notably, the United States. Local protective factors include the existing legal framework, the AEC's proactive approach to warning of disinformation's potential dangers and a relatively widespread community scepticism regarding statements made by politicians and political parties.

Looking forward, legislating for truth in political advertising is likely to remain a matter for debate in the next parliament. In late July 2025, Independent MP Zali Steggall and Independent Senator David Pocock introduced in their respective houses bills essentially identical to the government's lapsed bill, with the explicitly stated aim of putting the issue back on the public agenda. They reintroduced them in the first sitting weeks of the Forty-Eighth Parliament. Whether those bills will proceed, either as introduced or in an amended form, remains to be seen.

References

Arendt, Hannah. 1951. *The Origins of Totalitarianism*. New York: Harcourt Brace Jovanovich.

Australia Institute. 2025. 'Truth in Political Advertising.' [Project]. Canberra: The Australia Institute. australiainstitute.org.au/initiative/truth-in-political-advertising/.

Australian Associated Press (AAP). 2025. *AAP FactCheck*. [Online]. aap.com.au/factcheck/.

Australian Electoral Commission (AEC). 2024. *Corporate Plan 2024–25*. Canberra: Australian Electoral Commission. www.aec.gov.au/About_AEC/Publications/corporate-plan/files/2024/2024-corporate-plan.pdf.

Australian Electoral Commission (AEC). 2025a. *Authorisation Placement, Formatting, and Language: Better Practice Guide*. Canberra: Australian Electoral Commission. www.aec.gov.au/About_AEC/files/better-practice-guide.pdf.

Australian Electoral Commission (AEC). 2025b. *Electoral Integrity Assurance Taskforce*. Canberra: Australian Electoral Commission. www.aec.gov.au/about_aec/electoral-integrity.htm.

Australian Electoral Commission (AEC). 2025c. *Electoral Process Disinformation Register: 2025 Federal Election*. Canberra: Australian Electoral Commission. www.aec.gov.au/media/disinformation-register-2025.htm.

Australian Electoral Commission (AEC). 2025d. *Your Official Guide to the 2025 Federal Election: Saturday 3 May 2025*. Canberra: Australian Electoral Commission. www.aec.gov.au/election/fe25/files/official-guide/fe25-official-guide.pdf.

Carson, Andrea, and Max Grömping. 2025. 'Fake news and the election campaign—how worried should voters be?' *The Conversation*, 2 May. theconversation.com/fake-news-and-the-election-campaign-how-worried-should-voters-be-255514. doi.org/10.64628/AA.wr44u3gj6.

Carson, Andrea, Max Grömping, Timothy B. Gravelle, Simon Jackman, and Justin B. Phillips. 2025. 'Alert, but not alarmed: Electoral disinformation and trust during the 2023 Australian Voice to Parliament referendum.' *Policy & Internet* 17, no. 2: e429. doi.org/10.1002/poi3.429.

Digital Industry Group Inc. (DIGI). 2022. *Australian Code of Practice on Disinformation and Misinformation*. Sydney: DIGI.

Electoral Integrity Assurance Taskforce (EIAT). 2025a. 'Disinformation and misinformation.' Media release. Canberra: Australian Electoral Commission. www.aec.gov.au/About_AEC/files/eiat/eiat-disinformation-factsheet.pdf.

Electoral Integrity Assurance Taskforce (EIAT). 2025b. 'Election security environment overview.' Media release, January. Canberra: Australian Electoral Commission. www.aec.gov.au/About_AEC/files/eiat/election-security-environment-overview.pdf.

Electoral Integrity Assurance Taskforce (EIAT). 2025c. 'EIAT Board advice to the acting Electoral Commissioner on the 2025 federal election.' Media release, 1 July. Canberra: Australian Electoral Commission. www.aec.gov.au/About_AEC/files/eiat/Endorsed%201%20July%202025%20-%20EIAT%20Board%202025%20federal%20election%20post-event%20advice.pdf.

Evans v. Crichton-Browne [1981] HCA 14.

Garbett v Liu [2019] FCAFC 241.

Gauja, Anika, Marian Sawer, and Jill Sheppard. 2023. 'Watershed: The 2022 Australian federal election.' In *Watershed: The 2022 Australian Federal Election*, edited by Anika Gauja, Marian Sawer, and Jill Sheppard, 1–19. Canberra: ANU Press. doi.org/10.22459/W.2023.01.

Hill, Lisa, Max Douglass, and Ravi Baltutis. 2022. *How and Why to Regulate False Political Advertising in Australia*. London: Palgrave Macmillan. doi.org/10.1007/978-981-19-2123-0.

Joint Select Committee on Electoral Reform (JSCER). 1983. *First Report, September 1983*. Parliamentary Paper no. 227. Canberra: Government Printer.

Joint Standing Committee on Electoral Matters (JSCEM). 2023a. *Conduct of the 2022 Federal Election and Other Matters: Interim Report.* June. Canberra: Commonwealth of Australia. parlinfo.aph.gov.au/parlInfo/download/committees/reportjnt/RB000012/toc_pdf/Conductofthe2022federalelectionandothermatters.pdf.

JSCEM. 2023b. *Conduct of the 2022 Federal Election and Other Matters: Final Report.* November. Canberra: Commonwealth of Australia. parlinfo.aph.gov.au/parlInfo/download/committees/reportjnt/RB000172/toc_pdf/Conductofthe2022federalelectionandothermatters.pdf.

JSCEM. 2025. *From Classroom to Community: Civics Education and Political Participation in Australia.* January. Canberra: Commonwealth of Australia. parlinfo.aph.gov.au/parlInfo/download/committees/reportjnt/RB000363/toc_pdf/FromClassroomtoCommunity.pdf.

Kapterian, Gisele. 2025. 'Every vote counts.' Instagram post, 14 July. www.instagram.com/p/DMFZGI-pUMV/?hl=en.

Kessler, Glenn, Salvador Rizzo, and Meg Kelly. 2021. 'Trump's false or misleading claims total 30,573 over 4 years.' *The Washington Post*, 24 January. www.washingtonpost.com/politics/2021/01/24/trumps-false-or-misleading-claims-total-30573-over-four-years.

Maley, Michael. 2019. 'Home truths about political advertising.' *Inside Story*, 30 July. insidestory.org.au/home-truths-about-political-advertising/.

Maley, Michael. 2024. 'Truth rears its ugly head.' *Inside Story*, 21 May. insidestory.org.au/truth-rears-its-ugly-head/.

Ng, Yee-Fui. 2024. *Truth in Political Advertising Laws: Design, Operation, Effectiveness and Recommendations for Reform. Final Report.* 17 December. Melbourne: Monash University. apo.org.au/sites/default/files/resource-files/2024-12/apo-nid329295.pdf.

RMIT ABC Fact Check. 2024. 'Fact Check signs off today after 11 years at the ABC. Here's our guide to being your own fact checker.' *ABC News*, 28 June. www.abc.net.au/news/2024-06-28/fact-check-final-wrap-11-years/104033004.

Rushton, Gina. 2025. 'How checking facts got political.' *ABC News*, 16 March. www.abc.net.au/news/2025-03-16/fact-checking-partisan-media-meta-trump-politics/105046680.

Part 2.
Actors

10

The Australian Labor Party

Rob Manwaring and Emily Foley

Abstract

The Australian Labor Party's landslide victory in the 2025 federal election marks a historic moment. Anthony Albanese joins Gough Whitlam and Bob Hawke as one of only three Labor leaders to secure consecutive terms. This chapter analyses the drivers behind Labor's significant win, in the wider context of electoral volatility and long-term party adjustments. While exogenous factors such as the collapse of the Coalition and the Trump presidency played a role, we focus our analysis on three interconnected elements of Labor's performance: the repercussions from its 2019 defeat, its record in office from 2022 to 2025 and its disciplined campaign in 2025. Drawing on other recent centre-left governments, we also make some observations about the future of the Albanese government. While Labor's strategy was electorally effective, its ability to maintain a transformative policy agenda in the long term remains uncertain.

Keywords: Australian Labor Party; labourism; centre-left; policy; elections

An ALP win for the ages

On 3 May 2025, the ALP resoundingly won the federal election by a significant landslide. The party won an extraordinary 94 seats, reducing the Coalition to 43 seats in the 150-seat parliament. It was a Labor win for the ages. The last time a Labor leader won a second term in office was Bob

Hawke in 1984. The Albanese win dwarfs Labor's much more marginal win in 2010, when Julia Gillard secured a second term in office, albeit in minority government.

The scale of Albanese's win is starkly impressive, with 94 seats comfortably the highest number the ALP has *ever* won, easily surpassing the 86 seats that Hawke won in 1987. If we account for the growing size of the House of Representatives, the only Labor leader to win a higher proportion of available seats was John Curtin in his extraordinary performance during World War II at the 1943 election. Curtin won 49 of 74 seats (66.2 per cent of seats available), while Albanese secured 62.6 per cent of the available 150 seats. Labor's win was dominant, emphatic and, as Treasurer Jim Chalmers noted, it exceeded even the ALP's 'most optimistic expectations' (Mealey 2025).

The legacy and impact of the Labor win are significant—notably, the impact on their political rivals. On the left side of politics, Labor won three of the four seats held by the Greens, including leader Adam Bandt's seat of Melbourne. Prime Minister Albanese would also be pleased by the loss of Greens MP Max Chandler-Mather—a consistent thorn in the government's side during the 2022–25 term. On the right side of politics, the ALP saw the collapse of the Liberals, the defeat of the Opposition leader Peter Dutton and the temporary dissolution of the Coalition. That said, the full extent of Labor's win over the Liberals remains open to question. Famously, British Conservative Party leader Margaret Thatcher reflected that her greatest achievement was 'Tony Blair and New Labour. We forced our opponents to change their minds' (Burns 2008). While the Liberals face a long road back to power, the extent to which Labor has forced them to change their minds is less clear. The collapse in Liberal support owed more to the broader fragmentation of the centre-right (Bale and Kaltwasser 2021) than to the way a governing party had redefined the ideological and policy agenda.

The scale of Labor's win occurs against the trend of the declining vote share of the major parties. Labor's primary vote of 34.6 per cent was the first election in nearly 20 years in which Labor secured an increase on this metric. During the peak of the Hawke era, the party was comfortably assured of 40–45 per cent of the vote (Figure 10.1). The tectonic plates of Australian politics are shifting and the scale of the seat count risks masking these changes (Megalogenis 2024).

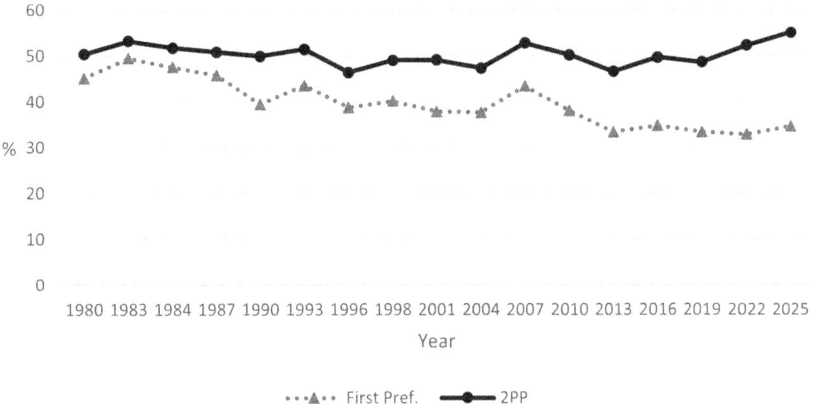

Figure 10.1 ALP vote share, 1980–2025
Source: Compiled by authors using AEC data.

An additional contextual factor was the timing of the election. As indicated by polling data (see Chapter 20, this volume), at the start of January 2025, the Coalition had a strong advantage over the ALP in both primary and secondary votes. Indeed, from the loss of the Voice referendum in October 2023 until the final few weeks of the short campaign in 2025, the Coalition led the ALP on both first preferences and two-party-preferred (2PP). With hindsight, the Queensland cyclone and floods and the 2025 (additional) Labor budget seemed to amplify the collapse in the Liberal vote. This timing reflects the broader fluidity in voting behaviour in Australia and situates the ALP's win within a more volatile political environment (Cameron and McAllister 2022: 18–24). Labor's win comes off a shrinking base, as only 12 per cent of all voters consider themselves 'stable' Labor voters (Cameron and McAllister 2022).

The focus of this chapter is on understanding the critical factors in Labor's performance, both during the campaign and more broadly. Clearly, external factors help explain the overall result (see Chapter 1, this volume). We highlight one external factor, or 'silence', which shaped the 2025 result and merits proper acknowledgement: the negligible influence of the Trumpet of Patriots' campaign. In 2019, the $60-million campaign by billionaire Clive Palmer's previous campaign party vehicle, the United Australia Party (UAP), was critical to Labor's disastrous election result (Orr 2020). The UAP scare campaign against Labor's supposed 'death tax' was a mobilising force against the ALP (but not *for* the UAP in terms of seats). In effect, the right and centre-right mobilised in tandem (not in coordination) against Labor and this played into longstanding voter perceptions of Labor as a party of 'tax and spend'. In 2025, Labor faced a wholly disorganised and incoherent electoral threat from the right.

In our analysis of Labor's performance, we attribute three critical elements to understanding Labor's extraordinary electoral win:

1. institutional learning—notably, the enduring influence of the 2019 election defeat
2. the ALP's record in office (2022–25)
3. the strategic focus and impact of the 'long' and 'short' electoral campaigns.

The impact of the 2019 election defeat remains a strong influence on Labor's campaigning and governing strategy (Emerson and Weatherill 2019; Wallace 2020). Albanese's policy reset, especially in terms of tax policy, was critical to Labor's victory. While not acknowledged in national secretary and campaign director Paul Erickson's (2025) address to the National Press Club on Labor's election performance, it shaped many of the key factors that he did raise. The strategic caution and incrementalism that marked Labor's time in office were contrasted with the party's framing of Peter Dutton as a 'risk' (Erickson 2025). Ultimately, the 2025 result reflects a two-term strategy by Labor, which, aside from the Voice referendum, had modest ambitions for its first term (Combet and Oshalem 2022). The ALP was 'building on the foundations', as Erickson (2025) described it, which enabled them to consolidate for a potential second term.

Labor's first term in government (2022–25)

Labor's first term in office since the troubled Rudd–Gillard era was challenging, and there was a strong risk that it would face an anti-incumbent backlash amid high inflation. The overall verdict on its first term chimes with a general perception that Labor was 'small target', incremental and lacking strong reformist ambition. That led respected economist John Quiggin (2024) to argue that Labor 'doesn't look like Labor anymore'. While we do not disagree with the 'small target' analysis, it fails to capture aspects of what the government aimed to achieve and indeed did achieve. Three core themes best capture Labor's agenda and first term:

- a central 'labourist' focus on improving wages and conditions and protecting key categories of workers
- a cautious, protective strategy, especially in areas of fiscal, tax and welfare policy, often with the intent to neutralise politically problematic issues
- competence and policy fixes, but often without a clear narrative or political success.

After some initial policy wins, Labor's agenda was dominated by the Voice referendum and the subsequent loss of political momentum. In the second half of 2024, the government ramped up its policy agenda (for example, the social media ban for minors) to reclaim the political initiative. We draw on Marsh and McConnell's (2010) 'policy success' framework to capture the key dynamics and themes of Labor's policy record. Simply put, this framework disaggregates 'success' and 'failure' across three main criteria: 1) process success—how well the policy was developed; 2) programmatic success—a focus on goal attainment; and 3) political success—partisan or other political achievements. To give an overview of Labor's first term, we condense the first two policy categories (process, programmatic) to make a proximate judgement about the overall policy coherence and impact of key signature policies.

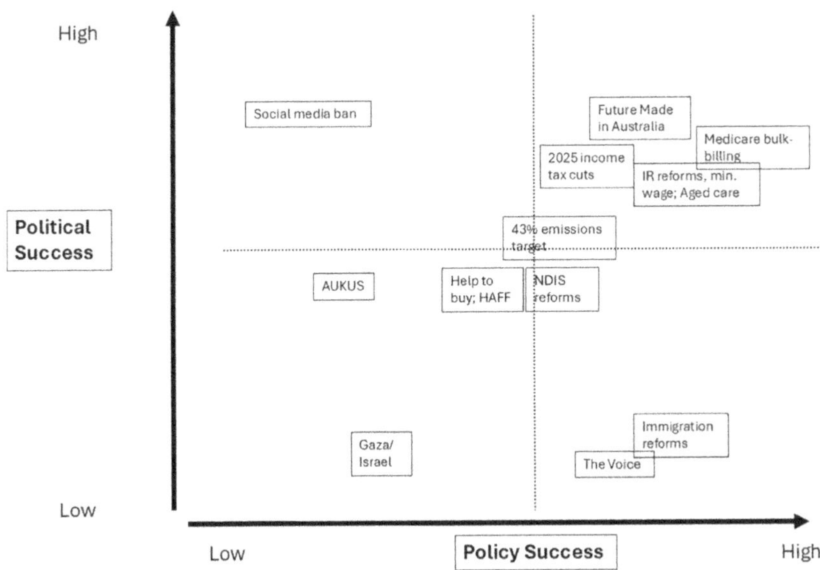

Figure 10.2 Political and policy success: ALP in office, 2022–2025

Notes: HAFF = Housing Australia Future Fund.

Source: Compiled by authors.

In Figure 10.2, we provide a proximate representation of these policies to capture the dynamics of Labor's agenda. We highlight a specific case to underscore why we have adopted the framework. In November 2024, the Labor government passed legislation banning those under 16 years of age from accessing various social media platforms. We judge this to have achieved a high level of political success and support, but with a relatively low level of policy success. While it was politically 'popular', particularly among parents, in terms of policy, it was far from an 'evidence-informed' approach. Experts and stakeholders, including the Australian Human Rights Commission (AHRC 2024), have expressed a range of concerns, including implementation shortcomings.

By and large, Labor delivered a set of policies that were reasonably successful, robust and coherent. One of the most high-profile was its 'Future made in Australia' policy framework, which set out priorities for specific industries and public infrastructure investment (Bathgate 2024). It was interventionist, seeking to meet the interests of both capital and labour, but also had a latent nationalism. We can broadly categorise many of these key initiatives as 'labourist'—seeking to give material uplift and protection to specific categories of workers and low-income-earners. Labor passed a suite of industrial relations reforms relatively uncontroversially (Hegarty 2025) and, for a brief period, seemed to have built momentum after its Hawke-inspired Jobs and Skills Summit.

An emblematic example of this more successful agenda was Labor's elevation of Medicare bulk-billing to the centrepiece of its 2025 campaign. This was both smart politics and smart policy. It is worth also contrasting this with Labor's extensive health spending plans in 2019, which included a $1.7-billion package to subsidise cancer treatments. In 2025, there was evidence of policy learning: recalibrating health spending to target obvious and tangible benefits for many voters.

A second cluster falls within the broader category of cautious, 'protective' policies, some of which also sought to neutralise political problems. Here, there is a group of policies with moderate levels of political and policy 'success'. The most positive of these might be the end to the 'climate wars' (or at least some reprieve), with Labor legislating its emissions reduction targets (Albanese 2022). This is a classic centre-left response; it identifies a significant policy problem and devises a policy to straddle 'pragmatism' with modest reforms. Labor's key housing policies (the 'right to buy' changes and the Housing Australia Future Fund) might also fall into this category. They reflect a defensive posture by Labor, especially after the electoral damage of its proposed reforms to negative gearing in 2019. The ongoing sparring with the Greens over this issue reflected the delicate balance the Albanese government was striving to achieve between reform and 'pragmatism'.

Within this subset of policies, it is critical to highlight Labor's reform of the Coalition's flagship 'stage 3' tax cuts. In opposition, Labor strategically supported the highly regressive tax changes, which removed a whole income tax bracket for middle-to-high income-earners. In January 2024, Labor legislated a suite of reforms, reversing the Coalition's policy, while also delivering further tax relief for low-income and middle-income-earners (Bennett 2024). Labor expended a good deal of political capital and cycled through two budgets before announcing the change. Ultimately, the change neutralised the issue for Labor, although it had to defend breaking an election promise. While Erickson and Labor strategists might see this as 'laying the ground' for future reforms, Labor only sought to neutralise the issue. It strongly resisted calls to consider making much deeper structural reforms. A range of voices, including the *Australian Financial Review* (*AFR*), a 'community' tax conference organised by think tank Per Capita and a Green Paper by Teal Independent Allegra Spender (2024) were all seeking to push the Albanese government to countenance a follow-up to Ken Henry's 2010 tax review under Kevin Rudd's leadership. The *AFR* (2024) argued that the ALP's changes had only served to 'highlight the unprincipled mess of Australia's tax system'. Politically, Labor will feel vindicated, as it enabled them to use this as a springboard for further pre-election income tax cuts, which wrong-footed the Opposition.

A third set of policies are those with merit but that have achieved little or no political success. A good example here are the issues and policy changes around immigration. In *Inside Story*, Peter Mares (2024) reviewed Labor's immigration reforms under minister Andrew Giles, noting Labor had 'significantly improved how the migration system works'. This chimes with other areas of policy, which, in Carol Johnson's (2024) view, reflects the ALP's 'narrative failure'. Labor often failed to provide a clear set of stories, visions or political messages to articulate what they were seeking to achieve.

In short, Labor's first term in office was generally a period of cautious, incremental government, largely overshadowed by the Voice referendum result. What this broad narrative misses, however, are the ways in which the ALP, especially through many of the measures from Jim Chalmers' budgets, implemented a range of targeted labourist strategies. Yet, in many policy areas, Labor either lacked a clear narrative or its efforts seemed unfocused. At the start of 2025, despite some achievements, their electoral prospects were not looking strong.

Labor's campaign strategy

Long campaign: November 2024 to March 2025

The Albanese government's re-election in 2025 marks a significant moment in Australia's political landscape, not so much for its drama or transformative promises, but rather for its disciplined execution of a centre-left campaign. Considering the troubling polls from January 2025, which hinted at the possibility of a minority government, the ALP had already begun to roll out its 'long' campaign. Albanese himself began flagging key campaign initiatives and policies by the second half of 2024 and, by November, had already started selecting Labor's campaign team. While Chapter 3 of this volume offers a more detailed examination of Labor's electoral strategy, broadly speaking, the ALP concentrated its campaign efforts on four key battleground States: Queensland, New South Wales, Victoria and Western Australia.

Labor entered the election campaign defending 14 seats with margins of less than 4 per cent (Tillett 2025). With just 79 seats at the end of its first term, the ALP's slim majority meant that losing as few as two seats could result in a hung parliament unless offset by gains elsewhere. Retaining marginal seats won in 2022 was a priority, particularly in Western Australia, where Labor had secured gains in Tangney, Hasluck and Pearce. Labor's campaign also focused on retaining mostly outer suburban electorates in Sydney and Melbourne, such as McEwen, Bruce and Hawke.

Queensland was critical for Labor, which aimed to regain ground in seats lost to the Greens in 2022, such as Brisbane and Griffith. For the first time, Labor established a dedicated team and worked with advertising agency The Shannon Group to target these electorates and counter the growing Greens vote. Electoral redistributions further complicated the landscape, making some seats more marginal. Bennelong in New South Wales and Wills in Melbourne were seen as increasingly favourable to the Liberals and Greens, respectively.

Despite concentrating its efforts on marginal electorates that Labor deemed vulnerable, the party managed to secure some unexpected wins, such as Petrie, in Brisbane's north, and Moore, in Western Australia (Truu 2025; Armstrong 2025). These victories helped reinforce Labor's position beyond the expected battlegrounds in what shaped up to be a successful campaign.

In one of Albanese's first pre-election 'vision' speeches, in November 2024, he highlighted Labor's first-term accomplishments, underscoring what would become central pillars of Labor's campaign agenda: health and education. This also signalled the beginning of Labor's substantive policy announcements with a commitment to legislate 100,000 annual fee-free TAFE places as well as wiping 20 per cent off student university HECS debts (Albanese 2024a). The following month, Albanese announced a second significant election commitment, this time within early childhood education, where Labor would establish a \$1-billion fund to build and expand childcare centres in outer suburbs and regional Australia (Albanese 2024b).

Anthony Albanese had begun travelling around Australia in campaign mode almost immediately after the summer break ended. By the second week of January, Albanese had already visited Queensland, the Northern Territory and Western Australia. This attempt to get moving early in the year can partly be attributed to Labor's weak position in public polling. However, by engaging early with voters across Australia, Labor's proactiveness could also be seen as a way to ensure that Albanese himself was well-practised and organised in the leadup to the official campaign, considering his track record in the previous election, which was marked by a number of gaffes and slip-ups.

By 12 March, Labor was poised to launch its formal campaign; however, the timing was complicated by Cyclone Alfred in Queensland. This was significant, given that a delay in calling the election date meant the ALP would be tasked with delivering one last Federal Budget before entering a caretaker period. In line with its broader first-term agenda, Labor utilised the Budget as an opportunity to position cost-of-living relief and reforms in health care, housing and education as central to a second-term ALP government. Importantly, Labor's emphasis that the Budget contained 'the single largest commitment to Medicare since its creation' (Chalmers 2025) positioned health care as central to Labor's election campaign and policy agenda.

Furthermore, the Budget included a commitment to introduce additional 'modest' tax cuts (Chalmers 2025) for taxable incomes between $18,201 and $45,000, entailing a 1 per cent cut in 2026, followed by a further 1 per cent cut in 2027. Labor's tax cuts were opposed by Opposition leader Peter Dutton, who called them a 'cruel hoax' (Lane 2025) and pledged to repeal the measures if elected. As both major parties began announcing their respective economic campaign agendas, it appeared odd that Labor would be campaigning on lowering taxes—an economic position historically held by the centre-right, economically conservative Liberals.

Short campaign: March to May 2025

Cyclone Alfred, while harrowing for Queenslanders, proved serendipitous for the ALP, enabling Albanese to display bipartisan crisis leadership alongside Queensland Premier David Crisafulli, while Coalition leader Dutton drew criticism for attending a fundraiser in Sydney as the cyclone approached. The delay also gave Labor time to refine its messaging and organise a streamlined, disciplined campaign in contrast to the Coalition's blunder-prone, incoherent effort. By the time Albanese called the election, the vision and strategy of the ALP's campaign for its second term were already abundantly clear. Albanese's press conference on 28 March announcing the election presented voters with a choice of visions for the nation. Albanese clearly articulated Labor's strategy as a choice to continue 'building Australia's future' in contrast with a Dutton-led Coalition government, which would take Australia 'back to the failures of the past' (Albanese 2025a). The rhetorical use of the slogan began to take more of a literal effect at Labor's campaign launch in Perth on 13 April, with the centrepiece of Albanese's speech a pledge to establish a $10-billion fund to build 100,000 new homes for first homebuyers across the nation (Albanese 2025b).

In Albanese's final speech in the last week of the election campaign, the overarching emphasis on health care was driven home. At a Labor rally in Sydney, Albanese continued to emphasise that Medicare and health were not only central to the Labor tradition, but also 'part of the Australian story and one of the most meaningful expressions of the fair go that we have' (Albanese 2025c). In announcing Labor's commitment to rebrand an existing healthcare telephone hotline into 1800 MEDICARE and substantially invest in its expansion, Albanese presenting his own Medicare card, as he had done throughout the campaign, reinforcing Australia's egalitarian history of universal health care and that Labor would protect it.

Labor's campaign narratives

To understand Labor's campaign strategy in 2025, we draw on Bartlett and Rayner's (2014) analysis of campaign narratives. Taking inspiration from Somers and Gibson's (1994) framework for understanding public narratives, Bartlett and Rayner identify four questions that are important for understanding the types of narratives employed by major parties in election campaigns. These questions are: 1) what are the main objectives and concerns of the parties (plot); 2) what is at stake (drama); 3) what is the arrangement of events and what causes are attributed to them (explanation); and 4) what are the types of framing or symbols that are employed (selective appropriation)?

In the 2025 campaign, the ALP utilised a combination of three separate but overlapping campaign narratives, contributing to their electoral success in forming a majority government. First, Labor drew heavily on what Bartlett and Rayner call the 'job isn't done' narrative throughout both its long and its short campaigns. This narrative is unique to incumbent governments in their bid to return to office. It is a largely optimistic vision that seeks to build on the party's track record from its first term, while juxtaposing the Opposition as committed to unravelling the hard-won gains and achievements made. Throughout the campaign, Labor consistently sought to position itself as a hardworking, high-achieving first-term government with a strong record of economic productivity and cost-of-living relief and a strong emphasis on social reforms. Labor's main slogan of 'Building Australia's future' drew on the party's record and achievements in its first term, while acknowledging the work still ahead.

The second narrative employed by the ALP during its campaign was that of 'experience versus inexperience', which again is commonly used by incumbent governments in presenting themselves as stable and capable. In contrast, leaders present the opposition party as a risk that would jeopardise progress. Following Labor's election victory, Erickson highlighted this narrative in his Press Club speech, reflecting that Labor sought to increase its electoral support by emphasising its track record as a 'responsible' government with an economic strategy that helped to bring down inflation without increasing unemployment or triggering a recession (Erickson 2025). In highlighting their responsible economic measures, Jim Chalmers and Minister for Finance Katy Gallagher would frequently emphasise that during a continued period of 'extreme global economic volatility … now is the worst time to risk a Dutton-led Coalition Government that would make Australians worse off' (Chalmers and Gallagher 2025). In campaign speeches, Albanese would highlight the Opposition's incompetence, stating that they would take the nation 'back to chaos and confusion, when this moment demands measured leadership and safe hands' (Albanese 2025b).

Finally, the 'fear' narrative functions to provoke strong negative emotions by warning voters that electing the Opposition would bring harm to them and their way of life. Within Labor's utilisation of the frame narrative, the threat posed by Peter Dutton was the centrepiece and focal point. Campaign slogans such as 'Don't risk Dutton' and 'Dutton cuts, you pay' successfully prosecuted the argument that Dutton as prime minister would involve 'cutting and wrecking' (Albanese 2025b) in areas such as health and education. Undoubtedly, the Trump presidency also played a part in stoking voters' fears of economic and political uncertainty.

Broadly, Labor's re-election strategy can be categorised as leaning into its incumbency, emphasising competence and stability during a period of ongoing domestic and global economic uncertainty, coinciding with slight national economic improvement. The party largely avoided contentious topics such as climate change, the war in Gaza, relations with China and Trump, instead foregrounding cost-of-living pressures and public services, projecting itself as a party of competent economic stewards. Integral to Labor's pitch was its clear ownership of health and education policies with values of egalitarianism and fairness that only a Labor government could protect and advance. Drawing on valence politics and issue ownership theory, Labor capitalised on its perceived strength in public health, successfully tying its campaign to the everyday concerns of voters. Perhaps most notable is Labor's growing emphasis on traditionally progressive areas, such as education and gender equity, while championing fiscal restraint. From fee-free TAFE to early childhood education subsidies aimed at increasing women's workforce participation, the ALP was attempting to reassert social policy leadership without alienating centrist voters.

The politics of stability: 'Thin' Labourism revisited

In our analysis of the 2022 federal election, we argued that the current Labor Party could best be understood through the prism of 'thin' labourism (Manwaring and Foley 2023), on which we have since elaborated. Our central argument was that while Albanese Labor is often described as 'small target', incremental and cautious, these descriptors fail to sufficiently capture the ideological aims and contours that shape a critical part of its agenda. Drawing on Michael Freeden's distinction between thick and thin ideologies, we identify a distinctive strand, 'labourism', which informs what the ALP seeks to achieve (Manwaring and Foley 2023: 190–91). Indeed, it has stronger descriptive qualities than Jim Chalmers' efforts to build a 'values-based capitalism'. Thin, or 'new', labourism also has a much stronger focus on securing gender policy gains, notably through Labor's focus on childcare reforms and targeting support for pay awards in key female-dominated parts of the care economy.

We make a few additional observations about the project of thin labourism. First, it reflects a general reticence by Labor to shift towards supporting broader social-democratic conceptions of equality (such as on grounds of race or sexuality) and it is generally defensive on cultural (rather than economic) policies (Karp 2023). Labor's post-Voice positioning on First Nations politics is emblematic here. This reticence to promote wider forms of social (and cultural) equality also dovetails with forms of conservative politics within the broader electorate (and the party's right faction). Third, the political economy of thin labourism is less ambitious in efforts to reform capitalist economic structures than thicker, older versions of social democracy (Bailey 2009), and less willing to tackle some forms of entrenched inequalities. Centre-left politics entails a compromise working with the market economy and labourism prioritises material gains over structural reform. The ALP's new version of labourism is a political project of systemic stability.

We can see further evidence of thin labourism with the emerging paradigm of what we term 'strategic unionism'.[1] Would the average Australian voter have noticed during the 2025 campaign that the Labor Party has a formal relationship with various trade unions? The short answer is: unlikely. Unions remain a critical source of revenue for the ALP and make up 50 per cent of delegates at its national conference. Yet, the trade unions and their peak body, the Australian Council of Trade Unions (ACTU), were largely absent from the public and media discourse during the election (for a complementary perspective, see Chapter 16, this volume). The trade unions' mostly low-profile influence can be seen through the lens of 'strategic unionism'—a political strategy whereby trade unions aim to secure crucial

---

1   We use the term 'strategic unionism' in a specific way in our analysis of the ALP's campaign, but it is useful to note that the term has been deployed in a different way in earlier works (see Irving 1994: 7).

gains for their members and certain categories of workers in a low-profile, anti-confrontational manner, most often through state institutions, to influence legislation with the ALP in office. The low-profile, yet important role of the unions can be attributed to several factors.

Most prominently, the scandal that engulfed the construction branch of the Construction, Forestry and Maritime Employees Union (CFMEU) cast a pall over labour politics and trade unions (Dunckley and Bachelard 2024). The allegations of criminal activity and links with organised crime led to the ALP suspending its affiliation with the CFMEU's construction wing (Remeikis 2024; Sakkal and Rooney 2024). This scandal, along with wider structural issues—notably, declining union density—poses legitimacy risks for both unions and the ALP.

In addition, many unions support Labor, but ideologically this is mostly through their opposition to the Coalition. As the ACTU (2025) noted after the election, 'Australians couldn't risk Dutton'. Unlike the WorkChoices campaign in 2007, the unions have since been mostly galvanised by opposing the return of the centre-right. Crucially, with the advent of a potentially long-running Labor government, unions see an opportunity to increase their representation in key economic institutions, including the Reserve Bank (Sakkal and Massola 2023). These gains mean that, aside from strategically cultivated dissent (mostly from the left-leaning unions and their concerns about AUKUS at the ALP National Conference in 2023), the unions remain quiet but important supporters of the Albanese government. Strategic unionism is, then, a component of the overall variant of labourism pursued by the Albanese government.

Conclusion: Future dilemmas for the Albanese government

As the Albanese government heads into a second, and potentially third, term of office, it would do well to reflect on the fortunes of other recent centre-left governments—notably, those in the United Kingdom, Germany and New Zealand. The demise of German chancellor Olaf Scholz's SPD 'traffic-light' coalition government (2021–24) is instructive (Münchau 2024). Ultimately, the failure at the heart of the Scholz government was the inability to oversee and build support for economic transition, especially in the era of deindustrialisation (Reuters 2024; Kampfner 2024).

A key tension for the centre-left is the difficulty in balancing calls for reform with the pursuit of a pragmatic labourist politics. In the United Kingdom, Sir Keir Starmer's Labour government attempted a series of deeply unpopular welfare reforms and caused itself much political damage with a series of policy U-turns (Smout and Ravikumar 2025). Albanese's Labor has also attempted welfare reform (for example, with the National Disability Insurance Scheme), yet reform measures fail when they are poorly explained or lack a clear rationale. Both governments have been criticised for not having a compelling governing narrative.

The fate of Jacinda Ardern's Labour government in New Zealand is the most pertinent for the Albanese government (Duncan 2025). It narrowly won office as a minority government in 2017, stormed to an extraordinary majority win in 2020, but lost office and momentum at the 2023 election. The Ardern government was undone for a range of reasons, but primarily due to an inability to 'deliver' or make significant policy inroads into a suite of core issues—notably, the housing crisis (Duncan 2025: 247). Historic political victories can prove short-lived with impatient electorates.

References

Albanese, Anthony. 2022. 'Australia legislates emissions reduction targets.' Media release, 8 September. Canberra: Office of the Prime Minister and Cabinet. www.pm.gov.au/media/australia-legislates-emissions-reduction-targets.

Albanese, Anthony. 2024a. 'Building Australia's future.' Speech, Adelaide, 3 November. anthonyalbanese.com.au/media-centre/building-australias-future-am-10-dpq.

Albanese, Anthony. 2024b. 'Building early education for Australia's future.' Speech, Brisbane, 11 December. anthonyalbanese.com.au/media-centre/building-early-education-for-australias-future.

Albanese, Anthony. 2025a. 'Press conference—Canberra.' 28 March. Transcript available: anthonyalbanese.com.au/media-centre/press-conference-canberra-280325.

Albanese, Anthony. 2025b. 'Address to Labor campaign launch—Building Australia's future.' Speech, Perth, 13 April. anthonyalbanese.com.au/media-centre/address-to-labor-campaign-launch-building-australias-future.

Albanese, Anthony. 2025c. 'A choice for the future.' Speech, Parramatta, 27 April. anthonyalbanese.com.au/media-centre/a-choice-for-the-future-parramatta.

Armstrong, Clare. 2025. 'Blueprint for a red wave.' *Daily Telegraph*, 10 May.

Australian Council of Trade Unions (ACTU). 2025. 'Australians couldn't risk Dutton.' Media release, 4 May. Melbourne: ACTU. www.actu.org.au/media-release/australians-couldnt-risk-dutton/.

Australian Financial Review (AFR). 2024. 'Tax summit would table all reform options.' *Australian Financial Review*, 1 February. www.afr.com/policy/tax-and-super/tax-summit-would-table-all-reform-options-20240201-p5f1je.

Australian Human Rights Commission (AHRC). 2024. *Human Rights Explainer: Proposed Social Media Ban for Under-16s in Australia.* Sydney: AHRC. humanrights.gov.au/sites/default/files/2024-11/AHRC_Social-Media-Ban-Explainer.pdf.

Bailey, David. 2009. *The Political Economy of European Social Democracy: A Critical Realist Approach.* London: Routledge. doi.org/10.4324/9780203867662.

Bale, Tim, and Cristóbal Rovira Kaltwasser, eds. 2021. *Riding the Populist Wave: Europe's Mainstream Right in Crisis.* Cambridge: Cambridge University Press. doi.org/10.1017/9781009006866.

Bartlett, David, and Jennifer Rayner. 2014. '"This campaign is all about …": Dissecting Australian campaign narratives.' *Communication, Politics & Culture* 47, no. 1: 51–68.

Bathgate, Becky. 2024. *New Industry Policy: A Future Made in Australia.* Budget Review Article, 2024-25, 25 June. Canberra: Parliamentary Library. www.aph.gov.au/About_Parliament/Parliamentary_departments/Parliamentary_Library/Research/Budget_Review/2024-25/NewIndustryPolicy.

Bennett, Ebony. 2024. 'Stage 3 tax changes: A win for Australians & sensible policy.' *The Australia Institute*, 4 February. australiainstitute.org.au/post/stage-3-tax-changes-a-win-for-australians-sensible-policy/.

Burns, Connor. 2008. 'Margaret Thatcher's greatest achievement: New Labour.' [Blog]. *Conservativehome/CentreRight*, 11 April. conservativehome.blogs.com/centreright/2008/04/making-history.html [page discontinued].

Cameron, Sarah, and Ian McAllister. 2022. *Trends in Australian Political Opinion: Results from the Australian Election Study 1987–2022.* Canberra: Australian Election Study, The Australian National University. australianelectionstudy.org/wp-content/uploads/Trends-in-Australian-Political-Opinion-Results-from-the-Australian-Election-Study-1987-2022.pdf.

Chalmers, Jim. 2025. '2025–26 budget speech, Parliament House, Canberra.' 25 March. ministers.treasury.gov.au/ministers/jim-chalmers-2022/speeches/2025-26-budget-speech-parliament-house-canberra.

Chalmers, Jim, and Katy Gallagher. 2025. 'Labor's costed plan to build Australia's future.' Media release, 28 April. Canberra: Australian Labor Party. alp.org.au/news/labors-costed-plan-to-build-australias-future/.

Combet, Greg, and Lenda Oshalem. 2022. *Election 2022: An Opportunity to Establish a Long-Term Labor Government*. Report of the review of Labor's 2022 Federal Election Campaign. Canberra: Australian Labor Party. alp-assets.s3.ap-southeast-2.amazonaws.com/documents/ALP+CAMPAIGN+REVIEW+2022.pdf.

Duncan, Grant. 2025. 'The making and breaking of Jacinda Ardern's Labour government, 2017–2023.' *The Political Quarterly* 96, no. 2: 246–54. doi.org/10.1111/1467-923X.13512.

Dunckley, Mathew, and Michael Bachelard. 2024. 'How the CFMEU scandal unfolded.' *The Age*, 19 November. www.theage.com.au/national/how-the-cfmeu-scandal-unfolded-20241119-p5krwx.html.

Emerson, Craig, and Jay Weatherill. 2019. *Review of Labor's 2019 Federal Election Campaign*. Canberra: Australian Labor Party. alp.org.au/media/2043/alp-campaign-review-2019.pdf.

Erickson, Paul. 2025. 'Campaign director's address: Paul Erickson, ALP National Secretary.' Speech, National Press Club, Canberra, 21 May. alp.org.au/national-secretary-media/250521-campaign-directors-address-to-the-national-press-club/.

Guardian. 2024. 'The Guardian view on Olaf Scholz's struggling coalition: Running out of time.' *The Guardian*, 23 September, [Updated 24 September 2024]. www.theguardian.com/commentisfree/2024/sep/23/the-guardian-view-on-olaf-scholzs-struggling-coalition-running-out-of-time.

Hartwich, Oliver. 2025. 'Scholz promised stability, but Germany got chaos instead.' *Australian Financial Review*, 21 February. www.afr.com/world/europe/scholz-promised-stability-but-germany-got-chaos-instead-20250220-p5ldr5.

Hegarty, Nicole. 2025. 'How Labor changed workplace laws and what the Coalition wants to change back.' *ABC News*, 1 May. www.abc.net.au/news/2025-05-01/industrial-relations-changes-federal-election/105235812.

Irving, Terry. 1994. 'Labourism: A political genealogy.' *Labour History*, no. 66: 1–13.

Johnson, Carol. 2024. 'Failure to launch: Why the Albanese government is in trouble.' *The Conversation*, 8 October. doi.org/10.64628/AA.3r657rdyh.

Kampfner, John. 2024. 'Scholz's leadership failure.' *Politico*, 22 November. www.politico.eu/article/germany-chancellor-olaf-scholz-social-democratic-party-spd-leadership-german-election-politics/.

Karp, Paul. 2023. 'Labor criticised for apparent "backtrack" on stronger LGBTQ+ legal protections.' *The Guardian*, 2 June. www.theguardian.com/australia-news/2023/jun/02/labor-criticised-for-apparent-backtrack-on-stronger-lgbtq-legal-protections.

Lane, Sabra. 2025. 'Tax cuts a "cruel hoax": Peter Dutton.' *AM*, [*ABC Radio*], 26 March. www.abc.net.au/listen/programs/am/tax-cuts-a-cruel-hoax-peter-dutton/105096562.

Manwaring, Rob, Grant Duncan, and Charlie Lees. 2024. '"Thin labourism": Ideological and policy comparisons between the Australian, British, and New Zealand labour parties.' *The British Journal of Politics and International Relations* 26, no. 1: 39–61. doi.org/10.1177/13691481221148326.

Manwaring, Rob, and Emily Foley. 2023. 'The Australian Labor Party.' In *Watershed: The 2022 Australian Federal Election*, edited by Anika Gauja, Marian Sawer, and Jill Sheppard, 181–202. Canberra: ANU Press. doi.org/10.22459/W.2023.09.

Mares, Peter. 2024. 'Poor at politics, strong on policy.' *Inside Story*, 2 August. insidestory.org.au/poor-at-politics-strong-on-policy/.

Marsh, David, and Allan McConnell. 2010. 'Towards a framework for establishing policy success.' *Public Administration* 88, no. 2: 564–83. doi.org/10.1111/j.1467-9299.2009.01803.x.

Mealey, Rachel. 2025. 'Win exceeds even most optimistic expectations: Jim Chalmers.' *AM*, [*ABC Radio*], 4 May. www.abc.net.au/listen/programs/am/win-exceeds-even-most-optimistic-expectations-jim-chalmers/105249940.

Megalogenis, George. 2024. 'Minority report: The new shape of Australian politics.' *Quarterly Essay*, no. 96: 1–72.

Münchau, Wolfgang. 2024. 'How Olaf Scholz lost Germany.' *New Statesman*, 7 February. www.newstatesman.com/comment/2024/02/how-olaf-scholz-lost-germany.

Orr, Graeme. 2020. 'Clive Palmer's "death tax" scare campaign isn't new. But it's still outrageous.' *The Guardian*, 28 October. www.theguardian.com/commentisfree/2020/oct/28/clive-palmers-death-tax-scare-campaign-isnt-new-but-its-still-outrageous.

Quiggin, John. 2024. 'It's time to give Labor's first term a scorecard—have we actually seen any transformative vision?' *The Conversation*, 16 May. theconversation.com/its-time-to-give-labors-first-term-a-scorecard-have-we-actually-seen-any-transformative-vision-230115. doi.org/10.64628/AA.7jhs9ha6u.

Remeikis, Amy. 2024. 'Labor suspends affiliation with construction arm of CFMEU.' *The Guardian*, 18 July. www.theguardian.com/australia-news/article/2024/jul/18/actu-had-no-idea-of-cfmeu-allegations-sally-mcmanus-says-as-labor-executive-meets-to-decide-next-step.

Reuters. 2024. 'Germany must forge new policy to save its industry, says Scholz.' *Reuters*, 16 October. www.reuters.com/world/europe/scholz-must-forge-new-policy-save-german-industry-2024-10-16/.

Sakkal, Paul, and James Massola. 2023. 'Union push for worker representatives on RBA and Future Fund.' *The Sydney Morning Herald*, 16 August. www.smh.com.au/politics/federal/union-push-for-worker-representatives-on-rba-and-future-fund-20230815-p5dwpc.html.

Sakkal, Paul, and Kieran Rooney. 2024. '"Dumping ground": Labor Senate team under spotlight for being union-heavy, minister-light.' *The Age*, 11 April. www.theage.com.au/politics/federal/dumping-ground-labor-senate-team-under-spotlight-for-being-union-heavy-minister-light-20240410-p5fipi.html.

Smout, Alistair, and Sachin Ravikumar. 2025. 'Britain considers ditching two-child cap on benefits.' *Reuters*, 27 May, [Updated 28 May 2025]. www.reuters.com/world/uk/britain-considers-ditching-two-child-cap-benefit-payments-2025-05-27/.

Somers, Margaret, and Gloria Gibson. 1994. 'Reclaiming the epistemological "other": Narrative and the social constitution of identity.' In *Social Theory and the Politics of Identity*, edited by Craig Calhoun, 37–99. Oxford: Blackwell.

Spender, Allegra. 2024. 'Tax reform that delivers for future generations.' [Media release]. Sydney: Allegra Spender MP, Federal Member for Wentworth. www.allegraspender.com.au/4821/tax.

Tillett, Andrew. 2025. 'Game on as PM gets the jump.' *Australian Financial Review*, 11 January.

Truu, Maani. 2025. 'How Labor pulled off a landslide no one saw coming.' *ABC News*, 25 May. www.abc.net.au/news/2025-05-25/how-labor-pulled-off-a-landslide-no-one-saw-coming/105325976.

Wallace, Chris. 2020. *How to Win an Election*. Sydney: NewSouth Publishing.

11

The Liberals go backwards again

Josh Sunman, Zareh Ghazarian
and Marija Taflaga

Abstract

The 2025 election was the worst result in the Liberal Party's history, compounding their previous worst result in 2022. These results were largely driven by urban and suburban decline, with the party driven out of metropolitan Perth and Adelaide. The Liberals' results were almost as poor in Melbourne and Sydney, while they suffered devastating and unexpected losses in Brisbane—home to Opposition leader Peter Dutton. The party entered the campaign with severe organisational impediments across the country. These organisational issues were patched over throughout Dutton's leadership with a set of opportunistic, ideologically incoherent policy priorities, ranging from heavily interventionist nuclear and gas programs, to 'sugar hit' cost-of-living relief, such as cutting the fuel excise. Buoyed by the failure of the Indigenous Voice to Parliament referendum, the party ran a chaotic campaign that failed to address the concerns of the electorate. These factors contributed to a devastating defeat for the Liberal Party.

Keywords: Liberal Party; party organisation; party ideology; policy agenda; election campaign

The 2025 election was a disastrous result for the Liberal Party of Australia (LPA), which went further backwards from its 2022 defeat and suffered its worst result since its formation in 1944. The scale and nature of this defeat have given rise to debates about whether the party faces an existential crisis and what this means for its organisational future.

The Liberals failed to gain significant ground in their former heartland where Teal Independents retained seats won in 2022, except Goldstein. This was largely expected, as the Dutton Opposition had spent the term seeking to target outer suburban areas at the expense of wresting back wealthier electorates. However, this appeal also fell dramatically short. The party lost ground contrary to expectations in Victoria, as well as unexpectedly losing several Brisbane marginals—most devastatingly, Dutton's own seat of Dickson. The party also had a worse performance than its 2022 nadirs in South Australia and Western Australia and was wiped out in Tasmania.

Dutton's strategy of courting Labor's traditional base in the outer suburbs was seemingly vindicated by the overwhelming 'No' vote in the Indigenous Voice to Parliament referendum, emboldening the Liberals' embrace of 'culture war' issues and its flirtation with right-wing populism. This strategy was only tempered by growing disquiet over the governing approach of US President Donald Trump in the final weeks of the Albanese government's first term. Despite having a broad political strategy, the Liberals entered the 2025 campaign with an underdeveloped policy envelope and the party organisation in a rundown state. The campaign appeared to lurch from one misstep to another, with party elder George Brandis later describing it as an exercise in 'running out of people to offend' (in Karvelas 2025). In the end, the results on the night laid bare how risky Dutton's gamble had been. This chapter will utilise Stuart Ball's framework of opposition success to assess the Liberals' campaign performance. It examines the pre-electoral context, with a focus on the LPA's strategic approach and organisational capacity, the shambolic campaign run by Dutton and the wider party and the scale of the LPA's defeat.

Pre-campaign context

Developing a strategy in the aftermath of 2022

It is helpful to assess the strategic approach of the Liberal Party through the lens of Stuart Ball's framework of opposition requirements. Ball's essential argument is that whether oppositions are successful in regaining office depends on five factors: the injection of 'fresh faces' into the leadership team, maintenance of party cohesion, the visibility of a new or distinctive agenda, an efficient party organisation and an overall adaptability—that is, a hunger for office that prevails over notions of ideological purity (Ball 2005). Tim Bale builds on this framework by offering two broad strategic approaches followed by successful oppositions: impressionism and pointillism. In essence, impressionism captures parties which signal broad intentions and values without specific details, whereas pointillism focuses on the outlining of specific and detailed manifestos (Bale 2015: 62).

Peter Dutton adopted an impressionistic strategy throughout his tenure as Opposition Leader, signalling values and intent rather than providing programmatic detail. In his first press conference as leader, Dutton promised 'strong policy to make the lives of Australians better'. In making this promise, Dutton (2022) signposted his key electoral focus, declaring that 'our policies will be squarely aimed at the forgotten Australians, in the suburbs, across regional Australia'. This is an adaptation of a core construct of Liberal Party politics in Australia, the so-called forgotten people of LPA founder, Robert Menzies. As pointed out by Judith Brett (1992), Menzies outlined the LPA's core constituency as the overlooked 'middle classes'— not extremely wealthy, but outside Labor's sectional focus on blue-collar workers. This construct is invoked in a ritual manner by most LPA leaders, but its meaning has changed over time to suit political circumstances and the electoral appeals of particular leaders. Dutton's invocation combines the language of Menzies with the culturally conservative and masculine appeals of John Howard and, later, Scott Morrison—a clear example of impressionistic signalling rather than a set of detailed policies.

The party's path to recovery from the 2022 result was hampered by lingering scandals from the Morrison government. These were the multiple-ministries scandal, the Robodebt Royal Commission and continued revelations from the Brittany Higgins case. The impact of these challenges was exemplified in the Aston by-election in 2023. This was necessitated by the resignation of former minister Alan Tudge, who had been implicated in the fallout from Robodebt and faced additional pressure over an extramarital affair. Aston was a historic defeat for the Opposition, with Labor claiming the seat on a 6 per cent swing and a final two-party-preferred vote total of 54 per cent. This represented the first time a government had won a seat from an opposition at a by-election since Kalgoorlie in 1920 (AEC 2023). These challenges speak to the Dutton Opposition's difficulty in establishing 'visibility' for their new priorities and breaking from the Morrison government. The challenge was exacerbated by a shortage of 'fresh faces' in the core leadership team, as most were veterans of the tarnished Morrison government (see Ball 2005).

At the time of the by-election, the Coalition was deliberating on how to approach the Albanese government's Voice referendum. The Nationals had pre-empted the Liberals, announcing their opposition in principle to the Voice in December 2022 (Karp 2022). Days after the Aston by-election, Dutton followed suit, announcing that the Liberal Party would also oppose 'the Prime Minister's Canberra Voice. It should be very clear to Australians by now that the Prime Minister is dividing our country, and the Liberal Party seeks to unite our country' (Dutton and Ley 2023). The tone of this statement was highly partisan and arguably populist, labelling the so-called Canberra Voice championed by Albanese a divisive and elitist institution (see Chapter 4, this volume). While opposing the Voice referendum was broadly supported in both party rooms, there was some notable dissent. Julian Leeser quit as the responsible shadow minister and Andrew Gee defected from the Nationals. Finally, Ken Wyatt, the former Indigenous Affairs Minister and a proud Nyungar man, quit the party in protest.

Dutton successfully used the 'No' campaign to build momentum, attack the standing of the Prime Minister and paint the government as distracted from the cost-of-living crisis—achieving a distinctive and visible policy position vis-a-vis the government (see Ball 2005). The referendum's defeat weakened Labor's and Albanese's confidence and boosted the Coalition's morale. In hindsight, it also bred complacency. Dutton and the wider party viewed the failure of the Voice referendum as a vindication of their suburban strategy and evidence of Labor's detachment from its traditional base, rather than a poorly prosecuted case for change through a referendum mechanism that has historically favoured the status quo.

A more prescient event that should have given the Opposition pause was the Dunkley by-election. Located in Melbourne's outer south, Dunkley was consistently held by the Coalition from 1996 to 2019 and its demographic profile meant it was exactly the kind of electorate on which Dutton had pinned his electoral hopes. Labor retained the seat in the 2024 by-election despite suffering a 3.6 per cent swing against it. This result reflected the average swing of 3.5 per cent against governments in by-elections since 1984. However, considering Dutton's stated suburban electoral strategy, the result was underwhelming (AEC 2024). Dunkley, as well as Aston, were both comfortably retained by the Albanese government in the 2025 general election and offered early warning signs that Dutton's impressionistic strategy perhaps needed further refinement and policy detail.

The Liberal Party organisation

At the organisational level, the LPA's party organs continued a downward decline, failing to demonstrate the efficiency and efficacy needed for electoral success (see Ball 2005). The party was out of office at the State level in New South Wales, Victoria, South Australia and Western Australia, compounding difficulties of resourcing, policy development, candidate selection and fundraising in those divisions. The South Australian and Victorian divisions remained riven by high-profile factional and leadership issues. The Tasmanian division held on to power in minority status, while the composite parties, the Liberal National Party (LNP) in Queensland and the Country Liberal Party (CLP) in the Northern Territory, had the most success, with both returning to government.

Ongoing conflict between Dutton's travelling campaign office and the main headquarters worsened throughout the campaign, with concerns throughout the party that Dutton's team was making 'on the fly' announcements without proper consultation and utilisation of central resources (Kehoe 2025). Likewise, Senator Jonathon Duniam of Tasmania later complained of disconnects between the central campaign and more localised needs, arguing that local campaign teams had been constrained by central directives (Moran 2025; Chapter 2, this volume).

Low morale and poor State-level results had seen members quit or fail to renew memberships, with a related decline in revenue. In Victoria, membership sits between 8,000 and 10,000 people, with an average age of 68 years. In New South Wales, membership is estimated to be between 8,000 and 12,000 (Kolovos and Belot 2025). The lack of party members, and therefore volunteers, saw the Liberal Party reportedly rely on the Exclusive Brethren to hand out how-to-vote cards at election booths (Bachelard and Maddison 2025). While it was argued during the campaign that this was spontaneous grassroots action, it was revealed after the election that Brethren support for Liberal campaigns went beyond ad hoc canvassing, with the party's Feedback voter-contact software having a package and log-in keys specifically for Brethren members (Maddison and Sakkal 2025). Additionally, a key Dutton advisor, Sam Jackson-Hope, had been allegedly tasked for much of the campaign proper to liaise between party campaign teams and Brethren supporters. It is estimated that in addition to on-the-ground campaigning, the Brethren made up to one million voter calls by the end of the election campaign (Maddison and Sakkal 2025).

The State divisions were also struggling to appear united. In the leadup to the election, the Victorian division was embroiled in damaging internal conflict after state Liberal MP Moira Deeming successfully sued the Victorian party leader John Pesutto for defamation (see Legg and Metzger 2025). In New South Wales, Peter Dutton ordered an intervention in that State's division, appointing two conservative Victorian elder statesmen, Alan Stockdale and Richard Alston, and former NSW MP Peta Seaton as a three-person administrative committee with the aim of tackling dysfunctional factional organisation (Karp 2025; Stockdale et al. 2025). The Liberal Party's Western Australian organisational decline continued, having been in a downward spiral after consecutive State landslide losses in 2017, 2021 and 2025. Likewise, the South Australian division had reached a new nadir after its 2022 State election loss, with its previous leader David Speirs resigning in disgrace after drug supply charges, and losing two by-elections to the Malinauskas Labor government (Sunman 2025: 319–20).

Considering the turmoil engulfing multiple State Liberal divisions, and the level of dysfunction present in the campaign, we argue that the Liberal Party's lack of organisational efficiency was a major contributing factor to their 2025 defeat. The party also struggled to offer 'fresh faces' to the electorate, with its core leadership team comprising Morrison government ministers. On the criteria of 'visibility', the party struggled to move past the toxic hangovers from its time in office and offer a distinctive policy vision for a future Coalition government.

The campaign issues and dynamic

The lack of a coherent policy agenda from the Coalition was a substantial contributor to the breadth and depth of the Opposition's defeat. Dutton and the wider frontbench failed to offer a set of clear, coherent policy pledges and principles and failed to 'adapt' their ideological preconceptions to the Australian electorate.

The Liberals' poor campaign was not solely due to policy, however, as the shadow of Trump also hamstrung Peter Dutton's natural style of campaigning. Initially from a police background, and with notable ministerial stints in

Defence and Home Affairs throughout the Liberals' previous terms in office, Dutton had developed a 'strongman' persona among the electorate (Blaine 2024; Long 2025; Chapter 2, this volume). This persona was ill-suited to an election held in the shadow of Trump and the machismo approach taken by his administration. This led to Dutton attempting to soften his image, which in turn seemed inauthentic and at times indecisive (Mizen 2025a). Dutton had run a tight, 'cohesive' Opposition—one that seemed to be well placed to defeat the government right up until the writs were issued. In the light of the campaign, this unity was revealed to be driven by a tightly controlled, highly centralised operation from the leader's office—one characterised by a distinct lack of visible policy development and ideological rigidity.

Taflaga (2023) noted that the 2022 Liberal campaign was distinctly masculine and based on Morrison's appeals to outer suburban electorates, although there was some effort from candidates in so-called Teal seats to offer a more socially progressive Liberal vision. In 2025 there was no concerted effort to offer different messaging to more up-scale traditional Liberal heartlands to reclaim seats from Teal Independents, with the party doubling down on the outer suburban strategy employed in 2022.

The party's campaign relentlessly targeted the seats of Hawke and McEwen on Melbourne's north-western fringe, Werriwa in Western Sydney and Whitlam, based in the Illawarra. Of these seats, McEwen and Werriwa recorded swings to the ALP below Statewide averages, Hawke no swing and Whitlam a rare swing to the Coalition. This suggests that, perhaps, had they been on track for a victory, these seats would have delivered the Coalition a majority. In hindsight, seemingly erroneous internal polling showing the Coalition highly competitive led to traditionally marginal seats such as Petrie being relatively undefended:

> [T]he whole polling was wrong … The messaging from the campaign and the leader's office was 'we're going to win additional seats, there's no way the Labor Party can increase their majority, they will go backwards into minority government and that's the best they can hope for'. (Howarth, cited in Elks 2025)

This misplaced optimism based on incorrect polling was arguably a large contributor to the Liberal campaign's laser-like focus on the outer suburbs and potentially explains its failure to correct course on several damaging policies.

Nuclear and gas

The Coalition advanced one 'big picture' policy proposal: the introduction of nuclear power into Australia's energy grid. However, the details of this major energy policy were left quite vague and it presented a big target for negative Labor campaigning. The Liberal plan touted the construction of seven nuclear power plants at the sites of former coal-fired power stations with a mixture of full-size and smaller modular plants (Dutton et al. 2024). Labor ruthlessly attacked this proposal, using the tagline 'He cuts, you pay', tying what they argued to be a $600-billion cost of construction to existing voter perceptions of the spectre of budget cuts to wider government programs and social services (see Chapter 3, this volume).

Internally, nuclear offered a somewhat clean solution to long-running disputes over energy policy in the Coalition. Conservative members of the Liberals, as well as the Nationals, had long opposed net-zero targets and the introduction of policies favouring clean and renewable sources of energy. These disputes were major contributing factors to instability in the Liberal leadership from 2009 to 2018 and Dutton's pledge to introduce nuclear largely assisted party and Coalition cohesion.

In ideological terms, however, this policy represented a dramatic departure from core Liberal principles. As noted by Brett (2024), the Liberal Party has always emphasised the role of private enterprise over government and the role of the States over Commonwealth centralisation. This new policy marked a dramatic break from both principles, with the policy proposing Commonwealth Government intervention in a largely private market and overruling State-level concerns about the imposition of nuclear energy. This contradiction was acknowledged post election by frontbench Senator James Paterson:

> The answer for the Liberal Party going forward on this is probably not … a government-initiated and managed and run program where taxpayers would finance and build them … [b]ut instead go for a more traditional Liberal … market-based approach, which is repeal the prohibition on nuclear power, and then leave it up to the energy industry. (cited in Coorey 2025)

The Liberals sidelined their nuclear proposals throughout much of the campaign (Cropp 2025), with gas receiving greater attention in terms of policy announcements. The centrepiece of the party's gas plan was the creation of an East Coast Gas Reserve, mandating that the three largest gas providers reserve 20 per cent of Eastern Australia's gas for the domestic market. This was proposed to be coupled with an Australian domestic gas security mechanism to force suppliers to offer gas to the domestic market at lower rates than gas exported to foreign markets. These measures were to be supported by a $300-billion critical gas infrastructure fund and a general policy of fast-tracking new gas projects (LPA 2025). Reaction from industry players was mixed, with Energy Producers Australia arguing the policy would lead to oversupply and deter investment, but companies such as Santos welcomed the approach (Greber 2025). Regardless of industry perspectives, this gas policy was highly interventionist, contradicting traditional Liberal approaches.

Cost of living and work conditions

This ideological incoherence was also reflected in the party's approach to cost-of-living issues. Rather than advancing a set of philosophically cohesive policies targeted at addressing inflation and lowering tax burdens, the Liberals opted for 'sugar hits' such as lowering the fuel excise by 25 cents per litre for 12 months and a promise of a $1,200 cost-of-living tax offset. Here, however, the Opposition found itself outmanoeuvred by the Albanese government into not supporting a tax cut in the lowest tax bracket. Once again, Senator Paterson offered some helpful post-election analysis:

> [W]e made some tactical errors which confused some of our supporters, for example, opposing a tax cut and going to an election saying we're going to reverse a tax cut … When people vote Liberal, one of the things they expect from us is lower taxes. (cited in Kehoe 2025)

The proposed unwinding of work-from-home arrangements for Canberra-based public servants was another ill-fated policy. Initially announced without shadow cabinet consultation by opposition finance and public service spokeswoman Jane Hume, and later backed by Peter Dutton, the announcement spiralled throughout the electorate. While targeted only at Canberra-based public servants, the proposal caused voters to doubt the Coalition's overall position on flexible working arrangements. Had the party paused to consider, it may well have realised the massive potential impact forcing remote workers back to the office could have on voters during a cost-of-living crisis (see Chapter 6, this volume). Dutton eventually backed down from the policy after public blowback, but not until after lasting electoral damage had been done.

Defence and immigration

The Liberals also suffered from their traditional 'home base' policy areas of defence and immigration being neutralised throughout the campaign. Defence was sidelined due to three factors: Dutton's overzealous 'verballing' of the Indonesian President over supposed deployment of Russian long-range aircraft to Indonesian airbases, Donald Trump's destabilisation of global affairs and disparaging comments from the party's candidate in Whitlam regarding women serving in the defence force, with shadow defence minister Andrew Hastie also sidelined due to similar past comments (Hannaford 2025). After the election, Hastie discussed his frustrations over the central campaign failing to announce developed policies in a timely manner— a critique supported by shadow education minister Sarah Henderson (Karvelas 2025).

Likewise, the immigration debate was won by Labor with their policy of international student caps—forcing the Opposition into a 'me too' position. The Liberal Party has traditionally 'owned' both defence and immigration as policy areas. That is, the Liberals are generally preferred by the electorate to handle these issues (Cameron and McAllister 2019). Labor, in contrast, has experienced a lot of political trauma from immigration in election campaigns, ranging from the Tampa affair in 2001 to the potent 'stop the boats' campaign in 2013. Fears of appearing to be 'Trump-like' also played a role in discouraging the Liberals from pursuing a hard immigration agenda; they sought to avoid comparison with Trump's tough-on-immigration approach involving mass deportations and denigration of minority groups (Butler 2025). These factors combined undermined the Coalition's ability to capitalise on their traditional areas of strength through high-profile policy proposals.

The overall policy agenda (or lack thereof) presented by the Liberal Party contributed to the severity of its defeat. It failed to advance a clear, visible agenda to the electorate. It gave into comfortable, but unpopular ideological impulses, contributing to the scale of its defeat.

Liberal Party results

The Coalition lost government in 2022 after the Liberal Party lost 16 seats and the LNP in Queensland lost an additional two seats. Combined, the Coalition held 58 seats in the House of Representatives in the Forty-Seventh

Parliament of Australia. In contrast, Labor won 77 seats in the 151-seat chamber, giving it a thin majority (increasing to 78 with the Aston victory). These numbers may have provided some hope to the Liberal Party that it could return to government, or at least force Labor into minority status after a single term, as it had in 2010.

There was a sense in the leadup to the 2025 election that the Coalition was making up ground and would improve its representation in the new parliament. In January and February 2025, for example, the Coalition led the government on a two-party-preferred basis, according to published opinion polling (Beaumont 2025). Despite such strong results, it was still unlikely that the Coalition could win enough seats to hold a majority in the House of Representatives. A minority government appeared to be inevitable.

Following this surge in support in early 2025, however, the Coalition's support appeared to slip (see Nicholas et al. 2025). By March, Labor had closed the gap, with the Coalition starting to trail as the election was called. As the campaign rolled on, Labor continued to attract support and polls showed it was on track to hold on to government. Nevertheless, Opposition leader Peter Dutton maintained that internal party polling was stronger for the Liberal Party than published polls (Nilsson 2025). As discussed above, these internals were based on flawed assumptions about voting behaviour, influenced by the Voice referendum result.

Any hope that the Liberal Party would regain seats it lost in 2022, and even win new seats off Labor, evaporated quickly on election night. Early results after the close of polling stations in Eastern Australia at 6 pm showed a swing against the party. By the time polling stations closed in Western Australia, the extent of the party's loss across the eastern States was clear. As a symbol of how bad the Liberal Party's performance was, Peter Dutton on the night delivered a concession speech not just for the party, but also for his own seat. Of the three parliamentary factions, the conservative 'National Right' remained the largest inside the parliamentary party, but its only 'new' member was Jacinta Nampijinpa Price, who defected from the Nationals. The Moderates, while still smaller as a proportion of the party room, gained two new members. The election of Sussan Ley (of the Morrison/Alex Hawke–aligned Centre-Right) over Angus Taylor from the National Right suggests that the Right's dominance has waned since Dutton's tenure, but the party room remains finely balanced (see Mizen 2025b).

House of Representatives results

The results across the country gave an indication of how the Liberal Party's policies failed to resonate with voters. As Table 11.1 shows, the party's primary vote was just 20.7 per cent. This indicated a 3.2 per cent swing against the party compared with the 2022 election. Moreover, the party managed to win just 28 seats—a net loss of seven seats compared with the previous election.

Table 11.1 Liberal Party primary vote at the 2025 election

State/Territory	Primary vote (%)	Primary vote change since last election (%)	Two-party-preferred (%)	Two-party-preferred change since last election (%)	Seats won	Seats won or lost since last election
National	20.7	-3.2	44.8	-3.1	18	-8
NSW	24.2	-4.1	44.7	-3.9	6	-4[a]
Vic.	27.6	-1.9	43.7	-1.5	6	0
Qld[b]	34.9	-4.7	50.6	-3.5	16	-5
WA	28.7	-5.5	44.2	-0.8	4	-1
SA	28.0	-7.3	40.8	-5.2	2	-1
Tas.	24.5	-8.4	36.7	-9.0	0	-2
ACT	21.2	-5.3	27.5	-5.5	0	0
NT[c]	33.8	4.4	45.7	-1.3	0	0

Notes: [a] The Liberal candidate for Bradfield, Gisele Kapterian, lost the seat by 26 votes, with the case being before the Court of Disputed Returns at the time of writing; [b] The Queensland result is for the LNP; [c] The NT result is for the CLP.
Source: Green (2025).

The strongest swing against the party occurred in Tasmania, where the Liberals held two of the five seats in the State. It suffered big swings—9.4 per cent in Bass and 15.2 per cent in Braddon—losing both to Labor emphatically, leaving the party without a lower house representative in the State. As Table 11.1 shows, the party's performance in other States was also poor. Its result in Queensland, where the Liberal and National parties merged in 2008, was particularly bad as it lost five seats rather unexpectedly, including that of Peter Dutton. Labor managed to win seats in Queensland that had not been particularly competitive since the homegrown advantage of Kevin Rudd in 2007.

As expected, the party's primary vote impacted its two-party-preferred result, which went backwards on both measures in all jurisdictions except the Northern Territory. At the national level, the Coalition won just 44.8 per cent and only managed to win more than 50 per cent in Queensland. In every other jurisdiction, the Coalition lagged Labor on a two-party-preferred basis. Further analysis of the Liberal Party's results indicates the party failed to resonate with voters from across metropolitan and non-metropolitan electorates (see Table 11.2). In metropolitan seats, the strongest swings against the party were in South Australia (7.8 per cent) and in Queensland against the LNP (5.51 per cent). The swing in metropolitan seats in Victoria against the Liberal Party was the lowest, at just 1.65 per cent. The CLP's vote went up significantly in the Northern Territory seat of Solomon, but the party was unable to repeat the strength of its Darwin vote in the 2024 Territory election.

Despite the loss of key marginals to Labor, there was a rare positive story for the Liberal Party in Victoria, where the party had lost previously safe seats to the so-called Teal Independents. Tim Wilson, the former MP for Goldstein, recontested the seat and defeated Independent Zoe Daniel by just 175 votes. In so doing, he became the first Liberal to win a seat off the Teals and demonstrated that the Liberal Party could attract support through a campaign that was focused on local matters and effectively marshalled local resources.

Table 11.2 Liberal Party primary vote in metropolitan and non-metropolitan electorates (per cent)

State/Territory	Metropolitan primary vote	Metropolitan primary vote change since last election	Non-metropolitan primary vote	Non-metropolitan primary vote change since last election
National	23.9	-3.4	16.2	-2.9
NSW	30.9	-4.6	6.1	-3.6
Vic.	28.6	-1.7	26.0	-2.4
Qld[a]	31.7	-5.5	37.4	-4.2
WA	27.8	-4.8	32.8	-8.4
SA	25.0	-7.8	35.0	-6.4
Tas.	16.42	-5.08	29.72	-10.6
ACT	21.16	-5.35	n/a	n/a
NT[b]	35.99	+10.28	30.99	-3.48

Notes: [a] The Queensland result is for the LNP; [b] The NT result is for the CLP.
Source: Compiled by authors from AEC (2025c, 2025d) data.

Senate results

The Liberal Party's fortunes were no better in the Senate. As Table 11.3 demonstrates, the party's vote fell in every jurisdiction, except in the Northern Territory, where it increased by 1 per cent. The party's vote fell most dramatically in Tasmania (with a swing of –8.48 per cent). In New South Wales, where the Liberal Party ran a joint ticket with the Nationals, the primary vote fell by 7.29 per cent. The party's result meant that it could not secure a third seat in the State (which, under the Coalition Agreement, caused the Nationals' Perin Davey to lose)—a result that was replicated in Victoria and Queensland. The party's performance in Western Australia, South Australia and Tasmania meant that it had to rely on preferences to achieve a second Senate quota. The net result of this election was that the Coalition lost one seat each in New South Wales, Victoria, Queensland, Western Australia and South Australia, leaving it 27 of the 76 seats in the new Senate.

Table 11.3 Coalition performance in the Senate

Jurisdiction	Primary vote (%)	Swing (%)	Quota
NSW	29.44	–7.29	2.06
Vic.	31.41	–0.88	2.20
Qld[a]	30.93	–4.30	2.16
WA[b]	26.61	–5.06	1.86
SA[b]	27.57	–6.36	1.93
Tas.[b]	23.54	–8.48	1.65
ACT[b]	17.76	–7.04	0.53
NT[c]	32.73	+1.03	0.98

Notes: [a] The Queensland result is for the LNP; [b] The Liberal Party ran a separate Senate ticket to the Nationals in Western Australia, South Australia, Tasmania and the ACT; [c] The NT result is for the CLP.

Source: AEC (2025b).

Conclusion

The 2025 election result was a low point for the Liberal Party. It represents the party's most comprehensive defeat at the federal level in its history. Beyond its paltry seat total, the party finds itself politically and institutionally adrift. While the election of Sussan Ley as the party's first female leader represents a significant milestone, much of her shadow cabinet comprises former Morrison government ministers in key portfolios—a distinct lack of 'fresh faces'. The greatest success of the Dutton Opposition was its outward projection of unity, even though this unity stifled the development of a visible and coherent policy agenda. Organisationally, the party is largely in chaos, with many of its State branches either moribund or in active factional disarray. It remains difficult to see how an 'efficient' party organisation can be rebuilt before an election due in 2028. The Dutton Opposition was ideologically rigid and failed to 'adapt' to the electorate on policy. A key test for Ley is whether she can recalibrate the party to appeal effectively to lost traditional Liberal voters, while successfully pursuing soft Labor voters in the outer suburbs.

References

Australian Electoral Commission (AEC). 2023. 'Aston, Vic.' *Tally Room: 2023 Aston By-Election*. [Updated 15 April 2023]. Canberra: Australian Electoral Commission. results.aec.gov.au/28791/Website/HouseDivisionPage-28791-197. htm.

Australian Electoral Commission (AEC). 2024. 'Dunkley, Vic.' *Tally Room: 2024 Dunkley By-Election*. [Updated 21 March 2024]. Canberra: Australian Electoral Commission. results.aec.gov.au/29778/Website/HouseDivisionPage-29778-210. htm.

Australian Electoral Commission (AEC). 2025a. 'First preferences by candidate.' *Tally Room: 2025 Federal Election*. [Updated 28 May 2025]. Canberra: Australian Electoral Commission. results.aec.gov.au/31496/Website/SenateStateFirstPrefs-31496-NSW.htm.

Australian Electoral Commission (AEC). 2025b. 'Senate: State and Territory results.' *Tally Room: 2025 Federal Election*. [Updated 30 May 2025]. Canberra: Australian Electoral Commission. results.aec.gov.au/31496/Website/Senate StateResultsMenu-31496.htm.

Australian Electoral Commission (AEC). 2025c. 'Metropolitan results.' *Tally Room: 2025 Federal Election*. [Updated 10 June 2025]. Canberra: Australian Electoral Commission. results.aec.gov.au/31496/Website/HouseDemographicFirstPrefsBy Party-31496-NAT-Metropolitan.htm.

Australian Electoral Commission (AEC). 2025d. 'Non-metropolitan results.' *Tally Room: 2025 Federal Election*. [Updated 10 June 2025]. Canberra: Australian Electoral Commission. results.aec.gov.au/31496/Website/HouseDemographic FirstPrefsByParty-31496-NAT-NonMetropolitan.htm.

Bachelard, Michael, and Max Maddison. 2025. '"Game On": The minute-long message that unleashed the Brethren's election machine.' *The Sydney Morning Herald*, 7 June. www.smh.com.au/politics/federal/game-on-the-minute-long-message-that-unleashed-the-brethren-s-election-machine-20250604-p5m505.html.

Bale, Tim. 2015. 'If opposition is an art, is Ed Miliband an artist? A framework for evaluating leaders of the opposition.' *Parliamentary Affairs* 68, no. 1: 58–76. doi.org/10.1093/pa/gsu017.

Ball, Stuart. 2005. 'Factors in opposition performance: The conservative experience since 1867.' In *Recovering Power: The Conservatives in Opposition*, edited by Stuart Ball and Anthony Seldon, 1–27. London: Palgrave Macmillan. doi.org/10.1057/9780230522411_1.

Beaumont, Adrian. 2025. 'Coalition has lead in most polls as Dutton gains five-point preferred PM lead in Resolve.' *The Conversation*, 23 January. theconversation.com/coalition-has-lead-in-most-polls-as-dutton-gains-five-point-preferred-pm-lead-in-resolve-248001. doi.org/10.64628/AA.nqg375hwt.

Blaine, Lech. 2024. 'Bad cop: Peter Dutton's strongman politics.' *Quarterly Essay*, no. 71.

Brett, Judith. 1992. *Robert Menzies' Forgotten People*. Sydney: Pan Macmillan.

Brett, Judith. 2024. 'With its nuclear energy policy, Peter Dutton seems to have forgotten the Liberal Party's core beliefs.' *The Conversation*, 2 July. theconversation.com/with-its-nuclear-energy-policy-peter-dutton-seems-to-have-forgotten-the-liberal-partys-core-beliefs-233444. doi.org/10.64628/AA.vvddtrgnm.

Butler, Josh. 2025. 'Donald Trump in the White House seemed like a plus for Peter Dutton. But after this week, maybe not so much.' *The Guardian*, 5 April. www.theguardian.com/australia-news/2025/apr/05/donald-trump-in-the-white-house-seemed-like-a-plus-for-peter-dutton-but-after-this-week-maybe-not-so-much.

Cameron, Sarah, and Ian McAllister. 2019. *The 2019 Australian Federal Election: Results from the Australian Election Study*. Canberra: School of Politics and International Relations, The Australian National University. australianelectionstudy.org/wp-content/uploads/The-2019-Australian-Federal-Election-Results-from-the-Australian-Election-Study.pdf.

Coorey, Phillip. 2025. 'Nuclear policy was at odds with Lib philosophy: Paterson.' *Australian Financial Review*, 2 June. www.afr.com/politics/federal/nuclear-policy-was-at-odds-with-lib-philosophy-paterson-20250602-p5m42i.

Cropp, Ryan. 2025. 'Why Labor won't stop talking about nuclear power.' *Australian Financial Review*, 2 May. www.afr.com/policy/energy-and-climate/why-labor-won-t-stop-talking-about-nuclear-power-20250428-p5luw4.

Dutton, Peter. 2022. 'Opening remarks at joint press conference, Canberra.' 30 May. Brisbane: Peter Dutton Media Releases. Transcript available: web.archive.org/web/20230308072500/https://www.peterdutton.com.au/transcript-opposition-leadership/.

Dutton, Peter, and Sussan Ley. 2023. 'Leader of the Opposition joint press conference with the Hon Sussan Ley MP, Deputy Opposition Leader, Canberra.' 5 April. Brisbane: Peter Dutton Media Releases. Transcript available: web.archive.org/web/20231028035234/https://www.peterdutton.com.au/22490-2/.

Dutton, Peter, David Littleproud, and Ted O'Brien. 2024. 'Australia's energy future.' Liberal Party of Australia, 19 June. www.liberal.org.au/2024/06/19/australias-energy-future.

Elks, Sarah. 2025. 'Swings and misses: Party's polling debacle.' *The Australian*, 23 May. www.theaustralian.com.au/nation/swings-and-misses-partys-polling-debacle-in-election-2025/news-story/b7cb8de97972f5f626227408bbbc2a57.

Ferguson, John. 2025. 'Libs split after Cormack Foundation fails to back embattled MP.' *The Australian*, 11 April. www.theaustralian.com.au/nation/politics/libs-split-after-cormack-foundation-fails-to-back-embattled-mp-over-crippling-court-costs/news-story/fdadb543806349d3a215f5bb599ff120.

Greber, Jacob. 2025. 'Energy expert slams Dutton's "populist anti-market" gas plan as self-defeating "betrayal".' *ABC News*, 29 March. www.abc.net.au/news/2025-03-29/leading-gas-expert-rips-dutton-plan/105110962.

Green, Antony. 2025. 'Party totals.' *ABC News*, 3 May, [Updated 8 June 2025]. www.abc.net.au/news/elections/federal/2025/results/party-totals.

Hannaford, Patrick. 2025. 'Andrew Hastie speaks out on being "sidelined" during campaign, responds to criticism of Coalition's defence policy.' *Sky News*, 15 May. www.skynews.com.au/australia-news/politics/andrew-hastie-speaks-out-on-being-sidelined-during-campaign-responds-to-criticism-of-coalitions-defence-policy/news-story/36c8813cac149a56e39bc0c790eff577.

Jervis-Bardy, Dan, and Anne Davies. 2025. 'Victorian octogenarians dumped from committee running NSW Liberal Party but federal intervention continues.' *The Guardian*, 17 June. www.theguardian.com/australia-news/2025/jun/17/nsw-liberal-party-federal-intervention-continues-state-branch.

Karp, Paul. 2022. 'Nationals MP Andrew Gee quits party citing its opposition to Indigenous Voice.' *The Guardian*, 23 December. www.theguardian.com/australia-news/2022/dec/23/nationals-mp-andrew-gee-quits-party-citing-opposition-to-indigenous-voice.

Karp, Paul. 2025. '"George Washington couldn't have saved it": NSW Liberals fume at feds.' *Australian Financial Review*, 15 May, [Updated 16 May 2025]. www.afr.com/politics/utterly-out-of-touch-nsw-liberals-fume-at-federal-takeover-202505 15-p5lzgk.

Karvelas, Patricia. 2025. 'Decimated and divided Liberal Party insiders at odds over what went wrong and what they stand for.' *ABC News*, 26 May. www.abc.net.au/news/2025-05-26/liberal-party-insiders-election-campaign-divided-four-corners/105313660.

Kehoe, John. 2025. 'Liberal admits "tactical errors" on tax and spending.' *Australian Financial Review*, 1 June. www.afr.com/policy/economy/liberal-admits-tactical-errors-on-tax-and-spending-20250530-p5m3jr.

Kolovos, Benita, and Henry Belot. 2025. 'Secret figures show Liberal Party's ageing membership in freefall in NSW and Victoria.' *The Guardian*, 31 May. www.theguardian.com/australia-news/2025/may/31/liberal-party-membership-levels-numbers-victoria-nsw.

Legg, Michael, and James Metzger. 2025. 'John Pesutto owes Moira Deeming $2.3m, but he doesn't have it. Can former premiers be forced to pick up the tab?' *The Conversation*, 6 June. theconversation.com/john-pesutto-owes-moira-deeming-2-3m-but-he-doesnt-have-it-can-former-premiers-be-forced-to-pick-up-the-tab-258059. doi.org/10.64628/AA.mj5qfypkd.

Liberal Party of Australia (LPA). 2025. 'Our plan to deliver Australian gas for Australians: We will drive gas prices down, bring on new supply and get gas to where it is needed most.' [Media release]. Canberra: Liberal Party of Australia. www.liberal.org.au/policy/our-plan-to-deliver-australian-gas-for-australians.

Long, Claudia. 2025. 'Peter Dutton is trying to change his "strongman" image, but who is it for?' *ABC News*, 16 January. www.abc.net.au/news/2025-01-16/peter-dutton-politics-campaign-teal-strategy/104821352.

Maddison, Max, and Paul Sakkal. 2025. 'Exclusive Brethren made nearly a million calls for Liberal Party in election campaign.' *The Sydney Morning Herald*, 14 May. www.smh.com.au/politics/federal/exclusive-brethren-made-nearly-a-million-calls-for-the-liberal-party-20250508-p5lxml.html.

Mizen, Ronald. 2025a. 'Dutton's political legacy will be a cautionary tale of what not to do.' *Australian Financial Review*, 4 May. www.afr.com/politics/federal/dutton-s-political-legacy-will-be-a-cautionary-tale-of-what-not-to-do-20250417-p5lsgi.

Mizen, Ronald. 2025b. 'How a crushing defeat shifted factional power in the Liberal Party.' *Australian Financial Review*, 29 May. www.afr.com/politics/federal/how-a-crushing-defeat-shifted-factional-power-in-the-liberal-party-20250526-p5m27u.

Moran, Jessica. 2025. 'Tasmanian Liberals reflect on how Coalition campaign didn't "read the tea leaves".' *ABC News*, 5 May. www.abc.net.au/news/2025-05-05/tasmanian-liberals-reflect-crushing-coalition-election-defeat/105252786.

Nicholas, Josh, Luke Mansillo, and Nick Evershed. 2025. 'Labor v the Coalition: Political opinion poll tracker.' *The Guardian*, 2 May. www.theguardian.com/australia-news/ng-interactive/2025/may/02/australia-election-polls-latest-aus-opinion-poll-tracker-results-current-polling-survey-labor-vs-liberal-dutton-albanese.

Nilsson, Anton. 2025. 'Was Dutton dishonest about his internal polling, or misled? Liberals believe it's the latter.' *Crikey*, 5 May. www.crikey.com.au/2025/05/05/peter-dutton-coalition-polling-ct-group-freshwater-strategy/.

Stockdale, Alan, Peta Seaton, and Richard Alston. 2025. 'For the Liberals to survive, NSW party reform is essential.' *Australian Financial Review*, 11 May. www.afr.com/politics/federal/for-the-liberals-to-survive-nsw-party-reform-is-essential-20250511-p5ly6h.

Sunman, Josh. 2025. 'Political chronicle: South Australia—July to December 2024.' *Australian Journal of Politics and History* 71, no. 2: 318–24. doi.org/10.1111/ajph.13051.

Taflaga, Marija. 2023. 'The Liberal Party of Australia.' In *Watershed: The 2022 Australian Federal Election*, edited by Anika Gauja, Marian Sawer, and Jill Sheppard, 203–22. Canberra: ANU Press. doi.org/10.22459/W.2023.10.

Tchetchenian, Charlie. 2025. 'Embattled NSW Liberal committee undergoes major shake-up, as moderates reassert dominance whilst fending off unexpected bid from Tony Abbott.' *Sky News*, 17 June. www.skynews.com.au/australia-news/politics/embattled-nsw-liberal-committee-undergoes-major-shakeup-as-moderates-reassert-dominance-whilst-fending-off-unexpected-bid-from-tony-abbott/news-story/0d0b2050ac7e842926216829270f2cb5.

12

The Nationals on the wombat trail

Richard Reid

Abstract

Compared with the stunning loss of seats by the Liberal Party, the Nationals had a more successful 2025 election. They held all their seats in the House of Representatives and two of three senators contesting were re-elected. However, the steadiness of the Nationals raises larger questions—first, about the party's future. While the Nationals were able to hold their seats and transition some of these to new MPs, they seem unable to expand. While in 2025 they showed more ambition than in 2022 there appear to be limited prospects for growth for the Nationals—besides a strong result in Bendigo. While holding 15–16 lower house seats ensures the Nationals' continued importance to Coalition hopes of forming government, guaranteeing frontbench positions and policy influence, it does raise questions about their claims to represent regional Australia while only holding about one-quarter of regional seats in the Federal Parliament.

Keywords: National Party; political representation; rural and regional Australia; parties; representative claims

The Nationals held all the House of Representatives seats they were defending. This differentiated them from their Coalition partners, who had a devastating defeat in the 2025 federal election. Not only did the Nationals hold all their lower house seats, but also, due to the Liberal Party's significant losses, they increased their proportional strength within the Coalition. This perhaps, at least in part, explains their bold negotiating style in the weeks after the election. This included a one-week split in the Coalition. This split was attributed by the Nationals to the Liberal Party's unwillingness to offer their continued commitment in four policy areas: the Regional Australia Future Fund, divestiture powers, universal service obligations for communications providers and nuclear power (see Nationals 2025b). Compared with the Liberals, the Nationals had a solid election result.

A danger is that, while attention focuses on the Liberal Party's need to rebuild, particularly in Australia's capital cities and with women voters, the broader implications of the results of the 2025 election for the Nationals will be underexamined. The Nationals' leader, David Littleproud (2025), has reflected that the 'overall election result was disappointing'. Prominent backbencher Colin Boyce called for Littleproud's resignation after 'what is a monumental political disaster for conservative politics' (see Scully and Holdsworth 2025). Clearly, the Nationals recognise that a Coalition defeat, even if the Nationals held all their lower house seats, is still a defeat.

While questions about the Nationals' survival have been quietened over recent elections, a new question has emerged: have the Nationals reached a ceiling in terms of their lower house representation? The party appears to be here to stay as a force in federal politics with their steady election results; however, this steadiness—only a movement in the range of one seat over the past five elections—could also be seen as evidence of an electoral ceiling, the implications of which are important for their ability to claim to 'represent the 9 million Australians who don't live in capital cities' (Senator Bridget McKenzie, quoted in Gould and Boscaini 2025).

In exploring the Nationals' 2025 election performance, this chapter is structured in four parts. First, it outlines the Nationals' campaign: 'the Wombat Trail'. Second, consideration turns to the election results where the Nationals were able to hold all their seats (except Senator Perin Davey in New South Wales) and, in several cases, had swings towards them, yet at the same time their inability to expand. The third part of the chapter explores the implications of the results and raises two questions: are the Nationals under an electoral ceiling and what does this mean for their claims to represent regional Australia? In considering the latter question, this chapter engages with the 'constructivist turn' in political representation (see Wolkenstein 2024) and, particularly, Michael Saward's (2010) representative-claims approach. There is a short conclusion that reflects on the next steps for research on the Nationals given the 2025 federal election results.

The campaign

The Nationals' campaign has long been known as the 'Wombat Trail'. This comprises the leader of the Nationals and other senior figures in the party making their way across rural, regional and remote Australia (see Ewart 2014). David Littleproud made this a feature of his campaign, travelling with a small wooden wombat, which was displayed in many of his campaign social media posts. As Littleproud posted on Instagram after the calling of the election, along with a video of himself collecting the wooden wombat and walking out of his office: 'It's on. See you on the Wombat Trail.' The symbolism is clear: the path for the Nationals is outside Australia's capital cities—the territory of the wombats.

In 2025, the Wombat Trail comprised visits to seats the Nationals were defending such as Cowper, which had faced a significant challenge from Community Independent Caz Heise in 2022 and who was running again in 2025 (see Gauja 2023; Hendriks and Reid 2023). In 2025, the Wombat Trail also involved Littleproud spending significant time in five main target seats for the Nationals: the newly created Bullwinkel in Western Australia, Lingiari in the Northern Territory, formerly Nationals-held Calare in New South Wales, Hunter in New South Wales and Bendigo in Victoria (the last of which proved the closest the Nationals came to expanding their number of seats). In addition to Littleproud, Victorian Senator Bridget McKenzie was a prominent feature of the Nationals' 2025 campaign, particularly in the key target seat of Bendigo in her home State of Victoria.

The National Party campaign focused on a range of policies. These included the Nationals' traditional focus on local infrastructure projects and grants—consistent with their slogan, 'Think local. Vote National'. Second was the Coalition's plan to halve the fuel excise for 12 months—a significant cost-saving for those living in regional Australia where there is a heavy reliance on private transport and longer driving distances. Third was the plan for a $20-billion Regional Australia Future Fund, which, it was argued, would provide an annual $1 billion to be spent in regional Australia, including on childcare, health care and infrastructure (Nationals 2025a). Fourth was the Coalition's policy to reduce energy prices through an East Coast gas reserve. And finally, tax cuts announced by Peter Dutton at the Coalition's campaign launch.

While the Nationals had been instrumental in driving the Coalition towards a nuclear energy policy, this featured less prominently in the campaign. Whether this was a result of strong campaigns against nuclear power or because the Nationals thought focusing on other policy areas would be more resonant in the seats they were contesting is unclear. What is clear is that during the campaign the Coalition policy of building seven nuclear reactors was not prominent in National Party election communications. However, this should not be read as signalling a lack of commitment to nuclear energy by the Nationals. Nuclear energy is one of the four policy commitments the Nationals wanted from the Liberal Party in the discussions over the post-election Coalition Agreement (see Nationals 2025b).

The election results

The House of Representatives

The Nationals held all the House of Representatives seats they were defending; they went into the election with 15 and held them all. This figure excludes Calare, which was won in 2022 by the Nationals' Andrew Gee, who subsequently left the party during the Forty-Seventh Parliament and who contested the 2025 election as an Independent incumbent. In these seats, the Nationals faced a variety of two-candidate-preferred challengers ranging from the Labor Party in most of their seats (13 of 15), to a Community Independent (in one seat) and Pauline Hanson's One Nation (one seat). Many Nationals seats are very safe and few incumbents were under any real pressure in this election. Illustrative of this is the fact that three Nationals seats were won on first preferences (Maranoa in Queensland, Gippsland in Victoria and New England in New South Wales) and nine of their 15 seats were won with more than 60 per cent of the two-candidate-preferred vote. The only concern for the Nationals was the seat of Cowper, with a strong Community Independent challenger from 2022, Caz Heise, running against Pat Conaghan again in 2025. The result was a very small swing to Conaghan (see Table 12.1).

Many Nationals MPs also had swings towards them in 2025, with the swings provided in this chapter based on the ABC's (2025) calculations, which factored in the effects of redistributions since the 2022 election. Four had positive first-preference swings (see Table 12.1). The swing to Sam Birrell in the Victorian seat of Nicholls, centred on the city of Shepparton, was largely the result of the absence of a Community Independent challenger in 2025 compared with 2022 when local businessman Rob Priestly mounted a significant challenge to the Nationals (see Hendriks and Reid 2023). In two-candidate-preferred terms, six Nationals had positive swings. However, in more than half the seats the Nationals were defending (nine of 15) there were two-candidate-preferred swings against them, the largest of which was in the western NSW seat of Parkes, where long-time member Mark Coulton was retiring.

Besides the swings to many Nationals MPs in an election that saw an overall swing to the Labor government, the other notable point was the transition to several new MPs in the Nationals' ranks. Three new MPs replaced retiring incumbents in, as mentioned earlier, Parkes and Lyne in New South Wales and Hinkler in Queensland. Prominent in local government, the new MP for Parkes, Jamie Chaffey, moved straight into the shadow assistant ministry (NSW Nationals 2025). Also significantly, David Gillespie in Lyne was replaced with Alison Penfold, increasing the representation of women in the Nationals' lower house numbers (a point discussed in more detail below).

Table 12.1 Election results in Nationals-held seats, 2025 (per cent)

Electorate	Nationals incumbent	Primary vote (swing from 2022)	Two-candidate-preferred vote (swing from 2022)
House of Representatives			
New England, NSW	Barnaby Joyce	52.2 (+1.4)	67.1 (+1.8)
Riverina, NSW	Michael McCormack	40.3 (–3.6)	62.6 (+2.9)
Cowper, NSW	Pat Conaghan	37.9 (–1.6)	52.5 (+0.1)
Parkes, NSW	Jamie Chaffey	39.9 (–9.0)	63.0 (–5.2)
Maranoa, Qld	David Littleproud	53.2 (–3.1)	70.1 (–2.0)
Page, NSW	Kevin Hogan	44.7 (–0.8)	59.3 (–1.4)
Gippsland, Vic.	Darren Chester	52.5 (–1.6)	69.4 (–1.2)
Nicholls, Vic.	Sam Birrell	46.3 (+21.9)	64.4 (–1.4)
Capricornia, Qld	Michelle Landry	36.6 (–2.9)	55.8 (–0.8)
Flynn, Qld	Colin Boyce	37.4 (+0.6)	60.2 (+6.4)
Wide Bay, Qld	Llew O'Brien	39.1 (–4.4)	57.6 (–3.7)
Dawson, Qld	Andrew Willcox	41.7 (–1.6)	61.8 (+1.4)
Lyne, NSW	Alison Penfold	36.2 (–7.3)	59.8 (–4.0)
Hinkler, Qld	David Batt	38.0 (–4.1)	56.3 (–3.8)
Mallee, Vic.	Anne Webster	49.7 (+0.6)	69.0 (+0.1)

Electorate	Nationals incumbent	Primary vote (swing from 2022)	Two-candidate-preferred vote (swing from 2022)
Senate			
NSW	Perin Davey	Defeated	
NT	Jacinta Nampijinpa Price	Re-elected	
Qld	Susan McDonald	Re-elected	

Source: ABC (2025).

The Nationals demonstrated ambition in seeking to expand at the 2025 election. For example, in the 2022 election, the Nationals contested only six House of Representatives seats that they did not already hold (see Gauja 2023: 227). In 2025, the Nationals fielded challengers in 12 electorates. These included five of the six they contested unsuccessfully in 2022 (excluding Indi): Hunter, Richmond, Lingiari, Barker and Durack. The Nationals significantly expanded their efforts in Western Australia, where, in addition to Durack, they also contested the Liberal-held seats of O'Connor and Forrest, and former WA Nationals leader Mia Davies ran in the newly created seat of Bullwinkel. In South Australia, the Nationals contested the Liberal-held seats of Barker and Grey. None of the National Party candidates in any of the six seats they contested in Western Australia or South Australia was in the final distribution of preferences. Their primary votes ranged from 1.74 per cent in Barker to 15.77 per cent in Bullwinkel. These results demonstrate the weakness of the National Party at the federal level in these two States. In Queensland, the LNP sought to unseat former Nationals MP and founder of Katter's Australian Party, Bob Katter, but had a swing against them in terms of both their primary and their two-candidate-preferred votes. The final two seats, along with Bullwinkel, were where the Nationals put most effort into the campaign: Calare in New South Wales and Bendigo in Victoria.

Since Independent Peter Andren retired in 2007, the Nationals had returned a member for Calare. It was held by John Cobb from 2007 to 2016 and, more recently, by former cabinet minister Andrew Gee. Following the Nationals' announcement of their opposition to a constitutionally enshrined Indigenous Voice to Parliament, Gee resigned from the Nationals to sit as an Independent. At the 2025 election, the Nationals sought to win the seat back from Gee with high-profile former NSW State minister Sam Farraway. While Farraway received more first-preference votes than Gee (see Table 12.2), he was unable to win the seat for the Nationals, with Gee securing 56.8 per cent of the two-candidate-preferred vote (and a 22.2 per cent swing away from the Nationals). Gee's re-election is evidence of a perennial problem for the Nationals of MPs resigning from the party and then holding their seats as Independents (for example, Bob Katter in Kennedy) or former members running as Independents against National Party incumbents (Tony Windsor in New England and Rob Oakeshott in Lyne, both in New South Wales).

In Victoria, where the Nationals hold three seats in the House of Representatives, there was heavy investment in challenging incumbent Labor backbench MP Lisa Chesters in the regional seat of Bendigo. The National Party preselected prominent local businessman Andrew Lethlean and senior Nationals Littleproud and McKenzie campaigned in the seat. While unable to defeat the incumbent, the Nationals outperformed the Liberal candidate in a three-cornered contest and managed to secure a large, 9.8 per cent swing against Labor in two-candidate-preferred terms (factoring in the redistribution since 2022), reducing Labor's margin to 2,983 votes. This result was a highlight for the Nationals, with McKenzie (2025) referring to the 'remarkable 10 per cent shift away from the government in Bendigo, where Labor's neglect of the regions has been acutely felt'.

Table 12.2 Election results in Nationals-contested seats, 2025 (per cent)

Electorate	Nationals candidate	Primary vote (swing from 2022)	Two-candidate-preferred vote (swing from 2022)
House of Representatives			
Bullwinkel, WA	Mia Davies	15.8 (+14.4)	–
Bendigo, Vic.	Andrew Lethlean	29.7 (+28.8)	48.6 (+9.8)
Calare, NSW	Sam Farraway	29.7 (–18.0)	43.2 (–22.2)
Hunter, NSW	Sue Gilroy	18.2 (–6.5)	–
Richmond, NSW	Kimberly Hone	24.6 (+1.2)	40.0 (–1.8)
Lingiari, NT	Lisa Siebert (CLP)	31.0 (–3.5)	41.9 (–6.5)
Kennedy, Qld	Annette Swaine	23.8 (–4.4)	34.2 (–2.7)
Barker, SA	Jonathan Pietzsch	1.7 (–0.6)	–
Grey, SA	Peter Borda	3.1 (+3.1)	–
Durack, WA	Bailey Kempton	13.6 (+4.2)	–
Forrest, WA	Cam Parsons	4.8 (+4.8)	–
O'Connor, WA	Heidi Tempra	12.8 (+12.8)	–

Electorate	Nationals candidate	Primary vote (swing from 2022)	Two-candidate-preferred vote (swing from 2022)
Senate			
Vic.	Glenn Arnold	Not elected	
SA	Monique Crossling Emma Azzopardi	Not elected Not elected	
WA	Paul Brown Jeremy Miles	Not elected Not elected	

Source: ABC (2025).

The Senate

In the Senate, the Nationals are largely constrained by Coalition agreements in New South Wales and Victoria and the merged party in Queensland (more on this below). In Queensland, shadow minister Susan McDonald was re-elected as the Nationals have second spot on the LNP ticket. However, the party's biggest disappointment in the election was the defeat of deputy leader Perin Davey. Due to the NSW Coalition Agreement, the Nationals were placed in third position on the Coalition joint ticket at the 2025 election (Davey, in Oriti 2025) and, due to the loss of support for the Liberal Party, the joint ticket could only secure two seats in the State— both Liberals. Davey (in Oriti 2025) reflected that she was 'shattered' by the result.

Jacinta Nampijinpa Price was re-elected for the CLP in the Northern Territory. However, days after the election, Price announced she would no longer sit within the Nationals party room in Canberra and would be joining the Liberal Party—a move that attracted significant criticism from Nationals MPs and senators who saw it in terms of disloyalty. Bridget McKenzie, while accepting it was a decision for Senator Price, commented: 'Loyalty is a rare commodity in politics but it's an essential one, and out in the bush, it's worth everything' (quoted in Aidone 2025). Lower-profile LNP (Nationals) MP Michelle Landry saw it in similar terms: 'We're all very upset that she's decided to move over to the Liberals and I just think that there's a lack of loyalty there' (quoted in Aidone 2025). Consequently, in the Forty-Eighth Parliament, the Nationals will have only four senators compared with the six they had in the previous parliament: Bridget McKenzie (Victoria), Ross Cadell (New South Wales), Matt Canavan (Queensland) and Susan McDonald (Queensland).

The Nationals were unable to win any new Senate seats. Glenn Arnold was in the unwinnable fourth spot on the joint Coalition ticket in Victoria. As part of the Victorian Coalition Agreement, it appears the Nationals are only given a winnable position (second) every second election. In South Australia and Western Australia, where the Nationals run separately from the Liberal Party in the Senate, they received very low first-preference votes—5,695 votes (0.5 per cent) and 58,043 votes (3.6 per cent), respectively—and were unable to secure any Senate seats.

Women's representation in the National Party

Of the 15 House of Representatives seats held by the Nationals going into the 2025 election, only two had women incumbents (Michelle Landry in Capricornia in Queensland and Anne Webster in Mallee in Victoria) and one a woman candidate (Alison Penfold in Lyne, NSW). While this was an increase from 2022 as Penfold was selected to replace David Gillespie in Lyne, following the election, only 20 per cent of Nationals MPs are women. The figure is higher in the Senate at 50 per cent (two of four) following the defection of Price and the defeat of Davey and includes the Nationals' Senate Leader, Bridget McKenzie. In the Forty-Seventh Parliament, 67 per cent of Nationals senators were women (four of six), including McKenzie as Senate Leader and Davey as the party's deputy leader. Following the defeat of Davey in the 2025 election, the deputy leadership of the Nationals moved to a man (Kevin Hogan), reducing the representation of women in the party's leadership group.

In terms of House of Representatives candidates in unheld seats, six of the 12 were women (50 per cent); this is a marked increase on 2022 when only four women in total were selected by the Nationals for the House of Representatives, including the two incumbents, Landry and Webster (Gauja 2023: 227). This is a significant development in terms of greater representation of women in the National Party's parliamentary team. However, it also reflects a well-known barrier to increasing women's representation: when women are selected, even in increasing numbers, they tend to be selected in less winnable seats. Hopefully, as incumbent male MPs retire, more women will be selected to replace them and, as the Nationals tend to hold quite safe seats, this will be an important pathway to increasing the representation of women within the Nationals in the House of Representatives.

Compared with the 2022 election, Bridget McKenzie played a prominent role in the Nationals' 2025 campaign and arguably has as high if not a higher national profile than the party's leader, David Littleproud. Senator Price, before her decision to sit with the Liberal Party, was another high-profile woman in the National Party. Her comments during the campaign to 'make Australia great again' received significant attention in the national media for their resonance with the campaign politics of US President Donald Trump (see Truu 2025; Chapter 4, this volume) and were seen to hurt the Coalition's campaign.

Coalition agreements

Following the election, the federal Coalition Agreement between the Liberal Party and the National Party received significant attention. However, the range of National Party House of Representatives candidates and the results in the Senate demonstrate the importance of State-level Coalition agreements and arrangements. In Western Australia (Durack and O'Connor) and South Australia (Barker), the Nationals challenged three incumbent Liberal MPs and ran separately in the Senate, whereas in New South Wales and Victoria, there was more collaboration, with the Nationals not challenging any sitting Liberals and running a joint ticket in the Senate. In Queensland and the Northern Territory, where the parties are united in one organisation at the subnational level, there were clearly no electoral challenges between the parties.

The convention for many years now has been that CLP senators from the Northern Territory sit in the Nationals' party room in Canberra. While they are not bound by this convention, it is the expectation. However, the LNP in Queensland is different. The issue is that at the State level there is one party (the LNP) but at the federal level there are two. While the Liberal Party and the Nationals are almost always in Coalition and meet in a joint party room, they retain two distinct identities at the federal level and have separate party rooms. For the Federal Parliament, Queensland's electorates have been divided between those who will sit in the Nationals' party room and those who will sit in the Liberals' party room in Canberra. The example of Ian Macfarlane, who attempted to move from the Liberals to the Nationals but was blocked by the LNP executive, shows that LNP MPs cannot choose in which party room they sit.

The arrangements, however, are not just about conflict or collaboration but also, in the Senate, about the ordering of joint tickets. As mentioned above, in Victoria the Nationals appear to be given a winnable spot every second election (not in 2025, with Glenn Arnold in the fourth position). On the NSW joint Senate ticket, in one election the Nationals are second and in the next third and so forth. In 2025 they were third, costing Perin Davey her seat because of the loss of support for the Coalition (see Davey, in Oriti 2025). The position of the Nationals is stronger in Queensland, where they have the second spot each election, basically guaranteeing a National Party senator is elected at every half-Senate election; spots on the Senate ticket are allocated based on with which party Senate candidates will sit in Canberra. More research on these State-level Coalition agreements would much enrich our understanding of these arrangements and their effects on not only State but also federal politics.

Implications of the results

Are the Nationals facing an electoral ceiling?

From the increased number of National Party candidates in 2025 compared with 2022, there is evidently an appetite for expansion within the Nationals. However, as shown in Table 12.3, the Nationals seem unable to move beyond 15–16 seats. In fact, while the Nationals dipped as low as 10 seats in 2007, they have not been able to regain their high of 18 seats, which they won in 1996. Some might see their 2007 low, and the ability to return between 15 and 16 MPs each election since 2013, as an electoral floor. The consistency of the Nationals' numbers and their ability to hold their seats raise important questions about how the Nationals, particularly compared with the Liberal Party, can keep their seats so safe from electoral challenge. There are potentially multiple explanations for this, including the National Party's organisation on the ground, all of which require further exploration.

A second interpretation of the consistent numbers of National Party MPs focuses less on an electoral floor and instead asks whether the Nationals are operating under an electoral ceiling. Further, while recognising that the Nationals have never held all rural and regional seats, what might the party be able to do to broaden their support across regional Australia? The result in Bendigo is important in this regard as it demonstrates that there is potential for the Nationals to expand into new territory where they can select a high-profile, locally prominent candidate and invest significant financial resources and the time of leading Nationals figures. However, there still seems to be something preventing the Nationals from appealing to a broader regional audience considering their poor performances in their other target seats—Bullwinkel, Hunter and Lingiari—and their inability to take back Calare from Andrew Gee.

Table 12.3 Nationals seats won in federal elections, 1996–2025

1996	1998	2001	2004	2007	2010	2013	2016	2019	2022	2025
18	16	13	12	10	12	15	16	16	16	15

Source: The author's calculations.

While the Nationals may eventually win back Calare, like they did Lyne from Rob Oakeshott, the question remains why is the party unable to expand their presence across rural and regional Australia? The Nationals now hold only 32 per cent of the electorates designated as rural by the AEC and only 12.5 per cent of provincial electorates (those outside capital cities but mostly in provincial cities). Taken together, the Nationals hold only 15 of the 62 House of Representatives seats outside capital cities (see Table 12.4). The Nationals hold no federal seats in Western Australia, where there are three rural electorates (the Nationals ran in all three in 2025); South Australia, where there are also three rural electorates (the Nationals ran in two in 2025, but not in Centre Alliance–held Mayo); or the Northern Territory, where there is one rural electorate currently held by the Labor Party's Marion Scrymgour.

Table 12.4 Rural and provincial electorates by party held, 2025

	Total	Nationals	Liberal Party	Labor Party	Independents and minor parties
Rural electorates	38	12	13	9	4
Provincial electorates	24	3	6	15	0
Total	62	15	19	24	4

Source: The author's calculations based on AEC profiles (see AEC 2025a).

The Nationals' representative claim-making

Central to the Nationals' claims to represent regional Australians is that they only hold rural or provincial (regional) seats. Yet, they hold only 24.2 per cent of rural and provincial seats and, as discussed earlier, they appear to be unable to expand into new territory. So, what does this mean for their claims to represent regional Australia—the '9 million Australians who don't live in capital cities' (McKenzie, quoted in Gould and Boscaini 2025)? Such claims were central to the Nationals' campaign and are, indeed, fundamental to their identity as a party (see Reid et al. 2024).

It is important to stress here that this is not to question the Nationals' sincerity in their claims. Nor does this chapter make any attempt to evaluate in any 'objective' or policy sense whether the Nationals do or do not represent regional Australians or do or do not represent regional Australians well. This is important to make clear. This chapter, engaging with the broader 'constructivist turn' in political representation, and in particular Michael Saward's (2006, 2010) representative-claims approach, rather focuses on an understanding of representation as claim-based, constitutive of political identities and dynamic.

This claim-making approach focuses on the importance of relevant audiences in assessing claims to represent, with the central question being whether they are aware of and then whether they accept or reject claims to represent (see Saward 2010). While the representative-claims approach moves away from elections as the arbiter of representation—'We need to move away from the idea that representation is first and foremost a given, factual product of elections, rather than a precarious and curious sort of claim about a dynamic relationship' (Saward 2006: 298)—it is contended here that elections provide one means for assessing the reception of claims to represent.

For the Nationals, it would be fair to argue that regional Australians are a key audience. So, the fact the Nationals seem unable to expand their electoral success with more regional Australians does appear to suggest that many regional Australians lack either awareness or acceptance of the Nationals' claims to represent them. There is always a supply dimension here—party offerings—and this is partly the result of State-level Coalition agreements, as discussed above. However, that the Nationals were unable to gain any new seats in the 2025 election at the same time as competing in more seats than in 2022 does suggest that, for whatever reasons, their claims to represent in 2025 were not accepted by many regional Australians.

This naturally goes to the heart of the challenge to claim to represent such a diverse people as *regional Australians*: people ranging from those who live in Wollongong or Townsville to those in remote parts of Western Australia and the Northern Territory, and every type of rural, regional and remote community in between. Again, the point here is not to make any assessment of the sincerity of the efforts of the Nationals or the effects of their policies or actions in pursuing their understanding of the interests of regional Australians. But, rather, to ask the question: why are so many regional Australians voting not for the Nationals but for the Liberal

Party, the Labor Party or for Independents and minor parties? The level of support for the Nationals among regional Australians and its causes are central questions for the Nationals moving forward. Indeed, exploring these questions will be crucial if the Nationals wish to move beyond what appears to be an electoral ceiling.

Conclusion

The aftermath of the 2025 election has proven tumultuous for the Coalition. The first split in the Coalition since the late 1980s (albeit only for a week), the defection of Senator Jacinta Nampijinpa Price and the challenge by Senator Matt Canavan to the leadership of David Littleproud—with the aim of putting pressure on the Coalition's commitment to net-zero by 2050 (see Coorey 2025)—highlight the wounds from the Coalition's defeat. While the Nationals fared better than their Liberal partners in holding on to their seats—a consistency that requires further examination—this chapter suggests that this should not distract from the serious questions for the Nationals and their claimed role as the representatives of regional Australians.

Building on these reflections on the 2025 election, the Nationals are an excellent case for a range of future research. Much more academic study of the Nationals is needed and would perhaps help to answer the questions posed in this chapter, particularly in terms of their organisation both centrally and in their electorates, the views of regional Australians on the Nationals, the party's claims to represent regional Australians and the reasons many regional Australians do not vote for the Nationals. Beyond the views of audiences, more research is also needed to understand the claims to represent of the Nationals and the understandings of Nationals MPs and senators of regional Australia, its interests and its values.

This chapter, in reflecting on the Nationals' results in the 2025 federal election, has raised two questions. First, what is the potential for growth for the Nationals in the federal parliament and, second, what are the implications of their current numbers for their claims to represent regional Australians? Due to their ability to hold their seats, the Nationals will remain an important part of any Coalition attempt to form government, ensuring continued access to power and influence over policy. However, while not evaluating whether the Nationals, in their actions, represent regional Australians, this chapter has drawn attention to important questions about the reception of the Nationals' claims to represent regional Australians.

These questions emerge when considering the election results using Saward's representative-claims approach, within the broader 'constructivist turn' in studies of political representation. Whether or not the Nationals reflect on these questions, the party remains a fascinating case for the study of contemporary political representation and party organisation in Australia.

References

Aidone, David. 2025. 'Ley in, Tehan out of Liberal leadership bid as rift over Price's defection emerges.' *SBS News*, 8 May, [Updated 10 May 2025]. www.sbs.com.au/news/article/liberals-set-date-for-leadership-vote-as-keating-criticises-albanese-cabinet-reshuffle/29m4fp8jl.

Australian Broadcasting Corporation (ABC). 2025. 'Federal election 2025—Australia votes.' *ABC News*. www.abc.net.au/news/elections/federal-election-2025.

Australian Electoral Commission (AEC). 2025a. 'Current electorate names.' *Electorate Finder*. Canberra: Australian Electoral Commission. www.aec.gov.au/profiles/.

Australian Electoral Commission (AEC). 2025b. 'House of Representatives—final results.' *Tally Room: 2025 Federal Election*. Canberra: Australian Electoral Commission. results.aec.gov.au/31496/Website/HouseDefault-31496.htm.

Coorey, Phillip. 2025. 'Coalition crisis worsens as Canavan mounts challenge.' *Australian Financial Review*, 9 May. www.afr.com/politics/federal/ley-declares-her-hand-price-defection-backfires-20250509-p5lxua.

Ewart, Heather. 2014. 'On the wombat trail: The history of the Nationals.' *ABC News*, 20 November, [Updated 21 November 2014]. www.abc.net.au/news/2014-11-20/ewart-on-the-wombat-trail-the-history-of-the-nationals/5905454.

Gauja, Anika. 2023. 'The National Party of Australia.' In *Watershed: The 2022 Australian Federal Election*, edited by Anika Gauja, Marian Sawer, and Jill Sheppard, 223–39. Canberra: ANU Press. doi.org/10.22459/W.2023.11.

Gould, Courtney, and Joshua Boscaini. 2025. 'Federal politics: Bridget McKenzie says Coalition needs a "deep" assessment of campaign—as it happened.' *ABC News*, 14 May. www.abc.net.au/news/2025-05-14/federal-politics-blog-albanese-ley/105288276.

Hendriks, Carolyn M., and Richard Reid. 2023. 'The rise and impact of Australia's movement for Community Independents.' In *Watershed: The 2022 Australian Federal Election*, edited by Anika Gauja, Marian Sawer, and Jill Sheppard, 279–304. Canberra: ANU Press. doi.org/10.22459/W.2023.14.

Littleproud, David. 2025. 'The Hon David Littleproud's June opinion piece.' Media release, 9 June. Dalby: David Littleproud. davidlittleproud.com.au/the-hon-david-littleprouds-june-opinion-piece/.

McKenzie, Bridget. 2025. 'Why the Nationals are forging their own path for Australia.' *Australian Financial Review*, 20 May: 39. www.afr.com/politics/federal/why-the-nationals-are-forging-their-own-path-for-australia-20250520-p5m0qv.

Nationals. 2025a. 'Coalition launches Regional Australia Future Fund.' *National Party of Australia*, 10 April. www.nationals.org.au/news-posts/coalition-launches-regional-australia-future-fund.

Nationals. 2025b. 'The Nationals forge their own path for regional Australia.' *National Party of Australia*, 20 May. www.nationals.org.au/news-posts/the-nationals-forge-their-own-path-for-regional-australia.

NSW Nationals. 2025. 'Nationals' new shadow cabinet.' *National Party of Australia for Regional NSW*, 28 May. www.nswnationals.org.au/new-shadow-cabinet/.

Oriti, Thomas. 2025. 'Breakfast with Thomas Oriti.' [Interview with Perin Davey]. *ABC News Radio*, 6 May. perindavey.com.au/abc-news-radio-breakfast-with-thomas-oriti/ [page discontinued].

Reid, Richard, Carolyn M. Hendriks, and Anika Gauja. 2024. 'Representing rural Australia: Political representation and rural discontent.' *Australian Journal of Political Science* 59, no. 3: 255–71. doi.org/10.1080/10361146.2024.2416180.

Saward, Michael. 2006. 'The representative claim.' *Contemporary Political Theory* 5, no. 3: 297–318. doi.org/10.1057/palgrave.cpt.9300234.

Saward, Michael. 2010. *The Representative Claim*. Oxford: Oxford University Press. doi.org/10.1093/acprof:oso/9780199579389.001.0001.

Scully, Jess, and Rachel Holdsworth. 2025. 'Nationals weigh up increased Coalition role after federal election.' *ABC News*, 5 May. www.abc.net.au/news/2025-05-05/nationals-push-more-shadow-ministries-liberal-election-result/105252704.

Truu, Maani. 2025. 'Jacinta Nampijinpa Price vows to "make Australia great again", accuses media of being "Trump obsessed".' *ABC News*, 12 April. www.abc.net.au/news/2025-04-12/jacinta-nampijinpa-price-trump-make-australia-great-again/105169348.

Wolkenstein, Fabio. 2024. 'Revisiting the constructivist turn in political representation.' *European Journal of Political Theory* 23, no. 2: 277–87. doi.org/10.1177/14748851211055951.

13

The Greens' campaign

Stewart Jackson and Josh Holloway

Abstract

The Australian Greens entered the 2025 federal election hoping to consolidate and expand their parliamentary representation, with the re-election of high-profile MPs such as Adam Bandt and Max Chandler-Mather seen as likely. While the party secured six Senate seats, as expected, its lower house performance fell short: Bandt lost Melbourne and two of the three Queensland-held seats also fell to Labor. Despite these losses, the national House of Representatives vote remained stable and the Senate result underscored the party's ongoing strength in proportional contests. This chapter argues that the Greens' campaign was constrained less by voter repudiation than by structural and strategic challenges: resurgent Labor support, competition from climate-focused Independents and the difficulty of converting national support into local victories. In highlighting both setbacks and signs of growth, particularly in outer suburban areas, the 2025 election offers insight into the party's evolving electoral terrain—and the recalibrations likely required for future success.

Keywords: Australian Greens; election; campaign; policy salience; results

The 2025 federal election offered the Australian Greens both significant opportunity and electoral risk. Following a period of growing influence in national politics, marked by three lower house wins in 2022 and a strengthened Senate presence, the party entered the 2025 campaign with significant ambitions. The Greens sought to not only retain current representation, but also secure decisive influence over a (Labor) minority government by way of expanded presence in the House of Representatives. Yet, soon after polling day, those ambitions had collapsed. The Greens lost two of their three Queensland seats and, most strikingly, party leader Adam Bandt's long-held seat of Melbourne. While the party maintained its Senate representation, the result prompted a flurry of media commentary describing the election as a repudiation of the Greens' political project.

This chapter takes a more tempered view. It argues that while the Greens' 2025 federal campaign did fall short of its lower house ambitions, this outcome is better understood as a product of structural constraints and strategic tensions rather than *widespread* voter rejection. The party's continued Senate success affirms a stable base of national support, while losses in the House point to the difficulty of replicating high-intensity local organising strategies, the challenge of adapting narrative and tactics in response to a resurgent Labor Party and growing competition from ideologically adjacent Independents. These results underscore the enduring tensions faced by policy-seeking minor parties operating within a preferential, majoritarian electoral system. This chapter therefore evaluates the Greens' performance not solely in terms of vote share, but also in relation to institutional context, interparty dynamics, policy consistency, narrative framing and organisational execution.

A distinctive feature of the Greens' recent strategy was emphasis on year-round local campaigning, mutual-aid initiatives and embedded grassroots organising. Yet, the 2025 election suggests this model has limitations. While powerful in electorates with existing activist networks and favourable demographics, its expansion into electorates with weaker campaign infrastructure and distinct political circumstances exposed limits to scalability. But even where this strategy was executed most successfully—indeed, where it was pioneered—in the electorates of Griffith and Melbourne, the party's support still receded. Simultaneously, the party struggled to distinguish its national narrative as the Coalition's campaign faltered and Labor's electoral prospects improved.

The chapter proceeds in four parts. It first reviews the inter-election period (2022–25), identifying patterns in the Greens' subnational performance and campaign development. The second section analyses the 2025 election results across the House and the Senate, drawing on both national trends and electorate-level data. The third section evaluates the campaign narrative, policy emphases, legislative positioning and organisational strategy, asking what worked, what did not and why. The concluding section reflects on the implications of these results for the Greens' future, identifying both the constraints they face and the paths available for strategic recalibration.

The inter-election period: 2022–2025

For the period 2022–25, encompassing all State and Territory elections, including for the Brisbane City Council, the Greens generally experienced increasing vote share and rising seat numbers in lower houses. The 2022 federal election, in which the party won three Brisbane inner-city seats, was seen as a high point in the period leading into the 2025 contest. State elections in Western Australia, New South Wales, Queensland, Victoria, the Australian Capital Territory and Tasmania, however, brought mixed results—although only the ACT saw a significant slide in vote share (see Table 13.1). The Greens defended incumbent seats in New South Wales and expanded their numbers in Western Australia and Tasmania due to changes to those States' electoral systems. In the Northern Territory, long considered one of the hardest jurisdictions for Greens breakthroughs, they succeeded in electing one MLA and came close to electing a second. However, both the ACT and Queensland brought reversals, even as the overall vote in Queensland remained steady. The ACT Greens, in particular, faced stiff competition from high-profile left-leaning Independents, and ultimately lost two seats.

Across the 2022–25 period, various campaign strategies and slogans were used by both the ALP and the Coalition to counter some of the more high-profile efforts supported by the Greens. There was general agreement among all parliamentary parties that Russia's invasion of Ukraine in 2022 was unlawful and should be strongly resisted (even as the details of how to do that varied). The war, however, compounded the lingering economic effects of the Covid-19 pandemic. Although the Australian economy appeared to have rebounded, housing affordability remained a serious problem, with the housing market continuing to outpace wages growth. The disruption caused by turning a major grain producer (Ukraine) into a net importer of food, combined with European sanctions on Russian gas, contributed to price rises across Europe. While Australia was somewhat insulated from these European shocks, the consumer price index continued to rise through 2022 and 2023, before declining to closer to the pre-Covid mean (ABS 2025).

Table 13.1 Greens vote and seat shares, Australian elections, 2022–2025

Year	State/ Territory/ national	House of Representatives (%)	+/– (%)	Seats won	+/–	Senate (%)	+/– (%)	Seats won	+/–
2022	SA	9.1	3	0	0	9.0	3.2	1	0
2022	Federal	12.2	1.8	4	+3	–	–	6	+3
2022	Vic.	11.5	0.8	4	+1	10.3	1.1	4	+3
2023	NSW	9.7	0.1	3	0	9.1	0.6	2	0
2024	Tas.[a]	14.4	4	5	+3	–	–	1	–
2024	[Brisbane City]	23.2	5	2	+1	–	–	–	–
2024	NT	8.1	4	1	+1	–	–	–	–
2024	ACT	12.2	–1.3	4	–2	–	–	–	–
2024	QLD	9.9	0	1	–1	–	–	–	–
2025	WA[b]	11.1	4	0	0	10.9	4.6	4	+3
2025	National[c]	10.9	1.8	22	+5	9.8	2.4	11	+6

Notes: [a] Tasmania changed the number of seats in the House of Assembly from 25 to 35 in 2022. The Tasmanian Greens also hold one of 15 Legislative Council seats (Hobart, elected in 2024) that are elected at intervals not necessarily coinciding with House of Assembly elections; [b] Western Australia abolished the previous six multi-member districts in the Legislative Council, replacing them with a single Statewide electorate; [c] The federal Senate and the Legislative Councils in New South Wales and South Australia hold election by half at each election. The elected total of Greens upper house members is twenty.

Source: Various electoral commissions.

The 7 October 2023 attack on Israel by terrorist group Hamas, which claimed the lives of more than 1,200 people—including civilians, military personnel and police—and saw 251 people taken hostage, brought widespread condemnation. However, the Israeli Government's retaliatory strikes and continuing war against Hamas, marked by a high civilian death toll, drew more divided political responses. This was particularly evident in Adam Bandt's decision not to support an ALP-sponsored motion condemning Hamas because it did not also condemn actions by the Israeli Defence Forces (Clarke 2023). The Greens' position became especially prominent when their senators staged a walkout from the chamber in protest at the Labor government's ongoing support for Israel despite mounting allegations of war crimes (Karp 2023). This move attracted sharp criticism from political opponents and media outlets (see Stone 2024) but also drew praise from sections of the party's activist base and aligned civil society groups. A consistent message from conservative media outlets was that the Greens were supporters of terrorist organisations such as Hamas, Hezbollah and the Islamic Revolutionary Guard Corps by endorsing rallies at which flags of these organisations were flown (Molan 2024; Hildebrand 2024). Though external to campaign mechanics, this episode likely shaped elements of the party's public image and media coverage leading into the 2025 election.

Importantly, a new set of campaigning ideas began to take hold within the Greens during this period. The rise of the party in Brisbane was foreshadowed by the success of Jono Sriranganathan in the Brisbane City Council elections, followed by State-level victories for Michael Berkman and Amy McMahon (the latter losing her seat in the 2024 Queensland election). The Greens' emphasis on inter-election doorknocking and community organising—including self-help and food delivery services during the Covid pandemic and the 2022 floods—proved successful in the 2020–22 period. The 2022 federal election campaign was explicitly modelled on these approaches, with potential Greens MPs campaigning early and intensely on local concerns. Max Chandler-Mather in Griffith and Stephen Bates in Brisbane focused particularly on renters' rights, aircraft noise and housing affordability.

The idea of the 'permanent election' was the basis of this organising, with the Greens identifying ongoing community contact as key to winning seats. This was most evident after the Brisbane floods, just before the 2022 federal election, when assisting people in need turned into garnering votes (Flenady 2022). While data-driven forms of campaigning have dominated recent electoral cycles (Kefford 2021), the Greens' approach marked a potential shift in party–community relations. However, community organising and election campaigning have different ends—one focused on issue outcomes, the other on electoral outcomes. These goals are not inherently incompatible, but nor are they always aligned (Powell 2023). The 2025 campaign would become a test of whether the Greens could successfully scale this local organising model and convert it into durable national gains.

Results

There is a risk of overinterpreting the Greens' election results. Opinion polling and expectations played a role in framing the outcome but, by the campaign's final weeks, a clear pattern had emerged. The Greens had polled steadily between 12 per cent and 13 per cent nationally—and occasionally as high as 14.5 per cent. The poll aggregator Australian Election Forecasts (AEF 2025) predicted a modest Labor majority, with the Greens on track to win between two and eight lower house seats, with four most likely. On election night, however, the party faced a significant setback. The Greens lost Adam Bandt's long-held seat of Melbourne, along with two of the three Queensland seats gained in the 2022 'Greenslide' (Griffith and Brisbane). Although the national House of Representatives vote remained stable, the loss of high-profile MPs created a powerful narrative of decline. The Senate outcome, however, was notably stronger. The Greens comfortably returned a senator in each State, maintaining their overall Senate numbers, and, in some cases, obtained close to or even exceeded a full quota on first preferences.

The divergence in the Greens' success across chambers is crucial. The 2025 election should not be seen as a repudiation of the Greens, but as an illustration of the structural constraints, strategic vulnerabilities and contested terrain the party must navigate, especially when expanding beyond its institutional heartland in the Senate. Indeed, there is considerable reason to doubt the narrative quickly emerging among media and political commentators that the results reflect a widespread repudiation of the party (Dalidakis 2025), mark a failed political project (Keane 2025) or should prompt an identity crisis akin to that now faced by the Liberal Party (Williams 2025). Some commentary seemed celebration masquerading as analysis, reading from the Greens' electoral shortfalls supposed voter feedback on singular policy issues (Dyrenfurth 2025). The Greens did suffer significant setbacks in the House of Representatives, and these should not be minimised. Yet, the 2025 election also appears to be a consolidation of the party's position and role in the upper house.

Lenses customarily used in evaluating the electoral performances of Labor and the Coalition often misidentify dilemmas faced by minor parties. First, the Greens are a policy-seeking, rather than purely office-seeking, party, making for goals quite distinct from those of major parties (Adams et al. 2006; Bischof and Wagner 2017). Second, the Greens' organisational structure, even following centralising change, still makes for an internal balance-of-power that constrains the behaviour of the parliamentary party (Jackson 2016). Third, the Greens occupy a peculiar space in Australia's electoral and legislative party systems. Unlike the Nationals, they lack any underpinning social cleavage capable of reliably corralling winning majorities. Unlike most successful Independents, the Greens advance a policy platform well left of the centrist ideological positions claimed by many Australians and cannot benefit from 'anti-party' sentiment. Except in Melbourne, when the Greens have won seats in the House, they have done so relying on precise ballot orders and party preference flows in complex multiparty contests. Predominantly, the Greens are a party of the Senate.

Figure 13.1 Greens vote share, House of Representatives and Senate, 1993–2025

Source: AEC.

Clearly the Greens have aspirations beyond the Senate. And voters did shift away from the party, including in lower house electorates previously represented by a Greens MP. Figure 13.1 charts the party's national share of first preferences in the House and the Senate in elections from 1993 to 2025. At this level, the Greens' 2025 performance is surpassed only by the 2022 and, for the Senate, 2010 elections. The Greens have never attracted sudden surges of support; rather, 2025 solidifies a long-term trend of gradual growth. But there is an apparent limit to their appeal, no matter the competitive conditions, at a share of roughly 12–14 per cent of the vote.

In some respects, though, nationally aggregated figures do not matter. At the subnational level there is only minimal variation, with sufficient support across States to reach a Senate quota either on first preferences (Tasmania) or relatively comfortably via distribution of preferences (all other States). At the House of Representatives electorate level, though, we see marked differences. Table 13.2 shows first-preference vote shares and absolute swings in electorates that: 1) were held by Greens MPs before the election (in bold); 2) were nominated by the party as target seats (italicised); or 3) recorded Greens support greater than 20 per cent in 2025. The Greens lost support in all four seats with incumbent MPs, though only marginally so in Griffith, Ryan and Brisbane. They meanwhile saw mixed success in their five 'target seats' of Wills, Richmond, Macnamara, Perth and Sturt (Australian Greens 2025). Given that the party also furnished considerable resources on other local campaigns, such as in Moreton (Smee 2025), it could be that the Greens' limited resources were stretched far too thin across disparate seats —some of which, such as Macnamara and Sturt, had only a limited chance of electing a Greens MP.

There is a limit to what electorate-level data can explain, but Table 13.2 does offer some initial insight. First, even accounting for the unfavourable boundary redistribution in Melbourne ahead of the election—doing so reduces the anti-Greens swing to –5.3 per cent—Bandt lost primary votes, and likely in large number to now-elected Labor candidate Sarah Witty. The Greens suffered swings against them even in suburbs long part of the electorate, while Labor increased its primary vote at nearly every booth. Booth-level results highlight that, for the Greens to regain Melbourne, they must significantly bolster their support in the eastern and southern sections of the electorate.

Outside Melbourne, though, Victorian results reveal a trend occurring in several States: the geographic patterns of Greens support are shifting. As votes declined in Melbourne (–5.3 per cent) and Macnamara (–4.2 per cent), they lifted significantly in Fraser (6.4 per cent), Lalor (4.9 per cent) and Maribyrnong (4.5 per cent). Likewise, in New South Wales, losses in Sydney and Wentworth were offset by gains in Page (6.7 per cent), Macarthur (5 per cent), Hughes (5 per cent) and Barton (4.9 per cent). In electorates such as Parramatta that had seen the Greens poll between 5 and 7 per cent from 2007 to 2019, the vote rose to more than 12 per cent. In the neighbouring seat of McMahon, the Greens' vote went from less than 3 per cent in 2013 to 9 per cent in 2025. While ultimately demonstrating positive voter recognition outside inner-city cores, many of these electorates offer little immediate chance of future seat gains.

Table 13.2 Greens vote share in key seats, 2016–2025 (per cent)

Seat	2025		2022		2019		2016	
	Primary vote	Absolute swing	Primary vote	Absolute swing	Primary vote	Absolute swing	Primary vote	Absolute swing
Melbourne	**39.5**	**–10.1**	**49.6**	**0.3**	**49.3**	**5.5**	**43.8**	**1.1**
Wills	35.4	7.1	28.3	1.7	26.6	–4.2	30.8	8.6
Griffith	**31.7**	**–2.9**	**34.6**	**11.0**	**23.6**	**6.5**	**17.1**	**6.8**
Ryan	**29.0**	**–1.2**	**30.2**	**9.9**	**20.3**	**1.6**	**18.7**	**4.3**
Richmond	26.5	1.2	25.3	5.0	20.3	–0.1	20.4	5.1
Brisbane	**25.9**	**–1.3**	**27.2**	**4.8**	**22.4**	**3.0**	**19.4**	**5.1**
Macnamara	25.5	–4.2	29.7	5.5	24.2	0.6	23.8	3.6
Fraser	25.3	6.8	18.5	10.2	8.3	–	–	–
Cooper	25.2	–2.2	27.4	6.3	21.1	–15.1	36.2	9.8
Grayndler	25.1	3.1	22.0	–0.5	22.5	0.3	22.2	0.2
Perth	24.5	2.3	22.2	3.3	18.9	1.8	17.1	5.1
Newcastle	22.2	2.1	20.1	4.5	15.6	1.9	13.7	1.7
Moreton	21.7	0.9	20.8	4.0	16.8	4.1	12.7	2.7
Sydney	21.6	–1.4	23.0	4.9	18.1	–0.7	18.8	0.5
Maribyrnong	21.2	4.9	16.3	1.5	14.8	5.2	9.6	–0.3
Cunningham	20.4	–1.3	21.7	6.6	15.1	0.4	14.7	2.9
Sturt	15.6	–0.8	16.4	5.2	11.2	4.1	7.1	–2.7
National	12.2	–0.05	12.2	1.8	10.4	0.2	10.2	1.6

Notes: 'Absolute swing' here is calculated as the shift in recorded primary support from one election to the next, not accounting for boundary redistribution; Seats held by Greens MPs after the 2022 election are in bold text; additional Greens target seats in the 2025 election campaign are italicised.

Source: AEC.

Queensland instead demonstrates the precarity of representation in electorates marked by close three-cornered contests. What's more, the LNP and ALP alike targeted Brisbane's three Greens-held seats aggressively, alongside well-funded campaigns from right-wing groups such as Advance Australia and Better Australia (Massola 2024; Martin 2025). Advance Australia was reported to have a $14-million war chest amassed to specifically target Greens and Teal candidates (West 2025). In 2022, Chandler-Mather won Griffith with favourable preference flows from Labor's Terri Butler after the latter failed to make the two-candidate-preferred count. In 2025, the order of primary votes shifted: the LNP dropped out earlier in the count and preferences flowed to Labor, unseating the Greens. In Brisbane, a minor drop in the Greens' vote removed Stephen Bates from the two-candidate-preferred count, again handing victory to Labor. Only in Ryan, where the LNP suffered a larger decline, did the Greens hold on. Certainly, in each seat, the Greens' vote went backwards. Yet, these modest losses do not warrant sweeping proclamations of outright repudiation of the party. Given that minor primary vote movement in these contests can be decisive, the Greens remain competitive in each.

What ought to concern the Greens, however, is the softness of their vote amid challenges from well-resourced Independents. That a significant portion of voters abandon the party when another viable non–major-party option is present has been evident since at least Nick Xenophon's entry into federal politics, yet Teal and Community Independents have spread this effect beyond South Australia. Table 13.3 lists Greens' primary votes and absolute swings in seats where Climate 200–backed Independents have won or attracted significant support in successive elections. A clear pattern is evident: where such Independents emerge, the Greens tend to lose vote share and struggle to regain it in subsequent elections. An element of 'strategic voting' may be at play here, where Independent challengers are perceived as having a greater chance of winning. Also likely is that Teal Independents in particular draw in part from a pool of issue-oriented and, especially, climate-oriented 'soft progressive' voters—whom the Greens cannot consistently claim as their own.

Table 13.3 Greens vote share in seats with Independents, 2016–2025 (per cent)

	2025		2022		2019		2016	
	Primary vote	Absolute swing	Primary vote	Absolute swing	Primary vote	Absolute swing	Primary vote	Absolute swing
Fremantle	**11.6**	–6.5	18.1	2.1	16	–1.7	17.7	5.8
Bean	**9.5**	–5.3	14.8	1.7	13.1	–	–	–
Curtin	7.8	–2.6	**10.4**	–4.9	15.3	1.3	14.2	–0.6
Bradfield	6.7	–2.6	**9.3**	–4.4	13.7	2	11.7	–1.2
Goldstein	7.2	–0.6	**7.8**	–6.3	14	–1.9	15.9	0
Clark[a]	13.2	–0.3	13.5	3.9	9.6	–	–	–
Mackellar	6.1	0	**6.1**	–5.4	11.5	–2.5	14.1	–0.1
Indi[b]	3.6	0	3.6	–0.6	4.2	0.4	3.8	0.4
Warringah	8.8	1.4	7.4	1.3	**6.1**	–6.1	12.2	–3.3
Kooyong	7.8	1.5	**6.3**	–14.9	21.2	2.7	18.9	2.3
Mayo	13.6	1.8	11.8	2.5	9.3	1.2	**8.1**	–6.1
Wentworth	10.2	1.9	8.3	0.8	**7.5**	–7.3	14.9	0.8
National	12.2	–0.05	12.2	1.8	10.4	0.2	10.2	1.6

Notes: 'Absolute swing' here is calculated as the shift in recorded primary support from one election to the next, not accounting for boundary redistribution; The election at which a strong Independent emerges is highlighted in bold; [a] Andrew Wilkie was first narrowly elected in 2010 in the then seat of Denison, with no effect on the Greens. However, in 2013, Wilkie won easily, with the Greens dropping from 18.98 to 7.92%. [b] Cathy McGowan was elected in 2013 with the Greens' vote dropping from 9.63 to 3.42%.

Source: AEC.

One further development was the emergence of Independents endorsed by The Muslim Vote (TMV) in three seats: Blaxland, Watson and Calwell. Although initially thought to split the Greens' potential gains among Muslim voters, the party's vote in those electorates instead largely held steady or increased slightly. In Blaxland and Watson, TMV candidates drew primarily from the major parties, with the greater share coming from Liberal candidates, with the Greens seeing modest increases. Nonetheless, before the election, the Greens had strongly supported action on Palestine and greater efforts for an enduring peace in the Middle East, so would have expected greater results for this stand, even as the TMV candidates pitched themselves as 'centrist'. Only in Calwell, in a complex and highly competitive seat with 13 candidates, did the Greens experience a small decline.

In sum, the 2025 results delivered a dual verdict. The Greens remain a stable and electorally viable minor party, with national support sufficient to retain considerable Senate influence. But results in the House of Representatives exposed the fragility of that support in local contests, particularly in crowded electoral fields. These dynamics will not mark the end of the Greens' lower house ambitions. Yet, they do underscore the need for a recalibrated strategy—one more attuned to the party's organisational limits, changing geographic strengths and the increasingly competitive terrain of left-of-centre politics in Australia.

The campaign: Narrative, policy, tactics

What might help explain these results? Several trite explanations appearing in post-election media coverage—the party has become too extreme, too obstructionist, too distant from an imagined single-issue environmentalist past—may nicely align with ALP (and Advance) campaign rhetoric but are nonetheless unpersuasive on the available evidence. If the Greens are now more 'extreme', it is an extremism shared by a significant and relatively stable proportion of Australians. Likewise, lacking individual-level data, it cannot be ruled out that the party's legislative tactics influenced voting behaviour. But the divergent swings across electorates suggest that voter response was far from uniform. Much has also been made of the supposed shift in party priorities away from the environment. Yet, the Greens, like their antecedent parties (such as the United Tasmania Group), are better understood as ecologically based, not ecologically focused. Their platforms have long encompassed a broad social-democratic agenda. In what follows, after a discussion of campaign narrative, we explore each of these points in turn.

Narrative

The Greens' campaign launched with a guiding narrative: 'Keep Dutton out and get Labor to act.' This framing likely suited a context in which a minority government appeared possible. Yet, as the Coalition's campaign faltered, the Greens failed to pivot to a narrative that clearly differentiated themselves from a resurgent Labor Party. Voters may have believed keeping Dutton out was more likely achieved by voting Labor, while the Greens' presence in the Senate would pressure Albanese towards progressive outcomes. Nonetheless, much of the Greens' campaign rhetoric remained focused on power-sharing in a minority government. Greens support for a Labor minority was premised on several core demands: adding dental to Medicare, reforming negative gearing and capital gains tax, capping rents, banning new fossil fuel projects and ending native forest logging (Dick 2025).

Yet, having ruled out (quite reasonably, given the ideological gap) supporting a Dutton-led Coalition, the Greens offered little public strategy for the more likely scenario: that Labor would win a majority and decline to engage with the party's demands. Here, the campaign seemingly lacked a backup plan. With Labor increasingly dominant in polling from April, the Greens' continued emphasis on a minority power-sharing frame may have sounded implausible or redundant to voters. What's more, apart from the environment and climate change, Labor advanced what was arguably a credible alternative set of positions in policy areas central to the Greens' campaign. Overall, this dynamic reflects a broader challenge for policy-seeking minor parties. Their success is a function of not just their own narrative or issue positions but also their ability to maintain distinctiveness as major parties respond (Meguid 2008).

Policy

Have the Greens become more 'extreme' (Dyrenfurth 2025)? Have they turned away from environmental issues to become a 'party of renters' (Roe 2025)? In a post-election edition of the *7am Podcast*, journalist Mike Seccombe summarised former Greens leader Richard Di Natale's view that the party's platform in 2025 was largely unchanged from previous elections:

> [I]n terms of substance, actually, the platform that they took to this election, which wasn't so successful, was the same as the one that they took to the previous election, at which they were very successful, and essentially the same as the one that they took to the election before that. (Seccombe 2025)

The evidence suggests that Di Natale is broadly correct. The policy positions, and salience afforded to different policy areas, in Greens' platforms show considerable consistency. Table 13.4 uses Manifesto Project (Lehmann et al. 2024) data—which code election platforms into quantifiable policy categories—to measure the degree of consistency in Greens, Labor and Liberal election platforms from 2004 to 2022 (as of writing, 2025 data are unavailable, but see the media release analysis below). The score for each party is the sum of absolute differences between the salience attributed to each policy category across a pair of elections, divided by two and then subtracted from 100, rendering a percentage of overlap. The higher the overlap figure, the greater is the consistency across a party's two platforms. The figures reveal, accordant with the policy-seeking orientation of the Greens (Adams et al. 2006), that the party maintains a more consistent platform, relative to the major parties, regardless of broader electoral conditions. Barely one-quarter of the Greens' policy emphases change from one election to the next.

Table 13.4 Intraparty policy overlap: Greens, Labor and Liberal, 2004–2022 (per cent)

Election platforms	Greens	Labor	Liberal
2022–2019	76.3	66.8	72.2
2019–2016	75.2	71.2	42.6
2016–2013	65.2	55.2	47.9
2013–2010	73.5	53.9	54.7
2010–2007	73.9	49.2	58.7
2007–2004	78.8	47.3	70.2

Source: Manifesto Project (Lehmann et al. 2024).

But what policy areas do Greens election platforms typically address? Figure 13.2 charts the proportion of Greens policy platforms dedicated to issue variables that, at any election from 2004 to 2022, made up at least 5 per cent of their platform. Darker shading corresponds with greater emphasis on a policy platform, while the top three most salient policy areas are highlighted with their percentage share. For example, in 2022, the top three most salient policy issues in the Greens' platform were welfare expansion, environmental protection (including from climate change) and anti-growth economics (mostly focused on sustainable development). Positive statements on unions and initiatives on enhancing equality closely followed. While precise salience figures shift from one election to the next, there is a 'typical' Greens platform from which the party rarely strays. The Greens' most successful elections, 2010 and 2022, are among the upper and lower ends of environmental issue salience; descriptively, at least, there seems to be little relationship between 'attention' given to the environment and electoral wins.

Lacking Manifesto Project data for 2025, we instead thematically code media releases distributed by the party's media list during the campaign. While media releases differ from election platforms, they nonetheless exhibit a policy focus, reflect with greater accuracy the initiatives pursued by the parliamentary party and allow us to address some pervading myths. Table 13.5 shows the results of a thematic coding process, whereby each media release was assigned one primary policy theme.[1] What is immediately obvious is that any claims of a minimisation of the environment in the Greens' campaigning should be treated as dubious at best.

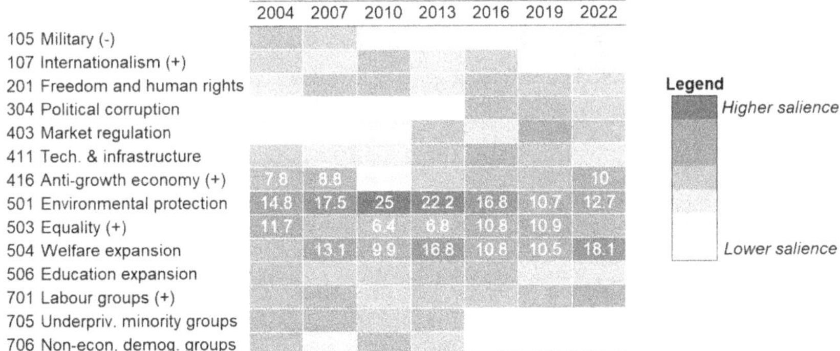

	2004	2007	2010	2013	2016	2019	2022
105 Military (-)							
107 Internationalism (+)							
201 Freedom and human rights							
304 Political corruption							
403 Market regulation							
411 Tech. & infrastructure							
416 Anti-growth economy (+)	7.8	8.8					10
501 Environmental protection	14.8	17.5	25	22.2	16.8	10.7	12.7
503 Equality (+)	11.7		6.4	6.8	10.8	10.9	
504 Welfare expansion		13.1	9.9	16.8	10.8	10.5	18.1
506 Education expansion							
701 Labour groups (+)							
705 Underpriv. minority groups							
706 Non-econ. demog. groups							

Figure 13.2 Policy salience in Greens election platforms, 2004–2022
Source: Manifesto Project (Lehmann et al. 2024).

---

1   Some careful interpretation is required with such coding, and there are policy initiatives announced in media releases that span multiple policy areas—for instance, advocating greater renters' rights around the installation of solar panels covers, *inter alia*, law reform, climate action, cost-of-living relief and energy costs. To address this complexity, coding is determined by language used, emphasis and the portfolio responsibilities of the Greens spokesperson responsible for the release.

Table 13.5 Greens media release themes

Policy theme	Count
Environmental protection	8
Campaign narrative and electioneering	7
Education expansion	7
Housing	6
Climate change	5
Public service	5
Energy and resources	4
Media and communications	4
Arts	3
First Nations	3
Health	3
Cost of living	2
Economic management	2
Trade	2
Women	2
Childcare	1
Foreign policy	1
Immigration	1
Industrial relations	1
Law and justice	1
Welfare expansion	1
Total	**69**

Source: Authors' calculations.

Environmental protection emerged as the most frequently cited theme (11.6 per cent), followed by education expansion, campaign narrative and housing. If we include releases specifically focused on climate change, the combined environment/climate share rises to 18.8 per cent—by far the highest combined thematic grouping. Other prominent areas included energy and resources, public service reform and arts policy. Some surprises emerge: while welfare expansion is a core policy area for the party, it was the primary theme in just one campaign release—curiously, given the party's voter base—on lifting the age pension. Likewise, while health policy was central to the Greens' demands for supporting a Labor minority government, it appeared late in the campaign and the party's spokesperson, Senator Jordon Steele-John, was absent from associated media releases. Conversely, the Coalition's proposed cuts to the public service gained repeated attention.

Both the distribution and the substantive content of the releases suggest a campaign focused on connecting key policy areas—the environment, housing, education and public services—with tangible cost-of-living concerns. In this sense, the Greens were not abandoning environmentalism or embracing a new economic agenda, but rather advancing a socially rooted green politics—one that attempts to integrate distributive and sustainability claims. This approach aligns with what Adam Bandt (2023) and others have termed a kind of 'green social democracy'.

Of course, media releases reveal only the 'supply side' of party communication. What voters heard—and internalised—may have differed. This divergence between intended and received messaging is especially significant for minor parties with limited earned media access. But if public opinion, or media reporting, shifted towards seeing the Greens as more radical or less environmentally focused, the available data suggest these were shifts in perception rather than reality. Policy content remained broadly stable and environmental themes retained significant salience. The more pressing question, then, is whether the balance and clarity of messaging were effective. In a campaign in which Labor surged, the Greens' policy offers— often veering into areas of traditional Labor 'ownership'—may have lacked clear anchoring in voters' minds, allowing other narratives to take hold.

Parliamentary tactics

Central to Labor's campaign was the portrayal of the Greens as obstructionist. This line of attack—while somewhat cynical, given Labor's routine refusal to negotiate—gained traction in part because it was grounded in basic facts, such as the Greens' role in delaying the government's housing policy agenda. Before the campaign, the Greens already deemed it necessary to defend their approach to the Forty-Seventh Parliament, with Bandt acknowledging 'we pushed hard this year, and pushing the government isn't always pretty' (Middleton 2024). The defensive stance continued into the campaign, as party rhetoric and releases alike emphasised the benefits of Labor–Greens cooperation. Negative campaigning, meanwhile, was more targeted towards Dutton and the Coalition.

Yet, the effects of this parliamentary record on voting behaviour are difficult to assess. Swings against the Greens occurred in some seats but not others; if the 'obstructionist' frame worked, it did so unevenly. More importantly, the Greens' parliamentary tactics appeared to lack a clear internal logic. Early in the Forty-Seventh Parliament, they backed Labor's climate safeguard mechanism, despite its inadequacies, after securing a cap on emissions (Macintosh and Butler 2023). Later, they extracted $3 billion in additional housing investment by holding up Labor's housing bill. But, over time, this assertiveness faded. The party eventually voted for numerous government bills after securing only minor concessions (Karp 2024). Late in the parliamentary term, the Greens even indicated willingness to support Labor's environmental protection reforms without a climate trigger, which was arguably a modest and symbolic ask, previously backed by Albanese himself.

This pattern suggests a party caught between its programmatic roots and its desire to influence. Minor parties often struggle to balance the competing imperatives of legislative impact and ideological distinctiveness (Pedersen 2011; Spoon 2011). For the Greens to frame a series of policy problems as crises, to maintain credibility, the party then needed to be seen as engaging in either principled opposition or constructive negotiation. Instead, the result may have been a muddled message to voters about what the party stood for in parliament, and why.

Conclusion

For the Australian Greens, the election was seen as a test of their newly adopted on-the-ground campaign techniques, which appeared to have limited impact in key seats where they were most actively deployed. The campaign result itself, particularly the loss of multiple lower house MPs, was widely seen as a failure for the party, even though the national House of Representatives vote share remained essentially unchanged. In contrast, six senators were re-elected relatively comfortably, despite a national swing of about 1 percentage point against the party. So, was this such a bad election?

The immediate aftermath of election night was sobering. Greens leader Adam Bandt began the evening confident of victory, only to see not just two of the three Queensland seats lost, but also his own seat of Melbourne fall to Labor. Other target seats came close but ultimately returned unsuccessful candidates. Even the Senate result was quickly overshadowed by the post-election defection of WA Greens Senator Dorinda Cox to the ALP. The subsequent election of Queensland Senator Larissa Waters to the party's leadership signalled a geographic shift in the party's centre of gravity—away from the traditional bases of Victoria and Tasmania and dramatically north. While the Tasmanian branch has experienced some renewed success at both State and federal levels, it can no longer be regarded as the undisputed core of the party. Likewise, the once-solid Greens stronghold in Melbourne—long a symbol of the party's inner-urban strength—now appears vulnerable.

Yet, despite the storm clouds surrounding the 2025 result, there is a silver lining. Greens campaigns outside the inner city performed relatively well, particularly in Western Sydney and suburban Melbourne, suggesting that the party's support base may be gradually shifting. The success of ongoing campaigns at the local and State levels, as well as strong alignment with key public concerns such as housing and climate, point to a viable future trajectory—even as the inner-urban foundation of the party's vote has softened. What the 2025 election revealed was not the collapse of the Greens' political project or widespread repudiation, but a set of structural and strategic challenges that now demand the party's attention.

References

Adams, James, Michael Clark, Lawrence Ezrow, and Garrett Glasgow. 2006. 'Are niche parties fundamentally different from mainstream parties? The causes and electoral consequences of Western European parties' policy shifts, 1976–1988.' *American Journal of Political Science* 50, no. 3: 513–29. doi.org/10.1111/j.1540-5907.2006.00199.x.

Australian Bureau of Statistics (ABS). 2025. *Consumer Price Index, Australia.* March Quarter 2025, 30 April. Canberra: Australian Bureau of Statistics. www.abs.gov.au/statistics/economy/price-indexes-and-inflation/consumer-price-index-australia/mar-quarter-2025.

Australian Election Forecasts (AEF). 2025. *2025 Federal Election—General Forecast.* Last updated 3 May. Australian Election Forecasts. www.aeforecasts.com/forecast/2025fed/regular.

Australian Greens. 2025. 'Greens hit go on biggest ever national campaign for minority government.' Media release, 28 March. Canberra: The Australian Greens. greens.org.au/news/media-release/greens-hit-go-biggest-ever-national-campaign-minority-government.

Bandt, Adam. 2016. 'Making progressive government happen.' In *How to Vote Progressive in Australia: Labor or Green?*, edited by Dennis Altman and Sean Scalmer, 179–202. Melbourne: Monash University Publishing.

Bandt, Adam. 2023. 'Adam Bandt: National Press Club address.' 26 April. Canberra: The Australian Greens. Transcript available: greens.org.au/news/speech/adam-bandt-national-press-club.

Beaumont, Adrian. 2025. 'Final polls give Labor a clear lead before the election.' *The Conversation*, 2 May. theconversation.com/final-polls-give-labor-a-clear-lead-before-the-election-255724. doi.org/10.64628/AA.n7djcgfh7.

Bischof, Daniel, and Markus Wagner. 2017. 'What makes parties adapt to voter preferences? The role of party organisation, goals and ideology.' *British Journal of Political Science* 50, no. 1: 391–401. doi.org/10.1017/S0007123417000357.

Clarke, Tyrone. 2023. 'Adam Bandt leads Greens MPs into voting against Anthony Albanese's motion to condemn Hamas terrorist attacks.' *Sky News*, 16 October. www.skynews.com.au/australia-news/politics/adam-bandt-leads-greens-mps-into-voting-against-anthony-albaneses-motion-to-condemn-hamas-terrorist-attacks/news-story/d67943bc670e92360899d73b6bb7ba15.

Dalidakis, Philip. 2025. 'The Greens crossed a line and Australians pushed back.' *Australian Financial Review*, 6 May. www.afr.com/politics/federal/the-greens-crossed-a-line-and-australians-pushed-back-20250506-p5lwxs.

Dick, Samantha. 2025. 'Here's what the Greens will prioritise in a minority Labor government.' *ABC News*, 30 April. www.abc.net.au/news/2025-04-30/greens-party-campaign-launch-federal-election-2025/105223228.

Dyrenfurth, Nick. 2025. 'Greens collapse is a voter revolt against radical politics.' *Australian Financial Review*, 7 May. www.afr.com/politics/federal/greens-collapse-is-a-voter-revolt-against-radical-politics-20250507-p5lxa0.

Flenady, Liam. 2022. 'Greens campaign manager: Brisbane Greenslide demonstrates power of combining social and electoral organising.' *GreenLeft*, 30 May, no. 1347. www.greenleft.org.au/content/greens-campaign-manager-brisbane-greenslide-demonstrates-power-combining-social-and.

Hildebrand, Joe. 2024. 'How did the Greens wind up getting so cozy with terror?' *The Daily Telegraph*, 14 October. www.dailytelegraph.com.au/news/opinion/how-did-the-greens-wind-up-getting-so-cozy-with-terror/news-story/5c6f7ded2247a6ccd13e2640ec3b1df2.

Jackson, Stewart. 2016. *The Australian Greens: From Activism to Australia's Third Party*. Melbourne: Melbourne University Press.

Karp, Paul. 2023. 'Greens stage Senate walkout over Labor's Israel–Hamas war response.' *The Guardian*, 6 November. www.theguardian.com/australia-news/2023/nov/06/greens-senate-walkout-over-labor-albanese-israel-hamas-war-response.

Karp, Paul. 2024. 'Senate moving through 31 bills in frantic end to year as Labor strikes deal with Greens.' *The Guardian*, 28 November. www.theguardian.com/australia-news/2024/nov/28/albanese-labor-senate-likely-to-pass-31-bills-guillotine-motion-greens.

Keane, Bernard. 2025. 'Bandt's project to change the Greens failed. Along the way, he helped wreck the appeal of minority government.' *Crikey*, 5 May. www.crikey.com.au/2025/05/05/election-2025-adam-bandt-greens-failure/.

Kefford, Glenn. 2021. *Political Parties and Campaigning in Australia: Data, Digital and Field*. Cham, Switzerland: Palgrave Macmillan. doi.org/10.1007/978-3-030-68234-7.

Lehmann, Pola, Simon Franzmann, Denise Al-Gaddooa, Tobias Burst, Christoph Ivanusch, Sven Regel, Felicia Riethmüller, Andrea Volkens, Bernhard Weßels, and Lisa Zehnter. 2024. *Manifesto Project Main Dataset (Party Preferences): Manifesto Project Dataset (version 2024a)*. Berlin and Göttingen: Wissenschaftszentrum Berlin für Sozialforschung and Institut für Demokratieforschung. doi.org/10.25522/manifesto.mpds.2024a.

Macintosh, Andrew, and Don Butler. 2023. 'The unsafe Safeguard Mechanism: How carbon credits could blow up Australia's main climate policy.' *The Conversation*, 10 November. doi.org/10.64628/AA.ey3wgx7es.

Martin, Josh. 2025. 'Liberal–National Coalition and Labor to target Brisbane's "Green Machine" during federal election.' *7News*, 28 March. 7news.com.au/news/liberal-national-coalition-and-labor-to-target-brisbanes-green-machine-during-federal-election-c-18189690.

Massola, James. 2024. 'Right-wing group targets Greens in million-dollar ad blitz.' *The Sydney Morning Herald*, 18 November. www.smh.com.au/politics/federal/right-wing-group-targets-greens-in-million-dollar-ad-blitz-20241115-p5kr0y.html.

Meguid, Bonnie M. 2008. *Party Competition between Unequals: Strategies and Electoral Fortunes in Western Europe*. Cambridge: Cambridge University Press. doi.org/10.1017/CBO9780511510298.

Middleton, Karen. 2024. '"Pushing isn't always pretty": Adam Bandt on why the Greens blocked Labor's agenda until last sitting day of the year.' *The Guardian*, 29 November. www.theguardian.com/australia-news/2024/nov/29/adam-bandt-greens-labor-bills-albanese-plibersek.

Molan, Erin. 2024. 'Greens slammed over Middle East stance.' *Sky News*, 2 November. www.skynews.com.au/opinion/greens-slammed-over-middle-east-stance/video/009ccbf3089d2d6f99a833dc8712de44.

Pedersen, Helene H. 2011. 'Policy-seeking parties in multiparty systems: Influence or purity?' *Party Politics* 18, no. 3: 297–314. doi.org/10.1177/135406881038 2940.

Powell, Matthew. 2023. 'A comparative study on grassroots community organising in New South Wales.' Unpublished PhD diss., University of Sydney.

Roe, Isobel. 2025. 'How the Greens rebranded from activists to the "party of renters".' *ABC News*, 30 April. www.abc.net.au/news/2025-05-01/greens-party-rebrands-ahead-of-federal-election-2025/105235682.

Seccombe, Mike. 2025. 'The Greens "stunning" election defeat.' *7am Podcast*, 12 May. 7ampodcast.com.au/episodes/the-greens-stunning-election-defeat.

Smee, Ben. 2025. 'How deep are the Greens' roots in Brisbane? Three seats will tell the tale in 2025.' *The Guardian*, 8 April. www.theguardian.com/australia-news/2025/apr/08/how-deep-are-the-greens-roots-in-brisbane-three-seats-will-tell-the-tale-in-2025.

Spoon, Jae-Jae. 2011. *Political Survival of Small Parties in Europe*. Ann Arbor: University of Michigan Press. doi.org/10.3998/mpub.3210669.

Stone, Deborah. 2024. 'Jewish organisations ask majors to dump Greens.' *The Jewish Independent*, 9 October, [Updated 10 October 2024]. thejewishindependent.com.au/jewish-organisations-campaign-against-greens.

West, Michael. 2025. 'Dark money. Hard-right Advance targets Greens, Teals with $14m warchest.' *Michael West Media*, 3 February. michaelwest.com.au/advance-warchest-targets-greens-teals/.

Williams, Paul. 2025. 'The Greens' identity crisis: Where to now for a party built on protesting against the status quo?' *The Guardian*, 8 May. www.theguardian.com/australia-news/commentisfree/2025/may/08/the-greens-identity-crisis-where-to-now-for-a-party-built-on-protesting-the-status-quo.

14

An electoral test for the Community Independents

Carolyn M. Hendriks and Richard Reid

Abstract

The 2025 election was a test for the Community Independents Movement (CIM): would it continue to expand or had its momentum peaked? The answer is mixed. On one hand, the movement has grown, with 37 Community Independent (CI) candidates standing for the House of Representatives and one in the Senate. Votes for CI candidates were also up from 2022. Yet, with only one additional seat won (Bradfield) and the loss of Zoe Daniel in Goldstein, the 2025 election represents a consolidation of the CIM's electoral position, rather than an expansion. To make sense of these mixed results, the chapter discusses three groups of CI candidates: incumbents, repeat challengers and newcomers. It argues that the CIM's diverse results reflect the localised nature of the movement, its appeal and the varying dynamics across electorates. The chapter considers issues facing the CIM going forward, including fatigue and campaign spending limits.

Keywords: Community Independents; Teals; Community Independents Movement; Climate 200; elections

The 2025 election was always going to be seen as a test for the Community Independents Movement (CIM). Could the CIM grow its presence in the parliament, building on the 2022 election results, when eight Community

Independents (CIs) were elected to the House of Representatives and one to the Senate, or would this election prove that the 'Teal wave' in 2022 was simply a rejection of the Morrison government? In the end, the 2025 results for the CIM were mixed. All CI incumbents except Zoe Daniel in Goldstein successfully held their seats and one new CI was elected (Nicolette Boele in Bradfield); however, more than two-thirds of the 38 CI candidates were unable to win. So, although more than a million Australians voted for an Independent candidate as their first preference (up 2.1 per cent from 2022) (ABC 2025b), this did not translate into a greater number of seats for CI candidates. Overall, the minority government that many had expected—with Independents and minor parties holding the balance of power in the House of Representatives—did not eventuate.

Although CI candidates did not perform as well as some had predicted, the movement remains optimistic about its ongoing capacity to have a positive impact on Australia's democratic system. This sentiment is encapsulated by the post-election words of defeated MP Zoe Daniel (2025): 'This is not the end. It's not even the end of the beginning. Community independent politics is alive. It is thriving. And together, we will keep shaping the future of our democracy.'

In this chapter, we consider the campaigns and electoral results of candidates who were part of the CIM at the 2025 election. We contend that the mixed electoral results for CI candidates reflect the localised nature of the movement, its appeal and the varying dynamics across electorates. In the 2025 election, CI candidates faced competition from diverse party candidates; many stood against a Liberal incumbent while others stood against either a Labor or a Nationals incumbent. A few faced three-cornered contests against well-known former party MPs running as Independents—for example, in Calare (NSW), Monash (Victoria) and Moore (WA).

We cannot do justice to the unique experiences of all CI candidates in this short chapter and we also recognise that the localised nature of the CIM makes it more difficult to provide general reflections compared with political parties. However, we offer a synthesis of key data by considering three distinct CI candidate groups: incumbents, repeat challengers and newcomers. In the discussion, we reflect on some of the issues that surfaced in the 2025 election and consider the future and challenges for the CIM.

The chapter is structured in seven short parts. The first is a brief overview of the CIM. Following this is consideration of the 2025 electoral context. The chapter then moves to focus on: the CI candidates, the CI campaigns and the CI results. In the sixth part, the chapter provides some reflections on the implications of these results for the CIM and its future. Following this is a short conclusion.

Community Independents: A localised model and a national movement

The CIM claims to offer an alternative form of political representation to the 'broken' party system (Johnson 2025). It champions a grassroots model whereby local candidates are nominated or endorsed by an electorate community group (Hendriks and Reid 2024a). This model first emerged in the electorate of Indi in the leadup to the 2013 federal election (Hendriks 2017). Similar community groups then emerged and stood CI candidates in the 2019 and 2022 elections, particularly in metropolitan seats in Sydney, Melbourne and Perth, but also in several regional electorates (Hendriks and Reid 2023). In 2022, the CIM received significant attention due to the success of six new 'Teal' MPs and one senator. They joined Helen Haines (Indi) and Zali Steggall (Warringah), both of whom were first elected in 2019.

The CI model continues to adapt and evolve. While there are local variations (a point to which we return in our broader reflections), the typical CI approach involves: 1) the formation of a local community electorate group; 2) the engagement of local constituents in discussions about what local representation should look like; 3) the recruitment, selection and/or endorsement of a local Community Independent candidate; and 4) a community-led political campaign (Hendriks and Reid 2024a).

Since the 2022 election, the CIM has expanded considerably, building on the high profiles of CIs in the House of Representatives and the Senate. By May 2025, around the nation there were 45 active local community electorate groups (CIP 2025b)[1] and numerous intermediary organisations, networks and platforms resourcing, advising and broadcasting CI candidates

---

1   Some of these groups cover multiple electorates. For example, Voices of Tasmania covers the five Tasmanian electorates of Bass, Braddon, Clark, Franklin and Lyons.

and their campaigns. At the 2025 election, there were 38 CI candidates: seven incumbent MPs,[2] one incumbent senator, seven recontesting CI candidates and 23 new CI candidates.

The 2025 electoral context for Community Independents

Going into the 2025 election the CIM had grand aspirations. CI candidates were seen to be strong possibilities in several regional seats such as Monash, Cowper, Wannon and Calare. Pollsters also predicted the CIs would do well. In his contribution to the Election Analysts Forum at the National Press Club on 22 April 2025, Shaun Ratcliff from the polling group Accent Research predicted that the Coalition would be 'bleeding' votes to Community Independents in metropolitan seats such as Bradfield and in rural seats such as Cowper, Calare, Monash and Wannon. He went on to argue that Labor would also be vulnerable to CIs. Similarly, reports of polling commissioned by the crowd-funding organisation Climate 200 (C200) predicted that CI candidates would win Cowper and Bradfield and would come close in Flinders and Forrest (Seccombe 2025a).

But the 2025 election would prove to be a highly unpredictable and complex political context for CIs. On the upside, CI candidates were a known, familiar and, to some, proven quantity. The public prominence and actions of the eight CI MPs and one CI senator in the Forty-Seventh Parliament offered voters at the 2025 election concrete examples of what a CI is and what they do. However, the challenges were that some of the key issues that shaped the 2022 election were notably absent in 2025 (such as strong anti–Scott Morrison sentiment and significant attention to climate change). In 2025, CI candidates (like their party counterparts) faced voters who wanted action from politicians on cost-of-living pressures, housing affordability and intergenerational (in)equity. Global affairs would also impact the 2025 election in ways very different from 2022, particularly concerns about instability in the world economy and international order following the inauguration of US President Donald Trump for his second term in January 2025.

---

2   Kylea Tink, who was elected to the seat of North Sydney in 2022, did not stand in the 2025 election as North Sydney was abolished in a 2024 AEC redistribution.

Plate 14.1 Corflutes on display in Goldstein seven months before the election

Photos: Carolyn Hendriks.

The movement had also changed since 2022. In this election, there were more local CI groups and candidates standing in diverse seats and their campaigns had longer lead times, were better resourced and supported and were able to attract more volunteers than in 2022. Major-party MPs and candidates had a greater understanding of the CIM and were in no way caught off-guard as they might have been in 2022. An illustrative example of this was in Goldstein, where former MP Tim Wilson successfully designed a long-planned local campaign to win back the seat from CI incumbent Zoe Daniel (see Ilanbey 2025). As shown in Plate 14.1, the public contest between Wilson and Daniel began well before election.

Since 2022 there had also been growth in third-party entities challenging and campaigning against CI candidates, especially incumbent CI MPs. For example, in the Melbourne seat of Goldstein, a group calling itself 'Repeal the Teal' was active throughout the 2025 election campaign with pamphlets, posters and T-shirts. Other third-party groups such as Advance and Better Australia had been active in multiple seats such as Wentworth (Bogle 2025) and Goldstein (Epstein 2025).

Overview of CI candidates

This chapter focuses on the candidates recognised by the Community Independents Project (CIP), a key body within the CIM founded by original members of Voices for Indi and Voices of Warringah. At the 2025 election, the CIP recognised 37 House of Representatives candidates and one Senate candidate.[3] Below we provide an overview of these candidates, listing them under three groupings: incumbents (CI MPs), repeat challengers (CI candidates standing again) and newcomers (CI candidates standing for the first time).

A distinct aspect of the 2025 election was the sheer diversity of electorates in which a CI candidate stood (as summarised in Tables 14.1, 14.2 and 14.3, and visualised in Map 14.1). This diversity somewhat debunked the popular myth that CIs only emerge in wealthy metropolitan seats. Indeed, in the leadup to the 2025 election, commentators gave considerable attention to several CI candidates running in rural and provincial (regional) seats, on the back of unsuccessful attempts in either 2019 or 2022, such as Alex Dyson in Wannon, Caz Heise in Cowper and Kate Hook in Calare (see, for example, Newlands 2025). There were also CI candidates in outer suburban seats that were once safe Labor electorates. Other noteworthy features of the CI candidates in the 2025 election include: as in 2022, they were predominantly women—only eight of the 38 CI candidates were men; most have work backgrounds in the professions or public or community sectors; and most of the newcomers sought a campaign colour that distinguished them from the 'Teals'.

---

3   The CIP list is broader than the candidates listed by C200 because not all 2025 CI candidates were financed by C200. Some candidates—most notably, Andrew Wilkie and Rebekha Sharkie—are increasingly associated with the CIM because they receive funding from C200. We do not include these candidates in this chapter, because either they are a minor-party member (in the case of Sharkie) or they are an Independent who does not claim 'community' status (in the case of Wilkie). For a discussion of other Independents, see Chapter 15, this volume.

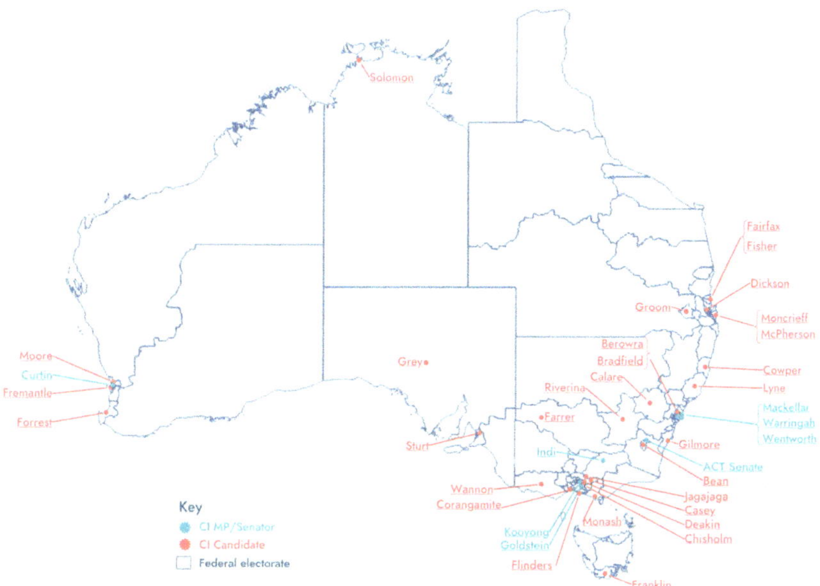

Map 14.1 Community Independent candidates and their electorates
Source: CIP (2025a).

It is also notable that apart from David Pocock in the ACT, there were
no other CI candidates standing for the Senate in 2025. This reflects the
fact that the electoral system used for the House of Representatives is
more favourable than the Senate's single transferable vote proportional
representation system. Pocock is the exception, partly reflecting the small
size of the ACT population.

Table 14.1 Community Independent incumbents (8)

Candidate	Electorate	Type of electorate	Gender
Kate Chaney	Curtin, WA	Metropolitan (inner)	Woman
Zoe Daniel	Goldstein, Vic.	Metropolitan (inner)	Woman
Helen Haines	Indi, Vic.	Rural	Woman
Monique Ryan	Kooyong, Vic.	Metropolitan (inner)	Woman
Sophie Scamps	Mackellar, NSW	Metropolitan (outer)	Woman
Allegra Spender	Wentworth, NSW	Metropolitan (inner)	Woman
Zali Steggall	Warringah, NSW	Metropolitan (inner)	Woman
David Pocock	ACT Senator	–	Man

Source: Compiled by authors from CIP (2025a) data.

Table 14.2 Community Independent repeat challengers (7)

Candidate	Electorate	Type of electorate	Gender
Nicolette Boele	Bradfield, NSW	Metropolitan (inner)	Woman
Alex Dyson	Wannon, Vic.	Rural	Man
Claire Ferres Miles	Casey, Vic.	Rural	Woman
Caz Heise	Cowper, NSW	Provincial	Woman
Suzie Holt	Groom, Qld	Provincial	Woman
Kate Hook	Calare, NSW	Rural	Woman
Deb Leonard	Monash, Vic.	Rural	Woman

Source: Compiled by authors from CIP (2025a) data.

Table 14.3 Community Independent newcomers (23)

Candidate	Electorate	Type of electorate	Gender
Nicole Arrowsmith	Moncrieff, Qld	Provincial	Woman
Nathan Barton	Moore, WA	Metropolitan (outer)	Man
Tina Brown	Berowra, NSW	Metropolitan (outer)	Woman
Sue Chapman	Forrest, WA	Rural	Woman
Verity Cooper	Sturt, SA	Metropolitan (inner)	Woman
Kath Davies	Chisholm, Vic.	Metropolitan (inner)	Woman
Kate Dezarnaulds	Gilmore, NSW	Rural	Woman
Peter George	Franklin, Tas.	Metropolitan (outer)	Man
Kate Hulett	Fremantle, WA	Metropolitan (inner)	Woman
Keryn Jones	Fisher, Qld	Rural	Woman
Chris Kearney	Jagajaga, Vic.	Metropolitan (outer)	Man
Anita Kuss	Grey, SA	Rural	Woman
Kate Lockhart	Corangamite, Vic.	Provincial	Woman
Jeremy Miller	Lyne, NSW	Rural	Man
Michelle Milthorpe	Farrer, NSW	Rural	Woman
Erchana Murray-Bartlett	McPherson, Qld	Provincial	Woman
Jess Ness	Deakin, Vic.	Metropolitan (outer)	Woman
Jessie Price	Bean, ACT	Metropolitan (inner)	Woman
Jenny Rolfe	Riverina, NSW	Rural	Woman
Phil Scott	Solomon, NT	Metropolitan (inner)	Man
Ben Smith	Flinders, Vic.	Rural	Man
Ellie Smith	Dickson, Qld	Metropolitan (outer)	Woman
Francine Wiig	Fairfax, Qld	Rural	Woman

Source: Compiled by authors from CIP (2025a) data.

CI election campaigns

Each CI candidate led a local community campaign. Many CI campaigns involved large volunteer numbers engaged in doorknocking and a variety of activities in the community to boost candidate visibility and attract supporters, as seen in previous elections (see Hayman 2024). Each CI campaign was shaped by the specific political dynamics of the electorate. This is reflected in the different policy issues CI candidates emphasised, the different colours they used and their different campaign approaches. As shown in Plate 14.2, some, like Jessie Price, followed Indi and opted for bright orange.

Compared with the 2022 election, CI candidates in the 2025 election had far more time to plan their campaign. In some cases, they had too much time and ran out of money (see Seccombe 2025b). The long campaign also presented challenges to campaign teams as they sought to maintain and sustain highly energised campaigns with hundreds of volunteers (we return to campaign fatigue below).

Plate 14.2 CI candidate Jessie Price and her volunteers in Bean, ACT
Source: Jessie Price.

The 2025 election followed AEC electoral redistributions in 2024 that resulted in the abolition of two seats (CI-held North Sydney and Labor-held Higgins in Victoria), the creation of a new WA seat (Bullwinkel) and, consequently, the redrawing of the electoral boundaries of a significant number of electorates. The impact of these boundary changes on CI candidates was variable. Importantly, for CI incumbents, their electorates were not the same as their constituencies during their term, particularly in Sydney and Melbourne. While the redistribution in New South Wales abolished one CI seat in North Sydney, the resulting boundary changes likely worked in favour of CIs in Bradfield and Warringah. In Melbourne, meanwhile, the abolition of Higgins seems to have worked against Monique Ryan in Kooyong and Zoe Daniel in Goldstein.

Some of the CI campaigns were especially confrontational and consequently attracted more national media attention than others. Examples of this include video footage emerging of CI MP Monique Ryan's husband removing a corflute of Liberal candidate Amelia Hamer in Kooyong (ABC 2025a) and tensions in Wentworth relating to the conflict in Gaza. In contrast to the 2022 election, many of the volunteers on the CI campaigns found the pre-polling particularly politicised and, in some instances, unsafe and scary. This seems to have been a broader experience of many volunteers in the 2025 election, not just those supporting CIs (see Tingle 2025).

In this election, CI candidates were taken more seriously by parties and, in many seats, parties launched strong attacks on CI candidates (especially incumbent CI MPs). Parties and their candidates had a better understanding of the CI approach (and electoral threat) and they used this knowledge to challenge CI candidates. As mentioned above, the key example of this was Tim Wilson in Goldstein, but also in other seats the parliamentary voting records of CI incumbents, particularly their votes with the Greens, were used in advertising attacking the 'independence' of CI MPs. In addition, according to key figures within the movement, such as Zali Steggall on ABC TV's *Insiders* program the day after the election, third-party groups such as Advance played a large role campaigning against CI candidates. The media covered several targeted attacks on CI candidates especially in metropolitan seats (for example, Tingle 2025d; Bogle 2025), but it is important to note that such attacks also surfaced in the regions. For example, as shown in Plate 14.3, posters were erected in rural areas such as Calare (NSW).

Plate 14.3 Negative attacks on CI candidate Kate Hook in Calare, NSW
Photo: Kate Hook.

Plate 14.4 Climate 200–funded mobile billboards for multiple CI candidates
Photo: Climate 200.

While the campaign dynamics were highly localised, there were some common elements across CI campaigns, particularly in terms of donations and support from C200 (see Plate 14.4). Of the 38 CI candidates who stood, 33 received part of their funding and other support from C200. From what we understand, five CI candidates did not receive C200 support during the election. This included newcomers Chris Kearney (Jagajaga), Kath Davies (Chisholm) and Kate Lockhart (Corangamite)—all contesting Labor-held seats. In addition, David Pocock (ACT Senator) and Zali Steggall (Warringah) publicly moved away from C200 funding. This served to create distance from the organisation and its founder, Simon Holmes à Court (Coorey 2025). Steggall is quoted as saying: 'I have received no funding from Climate 200 for the upcoming election … Suggestions that I'm beholden to Climate 200 or its founder are completely incorrect and overblown' (Cropp 2025a).

In this election, CI campaigns were also well supported by a growing and more sophisticated network of intermediaries providing practical advice and mentoring to CI candidates. For example, the CIP convenes an annual virtual conference and hosts a public website with information and resources. In addition to C200, other funding bodies have been established—for example, the Vida Fund (to support women Independent candidates running on strong gender equity platforms) and the Regional Voices Fund (to seed local community 'voices' groups in rural and regional electorates). The Australian Democracy Network also hosted public forums at which CI candidates were invited to speak, such as their National Integrity Policy Forum on 23 April 2025. This election also saw growth in the use of diverse media platforms and podcasts that CI candidates used to build their local and national profiles, such as C200's The Independents Podcast (hosted by Julia Zemiro) and the SpinProof podcast (hosted by Denise Shrivell).

As in 2022, CI candidates used a variety of colours in their campaigns, with many opting to not use teal shades.[4] Interestingly, some party challengers who were seeking to oust incumbent CI MPs were replacing their traditional party colours with a more 'teal' shade. For example, in the seat of Curtin (which was the most marginal of the CI incumbent seats going into the 2025 election), Liberal Party challenger Tom White adopted a softer 'teal-like' blue tone for his election campaign.

---

4   For more discussion of the CIM's use of colour, see Hendriks and Reid (2023).

Community Independents' election results

The election results for CI candidates were mixed; much depended on the specific political challenges that played out in each electorate.[5] Below we have collated the electoral results based on which candidates were successful, who made it into the final two and who did not make it into the final distribution of preferences.[6]

Table 14.4 Successful Community Independent candidates

Candidate	Electorate	Type of electorate	Result 2CP (%)	Swing first preference (%)	Swing 2CP (%)
Nicolette Boele	Bradfield, NSW	Metropolitan	50.0	+4.2	+2.5
Kate Chaney	Curtin, WA	Metropolitan	53.3	+2.5	+2.0
Helen Haines	Indi, Vic.	Rural	58.6	+1.6	–0.3
Monique Ryan	Kooyong, Vic.	Metropolitan	50.7	+3.1	–1.5
Sophie Scamps	Mackellar, NSW	Metropolitan	55.7	–0.5	+2.4
Allegra Spender	Wentworth, NSW	Metropolitan	58.3	+7.2	+1.6
Zali Steggall	Warringah, NSW	Metropolitan	61.2	–0.1	+1.8
David Pocock	ACT Senator	39.2% group vote (quota 1.17)	–	–	–

Note: 2CP = two-candidate-preferred.

Source: ABC (2025b).

The successful candidates are listed in Table 14.4. Six of the seven incumbents were re-elected: five CI MPs and one CI senator—most with stronger margins than in 2022. As seen in Indi and Warringah in previous elections, once a CI is elected, voters tend to hold on to their representative. A new CI MP, second-time challenger Nicolette Boele, was elected in the Sydney seat of Bradfield after waiting almost four weeks for counting to be finalised. The Bradfield result was a rollercoaster for all involved; on the first count, the Liberal candidate was ahead by 8 votes and, yet, after the recount, the

---

5   Whereas in 2022 the Australian Election Study (AES) Survey found that those voting for Community Independents were strategic voters seeking to oust Liberal candidates (McAllister 2023), we suspect the voting picture for 2025 is more complicated. The voting intentions for 2025 will be clearer once AES data are made available for the 2025 election.

6   The swings are based on the ABC's (2025b) calculations, which factored in the effects of redistributions since the 2022 election and consequently differ from the AEC's reported swings.

CI candidate won by 26 votes. Two months after the election, the Liberal Party lodged a petition to the Court of Disputed Returns contesting the Bradfield result.[7]

The two Melbourne CI incumbents, Zoe Daniel and Monique Ryan, had very close results after facing fierce competition from Liberal challengers, former Liberal MP Tim Wilson in Goldstein and Amelia Hamer in Kooyong. Both Ryan and Daniel had to wait more than three painstaking weeks to resolve their seats. Ryan was successful in Kooyong, with Daniel in Goldstein being the only incumbent CI MP to lose their seat in the 2025 election (after a partial recount that was called at her request).

The results indicate that, overall, the incumbent CIs did well. Four CI MPs had first-preference swings towards them, ranging from 1.6 per cent in Indi to 7.2 per cent in Wentworth. Four of the six also had two-candidate-preferred swings towards them. David Pocock was comfortably re-elected to the Senate. However, the Victorian incumbent CI MPs fared worse than those in other States and Territories. All three—Helen Haines, Monique Ryan and Zoe Daniel—had two-candidate swings away from them, and Daniel lost the seat of Goldstein (and is consequently included in Table 14.5).

Nine CI candidates made it into second place, as shown in Table 14.5. Three of these were repeat challengers, two of whom had small swings towards them in two-candidate-preferred terms: Dyson (Wannon) and Holt (Groom). Caz Heise in Cowper made it into the final two, but Nationals incumbent Pat Conaghan had a very small swing to him (+0.1 per cent).

Five newcomers made it into second place. Two came very close to unseating Labor incumbents in formerly safe seats: Jessie Price in Bean (ACT) and Kate Hulett in Fremantle (WA). Other newcomers, Ben Smith (Flinders), Michelle Milthorpe (Farrer) and Peter George (Franklin) also made it into the final two. All three were well-known local identities due to their professional backgrounds or community advocacy work.

---

7   This petition was ultimately unsuccessful.

Table 14.5 Community Independent candidates in second place

Candidate	Electorate	Type of electorate	Incumbent	Results 2CP (%)	Swing first preference (%)	Swing 2CP (%)
Zoe Daniel	Goldstein, Vic.	Metropolitan (inner)	Liberal	49.9	–0.6	–3.3
Alex Dyson	Wannon, Vic.	Rural	Liberal	46.7	+12.7	+0.5
Peter George	Franklin, Tas.	Metropolitan (outer)	Labor	42.2	+21.7	+5.9
Caz Heise	Cowper, NSW	Provincial	Nationals	47.5	+3.2	–0.1
Kate Hulett	Fremantle, WA	Metropolitan (inner)	Labor	49.3	+23.0	+16.2
Suzie Holt	Groom, Qld	Provincial	LNP	44.3	+8.9	+1.2
Michelle Milthorpe	Farrer, NSW	Rural	Liberal	43.8	+20.0	+10.2
Jessie Price	Bean, ACT	Metropolitan (inner)	Labor	49.7	+26.4	+12.6
Ben Smith	Flinders, Vic.	Rural	Liberal	47.7	+21.2	+3.9

Note: 2CP = two-candidate-preferred; Shaded rows indicate repeat challengers and incumbents.

Source: ABC (2025b).

The repeat challengers, overall, did well—in terms of votes. All repeat challengers increased their primary votes, except for Kate Hook in Calare. In the Sydney seat of Bradfield, Boele (discussed above) had a strong first-preference swing and a two-candidate-preferred swing of +2.5 per cent. In regional Australia, Suzie Holt (Groom in Queensland) and Alex Dyson (Wannon in Victoria) had swings towards them, building on their positive 2022 swings. In regional New South Wales, Caz Heise, while having a primary-vote swing of +3.2 per cent, had a small two-candidate-preferred swing away from her 2022 result of –0.1 per cent. However, and most importantly, only one CI repeat challenger managed to translate votes into seats at the 2025 election. All others were unsuccessful in unseating the incumbent MP (Cowper, Calare, Groom, Wannon, Monash and Casey). It is also worth noting that both incumbents and repeat challengers did not enjoy the same kind of preference flows they did in 2022. The presence of other Independents (especially ex-party MPs) made the task of election for some CI candidates especially difficult (for example, Hook in Calare).

The large group of newcomers (23) had diverse results. While by virtue of being first-time contenders all technically had primary-vote swings towards them, only five made it into the final distribution of preferences: Bean (ACT), Fremantle (WA), Flinders (Victoria), Farrer (NSW) and Franklin (Tasmania). Interestingly, and in contrast to the incumbent MPs and the repeat challengers, three of these were in traditionally safe Labor seats (Bean, Fremantle and Franklin). As elsewhere, local dynamics were incredibly important, with David Pocock's support, in addition to a strong local campaign, seen as a big vote-winner for Price in Bean; Hulett building on the back of a strong result in the preceding WA State election; and George, a well-known local media presenter, campaigned strongly on the issue of salmon farming in Tasmania (and was elected to the Tasmanian State seat of Franklin in July 2025). These strong results demonstrate the ability of CI candidates to be competitive outside Coalition seats. However, none of the newcomers was able to win the seat on their first attempt; they did, however, make some safe seats more marginal.

Of the CI candidates listed in Table 14.6, it is also noteworthy that a handful received significant numbers of first-preference votes and these were in rural seats—for example, Keryn Jones in Fisher (Queensland), Anita Kuss in Grey (South Australia), Sue Chapman in Forrest (Western Australia) and Jeremy Miller in Lyne (NSW). However, 10 CI candidates received fewer than 10,000 votes.

Table 14.6 Community Independent candidates not in final distribution of preferences

Candidate	Electorate	Type of electorate	Incumbent	First-preference votes	First-preference swing (%)
Nicole Arrowsmith	Moncrieff, Qld	Provincial	LNP	7,641	+7.6
Nathan Barton	Moore, WA	Metropolitan (outer)	Liberal	6,762	+6.3
Tina Brown	Berowra, NSW	Metropolitan (outer)	Liberal	13,135	+11.4
Sue Chapman	Forrest, WA	Rural	Liberal	18,206	+18.3
Verity Cooper	Sturt, SA	Metropolitan (inner)	Liberal	8,413	+7.2
Kath Davies	Chisholm, Vic.	Metropolitan (inner)	Labor	6,685	+5.9

Candidate	Electorate	Type of electorate	Incumbent	First-preference votes	First-preference swing (%)
Kate Dezarnaulds	Gilmore, NSW	Rural	Labor	8,371	+7.5
Claire Ferres Miles	Casey, Vic.	Rural	Liberal	11,590	+2.4
Kate Hook	Calare, NSW	Rural	Independent (formerly Nationals)	16,756	–4.6
Keryn Jones	Fisher, Qld	Rural	LNP	19,296	+16.3
Chris Kearney	Jagajaga, Vic.	Metropolitan (outer)	Labor	5,167	+4.6
Anita Kuss	Grey, SA	Rural	Liberal	18,745	+17.5
Deb Leonard	Monash, Vic.	Rural	Independent (formerly Liberal)	17,529	+6.4
Kate Lockhart	Corangamite, Vic.	Provincial	Labor	4,565	+4.4
Jeremy Miller	Lyne, NSW	Rural	Nationals	16,943	+15.5
Erchana Murray-Bartlett	McPherson, Qld	Provincial	LNP	13,366	+13.8
Jess Ness	Deakin, Vic.	Metropolitan (outer)	Liberal	8,253	+7.2
Jenny Rolfe	Riverina, NSW	Rural	Nationals	6,909	+6.5
Phil Scott	Solomon, NT	Metropolitan (inner)	Labor	7,501	+12.5
Ellie Smith	Dickson, Qld	Metropolitan (outer)	LNP	12,874	+12.2
Francine Wiig	Fairfax, Qld	Rural	LNP	13,085	+11.8

Note: Shaded rows indicate repeat challenger.

Source: ABC (2025b).

Broader reflections on the Community Independents Movement

While the number of CIs elected at the 2025 election was the same as the number of those holding seats going into the election, we offer a more nuanced interpretation of the CIM's impact on Australian politics at this point. Compared with 2022, the CIM is growing; there were more electorate groups, CI candidates and volunteers than in the 2022 election. CI candidates also attracted more votes.

The CIM continues to operate as a localised movement and not a party. Local electorate groups take differentiated pathways. Some begin with the slow, deep work of engaging local constituents in conversations about political representation, after which they might select a candidate and then support their campaign; other groups move faster by jumping directly into candidate selection and campaigning (see Hendriks and Reid 2024a). In relation to the diversity of local groups within the CIM, Alana Johnson, co-founder of Voices for Indi and the CIP, reflects that in the 2025 election the groups that went directly into campaign mode channelled community effort into a single moment, the election, but in so doing, they potentially missed broader opportunities to engage and empower local constituents to take ownership in strengthening political representation.[8]

The diverse election results of CI candidates reflect the localised nature of the movement. Each CI campaign was shaped by different levels of community input, resourcing and local political dynamics. The diverse results of the CI candidates also render visible the fact that the preferential voting system played out differently for CIs depending on the candidate list. The 2025 election also demonstrated that the CIM is not a one-off phenomenon nor is it solely an anti-Coalition one; Labor and Independent seats were also targeted. Moreover, many CI candidates made their seats more marginal and, in some cases, led to longer and more complicated counting processes.

The question of whether this is a predominantly urban phenomenon remains open. Half the CI candidates who stood were in what the AEC defines as rural or provincial seats (19 of 38). Yet, despite their number, CI candidates in rural and provincial seats struggled to make the same kinds of electoral gains as their metropolitan counterparts (such as in Bradfield,

---

8   Personal communication with the authors, 16 July 2025.

Bean and Fremantle). An analysis of booth-level voting patterns in rural and provincial seats by Cathy McGowan (with CIP) shows that CI candidates 'won' booths in some regional cities—for example, Albury and Toowoomba (see CIP 2025c).

The movement also continues to navigate tensions between its localised, largely leaderless approach and the reliance of many CI candidates on C200 for donations and campaign support. As was seen with the varying approaches of CI candidates to C200 funding, C200 generates challenges for the CIM. This is not just about its large financial contributions, but also about the media attention that C200 founder, Simon Holmes à Court, attracts. One CI insider is quoted as saying: 'Every time he sticks his head up, it creates negative media. It shouldn't be about him, it should be about the candidates' (Coorey 2025). In addition, former CI MP Kylea Tink, who stepped into a spokesperson role for the CIP in May 2025, is quoted as saying, in reference to the focus of a range of actors, including the media, on C200:

> Climate 200 at the moment is having an oversized share of the voice when it comes to what's really driving this movement ... That is very frustrating. This movement is far larger than Climate 200 and it's going to continue to get larger still. (Cropp 2025b)

Conclusion

The 2025 electoral journey of CI candidates serves as a reminder that Australia's electoral landscape remains dominated by the party system. For CI incumbent MPs, it is not always about smooth re-election, as Daniel and Ryan experienced in Goldstein and Kooyong, respectively. While in some seats, CI candidates are disrupting the party stranglehold, and in one case a new CI MP was elected, even after two or three attempts, most repeat challengers have been unsuccessful.

In the Forty-Eighth Parliament, the Labor Party's significant majority means that CI MPs, as part of the crossbench, are likely to have less influence than in the Forty-Seventh Parliament. When this proposition was put to Zali Steggall on ABC TV's Insiders program the day after the election, her response was that they would continue to play an important role in keeping the government accountable. This is even more significant in the Senate, where the Labor government will no longer need to work with

Independents and other minor parties if they can reach agreement with either the Coalition or the Greens. This will be a test for David Pocock, who had significant influence in the last parliament due to the Senate numbers.

Fatigue is also a significant issue for the movement; will repeat challengers and newcomers keep trying? Can candidates and their volunteers continue to sustain the electoral pressure? In addition, will donors keep supporting CI candidates? In Bradfield and Groom, Boele and Holt, respectively, maintained high profiles in their electorates over the past three years (see Hendriks and Reid 2024b) and this led to victory for Boele but not for Holt. In Wannon, 2025 was Dyson's third unsuccessful attempt. One repeat challenger, Caz Heise in Cowper, has already announced she will not be standing as a CI candidate at the next election. This speaks to the demands of political campaigning, particularly in the absence of the organisational supports of a political party.

The 2025 election might also prove something of a 'last' chance for new CI candidates to fund big campaigns that can compete with parties. This is the result of changes to election financing laws scheduled to come into force before the next election. It remains unclear what the effects of these changes and the response of the CIM will be. In the previous parliament CI MPs opposed aspects of these reforms (see Chaney 2024). While incumbent MPs will be advantaged, the challenge will be for new CI candidates to find ways to raise their profile and compete in the absence of large campaign spending. In a positive light, this might redouble the efforts of the CIM to engage widely and deeply with local communities, as it has done in Indi since 2013. While the results of the 2025 election as a test for the CIM are inconclusive, what is clear is that it remains extremely difficult to disrupt Australia's two-party system.

References

Australian Broadcasting Corporation (ABC). 2025a. 'Kooyong MP Monique Ryan, husband apologise after removing political rival's sign.' *ABC News*, 24 March. www.abc.net.au/news/2025-03-24/federal-mp-monique-ryan-and-husband-apologise-after-sign-removal/105088472.

ABC. 2025b. 'Federal election 2025—Australia votes.' *ABC News*. www.abc.net.au/news/elections/federal-election-2025.

Australian Electoral Commission (AEC). 2025. 'First preferences by party.' *Tally Room: 2025 Federal Election*. [Last updated 10 June]. Canberra: Australian Electoral Commission. results.aec.gov.au/31496/Website/HouseStateFirstPrefsByParty-31 496-NAT.htm.

Bogle, Ariel. 2025. 'Third-party groups targeting teals in key seats swarm pre-poll areas in NSW and Victoria.' *The Guardian*, 24 April. www.theguardian.com/ australia-news/2025/apr/24/teal-independents-nsw-victoria-better-australia-federal-election.

Chaney, Kate. 2024. 'Rather than banning big money, Labor's electoral changes will guarantee cash keeps flowing to the big parties.' *The Guardian*, 15 November. www.theguardian.com/commentisfree/2024/nov/15/labor-electoral-rules-changes-major-parties-donations.

Community Independents Project (CIP). 2025a. *About: CI Candidates in 2025.* [Online]. Sydney: Community Independents Project. www.community independentsproject.org/ci-mps-candidates.

Community Independents Project (CIP). 2025b. *About: Community Electorate Group Register.* [Online]. Sydney: Community Independents Project. www. communityindependentsproject.org/community-electorate-groups.

Community Independents Project (CIP). 2025c. *Election Debrief: The Independent Wave.* [Online]. Sydney: Community Independents Project. www.community independentsproject.org/cip-resources/election-debrief.

Coorey, Phillip. 2025. 'David Pocock leaves the Climate 200 mothership.' *Australian Financial Review*, 19 March. www.afr.com/politics/federal/david-pocock-leaves-the-climate-200-mothership-20250318-p5lkch.

Cropp, Ryan. 2025a. '"No funding": More teals play down Climate 200 links.' *Australian Financial Review*, 20 March.

Cropp, Ryan. 2025b. '"Headless movements fall": Can Holmes à Court maintain the rage?' *Australian Financial Review*, 17 April. www.afr.com/politics/federal/ headless-movements-fall-can-holmes-court-maintain-the-rage-20250406-p5lpie.

Daniel, Zoe. 2025. 'Statement to the people of Goldstein.' [News]. Zoe Daniel, 31 May. zoedaniel.com.au/2025/05/31/statement-to-the-people-of-goldstein/.

Epstein, Raf. 2025. 'Zoe Daniel says "lies and attacks" impacted election outcome in Goldstein.' *Melbourne Mornings*, [*ABC Radio*], 2 June. www.abc.net.au/listen/ programs/melbourne-mornings/zoe-daniel-on-losing-goldstein/105366164.

Hayman, Phoebe. 2024 'Doorknocks and dog bandanas: A new conception of field campaigning activities.' *Australian Journal of Political Science* 59, no. 1: 55–71. doi.org/10.1080/10361146.2024.2313717.

Hendriks, Carolyn M. 2017. 'Citizen-led democratic reform: Innovations in Indi.' *Australian Journal of Political Science* 52, no. 4: 481–99. doi.org/10.1080/1036 1146.2017.1374345.

Hendriks, Carolyn M., and Richard Reid. 2023. 'The rise and impact of Australia's Movement for Community Independents.' In *Watershed: The 2022 Australian Federal Election*, edited by Anika Gauja, Marian Sawer, and Jill Sheppard, 279–304. Canberra: ANU Press. doi.org/10.22459/W.2023.14.

Hendriks, Carolyn M., and Richard Reid. 2024a. 'Citizen-led democratic change: How Australia's community independents movement is reshaping representative democracy.' *Political Studies* 72, no. 4: 1609–31. doi.org/10.1177/ 00323217231219393.

Hendriks, Carolyn M., and Richard Reid. 2024b. 'Shadow representation: Making claims to represent better than the official representative.' *Representation* 60, no. 4: 685–702. doi.org/10.1080/00344893.2024.2386987.

Ilanbey, Sumeyya. 2025. 'Inside the campaign that brought Zoe Daniel down.' *Australian Financial Review*, 7 May. www.afr.com/politics/federal/inside-the-campaign-that-brought-zoe-daniel-down-20250505-p5lwnp.

Johnson, Alana. 2025. 'Doing politics differently: Safeguarding Australian democracy.' In *What's the Big Idea? 30 Years of The Australia Institute*, edited by Anna Chang and Alice Grundy, 90–93. Canberra: Australia Institute Press.

McAllister, Ian. 2023. 'Party explanations for the 2022 Australian election result.' *Australian Journal of Political Science* 58, no. 4: 309–25. doi.org/10.1080/1036 1146.2023.2257611.

Newlands, Maxine. 2025. 'Independents took cities by storm last election. This time they've got regional Australia in their sights.' *The Conversation*, 11 March. theconversation.com/independents-took-cities-by-storm-last-election-this-time-theyve-got-regional-australia-in-their-sights-250894. doi.org/10.64628/AA.7dc 655k4a.

Reid, Richard, Carolyn M. Hendriks, and Anika Gauja. 2025. 'An alternative to the party? Australia's movement for community independents.' *Party Politics*: July. doi.org/10.1177/13540688251356900.

Seccombe, Mike. 2025a. 'Polling shows teals support is growing in Coalition base.' *The Saturday Paper*, 22–28 March. www.thesaturdaypaper.com.au/news/politics/2025/03/22/polling-shows-teals-support-growing-coalition-base.

Seccombe, Mike. 2025b. 'Inside story: How Albanese's late election sent the teals broke.' *The Saturday Paper*, 29 March – 4 April. www.thesaturdaypaper.com.au/news/politics/2025/03/29/inside-story-how-albaneses-late-election-sent-the-teals-broke.

Tingle, Laura. 2025. 'Election volunteers say they experienced abuse and aggression at polling booths.' *7.30*, [*ABC TV*], 28 May. www.abc.net.au/news/2025-05-28/election-volunteers-say-they-experienced-abuse-and/105350306.

15

Independents and minor parties

Phoebe Hayman and Jill Sheppard

Abstract

Australian elections have long been characterised by Independent and minor-party challengers who struggle to get elected but influence the shape and colour of campaigns. In an era of disengagement from major political parties and electoral fragmentation, these candidates are increasingly important; though they rarely win, they influence campaign agendas and can seriously impact the distribution of preferences. The 2025 election saw low-spending candidates help keep housing and Gaza on the national agenda, incumbent Independents retain their seats with increased support and local candidates reverse the Labor tide in seats such as Calwell. Clive Palmer spammed the nation with text messages for zero return, while One Nation mostly laid low and doubled their presence in the Senate, rehabilitating their relationship with the Coalition along the way. Much more than in 2022 (when Teal candidates focused on Coalition seats), both major parties lost votes and attention to Independents and minor parties.

Keywords: Independents; minor parties; fragmentation; dealignment; preferences

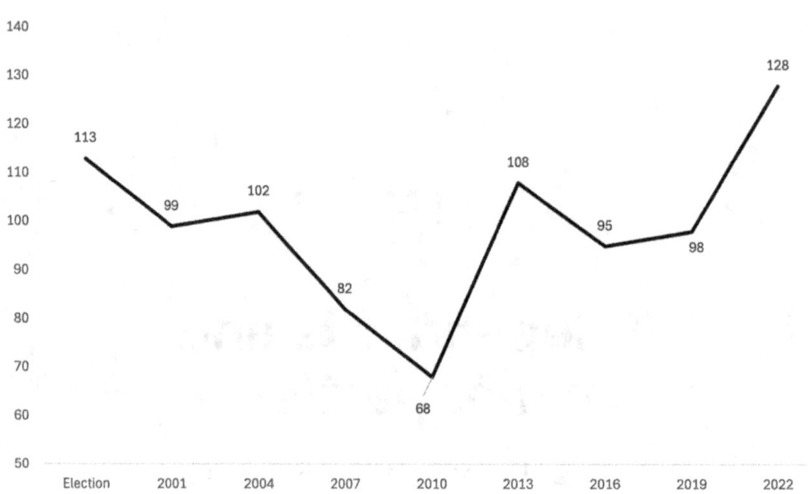

Figure 15.1 Count of Independent candidates contesting House of Representatives seats in federal elections, 2001–2025
Source: Compiled by authors using AEC data.

In the leadup to the 2025 federal election, a minority government seemed a very real possibility. The Albanese government had limped through the final year of its first term and, although the Liberal Party was ascendant, Opposition leader Peter Dutton's personal popularity and prospects in the inner-city seats won by 'Teal' Independents in 2022 appeared dubious. Independents and minor parties were (often quietly) multiplying and marshalling more resources and supporters than ever before. Some of these candidates—namely, Climate 200–backed Community Independents, generally known as 'Teals'—had access to millions of dollars and thousands of volunteers (see Chapter 14, this volume). At the other end of the resource spectrum, it is increasingly easy for any challenger to set up a campaign with the veneer of a professionalised and coordinated effort at a fraction of the price. This chapter discusses those Independents other than Community Independents who, from high-spending to shoestring, helped shape the 2025 federal election.

Of the 1,122 candidates who contested lower house seats in this election, 77 per cent were not from the major parties. This group comprised established minor parties such as the Greens and One Nation,[1] smaller minor parties, apostates from the major parties such as Andrew Gee and Ian Goodenough, established Independents such as Dai Le and Andrew Wilkie and newer

---

1   For discussion of the Greens' campaign, see Chapter 13, this volume.

entrants, including pro-Palestinian Independents supported by Muslim Votes Matter and Muslim Vote Australia. In total, 128 Independents ran in lower house contests across the country—the highest number in the two-party era (Figure 15.1).

The rise of Independents and minor parties is a direct response to major parties and their perceived failures, whether these failures are in achieving particular policy actions or representing their communities more generally.[2] Ghazarian (2012) charted the shift from secessionist to issue-based minor parties in the Senate from 1984 to 2012, as minor parties formed from social movements to take up the issue areas that major parties were failing to represent. These parties have championed national issues, such as the Greens' campaigning on the environment or Pauline Hanson's One Nation on immigration. In the same period, Independents were overwhelmingly men representing rural communities (Costar and Curtin 2004), although Riboldi et al. (2024) note the recent rise of party-like Independent women across State, Territory and the national parliaments. In 2025, we note two prevailing themes. First, although outsider candidates have previously been considered primarily expressions of local discontent, Independents and minor parties increasingly address both local and national issues. Voters' growing support for outsider candidates who contest on both national and local issues speaks to the growing gap in representation that voters are seeking to fill with something or someone new (Gauja and McSwiney 2019). Second, the majoritarian nature of Australia's electoral system obscures this story of dealignment, maintaining the tradition of Labor or Coalition governments, no matter the decline in major-party vote share. Despite a declining two-party vote, Australia's system remains stable, contrasting with the volatility seen elsewhere (Pildes 2021).

In this chapter, we capture the diversity and variety of these candidates who toil below the surface of Australian electoral politics. First, we consider the most enduring groups of outsider candidates: 'apostates' from the major parties and personalistic and regional Independent candidates. Next, we look at the Independent candidates outside the organised efforts associated with groups such as Climate 200 and discuss how local Independent campaigns appear increasingly professional. Despite gaining less national attention

---

2   Weeks' (2009) typology of Irish Independents provides familiar categories for Australians: community Independents (those elected on local issues), apostates (those who have left a political party through choice, exile or failure to win preselection) and ideological Independents (those elected to further a political cause or national issue).

than their Teal counterparts, these candidates are still the majority of Independents. Finally, we review the minor parties, distinguishing between those with significant campaign spending and those working within more modest budgets.

Incumbent Independents and minor-party members

Independents who were elected as party-endorsed candidates and defected mid-term have been the most enduring form of Independent candidate across Australian parliaments and were again well represented at this election. Andrew Gee (formerly Nationals) was the only 'apostate' to successfully retain their seat in 2025, winning Calare (NSW) with 57 per cent of the two-candidate-preferred (2CP) vote share (see also Chapter 12, this volume). Coming second on primary votes (behind Nationals candidate Sam Farraway), Gee benefited from the strong preference flows from repeat Independent candidate Kate Hook and Labor's Julie Cunningham. Other lower house apostates, Russell Broadbent and Ian Goodenough, were not re-elected.

In the Senate, David Van (Victoria) and Gerard Rennick (Queensland) stood for re-election after leaving the Coalition. Van was expelled from the Liberal Party in 2023 after several years of allegations of sexual misconduct (Grattan 2023). Years of positioning himself as a defence expert and friend to Ukraine were also undermined by allegations that he had misbehaved on a Defence Force–funded voyage in 2021 and accepted a trip to Ukraine funded by a drone manufacturer in 2022 (Elsworthy 2023). Van received 554 primary votes (0.0009 of a quota). Rennick left the LNP in 2024 after losing preselection for a winnable place on the Queensland Senate ticket. He formed the 'Gerard Rennick People First' party with a platform of lower taxes, withdrawal from international health and climate change treaties and calls for a referendum to enshrine freedom of speech in the Constitution. The party received 150,178 primary votes in Queensland but could not turn its 0.33 of a quota into an elected senator. Nonetheless, this primary vote result is significant in a State with a well-established One Nation support base and where Labor achieved a primary swing of 5.8 per cent.

The Forty-Seventh Parliament also comprised a core of well-established (and non–Climate 200–funded) Independent and smaller minor-party members: Dai Le (Fowler, NSW), Bob Katter (Kennedy, Queensland), Senator Jacqui Lambie (Tasmania), Andrew Wilkie (Clark, Tasmania) and Rebecca Sharkie (Mayo, SA). The first two have relatively low national profiles considering their huge electoral margins: in 2022, Wilkie won with 72 per cent of the 2CP vote and Sharkie (the sole member of the parliamentary Centre Alliance party) with 62 per cent of the 2CP. Wilkie was returned in 2025 with his margin unchanged. Sharkie received only 30 per cent of the primary vote, with a 2 per cent swing away from 2022, but benefited from strong preference flows from a wide range of candidates. Bob Katter (the lone Katter's Australian Party representative) was returned in Kennedy (Queensland) with only a 1 per cent primary-vote swing against him.

Le, who beat former NSW premier Kristina Keneally in 2022, formed her own party in 2023—originally the Dai Le & Frank Carbone Network (DLFCN), but renamed Western Sydney Community in 2024. The party appears to exist primarily to support local government candidates, as Le did not use the party endorsement in her parliamentary role nor run under the party name. The coordination between a federal parliamentarian (and former councillor) and a current local mayor is intriguing, however, and may inspire others to leverage local government popularity. In 2025 Le defeated Labor's Tu Le, gaining a 5 per cent swing on primary votes and a 1 per cent 2CP swing. While Labor was criticised for not nominating a Fowler local in 2022 (Sheppard 2023: 269–71), the party's decision to stand Tu Le, a daughter of Vietnamese refugees and community lawyer in Parramatta whom Labor overlooked at the previous election, did not bring voters back to the party.

Despite being in the Senate since 2013, Jacqui Lambie's primary vote has plateaued at about 8 per cent, or 0.6 of a quota in a half-Senate election. In 2025, she (as lead candidate for her eponymous party, the Jacqui Lambie Network) suffered a 1.4 per cent primary-vote swing against her in Tasmania but was elected in fifth place on the back of strong preference flows. There are two opposite but equally plausible interpretations of this result: given that Labor achieved an 8 per cent swing across the State, Lambie's primary vote held up quite well; on the other hand, conditions for Independent candidates are possibly as favourable as they will ever be and Lambie's inability to improve her primary vote above 8 per cent suggests a hard cap on her support. Either way, she cements her status as Australia's second-longest serving Independent senator.

Non–Community/C200 Independents

The seat of Calwell in Victoria, where retiring Labor member Maria Vamvakinou had a 2CP margin of 12.4 per cent, almost threw up the biggest surprise of 2025. Pre-election, the ABC's Antony Green described the seat as 'very safe' and could not find a headshot of Independent candidate Carly Moore—the eventual second-placed candidate—for his otherwise comprehensive election guide. Only Samim Moslih, an Independent candidate endorsed by pro-Palestine group Muslim Votes Matter, attracted serious media attention before 3 May (see, for example, Wedesweiler 2025). Neither Climate 200 nor Community Independents endorsed candidates in this seat.

Moore's candidacy in many ways reflects Dai Le's in 2022: both are former councillors within their electorates with political experience and strong local name recognition. Both were exercised by Labor's centralisation of preselection decisions: Moore's sister was overlooked to run in the seat, which was effectively gifted from Vamvakinou to her staffer Basem Abdo, while Le (arguably) benefited from Labor's preselection of former NSW premier Keneally in 2022. Moore quit the Labor Party and ran as an Independent with the support of disaffected Labor branch members (including her sister). Fellow Independent Joseph Youhana, a member of the local Assyrian community who ran on a noticeably anti-Labor platform, directed preferences to Moore. Despite a 14 per cent primary-vote swing against him, Abdo eventually won the seat to become the country's first Palestinian Australian parliamentarian.

The emphasis on preferences here is deliberate, speaking to the significance of even 'peripheral' candidates and parties (cf. Kefford 2017). While Moore benefited from a strong local profile (she won 82 per cent of the primary vote in her council ward in 2024), she also benefited from a large contingent of Independent and smaller minor-party candidates on the ballot (10 in total, plus Liberal, Labor and Greens). Buried at the bottom of an article on the complex vote count in Calwell was this revelation: 'Liberal MP Evan Mulholland, from Victoria's state upper house, was involved in negotiating several Independent candidates' preferences towards each other, which has kept them in the race' (Rooney 2025). This recalls 'preference whispering' in the Senate, where the election of candidates with as little as 0.5 per cent of the primary vote led to electoral reform in 2016 (Muller 2018). In the House of Representatives, though, voters are free to direct their preferences as they wish; the result in Calwell, where preference flows turned Moore's 11.9 per cent primary vote into 44.9 per cent 2CP, reflects voters' sincere distaste for major-party candidates.

Big-spending minor parties

Clive Palmer's Trumpet of Patriots

In what appears to be his final foray into Australian elections, mining billionaire and former MP Clive Palmer again spent big and won nothing. In 2022, Palmer's United Australia Party (UAP) nominated candidates in all 151 House of Representatives seats and in the Senate in every State. Expenditure of $131 million between 2019 and 2022 yielded one Senate seat in Victoria, with Ralph Babet elected on 4 per cent of the primary vote (0.28 of a quota). Unable to re-register the UAP name in 2024, Palmer took over the moribund Australian Federation Party, changed its name in December 2024 and unleashed on Australian voters Trumpet of Patriots and its AI-generated logo (comprising a trumpet-blowing lion and the motto '*Honor omnia*'). No Trumpet of Patriot candidates were elected, despite estimated campaign expenditure of about $60 million (Belot 2025).

The party launched its campaign with a live speech from American right-wing journalist Tucker Carlson and yellow caps with the slogan 'Make Australia great again'. In a campaign that ended with both prime ministerial aspirants trying to avoid being associated with Donald Trump, Trumpet of Patriots promised to create an Australian Department of Government Efficiency, 'prioritise migration from nations with compatible values', restore coal-fired power plants, 'get the woke agenda out of our schools' and 'bring back Australian manufacturing' (Wrightson 2025), as well as the obvious nod in the party's name.

Although Trumpet of Patriots nominated more candidates than did the UAP in 2022, the party was demonstrably disorganised and bad at vetting candidates. Only 44 candidates had been preselected four weeks out from the election, with the remainder announced during the campaign period. The party's candidate for Reid (NSW) had previously bought a fake PhD on the internet and posed as a qualified counsellor (Hair 2024). The candidate for Dickson had outstanding criminal charges for trespassing, possession of a knife, wilful damage, unlawful stalking and possession of unlawful weapons

(ABC 2025). The candidate for Wide Bay was previously imprisoned for fraud (Marie 2025). In Flinders, the party's candidate urged voters to put him last on their ballot paper in protest at receiving his how-to-vote cards and seeing his Teal opponent listed above more conservative candidates; Palmer said that the party had been 'hacked' and the cards printed incorrectly (Sharma 2025). Another candidate (in Makin, SA) resigned his nomination for several reasons, including the party's SMS-based advertising campaign and preference deals (McNamara 2025).

Trumpet of Patriots was not the only party to use mass text message advertising in 2025 but no other party was quite as egregious, with some voters receiving daily messages authorised by H. Fong, a longstanding friend of Palmer's. When asked why his name was used to authorise the messages, Fong said he did not know: '[Maybe] because my name is shorter than the rest' (Bogle 2025). In other media, Palmer maintained his party's disproportionately high expenditure with more than $24 million on television and YouTube advertisements (more than any other party) and an unspecified amount on countless billboards across the country and front-page newspaper advertisements. There did not seem to be a coherent strategy to the party's advertising expenditure; asked for comment, Palmer said 'money is made to spend' (Buckingham-Jones 2025). Post election, Senator Babet announced that he will not nominate for another term in 2028 and Palmer declared that he is 'getting too old for politics'. Certainly, the introduction of campaign expenditure caps in the next federal election would require Palmer to devise a strategy besides indiscriminate advertising buying.

Pauline Hanson's One Nation

One Nation maintained a relatively low profile in the leadup to the 2025 election. Despite campaigning on an extremely similar policy platform to Trumpet of Patriots—reducing government waste, lowering immigration, supporting local trades and manufacturing and a commitment to free speech—neither Pauline Hanson nor party members mentioned Trump even once during the election. In her one major foray into the campaign (an interview on ABC TV's *7.30* on 10 April), Hanson accused both major parties of 'stealing' her policies and claimed that both Dutton and Albanese refused to consult with her. Rather than trying to tap into pro-Trump sentiment, she and her party successfully aligned themselves with anti–major-party sentiment. In February, Palmer allegedly offered Pauline

Hanson $10 million to rename One Nation 'The Clive and Pauline Party' and grant him a majority of the party's executive positions (Mizen 2025). While Palmer insisted that Hanson's demand to be 'party president for life' killed the deal, One Nation countered that their party was 'not for sale' (Greber and Roe 2025).

More broadly, the party appeared to try to soften Hanson's image as a right-wing firebrand. In April 2024, the party announced that Hanson's daughter, Lee, was nominating for the Senate in Tasmania. Lee Hanson made no real attempt to differentiate herself from her mother, whom she described as 'one of the most tenacious, resilient and strongest women in Australia' (Duggan 2025). This characterisation followed Hanson crying in a television interview and having to 'rebuild her strength' after being found to have defamed Greens Senator Mehreen Faruqi (Crotty 2024).

Whether these were deliberate attempts to soften her public image or just an artefact of Hanson's newsworthiness, it paved the way for the party's reconciliation with the Coalition in the latter half of the campaign. In 2001, John Howard insisted that One Nation be listed last on Coalition 'how to vote' cards; in 2017, the WA Liberals dipped their toe in the water of One Nation deals by preferencing the party above the Greens. In 2025, the start of early voting on 22 April revealed that the Coalition was recommending voters place One Nation second or third in most House of Representatives seats. In return, One Nation recommended Coalition candidates over Labor and Teal Independents (but behind Trumpet of Patriots candidates) in every lower house seat (Martino et al. 2025). One Nation staffer James Ashby declared the preference deal would protect the Coalition from Teal challengers (Crabb 2025), while Liberal Senator James Paterson claimed that Liberal preferences would not go to One Nation candidates in practice, as One Nation candidates are eliminated in early rounds of counting (McIlroy 2025).

Both claims were partially correct. Nationally, 75 per cent of One Nation preferences flowed to the Coalition (compared with Labor), compared with 65 per cent in 2019. This aided the Coalition in seats such as Wannon (Victoria), where One Nation's 4.2 per cent primary vote helped the Liberals' Dan Tehan retain the seat with a 2CP margin of 3.3 per cent. Paterson was proven wrong in Hunter (NSW), where Trumpet of Patriots preferences pushed One Nation's Stuart Bonds ahead of the Nationals' candidate, leading to the distribution of Nationals' preferences to One Nation. Had Bonds been eliminated before the Nationals' Sue Gilroy, Labor's margin (currently

9 per cent) might have been halved. One Nation's self-belief was likewise justified: the party won Senate seats in Western Australia and New South Wales at the expense of Coalition incumbents. In Tasmania, Lee Hanson came eighth in final counting, but vowed to stand again at the next election (Wang 2025).

Low-spending minor parties

Smaller minor parties ran across Australia, representing single issues, local concerns and niche ideological perspectives. They more commonly came from the left of politics and were typically limited in their scope: contesting Senate positions in only some States or in a few lower-house seats in particular areas or States, such as the Victorian Socialists. Others focused on a single policy area—often reflected in the party's name, such as Legalise Cannabis. The prospect of minority government aided their efforts to get attention in 2025: parties such as the Better Together Party and Australia's Voice were announced in 2024 amid a flurry of media attention and enthusiasm that ultimately amounted to little real momentum or support.

Legalise Cannabis worked to build on its performance in 2022, when the party had enjoyed significant swings, most notably in Queensland. The party ran candidates in 41 House of Representatives seats in 2025 (an increase of 40), in a strategy often used by minor parties to gain visibility to increase Senate votes (White and Chung 2025). Among the leading Senate candidates were high-profile figures such as Victoria's Fiona Patten, previously leader of the Reason Party (formerly the Sex Party) in the Victorian Parliament. However, despite gaining ground in most States (amassing an average primary of more than 3.5 per cent), Legalise Cannabis again fell short of a Senate quota. After the election, party president Michael Balderstone spoke of his hopes that the party's strong support would encourage the government to legalise marijuana (White and Chung 2025).

Victorian Socialists

In addition to their efforts at Victorian State and, most successfully, local council elections, the Victorian Socialists have now contested three successive federal elections. The party nominated in just four Victorian seats (three in Labor-held electorates in Melbourne and one in the regional centre of Bendigo) and put forward their two most prominent candidates for the

Senate race. In 2025, the Senate ticket was led by Jordan van den Lamb, an outspoken advocate for renters' rights and housing affordability who has in recent years amassed more than 200,000 TikTok followers and almost 100,000 Instagram followers under the moniker 'Purple Pingers'. He has successfully attracted broadcast media attention for encouraging people to squat in vacant properties and for his website 'shitrentals.org', a public database on which tenants can review their rental properties and landlords (Bahr 2024). In an election in which the housing affordability crisis was in focus, van den Lamb's candidature attracted national media coverage for the Victorian Socialists. This attention was not necessarily positive in tone: links were established between van den Lamb and squatters who had stolen furniture from a property and he was called on to defend sharing the addresses of vacant properties on national television show *The Project* (Parkes-Hupton 2025).

Although none of the party's candidates was elected, the Victorian Socialists' primary vote did increase (from a very low base) in both houses. In the Senate, the party attracted a similar primary vote to the longstanding left-wing issue-based Animal Justice Party (1.5 per cent), but not enough to secure the sixth Senate spot. The party has since announced the establishment of State and Territory branches across Australia and the intention to form a federated national party (Puglisi 2025). In so doing, the Victorian Socialists would join a small list of parties that are registered in every State and Territory (including the majors, the Greens and the Animal Justice Party).

Unlike the rise of the Community Independents, political fragmentation to the left of Labor has primarily manifested itself in minor and issue-based parties. The Greens have been, and continue to be, the primary beneficiary of this splintering, but the recurring swings towards parties such as the Victorian Socialists, Legalise Cannabis and the Animal Justice Party indicate that some votes are shedding to smaller figures on the left. So far, the power of preferences and a majoritarian system have returned these votes to the Labor Party, but the pattern may impact electoral returns and suggests voters are exploring alternative options.

Better Together

Announced in early 2024, Better Together was formed by Lucy Bradlow and Bronwen Bock on the proposition that, if elected, they would job-share: splitting the hours and responsibilities between them. Originally intending to contest Higgins, the duo instead set their sights on the Senate.

Better Together was inspired by Community Independents and wanted endorsement and support from the movement. The campaign was supported by Kim Rubenstein, who ran unsuccessfully for an ACT Senate seat in 2022 with initial support from Climate 200 (Gannon 2025). Bradlow and Bock adopted the language of direct community representation, an interest in experimenting with modes and forms of political participation and a focus on women's issues.

The abolition of Higgins, followed by court challenges to regulations around nominating two individuals for one seat and, finally, Bradlow's dual citizenship conspired against them (Jeffery 2025). These issues scattered the momentum their original announcement created and forced Better Together to campaign Statewide rather than in a local seat—a deadly proposition for Community Independent–style offerings whose strengths and appeal typically derive from local connections and claims of local representation (see Chapter 14, this volume).

Gaza-focused parties and candidates

Muslim and Arabic communities critical of the Albanese government's response to the unfolding crisis in Gaza sought local candidates. These Independent candidates ran in traditionally safe Labor seats, including Watson and Blaxland in Sydney and Calwell in Melbourne (see also Chapter 5, this volume). For many Independent candidates, elections are not solely about winning (Brancati 2008): the goal may be getting a key issue on the agenda, affecting policy change or sending a message to the parties of government. Others may ultimately aim for electoral success, but common wisdom among Independents suggests this requires two successive election cycles (Hutchinson 2023). Whether the Independent candidates who ran in response to Gaza will run again remains to be seen, but their campaigns effectively drew attention to Muslim and Middle Eastern diaspora communities that Labor previously considered safe.

In addition to local organisations and pre-existing bodies such as the Australian Palestine Advocacy Network, two national bodies emerged to support candidates speaking out about Gaza: The Muslim Vote (TMV) and Muslim Votes Matter (MVM). These bodies were inspired by similar efforts in the United Kingdom that effectively shifted votes away from UK Labour in the 2024 general election and contributed to the election of five Independents (Wedesweiler 2024). UK success also contributed to media attention in Australia and speculation that Independents supporting greater pro-Palestinian intervention in Gaza may succeed in areas with significant Muslim populations, such as Western Sydney. As in the United Kingdom, any success would come at the cost of what were traditionally safe Labor seats.

TMV and MVM both supported Muslim Independent candidates but did so in different ways. TMV was the first launched and, in addition to its international sources, drew on the work of Climate 200 and 'Voices of' groups. TMV sought and endorsed candidates and, once the campaigns were launched, worked on fundraising, events, advertising and voter outreach. These efforts were pursued separately from, but in support of, the Independent candidates' campaigns. MVM's efforts more closely resembled those of issue-based third-party campaigning organisations in previous Australian elections. In addition to running voter contact and public events within communities, MVM developed how-to-vote guides and scorecards for candidates based on their stance on Palestine and Gaza, which their volunteers handed out a polling places in key seats. The organisation endorsed Senate candidates from Australia's Voice (discussed below) and 11 lower house candidates who had expressed support for Palestine, including several Greens. Greens candidates were notably only endorsed in the absence of a suitable Independent. TMV supported the efforts of only three Independents: Ziad Basyouny in Watson (NSW), Ahmed Ouf in Blaxland (NSW) and Samim Moslih in Calwell (Victoria).

Despite being motivated to run in response to global issues, these candidates remained remarkably local, as is typical of most Independents. They were notable figures in their communities, serving on the local council (Ouf) or working as a doctor (Basyouny). Prominent backgrounds such as these help Independents match some of the benefits associated with party membership, potentially affording them visibility and giving their campaigns access to community networks and potential supporters who may be recruited to campaign (Singleton 1996; Sharman 2002).

Although none of these Independent candidates made it across the line, their campaigns made an impact. In Watson, Blaxland and Calwell, the strong Independent primary vote (14.74, 18.76 and 6.85 per cent, respectively) was indicative of community support and often concentrated in polling booths with higher Muslim populations in the surrounding area. Basyouny and Ouf both finished in the 2CP count. As discussed, Calwell was a more fractured field, contested by 13 candidates including four Independents.

MVM and TMV have both since expressed their intention to continue. If it does take two elections to get an Independent elected, they may build on this success in 2028.

This was presumably also the thinking behind Senator Fatima Payman's Australia's Voice Party contesting Senate seats across the country for the first time in 2025, before Payman needs to re-contest in 2028. However, these campaigns gained less traction than those in the lower house. After her highly publicised exit from the Labor Party over disagreements about the government's response to Gaza, first-term Senator Payman employed 'preference whisperer' Glen Druery and founded Australia's Voice in 2024 (Karp 2024). Twelve candidates were nominated for Senate spots in Victoria, Queensland, New South Wales, South Australia and Western Australia. However, unlike the lower house Independent candidates, Australia's Voice candidates could not reap the benefit of strong community ties in the Senate race. In a crowded field of outsider candidates and competing issues, Australia's Voice did not manage to cut through. The party's primary vote was less than 1 per cent in most States contested. Payman herself will remain in parliament until the next Senate election, but this initial result was not promising.

Conclusion

The number of Independent and minor-party candidates, and the support they attracted, has continued to rise. Across the political spectrum, these candidates benefited from increased national media coverage, high-profile candidates, professionalised campaigning, supportive organisations and voter anger. The conditions in 2025 seemed particularly favourable and more candidates than ever before emerged in response. This may not be the case at the next federal election, once the new campaign spending regulations come into effect, preventing the type of campaign preferred by Palmer's Trumpet of Patriots and the fundraising that groups such as MVM coordinate.

While few Independent or minor-party candidates were elected in 2025, they influenced the election's key issues, how preferences flowed and where the major parties had to fight to retain seats. Independents and minor parties might be a longstanding feature of Australian politics, but they have never been so diverse or so visible. Some hope to amass enough votes to win a seat in parliament, but others instead aim to direct preferences or raise issues.

The wide range of 'other' options being explored by voters suggests the scale and diversity of voter dissatisfaction—encompassing local and international issues to the left and the right of the major parties. If voters continue to flake away from the major parties and towards these alternatives, the issues they raise and the preference deals they make will only become more important in shaping the national election agenda and the outcome of some of the most closely fought races. In 2025, however, Australia's majoritarian system won out, returning votes to major parties via preferences and maintaining the illusion of major-party dominance.

References

Australian Broadcasting Corporation (ABC). 2025. 'Trumpet of Patriots candidate Michael Jessop facing criminal charges.' *ABC News*, 14 April. www.abc.net.au/news/2025-04-14/michael-jessop-bail-serious-charges-federal-election-candidate/105174716.

Bahr, Jessica. 2024. 'Jordan went viral online exposing dodgy rentals. Now, he's entering politics.' *SBS News*, 26 August. www.sbs.com.au/news/article/jordan-went-viral-online-exposing-dodgy-rentals-now-hes-entering-politics/fmvciy4ur.

Belot, Henry. 2025. 'Clive Palmer's Trumpet of Patriots fails to pick up single lower house seat despite text spam and ad blitz.' *The Guardian*, 4 May. www.theguardian.com/australia-news/2025/may/04/clive-palmers-trumpet-of-patriots-fails-to-pick-up-single-lower-house-seat-despite-text-spam-and-ad-blitz.

Bogle, Ariel. 2025. 'Who is H Fong, the man authorising the flurry of annoying Trumpet of Patriots text messages?' *The Guardian*, 1 May. www.theguardian.com/australia-news/2025/may/01/who-is-h-fong-harry-trumpet-of-patriots-sms-text-messages-federal-election-ntwnfb.

Brancati, Dawn. 2008. 'Winning alone: The electoral fate of independent candidates worldwide.' *The Journal of Politics* 70, no. 3: 648–62. doi.org/10.1017/S002238160808080675.

Buckingham-Jones, Sam. 2025. 'Inside Clive Palmer's advertising strategy (if you can call it that).' *Australian Financial Review*, 7 April. www.afr.com/politics/federal/inside-clive-palmer-s-advertising-strategy-if-you-can-call-it-that-20250319-p5lkqw.

Cleal, Olivia. 2024. '"Politics has to evolve": The two women who want to make job-sharing in politics a reality.' *Women's Agenda*, 30 September. womensagenda.com.au/latest/politics-has-to-evolve-the-two-women-who-want-to-make-job-sharing-in-politics-a-reality/.

Copus, Colin, Alistair Clark, Herwig Reynaert, and Kristof Steyvers. 2008. 'Minor party and independent politics beyond the mainstream: Fluctuating fortunes but a permanent presence.' *Parliamentary Affairs* 62, no. 1: 4–18. doi.org/10.1093/pa/gsn035.

Costar, Brian, and Jennifer Curtin. 2004. *Rebels with a Cause: Independents in Australian Politics*. Sydney: UNSW Press.

Crabb, Annabel. 2025. 'Coalition cosies up to One Nation with preferences in ceasefire after 30-year war.' *ABC News*, 23 April. www.abc.net.au/news/2025-04-23/pauline-hanson-one-nation-preferencing-deal/105200748.

Crotty, Gemma. 2024. 'Pauline Hanson reveals she had to shut herself "away for a couple of days" after breaking down following Mehreen Faruqi defamation loss.' *Sky News*, 20 November. www.skynews.com.au/australia-news/politics/pauline-hanson-reveals-she-had-to-shut-herself-away-for-a-couple-of-days-after-breaking-down-following-mehreen-faruqi-defamation-loss/news-story/4907739a634586b81083f95df8f8f724.

Duggan, Josh. 2025. 'Lee Hanson, daughter of Pauline Hanson, hoping for Tasmanian Senate spot for One Nation.' *ABC News*, 25 April. www.abc.net.au/news/2025-04-25/lee-hanson-pauline-hanson-daughter-one-nation-candidate/105197404.

Elsworthy, Emma. 2023. 'Drone company sends Liberal drone to Ukraine.' *Crikey*, 13 February. www.crikey.com.au/2023/02/13/drone-company-liberal-senator-ukraine/.

Gannon, Genevieve. 2025. 'Job-sharing politicians: How two women want to change the system.' *The Australian Women's Weekly*, 12 February. www.womensweekly.com.au/news/job-sharing-politicians/.

Gauja, Anika, and Jordan McSwiney. 2019. 'Do Australian parties represent?' In *Do Parties Still Represent? An Analysis of the Representativeness of Political Parties in Western Democracies*, edited by Knut Heidar and Bram Wauters, 47–65. London: Routledge. doi.org/10.4324/9781351110952.

Ghazarian, Zareh. 2012. 'The changing type of minor party elected to parliament: The case of the Australian Senate from 1949 to 2010.' *Australian Journal of Political Science* 47, no. 3: 441–54. doi.org/10.1080/10361146.2012.704007.

Grattan, Michelle. 2023. 'Peter Dutton expels Senator David Van from Liberal Party room after more allegations against him.' *The Conversation*, 15 June. theconversation.com/peter-dutton-expels-senator-david-van-from-liberal-party-room-after-more-allegations-against-him-207826. doi.org/10.64628/AA.kypuj3d5s.

Greber, Jacob, and Isobel Roe. 2025. 'Clive Palmer, Pauline Hanson trade barbs over failed bid to unify parties.' *ABC News*, 19 February. www.abc.net.au/news/2025-02-19/clive-palmer-pauline-hanson-fail-unify-parties/104957330.

Hair, Jonathan. 2025. 'Clive Palmer's Trumpet of Patriots candidate David Sarikaya was banned from delivering health services.' *ABC News*, 16 April. www.abc.net.au/news/2025-04-16/trumpet-of-patriots-david-sarikaya-misrepresented-qualifications/105179728.

Hutchinson, Samantha. 2023. 'Independents got more votes than the National Party on March 25.' *Australian Financial Review*, 5 April. www.afr.com/politics/federal/nsw-election-laid-foundation-for-more-wins-climate-200-chief-2023 0405-p5cybo.

Jeffery, Stuart. 2025. 'Common(wealth) knowledge #115: "Job-sharing" Senate hopefuls defeated by South African dual citizenship.' *6 News Australia*, 30 March. www.6newsau.com/post/common-wealth-knowledge-115-job-sharing-senate-hopefuls-defeated-by-south-african-dual-citizens [page discontinued].

Karp, Paul. 2024. 'Ex-Labor Senator Fatima Payman appoints "preference whisperer" Glenn Druery as chief of staff.' *The Guardian*, 9 August. www.theguardian.com/australia-news/article/2024/aug/09/fatima-payman-glen-druery-chief-of-staff.

Kefford, Glenn. 2017. 'Rethinking small political parties: From micro to peripheral.' *Australian Journal of Political Science* 52, no. 1: 95–109. doi.org/10.1080/1036 1146.2016.1246650.

Marie, Johanna. 2025. 'Candidate nominations raise questions over Australian Constitution.' *ABC News*, 10 April. www.abc.net.au/news/2025-04-10/candidate-nominations-raise-questions-over-constitution/105147354.

Martino, Matt, Katia Shatoba, Thomas Brettell, Alex Palmer, and Mark Doman. 2025. 'How major parties want you to number the ballot in your electorate.' *ABC News Verify*, 1 May. www.abc.net.au/news/2025-05-01/how-to-vote-cards-in-your-electorates/105217758.

McIlroy, Tom. 2025. 'Peter Dutton's preference call on One Nation could hurt Coalition in at-risk seats, strategists warn.' *The Guardian*, 30 April. www.theguardian.com/australia-news/2025/apr/30/coalition-preferencing-one-nation-pauline-hanson-party-federal-election.

McNamara, Lauren. 2025. 'Trumpet of Patriots candidate quits over spam texts, "false promises".' *Mumbrella*, 29 April. mumbrella.com.au/trumpet-of-patriots-candidate-quits-over-spam-texts-false-promises-872513.

Mizen, Ronald. 2025. '"Clive and Pauline": Palmer sought One Nation deal before Trump pitch.' *Australian Financial Review*, 19 February. www.afr.com/politics/federal/make-australia-great-again-clive-palmer-launches-trump-style-agenda-20250219-p5ldd5.

Muller, Damon. 2018. *The New Senate Voting System and the 2016 Election*. Parliamentary Library Research Papers 2017–18, 25 January. Canberra: Parliament of Australia. apo.org.au/sites/default/files/resource-files/2018-01/apo-nid129 571.pdf.

Parkes-Hupton, Heath. 2025. 'Purplepingers defends vacant house list after woman's home broken into.' *News.com.au*, 17 April. www.news.com.au/finance/real-estate/purplepingers-defends-vacant-house-list-after-womans-home-broken-into/news-story/a1df32b21697edce02d57325bc663596.

Pildes, Richard H. 2021. 'The age of political fragmentation.' *Journal of Democracy* 32, no. 4: 146–59. doi.org/10.1353/jod.2021.0058.

Puglisi, Leonardo. 2025. 'Victorian Socialists to expand into every state and territory.' *6 News Australia*, 13 May. www.6newsau.com/post/victorian-socialists-announce-expansion-into-every-state-and-territory.

Riboldi, Mark, Ben Spies-Butcher, and Phoebe Hayman. 2024. 'Do independents like to party? The rise in independent and minor party MPs in Australian parliaments since 1970.' *Australian Journal of Political Science* 59, no. 3: 272–90. doi.org/10.1080/10361146.2024.2421519.

Rooney, Kieran. 2025. 'How a Labor power play turned Calwell into Australia's most unpredictable seat.' *The Age*, 8 May. www.theage.com.au/politics/victoria/how-a-labor-power-play-turned-calwell-into-australia-s-most-unpredictable-seat-20250507-p5lx92.html.

Sharma, Yashee. 2025. 'Clive Palmer claims his Trumpet of Patriots how-to-vote cards have been tampered with.' *9News*, 22 April. www.9news.com.au/national/federal-election-2025-clive-palmer-claims-his-trumpet-of-patriots-how-to-vote-cards-have-been-tampered-with/dfba639e-83d2-4468-a288-ec58c87696da.

Sharman, Campbell. 2002. *Politics at the Margin: Independents and the Australian Political System*. Papers on Parliament, no. 39. Canberra: Parliament of Australia. www.aph.gov.au/About_Parliament/Senate/Publications_and_resources/Papers_and_research/Papers_on_Parliament_and_other_resources/Papers_on_Parliament/39/sharman.

Sheppard, Jill. 2023. 'Independents and minor parties.' In *Watershed: The 2022 Australian Federal Election*, edited by Marian Sawer, Anika Gauja, and Jill Sheppard, 259–78. Canberra: ANU Press. doi.org/10.22459/W.2023.13.

Singleton, Gwyneth. 1996. *Independents in a Multi-Party System: The Experience of the Australian Senate*. Papers on Parliament, no. 28. Canberra: Parliament of Australia. www.aph.gov.au/About_Parliament/Senate/Publications_and_resources/ Papers_and_research/Papers_on_Parliament_and_other_resources/Papers_on_ Parliament/28/c05.

Voices for Indi. 2023. *The Indi Way*. Melbourne: Scribe Publications.

Wang, Jessica. 2025. 'Pauline Hanson's daughter Lee Hanson vows political comeback after failed Senate tilt.' *News.com.au*, 29 May. www.news.com.au/national/ politics/pauline-hansons-daughter-lee-hanson-vows-political-comeback-after-failed-senate-tilt/news-story/b2916b2ab962c11f07dba58ebb13d109.

Wedesweiler, Madeleine. 2024. 'Why the UK election's victorious pro-Palestinian candidates matter to Australia.' *SBS News*, 9 July. www.sbs.com.au/news/ article/why-the-uk-elections-victorious-pro-palestinian-candidates-matter-to-australia/o21nqftdf.

Wedesweiler, Madeleine. 2025. '"They're all useless": The battle to make alienated voters care about this election.' *SBS News*, 24 April. www.sbs.com.au/news/ article/theyre-all-useless-the-battle-to-make-alienated-voters-care-about-this-election/0y4i5sjls.

Weeks, Liam. 2009. 'We don't like (to) party. A typology of independents in Irish political life, 1922–2007.' *Irish Political Studies* 24, no. 1: 1–27. doi.org/ 10.1080/07907180802551068.

White, Robert, and Frank Chung. 2025. '"We'll win sooner or later": Legalise Cannabis party has high hopes after surprise election result.' *News.com.au*, 14 May. www.news.com.au/national/federal-election/well-win-sooner-or-later-legalise-cannabis-party-has-high-hopes-after-surprise-election-result/news-story/ c3ba6f81ca77969da28e845e3ebcbe6f.

Wrightson, Suellen. 2025. *Trumpet of Patriots Key Policies 2025*. [Online]. Gold Coast: Trumpet of Patriots. trumpetofpatriots.org/policies/.

16

Third-party campaigning

Mark Riboldi and Ariadne Vromen

Abstract

The 2025 election again saw interventions from third-party campaigners across the political spectrum. Although right-wing digital campaigning organisation Advance received significant attention, particularly from progressive media, the Australian Council of Trade Unions (ACTU) was the dominant campaigner. The ACTU outspent Advance in terms of digital advertising and, along with other anti-Coalition groups, outspent pro-Coalition groups at a rate of more than three to one. Further, analysis of TikTok data suggests that the ACTU was more successful in engaging potential voters outside their traditional supporter base. Meanwhile, the Australian Christian Lobby (ACL) and GetUp!—organisations with a significant presence in previous campaigns—dropped almost entirely off the map in 2025, with the ACL focusing on providing electoral education and GetUp! seemingly constrained by a lack of internal direction.

Keywords: Australian politics; third-party campaigning; Australian Council of Trade Unions; Advance Australia; GetUp!

Third-party influence over election campaigns and politics generally has a long history in Australia—historically dominated by the trade union movement and business interests, particularly those connected to mining and energy generation.[1] The rise and fall of former ALP prime minister Kevin Rudd are a case in point. The Australian Council of Trade Unions (ACTU) Your Rights at Work campaign was a key vehicle in electing Rudd in 2007 ahead of the Liberal–Nationals Coalition, as was the nascent digital-first campaigning organisation GetUp! (see Muir 2010; Vromen 2017). Just three years later, however, a public advertising blitz from the Minerals Council of Australia helped end Rudd's tenure as Prime Minister, along with his proposed tax on the super profits of mining companies (Bell and Hindmoor 2014). In 2025, third-party campaigners across the campaign were no less active when it came to issues of energy generation or workers' rights. However, the nature of which Australian third parties participate and how their campaigning connects with broader campaign trends have shifted over time.

In seeking to understand how third parties attempted to influence outcomes in the 2025 federal election campaign, this chapter analyses data from organisations' social media advertising spending, from their social media accounts generally, from the emails organisations sent to their supporters and from the mentions of selected organisations in print media. Continuing studies from previous Australian elections (for example, Vromen and Rutledge-Prior 2023), we focus on left-leaning organisations the ACTU and GetUp! and the right-leaning Australian Christian Lobby (ACL) and Advance Australia (Advance). We also include third parties engaged in large-scale digital advertising, including climate change and renewable energy–oriented Climate 200, which supported a variety of Community Independent 'Teal' candidates (see Chapter 14, this volume). Together, these data offer insights into how third-party organisations attempted to mobilise their supporters, influence voters and impact agenda-setting during the election campaign. Specifically, they reveal the scale of the union movement's campaigning against the Opposition leader Peter Dutton, contest around the Coalition's nuclear energy policy and the veritable disappearance of GetUp! from the Australian electoral landscape.

---

1   The AEC defines 'third-party' campaigners as actors that are neither candidates nor political parties. In other contexts, these might be referred to as interest groups, third-sector organisations or civil society organisations.

Third-party actors in Australian elections

Regulation of third-party actors in Australian elections is a shifting landscape that arguably fails to keep up with the reality of what these groups do. The AEC requires registration and reporting for *significant third parties*—organisations that spend more than $250,000 on electoral expenditure in a financial year, essentially covering content that 'seeks to influence' people's votes (AEC 2023). Additionally, organisations spending more than a disclosure threshold (currently $16,900) may elect to register as third parties for transparency purposes. Further, some organisations are separately registered as charities with the Australian Charities and Not-for-profits Commission (ACNC). ACNC registration can provide organisations with financial benefits such as access to public and philanthropic funding and deductible gift recipient status for private donations. However, these benefits typically come with restrictions on the kind of public advocacy in which organisations can engage—notably, a restriction on campaigning that endorses one candidate over another. Compared with non-ACNC registered organisations, which can campaign for or against a particular political candidate or party during elections, registered charities tend to present positions on issues, rather than candidates, requiring voters to draw the connections themselves.

We focus our analysis primarily on four organisations, Advance, the ACL, the ACTU and GetUp!, and, to a lesser degree, on a fifth, Climate 200. Unlike the other four organisations, Climate 200 exists primarily to support the election of political candidates, making them more a 'party-like' entity (Riboldi et al. 2024). Table 16.1 portrays these five organisations along with factors significant to the analysis: their 2023–24 income as reported to the AEC, as well as the number of followers they had on various social media platforms at the beginning of the official election campaign period.

Table 16.1 Key Australian third parties: Income and social media presence ahead of the 2025 election

Organisation	AEC-reported income (2023–24)	Facebook	Instagram	YouTube	TikTok
ACL	$6.2 million	305,000	18,000	99,000	–
ACTU	$27.7 million	202,000	32,000	3,000	10,000
Advance	$15.7 million	130,000	23,000	3,000	81,000
Climate 200	$5.9 million	9,800	19,900	425	3,500
GetUp!	$6.8 million	489,000	50,000	30,000	22,000

Sources: AEC; Facebook; Instagram; YouTube; TikTok.

The ACTU is clearly the most financially secure of the five, likely reflecting its long history and institutional role as the peak organisation for the trade union movement. Led in 2025 by Secretary Sally McManus, the ACTU's presence and following across social media channels are significant, though still generally less than digital-first campaigning organisation GetUp!. The ACTU is also the only organisation in this group with paid members: trade unions, which themselves have individual paid-up members. The large 'membership' claims of organisations such as Advance and GetUp! refer to the size of their email lists and are more accurately described as 'supporters' or 'subscribers', some of whom provide donations to fund these organisations.

Of the other organisations, the ACL is the most similar in 'type' to the ACTU. Founded in 1975, it is particularly active on socially conservative issues, having substantively opposed marriage equality, transgender rights and attempts to make abortion services safe and accessible. Unlike the other major third parties, the ACL is registered with the ACNC, meaning its political activities must focus more on their preferred policy issues, rather than directly advocating for or against a particular candidate, to maintain charitable status. Their CEO from April 2023 and during the election campaign was Michelle Pearse, a former Pentecostal pastor and former WA ACL State director.

GetUp!'s reported income in 2023–24 was on par with the ACL's: both about 20–25 per cent of the ACTU's $27.7 million. Founded in 2006 as a digital-first organisation focused explicitly on opposing the Coalition government, GetUp! rose to significance as a key actor in Australian elections, pioneering digital campaigning tactics that are now commonplace across the political spectrum (see Vromen 2017). Getup!'s 2022 election was noticeably lower profile than previous campaigns, corresponding with the rise of Climate 200, whose volunteer and donor bases—older, white and middle class—arguably have significant crossover. In August 2023, Widjabul Wia-bul woman Larissa Baldwin-Roberts became the first woman and first Indigenous CEO of GetUp!. However, Baldwin-Roberts left GetUp! in December 2024 in reportedly troubled circumstances, and the organisation entered the 2025 election campaign without executive leadership (McKinnon 2025; Wilson 2025a).

Advance began in 2018 as a conservative response to GetUp! and recorded more than twice as much income as GetUp! in 2023–24. The digital campaigning organisation received widespread attention for their work on the 'No' campaign in the Indigenous Voice to Parliament referendum in 2023 (Carson and Grömping 2024; Vromen et al. 2025). This activity led to accusations of circulating misinformation and disinformation and their reported international connections to the Atlas Network of right-wing think tanks (Walker 2023). Like the ACL, Advance went into the 2025 federal election campaign with a middle-aged white woman as their key spokesperson: former police officer Sandra Bourke.[2] This shift in public-facing leadership might be seen as a reaction to the breakthrough success of the Climate 200–backed Teal Independents in 2022, all of whom were middle-class, middle-aged white women; the Teals' success was partly attributed to the Coalition's poor track record in preselecting women in winnable seats and in appealing to women voters generally (see Hayman 2025).

Plate 16.1 An image from social media of Advance's anti-ALP advertising

Source: Advance, photo used with permission.

Data from the 2025 federal election campaign

To understand third-party activity and influence during the 2025 federal election, we collected data from publicly available sources such as the Meta Ad Library and the Google Ads Transparency Centre, direct observation of social media activity, organisations' media appearances via Factiva and Google Alerts, as well as subscribing to the publicly available supporter e-lists of various third-party organisations. This allowed us to examine activity from a variety of perspectives.

---

2   This was a change for Advance from both the 2022 election and the Voice referendum campaign. Matthew Sheehan was CEO and main spokesperson throughout this period. Former Advance (and Institute for Public Affairs) staffer Jacinta Nampijinpa Price, who later entered the Senate, was the Voice referendum 'No' campaign's chief spokesperson.

Digital advertising

Based on data from the Meta and Google political advertising libraries between 28 March and 3 May 2025, the three highest spending third-party organisations in the election campaign were the ACTU, Advance and Climate 200 (Table 16.2). Together, these three organisations accounted for almost half the $8 million spent by the top 20 spending groups. Where Advance and Climate 200 placed the bulk of their advertising on Meta platforms Facebook and Instagram, the ACTU spent twice as much on Google advertising (via Google Adwords and YouTube) as they did across Meta. For their part, GetUp! spent just $42,000 on Meta and the ACL $37,500, with no Google spending for either. Both organisations started their Meta spending in week four of the campaign (18–24 April), by which time Advance and the ACTU, respectively, had already spent $325,000 and $116,000 on Meta.

Table 16.2 Highest digital advertising spending by third-party campaigners, 28 March – 3 May 2025

Organisation	AEC status	Frame	Meta	Google	Total
ACTU	STP	Anti-Coalition	$477,000	$928,000	**$1,405,000**
Advance	STP	Pro-Coalition	$1,047,000	$296,000	**$1,343,000**
Climate 200	STP	Anti-Coalition	$896,600	$99,000	**$995,600**
Australian Taxpayers' Alliance	–	Anti-Greens/ Teals	$214,400	$296,000	**$510,400**
Liberals Against Nuclear	–	Anti-Coalition	$246,000	$156,000	**$402,000**
Australians for Prosperity	–	Anti-Greens/ Teals	$235,000	$159,000	**$394,000**
Climate Action Network Australia	TP	Anti-Coalition	$392,400	$0	**$392,400**
Hothouse Magazine	STP	Anti-Coalition	$287,700	$87,000	**$374,700**
Better Australia	STP	Anti-Greens/ Teals	$149,400	$153,000	**$302,400**
It's Not a Race	STP	Anti-Coalition	$187,700	$67,000	**$254,700**
Nuclear for Australia	–	Pro-Coalition	$236,500	$0	**$236,500**

Organisation	AEC status	Frame	Meta	Google	Total
United Workers Union	STP	Anti-Coalition	$149,400	$87,000	**$236,400**
Clean Energy Council Limited	–	Anti-Coalition	$209,300	$0	**$209,300**
Jobs for Mining Communities	STP	Anti-ALP	$164,600	$15,200	**$179,800**
Energy for Australians	–	Anti-ALP	$136,600	$16,900	**$153,500**
Greenpeace Australia Pacific	TP	Anti-Coalition	$150,600	$0	**$150,600**
The Climate Council	TP	Anti-Coalition	$122,100	$10,300	**$132,400**
Parents for Climate	–	Anti-Coalition	$122,600	$0	**$122,600**
Australians for Affordable Energy	–	Anti-Coalition	$110,600	$0	**$110,600**
Australian Conservation Foundation	STP	Anti-Coalition	$105,600	$0	**$105,600**
Total	–	–	**$5,641,100**	**$2,370,400**	**$8,011,500**

Note: STP = significant third party.

Sources: AEC; Meta Ad Library; Google Ads Transparency Centre.

Of the top 20 spending organisations across Meta and Google, about half were already registered with the AEC as significant third parties (STPs). Four of the 10 organisations that spent over the AEC's STP threshold of $250,000—on social media advertising alone—were not registered as STPs before the election: Australian Taxpayers' Alliance, Liberals Against Nuclear, Australians for Prosperity and Climate Action Network Australia. Two other organisations, Nuclear for Australia and the Clean Energy Council, likely also spent over the threshold when other costs are taken into account but were not registered as STPs. This suggests that the AEC's STP register could not necessarily indicate which organisations were significant actors before the election campaign, hampering transparency about where money is being spent to influence elections and to whose benefit.

Plate 16.2 An ACTU Facebook banner used during the campaign, spotlighting their 'Don't risk Dutton' frame

Source: ACTU, photo used with permission.

Comparing the primary frame of these third parties shows that anti-Coalition groups significantly outspent anti-ALP ones (Riboldi 2025). Anti-Coalition third parties include those with an anti-Dutton focus—such as the ACTU's 'Don't risk Dutton' slogan, which was picked up across the broad left, and the meme-oriented campaigning of Dan Ilic's It's Not a Race—as well as explicitly anti-nuclear groups. The last included most of the highest-spending environment and climate-focused organisations as well as Liberals Against Nuclear, which spent more than $400,000 across Meta and Google campaigning against their own party's signature energy policy. Collectively, the 13 anti-Coalition organisations in Table 16.2 spent close to $5 million on social media advertising alone during the election.

Right-wing third-party campaigning on social media was more disparate. Only Advance and Nuclear for Australia appeared explicitly pro-Coalition: Advance negatively targeted both the ALP and the Greens, and Nuclear for Australia supported Coalition policy. Together, these two organisations spent just over $1.5 million—more than three times less than the anti-Coalition organisations. Campaign messaging by other right-wing third parties was variously anti-Greens, anti-Teals or anti-ALP, but the disparate nature did not necessarily equate to a pro-Coalition message. Thus, while right-wing groups collectively spent more than $3 million on social media advertising, about one-quarter of this may have sent voters to candidates and parties other than the two Coalition parties.

TikTok and YouTube

On TikTok and YouTube, the primary third-party contest was again between Advance and the ACTU. Further, the ACTU's 'Don't risk Dutton' frame was more dominant than Advance's mixture of anti-ALP 'Weak, woke, sending us broke' and anti-Greens 'Greens truth' framing on TikTok, 30 per cent of whose global audience is aged 18–24, with about 70 per cent of Australian Millennials having TikTok accounts (MacFarlane 2025). For their part, GetUp! and the ACL appeared to be less prominent on these platforms than their counterparts, though for different reasons.

Plate 16.3 Advance billboard in Wickham Street, Fortitude Valley, Brisbane, January 2025

Photo: Courtesy of Headpress Pty Ltd.

Engagement on TikTok is commonly measured by the accumulation of 'likes', comments and 'pins' received on each post. While Advance and the ACTU (Australian Unions on TikTok) released a similar amount of TikTok content during the campaign, Advance had a significantly higher number of followers on the platform than the ACTU or GetUp! and garnered twice as many engagements per post, on average, compared with the ACTU (Table 16.3). The ACL did not use TikTok at the time of the election. Advance's most popular post was an attack on Australian Greens leader Adam Bandt: 'Australia could have a Deputy Prime Minister who refuses to stand in front of the Australian Flag. Can't vote Greens. Not this time.' Posted on 22 April, by polling day, the post had 12,174 engagements and had been viewed 150,500 times. Comparatively, the ACTU's most popular post—'It's not about making things better for us. You deserve better. #DontRiskDutton, #auspol'—posted on 21 April, had just 39,300 views and 2,900 engagements across a similar time frame.

Table 16.3 Third-party campaigner TikTok posts and engagement, 28 March – 3 May 2025

Organisation	Followers	Posts	Engagement	Engagement per post	Engagement per follower
ACL	–	–	–	–	–
ACTU	10,000	60	19,700	109	1.97
Advance	81,000	70	45,900	218	0.56
GetUp!	22,400	17	975	19	0.04

Source: TikTok.

While these engagement numbers appear to benefit Advance, looking at them as a factor of total account followers reveals a different story. In their TikTok posts during the campaign, the ACTU overall received about two engagements per follower, whereas Advance's rate was about one-quarter of this—a ratio of 0.56 of engagement to followers. This suggests that the ACTU posts were reaching people outside their follower base, which is vital for converting voters from one preference to another. Similarly, Advance's low engagement-to-follower ratio on TikTok supports anecdotal arguments from Coalition insiders that Advance's campaign operated 'in an echo chamber' (Koutsoukis 2025).

For their part, GetUp!'s 17 TikTok posts across the election period had an average of just 19 engagements per post and 0.04 as an engagement-to-follower ratio. Even considering a reported lack of donations flowing into the organisation, these numbers are surprisingly low. Because TikTok does not feature paid political advertising, it should have been an ideal platform for GetUp!—which started the campaign with twice as many followers as the ACTU—to attempt to influence the voting public, and especially younger voters, organically. Their most successful post of the period, on 31 March and receiving just 143 engagements, did not even relate to the election but to water contamination due to fracking near Borroloola in the Northern Territory.

GetUp!'s engagements on YouTube were similarly low (Table 16.4). Their most viewed video on the platform, 'Who is the real Dutton?', was released on 3 April and received a total of 8,243 views between then and polling day. The ACL's effort on YouTube was similarly humble, posting only one video throughout the campaign despite having almost 100,000 channel subscribers (see Table 16.1). Posted on 3 April, the ACL's video related to their primary election output, their 'Federal Election 2025 Australian Votes Website'. The three-minute video largely served an electoral education function. It recommended that people vote 'below the line' to ensure they know where their vote would go and that 'a vote for a minor party is never a wasted vote'. The video also advocated for people to vote 'according to truth' on issues such as 'biological reality'—presumably a coded reference to avoid voting for trans-supportive minor parties such as the Australian Greens.

Table 16.4 Third-party campaigner YouTube public videos and views, 28 March – 3 May 2025

Organisation	Videos	Views	Views per video
ACL	1	2,500	2,500
ACTU	–	–	–
Advance	25	4,655,000	186,200
GetUp!	4	9,000	2,250

Source: YouTube.

While from Table 16.4 it appears the ACTU produced no videos during the campaign, they spent more than $900,000 advertising on Google platforms, the primary one of which is YouTube, suggesting that, unlike Advance, the ACTU chose not to make their advertisements publicly viewable on their YouTube page. Instead, the ACTU's video ads, focusing almost exclusively on the 'Don't risk Dutton' frame, are registered but unviewable in the Google Ad Transparency Centre.

In contrast, Advance spent just under $300,000 on Google platform advertising, entirely on videos, suggesting that organic views of the ACTU's videos on YouTube could have been much higher than Advance's if they had chosen to make them public. Most of Advance's publicly available videos were 15 or 30 seconds long, suggesting that they were designed primarily as advertisements and for easy recirculation on other platforms. Of Advance's 25 videos, 12 attacked the Australian Greens and 13 the ALP, with total public views split fairly evenly at 2.38 million and 2.28 million, respectively. This broad equivalence between Advance's key frames suggests the organisation's public focus was roughly equal across the 'Greens truth' and the 'Weak, woke, sending us broke' campaigns. Whether either campaign was effective is a different question, despite Advance's post-election claim that their primary focus was always on 'destroying' the Greens (see Sheehan 2025).

Supporter emails

While public-facing social media channel campaigns try to reach and persuade voters, third parties' emails to existing supporters reveal how these groups try to activate and mobilise their base towards action. This includes the way these organisations 'claim and frame' election results. The key organisations studied here sent emails to supporters every two–three days across the campaign period, with a mixture of 'calls to action' that included asking supporters to make donations, register for webinars, sign e-petitions and volunteer for in-real-life campaign activities (Table 16.5). Furthermore, the frequency with which these organisations mentioned particular key words—'truth', 'Dutton', 'Greens' and 'Albo/Albanese'—provides insight into their electoral target.

Table 16.5 Third-party campaigner supporter emails, calls to action and keywords, 28 March – 10 May 2025

	ACL	ACTU	Advance	Climate 200	GetUp!
Total emails	13	13	19	16	18
Calls to action					
Donate	5	–	7	14	8
Register for webinar	4	2	–	–	–
Sign e-petition	–	–	4	–	–
Visit website	4	4	1	1	6
Volunteer on the ground	–	4	1	–	3
No call to action	–	3	6	1	1
Keyword mentions					
'Truth'	115	–	17	2	18
'Dutton'	2	58	–	16	121
'Greens'	35	–	118	–	–
'Albo/Albanese'	3	3	26	2	10

Source: Supporter emails.

Plate 16.4 An ACTU social media image highlighting union member on-the-ground campaigning during the election

Source: ACTU, photo used with permission.

Advance and GetUp! sent a similar number of emails, with a similar ratio of donation requests, whereas nearly all Climate 200's emails before polling day asked supporters for donations. The ACTU's emails involved no donation requests, potentially signifying a type of organisation that still has paid members rather than mainly supporters or subscribers. Through their 'calls to action', the ACTU and GetUp! also focused on activities that brought supporters into contact with the organisation, including calling for ground campaign volunteers.

When it comes to framing, the ACTU's supporter emails centred on their campaign slogan of 'Don't risk Dutton' (58 references to Dutton across 13 emails). GetUp!'s focus on mentioning 'Dutton' in their emails (121 mentions across 18 emails—almost seven times per email) mirrored the ACL's focus on 'truth' (nine per email) and Advance's on the Greens (six per email). In contrast to the other organisations, while the ACL's emails focused significantly on the idea of 'truth' and framing the Greens as opponents (mostly in relation to abortion law reform legislation in State parliaments), their emails were nonpartisan, focusing on electoral education and values reinforcement.

In terms of supporter emails after polling day, all five organisations sent at least one 'claim and frame' email, mostly announcing their supposed impact on the campaign. Advance, for example, claimed to have 'destroyed' the Greens while blaming the Coalition campaign for the ALP's election victory. The ACL's two emails in this period focused on framing the result as a desire for stability over change as well as highlighting opportunities to influence the new government. Both emails asked for donations (two of their total of five donation requests during the election period). GetUp! also asked for donations in a post-election email, in which they highlighted their activity during the campaign. Climate 200's initial post-election emails focused on the uncertainty in results—this was understandable, given that several of the results in Teal seats were close and votes were still being counted.

Newspaper attention

To examine the influence of third-party organisations on the election campaign, this chapter uses articles from the LexisNexis news database published from the beginning of March to the end of May 2025 for 12 main broadsheet and tabloid newspapers across Australia, including the *Guardian*. Incorporating only articles mentioning one of the four key third parties in the headline or lead paragraph resulted in a dataset of 21 articles: 10 Advance-related articles; nine ACTU articles; two ACL articles; and no GetUp! articles. This spread follows the broad levels of activity described above. Other Australian media outlets not in LexisNexis—mainly the *Saturday Paper* and *Crikey*—also ran feature articles on third-party campaigning groups during the election and we discuss some of these below.

Overall, more progressive newspapers (the *Guardian*, the *Saturday Paper* and *The Sydney Morning Herald*/Melbourne's *Age*) paid disproportionate attention to Advance, potentially exaggerating their electoral influence and impact. These articles were largely investigative, focusing on Advance's sources of funding and campaign tactics, and all labelled Advance as either a 'conservative' or a 'hard-right' organisation. Some of these articles placed Advance in a broader hard-right ecosystem internationally and nationally, describing links to the Conservative Political Action Conference (CPAC), the Atlas Network and the network of local anti-Teals and anti-renewables groups that emerged during the campaign. For example, *The Sydney Morning Herald*/Melbourne *Age* ran an extended 4,000-word feature on Advance in their *Good Weekend* magazine on 19 April. The article is written as an exposé, starting with: 'It claims to be a grassroots group promoting free speech and common-sense policy to ordinary Aussies but Advance's propaganda machine—and its deluge of disinformation—are linked to the far right in the US' (Elliott 2025).

Due to the focus on the money and political connections behind Advance and, to a lesser extent, the framing of its campaigns as 'Trump-like', there was little scrutiny of to whom Advance appeals or how it attempted to change votes. The more conservative newspapers—that is, the *Australian*, the *Australian Financial Review* (*AFR*) and News Corp–owned tabloids the *Daily Telegraph* and the *Herald Sun*—paid attention to Advance only with reference to the organisation's anti-Teal messaging and in articles that were mainly about Climate 200 and its influence on the election campaign.

In contrast, two conservative newspapers (the *Australian* and the *AFR*) were the main outlets to focus on the ACTU during the election, primarily portraying them as a pro-worker lobbyist campaigning on industrial relations law and raising the minimum wage. Only two of a total of nine articles make any overt mention of the ACTU as a political campaigner, either 'on the ground' or digitally (Hannan 2025; Marin-Guzman 2025). Both articles were published in conservative newspapers (the *Australian* and *Australian Financial Review*) and refer to the ACTU's electorate-based campaigning on workplace reforms, equal pay, health care and AI regulation. Both were largely sympathetic to the ACTU campaign, unlike coverage in other conservative and News Corp outlets, and did not offer views from business or other political actors to counter union claims. Beyond these examples, the role of the ACTU and union movement in organising and voter mobilisation appeared to be underestimated or simply ignored, especially by the more progressive newspaper outlets. Neither the *Guardian*, the *Saturday*

Paper nor *The Sydney Morning Herald*/Melbourne's *Age* published features on the prominence of Australian unions in the election campaign, let alone their role in helping the ALP to a historic electoral win (see also Chapter 10, this volume).

The near absence of news media attention to GetUp! during this campaign reflected the lack of election-related activities undertaken by GetUp! itself. This continues its decline since the 2022 election and is in contrast with the 2010 election campaign, when GetUp!'s successful challenge in the High Court over electoral enrolment was front-page news, and their 2016 election campaign against 'hard-right' candidates, which pioneered targeted Facebook advertising in Australia (Vromen 2017, 2018). Online news platform *Crikey* published two articles about GetUp!, both of which spoke to this shift. The first was published mid-campaign and entitled 'GetUp! CEO quietly departs as the group goes missing in action during election campaign' (Wilson 2025a; see also Wilson 2025b).

Implications and conclusions

Third-party campaigners are clearly significant actors in Australian elections, spending substantial amounts campaigning to mobilise their supporters and influence the public agenda and voter intentions. The 2025 election reveals three main conclusions and areas for future research on third parties in Australian politics. The first relates to how to better understand the electoral and political influence of these non-party actors. Elections are important focusing events in which all kinds of organisations can gain public attention. Many also have a stake in electing governments that will be more sympathetic to their issue agendas. The near-exclusive scholarly and media focus on political parties, election candidates and voters in Australia has come at the cost of systematic analysis of the electoral and political influence of non-party, civil society organisations in Australia. Third parties are too often wrongly conceptualised as 'partisans in disguise'—even the union movement is not always clearly partisan and there are ideological differences between unions. While the ACTU and the ALP have informal linkages and many individual unions are directly affiliated to the ALP, some are not. Further, union movement positions on workers' rights and industrial relations policy are rarely homogeneous. The ALP itself, with a declining and ageing membership, is increasingly reliant on a union member–driven ground campaign to deliver pro-ALP and anti-Coalition messages. Understanding the ACTU's—and other third parties'—issue agendas and campaign work is vital to properly appreciating their influence on Australian politics and policy agendas beyond mere support for one party over another.

Similarly, Advance's messaging and issue agenda might align with segments of the Liberal and National parties and be influential over some Coalition politicians, but post-election commentary suggests this was not necessarily connected to an organised pro-Coalition strategy (Koutsoukis 2025). Likewise, the climate movement's focus on opposing nuclear energy (that is, being anti-Coalition) potentially gave the ALP a free ride on the issue, to the detriment of the Greens and the Teals—neither of which, admittedly, ran a particularly strong pro-climate campaign (see Chapters 13 and 14, this volume).

The second question relates to whether existing regulation of election campaign fundraising and the spending of politically active third-party organisations is fit for purpose when it comes to digital campaigning and social media advertising. Only half the organisations that should register as 'significant third parties' and make funding and expenditure disclosures accordingly, based on social media spending alone, were registered before the election. Transparency around which organisations might plausibly influence an election campaign is important for the integrity and credibility of the system. To better capture and understand these organisations and their influence, 'live' disclosures and declarations of expenditure on campaign digital media advertising are needed. This would also bring Australia in line with countries such as Canada and the United Kingdom that focus less on third parties declaring donations and more on capping their election-specific expenditure (Lawlor and Crandall 2018), and, in Canada's case, also require third parties to file returns *during* the campaign period. In Australia, Meta and Google make online advertising spending data available, but the community currently relies on curious scholars and journalists to understand it, or else waits for the AEC declaration made up to 12 months later.

Relatedly, it may be time to re-evaluate the regulation of advocacy organisations and charities via the ACNC. Currently, registered charities are broadly permitted to advocate for and support policies that advance their interests, but they cannot be seen to support or oppose particular candidates or parties as it may result in the charity having engaged in a 'disqualifying political purpose'. For many Australian charities, especially organisations that campaign on environmental or international development issues, it has been risky to publicly advocate on issues of relevance to them during an election campaign. This real risk of losing charitable status may inhibit a range of organisations from advocating for causes in which they have legitimacy and expertise, reducing political campaigning to a smaller group of well-funded and often more polarised actors.

Third, this chapter suggests that part of the academic neglect of third-party campaigning organisations is the dauntingly complex ecosystem within which they operate. Organisations evolve over time and shift their activity depending on issue salience, the political landscape and their human and financial resources. For instance, how might we explain the non-action of once prominent groups in 2025? The ACL's transgender rights–related campaigning activity in 2025 appeared significantly more muted than in 2022 and largely focused on the Greens. It is possible the issue was less salient and thus less 'mobilisable' in religious communities than an issue such as marriage equality, yet the ACL's shift to a low-key 'electoral information' campaign, rather than one more aligned to a preferred major party, bears consideration.

It is also important to ask: what has gone 'wrong' with GetUp!? There were significant reports of internal problems and a massive decline in fundraising and staff resources (Wilson 2025a, 2025b), and suggestions of debilitating internal debates over priorities in their policy issue agendas, from the Voice referendum to the humanitarian crisis in Gaza to cost-of-living issues (McKinnon 2025). Post election, *Crikey* claimed GetUp!'s social media use and tactics were outdated and risk-averse and, somewhat ironically, suggested GetUp! could learn from Advance. GetUp! board chair Glen Berman was quoted saying:

> I'm not trying to suggest that I like Advance's campaigning, but I do think Advance is taking risks. And I think that's something we can really learn from. We know we need to rediscover that kind of ability to be humorous, be fun, to take risks. (Wilson 2025b)

There is clearly crossover between the donor and volunteer bases of GetUp! and Climate 200, but this does not entirely explain their decline in electoral significance. It will take more targeted research to better understand this notable decline.

Overall, for third-party campaigning organisations to maintain relevance in the electoral context, they need voter support, media and public attention and an ability to wield political influence. This is one area where the ACTU and associated unions have remained dominant, whereas other organisations, including the ACL and GetUp!, appear to have come in and out of the ecosystem depending on their agenda, resource base and capacity to mobilise.

References

Australian Electoral Commission (AEC). 2023. *Electoral Matter and Electoral Expenditure*. Fact Sheet, 22 February. Canberra: Australian Electoral Commission. www.aec.gov.au/parties_and_representatives/financial_disclosure/files/electoral-matter-and-electoral-expenditure-fact-sheet.pdf.

Bell, Stephen, and Andrew Hindmoor. 2014. 'The structural power of business and the power of ideas: The strange case of the Australian mining tax.' *New Political Economy* 19, no. 3: 470–86. doi.org/10.1080/13563467.2013.796452.

Carson, Andrea, and Max Grömping. 2024. *Influencers and Messages: Analysing the 2023 Voice to Parliament Referendum Campaign*. 22 April. Melbourne: LaTrobe University. osf.io/n2h5a/files/8nqg2.

Elliott, Tim. 2025. '"Copied the MAGA model": The "grassroots" lobby group funded by some of Australia's richest.' *The Sydney Morning Herald*, 19 April. www.smh.com.au/national/copied-the-maga-model-the-grassroots-lobby-group-funded-by-some-of-australia-s-richest-20250408-p5lq6k.html.

Hannan, Ewin. 2025. '"Just put Libs last": Unions go on defence amid drift from Labor.' *The Australian*, 28 March. www.theaustralian.com.au/nation/actu-urges-protesting-voters-to-put-coalition-last/news-story/4baea0c7c1b4fcf076bf586ddee92a3e.

Hayman, Phoebe. 2025. 'Political outsiders? A study of "Teal" independent campaign demographics in the 2022 Australian federal election.' *Journal of Australian Studies* 49, no. 2: 234–53. doi.org/10.1080/14443058.2025.2486854.

Koutsoukis, Jason. 2025. 'Inside story: Advance "siphoned" Liberal resources.' *The Saturday Paper*, 31 May. www.thesaturdaypaper.com.au/news/politics/2025/05/31/inside-story-advance-siphoned-liberal-resources.

Lawlor, Andrea, and Erin Crandall. 2018. 'Policy versus practice: Third party behaviour in Canadian elections.' *Canadian Public Administration* 61, no. 2: 246–65. doi.org/10.1111/capa.12266.

MacFarlane, Rebecca. 2025. 'Australian TikTok statistics to inform your strategy in 2025.' 12 May. Chicago: Sprout Social. sproutsocial.com/insights/tiktok-statistics-australia/.

Marin-Guzman, David. 2025. 'ACTU targets blue-collar seats to protect Labor, defend IR gains.' *Australian Financial Review*, 3 March. www.afr.com/work-and-careers/workplace/actu-targets-blue-collar-seats-to-protect-labor-defend-ir-gains-20250218-p5lcyn.

McKinnon, Alex. 2025. 'GetUp! In crisis—CEO ousting, job cuts and clash on Palestine prompt staff revolt.' *Deepcut News*, 21 May. www.deepcutnews.com/p/getup-in-crisis-ceo-ousting-job-cuts.

Muir, Kathie. 2010. '"Your Rights at Work" campaign: Australia's "most sophisticated political campaign".' *Labor History* 51, no. 1: 55–70. doi.org/10.1080/0023656 1003654735.

Riboldi, Mark. 2025. 'Follow the money: The organisations that spent the most on social media during the election.' *The Conversation*, 20 May. theconversation. com/follow-the-money-the-organisations-that-spent-the-most-on-social-media-during-the-election-256784. doi.org/10.64628/AA.nga6ksjah.

Riboldi, Mark, Ben Spies-Butcher, and Phoebe Hayman. 2024. 'Do independents like to party? The rise in independent and minor party MPs in Australian parliaments since 1970.' *Australian Journal of Political Science* 59, no. 3: 272–90. doi.org/10.1080/10361146.2024.2421519.

Sheehan, Matthew. 2025. Advance campaign election report. In supporters email, sent 20 June.

Vromen, Ariadne. 2017. *Digital Citizenship and Political Engagement*. London: Palgrave Macmillan. doi.org/10.1057/978-1-137-48865-7.

Vromen, Ariadne. 2018. 'GetUp! in election 2016.' In *Double Disillusion: The 2016 Australian Federal Election*, edited by Anika Gauja, Peter Chen, Jennifer Curtin, and Juliet Pietsch, 397–419. Canberra: ANU Press. doi.org/10.22459/DD.04. 2018.18.

Vromen, Ariadne, and Serrin Rutledge-Prior. 2023. 'Third party campaigning organisations.' In *Watershed: The 2022 Australian Federal Election*, edited by Anika Gauja, Marian Sawer, and Jill Sheppard, 305–31. Canberra: ANU Press. doi.org/10.22459/W.2023.15.

Vromen, Ariadne, Serrin Rutledge-Prior, and Michael Vaughan. 2025. 'Storytelling in the Australian 2023 Voice referendum campaign.' *The British Journal of Politics and International Relations*: doi.org/10.1177/13691481251317884.

Walker, Jeremy. 2023. 'Silencing the Voice: The fossil-fuelled Atlas Network's campaign against constitutional recognition of Indigenous Australia.' *Cosmopolitan Civil Societies: An Interdisciplinary Journal* 15, no. 2. doi.org/10.5130/ccs.v15.i2.8813.

Wilson, Cam. 2025a. 'GetUp! CEO quietly departs as the group goes missing in action during election campaign.' *Crikey*, 14 April. www.crikey.com.au/2025/04/14/getup-ceo-departs-group-missing-2025-election-campaign/.

Wilson, Cam. 2025b. 'Donations are nosediving and staff fleeing. But GetUp!'s chair is feeling optimistic—and wants to take risks.' *Crikey*, 21 May. www.crikey.com.au/2025/05/21/getup-campaigning-2025-federal-election-glen-berman/.

Part 3.
Results

17

The House of Representatives results

Ben Raue

Abstract

Labor won a landslide victory in the election for the House of Representatives in 2025 but did so with a primary vote not far above their lowest vote in modern Australian political history. The 2025 election was Labor's best result in terms of seats won and two-party-preferred vote share since 1943.

The House of Representatives electoral system has become increasingly complex as the vote for minor parties and Independents has increased. With more than one-third of votes cast for minor parties and Independents, an increasing number of seats have become contests involving a candidate outside the major parties in the top two, and several others are not far off. This chapter analyses trends in House of Representatives election results and house contests of interest at the 2025 federal election.

Keywords: House of Representatives; preferential voting; three-candidate-preferred; proportionality; electoral history

The 2025 federal election result was a landslide victory for Labor, the worst defeat for the Coalition in the history of the Liberal Party, but also an election in which the combined major-party vote reached a record low. While Labor's primary vote was nearly its lowest to date, the party won its largest share of seats in the House of Representatives since 1943. The Coalition was reduced to vote and seat shares not seen since before the formation of the Liberal Party during World War II.

The vote for minor parties and Independents reached a record high, exceeding one-third of the formal vote and higher than for the Coalition. Independent candidates posed serious threats in more seats than ever before, but the crossbench shrank slightly thanks to the Greens losing three seats to Labor. The declining major-party vote has also changed how the electoral system operates, with less certainty about which two candidates will poll highest in each seat and the need to pay more attention to the three-candidate-preferred (3CP) vote to determine which two candidates make the final preference count.

This chapter will analyse the House of Representatives results, with a particular focus on the decline in the vote for the major parties, how that declining vote is changing the way the electoral system operates, the impact of Independent candidates and minor parties and diverging trends between States and regions.

Table 17.1 Results of the 2022 federal election by party

Party	Votes	Percentage	Swing	Seats	Seat change
Liberal–Nationals Coalition	5,233,334	35.70	–5.74	58	–18
Australian Labor Party	4,776,030	32.58	–0.76	77	8
The Greens	1,795,985	12.25	1.85	4	3
Pauline Hanson's One Nation	727,464	4.96	1.88	0	0
United Australia Party	604,536	4.12	0.69	0	0
Liberal Democratic Party	252,963	1.73	1.49	0	0
Katter's Australian Party	55,863	0.38	–0.11	1	0
Centre Alliance	36,500	0.25	–0.08	1	0
Independents	776,169	5.29	1.92	10	7
Other	400,198	2.73	0.54	0	0

Source: Compiled by author from AEC (2025c) data.

Background to the election

The previous federal election in 2022 had brought Labor back into government after nine years out of power, with the party gaining eight seats for 77 in total. The outgoing Liberal–Nationals Coalition lost 18 seats, with seven new Independents and three new Greens MPs forming an enlarged crossbench. Labor won a clear majority of the two-party-preferred (2PP) vote—52.1 per cent, with a 3.7 per cent swing—but with the lowest Labor primary vote since the 1930s (32.6 per cent).

Between 2022 and 2025, House of Representatives electoral boundaries were redrawn in New South Wales, Victoria, Western Australia and the Northern Territory. The change in the Northern Territory was necessitated by seven years elapsing since the previous redistribution and the adjustment of the electoral boundary between the two NT divisions was relatively minor and uncontroversial (Raue 2024d).

The changes in the three larger States were necessitated by a change in each State's entitlement for members in the House of Representatives. This electoral cycle saw the most seats affected by such a redistribution since 1984, when the size of the parliament was increased. New South Wales's entitlement fell from 47 seats to 46 and the Independent-held seat of North Sydney was abolished (Raue 2024b). Victoria's entitlement was reduced from 39 seats to 38, with the Labor seat of Higgins abolished (Raue 2024c). Western Australia's entitlement increased from 15 seats to 16, with the new seat of Bullwinkel created on the eastern edge of Perth, with a notional Labor majority (Raue 2024a). These redistributions had other effects, which included the Labor seat of Bennelong in New South Wales redrawn with a notional Liberal majority and the Liberal seat of Menzies in Victoria redrawn with a notional Labor majority. Overall, redistributions resulted in no net change for Labor or the Coalition, but the number of seats held by crossbench members fell from 16 to fifteen.

Four federal by-elections were held during the 2022–25 parliamentary term. Three were triggered by the voluntary retirement of the sitting member, while the Dunkley by-election was triggered by the death of sitting Labor MP Peta Murphy. The first three by-elections were contested by both major parties. Labor won the Aston by-election off the Liberal Party—a very rare case of a government winning a seat from the Opposition mid-term.

The Coalition gained 2PP swings in the Fadden and Dunkley by-elections but failed to win Dunkley from Labor. Labor did not contest Cook and Liberal candidate Simon Kennedy easily retained the seat.

Table 17.2 By-elections held during the 2022–25 parliamentary term

Electorate	Date	Outgoing MP	Result	New MP
Aston	1 April 2023	Alan Tudge (Lib.)	+6.4% to ALP (2PP)	Mary Doyle (ALP)
Fadden	15 July 2023	Stuart Robert (LNP)	+2.7% to LNP (2PP)	Cameron Caldwell (LNP)
Dunkley	2 March 2024	Peta Murphy (ALP)	+3.6% to Lib. (2PP)	Jodie Belyea (ALP)
Cook	13 April 2024	Scott Morrison (Lib.)	+7.1% to Lib. (primary)	Simon Kennedy (Lib.)

Source: AEC (2025a).

The total number of candidates nominated for the House of Representatives declined slightly from a record in 2022, with 1,126 candidates nominating in 2025. There was one less electoral division, so the average number of candidates per division dropped from 7.97 to 7.51 (Raue 2025b).

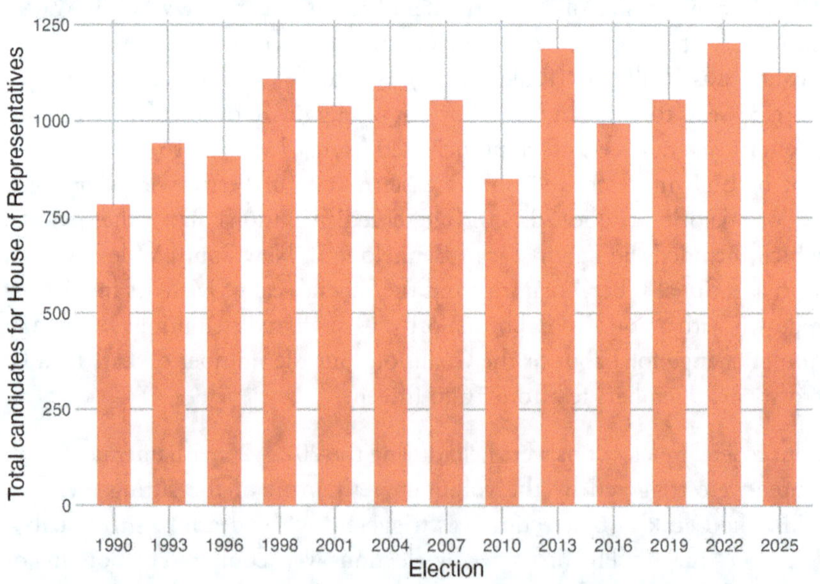

Figure 17.1 Total House of Representatives candidates per election, 1990–2025

Sources: Compiled by author from Carr (1998) and AEC (1998; 2025c) data.

The number of parties running candidates also fell in 2025: 34 parties nominated House of Representatives candidates in 2022, compared with 25 in 2025. This decline started after the 2016 Senate electoral reforms, while subsequent reforms to party registration rules have encouraged the consolidation of small parties. There was a significant increase in the number of Independent candidates running in 2025: 98 Independent or non-affiliated candidates stood in 2022, and this increased to 132 candidates in 2025 (see Chapter 15, this volume).

Labor and the Greens each ran candidates in every seat, while One Nation ran candidates in all seats except for the three in the Australian Capital Territory. The Liberal–Nationals Coalition ran at least one candidate in every seat. There were seven seats where the Liberal Party and the Nationals both ran. Clive Palmer's Trumpet of Patriots (see Chapter 15, this volume, for more detail) nominated just 100 candidates, while the party's two predecessors, the United Australia Party and Federation Party, had nominated 212 candidates between them in 2022. Legalise Cannabis had the biggest increase in candidates, having just one candidate in 2022 but running 42 candidates in 2025. The Libertarian Party (which was a new name for the former Liberal Democratic Party) ran 46 candidates, down from 100 candidates in 2022. The Animal Justice Party ran only 18 candidates, down from 48 in 2022.

National result

Labor won 55.35 per cent on 2PP—a swing of 3.22 per cent from 2022. On primary votes, Labor (34.6 per cent) gained a swing of 2.0 per cent, while the Coalition (31.8 per cent) suffered a swing of 3.9 per cent (AEC 2025c). This was the lowest primary vote for either major party since World War II and was the first time since 2007 that Labor polled a higher primary vote than the Coalition (Raue 2025c). The Greens suffered a very slight 0.05 per cent swing on the primary vote after polling a record high vote in 2022. One Nation gained a swing of 1.44 per cent. Independents' vote share increased by 2.06 per cent to a new high of 7.36 per cent.

Table 17.3 Results of the 2025 federal election by party

Party	Votes	Percentage	Swing	Seats	Seat change
ALP	5,354,141	34.56	+1.98	94	+17
Coalition	4,929,403	31.82	–3.88	43	–15
The Greens	1,889,978	12.20	–0.05	1	–3
Pauline Hanson's One Nation	991,815	6.40	+1.44	0	0
Trumpet of Patriots	296,077	1.91	–2.60	0	0
Family First	273,680	1.77	+1.77	0	0
Legalise Cannabis	186,335	1.20	+1.16	0	0
Katter's Australian Party	51,775	0.33	–0.05	1	0
Centre Alliance	37,453	0.24	–0.01	1	0
Independents	1,139,481	7.36	+2.06	10	0
Other	340,099	2.17	–0.56	0	0

Source: Compiled by author from AEC (2025c) data.

Seats changing hands

In total, 19 seats changed hands (based on pre-election estimates listing Liberal-held Menzies as notionally Labor and Labor-held Bennelong as notionally Liberal). Labor won a total of 13 seats from the Coalition and three from the Greens. The Liberal Party gained one seat from an urban Independent (in Goldstein) but lost Bradfield to an Independent. In New South Wales, Independent MP Andrew Gee retained Calare, which he had won in 2022 for the Nationals—technically an Independent gain.

Table 17.4 Seats that changed hands at the 2025 election

Seat	State	Incumbent	Winner	Margin (%)	New MP
Banks	NSW	Lib.	ALP	2.4	Zhi Soon
Bass	Tas.	Lib.	ALP	8.0	Jess Teesdale
Bennelong	NSW	ALP[a]	ALP	9.3	Jerome Laxale[a]
Bonner	Qld	LNP	ALP	5.0	Kara Cook
Braddon	Tas.	Lib.	ALP	7.2	Anne Urquhart
Bradfield	NSW	Lib.	Ind.	0.0	Nicolette Boele
Brisbane	Qld	Greens	ALP	9.0	Madonna Jarrett
Calare	NSW	Nats[b]	Ind.	6.8	Andrew Gee[b]
Deakin	Vic.	Lib.	ALP	2.8	Matt Gregg
Dickson	Qld	LNP	ALP	6.0	Ali France

Seat	State	Incumbent	Winner	Margin (%)	New MP
Forde	Qld	LNP	ALP	1.8	Rowan Holzberger
Goldstein	Vic.	Ind.	Lib.	0.1	Tim Wilson
Griffith	Qld	Greens	ALP	10.6	Renee Coffey
Hughes	NSW	Lib.	ALP	3.1	David Moncrieff
Leichhardt	Qld	LNP	ALP	6.1	Matt Smith
Melbourne	Vic.	Greens	ALP	3.0	Sarah Witty
Menzies	Vic.	Lib.*	ALP	1.1	Gabriel Ng
Moore	WA	Lib.	ALP	2.9	Tom French
Petrie	Qld	LNP	ALP	1.2	Emma Comer
Sturt	SA	Lib.	ALP	6.6	Claire Clutterham

Notes: [a] Bennelong was notionally a Liberal seat following a redistribution; [b] Calare was notionally a Nationals seat held by an ex-Nationals Independent.

Source: AEC (2025c).

Declining primary vote for the major parties

Labor's primary vote rebounded slightly in 2025 after dropping at six of the previous eight federal elections, but the Liberal–Nationals Coalition's primary vote dropped to a new low, of just 31.82 per cent. For the first time in modern Australian political history, the combined vote for minor parties and Independents exceeded one-third of the total (33.61 per cent) and exceeded one of the two major parties. The combined vote for the major parties experienced a significant drop in 2022, and declined slightly further in 2025, falling from 74.78 per cent in 2019, to 68.28 per cent in 2022 and 66.39 per cent in 2025 (Figure 17.2).

The declining primary vote for the major parties has meant that seats are more likely to be decided based on second and subsequent preferences, with fewer seats won with a majority of the primary vote; 2022 saw a surge in such contests, with a small increase for a total of 139 in 2025. While preferences can theoretically change the outcome in more than 90 per cent of contests, in most cases, the candidate with the most primary votes wins the seat. In 2025, there were 15 contests in which the winning candidate did not poll the most first-preference votes (a 'come from behind' win). This number has been steady in the previous five elections but is higher than the long-term trend: in the 21 elections before 2013, only four had more than 10 'come from behind' wins, with the previous record being 14 in 1972.

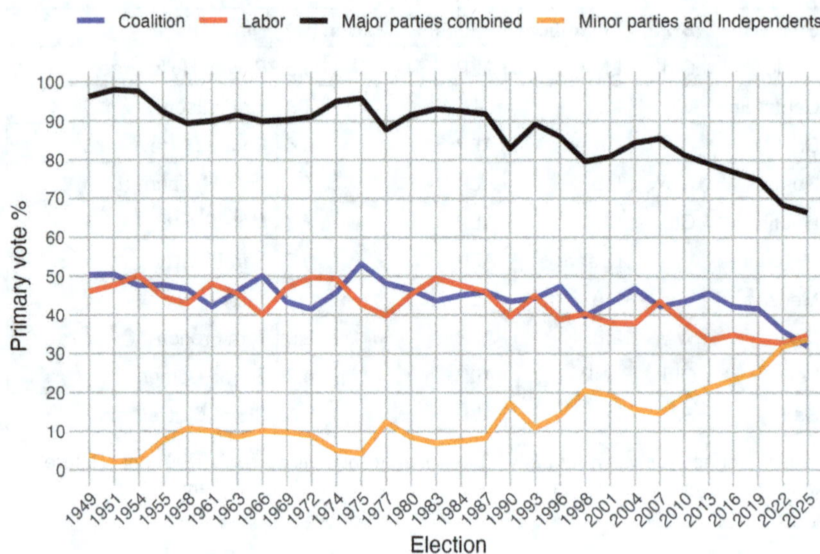

Figure 17.2 Primary vote for Labor, the Liberal–Nationals Coalition and all other candidates, 1949–2025

Sources: Raue (2025a) and AEC (2025c).

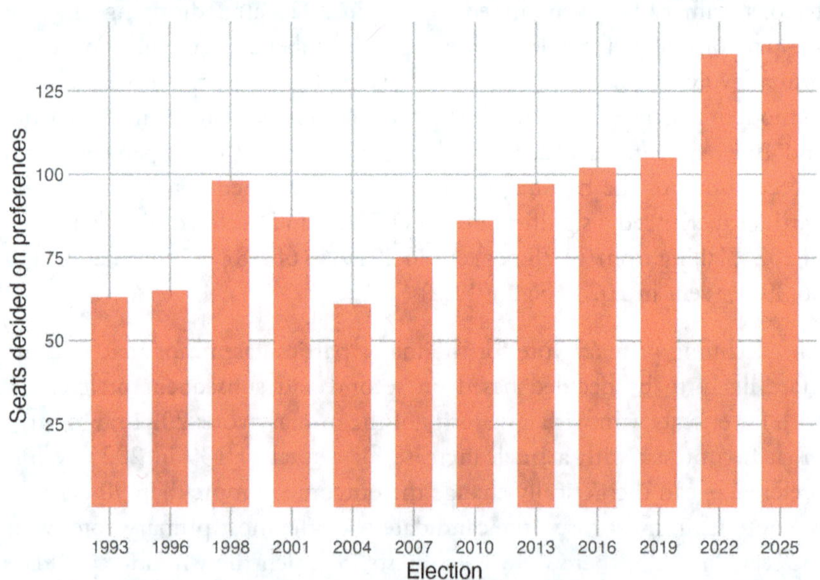

Figure 17.3 Seats decided on preferences, 1993–2025

Sources: Compiled by author from AEC (1998; 2025c) data.

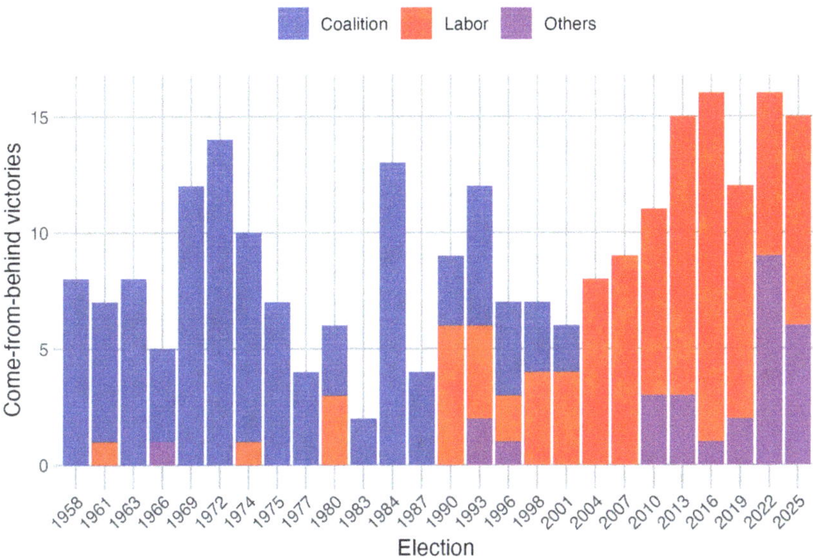

Figure 17.4 Seats in which the winning candidate did not poll the largest share of first-preference votes, by winning party, 1993–2025

Source: Compiled by author from various sources.

There has been a gradual shift in the partisan impact of preferences. In the mid-twentieth century, preference flows usually favoured Coalition parties, either due to Democratic Labor Party preferences or the common practice of two Coalition parties running and preferencing each other. This shifted later in the twentieth century, with Labor regularly winning seats from a trailing position since 1990. The Coalition has not won a single seat from such a position since 2001.

The past two elections have seen a rise in 'come from behind' wins (Figure 17.4). In 2025, Labor won from behind in nine seats, Independents in five seats and the Greens in one. Most of these seats had a Coalition candidate leading on first-preference votes; the only exceptions were Melbourne, where then Greens leader Adam Bandt topped the primary vote but was defeated by Labor, and Fowler, where first-term Independent MP Dai Le was re-elected. Le did increase her primary vote but still trailed Labor.

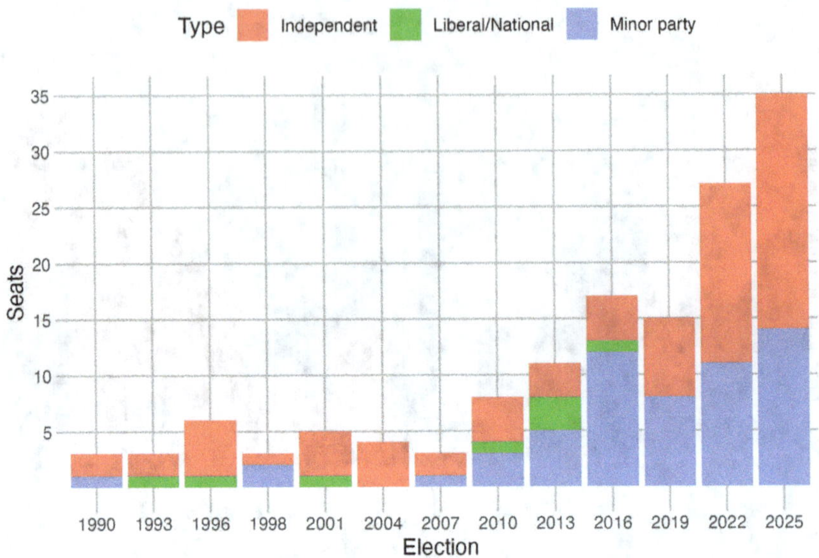

Figure 17.5 Non-classic contests in federal elections, 1990–2025

Sources: Compiled by the author from Carr (1990) and AEC (1998; 2025c).

There has also been an increase in the number of electorates in which the final two candidates after preferences are not from the major parties—also known as a 'non-classic' contest. The number of non-classic contests surged to 27 in 2022 and increased again, to 35, in 2025 (Figure 17.5). Most of that increase has been due to a larger number of seats with an Independent in the two-candidate-preferred (2CP) count, although the Greens made the 2CP count in 10 seats, One Nation in two seats and Katter's Australian Party and the Centre Alliance in one each.

Additionally, there are increasing numbers of seats in which there is uncertainty before the election, or even in the early stages of counting, about which candidates will make it to the 2CP count. When the AEC conducts a full distribution of preferences, there is a stage in which three candidates remain in the count. The third-placed candidate is then excluded and their preferences distributed to produce the final 2CP count. This stage is called the 'three-candidate-preferred' (3CP) count and is increasingly important. The average gap between the second and third-placed candidates at this stage of counting has been declining over the past 20 years (Figure 17.6), from more than 25 per cent of the total formal vote in 2007 to 15 per cent since 2022. This has also produced more seats with a very small gap between second and third on the 3CP: in 2022, just four seats had a margin below 1 per cent, compared with eight in 2025.

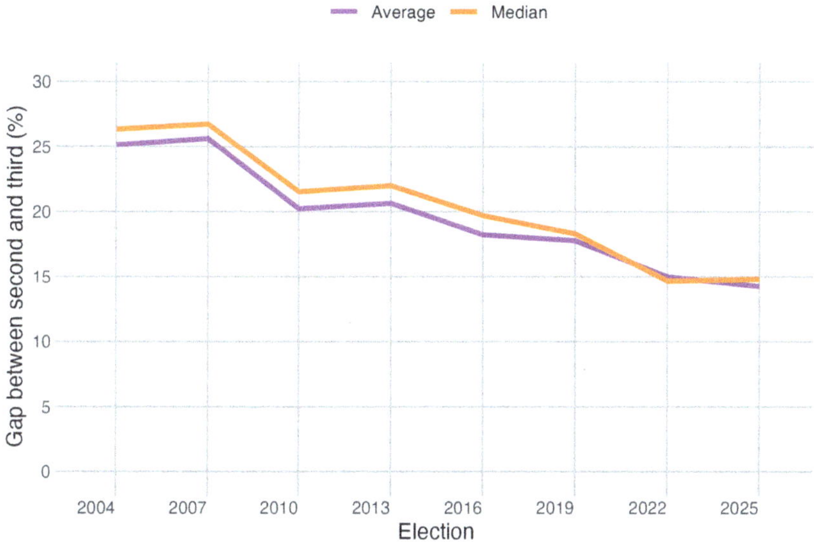

Figure 17.6 Gap between second-placed and third-placed candidates on the three-candidate-preferred count at federal elections, 2004–2025

Source: Compiled by the author from AEC (2025c) data.

In 2022, the AEC began conducting indicative 3CP counts in seats in which the likely final two candidates were not clear after early counting. In these cases, the AEC predicted which three candidates would likely be leading in the penultimate round of counting and distributed all formal votes to whichever of those three candidates had the highest-ranked preference. This procedure was conducted at least partially in four seats in 2022 and it was crucial to predicting outcomes in Brisbane and Macnamara before the final count was complete. In 2025, the AEC conducted this procedure in 13 seats, although some of these counts were abandoned when two clear leaders emerged. The 3CP count was crucial to predicting the outcome in Ryan, Fisher, Grey, Flinders, Forrest and Monash.

Ryan saw a close race for second place between Labor and Greens candidates. Whichever candidate came out ahead would easily defeat the LNP on the 2PP vote. In the end, the Greens' Elizabeth Watson-Brown narrowly outpolled her Labor rival, by a 0.78 per cent margin, and was re-elected. To take Ryan as an example, Watson-Brown defeated LNP candidate Maggie Forrest by a 3.3 per cent margin on the 2CP count. Yet, Labor candidate Rebecca Hack defeated Forrest by a 7.8 per cent margin on the 2PP count, suggesting that Labor would have comfortably won if they had overtaken the Greens. So, this seat is marginal between the Greens and Labor, but would also be considered a marginal seat in the final contest against the LNP.

In Fisher, Forrest and Grey, Independent candidates narrowly fell short of making the 2CP count and the Coalition defeated Labor after preferences. Based on the average rate at which Labor preferences flowed to Independents in other seats, Independent candidates may have won Fisher and Grey if they had made the 2CP count (Raue 2025f).

Disproportionality

The House of Representatives electoral system has never produced precisely proportional election results. The single-member system tends to favour the major parties and will usually result in the leading major party winning a larger share of seats than their share of primary votes. While it was previously common for a winning major party to win a seat share 30–40 per cent greater than their vote share, the Labor Party's victories in 2022 and 2025 have gone far beyond that range. In 2022, Labor's seat share was 56.5 per cent greater than their primary-vote share (Figure 17.7). In 2025, Labor won 34.6 per cent of the primary vote, but 62.7 per cent of House of Representatives seats—81 per cent higher than their vote share.

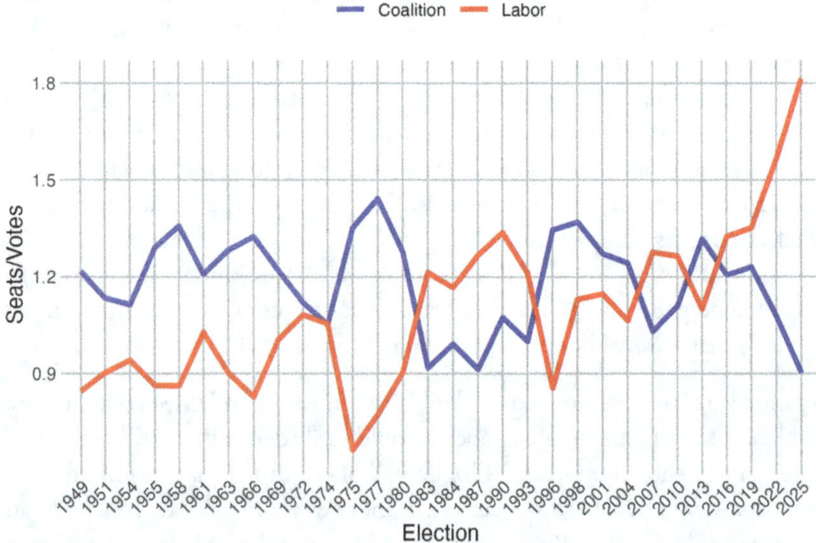

Figure 17.7 Ratio of House of Representatives seat share to vote share for major parties, 1949–2025

Source: Calculated by author.

Another way to view this trend is to look at the Gallagher index (Gallagher 1991), which measures the scale of disproportionality between votes won and seats won for each party. A score of zero indicates that each party won the identical proportion of seats as their share of the vote. This metric reached a record high index of 16.7 in 2022, but in 2025 it has reached 23.1 (Figure 17.8).

The widening urban–rural divide

The big story of the 2022 federal election was the collapse of Coalition support in inner metropolitan electorates, losing 12 of their 16 inner metropolitan (per AEC classification) seats while holding their rural seats (AEC 2025a). In 2025, the Coalition's losses were more focused in outer metropolitan electorates (Tables 17.5 and 17.6). The 2PP swing was similar in both inner and outer metropolitan seats, with an average 2PP swing of 4.16 per cent in inner metropolitan seats and 3.75 per cent in outer metropolitan areas. There was a swing to Labor in provincial and rural seats, but it was substantially less on average. The Coalition's seat losses were worst in outer metropolitan areas, where they lost eight seats—holding on to only seven. They did lose seats in every other region type, but on a smaller scale.

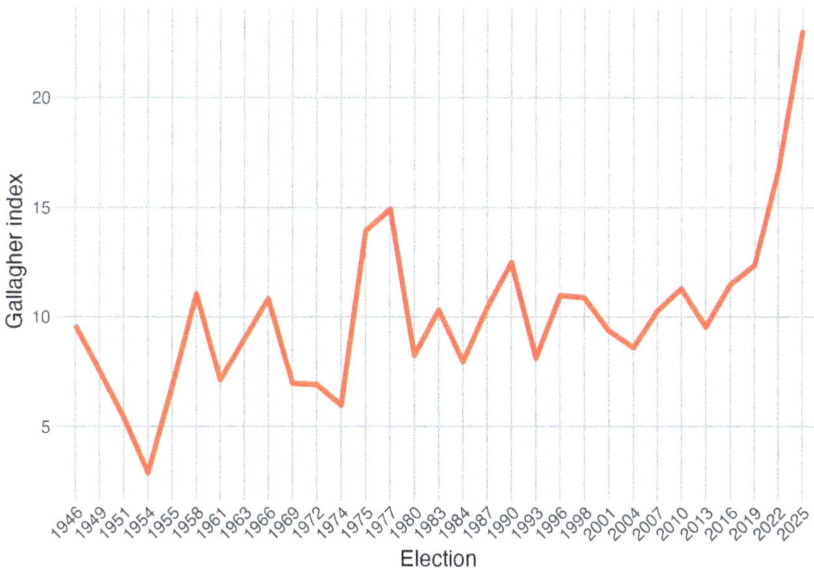

Figure 17.8 Gallagher index of disproportionality at Australian federal elections, 1946–2025

Source: Gallagher (2025).

Table 17.5 Two-party-preferred vote by geographical classification

State	Labor 2PP	Coalition 2PP	Swing to Labor
Inner metropolitan	63.46	36.54	4.16
Outer metropolitan	57.94	42.06	3.75
Provincial	53.50	46.50	1.83
Rural	43.95	56.05	1.98

Sources: Compiled by author from AEC (2025a and 2025c) data.

Table 17.6 Seats won by geographical classification

	Labor	Coalition	Crossbench
Inner metropolitan	35 (+4)	2 (–2)	6 (–4)
Outer metropolitan	35 (+10)	7 (–8)	3 (0)
Provincial	15 (+1)	9 (–2)	0 (–)
Rural	9 (+2)	25 (–3)	4 (+1)

Sources: Compiled by author from AEC (2025a and 2025c) data.

The crossbench is still relatively strongly concentrated in inner metropolitan areas, despite the Greens losing three inner-city seats and Zoe Daniel losing the seat of Goldstein (see Chapter 14, this volume). Independents made the 2PP count in seats such as Cowper, Groom and Wannon, or came close in seats such as Grey and Monash but were unable to break through. Looking at these trends over a longer period, the Coalition's relative strength in rural areas has grown over the past three elections while inner metropolitan areas have become much stronger for Labor on a 2PP basis. While Labor has usually won a clear majority of inner metropolitan seats and about half of outer metropolitan seats, they now hold large majorities in both seat categories. The Coalition lost some ground in rural areas, but Labor holds fewer seats there than when they won similar house majorities in 1993 and 2007.

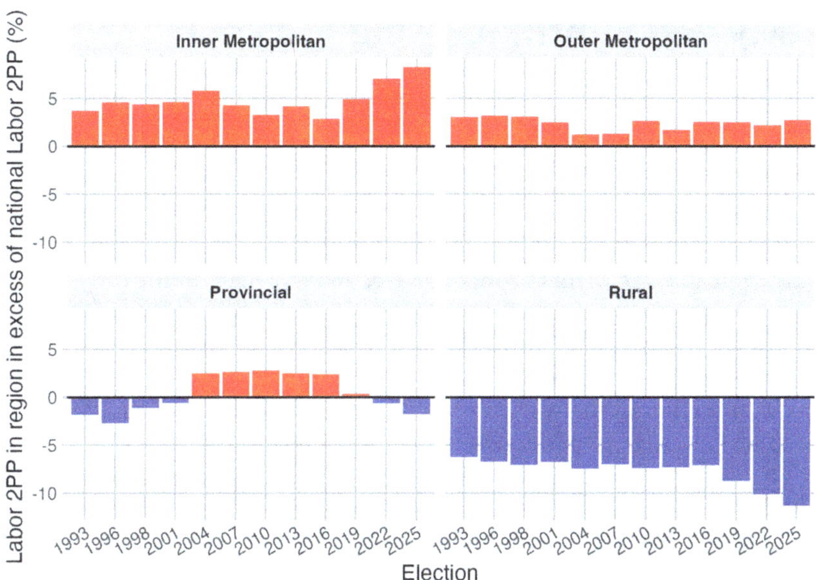

Figure 17.9 Difference between two-party-preferred vote for each regional classification and national two-party-preferred figures, 1993–2025

Sources: Compiled by author from AEC and Raue (2025f) data.

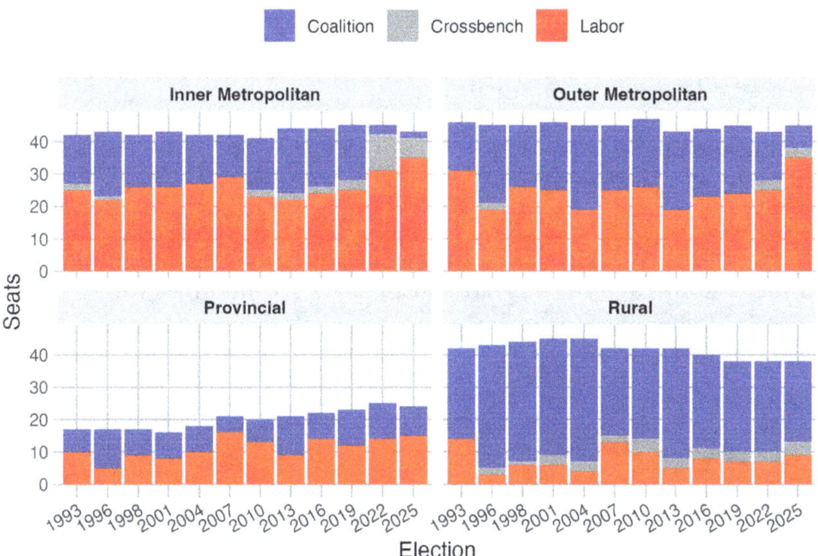

Figure 17.10 Seats won by regional classification, 1993–2025

Source: Compiled by author from AEC data.

Early and informal voting

The early vote (including postal voting)[1] made up a majority of the votes cast for the first time in 2022 but formed an even larger share of total turnout in 2025; fewer than 44 per cent of votes were cast on election day. Labor's swing was larger among election-day voters, producing an even larger gap between the two measures than in 2019 (Table 17.7). Labor's 2PP was 5.3 percentage points stronger on election day than on the early vote.

There was a slight increase in the informal vote in 2025, from 5.19 per cent to 5.60 per cent (Figure 17.11). The informal rate has been steady at recent elections, falling between 5 and 6 per cent at seven of the past eight elections. Informality partly reflects the size of ballot papers.

The informal rate generally increases with larger ballot papers and jumps noticeably when the number of candidates increases from seven to eight (Raue 2025e). Longer ballot papers require voters to mark more consecutive numbers without error for their vote to be formal and voters are advised to number 'at least 1 to 6' on their Senate ballot paper. A voter who follows those instructions for the House will have cast a formal vote in a seat with seven candidates, but not in one with eight candidates. Having said that, the overall rate of informal voting has not changed since the 2016 Senate voting system reform; it is possible some '1–6' informal votes have simply replaced other kinds of informal votes.

Informal voting is also higher in New South Wales than other States (Table 17.8). New South Wales uses optional preferential voting to elect its Legislative Assembly, which means a '1'-only vote is formal at State elections while informal at federal elections. The State had the highest informal vote in the country and the biggest increase in 2025. Informal voting fell in Victoria, Western Australia, Tasmania and the Northern Territory, barely changed in South Australia and the ACT and Queensland had a much smaller increase.

---

1   The AEC reports election results by different vote types. 'Ordinary' votes are those cast at polling places within the local electorate on election day, but they also include in-electorate pre-poll voting centres and some other vote categories such as mobile and hospital booths. 'Postal' votes cover all votes sent in by mail. 'Provisional' votes are a small number of other votes cast provisionally. 'Absent' votes are election-day votes cast outside the voter's home electorate. 'Declaration pre-poll' votes are votes cast at pre-poll voting centres outside the voter's home electorate. The 'early vote' label covers ordinary and declaration pre-poll votes, postal votes and some other ordinary votes such as remote mobile booths.

Table 17.7 Labor two-party-preferred vote before and on election day (per cent)

Election	ALP 2PP election day	ALP 2PP early	Difference	Percentage voting on election day
2001	49.44	45.14	4.30	89.72
2004	47.66	44.05	3.61	87.59
2007	53.23	49.76	3.47	85.32
2010	50.87	46.82	4.05	81.36
2013	47.76	43.22	4.54	72.06
2016	51.15	46.50	4.65	67.21
2019	50.64	45.50	5.14	57.72
2022	53.98	50.31	3.67	47.89
2025	58.23	52.97	5.26	43.58

Source: Compiled by author from AEC (2025c) data.

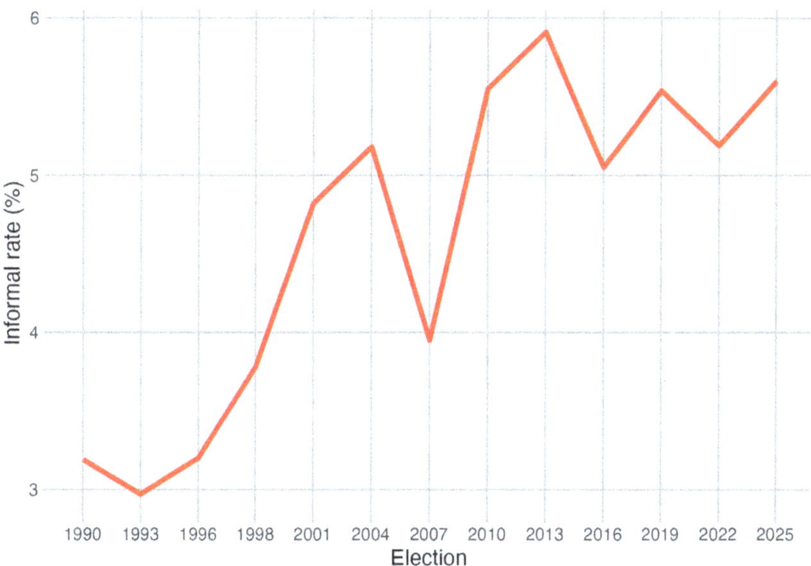

Figure 17.11 Informal voting rate at federal elections, 1990–2025

Sources: Compiled by author from Carr (1990) and AEC (1998; 2025c) data.

Informal voting is usually higher in multicultural electorates with large proportions of the population who speak a language other than English. Combined with the tendency for informal voting to be higher in New South Wales (Figure 17.12), this usually means that the seats with the highest rates of informal voting are in Western Sydney. Werriwa had the highest ever rate of informal voting at a general election for the House of Representatives, at 17.26 per cent. Watson was not far behind, at 17.01 per cent. Both seats recorded informal rates of about 10 per cent in 2022. The previous record high informal rate was Scullin in 1984: 14.09 per cent. Werriwa and Watson easily broke that record, with several other seats close behind.

Table 17.8 Informal voting rate by State or Territory (per cent)

State/Territory	Informal rate	Change in informal rate
NSW	8.06	1.84
Vic.	4.24	−0.47
Qld	4.93	0.76
WA	3.95	−1.57
SA	5.26	0.14
Tas.	4.25	−1.60
ACT	2.43	−0.03
NT	3.99	−1.32

Source: Compiled by author from AEC (2025c) data.

Figure 17.12 Informal voting rate compared with the number of candidates in each division, 2025 federal election

Source: AEC (2025c).

Results by State and Territory

There is considerable variation in both the 2PP vote and the swing from 2022 across States and Territories. Labor gained seats in all six States, with the most in Queensland, where they gained seven seats: five from the LNP and two from the Greens. The Coalition lost four seats in New South Wales; almost half the crossbench now represents seats in that State. Former Independent MP Kylea Tink's seat of North Sydney was abolished but another Independent, Nicolette Boele, narrowly won the seat of Bradfield, which had taken in large parts of Tink's former electorate. Independent Andrew Gee retained Calare after previously winning the seat for the Nationals.

Table 17.9 Two-party-preferred vote by State (per cent)

State/Territory	Labor 2PP	Coalition 2PP	Swing to Labor
NSW	55.47	44.53	4.05
Vic.	56.35	43.65	1.52
Qld	49.42	50.58	3.47
WA	55.84	44.16	0.84
SA	59.20	40.80	5.23
Tas.	63.34	36.66	9.01
ACT	72.49	27.51	5.54
NT	54.25	45.75	–1.29
Australia	55.35	44.65	3.49

Sources: AEC (2025c); Raue (2025f).

Table 17.10 Primary vote by State (per cent)

State/Territory	Labor	Liberal–Nationals	Greens	Others
NSW	35.20	31.53	11.06	22.21
Vic.	33.95	32.20	13.59	20.26
Qld	30.98	34.91	11.76	22.35
WA	35.59	31.54	11.97	20.90
SA	38.31	28.45	13.42	19.82
Tas.	36.60	24.50	11.12	27.78
ACT	47.53	21.16	15.06	16.25
NT	37.94	33.84	10.22	18.00
Australia	34.56	31.82	12.20	21.42

Source: AEC (2025c).

Table 17.11 Seats won by State

State/Territory	Labor	Coalition	Crossbench
NSW	28 (+2)	12 (–4)	6 (+1)
Vic.	27 (+3)	9 (–2)	2 (–2)
Qld	12 (+7)	16 (–5)	2 (–2)
WA	11 (+2)	4 (–1)	1 (–)
SA	7 (+1)	2 (–1)	1 (–)
Tas.	4 (+2)	0 (–2)	1 (–)
ACT	3 (–)	0 (–)	0 (–)
NT	2 (–)	0 (–)	0 (–)

Sources: Compiled by author from AEC (2024 and 2025c) data.

Most of Australia swung towards Labor on the 2PP vote, but some States swung more than others. In 2022, Labor gained a 2PP swing of more than 10 per cent in Western Australia, winning four Liberal-held seats. In 2025, Western Australia had the smallest swing to Labor, but the party still increased their 2PP vote compared with the record vote they polled in 2022. The swing was also relatively modest in Victoria, which has been one of Labor's best States at recent elections. Labor gained a 2PP swing in all six States and the ACT, ranging from 0.8 per cent in Western Australia to 9.0 per cent in Tasmania. The Country Liberal Party gained a 1.3 per cent swing in the Northern Territory. When comparing each State with the national figure (Figure 17.13), Tasmania is once again the most Labor-leaning State, after a swing of 9.0 per cent and a gain of two seats. Western Australia is now just slightly pro-Labor compared with Australia, but this is still very different to the historical trend of the State strongly favouring the Liberal Party.

Victoria has strongly favoured Labor at recent elections, but a modest swing in 2025 compared with Labor's bigger swings elsewhere means the State now has only a small pro-Labor lean. New South Wales has consistently been close to the national average in recent decades and 2025 was no exception. Labor's swing in Queensland only slightly exceeded the national trend, so, despite Labor's large haul of seat gains in this northern State, it still produced a stronger Coalition 2PP vote than Australia overall. Labor also gained a strong swing in South Australia, which means the State now has the strongest Labor lean since 1969.

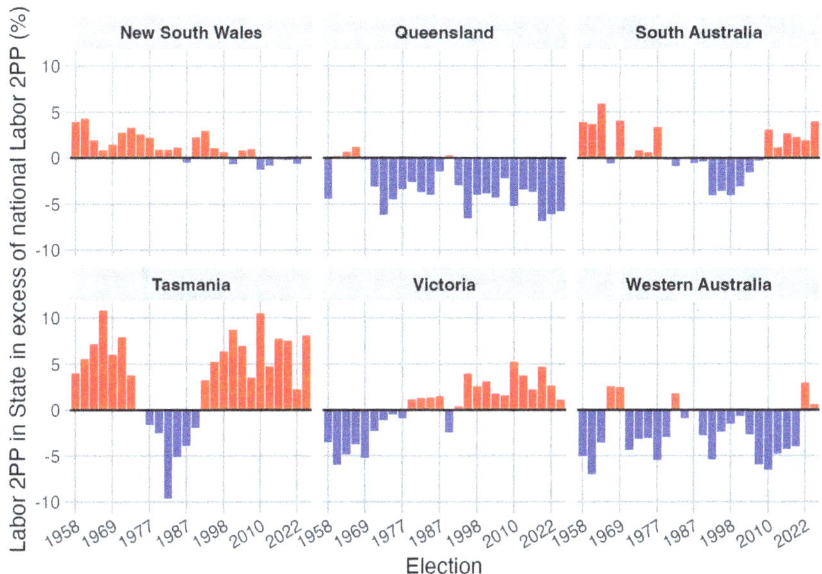

Figure 17.13 Difference between State two-party-preferred and national two-party-preferred figures per State, 1958–2025

Source: Compiled by author from various data sources.

New South Wales

Australia's most populous State saw four seats change hands. Labor won two seats off the Liberal Party: the neighbouring seats of Banks and Hughes in the south of Sydney. In Banks, Labor candidate Zhi Soon gained a 5.0 per cent 2PP swing to defeat Liberal shadow minister David Coleman with a 2.4 per cent margin. In Hughes, Labor candidate David Moncrieff defeated first-term Liberal MP Jenny Ware with a 6.5 per cent swing, finishing up with a 3.1 per cent margin. Andrew Gee, a former Nationals MP, was re-elected as an Independent in Calare with a 6.8 per cent margin against his former party.

Independent Nicolette Boele won the tightest race of the election, in Bradfield, defeating Liberal candidate Gisele Kapterian by just 26 votes after a full recount. Boele led Kapterian by 40 votes on first preferences but fell behind during the preference count (Figure 17.14). Kapterian was then the provisional winner by eight votes. The tight margin triggered an automatic full recount, which took from 26 May to 4 June and ended with Boele winning.

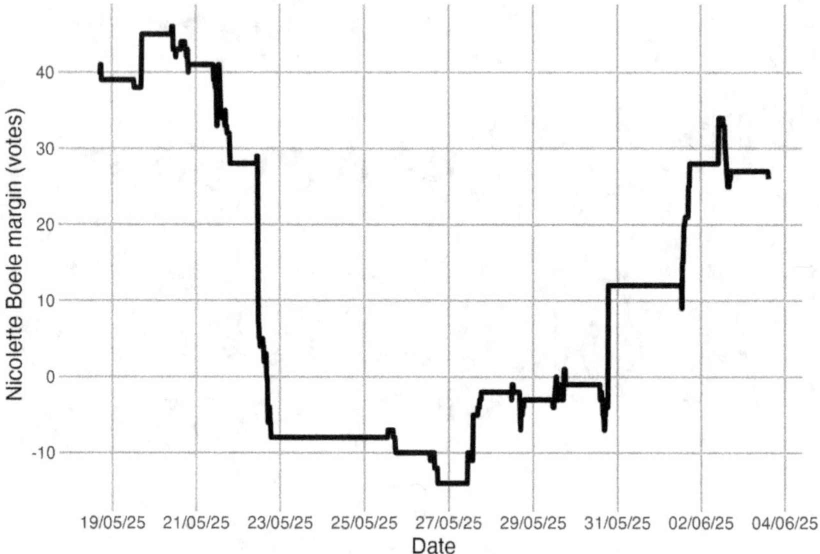

Figure 17.14 Two-candidate-preferred margin between Independent candidate Nicolette Boele and Liberal candidate Gisele Kapterian in the division of Bradfield during the distribution of preferences and recount, 19 May – 4 June 2025

Source: Compiled by author from AEC (2025b) data.

Victoria

In Victoria, Labor gained the eastern Melbourne suburbs seat of Deakin and won the neighbouring seat of Menzies, which was Liberal-held but had been redrawn as a marginal Labor seat. Labor candidate Matt Gregg gained a 2.8 per cent swing in Deakin, defeating long-serving Liberal MP Michael Sukkar. Sukkar's margin had been razor-thin, so Gregg ended up with a 2.8 per cent margin. Liberal MP Keith Wolahan lost the seat of Menzies to Labor candidate Gabriel Ng by a 1.1 per cent margin after a 0.7 per cent swing.

Labor prevailed in two close races against the Greens in inner-city Melbourne. Greens leader Adam Bandt lost his seat of Melbourne to Labor candidate Sarah Witty by a 3.0 per cent margin after a 9.5 per cent swing. Bandt's pre-election margin had been made smaller by redistributions that shifted Greens voters from Melbourne to the neighbouring seat of Wills. There, Labor MP Peter Khalil survived with a 1.4 per cent margin after a 3.2 per cent 2PP swing to former Victorian Greens State leader Samantha Ratnam.

The two sitting Independents both had tough re-election contests. In Kooyong, Monique Ryan held on by a 0.7 per cent margin after a 1.5 per cent swing to Liberal candidate Amelia Hamer. Fellow Independent Zoe Daniel was defeated in Goldstein, with her predecessor, Liberal MP Tim Wilson, regaining the seat by just 175 votes after a partial recount. Independents also performed strongly in three seats further afield. Liberal MP Dan Tehan retained Wannon by a 3.3 per cent margin against Alex Dyson. This was Dyson's third attempt and he gained only a 0.5 per cent swing compared with his 2022 performance. Ben Smith reduced Liberal MP Zoe McKenzie's margin to just 2.3 per cent in Flinders. In Monash, sitting MP Russell Broadbent contested the seat as an Independent after losing Liberal preselection, and came fourth. Fellow Independent Deb Leonard almost made the 2PP count, but eventually Liberal candidate Mary Aldred defeated Labor rival Tully Fletcher with a 4.1 per cent margin.

Queensland

Labor swept across South-East Queensland, gaining four seats from the LNP and two from the Greens. Labor candidate Ali France's defeat of Liberal leader Peter Dutton in Dickson was the most notable result, with France gaining a 7.7 per cent swing and winning with a 6.0 per cent margin. The LNP's Terry Young barely scraped by in the neighbouring seat of Longman by a 269-vote margin against Labor's Rhiannyn Douglas. Labor also gained the seat of Leichhardt in far north Queensland after the retirement of long-term member Warren Entsch; Matt Smith won the seat with a 9.5 per cent swing, defeating the LNP's Jeremy Neal by a 6.1 per cent margin. The Greens lost two of their three seats in inner-city Brisbane and came close in the third. Labor gained Max Chandler-Mather's seat of Griffith and Stephen Bates' seat of Brisbane. Greens MP Elizabeth Watson-Brown retained the seat of Ryan by a 3.3 per cent margin after outpolling Labor by just 0.8 per cent on the 3CP count.

Western Australia

Labor held on to all their 2022 gains in Western Australia and gained one more. Sitting MP Ian Goodenough resigned from the Liberal Party after losing preselection for his seat of Moore, recontesting the seat as an Independent. He came fourth, while Labor's Tom French defeated Liberal candidate Vince Connelly with a 2.9 per cent margin. Labor also narrowly won the newly drawn electorate of Bullwinkel, with Trish Cook elected by a slim 0.5 per cent margin despite a 2.8 per cent swing to the Liberal Party's Matt Moran. Liberal candidate Ben Smith narrowly retained the seat of Forrest by a 2.2 per cent margin against Labor's Tabitha Dowding after Dowding narrowly defeated Independent Sue Chapman by 0.8 per cent on the 3CP count. Chapman may have won if she had made the final preference count.

South Australia

Liberal MP James Stevens lost the seat of Sturt after a 7.1 per cent swing to Labor's Claire Clutterham, who won by a 6.6 per cent margin. This victory left Labor holding every seat in the Adelaide metropolitan region. Independent Anita Kuss fell just 2.1 per cent short of making the 2CP count in the seat of Grey, but Liberal candidate Tom Venning succeeded retiring Liberal MP Rowan Ramsey despite a 5.4 per cent swing to Labor after preferences.

Tasmania

Labor gained large swings across northern Tasmania, taking two Liberal seats. Labor candidate Jess Teesdale gained a 9.4 per cent swing in Bass, defeating Liberal MP Bridget Archer by an 8.0 per cent margin. In neighbouring Braddon, Labor Senator Anne Urquhart successfully switched to the lower house, gaining a 15.2 per cent swing after preferences to defeat Liberal candidate Mal Hingston by a 7.2 per cent margin after the retirement of Liberal MP Gavin Pearce. In the south-western electorate of Franklin, Independent Peter George won 21.7 per cent of the primary vote, cutting Labor MP Julie Collins' margin down to 7.8 per cent.

The Territories

The three electorates in the Australian Capital Territory are usually easy victories for Labor, but the southern seat of Bean proved more difficult in 2025. Independent Jessie Price won 26.41 per cent of the first-preference vote and came within 700 votes of defeating Labor MP David Smith on 2CP. The Northern Territory electorate of Solomon had the country's biggest 2PP swing to the Coalition: Lisa Bayliss gained a 7.1 per cent swing, reducing Labor MP Luke Gosling's margin to just 1.3 per cent.

Conclusion

In some ways, the 2025 federal election was very decisive. Labor won their biggest share of seats in the House in 80 years and gained a substantial 2PP swing. The Liberal–Nationals Coalition suffered a devastating defeat that has left the party with few seats in the Australian cities where most Australians live.

Yet, the story is more complex. More than one-third of votes were cast for minor parties and Independents, who were one of the two main contestants in almost one-quarter of seats and came close in several others. While the election was decisive, the complexity of multiparty politics cannot be ignored. Despite the record high vote for minor parties and Independents, the size of the crossbench fell in 2025, thanks to the Greens losing three seats. Labor achieved a record seat haul with one of their lowest primary votes, producing the most disproportional result in many decades.

The story of the Coalition's collapse is also the culmination of a long trend of the cities moving to the left. The Liberal Party is now more dominated than ever before by rural members, even before counting the rural Nationals members. Many Australian cities are now left with very few Liberal Members of Parliament. This will be a serious challenge for the Liberal–Nationals Coalition in coming years as they attempt to make their way back to power.

References

Australian Electoral Commission (AEC). 1998. *Election Statistics on CD-ROM*. [Online]. Canberra: Australian Electoral Commission. www.aec.gov.au/About_AEC/Publications/statistics/files/aec-1993-1996-1998-election-statistics.zip.

Australian Electoral Commission (AEC). 2025a. *Demographic Classification of Electoral Divisions. Current as at 4 March 2025*. Canberra: Australian Electoral Commission. www.aec.gov.au/Electorates/files/2025/demographic-classification-as-at-4-march-2025.xlsx.

Australian Electoral Commission (AEC). 2025b. *Australian Electoral Commission 2025 Federal Election Media Feed*. [Online]. Canberra: Australian Electoral Commission.

Australian Electoral Commission (AEC). 2025c. *Results: Tally Room Archive*. Canberra: Australian Electoral Commission. results.aec.gov.au.

Carr, Adam. 1990. 'Australian legislative election of 24 March 1990: The House of Representatives.' [Online]. *Psephos: Adam Carr's Election Archive.* psephos. adam-carr.net/countries/a/australia/1990/1990reps1.txt.

Gallagher, Michael. 1991. 'Proportionality, disproportionality and electoral systems.' *Electoral Studies* 10, no. 1: 33–51. doi.org/10.1016/0261-3794(91)90004-C.

Gallagher, Michael. 2025. *Election Indices.* [Online]. *16 June.* www.tcd.ie/Political_ Science/about/people/michael_gallagher/ElSystems/Docts/ElectionIndices.pdf.

Newton-Farrelly, Jenni. 2015. *Fairness and Equality: Drawing Election Districts in Australia.* Melbourne: Australian Scholarly Publishing.

Raue, Ben. 2024a. 'WA federal redistribution—Final margins.' *The Tally Room,* 28 September. www.tallyroom.com.au/56726.

Raue, Ben. 2024b. 'NSW federal redistribution—Final margins.' *The Tally Room,* 10 October. www.tallyroom.com.au/56992.

Raue, Ben. 2024c. 'Victorian federal redistribution—Final margins.' *The Tally Room,* 17 October. www.tallyroom.com.au/57084.

Raue, Ben. 2024d. 'NT federal redistribution drafts released.' *The Tally Room,* 18 October. www.tallyroom.com.au/57100.

Raue, Ben. 2025a. 'The declining two party system in federal politics.' *The Tally Room,* 7 April. www.tallyroom.com.au/60107.

Raue, Ben. 2025b. 'Nominations declared—The statistical wrap-up.' *The Tally Room,* 12 April. www.tallyroom.com.au/60187.

Raue, Ben. 2025c. 'Australia 2025—Wrap-up of the night.' *The Tally Room,* 4 May. www.tallyroom.com.au/60426.

Raue, Ben. 2025d. 'Pendulum—Australia 2025.' *The Tally Room.* www.tallyroom. com.au/aus2025/pendulumfed2025.

Raue, Ben. 2025e. 'Breaking down the informal vote.' *The Tally Room,* 27 May. www.tallyroom.com.au/60644.

Raue, Ben. 2025f. '3CP data sheds light on the close races.' *The Tally Room,* 24 June. www.tallyroom.com.au/60797.

18

The Senate results

Antony Green

Abstract

In contrast to Labor's landslide win in the House of Representatives, the use of proportional representation produced a less one-sided result and a larger crossbench in the Senate. The new Senate sees Labor with 29 senators and the Coalition down five seats to 27 seats. It was the Coalition's smallest representation since the expansion of the Senate in 1984 and the lowest Coalition vote share since the formation of the Liberal Party eight decades earlier.

The new Senate assembled with a record 20 crossbench members. For the third election in a row, the Greens elected a senator in each State, though defections had reduced its representation to 10 before the election. One Nation increased from two to four senators, recorded its highest vote since 1998 and, for the first time at a half-Senate election, returned senators from outside Queensland.

The Senate's electoral system continues to evolve in the wake of reforms introduced over the past decade. The Coalition's decision to recommend preferences for One Nation in all States for the first time greatly increased preference flows to the party. A higher Labor vote in the Senate compared with the House provides clear evidence of Labor supporters voting tactically for house Independents in traditional Coalition seats.

Keywords: Senate; preferential voting; proportional representation; preference flows; electoral reform

Campaigning for government in the House of Representatives defines the party contest in Australian elections, leaving the simultaneous Senate election campaign tethered in its wake. For major parties the Senate contest is an afterthought, but for minor parties it is the focus of a battle for seats and policy influence. Vote share by party for the two elections is strongly correlated but with variation due to the broader range of parties appearing on Senate ballot papers.

The 2025 result conformed to this pattern with Senate vote shares mirroring those in the House. Labor's vote rose while the Coalition's fell to its lowest level since the formation of the Liberal Party eight decades earlier. The combined vote for 'Other' candidates outpolled both Labor and the Coalition in 2022 but dipped in 2025 to fall short of Labor's increased support. The Greens elected a senator from each State for the third election in a row and support for Pauline Hanson's One Nation rose to 5.7 per cent— the party's highest vote since its first federal election in 1998. Excluding the Greens, One Nation, Independents and major parties, support for all other parties was 7.7 per cent in the House and 17.4 per cent in the Senate, where ballot papers presented a larger array of parties. Support for Independents in the Senate was just 0.2 per cent compared with an increased 7.3 per cent in the House.

Staggered Senate terms amplified the Coalition's seat losses. Facing election were positions last filled in 2019 when Liberal prime minister Scott Morrison led his government to a 'miracle' victory. The Coalition was defending three of the six seats facing election in the five mainland States. The 2025 result reduced the Coalition to two senators in all six States while the Liberal Party again failed to elect an ACT senator. Thirteen senators was the Coalition's worst result at a half-Senate election since the parliament's expansion in 1984, and losses over two elections reduced the Coalition to 27 senators—its worst representation in the same period. Having lost four seats in 2022, the Coalition lost a further five in 2025—three to Labor and two to One Nation.

The One Nation victories were significant for three reasons. First, One Nation had not previously elected senators outside Queensland at a half-Senate election. Two previous non-Queensland victories had been with the lower quota applying at the 2016 double-dissolution election. Second, both One Nation gains were from trailing positions—the first trailing wins in a half-Senate contest since changes to the Senate's electoral system in 2016.

Third, Coalition preferences played a part in both of One Nation's gains, with 2025 the first election in which the Coalition included One Nation in preference recommendations in every State.

Vote shares and seats won

Table 18.1 shows the Senate vote shares for parties polling more than 2 per cent in 2025. It also shows the change in vote share compared with 2022 and the 2019 election, when State senate positions were last elected. Over two elections, support for the Coalition declined 8.1 per cent while Labor's support rose 6.3 per cent.

Table 18.1 Senate result: Votes and seats, 2025

Senate as elected	Votes (%)	Change from 2022	Change from 2019	Seats won	Seats change
Labor	35.11	+5.03	+6.33	16	+3
Coalition	29.89	−4.33	−8.09	13	−5
Greens	11.72	−0.94	+1.53	6	0
Pauline Hanson's One Nation	5.67	+1.38	+0.27	3	+2
Legalise Cannabis	3.49	+0.15	+1.69	0	0
Trumpet of Patriots	2.60	−0.86	+0.24	0	0
Others	11.52	+0.20	−0.88	2	0

Notes: The Coalition total amalgamates votes for the four Coalition parties. While by registration a different party (see Chapter 15, this volume), the Trumpet of Patriots was backed by Clive Palmer and its vote share has been compared with support for Palmer's United Australia Party in 2019 and 2022.

Sources: Compiled by author from tables in AEC (2019a, 2022a, 2025a, 2025b).

Table 18.2 breaks down senators elected by party across two elections based on party affiliation at the election. The final line of Table 18.2 accounts for three senators changing affiliation since 2022. Victorian Senator Lidia Thorpe resigned from the Greens and became an Independent in February 2023. Two WA senators elected in 2022 also changed affiliation: Fatima Payman resigned from the Labor Party in July 2024 and formed her own Australia's Voice party, while Dorinda Cox resigned from the Greens and joined Labor after the 2025 election.

Table 18.2 Party composition and changes at the 2025 Senate election

Category (positions)	Labor	Coalition	Greens	One Nation	Others
2022 continuing senators (36)	13	14	6	1	2
Elected 2019 (36)	11	17	6	1	1
Elected 2025 (36)	14	12	6	3	1
Territory senators (2022, 2025)	2	1	0	0	1
Change	+3	–5	0	+2	0
2022–25 Senate as elected	26	32	12	2	4
2025–28 Senate as elected	29	27	12	4	4
Including membership changes	29	27	10	4	6

Sources: Compiled by author from tables in AEC (2019b, 2022b, 2025b).

In the new Senate, Labor (29) and the Greens (10) hold 39 seats—a majority to pass legislation in the 76-seat chamber. With only 27 seats, the Coalition needs both the Greens and other members of the crossbench to defeat Labor motions and legislation. An expanded crossbench of 20 members equals the previous record produced by the 2016 double-dissolution election.

In 2019 the Coalition polled between 2.51 and 2.96 quotas and elected a third senator after preferences in the five mainland States. Labor elected only one Queensland senator in 2019, with One Nation elected from 0.72 of a quota. One Nation polled between 0.20 and 0.41 of a quota in the other mainland States and was either the last excluded or the last remaining party after preferences.

The decline in Coalition support in 2025 reversed the position of One Nation and the Coalition in the race to elect senators. The Coalition's highest vote in quotas was 2.20 in Victoria and in three States it fell short of two quotas. The Coalition elected only two senators and had preferences distributed in most States. One Nation competed as the fourth party, with between 0.31 and 0.50 of a quota. Queensland dissolved into a battle of right-wing parties, with One Nation defeating Gerard Rennick's People First for the final seat. The Jacqui Lambie Network was the successful fourth-placed party in Tasmania. In the other four States, Labor's vote of between 2.43 and 2.66 quotas resulted in the party's third candidate competing with One Nation for a seat.

How the battle unfolded is outlined later in this chapter in a discussion of the results in each State and Territory. Labor was disadvantaged in some States by the Greens falling short of a quota, with preference flows from supporters of excluded left-wing parties filling Greens quotas rather than keeping Labor ahead of One Nation. With the Coalition excluded beyond two quotas in most States, One Nation faced little competition for preferences from supporters of right-wing parties. In a break with the past, the 2025 election was the first in which the Coalition included One Nation in its preference recommendations in all States. Coalition preferences helped to confirm One Nation's victories over Labor in New South Wales and Western Australia but could not stop Labor winning third seats in Victoria and South Australia.

Differences between the House and the Senate vote shares

As in 2019 and 2022, more than one-third of Senate votes were cast for groups other than Labor and the Coalition. Support for 'Others' was down from a record 35.7 per cent in 2022 to 35.0 per cent in 2025. Labor polled 35.1 per cent, ending a sequence of four elections with lower support than 'Others'—that is, Independent and non-Greens minor parties. For the second election in a row, support for the Coalition slipped below that for 'Others'. The three-way division of Senate party votes matches the path of recent House of Representatives elections, though support for 'Others' has been consistently a few percentage points higher in the Senate. Figure 18.1 uses the three-way division of party support to plot differences in support in the House and the Senate since 1984.

The additional minor parties contesting Senate elections have always seen some Labor and Coalition house voters drift to other parties in the Senate. The large 'Others' difference in 1984 was caused by the Nuclear Disarmament Party polling 7.2 per cent in the Senate but contesting few House of Representatives seats. The Australian Democrats regularly polled higher in the Senate than in the House—a gap of 4 per cent opening on the election of the Howard government in 1996. Elections between 2010 and 2019 were impacted by the proliferation of parties contesting Senate elections and the differences in vote shares have declined since changes to the electoral system (in 2016) and party registration (in 2022).

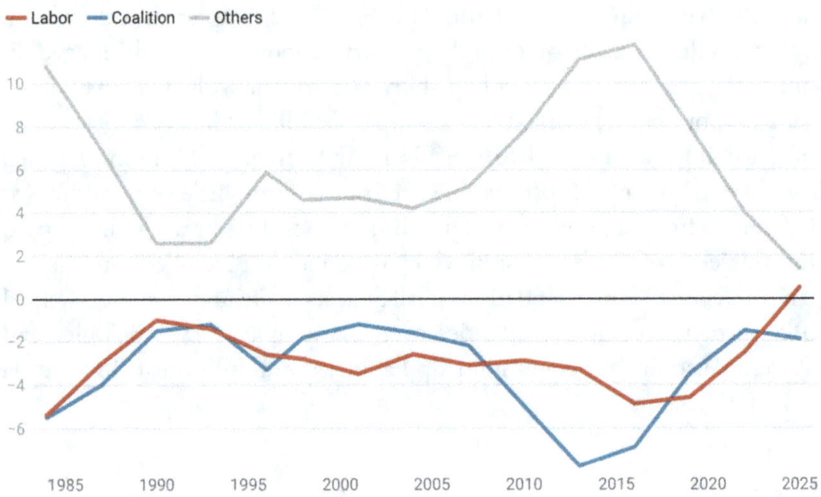

Lines represent House % Vote minus Senate % Vote by party. Points above the zero line represent where Senate % vote is higher, points below where House % vote is higher.

Figure 18.1 Difference in party support between the House and the Senate
Source: Compiled by author.

As Figure 18.1 shows, major parties consistently recorded lower support in the Senate until 2025 when Labor's Senate vote was 0.5 percentage points higher than its vote in the House. This is almost entirely due to votes in the 14 House of Representatives seats where Labor candidates were excluded in Coalition–Independent contests. In these seats, Independents polled 32.6 per cent in the House versus less than 0.5 per cent in the Senate, with Labor's House of Representatives vote in the same divisions 14.0 per cent compared with 29.5 per cent in the Senate. Overall, Labor recorded 249,727 more Senate votes in these 14 seats than in the House— a difference of 15.5 percentage points and a 2.34 ratio of Senate to House of Representatives Labor support. This is clear evidence of Labor voters casting tactical votes for Independents in traditionally safe Coalitions seats. These 14 seats account for almost all the difference between Labor's support in the two houses.

By contrast, in the 115 House of Representatives divisions that finished as Labor–Coalition two-party-preferred (2PP) contests, the Labor vote in the Senate was lower than in the House by 63,474 votes or 1.4 per cent—a ratio of Senate to House of Representatives vote shares of 0.98, which matches the traditional pattern of major-party split-ticket voting.

Candidates, parties and the evolution of the electoral system

Proportional representation by single transferrable vote (PR-STV) has been used to elect the Senate since 1949. A major change in 1984 divided the ballot paper with a thick horizontal line (see Plate 18.1) and introduced two voting options. Electors could vote for parties 'above the line' (ATL) or for candidates 'below the line' (BTL).

As originally introduced, the system meant electors could vote for only a single party above the line. The vote was imputed to be for the party's list of candidates as well as the party's full list of preferences for all other parties and candidates. These preferences were registered by a 'group voting ticket' (GVT). Voters wanting to choose between candidates or select their own between-party preferences were required to use the alternative BTL option, for which 90 per cent of candidate boxes had to be numbered.

The ease of ATL voting resulted in about 95 per cent of voters using that option between 1984 and 2013. This put more than 90 per cent of distributed preference votes under the control of GVTs. Even parties with low levels of support and minuscule campaigns could deliver tight preference flows using GVTs. Preferences became tradeable commodities and, over three decades, instances grew of parties with very low vote shares defeating higher-polling competitors via labyrinthine preference deals.

Reforms of the Senate's electoral system in 2016 ended GVT control of between-party preferences. A new form of ATL voting was introduced, allowing voters to complete a preference order for parties. Voters were instructed to mark at least six preferences for an ATL vote or 12 for BTL, introducing a form of optional preferential voting beyond minimum preferences.

As outlined in Green (2015) and McAllister and Muller (2019), the old system led to a proliferation of parties contesting elections as a tactic using GVTs to accumulate or 'harvest' preferences. The tactic was ended with the abolition of GVTs. Under the reformed system, only voters could determine between-party preferences. Parties actively campaigning and distributing how-to-vote recommendations could still influence preferences, but parties with little profile or campaign had no influence. A further change in 2022 increased from 500 to 1,500 the number of members required to register a party.

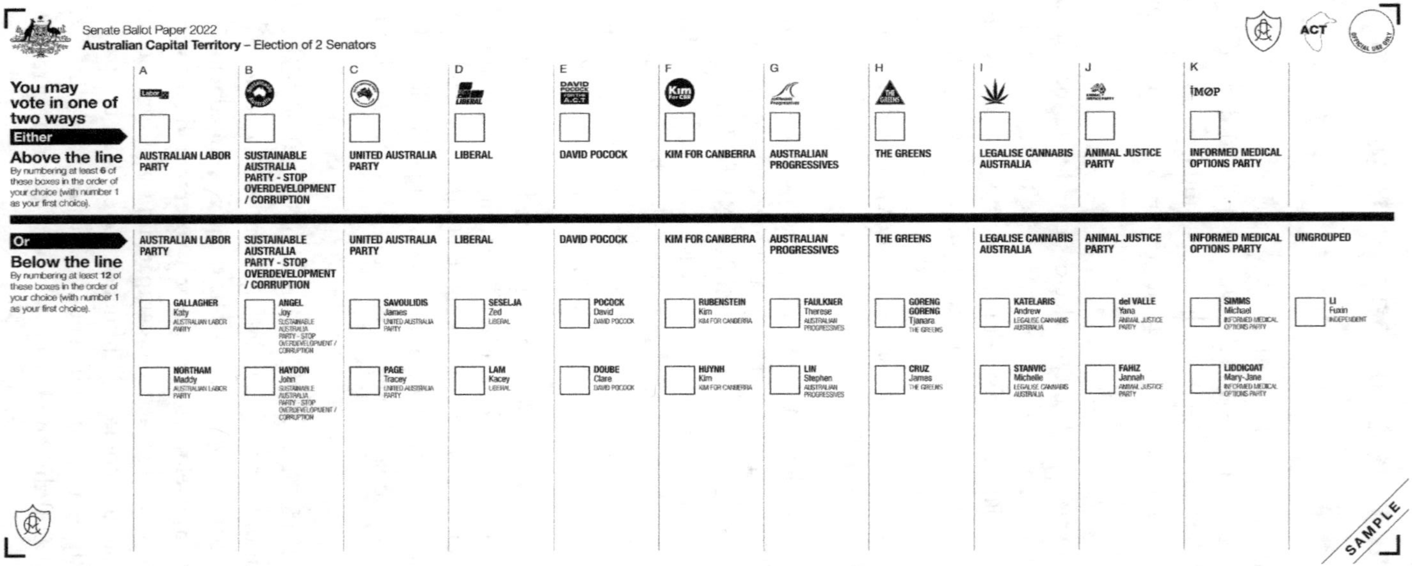

LANDSLIDE

Plate 18.1 Sample Senate ballot paper, 2022

Source: AEC.

The combined impact of these changes was to reduce both the number of parties contesting elections and the number of columns on Senate ballot papers. The last GVT half-Senate election, in 2013, was contested by 52 parties; the number of parties dipped to 48 in 2019, before the higher membership requirement reduced numbers further to 40 in 2022 and 28 in 2025. From an average of 7.7 groups per State in 1984, numbers surged to an average 33.7 at the last GVT election, before almost halving to an average of 17.2 in 2025. The result has been smaller ballot papers and a return to larger and more readable font sizes.

Abolishing GVTs and allowing preference exhaustion weakened preference flows and tipped the system in favour of parties that began the count with a significant quota or surplus quota of votes. It became harder for parties to win seats from trailing positions. At the last half-Senate election with GVTs, in 2013, there were nine candidates elected from trailing positions— in several cases, defeating candidates with many multiples more of first preferences (Green 2020).

The first election after the abolition of GVTs was the 2016 double-dissolution election at which a lower quota applied and only two senators were elected from trailing positions. There were no trailing wins when half-Senate elections resumed in 2019, and only one in 2022, with Independent David Pocock winning from behind in the two-vacancy ACT Senate election. The 2025 election produced two trailing wins—the first under the new rules at a half-Senate election, with One Nation candidates defeating third Labor candidates in New South Wales and Western Australia.

In New South Wales the third Labor candidate began the count with 0.63 of a quota to One Nation's 0.42 of a quota. In Western Australia Labor's third candidate held 0.53 of a quota to One Nation's 0.41 of a quota. One Nation's victory margin in both States was less than 0.03 of a quota. Labor's defeats were also the first under the new system in which a party had more than 0.5 of a quota and was defeated by a trailing candidate.

Is One Nation now established as Australia's fourth party?

Pauline Hanson was first elected to the House of Representatives as an Independent in 1996. She had been selected as a Liberal candidate, appeared on the ballot paper as a Liberal, but was disendorsed before polling day. After the formation of Pauline Hanson's One Nation in 1997, it had immediate success at the 1998 Queensland State election, polling 22.7 per cent and electing 11 MPs. Coalition preference recommendations had elected several One Nation members, but the Coalition joined Labor at the 1998 federal election in treating One Nation as a pariah party, placing it last in how-to-vote and Senate GVT preference recommendations. One Nation's Senate vote was 9 per cent in 1998; it elected a Queensland senator with a filled quota but was denied victories in other States by major-party preference deals.

One Nation continued to be placed last on major-party preference recommendations until the party faded from view a decade later. One Nation re-emerged in 2013 and contested the 2016 double-dissolution election in which a combination of name recognition, lower quotas and the abolition of GVTs saw the party elect four senators: two from Queensland and one each from New South Wales and Western Australia. The party has retained its Queensland Senate seat at three half-Senate elections since and, as already explained, added senators from New South Wales and Western Australia from trailing positions for the party's first half-Senate victories outside Queensland.

Importantly in 2025, the Coalition broke with past practice and included preference recommendations for One Nation in all States for the first time. Using the AEC's published ballot paper data, it is possible to calculate the proportion of Coalition ATL preferences that flowed to Labor, to One Nation or were exhausted at both elections. As Table 18.3 shows, the Coalition's decision on preference recommendations had a major impact on how Coalition preferences flowed.

In 2022 the Queensland LNP had included One Nation in its preference recommendations; the Coalition in New South Wales and Western Australia were doing the same but in selected seats. The Tasmanian Liberal Party recommended a preference of sixth for One Nation in 2022 but a more prominent second preference in 2025. As Table 18.3 shows, the Coalition's change in preference recommendations hugely increased the flows of preferences to One Nation.

Table 18.3 Distribution of Liberal preferences between Labor and One Nation, 2022 and 2025

State	2022 election			2025 election		
	ALP	PHON	Exhausted	ALP	PHON	Exhausted
NSW	23.9	30.5	45.5	18.2	65.6	16.3
Vic.	25.9	21.4	52.8	21.7	61.6	16.7
Qld	20.9	66.2	12.9	20.6	69.8	9.6
WA	28.4	34.4	37.2	22.8	64.2	13.1
SA	28.7	19.2	52.1	25.1	61.8	13.1
Tas.	37.7	42.0	20.4	33.4	57.4	9.2

Notes: While the preference flows between Labor and One Nation can be calculated, the order of candidate exclusion meant they were not involved in the distribution of preferences in Queensland or Tasmania.

Source: Calculations by author from ballot paper data files published by the AEC.

That One Nation elected senators was less about preferences and more a consequence of declining major-party vote share. In the House, a lower major-party vote creates more of what the AEC calls non-classic contests: counts that do not finish as Labor versus the Coalition after preferences. There were a record 35 non-classic contests in 2025. The consequence in the Senate is an increase in the number of contests in which one or both major parties find their vote below 2.5 quotas (35.7 per cent)—a rule-of-thumb level a party must reach to be in the running for a third senator.

Seven half-Senate elections between 1990 and 2007 produced 42 State contests. The Coalition averaged 2.98 quotas per contest in the period and Labor 2.60 quotas, leaving room for only one minor party to fill the sixth seat. Counting the Coalition as a single party, the 42 contests saw eight in which only the two major parties were elected, 31 three-party combinations split 3–2 to majors plus a minor party and only three contests in which four parties including a second minor party were elected.

That position has changed at half-Senate elections since 2019, with 18 contests in which the Coalition averaged 2.34 quotas, Labor 2.20 quotas and the Greens 0.86 of a quota. The 18 contests have seen nine that elected three parties in a 3–2–1 pattern, and nine that elected four parties. The Greens have elected a senator in all 18 contests, but a declining major-party vote has left open a second minor-party opportunity—filled by One Nation five times, the Jacqui Lambie Network three times and the United Australia Party (UAP) once.

Elections since 2013 have shown diminishing returns for parties associated with Clive Palmer, leaving One Nation as the highest-polling party to the right of the Coalition. In 2025 the Coalition faced a dilemma: did it break with the past and recommend preferences for One Nation or allow four States to finish with four left-aligned seats—three Labor plus a Greens? The Coalition acted in the hope of benefiting from One Nation preferences, but also to prevent Labor and the Greens winning four seats in the States. In making its preference decision, has the Coalition anointed One Nation as the main minor party of the right and established it as the fourth player at Australian elections? The answer may depend on how the party survives the day when Pauline Hanson retires from politics.

Results by State

New South Wales

Table 18.4 Senate result: New South Wales

Party	Vote (%)	Change	Quotas	Elected	Change
Labor	37.63	+7.19	2.63	2	0
Liberal–Nationals	29.44	–7.29	2.06	2	–1
The Greens	11.18	–0.28	0.78	1	0
One Nation	6.06	+1.93	0.42	1	+1
Trumpet of Patriots (versus UAP)	2.40	–0.98	0.17	0	0
Legalise Cannabis	3.49	+0.89	0.24	0	0
Others	9.79	–1.48	0.69	0	0

Note: Trumpet of Patriots change calculated versus 2022 United Australia Party result.
Source: Compiled by author from AEC (2025a) data.

The Coalition's 2025 vote share was its lowest since the formation of the Liberal Party eight decades ago. It resulted in the defeat of Nationals deputy leader Perin Davey, who was unfortunate under the Coalition Agreement to be occupying position three on the ticket in 2025. It was the first election since 1998 in which the Coalition failed to elect three senators, the 1998 election being the one in which Coalition preferences helped elect an Australian Democrat rather than a higher-polling One Nation candidate.

The Greens polled 0.78 of a quota and easily reached a quota on preferences, while Labor's 2.63 quotas re-elected its two sitting senators with enough surplus to compete for a third seat. Labor failed to win a third seat in a contest with One Nation, which began the count on 0.42 of a quota but attracted more preferences. At the final count, One Nation reached 0.89 of a quota to Labor's 0.87—a victory margin of just 17,326 votes, 0.35 per cent or 0.02 of a quota. Exhausted preferences represented 0.24 of a quota.

Labor missed the final seat due to two factors. First, the Greens, with a starting quota of 0.78, absorbed preferences from parties of the left that otherwise could have helped Labor. Picking apart the published ballot paper data, there were about 50,000 preferences for Labor from minor left-wing parties that instead helped fill the Greens' quota and so played little part in the eventual contest between Labor and One Nation.

Second, while the Coalition had a surplus of only 0.06 of a quota or about 45,000 votes, the decision to include One Nation in the Coalition's list of recommended preferences increased the flow of Coalition preferences to One Nation. As shown in Table 18.3, the percentage of Coalition preferences flowing to One Nation doubled, advantaging One Nation by about 18,000 votes—effectively the party's margin of victory over Labor.

Victoria

Table 18.5 Senate result: Victoria

Party	Votes (%)	Change	Quotas	Elected	Change
Labor	34.68	+3.23	2.43	3	+1
Liberal–Nationals	31.41	–0.88	2.20	2	–1
The Greens	12.45	–1.40	0.87	1	0
One Nation	4.44	+1.53	0.31	0	0
Legalise Cannabis	3.63	+0.63	0.25	0	0
Trumpet of Patriots (versus UAP)	2.52	–1.49	0.18	0	0
Others	10.87	–1.62	0.76	0	0

Note: Trumpet of Patriots change calculated versus 2022 United Australia Party result.
Source: Compiled by author from AEC (2025a) data.

As occurred in most States, in Victoria, the Coalition recorded its lowest vote share since the formation of the Liberal Party. The Coalition was defending three Senate seats from 2019, re-electing two sitting senators, but losing the third seat, which had been held by Liberal turned Independent David Van.

The Greens retained their traditional seat with 0.90 of a quota and, with Labor winning three seats for the first time since 2007, delivered four of the six Victorian seats to left-aligned parties. On first preferences, Labor's vote was 2.43 quotas against One Nation's 0.31 of a quota. This was a narrower lead than in New South Wales, but a higher Victorian Greens vote left preferences from the Animal Justice Party and Legalise Cannabis to boost Labor's total later in the count. Based on analysis of ballot paper data, Family First and Trumpet of Patriots delivered twice as many preferences to One Nation as to Labor, after which Labor's lead over One Nation had shrunk to 0.04 of a quota.

For the first time the Coalition in Victoria included One Nation in its preference recommendation. As shown in Table 18.3, the decision tripled the flow of Coalition preferences to One Nation, pushing One Nation to 0.73 of a quota ahead of Labor on 0.67 of a quota. The final act in the count was the distribution of preferences from former State MP Fiona Patten, the lead candidate of Legalise Cannabis. Having fallen behind One Nation by 32,505 votes at the previous count, Labor had a net gain of more than twice that to win the final seat by 32,041 votes, 0.05 of a quota or 0.8 per cent.

Queensland

Table 18.6 Senate result: Queensland

Party	Vote (%)	Change	Quotas	Elected	Change
Liberal National Party	30.93	−4.30	2.17	2	−1
Labor	30.48	+5.79	2.13	2	+1
The Greens	10.47	−1.92	0.73	1	0
One Nation	7.13	−0.27	0.50	1	0
Gerard Rennick People First	4.69	+4.69	0.33	0	0
Trumpet of Patriots (versus UAP)	3.65	−0.54	0.26	0	0
Legalise Cannabis	3.51	−1.86	0.25	0	0
Others	9.13	−1.60	0.64	0	0

Note: Trumpet of Patriots change calculated versus 2022 United Australia Party result.
Source: Compiled by author from AEC (2025a) data.

In 2019, the Queensland Senate election had returned the unusual combination of three LNP senators along with one each for Labor, the Greens and One Nation, with Labor polling only 22.6 per cent that year. Labor elected two senators in both 2022 and 2025. Labor's second seat at both elections was at the expense of a third LNP senator. For the third election in a row, Queensland elected two minor-party representatives with both Greens and One Nation senators.

The battle for the final seat did not involve the major parties. One Nation Senator Malcolm Roberts faced a challenge on the right from former LNP senator Gerard Rennick, who had formed his own party, Gerard Rennick People First, after being defeated for LNP preselection. Roberts began the count leading Rennick 0.50 to 0.33 of a quota. Analysis of the ballot papers reveals that Rennick had few political friends in the contest, with preferences from the LNP and Trumpet of Patriots heavily favouring Roberts. In a contest between two right-wing candidates, most left-wing voters made no selection between the two; final exhaustion rates calculated from ballot paper data were 81.8 per cent among Greens voters, 70.5 per cent among Socialist Alliance voters and 67.4 per cent among Labor voters. At the end of the count, 0.41 of a quota of votes had exhausted—higher than the rate in other States where more traditional left–right contests took place.

Western Australia

Table 18.7 Senate result: Western Australia

Party	Vote (%)	Change	Quotas	Elected	Change
Labor	36.17	+1.62	2.53	2	0
Liberal	26.61	–5.06	1.86	2	–1
The Greens	12.84	–1.42	0.90	1	0
One Nation	5.87	+2.38	0.41	1	+1
Legalise Cannabis	4.03	+0.65	0.28	0	0
Nationals	3.58	+3.58	0.25	0	0
Australian Christians	2.67	+0.50	0.19	0	0
Others	8.22	–2.25	0.58	0	0

Source: Compiled by author from AEC (2025a) data.

Liberal support in Western Australia plumbed new depths, falling to 26.6 per cent (under two quotas), with the party's second seat only achieved on Nationals preferences. Where the Liberal Party had easily elected three senators at 10 half-Senate elections between 1990 to 2019, the 2025 election was the second in a row in which the party elected only two senators. Labor elected two senators with a surplus of 0.53 of a quota, and the now traditional seat for the Greens was easily retained.

The contest for the final seat began with Labor on a partial quota of 0.53 versus One Nation's total of 0.41 of a quota. Preferences from several leftish parties helped fill the Greens quota while flows from a range of conservative minor parties aided One Nation. Ballot paper data show the combined preferences from Australian Christians, Trumpet of Patriots and People First split 61.9 per cent to One Nation, 22.3 per cent to Labor and 15.8 per cent were exhausted. The exclusion of the Nationals filled the Liberals' second quota and Liberal and Nationals preferences put One Nation far enough ahead of Labor to prevent preferences from Legalise Cannabis putting Labor back in the lead. At the end of the count, One Nation had reached 0.89 of a quota, Labor 0.86; One Nation's margin of victory was 8,397 votes or 0.5 per cent. A total of 56,967 votes, or 0.24 of a quota, had exhausted by the end of the count.

One Nation's victory was again aided by the Liberal Party's decision in all seats to include One Nation in preference recommendations, doubling the flow of Liberal preferences to One Nation. One Nation's narrow win would have been even narrower without Liberal preferences.

South Australia

Table 18.8 Senate result: South Australia

Party	Vote (%)	Change	Quotas	Elected	Change
Liberal	27.57	−6.36	1.93	2	−1
Labor	38.06	+5.80	2.66	3	+1
The Greens	12.90	+0.95	0.90	1	0
One Nation	5.34	+1.33	0.37	0	0
Legalise Cannabis	2.86	+0.54	0.20	0	0
Trumpet of Patriots (versus UAP)	2.84	−0.18	0.20	0	0
Jacqui Lambie Network	2.71	+2.71	0.19	0	0
Family First	2.02	+2.02	0.14	0	0
Others	5.70	−6.79	0.40	0	0

Note: Trumpet of Patriots change calculated versus 2022 United Australia Party result.
Source: Compiled by author from AEC (2025a) data.

The Liberal Party lost its third seat in South Australia with the party's support falling short of two quotas. The beneficiary of the Liberals' declining fortunes was Labor, winning a third seat in South Australia for only the second time since six-vacancy half-Senate elections began in 1990. The Greens elected a now traditional Senate seat, which, combined with Labor's three senators, resulted in left-aligned parties winning four of six South Australian half-Senate seats for the first time.

Labor's vote rose to 38.3 per cent—the party's equal highest level since the 1980s—and their 2.66 primary quotas were enough to elect Charlotte Walker to a third seat. Walker turned 21 on election day and set a record as the youngest person elected to the Senate. One Nation polled 0.37 of a quota and received strong flows of preferences from right-wing parties, but, with Liberal preferences playing no part, One Nation had only 0.80 of a quota by the time Labor's third candidate reached quota.

Tasmania

Table 18.9 Senate result: Tasmania

Party	Vote (%)	Change	Quotas	Elected	Change
Labor	35.23	+8.19	2.47	2	0
Liberal	23.54	−8.48	1.65	2	0
The Greens	16.31	+0.83	1.14	1	0
Jacqui Lambie Network	7.28	−1.36	0.51	1	0
One Nation	5.17	+1.29	0.36	0	0
Legalise Cannabis	3.40	+0.37	0.24	0	0
Trumpet of Patriots (versus UAP)	3.24	+1.61	0.23	0	0
Shooters Fishers Farmers	2.27	+0.37	0.16	0	0
Others	3.57	−2.82	0.25	0	0

Note: Trumpet of Patriots change calculated versus 2022 United Australia Party result.
Source: Compiled by author from AEC (2025a) data.

There was no change to Tasmanian party representation despite an 8-percentage-point shift in major-party support from Liberal to Labor since 2022. Compared with the 2019 elections, Labor's vote share rose 4.6 per cent, the Liberal Party's fell 7.9 per cent and the Jacqui Lambie Network's fell 1.6 per cent. The Liberal Party vote was the lowest on record, but the party turned 1.65 quotas into two seats on One Nation preferences. The Greens filled their usual quota, with few votes left over to help Labor turn 2.47 quotas into a third seat. Preferences from across the ballot paper favoured Jacqui Lambie, who was returned for another six years in the Senate. The 2025 election was the third in a row to elect two Labor, two Liberal, one Greens and a Jacqui Lambie candidate.

Australian Capital Territory

For the second successive election, the Liberal Party failed to elect an ACT senator. In 2022 Independent David Pocock caught and passed the Liberal Party on preferences to win the ACT's second seat. In 2025, Pocock increased his primary vote substantially to 39.2 per cent and won the first seat, achieving a quota in his own right. Labor polled just short of a quota with Finance Minister Katy Gallagher finally (and easily) elected on minor-party preferences. The Liberal Party again suffered a swing of more than 7 per cent, polling just over half a quota on 17.76 per cent.

The ACT Liberal Party's Senate vote did not drop below 30 per cent at 17 elections between 1975 and 2019. Over two elections since 2019, Liberal support has crashed from 32.4 per cent to 17.8 per cent. In the same period, Pocock's support in net terms has come at the expense of the Liberal Party (14.6 per cent), the Greens (9.9 per cent), Labor (7.6 per cent) and, finally, from others (7.0 per cent), largely due to fewer parties and Independents nominating in 2025.

Table 18.10 Senate result: Australian Capital Territory

Party	Vote (%)	Change	Quotas	Elected	Change
David Pocock	39.16	+17.98	1.17	1	0
Labor	31.74	–1.63	0.95	1	0
Liberal	17.76	–7.04	0.53	0	0
The Greens	7.78	–2.51	0.23	0	0
Others	3.56	–6.79	0.11	0	0

Source: Compiled by author from AEC (2025a) data.

Northern Territory

For the nineteenth election in a row, the Northern Territory elected one Labor and one Country Liberal Party (CLP) senator. Labor's Malarndirri McCarthy was re-elected for a fourth term with a quota on first preferences. CLP Senator Jacinta Nampijinpa Price fell just short of a quota but easily won a second term after a partial distribution of preferences.

Under the CLP's rules, elected federal members are permitted to sit in federal parliament as either Liberals or Nationals. CLP senators have traditionally joined the Nationals, as Senator Price did after her 2022 victory. Five days after the 2025 election, Senator Price announced she would take her new seat in the Senate as a Liberal; Liberal leadership aspirant Angus Taylor then announced Senator Price as his preferred deputy on 11 May. After Taylor's defeat by Sussan Ley in the leadership ballot, Price did not nominate for the deputy leadership ballot, to the annoyance of Taylor's supporters, according to reports.

Table 18.11 Senate result: Northern Territory

Party	Vote (%)	Change	Quotas	Elected	Change
Labor	34.97	+2.00	1.05	1	0
CLP	32.73	+1.03	0.98	1	0
The Greens	11.07	–1.20	0.33	0	0
One Nation	7.78	+7.78	0.23	0	0
Legalise Cannabis	5.34	–0.89	0.16	0	0
Others	8.12	–8.71	0.24	0	0

Source: Compiled by author from AEC (2025a) data.

Conclusion

The 2025 Australian Senate election produced a more proportional result than in the House, with Labor performing well but not enjoying a similar landslide. Labor won 16 of the 40 Senate seats up for election, increasing their Senate representation by three. The Coalition suffered its worst result since 1984, winning only 13 seats (down five seats from before the election). The result saw Labor with 29 seats in the full Senate, the Coalition 27 and the Greens ten. One Nation achieved its best result on the back of a preference deal with the Coalition, winning four Senate seats in total, including two from outside Queensland for the first time in a half-Senate election. Combined, Labor and the Greens can command a majority in the Senate with the crossbench potentially sidelined in legislative negotiations.

Two results stand out as particularly interesting. First, Labor performed much better in the Senate in electorates with Liberal–Independent two-candidate contests, suggesting that Labor voters are voting tactically to try to remove Liberal members of the House of Representatives. Second, the Coalition's preference deal with One Nation likely won One Nation the final Senate seat in New South Wales and increased the size of their win in the final WA seat. Although electoral reforms in 2016 and party registration restrictions in 2022 have reduced the number of candidates and groups contesting the Senate, the chamber continues to reflect fragmentation among the electorate generally.

References

Australian Electoral Commission (AEC). 2019a. 'First preferences by Senate group.' *Tally Room: 2019 Federal Election.* Canberra: Australian Electoral Commission. results.aec.gov.au/24310/Website/SenateStateFirstPrefsByGroup-24310-NAT.htm.

Australian Electoral Commission (AEC). 2019b. 'Party representation.' *Tally Room: 2019 Federal Election.* Canberra: Australian Electoral Commission. results.aec. gov.au/24310/Website/SenatePartyRepresentation-24310.htm.

Australian Electoral Commission (AEC). 2022a. 'First preferences by Senate group.' *Tally Room: 2022 Federal Election.* Canberra: Australian Electoral Commission. results.aec.gov.au/27966/Website/SenateStateFirstPrefsByGroup-27966-NAT.htm.

Australian Electoral Commission (AEC). 2022b. 'Party representation.' *Tally Room: 2022 Federal Election.* Canberra: Australian Electoral Commission. results.aec. gov.au/27966/Website/SenatePartyRepresentation-27966.htm.

Australian Electoral Commission (AEC). 2025a. 'First preferences by Senate group.' *Tally Room: 2025 Federal Election.* [Updated 30 May 2025]. Canberra: Australian Electoral Commission. results.aec.gov.au/31496/Website/SenateState FirstPrefsByGroup-31496-NAT.htm.

Australian Electoral Commission (AEC). 2025b. 'Party representation.' *Tally Room: 2025 Federal Election.* [Updated 30 May 2025]. Canberra: Australian Electoral Commission. results.aec.gov.au/31496/Website/SenatePartyRepresentation-31 496.htm.

Green, Antony. 2015. 'Explaining the results.' In *Abbott's Gambit: The 2013 Australian Federal Election*, edited by Carol Johnson and John Wanna, 393–410. Canberra: ANU Press. doi.org/10.22459/ag.01.2015.23.

Green, Antony. 2020. 'The Senate result.' In *Morrison's Miracle: The 2019 Australian Federal Election*, edited by Anika Gauja, Marian Sawer, and Marian Simms, 203–21. Canberra: ANU Press. doi.org/10.22459/MM.2020.10.

McAllister, Ian, and Damon Muller. 2019. 'Electing the Australian Senate: Evaluating the 2016 reforms.' *Political Science* 70, no. 2: 151–68. doi.org/10.1080/00323187.2018.1561153.

19

Turnaround: How Labor won voters

Simon Jackman

Abstract

Labor's turnaround leading up to the 2025 election was one of the most rapid in Australian electoral history, with two-party-preferred support rising by at least 4.3 percentage points (and possibly as much as 7.3 points) over just four months. This chapter analyses a unique four-wave survey panel conducted by The Australian National University, finding that Labor both retained its base and persuaded undecided and Greens voters as well as some Coalition voters. Voters who shifted to Labor were characterised by strong dislike of Peter Dutton and increasingly favourable perceptions of Anthony Albanese. The Coalition lost voters who supported the Voice referendum, as well as those with high educational attainment and who live in areas with high ethnic diversity. Neither gender nor age predicted voters' propensity to shift to Labor during 2025. The findings emphasise the importance of campaign strategy and party leadership in modern Australian elections.

Keywords: polling; persuasion; vote choice; strategy; campaigning

The 2025 election is historic in the magnitude of Labor's win and the depth of the Coalition's loss. But easily forgotten in the magnitude of Labor's win in May 2025 is just how parlous the party's position was just five months earlier. My average of public opinion polls had Labor on 48 per cent of the two-party-preferred (2PP) vote on New Year's Day 2025—its low point for the 2022–25 election cycle and close to Labor's 2019 election result. By election day on 3 May, that average of public polls had Labor on 52.2 per cent of the 2PP vote, replicating Labor's 2022 result and corresponding to a 4.2 per cent increase in the 2PP vote share in just four months. Yet, this final poll average was a full 3 percentage points below Labor's actual 2PP result of 55.3 per cent—easily Labor's best result in the post-1949 era (see Chapter 17, this volume).

Depending on when and how much the public polls were underestimating Labor's support, Labor recovered at least 4.3 points of 2PP vote share between January and May and possibly as much as 7.3 points (if early 2025 public polls were unbiased). Either way, this is one of the larger and more rapid movements in Australian voting intentions ever observed.

This chapter reveals the drivers of Labor's recovery and the Coalition's decline. I draw on a novel collection of data, a panel of survey data collected by Professor Nicholas Biddle of The Australian National University to explore the dynamics of voting behaviour in 2025. That is, individual respondents were reinterviewed at different stages of the campaign. These data and my analysis help us understand which voters changed their voting intentions between the start of 2025 and the election, and why.

The dataset is unique in Australia. There was no shortage of polling conducted in connection with the election. The flagship Australian Election Survey is a 'single-shot' or cross-sectional post-election survey. Commercial pollsters typically utilise cross-sectional designs, with short surveys probing little beyond voting intentions and the most basic demographics, and seldom make their unit-record data available (see Chapter 20, this volume). It is a similar story for the parties' internal polling which, while more extensive in scope, is not made available for scholarly analysis. Thus, for one of the first times in the study of Australian elections, we can systematically analyse opinion change over a pre-election period and, moreover, one of the more dramatic and rapid changes in voting intentions ahead of an Australian federal election.

The data reveal five key findings. First, Labor pulled votes from all over the political map: from those supporting Greens in January and February, especially from undecideds and from voters who entered 2025 intending to vote for the Coalition (see Table 19.2). The only group with whom Labor did not make significant inroads was those who started 2025 intending to support 'Other' parties or candidates, principally Independents or

One Nation. Almost one in four Greens supporters later reported voting for Labor and 36 per cent of voters saying they were undecided in early 2025 reported voting Labor in May. Labor also retained more than 80 per cent of its early 2025 support; the Coalition's retention rate was 76 per cent and the Greens' only 66 per cent.

Second, the longer the campaign wore on, and the more people saw of the leaders, the more Dutton's likeability ratings fell and Albanese's rose (Figures 19.1 and 19.2). And, the more a voter liked Albanese and the less they liked Dutton—or both—the greater was the probability of either a move to or staying with Labor (Figure 19.3). Labor's research revealed Dutton's low personal ratings as a key vulnerability for the Coalition. Labor's campaign was designed accordingly, and—as this analysis indicates—seems to have been effective.

Third, rather than wedging Labor voters, the Voice referendum appears to have wedged voters who as late as early 2025 were intending to vote for the Coalition (Table 19.3). Labor 'Yes' and Labor 'No' voters were equally likely to stay with Labor between early 2025 and the election. But Coalition 'Yes' voters were roughly three times more likely to have moved to Labor by the end of the campaign than Coalition 'No' voters.

Fourth, university-educated voters reporting themselves as undecided in early 2025 broke overwhelmingly for Labor: 51 per cent to 21 per cent for the Coalition and 20 per cent for 'Others' (Table 19.4). At the other end of the educational attainment continuum, among voters starting 2025 intending to vote Greens and with secondary school education, just 35 per cent remained with the Greens, with 57 per cent reporting a transition to a Labor vote in the May election. Similarly, Labor retained 88 per cent of its early 2025 supporters with secondary school levels of education.

Fifth, undecided voters from the more ethnically and racially diverse areas of the country were much more likely to transition to Labor than undecideds from less diverse areas (Figure 19.4).

Voting intentions

The data span four waves, from late 2024 to the May 2025 post-election wave. Table 19.1 shows estimated voting intentions at each wave. The May wave is when respondents report how they voted in the election; these responses let me weight the entire dataset to closely correspond to the election results (see the two rightmost columns of Table 19.1). Appendix 19.1 contains additional details.

Table 19.1 Voting intentions/recall in the 2025 election campaign, by wave of survey (per cent)

	December 2024		January/ February 2025		March 2025		May 2025 (post election)		
Voting intention	All	Voters	All	Voters	All	Voters	All	Voters	Actual
ALP	26.0	29.6	26.0	29.9	31.3	34.3	29.8	34.6	34.6
Coalition	35.2	40.0	34.3	39.5	33.5	36.8	27.4	31.8	31.8
Greens	13.1	14.9	11.9	13.7	13.6	15.0	10.5	12.2	12.2
Other	13.6	15.5	14.6	16.8	12.7	14.0	18.5	21.4	21.4
DK/NV/INF	12.1	–	13.2	–	8.8	–	13.8	–	–
Effective no.	1,211	1,236	1,080	1,132	1,135	1,115	1,093	1,440	–

Notes: DK = don't know; NV = didn't vote; INF = voted informal.
Source: ANU 2025 Election Monitoring Survey Series, Wave 1–4 (Biddle 2025).

As shown by public polls fielded at the time, Labor's estimated first-preference formal vote share in early 2025 was only 29.9 per cent, compared with 39.5 per cent for the Coalition. The Coalition lost almost 8 percentage points of vote share between these estimated January/February levels and the election, ultimately winning 31.8 per cent of formal first preferences. Labor's vote share improved by more than 5 percentage points from January/February to the election, from 29.9 per cent to 34.6 per cent.

Movers and stayers

The panel data allow us to track individual respondents' voting intentions over the course of the campaign. Here, I focus on voting intentions recorded in the January/February 2025 wave and the post-election May 2025 wave. Respondents interviewed in both waves supply a basis for estimating rates of 'moving' or 'staying' with respect to their vote.

We already know that Labor won more votes than it lost between January and May, and that the reverse is true for the Coalition. But Table 19.2 reveals the underlying sources of change and stability, containing estimates of the change in the electorate between early 2025 and the election, computing the distribution of reported voting in May by reported voting intentions in the January/February wave of the survey. Again, the data are weighted to closely correspond to the 2025 election results, bolstering confidence that these estimates validly characterise changes in voting intentions.

Table 19.2 Vote choice reported in May post-election wave by January/February voting intention (per cent)

May 2025, vote recall	January/February 2025				
	ALP	Coalition	Greens	Other	DK/NV/INF
ALP	81.4	12.1	23.8	8.6	35.6
Coalition	4.6	76.2	1.0	7.4	25.2
Greens	8.8	3.0	65.6	5.2	5.2
Other	5.3	8.7	9.5	78.8	34.0

Notes: DK = don't know; NV = didn't vote; INF = voted informal; Rows show post-election vote recollection. Columns show voting intention from January/February. Table excludes May 2025 'don't know', 'didn't vote' and 'voted informal' responses. Cell entries are percentages, summing to 100 within columns, so are interpretable as transition rates or the rate of voting for the party listed in row i of the table given a previously reported intention to vote for the party listed in column j; 'stay' rates appear on the diagonal of the table. Effective sample size = 871.

Source: ANU 2025 Election Monitoring Survey Series, Wave 1–4 (Biddle 2025).

Voting intentions are more fluid than conventional theories of voting behaviour would suggest: among the five voting categories utilised here, I estimate that 39 per cent of the electorate switched categories between early 2025 and the election. This 'switching' rate falls to 23 per cent if we exclude moves to or from the 'Don't know/No vote/Informal' category. Note that I have dropped from Table 19.2 respondents who reported in May not voting or voting informally. The population of non-voters and informal voters is very difficult to survey accurately, especially in this case of a four-wave panel study: conditional on responding to a multi-wave panel study about politics, few respondents report not voting or voting informally. I therefore focus on the four formal voting categories: ALP, Coalition, Greens and Others.

Among voters, Labor retained 81 per cent of its early 2025 supporters, while the Coalition retained only three-quarters. Meanwhile, 12 per cent of Coalition supporters from January/February reported a switch to Labor; just 5 per cent of ALP supporters from early 2025 made the opposite transition.

We also observe considerable churn in the Greens vote, with only two-thirds of January/February Greens supporters reporting in the post-election survey sticking with the Greens. Almost one in four Greens supporters (23.8 per cent) from early 2025 wound up reporting in May that they voted for Labor. Partially offsetting these loses were the 8 per cent of Labor supporters from early 2025 who transitioned to the Greens.

Labor also did well among the disengaged or undecided segment of the electorate, as measured in January and February. Among undecideds, those intending to not vote or vote informally, 36 per cent ended up reporting voting Labor, while just 25 per cent transitioned to Coalition support.

Thus, Labor not only retained more of its vote than any other party grouping but also was the single largest destination for vote switchers. Among those reporting a formal vote in May and switching from their early 2025 voting intention, 38 per cent landed on Labor, 17 per cent with the Coalition and 15 per cent with the Greens. The remaining 30 per cent of these switchers wound up transitioning to 'Others', such as Independents (including Teals), One Nation, Trumpet of Patriots, Family First, Legalise Cannabis and so on. In the voter conversion stakes—perhaps the single most important metric of campaign performance—Labor outperformed the Coalition by more than two to one, and the Coalition barely outpaced the Greens.

Diverging views about Albanese and Dutton

At each of the four rounds of interviewing, respondents were asked to rate the two major-party leaders, Peter Dutton and Anthony Albanese, on a zero to 10 likeability scale. Average scores for each leader in each round are shown in Figure 19.1.

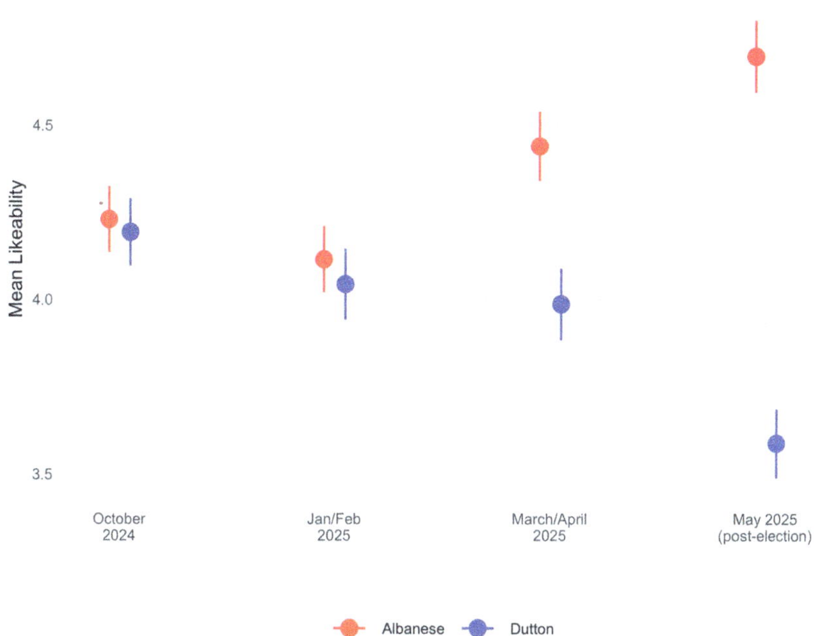

Figure 19.1 Anthony Albanese and Peter Dutton average likeability score, by wave (0–10 scale)

Note: Vertical bars cover 95 per cent confidence intervals.

Source: ANU 2025 Election Monitoring Survey Series, Wave 1–4 (Biddle 2025).

By late 2024, Dutton had drawn level with Albanese on likeability, with both leaders averaging about 4 on the zero to 10 scale. Albanese had been viewed more favourably than Dutton for most of the 2022–25 election cycle—an advantage that was slowly being muted as the cycle dragged on and cost-of-living pressures dominated the national conversation. Nonetheless, through 2023 and 2024, Labor strategists had repeatedly suggested to me that playing on Dutton's 'negatives'—heightening the political salience of Dutton and the contrast with Albanese, reminding voters about Dutton's past and current policies—was always going to be part of Labor's re-election campaign.

Labor's strategy—and its execution—clearly worked. Figure 19.1 shows that, after two years of Albanese's and Dutton's ratings slowly converging, these two indicators diverged markedly in the three months before the election. In the post-election wave, the two average scores were separated by a full point: 4.8 for Albanese and 3.6 for Dutton.

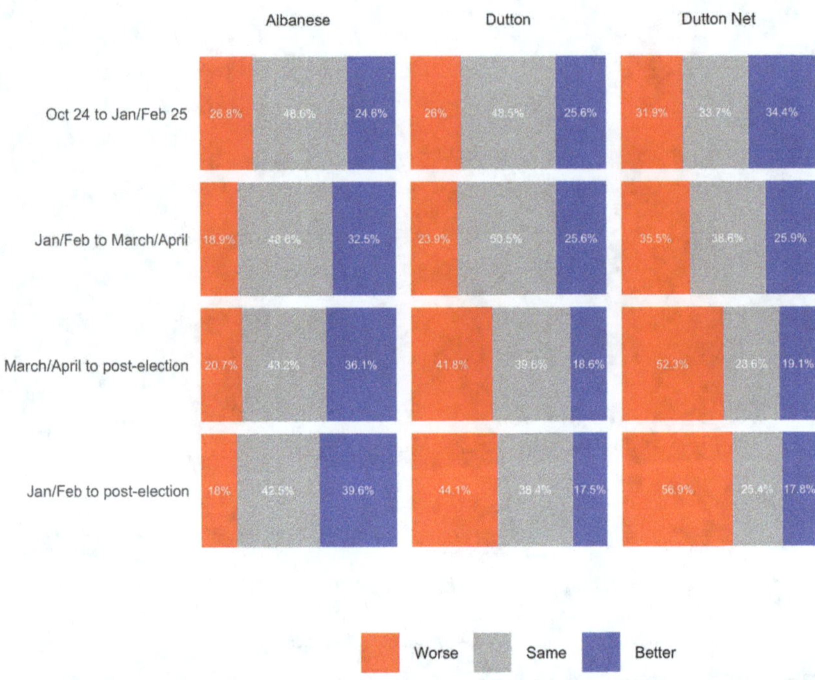

Figure 19.2 Change in Anthony Albanese's and Peter Dutton's likeability, by paired waves of the panel
Source: ANU 2025 Election Monitoring Survey Series, Wave 1–4 (Biddle 2025).

The panel data let us track the dynamics in evaluations of Albanese and Dutton over the months leading up to the election. Figure 19.2 examines wave-on-wave changes in Albanese's and Dutton's likeability, as well as the corresponding change in Dutton's net likeability (a respondent's Dutton likeability scores minus their Albanese likeability score). By the time of the May 2025 election, 40 per cent of the electorate found Albanese more likeable than at the start of the year, while 44 per cent found Dutton less likeable. Dutton's net likeability fell for 56.5 per cent of the electorate between early 2025 and the election, improving among a mere 17 per cent.

These asymmetries in likeability dynamics are especially pronounced in the formal campaign period itself, looking at the March/April to post-election comparisons presented in the third row of Figure 19.2. More than one-third (36 per cent) of respondents reported seeing Albanese as more likeable over this period, while just 20 per cent saw him as less likeable. For Dutton, 42 per cent of respondents reported a fall in their assessments of his likeability and just 18 per cent reported seeing him as more likeable. The result was that more than half the electorate reported Dutton's net likeability falling over the campaign period and only 19 per cent saw Dutton gaining in likeability vis-a-vis Albanese. Below, the chapter shows that changes in Dutton's net likeability between early 2025 and the election are strongly associated with changes in voting intentions over the same period.

Voice referendum

In the aftermath of the election, numerous commentators noted that the Coalition's emphasis on 'culture war' issues—Indigenous recognition chief among them—had backfired (Williams et al. 2025). My analysis of these panels reveals the full extent of this 'backfiring'.

Table 19.3 shows the transition in voting intentions between early 2025 and the election according to how respondents reported voting in the Voice referendum. Recalled Voice vote was asked well before the May post-election wave, so there is no chance that respondents were adjusting their recalled Voice vote to better 'match' their self-reported final vote. Labor 'stay' rates are statistically indistinguishable across Voice 'Yes' and 'No' voters. But this is not the case among other segments of the early 2025 electorate.

Table 19.3 Vote choice in May 2025 (rows), by January/February voting intention by Voice vote (per cent)

| | January/February 2025 by Voice vote | | | | | | | | | |
| | ALP | | Coalition | | Greens | | Other | | DK/NV/INF | |
Post-election vote	No	Yes	No	Yes	No	Yes	No	Yes	No	Yes
ALP	88	81	9	26	26	21	8	11	38	42
Coalition	3	3	83	52	3	0	8	7	42	9
Greens	2	11	0	12	55	71	0	20	0	17
Other	6	5	8	11	16	8	84	61	20	32

Notes: DK = don't know; NV = didn't vote; INF = voted informal; Voice vote shown in columns ('yes' and 'no'). Cell entries are percentages, effective sample size = 867. H_0 transition probabilities are independent of Voice vote, rejected at p < 0.01. DK/NV/INF on Voice and May 2025 vote choice are excluded.

Source: ANU 2025 Election Monitoring Survey Series, Wave 1–4 (Biddle 2025).

One-quarter of voters supporting the Coalition in early 2025 who recalled voting 'Yes' for the Voice wound up switching to Labor and only half this segment reported staying with the Coalition. Coalition 'Yes' voters were roughly three times more likely to flip to Labor than Coalition 'No' voters: 26 per cent to 9 per cent. Reminding voters of the Coalition's opposition to the Voice—or its claims that Welcome to Country ceremonies were 'overdone' and divisive—appears only to have driven votes *away* from the Coalition. Only one-half of 'Yes' voters reporting a Coalition voting intention in early 2025 reported sticking with the Coalition in their votes cast in May.

Among early 2025's undecided or non-voters, 42 per cent of 'Yes' voters wound up voting for Labor and a paltry 9 per cent for the Coalition. The Coalition fared better among undecided 'No' voters, picking up 42 per cent of this group, but this transition rate is nonetheless statistically indistinguishable from the 38 per cent of this group who ended up voting for Labor.

Of course, the usual correlation/causation caveats apply—namely, recalled Voice vote might be incorrect, proxying for other policy differences and evaluations of the parties since October 2023. Nonetheless, amid a broad net shift towards Labor between January and May, few variables identify 'movers' to Labor as well as one's recalled position on the Voice. Interaction effects are also apparent, with the Voice and low Dutton net likeability *combining* to nudge the probability of a Labor vote even higher, when averaged over the electorate.

Education

Educational attainment is a good predictor of the Greens to Labor transition (Table 19.4). More than half those reporting Greens support in early 2025 and secondary school education transitioned to Labor by May; university-educated Greens supporters display much more stability, with just 10 per cent switching to Labor and 79 per cent remaining with the Greens. University education also makes a Coalition to ALP transition more likely, as well as the 'Others' to Labor transition.

Table 19.4 Vote choice in May 2025 (rows), by January/February voting intention by educational attainment (per cent)

| | January/February 2025 voting intention by education | | | | | | | | | | | | | | |
| | ALP | | | Coalition | | | Greens | | | Other | | | DK/NV/INF | | |
Post-election vote:	HS	Trade	Uni.	HS	Trade	Uni.	HS	Trade	Uni.	HS	Trade	Uni.	HS	Trade	Uni.
ALP	88	81	77	10	9	15	57	28	10	5	2	15	25	38	51
Coalition	4	0	7	78	78	74	1	0	1	8	15	3	34	14	21
Greens	4	14	10	4	1	2	35	60	79	9	0	5	0	11	8
Other	5	4	6	7	12	9	7	12	10	78	83	77	41	37	20

Notes: DK = don't know; NV = didn't vote; INF = voted informal; HS = high school; Cell entries are percentages; effective sample size = 871. H_0 transition probabilities are independent of education, rejected at $p < 0.01$. DK/NV/INF on May 2025 vote excluded.

Source: ANU 2025 Election Monitoring Survey Series, Wave 1–4 (Biddle 2025).

A key insight into campaign dynamics comes via the way that educational attainment strongly structures where undecided voters end up. Of those reporting being unsure or planning to not vote or to vote informally in early 2025—and who went on to report a formal vote in the election—half those with tertiary education reported voting for Labor in May and just 21 per cent for the Coalition. The Coalition also trailed Labor in conversions among those with trade or technical qualifications in this segment, 14 per cent to 38 per cent. Only among secondary-school–educated undecideds did the Coalition win more conversions than Labor, with 34 per cent to Labor's 25 per cent.

This pattern is again consistent with a good portion of early 2025 undecideds comprising many Labor 'learners': those who perhaps voted for Labor in 2022 but, for a variety of reasons, reported being undecided at that stage of the electoral cycle. Labor's resurgence in support over the opening months of 2025 rested not just on flipping voters intending to vote for another party, but also on reactivating soft or dormant preferences for Labor. To the extent that educational attainment is correlated with 1) news consumption and attention to politics and 2) socially progressive policy preferences, Labor's outperformance among undecideds with tertiary education speaks to the differences in content of the major parties' campaigns. The statistical modelling that follows helps to disentangle the contributions of two correlated features, 'Yes' Voice votes and educational attainment, as sources of Labor gains over the 2025 campaign.

Modelling transitions to or from Labor over 2025

Statistical modelling can rigorously assess the contributions of leader likeability, position on the Voice and other factors to the probability of a Labor vote in May 2025, conditional on each respondent's voting intention as reported in the January/February 2025 wave.

Specifically, I model the binary outcome $y_i = 1$ if respondent i reported voting Labor in May 2025, and $y_i = 0$ otherwise. The inclusion of indicator variables for each voting intention reported in January/February—ALP, Coalition, Greens, 'Other' and 'Don't know/Undecided'—as predictors gives the model the interpretation as a *transition* model. That is, base rates of moving to a Labor vote (or staying with Labor) can be thought of as 'hardwired' into the model; these are reported in the top row of Table 19.2. Additional predictors tap into the extent to which 'move to Labor' or 'stay with Labor' rates vary around these base rates. A wide variety of model specifications was tested via cross-validation, guarding against over-fitting in this modestly sized sample; details appear in Appendix 19.1.

My model for the probability of a Labor vote in May 2025 includes the following predictors:

- Indicator variables for each voting intention reported in January/February 2025: ALP, Coalition, Greens, 'Other' and 'Don't know/Undecided', with the ALP category absorbed into the model intercept.

- Change in Dutton's net likeability between January/February 2025 and the post-election wave of the panel: a continuous variable ranging from −19 to 10, with 90 per cent of values between −6 and two.

- Voice vote: indicator variables for 'Yes', 'No' and 'Don't know'/'Didn't vote', with the last category absorbed into the model intercept.

- A three-level measure of highest level of educational attainment (as used in Table 19.4): high school (including less than high school), trade and technical education (Certificate III and IV) and tertiary education.

- A scale measure tapping the ethnic and racial diversity of postcodes, described in Appendix 19.1.

My preferred model is a random forest (Breiman 2001), of a collection of decision trees using these predictors in various combinations. These models do not produce parameter estimates and are inherently nonlinear. Accordingly, I compute predictions from the model and use tables or graphs to show the modelled effects of key predictors. Note, too, that characteristics such as age and gender that often appear in models of voting choice do not appear in this model of transitions from January/February voting intentions to post-election recalled vote; while age and gender do often predict voter intentions in the aggregate (for instance, the Coalition's repeated poor performance with women and young voters), I find no evidence that age or gender significantly shaped changes in voting intentions between early January and May 2025, which is the focus of this chapter.

Change in leader assessments

The growing gap in likeability assessments of the two leaders has a large effect on the probability of a move to or staying with Labor, as shown Figure 19.3. Each panel corresponds to a January/February 2025 voting intention. Changes in Dutton's net likeability are plotted against the horizontal axis, restricted to 90 per cent most commonly observed actual changes, ranging from –6 to 2 across the sample (and with very little variation in these 90 per cent bounds across the January/February voting intention segments); the grey vertical bars in each panel in Figure 19.3 show the distribution of changes in Dutton's net likeability, by January/February voting intention.

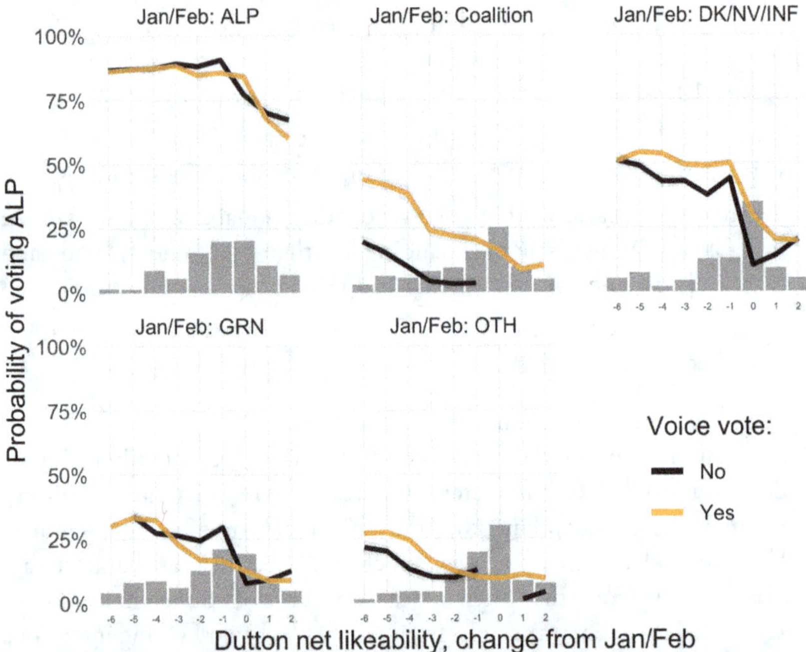

Figure 19.3 Modelled effect of change in Peter Dutton's net likeability between January/February 2025 and the post-election wave on the probability of an ALP vote, by January/February voting intention (each panel) and Voice vote (the orange and black lines, per panel)

Notes: Bars show the distribution of changes in Dutton's net likeability, by January/February reported vote. Most respondents reported a decline in Dutton's net likeability over the period, associated with a higher probability of either staying with or transitioning to a Labor vote over the campaign. Note, too, the significant interaction with the Voice vote for respondents who in January/February 2025 were intending to vote for the Coalition. Details on model fitting and construction of marginal effect profiles appear in Appendix 19.1.

Source: ANU 2025 Election Monitoring Survey Series, Wave 1–4 (Biddle 2025).

Clearly, where one stood in January/February 2025 is highly predictive of the vote one reported casting in the May election; this explains the large overall differences across the panels in Figure 19.3. Per Table 19.2, Labor retained more of its vote than the Coalition over this interval, and a large portion of Coalition transitions to Labor is concentrated among Voice 'Yes' voters.

But for all January/February voting intention segments, staying with or transitioning to Labor is strongly related to changes in the relative assessments of the two leaders. Recall that 44 per cent of voters liked Dutton less by May 2025 than they had in January/February—and 39 per cent liked Albanese more—resulting in 57 per cent of the sample scoring in negative territory on the change in Dutton's net likeability measure (Figure 19.2). As Dutton's net likeability falls, the probability of a transition to Labor (or remaining with Labor) rises; conversely, for respondents in January/February intending to vote for the Coalition, the probability of staying with the Coalition rises (the probability of a transition to Labor falls) as evaluations of Dutton vis-a-vis Albanese become more favourable. This is especially true for voters reporting as undecided in January/February, when there is an abrupt increase in the probability of a transition to Labor as changes in Dutton's net likeability fall from no change to negative.

Ethnic and racial diversity

The ethnic or racial diversity of a respondent's postcode also predicts the probability of a Labor vote in May 2025, as shown in Figure 19.4. For voters reporting an intention to vote ALP or Greens in early 2025, racial and ethnic diversity has modest predictive power with respect to staying with or moving to Labor by May. Labor's 'stay' rate rises over the least diverse 30 per cent of postcodes, but plateaus and may even taper slightly in the country's most diverse postcodes. Greens-to-Labor transitions are slightly more likely in the country's most diverse postcodes, reaching as high as 25 per cent for 'Yes' voters in the top decile of postcodes on this scale measure. As most Australians live in postcodes with no concentrations of people not speaking English at home, Muslim religious affiliation and other markers of ethnic and racial diversity (details on scale construction appear in Appendix 19.1), I plot the modelled effects as a function of the deciles of the scale.

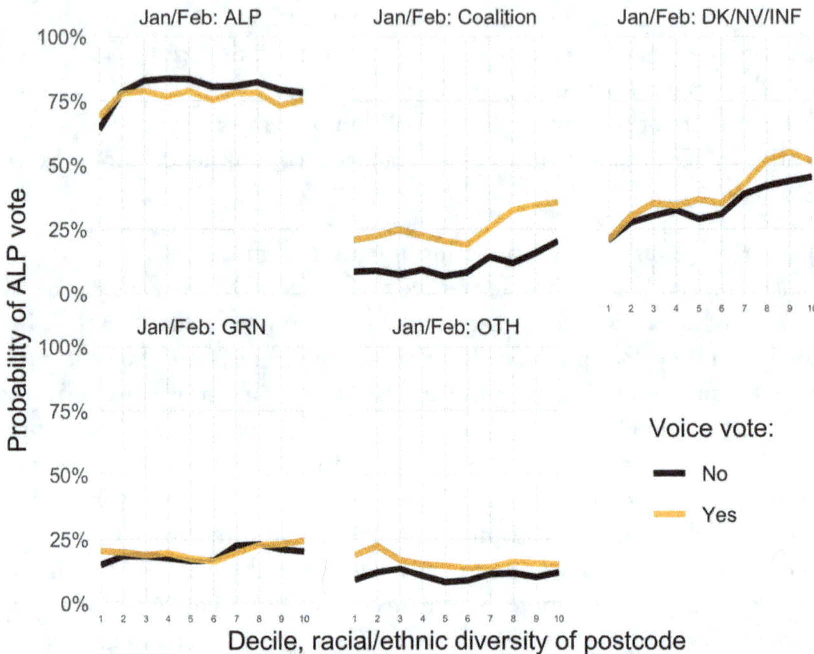

Figure 19.4 Modelled effects of racial and ethnic diversity change on the probability of ALP vote, by January/February voting intention (each panel) and Voice vote (the orange and black lines, per panel)

Notes: There is a significant interaction with Voice vote for respondents who in January/February 2025 were intending to vote for the Coalition. Details on the construction of the racial and ethnic diversity postcode level index and the effects plotted here are in Appendix 19.1.

Source: ANU 2025 Election Monitoring Survey Series, Wave 1–4 (Biddle 2025).

The most pronounced and interesting effects of racial diversity are among voters who entered 2025 either intending to vote for the Coalition or undecided. Coalition-to-Labor transitions were much more likely in racially and ethnically diverse postcodes, reaching as high as 35 per cent for 'Yes' voters in the top decile of postcodes on this measure and 20 per cent among 'No' voters. Labor's conversion of undecided voters increases almost linearly across the postcode deciles, ranging from a low of 21 per cent in the least diverse decile of postcodes to above 50 per cent for undecided 'Yes' voters in the 30 per cent most ethnically diverse postcodes, and in the mid-40 per cent range for 'No' voters.

Conclusion: Campaigns or context?

This analysis supports a popular narrative about the 2025 election: 1) that Labor was able to reframe the contest as between Albanese and Dutton and as less of a retrospectively oriented referendum on Labor's handling of cost-of-living pressures; and 2) given this framing, Albanese's greater popularity and likeability relative to Dutton would reconstitute the winning majority Labor enjoyed in 2022, shoring up Labor's core vote and persuading undecided voters to 'come back' or transition to Labor.

Of course, two external developments are also widely believed to have lent 'ecological' or 'contextual' validity to Labor's reframing strategy. The first was the decision by the Reserve Bank of Australia (RBA) to cut interest rates on 18 February, helping Labor advance the argument that the worst of the cost-of-living crisis was over. The second was the torrent of news from the second Trump administration, including deep and abrupt cuts to the US civil service, the threat of tariffs on Australian exports and complaints about mainstays of Australian public policy such as the Pharmaceutical Benefits Scheme. Dutton and the Coalition seemed remarkably ill prepared and flat-footed in responding to both Labor's reframing strategy and the extent to which Trump's dramatic opening months in office galvanised the Australian electorate, radically accelerating the reframing of the election already under way in early 2025. Trump's persona and his policies—and Dutton's inability to hose down dalliances with MAGA policies and rhetoric, by himself or Coalition colleagues—put Labor's reframing strategy on skates. In a remarkably brief window, the election was transformed: no longer *retrospection* about Labor's handling of the cost-of-living crisis, but rather a contemporaneous or prospective framing, grounded in assessments about which leader would be least like Trump and would be least likely to import Trump-like policies.

I offer these observations more as commentary than as conclusions supported by the data: the survey data I analyse in this chapter do not contain questions permitting me to rigorously test the causal connections between respondents' awareness of or reactions to these external events, changes in Dutton's likeability, changes in issue salience and changes in voting intentions.

The evidence I present here is, however, nonetheless consistent with Labor's reframing strategy succeeding, whatever role should be attributed to factors such as the RBA rate cut and Trump. We track a broad recovery in

Albanese's likeability over Dutton's across the five months leading up to the May election. These changes are strongly predictive of either staying with or transitioning to Labor.

It appears that Labor's campaign helped not only shore up the support it took into the calendar year 2025, but also recapture some of Labor's 2022 vote that was sitting with the Coalition, the Greens or in the undecided column in early 2025. A long vein of political science stresses that campaigns first reactivate dormant partisan dispositions before they persuade or convert (Campbell et al. 1960; Bartels 2000; Green et al. 2002). The evidence presented here is consistent with that view. The campaign generated outsized transitions to Labor among university-educated undecided voters, secondary-school–educated Greens supporters, those who voted 'Yes' for the Voice and those in Australia's more racially and ethnically diverse postcodes. Labor's campaign strategy—and the Coalition's underperformance—saw the party not only reassemble its winning 2022 electoral base, but also consolidate its support in sociodemographic segments already tending to vote Labor.

Longer-term extrapolations from analysis of a campaign are always fraught. My analysis does reveal the capacity for volatility in the electorate over short time frames. Some of this is to be expected in a regime of compulsory voting, where even the least politically engaged are legally obliged to turn out, and most do. Some of Labor's gains and the Coalition's losses may therefore be short-lived. This caveat aside, the more consequential finding is the consolidation of Labor support over the past two electoral cycles—and, by corollary, the extent of the erosion of Coalition support.

Labor won not just the campaign—and a massive electoral victory—but also a once-in-a-generation opportunity to govern with broad demographic support and, for now, deep reservoirs of political capital.

References

Bartels, Larry M. 2000. 'Partisanship and voting behavior, 1952–1996.' *American Journal of Political Science* 44, no. 1: 35–50. doi.org/10.2307/2669291.

Biddle, Nicholas. 2025. *Hope, Hardship, and Democratic Confidence: Social Wellbeing and Political Sentiment in Election-Year Australia—March/April 2025*. 17 April. Canberra: School of Politics and International Relations, The Australian National University. politicsir.cass.anu.edu.au/files/docs/2025/4/Hope-Hardship-and-Democratic-Confidence.pdf.

Breiman, Leo. 2001. 'Random forests.' *Machine Learning* 45, no. 1: 5–32. doi.org/ 10.1023/A:1010933404324.

Campbell, Angus, Philip E. Converse, Warren E. Miller, and Donald E. Stokes. 1960. *The American Voter*. Chicago: University of Chicago Press.

Green, Donald P., Bradley Palmquist, and Eric Schickler. 2002. *Partisan Hearts and Minds: Political Parties and the Social Identities of Voters*. New Haven: Yale University Press.

Hastie, Trevor, Robert Tibshirani, and J.H. Friedman. 2009. *The Elements of Statistical Learning: Data Mining, Inference, and Prediction*. 2nd edn. New York: Springer doi.org/10.1007/978-0-387-84858-7.

Stone, M. 1974. 'Cross-validatory choice and assessment of statistical predictions.' *Journal of the Royal Statistical Society: Series B* 36, no 2: 111–33. doi.org/10.1111/ j.2517-6161.1974.tb00994.x.

Williams, Carly, James Vyver, Stephanie Boltje, and Brooke Fryer. 2025. '"All the wrong lessons" from Voice referendum "backfired" on Coalition, analysts say.' *ABC News*, 6 May. www.abc.net.au/news/2025-05-06/first-nations-people-respond-to-election-result/105260222.

Appendix 19.1

Methodological notes

Data

The data come from a four-wave survey panel study commissioned and authored by Professor Nicholas Biddle of The Australian National University. The data were provided by an online panel provider and the surveys were self-administered online.

The bulk of the analysis presented here focuses on transitions from the second wave of the study, fielded in January/February 2025, to the final, post-election wave administered immediately after the election in early May 2025. The data are weighted to be representative of the Australian electorate, by raking on recalled 2025 House of Representatives vote, age, education and geography.

Since the dataset for analysis spans respondents completing both the January/February wave and the post-election wave, panel attrition produces a slightly different distribution on January/February voting intentions than observed in the original, standalone January/February wave. A final round of weighting ensures that the distribution of January/February voting intentions in the two-wave analysis dataset matches the distribution of voting intentions observed in the January/February wave. The resulting weights were trimmed to lie between 8 and 1/8 and to sum to the number of respondents completing both the January/February and the post-election waves (n = 1,832). This weighting is nonetheless reasonably aggressive, yielding weights with variance of 1.63, resulting in an effective sample size of approximately 1,832/(1 + 1.63) = 696. Paradoxically, some analyses reported in the body of the chapter have larger effective sample sizes, when filtering out respondents with especially large or variable weights.

Postcode-level racial and ethnic diversity

The index of postcode-level racial and ethnic diversity is constructed from 2021 census data, spanning 2,641 postcodes. A broad range of postcode-level census aggregates was assembled, spanning indicators of wealth and income, educational attainment, religious affiliation, housing tenure and type, occupational structure, age structure, language use and ancestry, tabulated with respect to adult citizens by usual place of residence or at the dwelling level.

The effects of these variables were assessed via a wide set of modelling approaches, including tree-based models, a variety of neural architectures and scale construction via factor analysis prior to modelling.

Table A19.1 displays loadings from a factor-analytic model fitting three orthogonal factors via maximum likelihood estimation with a varimax rotation, as implemented in the factanal function in R. The input to the factor analysis is the weighted correlation matrix of the postcode-level indicators, with weights equal to the number of enrolled voters in each postcode (constructed from AEC redistribution files and SA1 to polling place mappings from past elections and normalised to match division-level counts of enrolled voters).

As a model for these indicators, the three-factor solution is probably not sufficient. But cross-validation of the downstream transition models suggests that the second factor produced from this three-factor solution is preferred over other factor-analytic solutions. The point here is less to perform a rigorous factor analysis of postcode-level census data and more to produce a scale measure that has validated predictive power in the models of transitions in voting intentions over the 2025 campaign.

The second factor, labelled 'Factor 2' in Table A19.1, taps racial and ethnic diversity, with high loadings from indicators such as percentage of adult citizens speaking non-English languages at home, percentage identifying as Muslim and percentage speaking Chinese languages at home. Note also the large *negative* loading for the percentage of adult citizens reporting no religious affiliation and positive loadings on dwelling-level measures such as persons per household or persons per bedroom.

Table A19.2 lists the highest-scoring postcodes on this measure, 10 postcodes with scores close to the median score of 0.4 and the 10 lowest-scoring postcodes. Western Sydney dominates the upper end of this diversity index. The pronounced right skew in the constituent indicators passed through to the index itself: although normalised to have a mean of zero by construction, the index has a median score of –0.4, a minimum score of –0.9, but a maximum score of 5.1.

Model fitting

The model relied on in the body of the chapter is a random forest, an ensemble ('forest') of decision trees, each tree formed from a random sample of observations and a random selection of predictor variables when forming branches for individual trees. Splits (for categorical predictors) or cut-points (for continuous predictors) are chosen to best discriminate with respect to the outcome being modelled (in this case, a binary outcome, $y_i = 1$ if the respondent, i, reported voting Labor in the May post-election survey and 0 otherwise). The model's predictions are formed by averaging the predictions from individual trees.

This class of mode—and the configuration of the random forest—was selected from a wide set of candidate models by cross-validation (Stone 1974). A textbook treatment appears in Hastie et al. (2009: Ch. 7). In this case, the data are repeatedly repackaged into five, 80–20 splits of training data and test data, but are stratified to guarantee virtually identical distributions of y between test and training slices. Over the five 'folds' of the dataset, each observation takes a turn as an out-of-sample or 'test' observation. Model performance is assessed with respect to the average fit across the five batches of out-of-sample fitting—in this case, using a log-loss criterion (equivalent to maximising the log-likelihood of the out-of-sample observations, averaged over the five folds). This procedure to model selection guards against over-fitting and bolsters confidence in the generalisability of the model's predictions.

Table A19.1 Factor loadings from a three-factor solution to a broad array of postcode-level census indicators, with varimax rotation

Variable	Factor 1	Factor 2	Factor 3
Median total household income ($)	**0.934**	0.085	–0.097
Professional occupation (%)	**0.828**	0.045	**0.526**
Median monthly mortgage repayment ($)	**0.827**	0.222	0.091
Highest educational attainment: year 9 or below (%)	**–0.822**	0.165	–0.126
Highest educational attainment: year 10 or above (%)	**–0.820**	0.051	–0.440
Tertiary qualification (%)	**0.818**	0.159	**0.529**
Median weekly rent ($)	**0.779**	0.190	0.045
Voice, 'Yes' vote (%)	**0.624**	0.228	**0.568**
Socioeconomic advantage and disadvantage decile 8 (%)	0.449	0.010	0.108
Indigenous (%)	–0.300	–0.037	–0.111
Socioeconomic advantage and disadvantage decile 7 (%)	0.254	0.027	–0.092
Jewish religion (%)	0.215	–0.005	0.176
Language other than English spoken at home (%)	0.096	**0.992**	0.026
Muslim religion (%)	–0.087	**0.735**	–0.081
No religion (%)	0.110	**–0.669**	0.358
Average persons per bedroom	0.206	**0.626**	0.298
Chinese languages spoken at home (e.g., Mandarin, Cantonese) (%)	0.258	**0.587**	0.232
Median age (years)	–0.264	–0.438	0.074
Aged under 30 (%)	0.022	0.233	0.183
Average household size (persons)	0.242	**0.530**	**–0.742**
Dwellings that are flats, units or apartments (%)	0.302	0.184	**0.706**
Renting (%)	–0.033	0.287	**0.613**
Member of a same-sex couple (%)	0.231	–0.080	**0.598**
Non-traditional Christian religion (%)	–0.153	0.280	–0.397
Lived elsewhere in Australia five years before 2021 Census (%)	0.139	–0.221	0.290
Socioeconomic advantage and disadvantage decile 6 (%)	0.014	–0.057	–0.219
Aged over 70 (%)	0.083	–0.035	0.140

Notes: Loadings greater than 0.5 in absolute value are highlighted in bold. The second factor taps racial and ethnic diversity and is the postcode-level measure used in the transition models in the body of the chapter.

Source: ANU 2025 Election Monitoring Survey Series, Wave 1–4 (Biddle 2025).

Table A19.2 Ten highest-scoring postcodes on racial and ethnic diversity

Postcode	Locality	Division	Diversity score	Non-English language at home (%)	Muslim (%)	No religion (%)	Chinese languages (%)	Persons/ bedroom
2144	Auburn	Blaxland (NSW)	5.1	83.4	44.7	18.3	20.8	1.2
2166	Cabramatta	Fowler (NSW)	5.1	84.4	2.0	21.5	17.5	1.1
2195	Lakemba	Watson (NSW)	5.0	80.9	47.9	11.3	6.8	1.3
6799	Home Island	Lingiari (NT)	4.8	77.8	78.4	16.1	0.0	1.1
2165	Fairfield	McMahon (NSW)	4.7	78.8	8.0	14.4	8.1	1.1
2200	Bankstown	Watson (NSW)	4.7	78.9	27.3	14.3	6.6	1.1
0872	Yuendumu	Lingiari (NT)	4.7	77.8	0.1	24.6	0.1	1.4
4876	Bamaga	Leichhardt (Qld)	4.7	78.2	0.3	21.0	0.0	1.3
2177	Bonnyrigg	Werriwa (NSW)	4.6	78.3	5.0	15.0	7.6	1.0
3061	Campbellfield	Scullin (Vic.)	4.6	75.7	35.8	9.9	0.5	1.0
2372	Tenterfield	New England (NSW)	−0.4	3.4	0.0	30.8	0.1	0.7
2480	Goonellabah	Page (NSW)	−0.4	4.4	0.2	44.2	0.2	0.8
4340	Rosewood	Blair (Qld)	−0.4	3.6	0.0	37.1	0.1	0.8
6488	Trayning	Durack (WA)	−0.4	2.4	0.0	47.5	0.0	0.6
2898	Lord Howe Island	Sydney (NSW)	−0.4	4.5	0.0	48.4	1.0	0.9
7264	Gladstone	Bass (Tas.)	−0.4	2.7	0.0	49.6	0.0	0.8
6603	Wongan Hills	Durack (WA)	−0.4	3.5	0.5	42.4	0.0	0.7
2430	Taree	Lyne (NSW)	−0.4	3.6	0.1	35.5	0.2	0.7
6510	Moora	Durack (WA)	−0.4	3.5	0.0	39.3	0.5	0.7

Postcode	Locality	Division	Diversity score	Non-English language at home (%)	Muslim (%)	No religion (%)	Chinese languages (%)	Persons/bedroom
2444	Port Macquarie	Cowper (NSW)	−0.4	4.4	0.2	36.6	0.3	0.7
7175	Bream Creek	Lyons (Tas.)	−0.8	0.0	0.0	57.7	0.0	0.8
3704	Koetong	Indi (Vic.)	−0.8	0.0	0.0	66.7	0.0	0.7
6613	Buntine	Durack (WA)	−0.8	0.0	0.0	61.1	0.0	0.7
3893	Tambo Crossing	Gippsland (Vic.)	−0.8	0.0	0.0	21.7	0.0	0.8
6463	Benjaberring	Durack (WA)	−0.8	0.0	0.0	54.5	0.0	0.8
5138	Basket Range	Mayo (SA)	−0.8	0.0	0.0	66.0	0.0	0.9
3785	Tremont	Casey (Vic.)	−0.8	0.0	0.0	88.6	0.0	0.8
7024	Cremorne	Franklin (Tas.)	−0.8	0.0	0.0	61.7	0.0	0.8
3852	East Sale	Gippsland (Vic.)	−0.9	2.1	0.0	72.0	0.0	0.7
5150	Leawood Gardens	Boothby (SA)	−0.9	0.0	0.0	48.6	0.0	0.7

Note: Includes 10 closest to the median score and 10 lowest-scoring postcodes.

Source: ANU 2025 Election Monitoring Survey Series, Wave 1–4 (Biddle 2025).

20

The polls: Underestimating Labor, overestimating the Coalition

Murray Goot

Abstract

All 10 national opinion polls exaggerated the Coalition's position and underestimated Labor's. Had they predicted a Coalition victory, even a hung parliament, their performance would have generated more consternation. From one poll to another, there was little variation in the estimates for either Labor or the Coalition. For this, herding is one possible explanation. But there are others: survey errors, which are common to most of the polls; the treatment of the 'undecided'; and shared assumptions that, in a cost-of-living 'crisis', the Coalition's vote was likely to rise and that, if Labor won, it was unlikely to win by much. The attempt to predict the vote seat by seat using multilevel regression with post-stratification (MRP) was equally unimpressive. While Labor gained 11 seats from the Coalition, the MRP predicted that it would win only seven. The continuing success of the electoral pendulum in predicting seats shares, the rise of Independents notwithstanding, remains noteworthy.

Keywords: opinion polls; Australian elections; electoral pendulums; MRP; herding

In the media's coverage of campaigns, polling is central. The calling of the horserace generates considerable interest (not least among political journalists and politicians), controversy (different polls calling it differently) and widespread publicity—for the media that publishes them and for the pollsters who produce them. If getting the figures 'right' brings kudos, getting them 'wrong' causes handwringing, finger-pointing and reputational damage.

The 2025 campaign involved more pollsters than ever. The internet has made polling cheaper; online polls cost as little as one-third that of a telephone (computer-assisted telephone interviewing) poll, which was the usual polling mode until 2016. There were no formal barriers to conducting polls, no audits of any kind or disclosure rules; most pollsters were not members of the Australian Polling Council (2025), the only body that sets minimum disclosure standards. And publishing polls had never been easier: in the absence of a media contract, pollsters could always publish on the internet. Since pollsters can sponsor more than one poll (two did this time) and since they can invoke different ways of judging their performance— predicting which side will win or will come closest to winning (a hung parliament), predicting the 2PP vote or the parties' first-preference shares, and so on—participating may be worth the risk.

During the final days of the 2025 campaign no fewer than 10 pollsters published their predictions of the national vote. Some were published (though not always commissioned) by the print media: Newspoll in the *Australian*; Freshwater in the *Australian Financial Review*; Resolve in the *Age* and *The Sydney Morning Herald*; and RedBridge/Accent in News Corp's metropolitan mastheads. Some were published online: Essential in the *Guardian* and Ipsos in the *Daily Mail*—both British-owned mastheads. And some were published by pollsters with no assured media outlet: DemosAU, Roy Morgan, Spectre and YouGov. There were attempts also to measure the vote in individual seats (YouGov, especially its MRP; but also Compass, DemosAU, Freshwater, JWS, KJC, the *New England Times* and UComms) or in clusters of seats (DemosAU, RedBridge/Accent)—all except RedBridge/Accent's financed by the pollsters themselves.[1]

---

1   For additional information, I thank Jessica Elgood from Ipsos, George Hasanakos from DemosAU, Morgan James from Spectre, Julian McCrann from Roy Morgan, Shaun Ratcliff from Accent, Kos Samaras from RedBridge, John Scales from JWS, Paul Smith from YouGov, John Utting from Utting Research, Dorian von Freyhold from Compass and Campbell White from Pyxis. Freshwater did not respond to my requests and Resolve asked me not to make any. For their comments on an earlier draft, I thank Anika Gauja, Luke Mansillo and Jill Sheppard.

How well did the polls perform, collectively as well as individually, in estimating the distribution of first preferences and the 2PP vote? How good was the polling based on MRP? And which approach offered the better guide to the outcome: the approach that assumed that if Labor increased its national vote share it would be returned, the bigger any increase the more comfortable its majority; or the approach that assumed that with the rise of the Independents, in particular, the election was best understood as 150 separate contests, making the MRP one's best bet?

I start by sizing up the errors made in estimating the 2PP vote: most, it turns out, stemmed from the polls' failure to estimate each party's first preferences. In trying to explain this, I consider the importance of sampling and the handling of the 'undecided' vote, as well as how the polls allocated preferences. Different ways of measuring the errors produced different leader boards. In single seats, measures of success also vary, though some polls were poor by any measure. The third task, seeing whether the national polls' estimates of the two sides' seat shares outperformed the estimates offered by the MRP, proved the most straightforward task of all.

The national polls

How good were the national polls? Since elections are one of the few public tests they face, and they have much at stake in the outcome, pollsters are keen to set the terms of these tests, to indicate how they should be applied and to make sure their own judgements about best and worst prevail. This means getting in early; first impressions can be lasting ones.

Weeks before the official count was finished, several pollsters had issued their own assessments of how they had done, and sometimes of how their competitors had done. Others did so in response to journalists' questions. The focus was on how well they had called the 2PP vote. Doing this better than anyone else meant winning 'line honours', as *The Poll Bludger*'s William Bowe (2025a) put it. The question of how well the polls had estimated first-preference votes was a secondary matter.

The two-party-preferred vote

Announcing, three days after the election, that it had 'aced' the election, Roy Morgan made it clear that its polling would come out well no matter the final vote. That the Albanese government would be 're-elected with an increased majority' was an outcome Roy Morgan had 'predicted last week and for the previous seven weeks since mid-March when the ALP took a decisive lead'. Its final poll 'showed the ALP ahead 53% to 47% based on respondent allocated preferences' but 'ahead 54% to 46%'—'in line with the projected final result', it emphasised—'based on how [preferences] flowed at the previous Federal Election'. With 63 per cent of the vote counted, Labor was ahead 54.6 to 45.4, and the result was expected to be 'close to' 54–46 (Roy Morgan 2025b); the actual result would be different: 55.2–44.8 per cent.

Roy Morgan had not tipped a 54–46 result. Guided by how respondents said they would allocate preferences, it had tipped a 53–47 result. Readers had to read to the end of Roy Morgan's press release to learn that 'based on how Australians voted at the 2022 Federal Election', the 2PP result favoured Labor, 54–46 (Roy Morgan 2025a). Not only did Roy Morgan's final report privilege respondent allocation over the 2022 allocation; so, too, over the previous seven weeks did every one of its reports. Roy Morgan's decision to publish two sets of figures bought it cover: it allowed it to cite whichever set of figures came closer to the real result. Publishing two or more sets of figures, based on different preference allocations (Goot 2021: Appendix) or different survey modes (Mansillo and Jackman 2020: 138), was a practice Roy Morgan had used in the past.

Resolve's Jim Reed was another pollster keen to jump in. With 77 per cent of the vote counted, and the 2PP vote favouring Labor 54.1–45.9, Reed declared that Resolve and RedBridge had produced the two most accurate estimates of the 2PP vote; overlooked were the Roy Morgan poll (described as 'unpublished') and the Spectre poll, both of which had produced the same estimates. The 'two least accurate' were Freshwater (51.5–48.5) and Ipsos (51–49).

According to Reed (2025), it was 'those polls taken a week out that [had] proven most accurate'. Singled out were 'the Resolve Political Monitor and RedBridge, both of whom called the TPP result within their error margins'. Since the five polls conducted three-to-six days out from the election produced an average 2PP vote of 52.6–47.4, and the five polls conducted one or two days out produced an average 2PP vote of 52–48, there was not much in it; with 'error margins' included, there was nothing in it. 'Pollsters left red-faced by Labor's powerful late surge' was the very different headline over *The Sydney Morning Herald*'s post-election review (Knott 2025). By the end of the count (55.2–44.8), all the polls had proved to be out by much more than Reed had imagined (Table 20.1).

Table 20.1 Accuracy of the national polling, House of Representatives, 2025 (per cent)

| Poll | Fieldwork | Days to election | Sample size | Mode | ALP | Coalition[a] | Greens | PHON | TOP | Other | DK[b] | Error (primary) | | | Error 2PP (ALP) | |
												ALP–Coalition	Avg. (5)[d]	RMSE (5)[d]	Est.	Error
Roy Morgan	28 April– 2 May	1	1,368	I+CATI +FtF	33.0	34.5	13.5	6.5	2.0	10.5	[5]	–4.3	**1.6**	**3.56**	53	**–2.2**
Freshwater	29 April– 1 May	2	2,055	I	33.0	37.0	12.0	8.0	n.a.	10.0	n.a.	–6.8	2.8	*11.60*	51.5	–3.7
Ipsos	28 April– 1 May	2	2,574	I+CATI	29.5	34.7	12.6	8.4	2.1	12.6	[5]	–8.0	2.1	*7.73*	51	–4.2
Newspoll (Pyxis)	28 April– 1 May	2	1,270	I	33.0	34.0	13.0	8.0	n.a.	12.0	[4]	–3.8	1.8	**3.92**	52.5	–2.7
YouGov	24 April– 1 May	2	3,003	I	31.1	31.4	14.6	8.5	2.5	11.9	n.a.o.	**–3.1**	1.8	4.40	52.2	–3.0
DemosAU	27–30 April	3	4,100	I	31.0	33.0	12.0	9.0	n.a.	15.0	[7]	–4.8	**1.5**	4.24	52	–3.2
RedBridge/ Accent	24–29 April	4	1,011	I	34.0	34.0	12.0	8.0	n.a.	12.0	[5]	**–2.8**	**1.5**	**3.36**	53	**–2.2**
Spectre	24–28 April	5	2,000	I	31.0	34.0	14.5	9.5	n.a.	11.0	[9]	–5.8	*3.0*	9.74	53	**–2.2**
Resolve	23–28 April	5	2,010	I+CATI	31.0	35.0	14.0	7.0	n.a.	13.0	n.a.o.	–6.8	2.2	6.16	53	**–2.2**
Essential[c]	24–27 April	6	2,163	I	32.0	34.0	13.0	10.0	2	9.0	[5]	–4.8	2.6	8.24	52.1	–3.1

| Poll | Fieldwork | Days to election | Sample size | Mode | ALP | Coalition[a] | Greens | PHON | TOP | Other | DK[b] | Error (primary) | | | Error 2PP (ALP) | |
												ALP–Coalition	Avg. (5)[d]	RMSE (5)[d]	Est.	Error
Average	–	–	–	–	31.9	34.2	13.1	8.3	–	12.6[e]	–	–	–	–	52.3	–
Election	3 May	–	–	–	34.6	31.8	12.2	6.4	1.9	13.1	–	–	–	–	55.2	–
Error	–	–	–	–	-2.7	+2.4	+0.9	+1.9	–	-2.4[e]	–	–	–	–	-2.9	–

Notes: n.a. = not available; n.a.o. = not an option; RMSE = root mean squared error; I = internet panels (Roy Morgan, 33 per cent; Ipsos, 67 per cent; Resolve, n.s.); CATI = computer-assisted telephone interviewing (Roy Morgan, 33 per cent; Ipsos, 33 per cent; Resolve, n.s.); FtF = face-to-face (Roy Morgan, 33 per cent). [a] Liberal Party plus Liberal National Party (Queensland) plus National Party plus Country Liberal Party (Northern Territory). [b] Respondents 'undecided' about their first preference after the 'leaner', subsequently deleted or distributed. [c] Undecided (4.8 per cent) on the two-party vote ignored for purposes of comparability; Essential's two-party figures were Labor, 49.6 per cent; Coalition, 45.6 per cent; and undecided, 4.8 per cent. [d] Based on five blocks of respondents: ALP, Coalition, Greens, PHON, TOP and Other. [e] Includes TOP; Figures in bold text are the best scores on this measure; those in italics are the worst scores on this measure.

Sources: AFR (2025); Beaumont (2025a); Butler (2025); Crowe (2025); DemosAU (2025); Ipsos Australia (2025); Pyxis Polling and Insights (2025); Roy Morgan (2025a); Spectre Strategy (2025); Wikimedia Foundation (2025); YouGov (2025b).

Immediately after the vote, Michael Turner, CEO of Freshwater, conceded that he had underestimated Labor's 2PP vote, but insisted that there had been 'a late swing among "soft" or undecided voters' that his poll and others found 'hard to pick up' (Turner 2025). But the evidence he adduced suggests otherwise. Of the polls he thought best—RedBridge, followed by Roy Morgan and Resolve—RedBridge had completed its fieldwork two days earlier than Freshwater, Morgan had completed its fieldwork a day later and Resolve, a day earlier (Table 20.1).

Writing for the masthead that had commissioned the Freshwater poll, journalist Michael Read recycled Turner's views. As for the almost equally wayward Ipsos poll, Read relied on the words of the company's research director: after being 'a little too progressive in the two-party preferred' in 'a couple' of earlier elections, Ipsos had 'overcorrected' (Read 2025).

Preferences

How the polls allocated preferences was widely seen as the key to their errors. In allocating preferences, different pollsters adopted different methods. RedBridge/Accent used the preference flows from 2022. Newspoll and Essential used flows from 'previous elections', including State elections. Ipsos, Roy Morgan, Resolve and Essential made two separate calculations— one based on preference flows in 2022; the other based on the respondents' own allocations—though they did not always publish the two. YouGov and Spectre 'blended' the two. RedBridge/Accent did as well, but only in relation to the Trumpet of Patriots (TOP); otherwise, it says, it based its allocation on the 2022 flows.

Did any of this make any difference? Roy Morgan's figures did vary, depending on whether it used respondent allocation or the 2022 flows. Ipsos and Essential, however, reported no difference. When the *Conversation's* psephologist Adrian Beaumont plugged the 2022 preference flows into 2025's first preferences, he came up with 'a Labor two-party lead of 55.3– 44.7, [virtually] the same as the actual result' (Beaumont 2025b).

The extent to which the pollsters did what they said they did is difficult to determine. Subtracting Labor's 2PP vote from its first-preference vote and dividing this number by the proportion of respondents who voted for someone other than Labor or the Coalition show that every pollster's allocation favoured Labor; since the Greens' vote accounted for more than one-third of all the preferences, this is not surprising. On YouGov's figures, 56 per cent of all preferences went to Labor; on Resolve's figures, it was

65 per cent. But given that YouGov was distributing the preferences of 37.5 per cent of its sample (those who were not giving their first preference to Labor or the Coalition), and Resolve was distributing the preferences of 34 per cent, the difference between the two in 2PP terms amounted to just 1 percentage point. These were the two outliers. Among the others, the range was narrower: 58 per cent (DemosAU) to 63 per cent (Spectre). On the day, Labor won just over 61 per cent of the second preferences (derived from Table 20.1), the midpoint of the polls' estimates.

Regardless of when they were conducted or how they allocated preferences, all the polls underestimated Labor's share of the 2PP vote (Table 20.1). On average, the error was not 'almost' as great as it was in 2019 (Beaumont 2025b), when all the polls picked the wrong winner; the average was just as great. Two of the polls' estimates would have seen Labor's 2PP vote slip back to 51 per cent (Ipsos) or 51.5 per cent (Freshwater) from 52.1 per cent, its 2022 level; one would have seen it stay the same (Essential); the others would have seen it increase to 52 per cent (DemosAU), 52.2 per cent (YouGov), 52.5 per cent (Newspoll) or 53 per cent (Roy Morgan, RedBridge/Accent, Spectre, Resolve).

Underestimates of Labor's 2PP share (55.2 per cent) ranged from 4.2 to 2.2 percentage points—from estimates that might have seen Labor lose its majority to estimates that might have seen its majority increase. By this measure, line honours were shared. Only by going to a second decimal point—mercifully, avoided—would the stewards have been able to separate Roy Morgan from RedBridge/Accent, Resolve or Spectre. But even a best of 2.2 was not particularly good (Goot 2021: Appendix).

One way of rescuing the reputation of the polls, or at least some of them, Beaumont (2025b) suggests, is to look through their back catalogue for figures that were closer than their final figures. This is a suggestion best ignored. Polls are time sensitive: 'right at the time', as pollsters like to say, not necessarily right sometime later. Beaumont's suggestion would open the way to cherry-picking. What if another pollster had produced a poll, say, four months earlier that was close to the result? Would their earlier poll have made them one of the best, regardless of their subsequent polls? His suggestion would also mean that changes in the polls could not be used as evidence of a shift in the final week.

Before 2PP became the dominant metric, honours may have been decided by which poll best estimated the gap, on first preferences, between the government and the Opposition (Beed 1977: 222). On this measure, the winner would have been RedBridge/Accent: it had the two level-pegging, in a photo finish with YouGov (the Coalition 0.3 of a point ahead); Roy Morgan (which had the Coalition 1.5 points ahead) would have come fourth, Spectre (three points) ninth and Resolve (four points) last (Table 20.1).

For the pollsters, the 2PP vote has been a boon (Goot 2021: 53). As Table 20.1 shows, the error based on how close each of the polls came to estimating the gap in first preferences between Labor and the Coalition was larger than the error based on the gap in the 2PP. For Roy Morgan, Freshwater and Ipsos, the error on first preferences was more than twice as large; for Spectre and Resolve, it was more than three times as large.

First preferences

The most important reason for Labor's 2PP vote being underestimated was not the formula used for allocating preferences; it was that Labor's first-preference vote was underestimated. The Coalition's vote was overestimated. These errors were compounded by the overestimation of the vote for Pauline Hanson's One Nation (PHON), only partly offset by overestimates for the Greens.

By the end of counting, Labor had secured 34.6 per cent of the first preferences. The average estimate across the polls was 31.9 per cent—an underestimate of 2.7 points. Not a single poll estimated a Labor vote higher than 34.6 per cent. While the Coalition secured 31.8 per cent of the first preferences, the polls' average estimate was 34.2 per cent—an overestimate of 2.4 points. Only YouGov (31.4 per cent) came close to estimating the Coalition's vote. The median error in estimating the gap between Labor and the Coalition's first-preference vote was 4.8, which is roughly in line with the performance of the polls since the 1940s internationally (Jennings and Wlezien 2018: 280, Fig. 2c).

According to Bowe (2025b), a 'large component of the pollsters' failure' to estimate Labor's share of the 2PP vote 'lay in an expectation … that preference flows to Labor would not match those of 2022'. Not so. Since the polls underestimated Labor's first preferences by 2.7 points, on average, and its share of the 2PP vote by 2.9 points, the error in estimating Labor's 2PP vote was almost entirely due to the errors in estimating its first-preference vote.

In addition to showing how well the polls estimated the first preferences of the parties of government, Table 20.1 shows how well the polls estimated the vote for the Greens, PHON and 'Others'—the other parties and Independents on which each of the polls reported. The best-performed polls were those by RedBridge/Accent and DemosAU; their average error, across each of the five, was 1.5 percentage points. Next came Roy Morgan (1.6). The worst performed, with errors up to twice as large, were Spectre (3.0), Freshwater (2.8) and Essential (2.6). Internationally, since the 1940s, average errors have been less than two points (Jennings and Wlezien 2018: 278).

Another measure, less widely used, is the root mean squared error of these errors. This punishes polls for big errors and rewards polls for errors that are only small. Here, honours again go to RedBridge/Accent (with a score of 3.36 percentage points), followed by Roy Morgan (3.56) and Newspoll (3.92). The wooden spooners are Essential (8.24), Spectre (9.74) and Freshwater (11.60).

While two of the four (Roy Morgan and RedBridge/Accent) that did best on the 2PP vote were also among the best on these two measures, Resolve and Spectre were among the best on neither of these measures.

Sampling errors and handling the 'undecideds'

Since almost all the polls erred in the same ways, what are the likely sources of these errors? *Coverage error* is one. The sampling frames used by online panels may not include all the relevant population—most obviously, voters who are not online. They recruit potential respondents by invitation, and the numbers recruited are tiny (Pennay et al. 2019: 48). To mitigate these problems, some pollsters added sampling frames: Ipsos and Resolve used telephone interviews; Roy Morgan, telephone and face-to-face interviews. The success of these strategies is unclear (Pennay et al. 2019: 49–50).

Another source of error—the only one that pollsters are happy to flag—is *sampling variance* ('sampling error'): the figure ('±3.2 per cent', depending on sample size) that assures readers that 95 per cent of the time polls come within a few percentage points of the real figures. These calculations, however, assume probability sampling, in which every voter has an equal (or at least known) chance of being selected. However, from already unrepresentative online panels, pollsters select not at random but by quota: a certain age distribution, equal numbers of men and women, and on so (Pennay et al. 2019: 50).

If sampling variance explained the errors, instead of all the polls underestimating Labor's 2PP vote, roughly as many polls would have overshot the real figure as undershot it. It was a similar case for estimates of Labor's first preferences (all too low), the Coalition's (all but one too high), One Nation's (all but one too high) and Others' (all but one too low). While some estimates of the Greens' vote were correct, and some too high, none was too low. It is this lack of 'dispersal' that shows that sampling variance is not the answer.

Non-response is a third potential source of error. Even if the samples drawn from the panel providers (or other sources) appear to be representative, those who agree to participate may not be; among respondents, young voters, for example, especially men, are likely to be underrepresented (Pennay et al. 2019: 52–53).

Since some groups will be underrepresented and others overrepresented, pollsters' post-weight their samples. Which variables they used, neither Freshwater nor Resolve disclosed. Pollsters who did disclose, or did so subsequently, used at least two weights: gender (sex) and age (including age times sex). Most also weighted by education—ignored in 2019 (Pennay et al. 2019: 86)—region (including sex times region) and vote at the 2022 election (recalled). Half the polls were weighted by income (sometimes household, sometimes personal), one by housing tenure and one by religion (Table 20.2). How some of these were measured is another question.

These were not the only weights. Freshwater weighted its data by how respondents recalled voting in the 2023 Voice referendum, as did YouGov and Spectre (Table 20.2). According to Turner (2025), '"Labor-No" voters just didn't switch over to the Coalition in the big numbers [we] estimated.' But this may be only half the story. Polling conducted by The Australian National University between early 2025 and the election suggests that, while intending Labor voters who recalled voting 'No' were as likely to stay with Labor as those who recalled voting 'Yes', intending Coalition voters who said they had voted 'Yes' were 2.5 times more likely than 'No' voters to have moved to Labor (see Chapter 19, this volume). Were Freshwater's figures different?

Table 20.2 Variables used to weight data, by poll, 2025

Poll	Sex	Age	Area	Education	Housing	Income	Religion	Vote 2022 election	Vote 2023 referendum
Roy Morgan	✓	✓	✓	–	–	–	–	✓	–
Freshwater*	–	–	–	–	–	–	–	–	–
Ipsos	✓	✓	✓	✓	–	household	–	✓	–
Newspoll	✓	✓	✓	✓	–	✓	–	✓	–
YouGov	✓	✓	✓	✓	–	household	–	✓	✓
DemosAU	✓	✓	✓	✓	✓	✓	–	✓	–
RedBridge/Accent	✓	✓	✓	✓	–	–	✓	–	–
Spectre	✓	✓	–	✓	–	✓	–	✓ State	✓
Resolve*	–	–	–	–	–	–	–	–	–
Essential	✓	✓	✓	✓	–	–	–	✓	–

Note: * Not disclosed.

Sources: Methodology disclosure statements from Australian Polling Council members (Ipsos, Pyxis, YouGov, Essential); personal communications (others).

The assumption behind weighting is that those who do not respond and those who do are the same in all relevant respects—'ignorable' nonresponse. But they may not be the same; hence, '"nonignorable" nonresponse' (Bailey 2024: Ch. 5). Where respondents and non-respondents hold different views—when they are not the same in all relevant respects—weighting may compound the error. Those 'who speak English poorly or not at all, those with low levels of literacy, and those with little digital affinity' are likely to be underrepresented; so, too, are those with little interest in politics (Pennay et al. 2019: 53–57). Which of these is 'ignorable' and which 'non-ignorable' may be difficult to determine.

Post-survey errors may not be ignorable either. Those respondents classified as 'undecided' pose the most obvious problem. Respondents were classified as 'undecided' if they expressed no preference (Roy Morgan, RedBridge) or said 'undecided'/'don't know' even after being asked a 'leaner'—a question to see whether there was a party (or candidate) towards which they were leaning even if it was not the party they were prepared to nominate when first asked how they would vote. Only Resolve and YouGov did not allow an 'undecided' response.

Table 20.3 Treatment of 'undecided' voters, by poll, 2025

Poll	Treatment
Roy Morgan	Like to see win
Freshwater	Not stated
Ipsos	Past vote
Newspoll	Excluded after leaner
YouGov	Not allowed
DemosAU	Excluded after leaner
RedBridge/Accent	Excluded after leaner
Spectre	Excluded after leaner
Resolve	Not allowed
Essential	Not allocated

Sources: AFR (2025); Beaumont (2025a); Butler (2025); Crowe (2025); DemosAU (2025); Ipsos Australia (2025); Pyxis Polling and Insights (2025); Roy Morgan (2025a); Spectre Strategy (2025); Wikimedia Foundation (2025); YouGov (2025b); Personal communications.

How did pollsters handle the 'undecideds'? Where respondents did not respond positively to the 'leaner', DemosAU, Newspoll, RedBridge/Accent and Spectre dropped them—equivalent to assuming that they would divide in the same way as other respondents; that these three were among the polls that most accurately estimated the first preferences suggests that this was a reasonable move. Morgan, the other poll to score well on this measure, asked the 'undecided' which side they would like to see win—a question that ignored strategic voting and made sense only in relation to the 2PP vote. Ipsos, one of the least accurate, distributed the 'undecideds' according to how they said they had voted in 2022 (Table 20.3). Whether any of this mattered is unclear.

Single seats and clusters of seats

While most election-watchers may have been pondering the polls' failure to predict the size of Labor's victory, and searching for reasons, YouGov (2025c) declared that it 'alone' had 'predict[ed] a historic win for Labor' and was the only poll 'to measure the scale of the Labor win'—a reference not to its final standard poll, conducted from 24 April to 1 May (Table 20.1), but to its very large MRP poll, completed two days earlier. Its previous (January–February) MRP, in sharp contrast, had suggested the Coalition might not only win but also do so without winning back any of the seats lost in 2022 to the Teals and the Greens (Goot 2025).

The enduring appeal of the MRP is twofold: its potential to overcome the limitations of national polling that does not use representative samples (Wang et al. 2015) and its promise to predict the outcome not only nationally but also seat by seat—Coalition seats, Labor seats and seats held by Independents and the Greens.

Based on its MRP, conducted 1–29 April, YouGov (2025a) estimated that both Labor and the Coalition would 'get lower primary votes than at the last election'. The Coalition's vote share, 31.8 per cent, came close to YouGov's estimate of 31.1 per cent. Labor's vote share, however, did not; it wasn't 31.4 per cent, as YouGov estimated, but 34.6 per cent—two points higher than in 2022. From both its MRP and its standard polls, YouGov expected a 2PP swing to Labor (measured to the second decimal point) of 0.07 points. But it was based on its MRP, not its standard poll, that YouGov predicted a 'Labor majority government' (YouGov 2025a, 2025b).

The most likely result, the MRP reported, using a credibility interval of 90 per cent, was Labor winning 84 seats (an upper limit of 85, well short of the 94 seats that Labor actually won), the Coalition 47 (a lower limit of 45),

Independents 14 (a lower limit of 13, not the 10 seats they did win) and the Greens three (a lower limit of two, not one). In short, the Labor majority YouGov envisaged was no higher than 20 seats; the majority Labor achieved, 38 seats, was nearly twice that.

How well did YouGov's seat-by-seat projections fare? In the 124 seats it expected to be 'classic contests'—in which the final two candidates in the count represented Labor and the Coalition (the Liberal Party, the Nationals or the LNP)—YouGov had Labor improving on its 2022 2PP vote in 69 but losing ground in 52 seats. In fact, Labor's position improved in 102 of the 121 contests that were 'classic', losing ground in just 19 seats.

Among an anticipated 29 'non-classic' contests—in which at least one of the final two candidates in the count did not represent a major party— there were 24 in which YouGov overestimated how well the Greens or Independent candidate would do, including 12 in which the overestimates exceeded 10 percentage points; in four, the contest turned out to be not 'non-classic' at all (Table 20.4).

Another way of judging an MRP is by calculating the absolute average error, seat by seat, in the 2PP/2CP (full tables available in Appendix 20.1). In the 'marginal' seats (seats requiring a swing of less than 6 percentage points), these errors were particularly high: a mean of 6.5 and a standard deviation of 7.54 in Coalition seats with a mean of 4.9 with a standard deviation of 3.77 in Labor seats. In 'fairly safe' seats for the Coalition, the figures are 3.7 and 5.37, respectively, and, for Labor, 5.1 and 4.94, respectively. In 'safe' Coalition seats, the figures are 3.0 and 3.16; in 'safe' Labor seats, 5.5 and 4.62, respectively.

One reason the MRP did not do well was because it was conducted over too long a period—out of the field close to election day having entered the field nearly five weeks earlier. As a comparison with the earlier MRP shows, and other polling confirms (see Chapter 19, this volume), Labor's position improved substantially during the campaign. Being in the field for a month and not reporting on how opinion shifted over this time was a strategic error. Labor's vote share was underestimated in 90 of the two-party contests (including 25 Coalition seats) and overestimated in just 34 (eight of them Labor seats). Since nominations were not declared until Friday, 11 April, when the MRP was launched, respondents could not be told candidates' names or even presented with an official list of the parties contesting the seats and it appears that this did not change.

Table 20.4 Non-classic contests as expected by the AEC, YouGov or both: YouGov MRP, 1–29 April 2025 (per cent)

State/Territory	Electorate	Incumbent	AEC 2CP	ABC 2CP	YouGov-predicted 2CP				Post-election 2CP				Error
					Ind.	GRN	Coalition	ALP	Ind.	GRN	Coalition	ALP	
NSW	Bradfield	Lib.	53.4	52.5	64.1	–	35.9	–	50.0	–	50.0	–	14.1
	Calare	Nats	59.7	59.7	53.1	–	46.9	–	56.8	–	43.2	–	–3.7
	Cowper	Nats	52.4	52.4	63.2	–	36.8	–	47.5	–	52.5	–	15.7
	Fowler	Ind.	51.8	51.1	63.0	–	37.0	–	52.7	–	–	47.3	10.3
	Grayndler	ALP	64.0	67.3	–	34.7	–	65.3	–	33.1	–	66.9	1.6
	Mackellar	Ind.	51.8	53.3	60.8	–	39.2	–	55.7	–	44.3	–	5.1
	Richmond	ALP	58.2 (2PP)	58.2 (2PP)	–	47.4	–	52.6	–	–	40.0	60.0	–
	Sydney	ALP	66.2	66.5	–	32.5	–	67.5	–	29.1	–	71.0	3.4
	Warringah	Ind.	60.3	59.4	63.5	–	36.5	–	61.2	–	38.8	–	2.3
	Wentworth	Ind.	50.6	56.8	58.4	–	41.6	–	58.3	–	41.7	–	0.1
Vic.	Cooper	ALP	58.9	57.8	–	39.8	–	60.2	–	40.3	–	59.7	–0.5
	Goldstein	Ind.	51.8	53.3	63.5	–	36.5	–	49.9	–	50.1	–	13.6
	Indi	Ind.	58.9	58.9	66.1	–	33.9	–	58.6	–	41.4	–	7.5
	Kooyong	Ind.	52.5	52.2	60.1	–	39.9	–	50.7	–	49.3	–	9.4
	Melbourne	GRN	55.6	56.5	–	56.1	–	43.9	–	47.0	–	53.0	9.1
	Monash	Lib.	52.9 (2PP)	52.9 (2PP)	54.1	–	45.9	–	–	–	54.1	45.9	–
	Nicholls	Nats	53.4	53.4	–	–	66.4	33.6	–	–	64.4	35.6	–
	Wannon	Lib.	53.5	53.8	61.9	–	38.1	–	46.7	–	53.3	–	15.2
	Wills	ALP	59.0	54.6	–	44.5	–	55.5	–	48.6	–	51.4	–4.1

State/ Territory	Electorate	Incumbent	AEC 2CP	ABC 2CP	YouGov-predicted 2CP				Post-election 2CP				Error
					Ind.	GRN	Coalition	ALP	Ind.	GRN	Coalition	ALP	
Qld	Brisbane	GRN	53.7	53.7	–	–	41.4	58.6	–	–	41.0	59.0	–
	Griffith	GRN	60.5	60.5	–	52.0	–	48.0	–	39.4	–	60.6	13.6
	Groom	LNP	56.9	56.9	–	–	57.3	42.7	44.3	–	55.7	–	–
	Kennedy	KAP	63.1	63.1	72.5	–	27.5	–	65.8	–	34.3	–	6.7
	Maranoa	LNP	72.1 (2PP)	72.1 (2PP)	33.8	–	66.2	–	29.9	–	70.1	–	3.9
	Ryan	GRN	52.7	52.6	–	52.0	48.0	–	–	53.3	46.7	–	–1.3
WA	Curtin	Ind.	51.3	51.3	55.7	–	44.3	–	53.3	–	46.7	–	2.4
SA	Mayo	CA	62.3	62.3	69.7	–	30.3	–	64.9	–	–	35.1	4.8
Tas.	Clark	Ind.	70.8	70.8	71.9	–	–	28.1	70.4	–	–	29.6	1.5
ACT	Bean	ALP	62.9 (2PP)	62.9 (2PP)			38.0	62.0	49.7			50.3	
	Canberra	ALP	62.2	62.2	–	39.9	–	60.1	–	30.5	–	69.5	9.4
Mean|median													6.6|4.6
Std dev.													5.97

Notes: CA = Centre Alliance; KAP = Katter's Australian Party; Shaded result was predicted to be a non-classic contest but was a classic contest (AEC/ABC: Brisbane, Nicholls; YouGov: Richmond, Monash); or was predicted to be a classic contest but was a non-classic contest (Maranoa, Groom, Bean).

Source: ABC data from Green (2025).

Based on its MRP, YouGov expected 11 seats (10 Coalition, one Greens) to change hands. All but two did: Cowper and Wannon, predicted to go to Independents, stayed Liberal. Another eight also changed: seven from the Coalition to Labor (Hughes, NSW; Deakin, Victoria; Dickson, Forde and Petrie, Queensland) or to an Independent (Bradfield, NSW); one from the Greens to Labor (Melbourne, Victoria); and one from Independent to Liberal (Goldstein, Victoria). Of the 20 seats that changed, YouGov's polling identified less than half.

In another poll—not an MRP—conducted 17–24 April, YouGov estimated vote shares in 10 classic regional contests and two non-classic contests. Again, results were calibrated to the second decimal point. In two of the classic contests (Dickson, where it was out by 11 points, and Bullwinkel, out by two), YouGov tipped the wrong winner. Across all 10 seats, the absolute error on 2PP averaged four points with a standard deviation of 4.53 (see Appendix 20.1 for seat-by-seat figures)—hardly an improvement on its MRP.

In other classic contests, polls also finished with large errors (10 points or more): KJC in Hunter, Richmond, Blair and Tangney, though the real size of its errors are difficult to judge; UComms and Freshwater in Dickson, with the Freshwater poll said to have misled the Liberal Party into thinking that its leader, Peter Dutton, was not in danger; DemosAU in Adelaide (a safe seat misdescribed as marginal); UComms, in Lyons, and in Forrest, where it failed to anticipate who the last two candidates would be; the *New England Times*, in New England; and a Compass poll in McMahon, which had Labor's Chris Bowen (who went on to win 45.5 per cent of the first-preference vote) losing to an Independent, Matthew Camenzuli (who secured just 9.8 per cent of the vote)—with Camenzuli listed first on the ballot (Bowen's spot) with a tick next to his name, but the APC reluctant to condemn it (ABC 2025). The only poll able to withstand similar scrutiny was the EMRS in Franklin.

Non-classic contests also threw up some 'stinkers' (Beaumont 2025b). In Bradfield, YouGov underestimated the Liberals' two-candidate vote by 14.1 points, in Wannon by 15.2 and in Cowper by 15.7 points. In Ryan, retained by the Greens, JWS forecast a classic contest; in Griffith, where Labor beat the Greens 60.6–39.4, JWS had Labor leading the LNP 51–49, as though it were also a classic contest; and in Brisbane, where JWS had Labor ahead 51–49 against the LNP, Labor prevailed 59–41 per cent.

Table 20.5 Contests in clusters of seats, 31 March – 3 May 2025 (per cent)

Pollster	Dates	Electorates	n		First preferences					2PP
					ALP	Lib./Nats	GRN	PHON	Other	(ALP)
DemosAU	7–15 April	Brisbane, Griffith, Ryan (Qld) [held by Greens]	1,087	Est.	29.0	36.0	29.0	3.0	3.0	56.0
				Vote	31.7	31.8	28.8	2.5	5.2	n.a.
				Error	–2.7	+4.2	+0.2	+0.5	–2.2	
DemosAU	13–22 April	Bruce, Dunkley, Hawke (Vic.) [Melbourne Labor marginals]	924	Est.	32.0	31.0	13.0	10.0	14.0	53.0
				Vote	40.9	28.5	11.2	8.2	11.2	59.8
				Error	–8.9	+2.5	+1.8	+1.8	+2.8	–6.8
DemosAU	18–23 April	Bonner, Dickson, Forde, Longman, Petrie (Qld) [Brisbane LNP outer metropolitan]	1,053	Est.	27.0	40.0	13.0	7.0	13.0	47.0
				Vote	35.8	35.0	10.6	7.1	13.3	52.6
				Error	–8.8	+5.0	+2.4	–0.1	–0.3	–5.6
DemosAU	13–27 April	Parramatta, Reid, Werriwa (NSW) [Sydney Labor marginals]	905	Est.	36.0	28.0	10.0	4.0	22.0	56.0
				Vote	45.9	31.1	11.6	3.0	8.4	60.6
				Error	–9.9	+3.1	–1.6	+1.0	+13.6	–4.6
RedBridge/ Accent	24–30 April	Bennelong, Dobell, Gilmore, Lindsay, Paterson, Robertson, Werriwa (NSW); Aston, Casey, Chisholm, Corangamite, Menzies (Vic.); Blair, Forde, Leichhardt, Longman (Qld); Bullwinkel, Tangney (WA); Sturt (SA); Lyons (Tas.) [20 'key seats': 13 Labor, 7 Coalition]	1,004	Est.	33.0	34.0	12.0	6.0	16.0	53.0
				Vote	37.3	33.8	10.9	5.9	12.1	55.7
				Error	–4.3	+0.2	+1.1	+0.1	+3.9	–2.7

Sources: Publicly reported estimates; AEC (2025a); author's calculations.

One of the things that JWS got wrong in these seats—and in others, such as Whitlam and Werriwa, which were not fully reported—were preference flows. Some 80–90 per cent of the preferences from the small right-wing parties (One Nation, Family First, Trumpet of Patriots) were likely to flow to the Coalition, it said, not the two-thirds or so that flowed in 2022 (Coorey 2025a).

In other polls, seats were clustered. DemosAU polled the three Brisbane seats held by the Greens (7–15 April), where its estimate of the 2CP vote assumed either an overall Labor versus LNP or Greens versus LNP contest (in Griffith, it turned out to be Greens versus Labor); three Labor marginals in Melbourne (13–22 April); five outer metropolitan seats in Queensland held by the LNP (18–23 April); and three Labor marginals in Sydney (13–27 April). In every case, the final Labor vote was underestimated—its first-preference vote more markedly than its 2PP share, with the 2PP share more accurate the closer the poll was to election day (Table 20.5). There was also a RedBridge/Accent poll of 20 'key seats'—13 Labor, seven Coalition—conducted six times, most recently on 24–30 April; all but three were marginals. It, too, underestimated Labor's first preferences and (more narrowly) Labor's share of the 2PP vote.

National polls versus the seat-by-seat count in the MRP

To focus on national polls rather than polls in particular seats is to assume a close relationship between changes in total vote share and in seat shares: seats won by the parties of government—hence, the electoral pendulum (Green 2024). As Phil Coorey (2025b) observed, if the 2PP 'swing against Labor of 0.6 percentage points'—the swing predicted by the Freshwater poll—'was applied across all electorates', Labor would be reduced from 78 seats to 'a bare majority' of 76, with the Coalition increasing its share from 57 to 59 seats. For this to be valid, swings did not need to be uniform; all that was required was that seats lost despite requiring a greater than average swing were matched by seats gained despite requiring a smaller than average swing.

Given the rise of the Independents, and the growing view that the pendulum had passed its use-by date, the performance of the pendulum was remarkable. A swing of 3.2 points might have been expected to deliver 13 seats from the Coalition to Labor (derived from Green 2024). In fact, the swing delivered

11 seats to Labor from the Coalition, just two seats short. (Aston, counted by the AEC [2025b] as a Labor gain, was Labor already, following the 2023 by-election; Bennelong, notionally a Labor gain, was already regarded as Labor after the 2024 redistribution.)

By contrast, the MRP fared poorly. It predicted a 2PP vote of 52.9 per cent—a swing to Labor of just 0.8 of a point. On the pendulum, this might have been expected to have shifted three of the Coalition's seats to Labor. The MRP's seat-by-seat predictions—the rationale for conducting an MRP—had Labor gaining seven seats from the Coalition, six of them marginals, with the other (Braddon) 'fairly safe'. All seven did fall to Labor, but another six fell as well.

Conclusion

The national polls exaggerated the Coalition's position (and One Nation's) and underestimated Labor's. This was true for most of the other polls as well. As in 2019, when the average error in the national polls was the same, 2025 was not a 'miss', explained by a late swing, but a 'failure', due to pollsters' errors (Durand and Blais 2020). Misses are uncommon, failures are not (Goot 2021). Had the polls predicted not a Labor majority but a Coalition victory or even a hung parliament, their performance would have generated more concern. In 2019, when the polls picked the wrong winner, the Market Research Society commissioned an inquiry (Pennay et al. 2019); after the 2025 election, because no poll suggested that the Coalition would win, no-one called for an inquiry.

Possible explanations for the polls' failure include survey errors (notably, non-ignorable nonresponses) and post-survey errors, including the treatment of the 'undecideds'. Might herding have played a part—even the dominant part—with pollsters making sure their poll was not too different from that of their rivals, being in wrong company preferable to being out on one's own? After the 2019 debacle, one pollster said he had not published his figures because they were at odds with those published by others (Mansillo and Jackman 2020: 137); what his figures were, he never disclosed.

In 2025, it is more likely that pollsters simply subscribed to a common assumption—widely shared by politicians and political journalists—that, in a cost-of-living 'crisis', if Labor were to win, it would not be by much. This proved mistaken: Labor won in a landslide.

References

Australian Broadcasting Corporation (ABC). 2025. 'Poll position.' *Media Watch*, [*ABC TV*], 28 April. www.abc.net.au/mediawatch/episodes/poll/105225644.

Australian Electoral Commission (AEC). 2025a. 'House of Representatives—Final results.' [Updated 10 June 2025]. *Tally Room: 2025 Federal Election*. Canberra: Australian Electoral Commission. results.aec.gov.au/31496/Website/House Default-31496.htm.

Australian Electoral Commission (AEC). 2025b. 'Seats that changed hands.' [Updated 10 June 2025]. *Tally Room: 2025 Federal Election*. Canberra: Australian Electoral Commission. results.aec.gov.au/31496/Website/HouseSeatsWhich ChangedHands-31496.htm.

Australian Financial Review (AFR). 2025. 'Explore the latest Freshwater strategy poll.' *Australian Financial Review*, 23 February. [Updated 1 May 2025]. www. afr.com/politics/federal/freshwater-strategy-poll-20250128-p5l7p3.

Australian Polling Council. 2025. *Code of Conduct*. [Online]. www.australianpolling council.com/code-of-conduct.

Bailey, Michael A. 2024. *Polling at a Crossroads: Rethinking Modern Survey Research*. Cambridge: Cambridge University Press. doi.org/10.1017/9781108697798.

Beaumont, Adrian. 2025a. 'Major YouGov poll has Labor easily winning a majority of seats in election.' *The Conversation*, 1 May. doi.org/10.64628/AA.puwm55w3g.

Beaumont, Adrian. 2025b. 'Final counting shows polls underrated Labor in 2025 election almost as much as they overstated it in 2019.' *The Conversation*, 5 June. doi.org/10.64628/AA.cpjyxwpwu.

Beed, Terence W. 1977. 'Opinion polling and the elections.' In *Australia at the Polls: The National Elections of 1975*, edited by Howard R. Penniman, 211–55. Canberra: Australian National University Press.

Bowe, William. 2025a. 'Federal election plus one week (open thread).' [Online]. *The Poll Bludger*, 11 May. www.pollbludger.net/2025/05/11/federal-election-plus-one-week-open-thread/.

Bowe, William. 2025b. 'Federal politics: Roy Morgan poll and preference flow data (open thread).' [Online]. *The Poll Bludger*, 25 June. www.pollbludger.net/2025/06/25/federal-politics-roy-morgan-poll-and-preference-flow-data-open-thread/.

Butler, Josh. 2025. 'Guardian Essential Poll: Labor leads Coalition in final pre-election poll as Dutton's approval rating slips further.' *The Guardian*, 29 April. www. theguardian.com/australia-news/2025/apr/29/guardian-essential-poll-labor-leads-coalition-in-final-pre-election-poll-as-duttons-approval-rating-slips-further.

Coorey, Phillip. 2025a. 'One Nation gives Dutton a poll boost.' *Australian Financial Review*, 30 April.

Coorey, Phillip. 2025b. 'Final poll: Labor fighting to retain majority government.' *Australian Financial Review*, 1 May. www.afr.com/politics/federal/labor-fighting-to-retain-majority-government-20250501-p5lvkp.

Crowe, David. 2025. 'Labor holds clear lead as time runs short for a Coalition rebound, poll reveals.' *The Sydney Morning Herald*, 29 April. www.smh.com.au/ politics/federal/labor-holds-its-lead-as-time-runs-short-for-a-liberal-rebound-poll-reveals-20250429-p5luz8.html.

DemosAU. 2025. *Final Poll: 2025 Australian Election*. [Report]. 2 May. demosau. com/wp-content/uploads/2025/05/DemosAU-Report-Final-Poll-May-2025-Australian-Election-1.pdf.

Durand, Claire, and André Blais. 2020. 'Quebec 2018: A failure of the polls?' *Canadian Journal of Political Science* 53, no. 1: 133–50. doi.org/10.1017/S000 8423919000787.

Goot, Murray. 2021. 'How good are the polls? Australian election predictions, 1993–2019.' *Australian Journal of Political Science* 56, no. 1: 35–55. doi.org/ 10.1080/10361146.2020.1825616.

Goot, Murray. 2025. 'A poll that answers Dutton's dreams …'. *Inside Story*, 10 March. insidestory.org.au/a-poll-that-answers-duttons-dreams/.

Green, Antony. 2024. *2025 Federal Election—New Electoral Pendulum*. Version 1a, December 2024. Sydney: ABC Election Unit. www.abc.net.au/dat/news/ elections/federal/2025/guide/FED2025_PostRedistPendulum.pdf.

Green, Antony. 2025. 'FED2025—Tracking the early vote.' *Antony Green's Election Blog*, 27 April. antonygreen.com.au/fed2025-tracking-the-early-vote/.

Ipsos Australia. 2025. 'Long methodology disclosure statement: Ipsos Australian national poll.' Media release, 2 May. Sydney: Ipsos Australia. www.ipsos.com/ sites/default/files/2025-05/Ipsos%20-%20APC%20Long%20Methodology%20 Disclosure%20Statement_Poll%20%233.pdf.

Jennings, Will, and Christopher Wlezien. 2018. 'Election polling errors across time and space.' *Nature Human Behaviour* 2: 276–83. doi.org/10.1038/s41562-018-0315-6.

Knott, Matthew. 2025. 'Pollsters left red-faced by Labor's powerful late surge.' *The Sydney Morning Herald*, 6 May.

Mansillo, Luke, and Simon Jackman. 2020. 'National polling and other disasters.' In *Morrison's Miracle: The 2019 Australian Federal Election*, edited by Anika Gauja, Marian Sawer, and Marian Simms, 125–48. Canberra: ANU Press. doi.org/10.22459/MM.2020.07.

Pennay, Darren, Murray Goot, Dina Neiger, Dennis Trewin, Paul J. Lavrakas, John Stirton, Phil Hughes, Jill Sheppard, and Ian McAllister. 2019. *Report of the Inquiry into the Performance of the Opinion Polls at the 2019 Australian Federal Election*. Association of Market and Social Research Organisations and the Statistical Society of Australia.

Pyxis Polling and Insights. 2025. 'Methodology statement: Newspoll.' Media release, 2 May. Sydney: Pyxis Polling and Insights. www.pyxispolling.com/ws/media-libr ary/906f8ff5e6c511d2ba153b238bc19646/newspoll-methodology-statement-2-may-2025-by-pyxis.pdf.

Read, Michael. 2025. 'This is why some pollsters missed the Labor landslide.' *Australian Financial Review*, 4 May. www.afr.com/politics/this-is-why-some-pollsters-missed-the-labor-landslide-20250504-p5lwet.

Reed, Jim. 2025. 'With 77% of the vote now counted, we thought it was time to run an initial analysis of the polling data.' LinkedIn post. www.linkedin.com/feed/update/urn:li:activity:7324957787187269633/.

Roy Morgan. 2025a. 'ALP set to win federal election with an expanded majority—ALP 53% cf. L-NP 47%.' Article no. 9886, 2 May. Melbourne: Roy Morgan. roymorgan-cms-prod.s3.ap-southeast-2.amazonaws.com/wp-content/uploads/2025/05/02093140/9886-Federal-Voting-Intention-Final-Pre-Election-May-2-2025.pdf.

Roy Morgan. 2025b. 'Roy Morgan update May 6, 2025: Roy Morgan aces election, consumer confidence and business confidence.' Finding no. 9869, Press release, 6 May. Melbourne: Roy Morgan. www.roymorgan.com/findings/roy-morgan-update-may-6-2025.

Spectre Strategy. 2025. *Australian Election Vote Forecast 2025*. [Online]. 1 May. www.spectrestrategy.com/blog-3-1/auselectionvoteforecast.

Turner, Michael. 2025. 'Three reasons we missed Labor's landslide.' *Australian Financial Review*, 4 May. www.afr.com/politics/federal/three-reasons-we-missed-labor-s-landslide-20250504-p5lwf8.

Wang, Wei, David Rothschild, Sharad Goel, and Andrew Gelman. 2015. 'Forecasting elections with non-representative polls.' *International Journal of Forecasting* 31, no. 3: 980–91. doi.org/10.1016/j.ijforecast.2014.06.001.

Wikimedia Foundation. 2025. 'Opinion polling for the 2025 Australian federal election.' *Wikipedia*, [Updated 19 August 2025]. en.wikipedia.org/w/index.php?title=Opinion_polling_for_the_2025_Australian_federal_election&oldid=1306694375.

YouGov. 2025a. 'Labor to win with an increased majority in YouGov's final MRP of the election.' *YouGov Australia*, 1 May. au.yougov.com/politics/articles/52098-labour-to-win-with-an-increased-majority-in-yougovs-final-mrp-of-the-election.

YouGov. 2025b. 'Labor on track for victory as Dutton records lowest satisfaction rating on record.' *YouGov Australia*, 2 May. au.yougov.com/politics/articles/52103-labor-on-track-for-victory-as-dutton-records-lowest-satisfaction-rating-on-record.

YouGov. 2025c. 'YouGov accurately calls historic Labor landslide in Australian federal election.' *YouGov Australia*, 7 May. au.yougov.com/politics/articles/52115-yougov-accurately-calls-historic-labor-landslide-in-australian-federal-election.

Appendix 20.1

Table A20.1 The MRP poll in 'marginal' seats, by order of marginality: YouGov, 1–29 April 2025 (per cent)

| | | Coalition 2PP/2CP | | | | | | Labor 2PP/2CP | | |
Electorate	State	Margin	Predicted	Actual	Error	Electorate	State/Territory	Margin	Predicted	Actual	Error
Deakin[a]	Vic.	0.0	49.3	47.2	+2.1	Gilmore	NSW	0.2	51.2	55.1	−3.9
Bennelong	NSW	0.0	49.0	40.7	+8.3	Menzies	Vic.	0.4	50.3	51.1	−0.8
Sturt	SA	0.5	49.3	43.4	+5.9	Lyons	Tas.	0.9	52.3	61.6	−9.3
Moore	WA	0.9	49.7	47.1	+2.6	Lingiari	NT	1.7	58.0	58.1	−0.1
Canning	WA	1.2	50.2	56.6	−6.4	Robertson	NSW	2.2	50.9	59.4	−8.5
Bass[a]	Tas.	1.4	52.2	42.0	+9.8	Paterson	NSW	2.6	51.8	56.9	−4.9
Casey	Vic.	1.4	52.7	52.9	−0.2	Tangney	WA	2.8	53.5	57.0	−3.5
Dickson[a]	Qld	1.7	50.2	44.0	+8.2	Boothby	SA	3.3	51.9	61.1	−9.2
Cowper[b] vs Ind.	NSW	2.4	36.8	52.5	−15.7	Chisholm	Vic.	3.3	53.1	55.7	−4.6
Bradfield vs Ind.	NSW	2.5	35.9	50.0	−14.1	Bullwinkel	WA	3.3	54.1	50.5	+3.6
Banks	NSW	2.6	49.4	47.6	+1.8	Aston[b]	Vic.	3.6	48.0	53.4	−5.4
Monash	Vic.	2.9	45.9	54.1	−8.2	Parramatta	NSW	3.7	56.3	62.6	−6.3
Longman	Qld	3.1	54.2	50.1	+4.1	McEwen	Vic.	3.8	53.2	55.8	−2.6
Bonner	Qld	3.4	48.8	45.0	+3.8	Wills vs GRN	Vic.	4.6	55.5	51.4	+4.1
Leichhardt	Qld	3.4	52.8	43.9	+8.9	Hunter	NSW	4.8	55.0	59.5	−4.5
Nicholls	Vic.	3.4	66.4	64.4	+2.0	Reid	NSW	5.2	57.4	62.0	−4.6
Hughes[a]	NSW	3.5	54.6	46.9	+7.7	Blair	Qld	5.2	54.5	55.7	−3.2

		Coalition 2PP/2CP						Labor 2PP/2CP			
Electorate	State	Margin	Predicted	Actual	Error	Electorate	State/Territory	Margin	Predicted	Actual	Error
Flynn	Qld	3.8	52.8	60.2	–7.4	Bruce	Vic.	5.3	55.2	64.6	–9.4
Wannon vs Ind.	Vic.	3.8	38.1	53.3	–15.2	Werriwa	NSW	5.3	53.3	56.8	–3.5
Forrest	WA	4.2	53.9	52.2	+1.7	Mean|median					4.9|–4.6
Forde[a]	Qld	4.2	52.5	48.2	+4.3	Std dev.					3.8
Petrie[a]	Qld	4.4	53.4	48.8	+4.6						
Durack	WA	4.7	54.9	60.2	–5.3						
Bowman	Qld	5.5	51.4	52.4	–1.0						
Mean|median					5.5|+2.1						
Std dev.					7.5						

Notes: Marginal = seats requiring a 2PP swing of less than 6 percentage points to change hands. Error = predicted minus actual. Seats in bold text changed hands; [a] Seat changed hands but not predicted to change hands; [b] Seat predicted to change hands but did not change hands.

Sources: Green (2024); YouGov (2025a); AEC (2025a); author's calculations.

Table A20.2 The MRP poll in 'fairly safe' seats, by order of marginality: YouGov, 1–29 April 2025 (per cent)

		Coalition 2PP						Labor 2PP			
Electorate	State	Margin	Predicted	Actual	Error	Electorate	State/Territory	Margin	Predicted	Actual	Error
Lindsay	NSW	6.1	55.1	52.8	+2.3	Shortland	NSW	6.0	55.6	61.5	–3.9
Flinders	Vic.	6.2	54.9	54.8	+0.1	Eden-Monaro	NSW	6.1	54.9	57.2	–2.3
Capricornia	Qld	6.6	55.8	55.8	0.0	Macquarie	NSW	6.3	54.9	57.7	–2.8
O'Connor	WA	6.7	55.1	63.3	–8.2	Dobell	NSW	6.6	55.5	59.4	–3.9
Hume	NSW	6.9	59.2	58.1	+1.1	Dunkley	Vic.	6.8	57.5	57.1	+0.4

		Coalition 2PP						Labor 2PP			
Electorate	State	Margin	Predicted	Actual	Error	Electorate	State/Territory	Margin	Predicted	Actual	Error
Groom vs Ind.	Qld	6.9	57.3	63.4	–6.1	Holt	Vic.	7.1	55.1	64.0	–8.9
Berowra	NSW	7.6	53.8	51.6	+2.2	Hawke	Vic.	7.6	54.1	57.6	–3.5
Braddon[a]	Tas.	8.0	57.0	42.8	+14.2	Cooper	Vic.	7.8	60.2	78.5	–18.3
La Trobe	Vic.	8.4	56.3	52.1	+4.2	Corangamite	Vic.	7.8	57.5	58.1	–0.6
Fisher	Qld	8.7	55.3	56.0	–0.7	Greenway	NSW	7.9	59.4	63.8	–4.4
Fairfax	Qld	9.0	55.8	53.2	+2.6	Richmond	NSW	8.2	52.6	60.0	–7.4
McPherson	Qld	9.3	55.1	54.4	+0.7	Whitlam	NSW	8.3	59.2	56.3	+2.9
Riverina	NSW	9.7	57.4	62.6	–5.2	Solomon	NT	8.4	59.7	51.3	+8.4
Calare vs Ind. MP	NSW	9.7	46.9	43.2	+3.7	Pearce	WA	8.8	56.0	56.4	–0.4
Mean|median					3.7|0.9	Hindmarsh	SA	8.9	60.4	66.4	–6.0
Std dev.					5.37	Rankin	Qld	9.1	59.4	65.6	–6.2
						Moreton	Qld	9.1	59.9	66.1	–6.2
						Swan	WA	9.4	58.5	64.0	–5.5
						Isaacs	Vic.	9.5	60.0	64.3	–4.3
						Macarthur	NSW	9.8	59.1	65.6	–6.5
						Cowan	WA	9.9	59.4	63.6	–4.2
						Mean|median					5.1|4.2
						Std dev.					4.94

Notes: Fairly safe = seats requiring a 2PP swing of between 6.0 and 9.9 percentage points to change hands; Error = predicted less actual; Seats in bold text changed hands; [a] Seat changed hands but not predicted to change hands.

Sources: Green (2024); YouGov (2025a); AEC (2025a); author's calculations.

Table A20.3 The MRP poll in 'safe' seats, by order of marginality: YouGov, 1–29 April 2025 (per cent)

		Coalition 2PP						Labor 2PP			
Electorate	State	Margin	Predicted	Actual	Error	Electorate	State/Territory	Margin	Predicted	Actual	Error
Grey	SA	10.1	57.2	54.6	+2.6	Gorton	Vic.	10.0	56.2	60.3	–4.1
Hinkler	Qld	10.1	56.2	56.3	–0.1	Hasluck	WA	10.0	66.0	66.0	0.0
Dawson	Qld	10.4	59.0	61.8	–2.8	McMahon	NSW	10.5	60.8	59.0	+1.8
Mitchell	NSW	10.5	56.5	53.8	+2.7	Lilley	Qld	10.5	62.5	64.5	–2.0
Fadden	Qld	10.6	55.9	56.9	–1.0	Makin	SA	10.8	61.5	64.7	–3.2
Page	NSW	10.7	58.0	59.3	–1.3	Bendigo	Vic.	11.2	60.9	51.4	+9.5
Wright	Qld	10.9	58.6	58.0	+0.6	Gellibrand	Vic.	11.2	62.3	65.1	–2.8
Moncrieff	Qld	11.2	58.1	58.8	–0.7	Hotham	Vic.	11.6	63.6	66.9	–3.3
Wide Bay	Qld	11.3	54.5	57.6	–3.1	Oxley	Qld	11.6	62.7	69.2	–6.5
Cook	NSW	11.6	59.0	57.2	+1.8	Adelaide	SA	11.9	61.9	69.1	–7.2
Herbert	Qld	11.8	59.4	63.4	–4.0	Barton	NSW	12.0	64.1	66.0	–1.9
Lyne	NSW	13.8	54.9	59.8	–4.9	Macnamara	Vic.	12.2	58.0	61.8	–3.8
New England	NSW	15.2	61.2	67.1	–5.9	Jagajaga	Vic.	12.2	60.8	62.9	–2.1
Farrer	NSW	16.3	59.3	62.9	–3.6	Canberra vs GRN	ACT	12.2	60.1	76.4	–15.3
Barker	SA	16.6	60.7	63.0	–2.3	Calwell	Vic.	12.4	58.5	64.7	–6.2
Parkes	NSW	18.2	62.7	63.0	–0.3	Corio	Vic.	12.5	60.2	63.2	–3.0
Mallee	Vic	19.0	64.6	69.0	–4.4	Lalor	Vic.	12.8	59.5	63.2	–3.7
Gippsland	Vic.	20.6	61.5	69.4	–7.9	Spence	SA	12.9	59.9	65.3	–5.4
Maranoa vs PHON	Qld	22.1	66.2	74.0	–7.8	Bean	ACT	12.9	62.0	69.3	–7.3
Mean|median					3.0|–2.3	Ballarat	Vic.	13.0	61.6	60.7	+0.9
Std dev.					3.16	Maribyrnong	Vic.	13.0	63.5	62.7	+0.8

	Coalition 2PP						Labor 2PP			
Electorate	State	Margin	Predicted	Actual	Error	Electorate	State/Territory	Margin	Predicted	Actual	Error
						Blaxland	NSW	13.0	63.4	71.9	−8.5
						Burt	WA	13.3	63.3	65.7	−2.4
						Kingsford Smith	NSW	13.3	65.2	67.2	−2.0
						Chifley	NSW	13.6	62.3	69.8	−7.5
						Franklin	Tas.	13.7	58.6	69.4	−10.8
						Perth	WA	14.4	56.6	66.5	−9.9
						Cunningham	NSW	15.1	62.2	67.5	−5.3
						Watson	NSW	15.2	64.7	72.9	−8.2
						Scullin	Vic.	15.4	62.1	64.3	−2.2
						Fenner	ACT	15.7	66.6	72.1	−5.5
						Kingston	SA	16.4	64.2	70.7	−6.5
						Sydney vs GRN	NSW	16.5	67.5	78.1	−10.6
						Fraser	Vic.	16.6	63.3	72.0	−8.7
						Fremantle	WA	16.9	62.2	68.7	−6.5
						Brand	WA	17.1	65.9	66.9	−1.0
						Grayndler vs GRN	NSW	17.3	65.3	80.2	−14.9
						Newcastle	NSW	17.9	64.7	70.8	−6.1
						Mean|median					5.5|−4.4
						Std dev.					4.62

Note: Safe = seats requiring a 2PP swing of more than 10 percentage points to change hands.

Sources: Green (2024); YouGov (2025a); AEC (2025a); author's calculations.

Table A20.4 Classic contests in single electorates, 31 March – 3 May 2025 (per cent)

Electorate	Incumbent; margin	Pollster	Date(s)	n		First preferences						2PP (ALP)
						ALP	Coalition	GRN	PHON	Ind.	Other	
NSW												
Eden-Monaro	ALP (McBain); 6.1	YouGov	17–24 April	268	Est.	42.2	26.0	10.9	7.0	10.6	3.3	61.0
		–			Vote	43.0	31.9	10.0	7.0	3.9	4.2	57.2
Gilmore	ALP (Phillips); 0.2	YouGov	17–24 April	255	Est.	36.2	33.5	11.1	6.0	8.5	4.7	54.0
		–			Vote	38.1	34.5	7.1	5.0	7.5	7.8	55.1
Hunter	ALP (Repacholi); 4.8	KJC Research	20 April	600	Est.	–	–	–	–	–	–	45.0*
		YouGov	17–24 April	224	Est.	35.8	14.6	8.8	25.3	0.5	15.0	59.0
		–			Vote	43.5	18.2	7.4	16.1	–	14.8	59.5
McMahon	ALP (Bowen); 10.5	Compass	8 April	1,003	Est.	19.0	20.0	–	–	41.0	–	–
		–			Vote	45.5	26.8	9.1	8.7	9.8	–	59.0
New England	Nats (Joyce); 15.2	New England Times	9–23 April	426	Est.	24.1	43.6	12.2	6.8	2.4	3.8	42.7
		–			Vote	20.3	52.2	7.9	10.0	3.7	5.9	32.9
Paterson	ALP (Swanson); 2.6	YouGov	17–24 April	302	Est.	30.9	25.9	11.5	14.2	15.9	1.6	55.0
		–			Vote	37.0	27.2	7.6	7.6	12.1	8.4	56.9
Richmond	ALP (Elliot); 8.2	KJC Research	24 April	600	Est.	–	–	–	–	–	–	34.0*
		–			Vote	30.4	24.6	26.5	5.4	2.6	10.5	60.0
Vic.												
Ballarat	ALP (King); 13.0	YouGov	17–24 April	217	Est.	38.5	23.8	17.7	9.8	6.1	4.1	62.0
		–			Vote	42.3	28.6	14.3	7.7	2.8	4.3	60.7

Electorate	Incumbent; margin	Pollster	Date(s)	n		First preferences						2PP (ALP)
						ALP	Coalition	GRN	PHON	Ind.	Other	
Qld												
Blair	ALP (Neumann); 5.2	KJC Research	24 April	600	Est.	–	–	–	–	–	–	41.0*
		–			Vote	–	–	–	–	–	–	55.7
Dickson	LNP (Dutton); 1.7	Freshwater	10 April (pub.)	–	Est.	–	–	–	–	–	–	43.0
		UComms	9–10 April	854	Est.	24.2	37.6	10.9	–	12.0	4.6	52.0
		YouGov	17–24 April	253	Est.	24.2	40.3	7.6	5.4	16.5	6.0	45.0
		–			Vote	33.6	34.8	7.6	4.2	12.2	7.6	56.0
WA												
Bullwinkel	ALP (notional); 3.3	YouGov	17–24 April	238	Est.	31.6	40.6	11.1	6.1	0.6	6.6	48.5
		–			Vote	32.0	40.1	11.2	8.6	–	8.2	50.5
Forrest	Liberal; 4.2	UComms	9–10 April	c.1,000	Est.	–	34	–	–	20	–	49.0 (Lib.)
		–			Vote	22.6	36.0	7.9	8.7	18.3	6.6	52.2 (Lib.)
Tangney	ALP (Lim); 2.8	KJC Research	24 April	600	Est.	–	–	–	–	–	–	45.0*
		–			Vote	42.5	34.3	13.0	4.1	–	6.2	57.0
SA												
Adelaide	ALP (Georganas); 11.9	DemosAU	27–29 April	1,974	Est.	29	32	12	9	–	18	51
		–			Vote	46.5	24.2	19.0	4.0	–	6.4	69.1
Boothby	ALP (Miller-Frost); 3.3	YouGov	17–24 April	250	Est.	32.1	30.7	14.9	9.0	0.4	12.9	52
		–			Vote	42.6	32.5	17.1	3.0	–	4.8	61.1

| | | | | | | First preferences | | | | | | |
Electorate	Incumbent; margin	Pollster	Date(s)	n		ALP	Coalition	GRN	PHON	Ind.	Other	2PP (ALP)
Tas.												
Braddon	Liberal; 8.0	YouGov	17–24 April	419	Est.	33.2	30.6	9.7	4.6	15.7	6.2	54
		–			Vote	39.5	31.7	8.4	7.6	8.3	4.5	57.2
Franklin	ALP (Collins); 13.7	EMRS	9–10 April	430	Est.	38	19	13	–	20	–	–
		–			Vote	39.0	18.8	10.5	5.0	26.7	–	57.8
Lyons	ALP; 0.9	UComms	10 April (pub.)	712	Est.	27.2	29.5	14.6	4.1	–	5.8	50.9
		YouGov	17–24 April	446	Est.	33.4	27.8	13.0	4.4	9.3	12.1	56
		–			Vote	43.3	26.4	10.6	6.8	3.2	9.7	61.6

Note: * Two-party vote adds to less than 100.

Sources: Publicly reported estimates; YouGov, Personal communication; AEC (2025a).

Table A20.5 Non-classic contests in single seats, 31 March – 3 May 2025 (per cent)

| | | | | | | First preferences | | | | | | |
Electorate	Incumbent; margin	Pollster	Date(s)	n		ALP	Coalition	GRN	PHON	Ind.	Other	2CP (Ind.)
NSW												
Calare	Gee (Ind.); 9.7 vs Nats	YouGov	17–24 April	184	Est.	8.2	25.1	5.1	13.9	38.9	8.8	57.0
		–			Vote	10.4	29.7	3.5	7.7	39.4	9.3	56.8
Wentworth	Spender (Ind.); 6.8 vs Lib.	UComms	9 April (pub.)	1,015	Est.	12.2	32.9	–	–	32.5	–	58.0
		Compass	18 April (pub.)	627	Est.	15.0	47.0	10.0	–	28.0	–	–
		–			Vote	13.4	36.4	10.2	2.4	37.7	–	58.3

Electorate	Incumbent; margin	Pollster	Date(s)	n		First preferences						2CP (Ind.)
						ALP	Coalition	GRN	PHON	Ind.	Other	
Vic												
Wannon	Liberal (Tehan); 3.8 vs Ind.	YouGov	17–24 April	246	Est.	12.2	33.2	5.2	6.9	35.7	6.8	57.0
		–			Vote	10.6	43.7	3.1	4.2	32.1	6.3	46.3
Qld												
Brisbane	Greens (Bates); 3.7 vs LNP	JWS Research	8–9 April	834	Est.	29.0	43.0	29.0	–	–	–	51 (ALP)
		–			Vote	32.2	34.3	25.9	2.5	–	5.2	59.0 (ALP)
Griffith	Greens (Chandler-Mather); 0.9 vs ALP (primary)	JWS Research	8–9 April	888	Est.	28.0	38.0	23.0	–	–	–	51(ALP 2PP)
		–			Vote	34.5	26.6	31.7	2.5	–	4.8	60.6 (ALP)
Ryan	Greens (Watson-Brown); 2.6 vs LNP	JWS Research	8–9 April	825	Est.	30.0	46.0	13.0	–	–	11.0	57 (LNP 2PP)
		–			Vote	28.2	34.6	29.0	2.3	–	5.9	53.3 (GRN)

Sources: Publicly reported estimates; JWS, Personal communication; AEC (2025a); Green (2024).

9 781760 467258

AMAZON Version ONLY

Ebook/Print Cover: CAROL MARQUES DESIGNS
Editing, Proofing, backgrounds, & Formatting: Dirty Sexy Words/ Storm shield Editing/Little Tailfeather Publishing
Cassandra's logos: Pretty in Ink Creations/Artlogo
Goosebusters Alpha team: Kat Silver, Becky Ross, Erica Taryn
Duckhunters Proofing Team: Jackie H, Jaemi Serrano
Sensitivity Readers: Brit Mason, Gail Jericho
Translation Consultant: Mo Jacobs
Legal Services: Joshua Farley, esq.
Agent: Laura Pink at SBR Media
Images/Fonts: Depositphotos, Shutterstock, Canva, & Photoshop

No GenAI was used within this book. All errors and greatness are by an ADHD muppet.